THE SCHOLEMS

THE SCHOLEMS

A Story of the German-Jewish Bourgeoisie from Emancipation to Destruction

Jay Howard Geller

CORNELL UNIVERSITY PRESS
Ithaca and London

First published 2019 by Cornell University Press

Printed in the United States of America

Library of Congress Cataloging-in-Publication Data

Names: Geller, Jay Howard, author.
Title: The Scholems : a story of the German-Jewish bourgeoisie from emancipation to destruction / Jay Howard Geller.
Description: Ithaca : Cornell University Press, 2019. | Includes bibliographical references and index.
Identifiers: LCCN 2018029901 (print) | LCCN 2018033456 (ebook) | ISBN 9781501731570 (pdf) | ISBN 9781501731587 (epub/mobi) | ISBN 9781501731563 | ISBN 9781501731563 (cloth ; alk. paper)
Subjects: LCSH: Scholem, Gershom, 1897–1982. | Scholem, Gershom, 1897–1982—Family. | Jewish scholars—Germany—Biography. | Jews—Germany—Biography. | Jews—Germany—History—20th century. | Middle class—Germany—History—20th century.
Classification: LCC BM755.S295 (ebook) | LCC BM755. S295 G45 2018 (print) | DDC 305.892/40430922 [B]—dc23
LC record available at https://lccn.loc.gov/2018029901

Cover images:
Top: The Scholem family, courtesy of the National Library of Israel, ARC. 4*1599/10/08, 003800443
Bottom: The Brandenburg Gate in Berlin, courtesy of the Library of Congress, LOT 14184, no. 257 (P&P)

Contents

Map of the Scholems' Berlin in the 1920s vii

Members of the Scholem Family ix

Introduction   1

1. Origins: From Glogau to Berlin   14

2. Berlin Childhood around 1900: Growing
   Up in the Growing Metropolis   32

3. Things Fall Apart: The First World War   47

4. Life in the Time of Revolutions:
   The Early Weimar Republic   73

5. The Gold-Plated Twenties and Beyond:
   Promise, Prosperity, and Depression
   in Interwar Germany   96

6. In the Promised Land: A New Home
   in Jerusalem   127

7. The Maelstrom: Jewish Life in Nazi
   Germany   142

8. Cresting of the Fifth Wave: Gershom
   Scholem's Palestine in the 1930s   172

9. Afterlives: Sydney and Jerusalem   193

Conclusion   209

Acknowledgments   *219*

Notes   *223*

Bibliography   *291*

Index   *321*

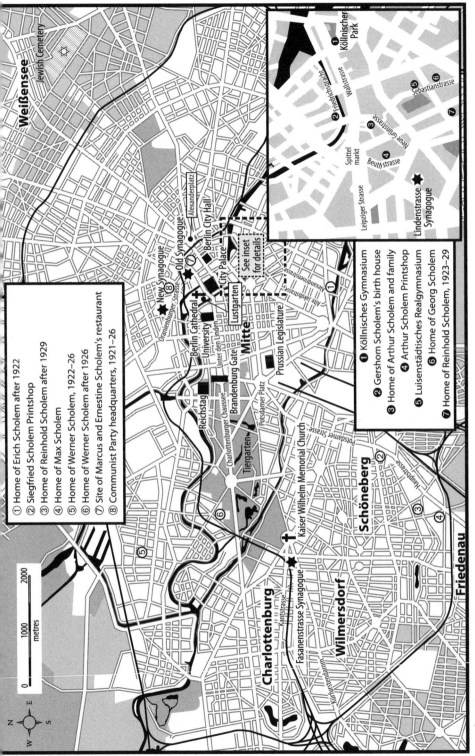

Weißensee

Jewish Cemetery

① Home of Erich Scholem after 1922
② Siegfried Scholem Printshop
③ Home of Reinhold Scholem after 1929
④ Home of Max Scholem
⑤ Home of Werner Scholem, 1922–26
⑥ Home of Werner Scholem after 1926
⑦ Site of Marcus and Ernestine Scholem's restaurant
⑧ Communist Party headquarters, 1921–26

New Synagogue
Old Synagogue
Oranienburger strasse
Berlin Cathedral
University
Unter den Linden
Brandenburg Gate
Reichstag
Charlottenburger Chaussee
Tiergarten
Potsdamer Platz
Alexanderplatz
Berlin City Hall
City Palace
Lustgarten
Mitte
Alte Jakobstrasse
Alexandrinenstrasse
Prussian Legislature
Potsdamer Strasse

See Inset
for details

① Köllnisches Gymnasium
② Gershom Scholem's birth house
③ Home of Arthur Scholem and family
④ Arthur Scholem Printshop
⑤ Luisenstädtisches Realgymnasium
⑥ Home of Georg Scholem
⑦ Home of Reinhold Scholem, 1923–29

Charlottenburg
Fasanenstrasse Synagogue
Kantstrasse
Kurfürstendamm
Kaiser Wilhelm Memorial Church
Wilmersdorf
Schöneberg
Hauptstrasse
Friedenau

N
W — E
S

0   1000   2000
         metres

Inset:
Köllnischer Park
Friedrichsgracht
Wallstrasse
Sebastianstrasse
Neue Grünstrasse
Beuthstrasse
Spittel markt
Leipziger Strasse
Lindenstrasse Synagogue

The Scholems' Berlin in the 1920s

MEMBERS OF THE
SCHOLEM FAMILY

Marcus Scholem: Born in Glogau in the late 1700s, moved to Berlin after 1812

Ernestine Scholem (née Esther Holländer): Wife of Marcus

Siegfried Scholem: Son of Marcus and Ernestine, born in Berlin in 1837, founder and owner of a printshop

Amalie Scholem (née Schlesinger): Wife of Siegfried

Arthur Scholem: Oldest son of Siegfried and Amalie, founder and owner of a printshop

Betty Scholem (née Hirsch): Wife of Arthur, devoted correspondent with Gershom

Reinhold Scholem: Oldest son of Arthur and Betty, coproprietor of the Arthur Scholem printshop, a German patriot and national liberal

Käthe Scholem (née Wagner): Wife of Reinhold

Erich Scholem: Second son of Arthur and Betty, coproprietor of the Arthur Scholem printshop, a liberal democrat

Edith Scholem (née Katz): First wife of Erich

Hildegard "Hilde" Scholem (née Samuel): Second wife of Erich

Werner Scholem: Third son of Arthur and Betty, a Communist politician

Emmy Scholem (née Wiechelt): Wife of Werner, non-Jewish, a Communist

Gershom (or Gerhard) Scholem: Youngest son of Arthur and Betty, a university professor and scholar of Jewish mysticism, a Zionist

Elsa "Escha" Scholem (née Burchhardt): First wife of Gershom, second wife of Hugo Bergmann

Fania Scholem (née Freud): Second wife of Gershom, former student of Gershom

Theobald Scholem: Second son of Siegfried and Amalie, coproprietor of the Siegfried Scholem printshop, a Zionist

Hedwig "Hete" Scholem (née Levy): Wife of Theobald, a Zionist

Eva Scholem: Daughter of Theobald and Hedwig, a physician

Dina Waschitz (née Scholem): Daughter of Theobald and Hedwig

Max Scholem: Third son of Siegfried and Amalie, coproprietor of the Siegfried Scholem printshop

Helene "Lene" Scholem (née Grund): Wife of Max

Herbert Scholem: Son of Max and Helene, a printer

Therese "Esi" Lacher (née Scholem): Daughter of Max and Helene

Georg Scholem: Fourth son of Siegfried and Amalie, a physician

Sophie "Phiechen" Scholem (née Sussmann): Wife of Georg

Ernst Scholem: Son of Georg and Sophie

Kurt Scholem: Son of Georg and Sophie

THE SCHOLEMS

Introduction

Monday, 21 February 1938. It is a cold, clear morning as the RMS *Queen Mary* sails up the Hudson River at the end of its five-day journey from Cherbourg, France. Among the passengers waiting to disembark at the West 50th Street pier in New York City is a lanky man in a suit and tie, outwardly unremarkable, save for his exceptionally prominent ears. The Immigration and Naturalization Service notes that he is a Palestinian citizen of the Hebrew race, born in Berlin, Germany, and he has come to the United States to give lectures.

His name is Gershom Scholem.

It is his first trip to America, a country that he regards with curiosity and some degree of suspicion. Over the next few weeks, he will speak to large crowds, visit research libraries, and rekindle old acquaintances among the emigrated German-born Jewish intelligentsia. His lectures will form the basis of a book that will fundamentally change the way the public thinks about Jewish mysticism and will help create an entirely new field of study. He will become the most important academic scholar of Judaism in his era and arguably Israel's preeminent public intellectual. But as Gershom Scholem descends the gangway on that winter morning, he is primarily excited about the prospect of studying rare manuscripts in New York and exploring the strange world that is America.

*

Friday, 1 July 1938. While Gershom savors his time in New York and basks in the glow of his successful lectures, a different ship brings his brothers Reinhold and Erich to their new life. The *Aorangi* sails into Sydney harbor, having crossed the Pacific Ocean from Canada. Reinhold, an unapologetic German patriot, and Erich, a disaffected liberal democrat, have completed a flight from Nazism that has taken them from Berlin to Southampton, Montreal, Vancouver, and Sydney. After six weeks of traveling, they are exhausted, but safe.

In contrast to Gershom's arrival in New York, they are not greeted by members of the local Jewish intelligentsia, and there is no large honorarium reserved for them. In fact, they have no jobs or apartments waiting for them. They plan to lodge in a residential hotel until they get established. Without relatives or friends in Australia, they report to the Australian immigration inspector that their only contact is the Jewish Welfare Society.

For decades, they were prosperous printshop owners, until they were deprived of their livelihood by the Nazis. They were lifelong Berliners, but they can no longer remain in Germany, and soon, the Nazi government will strip them of their German citizenship, rendering them officially stateless. They will spend years struggling to reestablish the affluence and sense of belonging they once had. And now, as Reinhold and Erich Scholem glimpse the iconic Sydney Harbour Bridge for the first time, they are immigrants in a strange land.

Saturday, 17 September 1938. While Reinhold settles into a new apartment in Sydney and fills out Australian immigration papers for his mother, a consignment of prisoners arrives at the Buchenwald concentration camp: Jews, Communists, and others considered enemies of the Nazi state. They sign forms and confirm the handover of their personal effects. Perhaps the most infamous among the inmates is Werner Scholem, a former representative in the German Reichstag, member of the Communist Party central committee, and editor of the Communist Party's official newspaper. He is also the brother of Gershom, Reinhold, and Erich.

He is already familiar with the world of the concentration camps, having been imprisoned since April 1933, shortly after the Nazis came to power. Over the last five years, he has been in Columbia-Haus, Lichtenberg, and Dachau. In each camp, his notoriety has exacerbated his situation, with both the guards and his fellow prisoners. Meanwhile, the Nazis have accused him of subverting the German army, singled him out as a mastermind of the Communist press, and exhibited him as a paragon of stereotypical Jewish physical features.

Though his health has suffered and he exudes unremitting pessimism, he yearns to join his family abroad. They have appealed to welfare boards, non-Jewish religious organizations, and political activists on his behalf. Some of his acquaintances inside the camps have been released to emigrate, giving his family hope. However, as Werner Scholem steps off the transport vehicle in Buchenwald, he does not know that this has been his last journey.

Wednesday, 9 November 1938. While Werner sits in Buchenwald, a storm of antisemitism erupts in cities and towns across Germany. It is Kristallnacht. In a sudden escalation in the violence against the Jews, Nazi storm troopers and their helpers smash the windows of thousands of Jewish-owned businesses. Tens of thousands of Jewish men are arrested and sent to jails and concentration camps. Hundreds of synagogues are burned down or partially destroyed, including the interior of the Berlin Lindenstrasse synagogue, where Betty Scholem occasionally worships with her family.

As the massive extent of the damage becomes clear, Betty Scholem is in a panic. She had wanted to stay in Germany to advocate for Werner's release, but Werner's wife, safe in London, urges Betty to flee immediately. She would leave that day if she could, but she is still waiting on an exit permit and her passport. From Australia, Reinhold sends his mother an Australian entry permit via air mail. There is no time to lose. It is clear that every Jew who can leave Germany must do so without delay. Facing this dire situation and ensnared in a bureaucratic tangle, she has a nervous breakdown. It is unclear if she will be able to travel, and if so, where she can go.

Four brothers, whose vastly different fates stem from choices made decades before, and their mother, in the middle of this disintegrating family.

What led them to this point? It would seem natural that siblings, raised in the same house under identical circumstances, would have the same or similar political views.[1] Moreover, political convictions frequently reflect a set of cultural and social practices: how people live, how they socialize, how they view the world, and what values they hold. Therefore, it is all the more unusual that the members of one family illustrate the diversity of political opinion and social choices among middle-class German Jews in the early twentieth century. Yet the Scholems, encompassing so many trends, were broadly representative of German Jewry in this era. Looking back on his youth, Gershom commented, "Perhaps one can say that the very different directions in which we four brothers developed in the ensuing years were typical of the world of the Jewish bourgeoisie and demonstrated what little influence a seemingly common environment has on the path taken by an individual young person."[2] The historian Shulamit Volkov has written, "Jews reacted to the waves of anti-semitism in the last quarter of the nineteenth and early twentieth centuries in four major ways." They were: a re-avowal of their faith in liberalism, usually accompanied by allegiance to the dominant nationalism of their country; a rejection of any nationalism and an embrace of socialist internationalism; an attempt to assert Jewish particularity while remaining Europeans; and Zion-ism.[3] Though she does not mention the Scholems as exemplars, they largely fit her paradigm.

Werner Scholem—who became a leader of the German Communist Party, member of the Reichstag, and rival of Joseph Stalin—made stark choices in response to the inequity of German society and the perceived hypocrisy of the German-Jewish bourgeoisie. Gershom Scholem was an extraordinary figure as an academic scholar of Judaism and Israeli public intellectual with an international reputation, yet his life course was shaped by the choices he made as a young man as he observed the situation of German Jewry and per-sonally reacted to it. Additionally, they were not alone in identifying as Com-munists or Zionists, and they remained embedded in a circle of like-minded Jews. In the radical, internationalist workers' movement, Werner's circle consisted largely of Communist intellectuals from Jewish backgrounds. After Gershom moved to Palestine, he circulated disproportionately among central European–born, German-speaking Jewish intellectuals, and even as a youth in Germany, he sought out other Jews who primarily emphasized their Jewish identity. But that group remained exceptional. As Reinhold recalled during an exchange with Gershom, "It seems to me that your feelings and views do not coincide with the majority of German Jews. . . . Conversely, you walked away [from Germanness] for Jewishness or Israeliness, and the Jews did not follow in the desired mass."[4] Politically, culturally, professionally, and even religiously, the brothers Reinhold and Erich were more typical of Ger-man Jewry, and they, too, made conscious choices as Jews and Germans as they reacted to the environment of Wilhelmine Germany, World War I, and the Weimar Republic. Their choices were indicative of how most members of the German-Jewish middle class viewed their world during these years of transition and, ultimately, peril. Moreover, the Scholem family consisted of more than the four brothers. There were parents, aunts and uncles, cousins, grandparents, and others who navigated the same shoals. In following the Scholem family's story, it is possible to learn much about the experience of the German-Jewish bourgeoisie and German-Jewish identities in the nine-teenth and twentieth centuries.

In fact, long before its dispersion throughout the world or destruction inside Hitler's Europe, the Jewish middle class in Germany formed a unique subculture. What were the characteristics of the German-Jewish bourgeoisie? As religious observance diminished over time, what elective affinities bound Jews together in Germany, and particularly in Berlin? In looking at this specific group through the lens of a single family, the Scholems, this book indicates the variety of Jewish involvement in German politics and the diversity of the internal life of the German-Jewish community. Generally speaking, the progress and success of liberalism in Germany widened the avenues for Jewish participation in German politics, but liberalism and Jewish involvement remained highly contested. Within the Jewish community, Zionists clashed with acculturists for the devotion and the electoral support of German Jews. Advocacy groups sought to define the place of Jews in German society, while protofeminist groups sought to redefine the place of women in the organized Jewish community.[5] Notably, these battles were fought not only at the communal level, but also within families, such as the Scholems. Additionally, German Jews frequently followed a certain set of educational and professional trajectories that differentiated them from other Germans.[6] Even more striking were patterns of socialization, identity formation, and cultural preferences, forged in the course of the nineteenth century and refined during the years of the Weimar Republic.[7] In so many ways, the acculturated German-Jewish bourgeoisie had its own specific way of being German and being Jewish and contributing to both worlds.[8] The Scholems were exemplars of this microsociety within German society and within European Jewry.

Studying German-Jewish society before 1933 illuminates the world that the Nazis destroyed. Not only did they compel Albert Einstein, Erich Mendelsohn, and Kurt Weill into exile, but also hundreds of thousands of less famous German Jews, many of whose families had lived in the German lands for centuries. Indeed, the Jews were an important part of the German bourgeoisie before 1933. Despite their relatively small proportion of the total German population, they had a special place in urban life in Germany before the Second World War. They were among the chief producers and consumers of modern culture in Germany. The Jewish middle class was central to journalism, the business community, and the professions of law and medicine in German cities before the Nazi era. Going beyond a review of their contributions to German society, this book elucidates the experiences of Jewish individuals and families within their own milieu and then the place of the German-Jewish microsociety in German society as a whole, and ultimately the world of the German-Jewish bourgeoisie in exile.

In this book I ask readers to re-approach the history of the Jews in Germany. While some writers, including Amos Elon, have thought of the German-Jewish epoch as commencing with Moses Mendelssohn's arrival in Berlin in 1743 or the *Haskalah* (Jewish Enlightenment) in the late eighteenth century, it is only with Jewish emancipation that the door to modernity and Germanness truly opened for Jews living under Prussian rule.[9] In 1812 King Frederick William III issued his "Edict Concerning the Civil Status of the Jews in the Prussian State," which granted rights to ordinary Jews, fostered their adoption of German culture, and permitted their eventual integration into German society. Furthermore, were it not for Frederick William's decree, which was largely a reaction to Napoleon, the Scholems and thousands of Jews like them would not have traveled from the eastern provinces to Berlin and other sites of modernity—a fact that young Gershom Scholem emphasized in his own diary.[10] Thus, it is necessary to commence the discussion of modern German Jewry with emancipation.

In considering the parameters of the modern German-Jewish epoch, it is equally important to reconsider when the curtain descended on the history of German Jewry. It is natural to posit that German Jewry's existence ceased during the Nazi era, and most studies of the topic conclude either with the rise of the Nazi state in 1933 or with the end of the Holocaust in 1945.[11] However, the de-emancipation of the Jews was neither complete nor inevitable in 1933, and, with a few small exceptions, Jewish life in Germany had ended long before 1945. The Nazis disenfranchised the Jews, expunged Jewish contributions from German culture, and placed the Jews in a metaphorical ghetto even before embarking on their genocidal campaign. As Saul Friedländer has noted, by January 1939, there was no longer "any remaining possibility for Jewish life in Germany or for the life of Jews in Germany."[12] Their epoch had ended.

Historians of modern Europe speak of a long nineteenth century, which began with the French Revolution and ended 125 years later with the First World War. Similarly, it is possible to speak of a long German-Jewish century that began with Prussia's emancipation of the Jews in 1812 and ended with the de-emancipation that presaged the Holocaust. By legislating civil rights for the Jews, the Prussian government encouraged the transformation and, ultimately, the integration of German Jewry. By legislating the abolition of civil rights for the Jews, the Nazis removed the Jews from German society. This long century provides the framework for a longitudinal study of German-Jewish history.

However, the situation is more complex, and there was a coda to the German-Jewish epoch. While Nazis did extinguish Jewish life in Germany,

German-Jewish civilization had an afterlife in emigration. The social and cultural history of the German Jews continued as refugees such as the Scholems took their interpersonal connections, cultural practices, and religious traditions with them to new homes. It was an extraordinary transnational development. The situation of German Jews in Palestine (later Israel) has gained scholarly attention in recent decades,[13] but the German Jews' cultural preservation and their contributions to life in other lands, where they were again part of a minority, have only begun to receive greater attention.[14] German Jews, including the Scholems, established themselves in Australia, Brazil, Britain, South Africa, and the United States, among other destinations. This study follows Betty, Reinhold, and Erich to Australia and Gershom to Palestine, where their habits and predilections reveal how they continued to live as Jews and Germans and how they variously defined both identities.

There are many ways to explore the history of German Jewry, particularly when focusing on transformations over the long term. Studies of institutions or select themes illustrate the structures of communal life and specific aspects of German Jewry, but they are frequently depersonalized and say little about the lived experience of individuals.[15] By contrast, Marion Kaplan has helped pioneer fine-grained social history of the Jews in Germany. In examining both the imperial era and the Nazi era, she has explicated the changes wrought on Jewish families, gender dynamics, and interpersonal relations with non-Jewish Germans.[16] Rather than assemble a comprehensive picture from a myriad of unconnected witnesses, I invite readers to follow one family's story, embedded in the broader narrative of the rise, development, and decline of the Jewish bourgeoisie in modern Germany. Considering a single family over the course of several generations provides narrative continuity, and there are many such studies of German-Jewish families.[17] As compelling as several group biographies of the Cassirer, Mosse, Warburg, and Wertheim families are, they speak to the experience of the wealthy and powerful elites. This exposition focuses on the German-Jewish middle class. The Scholems were not grandees of the community or uncommonly famous, but neither were most Jewish families in Germany.

Deborah Hertz has written a history of conversion and assimilation in Berlin, entitled *How Jews Became Germans*. Her study, however, focuses on the years 1770 to 1833, before migrant Jews from Prussian Silesia and Posen, or their descendants, fully engaged with Germanness and Liberal Judaism. Thus, she largely elides the notion of becoming German while staying Jewish, something achieved by generations of Scholems and hundreds of thousands of other Jews. Through their adoption and adaptation of German culture, they became Germans on their own terms and without converting to Protestantism—though true acceptance by their Christian, German neighbors was another matter.

Bourgeois German Jews, such as the Scholems, were anchored in a constellation of common practices and assumptions regarding religion, politics, and culture, though there were also many outliers. However, even outliers such as the Communist Werner Scholem and the Zionist Gershom Scholem still bore the marks of the German-Jewish bourgeoisie whence they came. Additionally, the Jewish bourgeoisie's communal sensibility changed under the impact of external circumstances. Yet, as Marion Kaplan has noted, members of the established Jewish middle class in Germany, and particularly Berlin, were very interconnected. Ties of kinship facilitated business connections, socializing, and marriage brokering. Shared cultural practices, political views, and prejudices regarding the outside world, to say nothing of external antisemitism, helped perpetuate the nature of this milieu. However, not all scholars share this view of the German-Jewish past. Till van Rahden posits that rather than forming a specific German-Jewish subculture, "a kind of civil society parallel to the society of the 'majority culture,'" Jews in Germany exhibited "situational ethnicity." They felt particularly Jewish "in specific situations, such as family life or participation in ethnic associations" and less Jewish in other situations, where "other feelings of belonging" took priority.[18] While it is true that the Jewish identity of bourgeois German Jews mattered less at some times than others, in many of the patterns of their domestic lives and public habits, they were clearly distinct from other Germans. The Scholems and their circle seem to have socialized little with non-Jews, but in a history of his own family, who lived in Breslau, the historian Fritz Stern writes, "Whatever silent prejudices they harbored, Christians and Jews intermingled socially," even in the 1920s.[19] The disparity between the Sterns' experience and the Scholems' experience might be attributable to nuanced differences within the bourgeoisie. For three generations, the Sterns had been prominent physicians and medical researchers and, thus, belonged to a higher social stratum than the Scholems, who were merely printshop owners and only a few generations removed from poverty. Indeed, in Berlin, where Jews made up a considerable part of the wealthiest stratum of society, the Jewish haute bourgeoisie had numerous ties to the aristocracy and even the officer corps, though almost never to the royal court. Nonetheless, members of the Jewish haute bourgeoisie retained their sense of identity. Their closest ties were with each other as friends, relatives, and business associates.[20]

This is more than a social history of German Jewry. It is also a biography of specific individuals, most notably Gershom Scholem, possibly the greatest Judaic studies scholar of the twentieth century and a public intellectual with an international reputation. The prefame lives of famous people are often objects of curiosity, but what differentiates Gershom Scholem from most other renowned German-born Jews is that he, too, had a preoccupation with his early life, which deeply affected his intellectual formation and political proclivities. This fascination with his own biography was matched by his obsession with the historical experience of the Jews in Germany. In the 1960s, he spoke publicly about these topics, and by the 1970s, he had begun publishing reminiscences of his youth, which culminated in the book *From Berlin to Jerusalem*, which Scholem revised and expanded as it appeared in translated editions.[21]

Gershom Scholem's compelling memoir chronicles his family's history and recounts events in his own life from his earliest years until he became a university lecturer in Jerusalem at the age of twenty-seven. Beyond that, it explores and critiques the nature of the German-Jewish bourgeoisie. Cynthia Ozick claimed, "And it is these Jews—this pitiable phenomenon of a passionately loyal citizenry only longing to be good and peaceable Germans—who comprise the furious hidden text of *From Berlin to Jerusalem*."[22] One cannot help but think that this memoir, written after the Holocaust extinguished the German Jews' world, was intended to settle scores with those who did not share Gershom's sentiments on Jewish life in Germany and perhaps even to gloat about his prescience at having left Germany long before the Nazi era. The Jewish community of Germany, and the extended Scholem family itself, was diverse and complicated, but so long as German Jews sought an enduring place in German society—whether they were liberals, like Gershom's parents, or Socialists, like his brother Werner—he regarded them with a combination of condescension, disdain, and some degree of pity. Indeed, Ozick commented, "It is more than an irony, it is an ongoing wound, that *From Berlin to Jerusalem*, incontestably a Zionist book, continues the fraternal drama."[23] The Scholem family and their peers have entered history in an account marked by a framework of post-Holocaust hindsight and a Zionist agenda.[24]

Nonetheless, *From Berlin to Jerusalem* has achieved enormous influence. Nearly every examination of Gershom Scholem's life and work references it, and some studies lean heavily on it. Incidentally, scholars first turned their attention to Scholem's life and its relation to his work right about the time that he was writing *From Berlin to Jerusalem*.[25] Since his death, the scholarly literature on Gershom Scholem has grown large and continues to grow as new generations of scholars encounter him as a historian of religion, philosopher and theologian, literary figure, or eyewitness to German-Jewish history.[26] Additionally, the enduring fascination with the pre-Holocaust German-Jewish intelligentsia, including Walter Benjamin and Hannah Arendt, has also brought attention to Gershom Scholem.[27] In the past few years alone, Gershom Scholem has been the subject of several biographies.[28] Noam Zadoff's study focuses largely on Gershom's intellectual development and inner life, and his family has almost no presence in the narrative. Biographies by Amir Engel and David Biale link Gershom's scholarly work and thought with his life experiences, including his political activism, and provide a context for some of his most important works. Biale, in particular, explores the familial background and milieu that was so important to Gershom Scholem's intellectual, cultural, and social development, but ultimately they remain mainly background for Gershom's life. Here, his family and their world are the story. While Gershom is a critical part of that narrative, the story is not his alone. In fact, Gershom Scholem remained tied to the German-Jewish bourgeoisie, or some aspects of it, long after his emigration, if not for the rest of his life. He was not just *from* the German-Jewish bourgeoisie; he was *of* the German-Jewish bourgeoisie.

While many scholars have researched the life and work of Gershom Scholem, only a few scholars have undertaken examinations of his Communist brother Werner.[29] Mirjam Zadoff looks at Werner, taking his family and his German-Jewish background into consideration. While Ralf Hoffrogge has also contextualized Werner's life and work, his examination largely centers on Werner's experience as a left-wing Socialist and Communist. Additionally, Hoffrogge has a far more judgmental perspective on the past, including the democracy of the Weimar Republic and the comportment of other Scholems, than does my study.

Gershom Scholem lived for most of the twentieth century. He was born in Berlin in 1897 and died in Jerusalem in 1982. However, the thread of his family's story extends much further back, through the Berlin of Kaisers Wilhelm I and Wilhelm II and the founding years of the German Reich, through the Revolution of 1848 in the Prussian capital and the Era of Reaction that preceded it. Before the Napoleonic era and well into the eighteenth century, it stretched to the Prussian province of Silesia, where the Scholems had lived for generations. Gershom was deeply conscious of the Scholems' position as an old Berlin Jewish family and intrigued by their roots in the East. A few weeks after his fifteenth birthday, he wrote the opening lines of his diary: "I am descended from Glogau Jews." Sixty years later, on the first page of his memoir, he noted, "I am descended from a Berlin Jewish family that resided in Glogau in Lower Silesia ('Greater Glogau') until the second decade of the previous century."[30] His story—and their story—was one of long-established Berlin Jewry and migration. For him, the tale ended in Jerusalem, but it did not truly commence in Berlin. It started in the Silesian city of Glogau. And it is there that my narrative begins.

Shortly after gaining basic civil rights, Gershom Scholem's direct ancestor left Glogau for Berlin, where he joined a growing community of religiously traditional Jewish migrants living just steps away from the city's sole synagogue. Life in Berlin, particularly after the emancipation edict of 1812, could not compare to life in provincial Glogau under the old regime. Broader horizons and new opportunities presented themselves. How did decisions about where to live, what occupation to have, and how to raise children denote the development of a German identity and the transformation of a Jewish identity? By the end of the century, after eighty years and three generations in the German capital, the Scholems were unqualifiedly part of the German-Jewish bourgeoisie.

It was into this milieu that Gershom Scholem and his brothers were born. What did their schooling and preprofessional trajectories, religious life, military service, political awakening, and confrontation with antisemitism indicate about how they viewed their world and its opportunities? In answering these questions, it is significant that they were Berliners. They grew up in a city that was expanding in size, wealth, power, and prestige, and not just in terms of general affairs, but also for the Jewish community. Berlin dominated German Jewry, and Berlin Jews were central in shaping the contours of modern Jewish life.[31] New forms of urban life and new possibilities for the Jewish bourgeoisie accompanied the dawn of a new century. Reinhold, Erich, Werner, and Gershom, the sons of Arthur and Betty Scholem, truly had a "Berlin Childhood around 1900," in the words of Walter Benjamin.

Despite the external stability of their world, life in the Scholem household was trying. Arthur, quick-tempered, self-righteous, and domineering, clashed with both his own father and his children. The eldest two sons, Reinhold and Erich, shared many, though not all, of their father's views on politics, society, and religion and would follow in his professional footsteps. By contrast, the youngest two sons, Werner and Gershom, shared their father's temperament, but disdained his politics and views on religion. As they grew to maturity, they did not refrain from sharing their opinions, heightening the tensions at home. How did this experience of opposition and conflict shape them? Though Betty and other relatives tried to maintain peace in the family, the Scholems had a tumultuous domestic life while inhabiting a bourgeois world of security.

And then came the First World War. As Germans rejoiced in the streets in August 1914, Jewish leaders hoped that the atmosphere of national unity would eradicate vestigial prejudices. In the liberal Jewish newspapers that Betty read and even in the Zionists newspapers that Gershom read, there were calls for Germany's Jews to rush to the colors. In fact, Reinhold and Erich were among the young men marching off to war, while Werner, already a Socialist, and Gershom, an incipient Zionist, openly resisted calls for patriotic sacrifice. Eventually, the spirit of 1914 could no longer withstand the experience of prolonged bloody warfare and deprivations on the home front. How did this war against France and Russia end up pitting non-Jewish German against Jewish German and Scholem against Scholem?

The Scholems survived the trenches, trials, food shortages, and influenza pandemic. As the war came to an end, they and so many other Germans looked forward to a return to order. Instead, they experienced five years of disorder: civil war, insurrection from Left and Right, punitive reparations, hyperinflation, and the first stirrings of fascism. However, they also experienced the birth of Germany's first egalitarian democracy. Jews like the Scholems enjoyed unprecedented freedoms *and* encountered more overt antisemitism than ever before. Under these circumstances, coming on the heels of a devastating and futile war, how did German Jews cope and what choices did they make? Indeed, it is here that the political paths of the four Scholem brothers definitively diverged. Eventually, those political choices, accompanied by social and professional choices, sealed their fates in ways that no one could have imagined in 1920.

Yet quotidian life continued, and while there was no return to the halcyon days of the prewar era, a new equilibrium was established in the mid-1920s. What did Germany's political and economic situation mean for the Jewish middle class? In this era of freedom, did bourgeois Jews opt for true assimilation or seek new ways of identifying as Jews and Germans? Among the Scholems, Reinhold, Erich, Werner, and Gershom came into their own, embarking on careers that would define their lives. Two sons stepped into their parents' shoes, taking over the family printing business and continuing the cultural practices that had long characterized the German-Jewish bourgeoisie, particularly in Berlin. By contrast, another son looked to Communist universalism in Germany and saw his future in politics, and yet another son devoted himself to an idiosyncratic form of Jewish particularism, built a home in Palestine, and sought a life of the mind. However, it was by no means clear which path was the surest in 1925, and by the 1930s, the Great Depression and political conflicts—between the German Left and Right, between Stalinist Communists and anti-Stalinist Communists, between

Arabs and Jews—threatened the achievements of the Scholem family and the Jewish middle class.

The looming storm finally broke in 1933 as the Nazis came to power. A reign of terror endangered the livelihoods and the lives of the Jews in Germany, and the Scholems were not spared. What options did they see open to them as the walls closed in around them politically, economically, and socially? More than ever, their long-established paths determined who would live and who would die, who would rest and who would wander. By 1940, as war raged across Europe and around the world, neither the Scholem family in Berlin nor the established Jewish bourgeoisie of Germany would exist any longer.

With limited capacity to help, Gershom Scholem watched his family's plight from afar and the influx of German-Jewish refugees to Palestine up close. As a young man, he had left behind the world of the German-Jewish bourgeoisie and spent the following ten years building a new Jewish home in Palestine. However, in the 1930s, thousands of middle-class German Jews came to Jerusalem, Tel Aviv, and Haifa. They directly transformed the *Yishuv* (the Jewish settlement in Palestine) and indirectly changed the dynamic of Arab-Jewish relations in Palestine. Moreover, as the Scholems of Berlin were brought low by persecution, Gershom Scholem was exalted, winning accolades in academia and notoriety in Zionist political circles.

The Scholems' old world, that of the Jewish bourgeoisie in Germany, dissipated, and in time, they became Israelis and Australians, but with an unmistakable trace of Germanness. Moreover, as the past receded farther away, it became a concern, if not an obsession, for the surviving family members. Reinhold, Erich, and, above all, Gershom Scholem critically engaged with their history, which they variously viewed with nostalgia, bitterness, or even contempt.

This book examines one family and revisits the German-Jewish bourgeoisie on their own terms, within the context of their era, without post-Holocaust hindsight, but it is also an exploration of choices that later had significant consequences. While this story ultimately took its central figures from Berlin to Jerusalem and destinations around the world, as well as to concentration camps within Europe, the heart of this tale is a journey from Glogau, Breslau, and other cities to Berlin, as well as movement within the modernizing metropolis of Berlin. It is a journey of acculturation, class advancement, and refinement. It is about the apogee of the German-Jewish bourgeoisie's unique subculture and the forces that challenged it and occasioned its demise, ending the German-Jewish century.

CHAPTER 1

Origins

From Glogau to Berlin

The city of Głogów sits astride the Oder River in the contemporary Polish province of Lower Silesia. The old town is only an approximate reconstruction of the once beautiful city that was known to the Germans as Glogau. Empty lots from the aftermath of the Second World War still mark parts of the inner city. And while Głogów is a county seat today, it has neither the importance nor the diversity that it once had. There are no indigenous Germans or Jews living there. Only a plaza and memorial plaque mark the site of the synagogue destroyed by the Nazis, and nothing remains of the city's Jewish cemeteries.[1] But it was here that the story of the Scholems began.

In 1742 the Prussian king Frederick II acquired most of the region of Silesia from Austria. Though under Austrian Habsburg rule since 1526, Silesia was largely Polish-speaking. Additionally, with the annexation of Silesia came thousands of Jews. Three more times in the late eighteenth century, Prussia enlarged its Jewish population with the acquisition of territory from Poland. By the time that Poland disappeared from the map of Europe in 1795, divided between Prussia, Austria, and Russia, over two hundred thousand Jews lived under Prussian rule.[2]

Jews living in Prussia were subjects of the king and not full citizens. As such, they were strictly limited in their choice of professions, and Jewish merchants were not even allowed to trade certain commodities. Jews had to deliver silver to the royal mint, had to pay a quarterly protection fee, and were subject to a grievous tax regimen. Jewish communities were held collectively responsible for any damage caused by a Jewish bankruptcy or the acceptance of stolen goods as collateral. Prussian law categorized the Jews into six classes, whose application found its apotheosis in Berlin. The rare few in the highest class, the "generally privileged," could settle freely and could buy houses and land. Jews in the next two classes, both categories of "protected Jews," could not reside wherever they wished and could pass on their rights to only one child. Their other children were among the "tolerated Jews," who needed the patronage of a protected Jew to reside in Berlin and who could only marry Jews from the highest two classes. The next class comprised Jewish community employees, and the lowest class comprised the servants of generally privileged Jews, who could remain in Berlin strictly for the duration of their employment. These regulations served to limit the growth of the Jewish population in Berlin and to exploit the Jews economically.[3] This arrangement suited Prussia's rulers, and there seemed little prospect of changing it as the eighteenth century ended. And then came Napoleon.

In the autumn of 1806, the Kingdom of Prussia went to war against Napoleon's French Empire. At the twin battles of Jena and Auerstedt in October, Napoleon's forces decisively defeated the Prussians, and a few days later the French occupied Berlin. This humiliating defeat convinced many officials in the Prussian government of the need to enact reforms that would strengthen society and make the state more efficient. Over the next few years, serfdom was abolished, freedom of occupation was legislated, and equality before the law was enacted. Modern schools and universities were founded to provide a well-educated citizenry that could serve the state. The reformers hoped to change the fundamental relationship between the people of Prussia and their state.

It was not long before the government's attention turned to the Jews. On 11 March 1812, King Frederick William III issued the "Edict Concerning the Civil Status of the Jews in the Prussian State." Jews in his kingdom could apply for citizenship, which granted them the same civil rights as Prussian Christians. They could reside freely, purchase property, practice any trade, hold teaching positions, and serve in public offices. They would no longer face special taxation, and they were free to marry other Jewish citizens without regulation. In exchange for these rights, Jews were required to bear a fixed surname, needed to use German for business and legal records, and were eligible for military conscription.[4] A new era had begun for the Jews in the German lands. It would last nearly 125 years.

After Napoleon's final defeat in 1815, the Prussian government did not extend the edict's jurisdiction to territories acquired or reacquired by Prussia during and after the struggle against Napoleon. It remained valid only in those areas that were part of Prussia in March 1812, including Brandenburg and Silesia, but excluding Posen, which had a large Jewish population. A patchwork of varying restrictive regulations governed Jewish life in Prussian regions not covered by Frederick William's edict, which was revised and supplemented several times before its replacement in 1847. As late as the 1840s, most Prussian Jews still lacked full civil rights.[5] Nonetheless, the edict was the first step on the path to true emancipation.

A critical requirement for those Jews applying to become Prussian citizens was the use of fixed last names. Historically, Jews had been known by their Hebrew patronymics. For example, Avraham, the son of Moshe, was simply known as Avraham ben Moshe. Avraham's son Nathan was Nathan ben Avraham. While last names were already common among some Jews in this era, many traditional Jews still retained the ways of their ancestors. However, in exchange for civil rights, the Jews of Prussia would now take last names. And so, as the story goes, one day in the late spring or summer of 1812, Scholem, the son of Elias, went to register with the Prussian state authorities in Glogau. When asked what his name was, he replied, "Scholem," a variant of the Hebrew name Shalom. When asked what his first name was, the perplexed Jew replied, "Scholem." Thus, he became known as Scholem Scholem, and a dynasty of German Jews was created.[6]

While this story has entered Scholem family lore, it is apocryphal. The precise origins of the Scholem family name are lost to history. Gershom Scholem believed that it was his great-great-grandmother, Zipporah, along with her five surviving children, who took her late husband's first name as their last name when required to choose one, and a "Scholem, Zipore, Wwe [widow]" was listed among the Jews living in Glogau on 24 March 1812.[7] However, the family may have acquired the surname earlier. Scholem family genealogists note an Abraham Scholem, born in Krakow in 1680, and Prussian archives have record of a protected Jew named Abraham Scholem in Brandenburg in the mid-1700s.[8]

Regardless, before Frederick William changed the fate of Prussia's Jews, Scholem and his wife, Zipporah, lived alongside the 1,500 Jews of Glogau. Jews had lived in Glogau continuously since the Middle Ages, and though their presence was not always welcomed, by 1800, they made up 15 percent of the city's population, making it percentage-wise one of the most Jewish cities in Europe west of the Oder River.[9] Scholem worked as a wagoner or a hauler, and Zipporah worked as an attendant for women who had recently given birth.[10] Other common occupations among their Jewish neighbors were traders or petty merchants and managers of distilleries or breweries owned by local nobles. Some worked as Jewish communal employees, such as teachers, but even they were often compelled to engage in trade on the side to make ends meet. Glogau, where government institutions and the military garrison dominated civic life, offered limited economic opportunities for young Jews. Scholem's son Marcus, born between 1789 and 1800, apprenticed as a baker, and at some point in the years that followed Napoleon's defeat, he made his way to Berlin, capital of the growing Prussian kingdom. Another son, Mathias, born in 1796, also went to Berlin in 1817, and a third son, Lazarus, born in 1808, became a goldsmith in Breslau (today Wrocław, Poland), the Silesian provincial capital.[11] They were just three of the many small-town Jews who left their homes for the possibilities offered by large cities. By the middle of the nineteenth century, approximately 950 Jews remained in Glogau, where they made up only 6.2 percent of the population. By contrast, the Jewish populations of larger cities had increased dramatically. Berlin's Jewish community had grown from 3,300 to 9,600 between 1800 and 1848, and Breslau's had increased from 2,900 to 7,380.[12] Economics and legal reforms had facilitated a centripetal process that would massively expand the size of the Jewish communities in large cities, while those in towns and smaller cities diminished.

Berlin may have been a magnet for those seeking their fortunes, but by European standards, it was not an old or a glamorous city. It had neither the charm of Vienna nor the pedigree of Rome. Compared to many other European capitals, it was considered dour and staid. Founded around the year 1237, it was best known as a royal city, serving since the fifteenth century as the seat of the margraves of Brandenburg and later residence for the kings of Prussia. They transformed Berlin into the administrative center of their kingdom, and the local economy focused on the court. It became a significant garrison town for the Prussian army, and the government encouraged the development of manufacturing industries. Beginning in the late seventeenth century, the city expanded rapidly, increasing from 6,500 residents in 1661 to 61,000 in 1712 to nearly 120,000 in 1763 and over 144,000 in 1783.[13] Because of its rapid growth, the city did not have an entrenched patrician class. It was a city of immigrants. Thousands of settlers came from Bohemia and Holland, but the most prominent immigrant group was the Huguenots, Reformed Protestants who fled Catholic persecution in France and became a major presence in Berlin.

Jews also took their place among the new groups in the city. After having been banished in the 1570s, Jews were readmitted in 1671. Frederick William, ruler of Brandenburg-Prussia, allowed fifty Jewish families, recently expelled from Vienna, to settle in the Brandenburg region, which included Berlin. He hoped that they would help revive the local economy after the devastation of the Thirty Years' War; however, they were not welcomed with enthusiasm. In contrast to the Huguenots, Jews did not receive financial assistance from the state, could not erect houses of worship, and were not granted the right to settle in perpetuity.[14]

Nonetheless, the Jewish community grew and established itself. In 1712 the king finally permitted the construction of a public synagogue, which opened for Rosh Hashanah in 1714. Located at the corner of Heidereuter-gasse and Rosenstrasse, two back streets, the building was not permitted to be higher than the houses around it. As a result, the ground floor was situated below street level. Though the building's exterior was relatively unadorned, the sanctuary featured a soaring ceiling and an ornate baroque Torah ark that resembled a contemporary church altarpiece.[15]

In 1743, the year that Moses Mendelssohn arrived in Berlin, fewer than 2,000 Jews resided in this city of 98,000 inhabitants.[16] Until the 1820s, less than 3,500 Jews lived in Berlin, approximately 2 percent of the city's popula-tion. While most were not wealthy or famous, some did achieve notoriety. Starting in the 1750s, Veitel Heine Ephraim and Daniel Itzig helped finance Frederick the Great's wars, which massively increased Prussia's size. The phi-losopher Moses Mendelssohn was the intellectual guiding light behind the *Haskalah* (the Jewish Enlightenment), which promoted the modernization of Judaism and the integration of Jews into the surrounding society. In the years after the Enlightenment, David Friedländer, son-in-law of Daniel Itzig and a student of Mendelssohn, mediated between the Jewish community and Christian society and lobbied for increased rights for the Jews in Prus-sia. Mendelssohn's sons Joseph and Abraham were among the era's leading bankers. Their sister Brendel (later known as Dorothea) consorted with the leading figures of literary Romanticism and married the philosopher Fried-rich Schlegel. Around the turn of the nineteenth century, Rahel Varnhagen von Ense (née Levin) and Henriette Herz (née de Lemos) became famous for organizing salons where Jews and educated Christians, including Jewish apostates, could meet and discuss contemporary issues in a neutral arena.[17]

From the perspective of traditionalists, the Berlin Jewish community was in the throes of a crisis in the early 1800s. Orthodox religious institutions were increasingly unpopular. Israel Jacobson, who had already founded Reform Jewish temples in Seesen and Kassel, established a Reform prayer house in Berlin, drawing hundreds to his services. When the modernized services moved to a private temple in the home of Jacob Herz Beer, over one-quarter of the city's Jewish population attended. David Friedländer also actively promoted significant changes to Jewish religious practice. Romanticism influenced young Jews to oppose traditional conventions on social comportment, and romantic relationships between modernizing Jews and Christians were not unheard of. Many Berlin Jews ceased to observe Jewish dietary laws and Shabbat, the Sabbath. Some who no longer found meaning in the rituals of their ancestors, but who were nonetheless excluded from high society and professional opportunities, simply converted to Christianity. At the time, Jewish leaders spoke of an epidemic of baptisms among Berlin Jews.[18] With a growing schism between older traditionalists and the young generation, the long-term fate of the community was called into question. Traditional Judaism was on the defensive. However, this trend was soon reversed as Orthodox Jewry reasserted itself with the assistance of King Frederick William III.[19]

The king learned of a private, Reform temple and expressed his disapproval, not because it was Reform, but because it was private. He was suspicious of any private meetings and sects, and this inclination opened the door for Jewish traditionalists to press their case. Orthodox Jews objected to the use of the German language and an organ during a religious service. Although Jewish community leaders and the Prussian interior minister Friedrich von Schuckmann had approved the changes, the traditionalists appealed to the king, who, in December 1823, forbade any Jewish religious innovations. Not coincidentally, the reactionary king also restricted many of the freedoms gained by Jews in 1812. Teaching positions and government posts were definitively closed to Jews, including army veterans and university graduates. One result was an upsurge in the number of conversions in the 1820s, particularly among modernizing young men from the provinces who came to Berlin only to find their professional ambitions thwarted by anti-Jewish legislation. Frustrated by the prohibition on liturgical innovations, many Berlin Jews became indifferent to religion, docilely conformed to Orthodoxy, or even converted to Christianity. At the same time, an influx of migrants from Prussia's eastern provinces increased the number of traditionalists.[20] Marcus and Mathias Scholem from Glogau in Silesia were among the newcomers.

Certain aspects of their lives reflected the new realities for Jews in Prussia and Berlin. One or possibly both of them lived in Heidereutergasse, adjacent to the city's synagogue.[21] While there was no single Jewish neighborhood, Orthodox Jews tended to be poorer and to live on the less prestigious streets where Jews had lived for generations. Among these were Jüdenstrasse, Rosenstrasse, and Heidereutergasse, the latter two being the cross streets of the synagogue.[22] In exchange for gaining citizenship, Jews were now eligible for army service, and Mathias spent one year in the Second Guards regiment of the infantry, a unit originally formed to fight against Napoleon.[23]

Additionally, both brothers married in Berlin. In February 1821, Mathias married a woman named Feile Isaac, whose father worked as a messenger. In February 1832, Marcus married Esther Holländer. Her father, Abraham, had been a merchant in Auras (today Uraz, Poland), a village fifty miles away from the Scholems' hometown of Glogau and less than fifteen miles from Breslau, where their younger brother lived.[24] Since most marriages in this era were arranged, it should be no surprise that Marcus married a woman whose family came from his home region. Moreover, she was twenty-eight or twenty-nine when they married and he even older. Such late marriages were common among Berlin Jews, especially those who were not wealthy. In this era, nearly one-quarter of Jews over fifty remained unmarried, and most of the unmarried men were migrants to Berlin who worked as commercial employees.[25] The Scholems were not the self-employed, Berlin-born elites of the local Jewish community. They were among the masses—at the lower end of the socioeconomic spectrum, religiously traditional, and still maintaining and relying on ties to Jews from their home region.

Mathias worked for the Jewish trader Hirsch Simon Glaser. Published records list "M. Scholem" variously as a trader (*Handelsmann*) or a dealer in second-hand goods (*Trödler*).[26] Despite the official freedom of occupation granted by the king's edict in 1812, the options for Jews could be limited. The government, responding to the complaints of Christian citizens, banned Jews from holding public office or taking up professions that were sponsored by the government. Jews were not permitted to exercise authority over their Christian fellow citizens, whether it be in the town hall, the courthouse, or the schoolhouse. Craft guilds still refused membership to Jews. However, in contrast to many other German cities, Berlin's commercial bourgeoisie was relatively open to Jews, and affluent Jews could join professional organizations. Indeed, trade—loosely defined and at different levels—remained the primary Jewish occupation, but a process of diversification and embourgeoisement was under way. By the middle of the nineteenth century, roughly half of the Jews in the German lands engaged in some form of trade, but the number of Jews who made their living as itinerant traders had diminished considerably.[27] Ever more Jews opened businesses at fixed locations. This was the Scholems' experience, too.

Sometime around 1841 Marcus and his wife opened a kosher restaurant on Klosterstrasse, in the premodern heart of the rapidly growing metropolis. It was quite common for Jewish husbands and wives to work together side by side in a family business, and Esther, calling herself Ernestine, continued the restaurant after her husband's death in February 1845.[28] That their restaurant was kosher, more then twenty years after leaving Glogau, is indicative of the slow pace of acculturation in the mid-nineteenth century. According to Gershom Scholem, the restaurant also became a locus for migrant Jews newly arrived from the provinces, including more than one future relative-by-marriage.[29] Indeed, Berlin was becoming a magnet for Jewish migrants, especially unskilled or semiskilled workers such as Marcus and Mathias had been.

Even in the metropolis, they retained many, if not most or all, of their traditional religious and cultural values.[30] And they existed in the stratum of the lower middle class. By contrast, their children, though raised in the ways of their parents, would make the transition to Western modernity and Germanness. Additionally, they greatly advanced their families' progress toward the upper middle class.

The oldest child of Marcus and Ernestine was born on 16 June 1833. Following Jewish tradition, he was named for his deceased grandfather, Scholem; however, Prussian officials, who had to approve and register each newborn's name, refused to accept the name Scholem Scholem. Thus, the child was legally named Solm Scholem. He had a sister, Jeanette, and a brother, Abraham. Eventually, Solm Scholem adopted the name Siegfried Scholem, and his brother Abraham became Adolph—highly visible manifestations of their transition to German culture—even as some "German" names, including Siegfried and Siegmund, came to be seen as "Jewish" names.[31] In contrast, their parents determined their schooling, which still leaned toward the traditional. While most Jewish children in Berlin in the 1840s attended non-Jewish schools—which, incidentally, accelerated their adoption of German culture, including the German language—young Solm attended the Berlin Jewish community's school for boys, led by the pedagogue Baruch Auerbach since 1829. However, Berlin may have been an exception among Jewish communities. As late as 1864, nearly half of all Jewish children in Prussia still attended Jewish schools.[32]

The climb to secure middle-class status was difficult. By midcentury, half of German Jewry was still poor, with one-third to one-quarter in the lowest tax brackets. Only 15 to 30 percent had reached the middle and upper tax brackets.[33] Any reversal of fortune could wipe out years of effort. Marcus Scholem's death in 1845 left his family in difficult circumstances, and two years later, at the age of fourteen, Siegfried left school. During this era, for both political and economic reasons, community leaders discouraged Jewish men from entering commerce and steered them into crafts.[34] Siegfried's guardian had intended for him to take a position working for the fashion house of Hermann Gerson, but he ended up taking an apprenticeship with the publisher Julius Sittenfeld. For five years, Siegfried learned the printer's trade and became a typesetter, working at various printshops in Berlin and Breslau. To become a journeyman printer, he set in type a collection of German poems. He ultimately passed the required examination to become a licensed lithographer.[35] Siegfried's choice of profession placed him at the center of a crucial development in the history of Germany: the proliferation of German-language print culture.

Siegfried began his apprenticeship in 1847. One year later, the Revolution of 1848 led to a massive increase in the number of newspapers, pamphlets, and posters, which helped shape public opinion and the spread of information. Additionally, in the late nineteenth century, newspapers helped newcomers comprehend and navigate life in the metropolises. By the time Siegfried died in 1901, Berlin was a city saturated by print media. Moreover, with modernity, all sorts of new niches emerged in the print market, including work for the expanding government, the publication of new scientific literature, and printing for modern corporations. Siegfried's first employer, Verlag Julius Sittenfeld, was a part of this process. It was known for publishing medical literature and print work for the Berlin city administration. In the mid-nineteenth century, Sittenfeld's firm also printed Jewish religious books.[36]

The rising German-Jewish middle class formed a discrete and endogamous community within the broader German society. Socially mobile German Jews strove to dress and speak like members of the educated, non-Jewish German bourgeoisie, but they almost always married other Jews. Some Jews converted to Christianity and married in the church, but they tended to belong to the economic and cultural elite, and even so, the number of Berlin Jews who became Christians stopped growing in the 1830s and declined precipitously after a spike around 1840.[37] When Siegfried married on 21 October 1860, it was to Amalie Schlesinger, whose family background was rather similar to his own. Marriages were still brokered, if not completely arranged, and spouses were selected based on financial and familial considerations.[38] Amalie was born into a religious Jewish family in the Silesian town of Beuthen (now Bytom, Poland) in 1837. Her father, David, originally from the province of Posen, had been a clockmaker in Beuthen and Lissa (now Leszno, Poland) before becoming a wool dealer on Berlin's Jüdenstrasse.[39]

Siegfried was not a man content to work for others, and on 1 April 1864, using a loan of 200 thalers, he and Amalie founded their own printshop: Siegfried Scholem, Book and Lithograph Printers. It was almost an expected step, as roughly 70 percent of Berlin Jews were self-employed, compared to 38 percent of the non-Jewish population.[40] A typical Jewish enterprise in

Berlin was a small family business, like Siegfried's. But self-employment was no guarantee of success. In fact, for many years, his firm struggled. Health problems and the impact of Otto von Bismarck's wars strained the print-shop.[41] However, immediately following the German victory over France in 1871, Siegfried prepared and published a program to accompany the victory parade of the Prussian army through the streets of Berlin.[42]

Eventually, Siegfried Scholem achieved a notable level of prosperity. He, like 60 percent of all German Jews in this era, belonged to the middle or upper tax bracket.[43] Indeed, this was a time of economic growth for Germany. French reparations from the Franco-Prussian War fueled a boom in Germany. Even after the boom collapsed in 1873, the German economy generally continued to grow, though growth rates were diminished. The service sector—which included many Jewish entrepreneurs and service providers—significantly outpaced the agricultural and industrial sectors between 1873 and 1895.[44]

As the Scholems attained prosperity, their lives took on the trappings of middle-class life. Amalie Scholem took vacations at European spas such as Karlsbad.[45] And, like many Jews in the 1880s, Siegfried and his family moved outside of Old Berlin, the area enclosed by the city's fortification moat. Considerable numbers of Jews now lived in the Stralauer District, Spandauer District, Friedrichstadt, and Luisenstadt, neighborhoods that ringed the old town. After several intermediate stops, around 1890 the Scholems settled at Sebastianstrasse 20, in the Luisenstadt, which had a mix of residential and commercial buildings. The Scholems' residence was indicative of their nascent upper-middle-class status. It was a grand four-story, stone building. The upper floors housed apartments and offices, while the ground floor contained various shops, including, conveniently, a printer's supply store. Surrounding the entrance to the building was a number of royal warrants for a silversmith's firm.[46]

In time Siegfried and Amalie had four sons: Arthur, born in 1863; Theobald, born in 1873; Max, born in 1875; and Georg, born in 1877. Their generation would complete the process of modernization begun by their father. At the same time, they pondered mutable German and Jewish identities. Even with the embrace of German culture, complete abandonment of Judaism was rare. Most German Jews strove to achieve a synthesis between these two identities.[47] Over time, as a bourgeois German-Jewish subculture developed, its members had a shared understanding of what it meant to be German and Jewish.

Siegfried had received his elementary education from the Jewish community in the shadow of the Old Synagogue. His sons received their education from the state, along with 62 percent of Jewish children in Prussia in their era.[48] One by one, the Scholem boys attended a *Gymnasium*—a university-preparatory secondary school—namely, the Luisenstädtisches Realgymnasium. In the nineteenth century, very few boys attended secondary school, and even fewer finished. One reason was the sheer expense of education. State schools were not free. Educating three or four sons could be a major expense for the middle class. In the year 1895–1896, Georg's school fees were 130 marks. At this time, a senior teacher in a Gymnasium made as little as 2,700 marks; a stationmaster, second-class, made a minimum of 1,800 marks; and a building inspector earned between 3,600 and 5,700 marks.[49] Naturally, a laborer earned much less. Nonetheless, many Jewish families undertook the expense, even if their sons never intended to complete the course of study. Gymnasium attendance was often more about gaining the general education and cultural refinement that characterized a member of the German upper middle class than eventual admission to university. In 1886–87, when Max Scholem started at the Luisenstädtisches Realgymnasium, 22 percent of Jewish boys in Prussia attended higher secondary schools as compared to less than 5 percent of non-Jewish boys.[50] In fact, in 1886, 86 out of 526 pupils at Max's school were Jewish, and the school began offering Jewish religious instruction. Fifteen years later, the student body was nearly 25 percent Jewish.[51]

The Scholems' educational attainments were very much in line with the German-Jewish bourgeoisie of their generation. Arthur, Theobald, and Max all studied at the Luisenstädtisches Realgymnasium, but they did not reach the final year of secondary education. Since they were destined to follow their father into the printer's trade, and presumably take over his business one day, they left school early to apprentice as printers.[52] Arthur spent a year working for a printer in London while living with an uncle, and returned to Germany in 1883. In England he supposedly learned English well enough to read the *Manchester Guardian*, a newspaper where his son apprenticed as a printer a generation later.[53]

Siegfried's youngest son, Georg, took a different path: he became a physician. It was not uncommon in rising Jewish families, such as the Scholem family, for the older sons to sacrifice their own educational ambitions so that the youngest son might attend a more prestigious secondary school and study at university. Similarly, older sons might support the educational and professional aspirations of the youngest son after having attained their own success, as was the case in the family of the professor and famous diarist Victor Klemperer. In part, this was because having a "Doktor" or "Herr Professor" in the family was a mark of prestige.[54] Georg Scholem's brothers attended a *Realgymnasium*, a high school that did not require ancient Greek and offered considerably less Latin than a humanistic Gymnasium. Though they did not earn their diplomas, if they had gone on to university study, they would have found that their choice of curriculum was limited. Realgymnasium alumni were not eligible to study medicine, the most popular subject of study for Jewish university students until the late nineteenth century.[55]

As a result of this restriction, Georg Scholem needed a different education. He began his schooling at the Luisenstädtisches Realgymnasium, but at the age of twelve he transferred to the more elite Köllnisches Gymnasium, where he studied Greek and Latin, among other subjects. He took his school-leaving examination (*Abitur*) in September 1895.[56] Passing this examination placed him in the top 1 to 2 percent of boys his age in Prussia. In his class of fourteen, there were six Jews. Three, including Georg, were going to study medicine, two engineering, and one law. In contrast, their non-Jewish classmates were going to study law, military medicine, philology, forestry, or theology.[57] After graduation, Georg enrolled at the University of Berlin, where he studied for a time with Rudolf Virchow, founder of the field of cellular pathology and a pioneer of modern medical education. For most, if not all, of his student years, Georg lived at his parents' home, and he did not join a fraternity, even though that was popular among fun-loving and connection-seeking students. It is not clear whether this was by choice or because the Scholems could not afford or did not approve of such frivolity. Nonetheless, in 1901, he completed his medical studies with a dissertation on a mercury-based treatment for syphilis. It was dedicated in gratitude to his parents. Georg's studies were followed by a stint as a ship's doctor. His most notable souvenir from this era was a talking parrot named Pedro who returned to Berlin with him.[58]

Siegfried died in 1901, and he left his printing firm to his sons Theobald and Max. By that point, Arthur already had his own printshop, and Berlin had two Scholem printing firms. It was not supposed to have been this way. After completing his apprenticeship and *Wanderjahr*, Arthur returned to Berlin and entered his father's firm, but it was a stormy association. Both men had strong wills and quick tempers, and in 1892 Arthur started his own printshop, which he ran with considerable help from his wife, Betty Hirsch, whom he had married in 1890.

In contrast to Arthur's family background among the commercial bourgeoisie, Betty's siblings were intellectuals, and some of her relatives were quite wealthy. Both her brother, Hans, and her sister, Käte, had doctorates, his in chemistry and hers in medicine. Their brother-in-law Arthur Scholem printed both dissertations.[59] After his graduation, Hans entered the clay industry and became prominent in German ceramics.[60] Käte, who graduated from the University of Freiburg in 1904, was among the earliest female university graduates in Germany. Freiburg, in the relatively liberal German state of Baden, was the first German university to permit regular enrollment of women, most of whom were aspiring physicians. Most Jewish female university students enrolled to study one of the sciences or mathematics, with medicine being exceptionally popular as it seemed to offer the best career prospects. Nearly 30 percent of all female doctors were Jewish.[61] Käte's most famous patient may have been Elly Heuss-Knapp, a liberal politician, social reformer, former Freiburg University student, and wife of the future West German president Theodor Heuss. Heuss credited "Miss Dr. Käte Hirsch" with saving the life of his wife and newborn son after a complicated birth.[62] Betty's maternal uncle was photographer to the royal court and very wealthy.[63] While Betty did not study at a university, she was an intelligent woman. Not only did she help manage the family business, but she also wrote plays for amateur performance.[64] The Hirsches were also more connected to the Jewish community than the Scholems. Arthur's father had been a dues-paying member of the Jewish community, but Betty's father, Hermann Hirsch, had worked as a Jewish communal employee in various small towns before moving to the metropolis, where he donated land for a synagogue in Charlottenburg, an upper-middle-class town immediately adjacent to Berlin. Dedicated in 1889–90, it had seats for 280 people. At the time of his death, Hirsch was the sole owner of the synagogue's building, and the Jewish community of Berlin did not take over the property until 1937.[65]

While Arthur Scholem saw himself as Jewish, he had an attenuated connection to Jewish religious tradition. He celebrated Passover seders and Friday night dinners at home or, more commonly, at the home of one of his brothers; however, his observance entailed "deliberate mockery," as Gershom Scholem later recalled. The family would recite the *Kiddush* blessings, but the Shabbat candles were used to light cigarettes and cigars. During Passover, matzo and bread were kept next to each other in adjacent baskets.[66] If Friday night dinner did not signify the beginning of the day of rest, it was at least a sort of "gastronomic Judaism."[67] By contrast, Arthur treated Yom Kippur as any other day, going to work and eating regularly rather than fasting.[68]

Moreover, many German Jews, including the Scholems, celebrated Christmas. In December a Christmas tree adorned the living room of their family's home. On Christmas Eve, carols were sung and a goose or hare consumed. Christmas was so integrated into their routine that Arthur and Betty Scholem failed to note the dissonance in their celebrating it. For example, they gave Gershom a framed portrait of the Zionist leader Theodor Herzl for Christmas in 1911. To them, it seemed like a perfect gift for their son, considering his Zionist proclivities.[69] The holiday had become such a part of Jewish life in Germany that in 1904 the satirical magazine *Schlemiel* featured a cartoon with a nine-branched menorah metamorphosing into a multibranched Christmas tree. In the twenty-first century, the Jewish Museum Berlin included in its permanent exhibition a model living room of a late nineteenth-century, bourgeois Jewish home, complete with a Christmas tree.[70] For the Scholems and other similar German Jews, Christmas was considered a German national or German ethnic holiday, disassociated from its religious origins.[71]

Despite Arthur's celebration of Christmas, his brother Theobald rejected the holiday. At his home, Hanukkah was celebrated, and he gave gifts of challah bread rather than *Stollen*, the traditional German Christmastime fruitcake. It was Theobald who read the Hebrew Haggadah at the Scholems' Passover seders. Exceptionally for his time, Theobald was also a Zionist. He was involved in Jewish sporting organizations and attended Zionist conferences. In his home, he had a collection box for the Jewish National Fund, and under his leadership, the family firm printed the Zionist newspapers *Jüdische Rundschau* and *Die Welt*.[72] Theobald's wife, Hete, had even more pronounced Zionist sympathies. She studied Hebrew, followed events in Palestine, and attended Zionist conferences. In later years, she became a sounding board for young Gershom on Jewish matters.[73]

Even as most German Jews ceased observing traditional rituals, they retained some practices, which were modified or personalized. The Scholems' Shabbat evening dinner was not Orthodox, but it remained an important family ritual. Indeed, many urban German Jews no longer celebrated holidays in the traditional manner, but they continued to recognize them, and family gatherings anchored their secular or semisecular Judaism.[74] Many Jews attended synagogue only in observance of Rosh Hashanah and Yom Kippur, earning them the sobriquet "three-day Jews."[75] Though Betty did not fast, she did accompany her own mother to synagogue, unlike her husband.[76] Indeed, assimilating women generally retained an attachment to ritual in their sphere—the home—longer than assimilating men did in theirs—the office and the synagogue. Nonetheless, all four Scholem brothers voluntarily remained dues-paying members of Berlin's Jewish community, and Arthur's family nominally affiliated with the Liberal synagogue on Lindenstrasse.[77] Arthur, possibly the least religious of his brothers, proudly considered himself a Jew. Gershom Scholem recalled: "Once or twice a year my father used to make a speech at the dinner table in praise of the mission of the Jews, which, according to him, was to proclaim pure monotheism and a purely rational morality to the world. Baptism was unprincipled and servile."[78]

While conversion to Christianity was exceptionally rare in the Scholem family, mixed marriages were not unknown. Approximately 13 percent of Prussian Jews married non-Jews around 1910, with the mixed marriage rate in Berlin around 18 percent. In the second half of the 1910s, over 20 percent of Prussian Jews and a full third of Berlin Jews married non-Jewish partners.[79] It was inevitable that this trend would affect the Scholems' family circle. In 1911, at the age of thirty-eight, Betty's sister, Dr. Käte Hirsch, married a colleague, Walter Schiepan. Although no one in Arthur's family showed the man hostility, he was never truly treated as part of the family, according to Gershom. Arthur was sure that the marriage would not last. The issue of intermarriage drew closer to home during the First World War, when, to his father's great consternation, Werner married a non-Jewish, working-class girl, and Reinhold allegedly had a relationship with the daughter of a high-ranking, but impecunious official who was not Jewish.[80]

Among a certain stratum of society, Christians and Jews mixed quite readily in Berlin. Indeed, the Jewish haute bourgeoisie played a critical role in the economic, cultural, and civic life of the German capital. In the years before World War I, twelve of Berlin's twenty wealthiest men were of Jewish ancestry, though few were practicing Jews. Jews made up the majority of the city's leading businessmen's organization.[81] Jewish Berliners were responsible for the vast majority of endowments bestowed on local museums, and Jewish grandees helped found the Kaiser Wilhelm Society for the Advancement of Science (Kaiser-Wilhelm-Gesellschaft zur Förderung der Wissenschaften). Renamed the Max Planck Society in 1946, it remains Germany's leading center for scientific and scholarly research. Affluent and educated Jews supplied a vastly disproportionate share of the creators and consumers of art in Berlin. In the words of one historian, "It is often difficult to distinguish clearly between what was 'cosmopolitan city-style' and what was Jewish."[82] Theodor Fontane, nineteenth-century Germany's greatest novelist and chronicler of Prussian society, wrote that "all our liberty and higher culture, at least here in Berlin, are being predominantly transmitted by wealthy Jewry."[83]

Even the Scholem family, part of the middle class, participated in non-Jewish or nonsectarian civic life. As a part of their acculturation to German society, the Scholems engaged in the most German of sports in the nineteenth century: gymnastics. Born of the German nationalist uprising against Napoleon, gymnastics was long associated with German patriotism. There is no doubt that, in the early nineteenth century, the movement's leaders exhibited clear anti-Jewish sentiments, yet in the course of the nineteenth century, thousands of acculturated young Jews, sharing a vision of German patriotism, entered the movement.[84] Their participation attested to

their love of Germanness and underscored their virility in the face of antisemites' claims that Jews were weak and unmanly. As a young man, Arthur
Scholem edited a book entitled *Allerlei für Deutschlands Turner* (Miscellany for
Germany's Gymnasts). His brothers Theobald and Max were even greater
gymnastics enthusiasts. Both were members of the Berliner Turner-Verein
(Berlin Gymnastics Association). They served as club officers for many years,
and Theobald wrote and published the special commemorative book for the
club's fiftieth anniversary in 1900. Max remained a member for thirty-six
years, until his death in 1929, and was feted by the club on the silver anniversary of his membership. For many years, religious affiliation seems to
have had no role in membership. The club registry had no entry space for
members' religion, and the membership rolls were dotted with surnames
such as Blumenthal, Goldstein, and Israel. One of the club's most celebrated
members was Gustav Felix Flatow, a German Jew who won two gold medals
at the Olympic Games in 1896 and participated in the 1900 games.[85]

By the turn of the twentieth century, antisemitism pervaded gymnastics
organizations in Germany, and specifically Jewish gymnastics organizations
were established. Theobald Scholem left the Berliner Turner-Verein on 7
April 1904, twelve years after joining, and became an avid participant in the
new Jewish-national sporting groups.[86] He helped found the Bar Kochba
club of Berlin, the oldest Jewish sports club in Germany, and from 1905 to
1907 he was chairman of the Jewish Gymnastics Association (Jüdische Turnerschaft), the umbrella organization for all Jewish gymnastics clubs in the
German-speaking world. His ideas led this group to resolve that its goal was
"the cultivation of gymnastics as a means of elevation of the Jewish tribe
[des jüdischen Stammes] in the sense of the Jewish national idea."[87]

The relationship between German Zionism and Jewish gymnastics
changed over time. In 1905 the organization proclaimed, "Zionism and the
Jewish gymnastics movement rest on the same basis; however, their goals
are not congruent." Indeed, at that time, the Jewish Gymnastics Association
abjured politics: "Our association fundamentally withdraws from politics.
Its goal is qualified and limited to the Jewish-national principle. The means
of achieving this goal is gymnastics."[88] That differentiation notwithstand-
ing, many Zionists, including Max Nordau, one of Theodor Herzl's chief
acolytes, considered gymnastics to be a vital means to regenerate the body
of the Jewish nation (metaphorically) by regenerating the bodies of Jews
(literally).[89] By the time of the First World War, approximately 9,300 Jews
participated in Jewish gymnastics organizations, making them a presence in
central European Jewish life and providing a space where Jews could engage
in sports without antisemitism.[90]

Organizational life was very important to the German middle class, with a myriad of clubs and associations for every social, cultural, and political interest. In promoting their own causes, members of the Jewish bourgeoisie replicated this pattern. This was an era that saw a proliferation of specifically Jewish organizations in Germany. The Central Association of German Citizens of the Jewish Faith (Central-Verein deutscher Staatsbürger jüdischen Glaubens), founded in 1893, fought for Jewish rights and against antisemitism. It appealed to people's reason and not infrequently the courts in its efforts. Jews also had their own student fraternities and sports clubs. The League of Jewish Women (Jüdischer Frauenbund) served as a vehicle for Jewish social welfare and the preservation of Jewish culture, alongside its activist work to combat sex trafficking. B'nai B'rith lodges were founded in Germany in 1882, and 12 lodges with 1,150 members were incorporated in 1885. By 1912, 79 lodges had 8,610 members. These organizations were not only a reaction to the antisemitism that precluded Jews from joining certain groups, but also a conscious effort to create Jewish social space. Most German Jews belonged to the liberal middle class, and clubs and associations were central to their social life.

Even if Arthur and Betty Scholem did not share the Jewish national outlook of some of their peers, they did share their peers' German liberal political views. In an era when most newspapers had a strong political orientation and one's choice of newspaper said much about one's worldview, Arthur Scholem read the *Berliner Tageblatt* and the *Manchester Guardian*.[91] The *Berliner Tageblatt* was owned by the Jewish newspaper magnate Rudolf Mosse and his family and was edited by the Jewish journalist Theodor Wolff. It represented the views of the politically liberal, sophisticated, urban bourgeoisie, which was, incidentally, disproportionately Jewish.[92] The only newspaper in Berlin that could rival the *Tageblatt* in its level of sophistication and influence among the city's white-collar elite was the *Vossische Zeitung*, owned, starting in 1914, by the Jewish Ullstein family. This two-hundred-year-old grand dame of German journalism was known to its loyal readers, including Betty Scholem, as "Aunt Voss," and it, too, represented a liberal political perspective.[93]

The Scholems' interest in newspapers was more than passive. As printers, they were deeply tied to Berlin's vibrant press. Many newspapers outsourced their printing to private printshops, such as the Scholem family firms, and newspaper publishers had warm relations with the Scholems.[94] Nonetheless, Arthur's firm struggled to establish itself in its early years, and middle-class prosperity was by no means certain. In November 1899, the firm entered into bankruptcy proceedings, which compelled Arthur to transfer management to Betty temporarily.[95] The following year, the firm recovered, and Arthur eventually found a number of market niches that would secure his future.

Jewish merchants were at the forefront of many trends in modern commerce, including offering new products, advertising widely, and selling via mail order. The Schocken department store chain, with branches across Germany, was known for its innovations in marketing, quality control, and consumer or test market research.[96] However, Arthur Scholem was also a commercial pioneer. When phonographs became popular, he became a leading printer of record labels, with customers all over Europe and the Middle East. His firm received orders by telegraph, making reference to examples in catalogues that had been previously distributed. Orders received on Thursday were shipped out on Saturday and arrived only a few days later. The quick turnaround enabled Arthur to compete successfully with printers in London for the English market until World War I cut the Scholems off from their customers. Arthur Scholem's other innovation, preprinted forms, led to a booming trade and the creation of a separate firm called Formular-Verlag. With the increasing regulation of modern life, there was a huge demand for forms that could be filled in easily. Arthur, who had long been active in the insurance association for printers and who was known in his industry as an expert on insurance matters, recognized the potential in exploiting this growing bureaucratization. He sent insurance companies a book on efficient management as well as samples of his forms. Soon, the orders came pouring in.[97] Thus, the Scholems, practitioners of an old modern trade—printing—became agents of an important aspect of the new modernity—standardization.

When Scholem ben Elias died in Glogau in 1809, Germany was overwhelmingly agrarian and rural. Exclusive guilds dominated the manufacturing economy, while the aristocracy dominated politics and culture, and less than twenty-five million people lived in the German lands. When his grandson Siegfried died in Berlin in 1901, over fifty-five million people lived in Germany. The country was rapidly urbanizing and industrializing, and the urban bourgeoisie of education and property had become the dominant class in society. A consumer-oriented economy, served by a modern service sector, was emerging and overtaking the older economy. Life was becoming increasingly urbanized, standardized, and secular. Jews were both harbingers and conveyors of this modernization process, and Arthur Scholem's life exemplified this ongoing transition. His four sons, born in the 1890s, were undoubtedly modern German Jews and the beneficiaries of life in Berlin at the apogee of the Belle Époque.

CHAPTER 2

Berlin Childhood around 1900

Growing Up in the Growing Metropolis

In 1900 Germany seemed to be a land of tre-
mendous opportunities. The country had been united for almost thirty years,
and it had been largely at peace the whole time. Its population was rapidly
growing through improvements in public health. National income and per
capita income were steadily rising. In less than two generations, Germany had
gone from an economic backwater to one of the world's three leading industrial powers, and it soon rivaled Britain for economic domination in Europe.[1]

Berlin, the German capital, was known for its dynamism. It was home
to burgeoning modern industries, including internationally known electrical
firms such as AEG and Siemens & Halske, and migrant workers from Prussia's largely Polish eastern provinces and other parts of Germany streamed
into the city to work in the new factories. Along the boulevards of the city
center and soon in the new western suburbs, modern department stores
catered to the tastes of the bourgeoisie. By 1910 Berliners could travel on an
underground rail system or in double-decker motor busses. Berlin was considered a place of innovation that drew scientists, artists, and entrepreneurs.
The Austrian writer Stefan Zweig recalled:

> In fact, I came to Berlin [in 1901] at a very interesting, historical
> moment. . . . Vienna above all, with its century-long tradition, its
> concentrated power, and its natural talent, was until then still vastly

superior to Berlin. However, in recent years, with the rapid economic rise of Germany, the page was turning. The large companies and the wealthy families moved to Berlin, and new wealth, paired with a strong sense of daring, opened to architecture and theater greater opportunities than in any other German city. . . . Vienna, tied to the old, worshipping its own past, proved to be cautious and non-committal towards young people and bold plans. But in Berlin, which wanted to develop quickly and individualistically, one looked for the new. So it was only natural that young people from throughout Germany and even from Austria thronged to Berlin, and the results proved to the talented among them that they were right.[2]

Once known as "Athens on the Spree" for its cultural and educational institutions, this city of two million residents was now called "Chicago on the Spree" for its growth and bustling economy.[3] It was the city of the future.

Berlin was also home to Germany's leading Jewish institutions. Living in close proximity to the centers of political, economic, and cultural power, the leaders of Berlin's Jewish community were in a position unlike any other in Germany. While Jewish notables in other regions grumbled about the arrogance of their coreligionists in the capital and resented Berlin's leadership, they generally acquiesced to it. Additionally, Jewish Berliners were often at the forefront of many trends of modernization. Indeed, as both Jews and Berliners, they were the vanguard of the vanguard in numerous cases.[4]

Even though Jews made up only 4 percent of the city's population, their absolute numbers were growing rapidly. In 1871, the year that the German Empire was founded, 36,015 Jews lived in Berlin. Only twenty-eight years later, 108,044 Jews lived in the Berlin area. By 1910, 143,975 lived in Greater Berlin.[5] Many neighborhoods had a marked Jewish character. This was particularly true of the Scheunenviertel (literally "Barn Quarter") and the adjacent area around Oranienburger Strasse, just a few blocks north of the Old Synagogue. In the seventeenth century, the barns that stored hay for the city's horse market were located here. Less than two hundred years later, it was a densely populated inner-city neighborhood and home to the city's leading Jewish institutions.[6]

As the city grew over time, wealthier Jews moved away from the old neighborhoods. Poor Jews from Posen, Silesia, Galicia, and even Russia came to the city, seeking economic opportunity or simply more freedom. They often lived near the numerous prayerhouses, schools, libraries, and kosher facilities in the Scheunenviertel. Meanwhile, in the 1880s, acculturated Jews increasingly moved to neighborhoods just outside the original old city and in the 1910s to the suburbs outside Berlin's historic city limits. In 1885 less than 2 percent of Berlin-area Jews lived outside Berlin proper. By 1905 more than 20 percent lived in the western suburbs, and in 1910, more than 30 percent did.[7] Near rectilinear boulevards with new cafés, department stores, and eventually cinemas, they founded liberal synagogues. In contrast to many other Jews who left the city core, however, Arthur Scholem did not move his family farther west. They remained in central Berlin, not far from the decrepit houses and narrow alleyways of the Fischerkietz (literally "Fishermen's Neighborhood") and the palaces along the Unter den Linden boulevard. It was here, in a comfortable middle-class home, only a few blocks from where Arthur grew up, that Arthur and Betty raised their sons Reinhold (born 1891), Erich (1893), Werner (1895), and Gerhard (1897), later known as Gershom. While it is impossible to know for certain why they remained there when others moved to the suburbs, it is likely that the close proximity to Berlin's newspaper district was the reason. Both the family home and their printshop were only a short walk from the headquarters of Berlin's leading newspapers.

Although nearly two million people inhabited Berlin in 1900, the city could feel like a small town, especially for Arthur Scholem's family, whose social networks were circumscribed and whose places of business and schools were in a small area. In fact, Betty Scholem quipped, "The world is small and Berlin a village."[8] The Scholems' circle of acquaintances was deeply rooted in the Jewish bourgeoisie of the city. These were families whose grandfathers had been poor peddlers, but in this era, they enjoyed affluence as small-time manufacturers, businessmen, and professionals. Even without always consciously recognizing it, the Scholems circulated among assimilated, middle- and upper-middle-class Jewish families like themselves, in a world where it could seem that everyone was somehow related or connected through business. In Berlin and other cities, the Jewish bourgeoisie formed its own class within a class with its own culture, characterized by similar views on politics and religion, employment in certain industries, and membership in specific clubs.

Moreover, Gershom and his brothers' spatial world was limited. Rather than the expansive boulevards of suburban Charlottenburg and Schöneberg, their immediate surroundings were the Luisenstadt and the twin neighborhoods of Fischerinsel and Neukölln am Wasser, on both sides of a narrow branch of the Spree River. Locals spoke a thick Berlin dialect and seemed provincial despite living in a world city.[9] From the windows of their home on the Friedrichsgracht quay, the Scholem brothers could watch barges laden with coal drift by. Gershom even recalled leaning out the window and spitting seeds into the river. Around the time he was nine years old, the family moved just across the river, to Neue Grünstrasse. Near their home, the Scholem boys could play in the Köllnischer Park and visit the Märkisches Museum, which chronicled the history of Berlin and its environs in a historicist red-brick building that echoed the region's traditional architecture.[10] Leaving the neighborhood, barely a mile away, one could quickly reach the exquisite museums of Berlin's Museum Island, the pomp of the royal City Palace and Armory, and the culture of the opera house and royal theater. Arthur's printshop was close to the family's apartment, and the bustle and business of the newspaper district was a five-minute walk away. Equally importantly for Gershom and his brothers, their grandmother Amalie lived two blocks from their home.

However, the suburbs increasingly appealed to the rising Jewish bourgeoisie. Not only did newer, more modern neighborhoods provide an alternative to the congestion and dated amenities of the city center, but they also offered new social and psychological vistas. Rather than living among the working class or the aristocracy, upper-middle-class bourgeois Berliners could live in districts that they might dominate. They could disproportionately influence the culture and even the politics of these areas.

Unlike Arthur and Georg, who remained in the neighborhood where they grew up, their brothers Theobald and Max moved their printshop and their homes to the suburbs a few years after the turn of the century. Siegfried Scholem, Book and Lithograph Printers, was located at one end of Hauptstrasse (literally "Main Street") in the suburb of Schöneberg, while Theobald made his home near the other end of Hauptstrasse, in the suburb of Friedenau. Max lived in between, also near the Schöneberg Hauptstrasse, and Betty Scholem's siblings were neighbors, as well. Once a small village a few miles from the Prussian capital, in the first decades of the twentieth century, Schöneberg was a thriving city immediately adjacent to Berlin and a part of the larger metropolis. Farmers' fields had given way to grand apartment buildings and tenements. Between wide avenues, smaller streets framed lots with new construction sites. In the years before World War I, Schöneberg built a city hall to rival Berlin's, and its citizens could travel on their city's modest subway system: one line with five stations.[11] The city was also home to an increasingly large Jewish population by 1910, numbering 11,641 people, 6.7 percent of the city's total population.[12] While he worked in Schöneberg, Theobald lived in Friedenau. Unlike many Berlin suburbs, which traced their origins to medieval villages, Friedenau was a new town, founded in the 1870s. Its residents were generally well-off and often lived in single-family homes or five-story buildings with elevators and spacious apartments. The town was popular with politicians, entrepreneurs, and successful artists who commuted by rail to Berlin.[13] Nonetheless, Friedenau had only a small Jewish population before World War I: 870 people, 2.5 percent of the total population.[14] In April 1920, Berlin annexed its immediate suburbs, including Schöneberg and Friedenau, which were then merged into a single city district, Berlin-Schöneberg.

For German Jews, extended families provided connections, financial assistance, and emotional support and were often their primary social circle. This was certainly true of the Scholem family, whose members socialized frequently with each other despite the miles between them and the competition between their printing firms.[15] They celebrated family milestones in grand style, with banquets accompanied by skits and singing. Befitting a family of printers, beautifully designed and printed programs were distributed at the parties. At the wedding of Theobald Scholem and Hedwig ("Hete") Levy, in 1904, Arthur's four sons performed a play that made light of Theobald's interest in exotic lands and his Zionist proclivities. Reinhold dressed as an Arab, Erich as a Chinese, Gerhard as an Indian, and Werner as a Jewish shepherd.[16] Two years later, when Georg married Sophie ("Phiechen") Sussmann, Betty wanted her sons to perform another play, but Gershom fell ill, and without the full cast, she cancelled the performance. For the same event, Theobald and Max printed a humorous biography of the young couple, written in rhyme; and at Amalie's seventieth birthday in 1907, the family sang old Prussian songs rewritten with special lyrics in praise of Amalie. To ensure that everyone knew the lyrics, Theobald and Max distributed booklets lavishly decorated with art nouveau decorative motifs and Amalie's portrait.[17] At Arthur's fiftieth birthday party, Reinhold and his friends belted out comic songs while fifteen-year-old Gershom, to his utter embarrassment, circulated among the guests dressed as a sausage salesman from the Tree Blossom Festival in Werder, a town just outside of Berlin.[18] The family's last major celebration before the outbreak of World War I was on 5 April 1914, for the fiftieth anniversary of the Siegfried Scholem firm. Family members, company employees, and friends convened in a lavish Schöneberg banquet hall and sang tunes from specially prepared songbooks. These festive occasions, celebrated by the extended family and closest friends with organized gaiety, typified the Scholems' social life, and the specifics of the merrymaking—Prussian songs, a salesman from the Werder Tree Blossom Festival, theatrical references to Zionism and Jewish shepherds in Palestine—indicate how rooted the Scholems were both in the culture of Berlin and in a Jewish milieu.

Though not quite members of the haute bourgeoisie, the Scholems' lifestyle had many of the hallmarks of the upper middle class in the decades before the First World War. They had a maid who took care of the house and cooked many of their meals. They also hired a Swiss woman to teach Gershom to speak French and to play the piano, while Reinhold took adult education classes and Berlitz language courses in his free time. The Scholems had sufficient funds to purchase an automobile, and they also took frequent vacations abroad, particularly to resort towns in Switzerland.[19] Arthur considered it important that his sons have foreign experience, and Reinhold and Erich apprenticed abroad for several years. As Reinhold recalled many years later, "I am still grateful today to Father that for three years he sent me abroad, where the experiences of the various environments made a lasting impression on me. Back then the differences between the individual countries were much greater than today."[20]

For bourgeois Jews, high culture and the familiarity with it that befit their class status became an integral part of their identity. They wholly embraced the German notion of *Bildung*, cultivation of the self through education and cultural refinement that led to spiritual betterment. Betty Scholem took her youngest son to see plays and operettas at Berlin's numerous theaters, though he preferred the cinema, a new feature in urban life. Cultured Jews, including Betty, revered German poetry, especially that by Friedrich Schiller. In fact, one historian has written that the Jews' "relationship with the works of Friedrich Schiller . . . was more real to them than the encounter with their [actual] German contemporaries."[21] Indeed, as Jews became "Germans" in the course of the nineteenth century, they adopted a very specific, even idealized version of German culture, which they grafted onto or blended with their Jewish culture. There was a reverence for the German classics. Middle-class and upper-middle-class German Jews, while fully cognizant of their history and identity as Jews, wished to transmit German high culture to their children. Not coincidentally, exceptionally wealthy German Jews, such as James Simon and Eduard Arnhold, were among the chief patrons of the arts in Germany and in Berlin in particular.

Naturally, formal education was also critical to the Jewish bourgeoisie's world, serving both as an end in itself and as a means of class advancement or consolidation. Enrollment in a Gymnasium—either a traditional, humanistic Gymnasium or a modern Realgymnasium—conferred prestige. Therefore, all four Scholem brothers attended a Gymnasium, a fact that was normal for a middle-class German-Jewish family, but quite exceptional within the general German population. In 1906–07, only 8 percent of all children in the German state of Prussia went past elementary school, but 59 percent of Jewish children in Prussia did and 67 percent of Jewish children in Berlin. In Hamburg, nearly every Jewish child received some secondary education.

That same year, Jews made up 6.5 percent of all Gymnasium students in Prussia. In Berlin, Jewish boys accounted for nearly 25 percent of all Gymnasium and Realgymnasium students before World War I. Even Jewish girls in Berlin had very high rates of education, with 42 percent of them attending one of the city's secondary schools for girls, accounting for 30 percent of the student body.[22] In certain neighborhoods, the percentage of Jewish students in public schools could be much higher. For example, in 1910 the vast majority of students in the youngest class at the Mommsen-Gymnasium in the upper-middle-class suburb of Charlottenburg was Jewish.[23]

During their youth, Gershom Scholem and his brothers enrolled at the Luisenstädtisches Realgymnasium as the previous generation of the family had. Reinhold started school in 1897 at the age of six. Four years later, he was joined by Erich. Next came Werner in April 1902 and Gershom in April 1904.[24] Eventually, all four brothers left the Luisenstädtisches Realgymnasium before graduation. Werner and Gershom continued their education elsewhere, while Reinhold and Erich began apprenticeships in the printing industry.

Enrollment at a Gymnasium was not just about preparation for a career in business or university study. After a certain level, students could serve as one-year volunteers in the army rather than two- or three-year conscripts, and young Jews frequently remained in school until that point.[25] For example, Gershom's good friend Karl Türkischer was among those young Jews at the local Luisenstädtisches Realgymnasium who received the certificate enabling him to serve as a one-year volunteer and potential reserve officer candidate in the army.[26] Nonetheless, Jews stood virtually no chance of being promoted to officer rank after completing their year of service, despite their education and occasional enthusiasm for service. Such was the antisemitism in the Prussian officer corps.[27]

School also brought young Jews into social contact with non-Jews. In many cases, interfaith friendships formed; in other cases, the Jewish students endured social exclusion and even exposure to overt antisemitism, especially in the advanced grades. As Jewish children grew older, their social circles seemed to become increasingly concentrated on other Jews, just as their parents' social circles were. Part of this development was cultural affinity, and part was self-defense in an environment permeated by social antisemitism.[28] For a rare few, including Gershom Scholem, withdrawal from non-Jewish society in Germany had less to do with self-defense or imitation of long-standing trends than with the cultivation of an intensely and exclusively Jewish identity.[29]

By the early twentieth century, German-Jewish family life was in transition. Jews had adopted the general society's sensibilities regarding culture and child-rearing, but at the same time maintained clear differences from non-Jewish households. With four children, Betty and Arthur had a larger family than most Jews in Prussia. Four children or more was the norm in 1871, but the average was nearly two children by the early 1900s. In contrast, non-Jews still tended to have larger families.[30] In bourgeois families, children were often allowed to be children, but at other times, they were expected to comport themselves like small adults. Young Gershom played marbles and went roller-skating, but he was expected to join his mother on social calls and at the theater. Nor was it unusual for relatively young children to learn Latin and to recite poetry for their families.[31]

Husbands and wives also had a more egalitarian relationship in Jewish families than in non-Jewish families, and mothers had authority over matters in the home. It was their sphere.[32] They supervised the household and took responsibility for inculcating their children with the proper values, even if they were not always present. While most Jewish mothers in this era did not have paid employment outside the home, many middle-class Jewish women—including Betty Scholem—worked without remuneration in small, family-run businesses.[33] Even then, they did not relinquish their authority over their domain, and Betty maintained "a very strong presence" in her children's home life, as Gershom recalled. She went to the printshop after the children had gone to school, but every morning before departing, she gave the cook instructions for the three-course meal to be served at lunchtime. She came home for lunch and usually went back to work for a few hours.[34]

Though Reinhold, Erich, Werner, and Gershom grew up in the same household under nearly identical circumstances, they took significantly different paths. Reinhold and Erich generally shared their father's political and religious outlook, and they were destined to enter their father's business and inherit his social world. Werner shared his father's quick temper and propensity to sermonize, but strongly differed from him on political matters. As Werner grew up, he drifted further to the left and became a Socialist and later a Communist. Gershom rejected the way that his family specifically related to Judaism. At a relatively young age he began an intensive study of Jewish topics and embraced a wholly Jewish identity.

Reinhold and Erich intended to join Arthur's firm; therefore, they left school before taking the university admission examination.[35] Instead of pursuing higher education, they undertook a series of apprenticeships in the printing trade. It was quite common for the sons of German-Jewish middle-class families to use their relatives' connections to gain professional training and employment.[36] Reinhold first worked for his father and his uncles and went abroad in 1909, training in London, Paris, and Turin. Starting in 1912, Erich worked as a printer for the *Manchester Guardian*, as his father had done, before taking a position in Paris the following year. Reinhold made the most of his time abroad, both learning the printing business and visiting countless museums, operas, and concerts. After returning from their apprenticeships abroad, they were ready to enter Arthur's business, but not before performing their military service.

Having entered the upper grades of the Gymnasium, they were eligible to serve as one-year volunteers in the army, which released them from longer conscription service. From October 1912 to October 1913, Reinhold served in Telegraph Battalion no. 1 of the Prussian army, stationed in the Berlin suburb of Treptow. After his service, he moved back into his parents' home and went to work with his father. Erich completed foreign apprenticeships and returned to Berlin in the summer of 1914. He intended to spend his military service with a Bavarian field artillery regiment in the city of Fürth starting in October of that year, but fate intervened. Before he could join his prospective regiment, Germany declared war on Russia and France, and he was assigned to an aviation equipment group.[37]

It was virtually expected that sons such as Reinhold and Erich would join their family business. Not only did their participation assure continuation of the firm, but also fathers often felt that they were building a business to bequeath to their children. Sons were being given a career. In the twenty years before the First World War, approximately 55 percent of German Jews were involved in commerce, while less than 13 percent of non-Jews were; however, the number of self-employed Jews was decreasing and probably was less than 50 percent by 1914. More and more Jews were taking salaried jobs working for larger enterprises.[38] Nonetheless, for those Jews engaged in commerce, ties of kinship and friendship fostered business relations, including finding apprenticeships for one's sons who would ultimately inherit a business.

Werner and Gershom were completely different from their older brothers. They were both more intellectual and more alienated from their family's political and cultural sensibilities. This may, in part, have been a result of frustration with their parents' continued response to changed circumstances. In the 1860s and 1870s, when their parents were young, new laws abolished the last vestiges of legal religious discrimination. For the first time, a handful of unbaptized Jews received judicial appointments. Increasing numbers of Jews served in the national parliament and state legislatures, primarily for the various liberal parties. Jews in Prussia could still be commissioned as reserve army officers.[39] Social antisemitism still existed, but it seemed on the wane. An era of enlightened national liberalism seemed at hand. One generation later, German Jews faced renewed, virulent antisemitism.

In the early twentieth century, some political parties and organizations that had supported Jewish emancipation, or at least had been neutral, adopted the antisemitic rhetoric that was gaining currency. For many non-Jewish Germans who opposed liberalism and modernization, antisemitism evolved into a cultural code.[40] Jewish contributions to German culture and society, which were numerous and important, were frequently dismissed or denigrated. Antisemitism, and even anti-Jewish violence, seemed to be on the rise at German universities, pushing educated Jews into increasingly parochial circles and inculcating many future non-Jewish German elites in exclusionary antisemitism.[41] Moreover, in addition to strictly economic, religious, or social antisemitism among many Germans, Jews had to contend with a smaller group of racial antisemites, who regarded Jews as an alien race that had settled among the German people and that was exploiting the Germans' hospitality.[42] Despite the altered political and social landscape, the leaders of German Jewry placed their faith in liberalism and rationalism.[43]

These ideologies no longer appealed to the younger Scholem brothers. Moreover, they, like their father, had a propensity to be self-righteous and argumentative. Werner bitterly quarreled with his parents—so much so that Gershom confided to his diary, "If I were Werner, I would have already run away ten times and would have tried to pull through without the 'family.' "[44] Werner left the local Gymnasium in 1909, at the age of thirteen, and his parents sent him to the Samson School, a nominally Jewish, patriotically oriented boarding school in Wolfenbüttel near Braunschweig. There, he experienced a highly regimented, highly supervised life and received an education designed to prepare boys for commerce or similar professions rather than university study.[45] Gershom recalled that Werner was repulsed by the "religious hypocrisy and false patriotism" that he allegedly experienced there. During school vacations, when both brothers were home in Berlin, Werner angrily and cynically shared his experiences with Gershom.[46] Eventually, Arthur reenrolled his son in a Berlin school.

Dissatisfied with his parents' bourgeois liberalism, Werner investigated other political worldviews. At first he considered Jewish nationalism and affiliated with a Zionist youth group—later calling himself a *rachmones* ("mercy" or "pity") Zionist—but he was ultimately drawn to Marxian socialism. He informed his Zionist colleagues that he had "found something broader than the narrow little thing called Jewish nationalism." He had discovered "Humanity."[47] As an enthusiastic devotee of August Bebel and Karl Kautsky, Werner joined the socialist youth movement in 1912 and the Social Democratic Party in 1913.[48] In fact, as the Social Democratic Party became more moderate in deed, if not in word, ever more Jews supported the party—roughly one in five Jewish voters in 1912 during the last prewar election. Jews also made up a significant portion of the party intelligentsia, leading to a vastly disproportionate share of parliamentary mandates and party journalist positions.[49] Nonetheless, the increasing respectability of Social Democracy and its popularity with Jews did not endear it to Arthur. According to Gershom, one day a politically leftist typesetter gave Arthur a newspaper report about "Comrade Werner Scholem." Enraged, once more Arthur sent Werner to boarding school.[50] This time it was the Gildemeistersches Institut in Hanover. However, exile from the capital did not prevent Werner's political activity. He became active in local Social Democratic politics, and soon he had a non-Jewish, working-class, Socialist girlfriend—another source of tension with his parents.[51] Incidentally, among Werner's classmates at the Gildemeistersches Institut was Ernst Jünger, who went on to become a hero in World War I and a famous right-wing author.[52]

Gershom's rebellion against his parents and their culture took the form of a reembrace of the family's Jewish heritage. The Scholems were consciously Jewish, but not truly observant. Arthur worked on the High Holidays, while Betty accompanied her own mother to synagogue. The family did not keep kosher or refrain from eating bread during Passover. The Scholem brothers received obligatory religious instruction in their public school, but they did not attend the voluntary religious schools operated by the Jewish community. All four brothers had bar mitzvah ceremonies when they were thirteen years old, as was common for virtually all Jewish boys. However, in contrast to the usual convention, the Scholems had theirs at the end of their thirteenth year instead of immediately after turning thirteen.[53] The Scholems, like so many other German Jews, celebrated Christmas, complete with a special dinner and an exchange of gifts.[54] However, it was exactly this sort of practice that drove Gershom, then still called Gerhard, toward Judaism.

Jewish students in state schools, including the Luisenstädtisches Realgymnasium, had a required class on Judaism, but Gershom found the lessons devoid of meaningful content. He also found the Jewish community's religious schools to be woefully inadequate. Instead, he turned to the large Jewish communal library on Oranienburger Strasse, and it was there, through the agency of Heinrich Graetz's *History of the Jews*, that he discovered Jewish history. Already at the age of twelve, with a growing interest in Jewish matters, he secretly began learning Hebrew with a teacher. He wanted to be able to speak, or at least read, the holy language at his bar mitzvah, in contrast to his brothers who simply read a transliteration of Hebrew. Even after his bar mitzvah, he continued to attend services, but not at the Liberal Lindenstrasse synagogue near his family's home. He went to the Old Synagogue, which first opened in 1714. Two hundred years later, it was one of the few Orthodox synagogues in the city. Congregants actively participated in the service, and there was no organ. Some Liberal synagogues were so decorous as to resemble a theater, with a finely attired audience listening to a cantor or a choir accompanied by an organ. Gershom rejected this sort of Judaism and wanted something more. With exhilaration, Gershom read *Chorew: Versuch über Jisraels Pflichten in der Zerstreuung* (Horeb: Essays on Israel's Duties in the Diaspora) by Samson Raphael Hirsch, the nineteenth-century German rabbi who was known as the father of neo-Orthodoxy, a religious movement that demanded strict adherence to Orthodox practices while striving for the adoption of Western culture and participation in modern society. "If Judaism had always been this way, as it should be according to Samson Raphael Hirsch, there would be no antisemitism in the world," Gershom exclaimed in his diary.[55] Gershom even joined the anti-Zionist, Orthodox Jewish organization Agudat Yisrael, but it was not for him in the long run. The group's other members felt that Gershom was insufficiently religious and removed him from the leadership. Soon, he ostentatiously quit the organization altogether, a decision he still felt compelled to defend six decades later.[56]

Gershom's personal adherence to Orthodoxy lasted scarcely a year. Nonetheless, he retained an unquenchable thirst for Judaic knowledge. Looking for study material, he frequented the Jewish used bookstores of the Scheunenviertel and its neighboring streets, which were home to many of Berlin's traditional Jews, especially recent arrivals from eastern Europe. He spent his meager savings on Judaic books. He passed his free time studying Hebrew and important Jewish religious texts, including the Talmud, under the guidance of Isaak Bleichrode, an Orthodox rabbi and descendant of the great rabbi Akiva Eger.[57]

In his thirst for Judaic learning and experiences, Gershom was not alone. He circulated among other sons of the German-Jewish bourgeoisie who were seeking greater Jewish content in their lives. Many members of his generation turned toward Jewish organizations as a way of self-identifying with the Jewish people in contrast to their parents. Among the best-known groups was Blau-Weiss (Blue-White), modeled on German nationalist outdoors clubs that glorified nature and stressed ethnic community. Other groups emphasized competitive sports as a means to prove Jewish vigor. Gershom, who was unathletic or even antiathletic, joined a Zionist club called

Jung Juda (Young Judah). He and his comrades were intensely intellectual and extremely serious, despite being mere teenagers. While other young Jews went on hiking trips or simply drank beer together, they sat in cafés, debating the various issues that divided the Zionist movement and dissecting the writings of German authors such as Jean Paul and Stefan George. Many of Gershom's peers had a fascination with the Jews of eastern Europe, who seemed more authentic to them, especially in comparison to their own assimilated families. The philosopher and essayist Martin Buber, who wrote about Hasidic Jews and who presented spiritual alternatives to mainstream German Judaism, was their intellectual guide. Even Gershom, who soon disagreed with Buber over the latter's view of Hasidism and his philosophy of mystical inner experience (*Erlebnismystik*), was enchanted by his writings at the time.[58]

Along with a passion for Jewish history and a scholarly interest in Jewish religion, Zionism was a central aspect of Gershom's Jewish identity. The modern Zionist movement had been formally organized in 1897, under the direction of the Austrian journalist Theodor Herzl. Its stated goal was the establishment of a Jewish national homeland in Palestine, recognized under international law. Herzl attempted to achieve this goal through diplomacy with government leaders and financiers of world import. Other Zionist leaders wanted to achieve Jewish predominance in Palestine from below, rather than from above.[59] They established settlements, chiefly agricultural, to obtain land for the Jews and to train them in the various professions that they would need in their own state. While Zionism attained a mass following among the Jews of eastern Europe, most German Jews saw their place in the German nation. Some, including members of the acculturist Central Association of German Citizens of the Jewish Faith, actively opposed Zionism.[60] The Berlin Jewish community suspended Rabbi Emil Bernhard Cohn because of his open support for Zionism.[61]

However, it is important to note the specific character of German Zionism. Proto-Zionist activity began in Germany even before Herzl's movement coalesced. Max Bodenheimer, a Jewish lawyer in Cologne, had organized the National-Jewish Association (National-jüdische Vereinigung) seven weeks before Herzl's inaugural Zionist Congress met in late August 1897. In October, the National-Jewish Association renamed itself the Zionist Federation of Germany (Zionistische Vereinigung für Deutschland). Additionally, the establishment of Zionist fraternities at German universities buoyed the movement. Since most German Jews were not going to immigrate to Palestine or even seriously consider doing so, early German Zionism took on largely philanthropic and cultural orientations. German Jews would help oppressed Russian Jews seek refuge in Palestine, while they would experience a revitalization of their own Jewish identity. In the years before the First World War, however, a movement led by Kurt Blumenfeld emerged within German Zionist circles to endorse the goal of emigration. Most German Jews favored German acculturation, if not assimilation, and did not share even the moderate Zionists' outlook. Many of them considered the Zionists' publicity to be a threat to their own position in Germany, including their claims to belong unreservedly to the German nation. As a result of Jewish communal protests, for example, Theodor Herzl had to hold his first Zionist Congress in Basel rather than Munich.[62] Regardless, the movement had only a small following in Germany before 1933. From 4,300 members in 1903, it grew to 9,800 in 1914, with possibly only one-third of those truly active.[63]

Among many young Zionists in Berlin, the political Zionism of Herzl was not initially popular. For them, Zionism was a cultural and spiritual force that promoted the creation of a Jewish identity as they reembraced Jewish history and traditions. This renewed identification would then lead to a spiritual and moral regeneration of the Jews living in the Diaspora. Once young Gershom Scholem was drawn to Zionism, he became a leading voice for cultural Zionism; however, he took it one step farther. While some of his peers' rejection of political Zionism led to a de-emphasis of the Land of Israel, he regarded it as central to Jewish identity. Moreover, Zion was something onto which he could project his desires as he yearned to escape his family's world.[64] Also, while he advocated a Jewish cultural and social renaissance emanating from the Land of Israel, he did not endorse the creation of an independent Jewish political entity in Palestine.[65] Ultimately, the return to Zion would become a literal endeavor for Gershom, not merely a figurative or spiritual one.[66]

Gershom became ever more involved in Zionist debates, first in the cafés and later in the pages of Zionist newspapers. His involvement in the movement, though not typical of German Jewry as a whole, was certainly not unprecedented and, to some degree, was representative. Cultural Zionism had particular appeal to young Jewish intellectuals in Berlin. However, during the decade between his embrace of Zionism and his immigration to Palestine, he grew increasingly strident and unrelenting, marking him as an extremist. Indeed, his idiosyncratic views and argumentative nature won him both friends and adversaries among young German Zionists.

Not only did Gershom adopt a vigorous Jewish identity, but he also claimed to reject Germanness. Years later, he wrote that he "turned away from a German feeling with full consciousness." He told his brother Reinhold, "I still recall the torments I suffered from the speeches you gave as a one-year military volunteer in 1913 . . . during your visits home. I reacted to them with complete silence as I did anyway to everything that was said about such topics, especially from Father, in my (!) parental home."[67] Gershom considered the German Jews to be living in a state of delusion about their place in Germany. In his diary he mentioned an encounter between a Socialist politician and his liberal, proudly German rival, who was Jewish. The anti-nationalist Socialist taunted the Jewish liberal by shouting, "Without Napoleon, you would still be in the ghetto!" Gershom found the liberal's "patriotic" retort—that Prussia's leaders would have liberated the Jews anyway—to be absurd.[68]

Already in the years before the First World War, German Jewry faced new challenges. Social and economic antisemitism, which had seemed to be declining decades earlier, was resurgent. Some Jews questioned their place in society and the nature of German-Jewish identity. Under these pressures, Germany's Jewish community began to divide socially and politically, and developments within the Scholem family were a microcosm of the changed circumstances. When war broke out in 1914, German Jews hoped that the mood of national unity would eliminate discrimination, but tensions escalated under the impact of wartime deprivation and seemingly endless conflict. Some Jews, including members of the Scholem family, held fast to their vision of an inclusive German nation, while others, including the youngest two Scholem brothers, looked for alternatives to the worldview presented to them by their liberal, bourgeois parents.

CHAPTER 3

Things Fall Apart

The First World War

On 28 June 1914, Gavrilo Princip, a Bosnian-born Serbian nationalist, acting with the support of rogue Serbian military intelligence officers, assassinated the Austrian archduke Franz Ferdinand. The murder of the heir to the Habsburg throne plunged Europe into a diplomatic crisis. However, the prospect of war unleashed a thunderbolt of excitement among many ordinary Europeans. Jubilant crowds filled the streets of central Berlin and erupted into song when Serbia turned down Austria's full demands for redress. With each passing day before the formal declaration of war, the demonstrations grew larger and more boisterous.[1]

In the raucous atmosphere of unbounded patriotism, previous divisions within society seemed to dissipate. Berlin's leading liberal newspaper reported, "While singing 'Wacht am Rhein,' the procession, in which workers, students, soldiers, and businessmen walked arm-in-arm, side-by-side, in unison, hurried itself to the palace." Further: "German and Austrian, student and soldier, businessman and worker felt the brotherly togetherness of a single heart and a single purpose in a fatefully serious hour."[2] After Germany declared war on Russia and France, the kaiser himself proclaimed, "I no longer recognize parties. I recognize only Germans!" Speaking to members of the Reichstag, he said, "As a sign that you are determined to persevere with me through thick and thin, through adversity and death, without difference of party, tribe, or religion, I call upon the chairmen of the parties to step forward and pledge that to me."[3] There was to be a suspension of the domestic political and economic conflicts that had roiled Germany, and all sides accepted this civic truce, known in German as the "Burgfrieden" (literally "fortress peace"). Under these new circumstances, the community of the nation seemed open to Jews.

In this heady atmosphere of national solidarity and patriotism, the Central Association of German Citizens of the Jewish Faith addressed the German Jews:

> We call upon you to dedicate your energies beyond the measure of duty to the Fatherland! Hurry voluntarily to the colors! All of you—men and women—put yourself in the service of the Fatherland through personal assistance of every sort and the donation of money and goods![4]

For the Central Association, the war was an opportunity for the Jews to be completely integrated into the unity of the German nation. The Zionist Federation of Germany also supported the war. It wrote to its members:

> German Jews! In this hour, it is for us to show once again that we Jews, proud of our tribe, belong to the best sons of the Fatherland. The nobility of our 4000-year history obliges us. We expect that our youth will voluntarily rush to the colors with a joyful heart. German Jews! We call upon you in the sense of the old Jewish obligation to the commandments to give yourself up to service to the Fatherland with your whole heart, whole soul, and whole fortune.[5]

For many German Jews, the war was a chance to prove their devotion to the Fatherland and to earn the true equality they had wanted. Moreover, they regarded the war as a crusade against benighted, antisemitic tsarist Russia.[6]

In total, approximately a hundred thousand Jews served in the German armed forces in the First World War, including the four Scholem brothers. Even German Jews who were unable to join the fight supported the cause. Intellectuals such as the painter Max Liebermann; the theater director Max Reinhardt; Paul Ehrlich, winner of the Nobel Prize for medicine in 1908; and the future winner of the Nobel Prize for chemistry Fritz Haber signed an explicitly prowar manifesto.[7] "Deutschland, Deutschland über Alles" rang out in Liberal synagogues in August 1914.[8] However, devotion to the cause was not confined to assimilated German Jews or those who were inclined to Liberal Judaism. Even strictly Orthodox Jews overtly prayed for Germany's victory, though they expressed their devotion differently from Liberal Jews, preferring traditionally Jewish forms rather than secular or even Christian symbolism.[9]

Betty and Gershom Scholem were on vacation in Switzerland when the war broke out.[10] Though Gershom was still too young for military service, his brothers were not. Reinhold, who had already performed his military service and was now working full-time, was recalled to service as early as 4 August 1914.[11] Erich, who earlier had planned to serve as a one-year volunteer with an artillery regiment, was assigned to a technical equipment unit providing service for German aviators.[12]

When the war broke out, Werner was a student at the Gildemeistersches Institut in Hanover. His classmate Ernst Jünger still remembered young Werner and his cynical, antiwar attitude sixty years later. Shortly after the declaration of war, most of the students left school to volunteer for the army. Jünger recalled, "I came back from the barber that day, and he remarked with a skeptical smile, 'Before battle, the Germanic youth anoints his hair.'"[13] Jünger enlisted, but Werner refused to join up despite his father's express wishes. Furthermore, Werner blamed the war on Russia and on Austria's policies in the Balkans, which Germany had supported.[14] His refusal to volunteer was not only a negative commentary on German nationalism, but also in the historic spirit of European socialism.

The Social Democrats had preached international brotherhood before the war, but when asked to prove their patriotism by voting to approve funding for war, they did so. In the early months of the war, even the "reddest of Reds volunteered" for the war, and at an assembly of socialist youth, Werner was labeled a "crazy fanatic" and a "coward" because he refused to enlist for military service. However, a small group within the Social Democratic Party, led most prominently by Karl Liebknecht and Rosa Luxemburg, opposed the war from the start. At first, they expressed their opposition only privately, but on 2 December 1914, Liebknecht voted openly in the Reichstag against additional funding for the war and, thus, against the war itself. Werner expressed his glowing admiration for Liebknecht.[15]

While Werner was away in Hanover and Gershom still at home in Berlin, the two carried on a lively correspondence about Marxism, Judaism, and anarchism. Werner characterized himself as a revolutionary Socialist along the lines of Rosa Luxemburg. He understood the real-world needs and moderation of the trade unions, but he embraced the radicalism of the socialist youth movement. Gershom, by contrast, could not accept historical materialism as a worldview, which was the basis of Marxist thought.[16] While he sympathized with the Socialists' program, in 1914, he was unable to join the party because he did not like organizations, likening them to "a turbid lake into which the beautiful, powerful storm of ideas flows and doesn't let it go out again. Organization is a synonym (!) for death." Werner replied,

"Every thinking Jew becomes a Socialist, which you now are," as Gershom already supported the party program. Nonetheless, despite his long, detailed argumentation about socialism, Werner advised Gershom not to follow his path to the workers' movement: "In the process, one suffers shipwreck and eventually goes meshuga [crazy], which, mind you, is not a blissful state."[17] Eventually, Werner took Gershom to secret socialist antiwar meetings at the Karlsgarten beer hall in the working-class Berlin district of Neukölln. It was not long before Gershom considered joining the Social Democratic Party. In December 1915, he made it as far as the local party office, but the treasurer was out and thus unable to take Gershom's dues. Later, Gershom realized that he could not in good conscience join the party, and he did not return.[18]

In the autumn of 1914, Werner lived with his "mother-in-law," as he called her.[19] In fact, Werner had become engaged to Emmy Wiechelt, a non-Jewish, working-class woman whom he had met in a socialist youth group. The illegitimate daughter of a domestic servant and a Protestant minister's son, Emmy was raised by her single mother in Linden, then an industrial, working-class suburb of Hanover. The engagement enraged Arthur Scholem, who disapproved of Emmy's religious background and social class.[20] Incidentally, during this time, Werner managed to complete his interrupted education by taking his school-leaving exam (*Abitur*) as an external examinee at Berlin's Luisenstädtisches Realgymnasium, where the Scholems had studied for two generations.[21]

Only sixteen years old when the war started, Gershom was still in school; however, he could not escape the militaristic atmosphere that pervaded wartime Germany. His Gymnasium formed a military company for students sixteen and older "to steel their powers, sharpen their senses, [and] prepare them for eventual service in the army," as the school director explained it.[22] The military drills and jingoistic tone of school life disgusted Gershom. He told Werner that their father taunted him because "I have shown myself to be such a 'coward' and do not want to feel absolutely any noble stirrings of the heart."[23]

Additionally, Gershom rejected the war expressly as a Jew, running counter to the prevailing trend. In November 1914, he wrote in his dairy, "You are Orientals and not Europeans. You are Jews and people, not Germans and degenerates. . . . Therefore you should not walk along their path."[24] He felt that "it is not *permitted* to sacrifice *Jewish souls*."[25] Even though prominent Jews and Zionists in Germany, including Martin Buber, endorsed the war, Gershom rejected it expressly from a Jewish perspective. In February 1915, he was outraged when he read an article in the Zionist newspaper *Jüdische Rundschau* that concluded, "It seems that we went to war because we are

Zionists, not, however, despite the fact we are Jews."[26] Indeed, Zionist leaders hoped that their support for the war would lead to the realization of their goals in the event of a German victory. Eventually, their good ties to German Foreign Office officials did prove useful when they wished to alleviate the wartime plight of Jews living in Palestine, then under the rule of Ottoman Turkey, a German ally.[27] Additionally, many Zionists supported the war in order to free their coreligionists from the yoke of tsarist Russian oppression.

By contrast, Gershom Scholem did not see the war as serving Jewish interests and despaired about the loss of Jewish lives in the service of non-Jewish powers. In response to the *Jüdische Rundschau* article, Gershom and a group of his friends composed a letter to the newspaper's editors. They directly claimed, "Germany's cause is just as little ours as that of any other country in the world."[28] While they ultimately did not publish the letter, it was to change Gershom's life.

He secretly brought the letter with him to school to gather an additional signature. A patriotically inclined fellow student found the letter among Gershom's belongings and denounced him to the school authorities. This led to an investigation and trial. As Gershom described it: "Some marvelous circumstantial evidence of my 'anti-national' ideology was produced, which was made much easier by my open advocacy of Judaism and my propaganda directed against the youth [military training] company that had expelled all its Jews. . . . In the end, I was removed."[29] In order to take the school-leaving examination that would permit regular university study, he would have to find another school.

Soon the shadow of the war loomed too great for Gershom to ignore. Fearing that he would be conscripted into the infantry, he volunteered for service. Under these exceptional circumstances, his Aunt Hedwig, one of his confidantes in the family, hoped that he could take the school-leaving exam on an emergency basis, which was common for advanced secondary school students entering military service.[30] Indeed, that is exactly what happened. To avoid conscription into the infantry, Gershom enlisted, which would have afforded a choice of army branch. Moreover, his enlistment allowed him to take the school-leaving exam as a visitor at the Königstädtisches Realgymnasium. He later recalled that his oral examiners expressed their curiosity as to why he had left his own school before his final year. Gershom knew that telling the truth—saying that he had been expelled for being unpatriotic in time of war—might doom his chances. So he said nothing. A teacher replied, "Oh, I understand . . . trouble with a girl." And, thus, Gershom completed his secondary education.[31] Nonetheless, enlistment had been the price for this opportunity, and in November 1915, he reported for duty. During the medical examination before basic training, he announced that he had a history of nervousness and spells of physical weakness during long marches. The army doctor declared him unfit for service.[32]

Despite his father's threats to send him off to a provincial city to work as a grocer's apprentice, Gershom could commence university study in Berlin even without a school-leaving certificate. A little-known regulation permitted advanced schoolboys, who were otherwise eligible to volunteer as one-year officer candidates in the army, to enroll for four semesters of university study. Even though Gershom had no intention of volunteering as an officer candidate, he took advantage of this loophole, which allowed nongraduates of secondary schools to study at university. As a student at the University of Berlin, Gershom focused on mathematics, with additional courses in philosophy and religion. Among his professors was the famous Protestant theologian and liberal politician Ernst Troeltsch, and he took one course on Buddhism, taught by the orientalist Hermann Beckh. More out of character for straightlaced and pacifist Gershom, he also took courses entitled "Hygiene of the Male Sex Life," and "State, Nation, Fatherland," both of which were presumably required.[33] Incidentally, from the autumn of 1915 through 1919, Arthur Scholem's firm printed the university's directory of students and staff.[34]

After a stint at the University of Berlin, Gershom spent time in Heidelberg, where he delved into a world of Judaic study. He studied the Talmud privately with an Orthodox scholar, and he befriended Jewish women students, who, like him, were reengaging with Judaism despite their family backgrounds. He also spent time with Martin Buber, who, though born in Vienna and raised in Austrian Galicia, now made his home in Heppenheim, only eighteen miles from Heidelberg. Buber's belief in revitalizing Jews and Judaism through an emphasis on the mythic rather than the rational deeply inspired Gershom in the early 1910s, as he sought spiritual vitality and intellectual sustenance through Judaism. The prose of his diaries from those years borrowed heavily from Buber.[35] Even after Gershom's initial ardor cooled, Buber remained a friend, ally, and frequent ideological opponent for him. They collaborated on Buber's journal, Der Jude, and expressed mutual sympathy, yet Gershom, disagreeing with Buber's political position on the war and his intellectual position on the German Jews' relationship to eastern European Jewry, called him a "False Teacher" and complained about his influence on German Zionism.[36] Regardless of his tone, Gershom was correct that Martin Buber greatly inspired those German-Jewish youths who sought a revitalized engagement with Judaism.

Inspired by Buber, his *Erlebnismystik*, and his romanticization of eastern European Jewry, young German Jews established a Jewish cultural center in a working-class area of Berlin. During the war, they did relief work for displaced eastern Jews or cared for the easterners' children while the parents worked all day. In the evening, these young German Jews held discussions or study groups on Jewish topics. Buber directed Gershom to visit this popular center. Gershom admired the idea behind the project, but he criticized its execution in excoriating terms. After visiting the center's devotees, he derided their ignorance of the Torah and Hebrew and—in his opinion—insufficient efforts to study both. He claimed that they were not willing to work hard to acquire Jewish knowledge. He attacked their seeming lack of burning concern with Jerusalem as the focal point of all Zionism. They were "heretical" as far as he was concerned. He even called the center's director, Siegfried Lehmann, "dishonest" and "immoral."[37] Moreover, since the program was inspired by Buber, Gershom directed his ire against Buber as well. He wrote, "I must be, and am, at my core against him. It has become clear to me that in the final analysis, Buber is not Jewish, but modern, considering all Jewishness. And Buber's philosophy of history is fundamentally wrong, *even* refutable." In his rage, Gershom added that, through his interactions "with some Buberians," he "saw completely clearly that this road is dangerous and pernicious."[38] Scholem, only nineteen years old, did not shy away from unleashing furious criticism at those who pursued Zionism differently than he did, those who held a different interpretation of German-Jewish history, or even those who translated Yiddish incorrectly, in his view.[39] Such a passionate and unremitting critique of his adversaries would be a hallmark of Gershom's style throughout his life.

Even for his times, when young people dedicated themselves to intense intellectual endeavors, debate, and introspection in the neo-Romantic tradition, Gershom was an exceptionally serious young man. While on vacation in the Bavarian Alps, he wrote, "This whole time, I have been doing nothing other than rebuilding myself . . . and I am building up my Zionism so strongly that I will be able to build my life on it without fearing that it could ever be shaken."[40]

As thousands of his peers, including his brothers, enlisted or were called up for military service, Gershom remained distant from the ongoing conflict. He told his friend Harry Heymann, "You are really right when you say that your military activity does not interest me (in so far as you are not sick!), for all of this is worlds away from me."[41] He made little secret of his opposition to the war, and for the most part he wrapped himself in a cocoon of Zionism and Judaic learning. He explained to his friend Edgar Blum that, for people like him, fixated solely on Zionism, "the problem of the war no longer exists for us."[42] During his free time, Gershom immersed himself in the study of classical Jewish texts, such as the Talmud, and works on the Kabbalah, a field with a rich history, though one not taken seriously by academic scholars at the time.

But on occasion, the tragedy of the war invaded Gershom's sphere, and he was forced to deal with it in some way. His close friend Edgar Blum died of war wounds in November 1916—literally only days after Gershom wrote to Blum about how little the war meant to him. Together, they had "immigrated into the empire of the spirit, where more noble wars than this one are conducted," Gershom wrote. He described Blum as a genius, with interests in mathematics and Judaics. He wrote, "I consider myself to be my friend's spiritual heir, and I have the obligation to accomplish what he was prevented from accomplishing." Blum's memory also inspired Gershom to pursue his own work more intensely.[43] And thus, while millions died and tectonic shifts in European politics were under way, his main interests remained studying Jewish texts and participating in Zionist debate. Only when a British army was on the cusp of conquering Palestine did Gershom evince a notable interest in the war. "For the first time in the war, I am eagerly following the military reports: I really hope that *Eretz Yisrael* will be free *bimhera b'yamenu* [speedily in our days]."[44]

Hand in hand with Gershom's Judaic study was his preoccupation with the Jewish, or Zionist, youth movement. There were many Jewish youth organizations, but in Gershom's opinion, no movement that young people would truly find to be Jewish. There were discussions, lectures, and programs, but "nothing effective and alive."[45] He despised youth congresses with their speeches and singing of songs in German, Hebrew, and Yiddish. All this he judged as superficial, unserious, and even unnecessary.[46] So weak was the movement "that in the decisive hours, our youth is inferior to the war," he opined.[47]

A particular object of his invective was the best-known Zionist youth group: the Blau-Weiss movement. Not lacking in self-confidence, Gershom attacked Blau-Weiss in its own newspaper. He criticized the group as insufficiently Jewish, citing its lack of emphasis on learning Hebrew and its culture of hiking, which imitated non-Jewish youth groups.[48] When encouraged to show tolerance toward other types of Zionists, he exclaimed, "How should we be 'tolerant' when we know what the truth is and the others partially put out absolute lies or at least something other than the truth? How can we call people Zionists who do not aspire in any way to what in truth is called Zionism? That really goes too far!"[49]

He encouraged his acquaintances to quit Blau-Weiss and intervened in the group's internal affairs to rectify matters, as he saw them.[50] In his diary, he strongly attacked Theodor Herzl and Herzlian Zionism: "We reject Herzl. It is his *fault* that contemporary Zionism does not look forward, but rather backwards, that it is an organization of shopkeepers, that it crawls on its hands and feet before anyone in power! Yid, that is Zionism!" Herzl had wanted a state for the Jews. Gershom wrote, "And we reject that . . . we do not want a state, but rather a free society."[51]

In contrast to mainstream Zionism and Blau-Weiss was Jung Juda, the Zionist circle of Gershom and his teenage friends. They sought a personal and even spiritual renewal of the Jewish people through Zionism. Gershom wrote that "Jung Juda is not an organization, but rather an idea," and they rejected traditional models of Zionist association.[52] They fancied themselves to be revolutionaries and anarchists, who opposed the hierarchical, formalized world of institutional Zionism. Gershom expressly rejected traditional youth group work: "I want to be a Zionist and nothing else, not a 'youth movement member.' I renounce my youth."[53] Unlike other German-Jewish youth groups, which engaged in supposedly regenerative physical activities such as hiking and gymnastics, Jung Juda was overtly intellectual. Its members focused on Judaic study, either of texts or through discussions and lectures. They published a newsletter entitled *Die Blauweiße Brille* (The Blue-White Spectacles) to promote their views.

The short-lived newspaper featured stirring appeals and editorials by Gershom and his collaborators as well as highly stylized illustrations, including portraits of Martin Buber, Max Nordau, and Ahad Ha'am. The articles regularly critiqued the Jewish youth movement in Germany: "We do not have a Jewish youth movement, but rather a lack of movement. Three words, and one is always missing: Jewish movement without youth, Jewish youth without movement, youth movement without Judaism."[54] Gershom and his friends decried the paucity of "ideology" behind contemporary Zionism as well as the emphasis on politics over cultural work.[55]

Not everyone applauded or even tolerated Gershom's uncompromising view of Zionism and its youth movement. Scholem found himself attacked in the pages of Blau-Weiss's publications. He was accused of negating life in favor of dogma, of wanting soldiers or monks and not people.[56] In a public address, one opponent decried "Scholemism," which "confines a person in the four walls of his study and fills up the brain with [Hebrew] vocabulary words at any cost!"[57] Gershom sent copies of *Die Blauweiße Brille* to a young Zionist woman named Julie Schächter, who replied that, contrary to his assertions, there actually was a Jewish youth movement, which included

Blau-Weiss and the Herzl Club. She added that Gershom might not be suited for these organizations simply because his personality was more suited to solitude.[58] Jung Juda's condescending attitude toward other Zionist groups could be counterproductive. The Herzl Club limited access to its rooms for Jung Juda members and banned copies of *Die Blauweiße Brille* on its premises.[59] The Zionist Federation of Germany did not invite Jung Juda members to a meeting on youth matters.[60]

One adult, however, did not find Gershom's attitude thoroughly annoying: Hedwig Scholem. He sent his aunt copies of *Die Blauweiße Brille* for her comments. While she offered critical comments about some specific articles, she generally agreed with much of what she read.[61] Occasionally, she wrote to him in Hebrew, and she asked for his advice on Hebrew-German dictionaries. They corresponded about book recommendations and philosophy, as well as news about Palestine.[62] Interestingly, Gershom and Martin Buber also developed a growing friendship and collaboration, even though Gershom criticized Buber in the pages of *Die Blauweiße Brille*.[63]

As the war, university study, health problems, and family matters scattered the core members of Jung Juda away from Berlin, the group lost momentum and effectively dissolved. *Die Blauweiße Brille* ceased publication after three issues. Meanwhile, Gershom Scholem maintained a number of very warm friendships with various young women. Most of them were study partners during his time in Berlin, and later in Heidelberg and Jena. He gladly tutored some in Hebrew and shared his Judaic wisdom with them. However, in 1915, a schoolgirl named Stephanie Rothstein became especially fond of Gershom, and her letters to him quickly grew less formal and more personal. She asked him to pay her social calls at home, loan her books, and accompany her on a school trip through Old Berlin. In the spring of 1916, she offered to send him a care package of marzipan when he went to Bavaria and then expressed her distress that her mother had intercepted and read his letters to her. Unfortunately, Gershom did not keep copies of his letters to Rothstein, so it is not known how he felt about her.[64]

While teenage Gershom argued about the future of Zionism and continued his studies in Berlin, the war became an inescapable reality for his brother Werner. Despite their differing motivations, Werner shared Gershom's disdain for the war, but he was conscripted in June 1915.[65] Subsequently, he saw action on the Serbian front and the Russian front as a private in the infantry. In the spring of 1916, the Russians launched an attack near Lake Narach [*sic*] in Belarus with the hope of retaking German-occupied Vilna (today Vilnius, Lithuania). Known as the Lake Naroch Offensive, 350,000 Russians faced only 75,000 Germans. Despite their numerical superiority in men and guns, the Russians' artillery bombardment and infantry attacks proved ineffectual against the entrenched Germans.[66] The offensive ended barely ten days after it began, but not before Werner received a shrapnel wound on his right foot. For two months he recovered in the infirmary of the German fortress of Graudenz (today Grudziądz, Poland) and was then sent to a Berlin hospital, where his Uncle Georg, a military physician, helped him manage. Werner called it "nepotism in its purest form!" During his convalescence, he could rest at his parents' home, where he made use of Gershom's library, and he hoped to attend university classes.[67] When military doctors judged Werner fit for light duty in late August 1916, he received a pass for a fourteen-day leave, which he promptly spent with Emmy in Hanover.[68] Later, he continued his recovery in the city of Halle and enrolled at the local university. Still, his view of the war grew ever dimmer. He foresaw no end to the war before 1917 and predicted further waves of conscription, which might involve Gershom. He wrote that either he or Gershom had to survive the war so as to continue the Scholem family line.[69]

During these days, Werner's relationship with his family remained fractious, in part because of his attitude toward the war. His father forbade him to visit relatives, lest he embarrass the family or do something stupid. Twice already he had caused uproars: once by mocking Reinhold's Iron Cross award and another time by openly reading the socialist newspaper *Vorwärts* while in a military hospital.[70] Nonetheless, he wanted more money from his parents and asked Gershom to have their mother send it to him.[71]

Werner remained politically aware during his war service. He followed internal Social Democratic Party debates closely, and he wished that the party would have the spirit of Karl Liebknecht and the leadership of Hugo Haase—the former being the first Reichstag representative to oppose the war openly and the latter being the leader of the party's left wing.[72] In addition to subscribing to *Vorwärts*, while continuing his recovery in Halle, he read the *Volksblatt*, a left-wing local newspaper. He watched local and regional election results with great interest.[73]

Werner became increasingly politically radical under the impact of the continuing war. On 27 January 1917, he joined other young Socialists in disrupting a rally celebrating the kaiser's birthday. They shouted, "Cheers for Liebknecht! Down with the war!" Moreover, Werner protested while wearing his army uniform. The police were unable to catch the fleeing demonstrators, but an anonymous witness denounced Werner as a participant, and he was later arrested.[74] Fortunately for him, the charge of treason was reduced to lèse-majesté. Werner's military trial and appeal dragged on, and in his correspondence with Gershom, Werner expressed little remorse. In fact, as he did throughout his political life and his repeated brushes with the legal system, Werner adopted an unapologetic tone of disdain and cynicism. He touted his own comportment before the court. He announced that his defendant's statement would prove to the world that his behavior was not "unsocialist." His main goal was not to avoid prison; it was to save his political reputation, both in the eyes of his comrades and his younger brother. Before the Superior Military Tribunal, Werner made a "roaring speech that one should have been able to hear throughout the whole building," as he described it. He found it highly amusing that he delivered his remarks in imitation of the French revolutionary Danton. Werner's attorney found the speech less amusing and said that it would add at least two months to his sentence.[75] Ultimately, he received a nine-month prison sentence, including time already served.[76] Upon his release from prison, he was also expelled from the University of Halle, where he had been studying.[77]

In April 1917, the Social Democratic Party split over the issue of continuing support for the war, with the left faction calling itself the Independent Social Democratic Party (Unabhängige Sozialdemokratische Partei Deutschlands). Werner supported this new, antiwar group, and in June he wanted to know if Gershom would join. He was disappointed at how few of his friends had thus far enrolled.[78] He reminded Gershom that he had previously said he would join with the leftists if the party split, and when Gershom was finally conscripted, Werner expressed his hope that Gershom's experience in the army would bring him to socialism.[79] Additionally, the scandal surrounding his arrest, trial, and imprisonment caused the final rupture between Werner and his father, Arthur. After Werner's release from prison in December 1917, he distanced himself further from his family background.

On the eve of 1918, immediately after turning twenty-two years old, he married his longtime girlfriend Emmy Wiechelt.[80] He described it as his final break with the bourgeoisie. His parents were aghast, and no one from his family was at the wedding, though Gershom was invited and did not attend for lack of train fare.[81] Werner was quite pleased with his bride. One year earlier, he had written, "She can really be considered worthy of bearing my children. She is free of Christian spirit and free of Germanic flaws." Later, he added, "for she has neither the disadvantages of a Jewish girl from Berlin nor those of a plant grown in working-class Linden. She is well-built inside and out, and when she has learned something, she will be a very good mother." She would even convert to Judaism if he wanted her to, though he wondered what for.[82]

Cut off from his family and still ailing from his war wound, Werner had hoped to continue his university studies with Emmy's support, even if it meant moving to Zurich. He could no longer count on his parents for financial support.[83] But he did not escape from the dictates of the German military, which immediately assigned him to a unit based in Halle. Werner's imprisonment did little to tame him, and according to his wife, the authorities were determined as ever to break him. She claimed that they wanted to put Werner on trial for making antiwar speeches, but there was a lack of evidence. Therefore, to make him "harmless," he had been declared fit for service and would be sent immediately back into battle. Emmy called it "nothing other than chicanery, for Werner has not been fit for infantry service for a long time. He is not in the least capable of withstanding long marches, etc."[84] His unit, the Thirty-Sixth Fusilier Regiment, regularly saw action on the Western Front. Emmy and Werner's fears were temporarily allayed after Werner visited the battalion's doctor and received an assignment to work as a driver and later as a scribe. He also worked in the kitchen, had much free time, and, despite his attenuated connection to Judaism, happily took advantage of festive meals provided to Jewish soldiers by the local Jewish community in Halle.[85]

But in the spring of 1918, Werner really wished that he could join a Red Guard unit in the nascent Russian Civil War. "It would be my great delight to behead Baltic barons," he wrote to Gershom.[86] Indeed, Werner's radicalization and cynicism shocked and even alienated Gershom, virtually the only member of the family who still maintained contact with him: "If he were not my brother, I would never be connected with him. Those are precisely the people who always make the revolution fail (or more precisely a priori *impossible*). For Werner, it is enough to be famous as a demagogue. He is political in a bad sense."[87] Perhaps Werner's own wife perceived the situation somewhat similarly. After the war, Emmy Scholem wrote to Gershom, "To me, you are the dearest person of all. You are dearer to me as a person than Werner, and that has nothing to do with the fact that Werner is my husband."[88]

Halle had become a home of sorts for Werner, who had been stationed there for a long time. Eventually, when he was transferred to the Seventy-Fifth Field Artillery Regiment, he breathed a sigh of relief since his new unit was based in Halle. He had worried that he might be transferred to the transport corps—a less dangerous assignment in the long term, but involving an immediate move to Magdeburg. He was looking forward to living outdoors, and to his satisfaction, his fellow artillery trainees were not new recruits, but rather other veterans transferred from the infantry.[89] A few days later, he was sent to the front with the duty of bringing munitions from the rear to the artillery positions. But even this assignment did not last, and he went from unit to unit "since no one will have me," as he put it in a letter to his brother.

Among the odd duties he performed was telephone service at regimental headquarters. Eventually, he ended up with an artillery unit in a forward position and participated in fierce combat in the Champagne region, with many comrades wounded.[90]

Soon, he had an additional concern: Emmy was pregnant. At first, Werner did not want the child at all. As he wrote to Gershom, "Yes, what should one say about this fact?! At first, I demanded that this matter should disappear, that is, naturally, at the very beginning of the pregnancy. But my wife's maternal feeling became too strong, and one cannot rebel against that."[91] Werner wanted a girl, but Emmy hoped for a boy, and she gave birth to a little girl named Edith on 27 September 1918. Emmy described the baby as "a little dainty black thing, a complete 'Scholem.' " She was compelled to return to full-time work only two weeks after the birth, and she anxiously awaited Werner's return from the war.[92] Later, Werner allegedly had the girl registered as Jewish, "so as to give her an oppositional position from the outset," even though she was not halakhically Jewish, having a non-Jewish mother.[93]

Similar to Werner's wartime experience, Gershom experienced personal crises, intellectual and political development, and longings for a future very different from his childhood. As a result of his Zionism and opposition to the war, he was expelled from school. Soon, a new crisis changed his life again. A few days after Werner's arrest on charges of treason, with Arthur still agitated, Gershom dared to disagree with their father during a lunchtime discussion. Arthur responded by evicting Gershom from the Scholems' home. On 15 February 1917, Arthur mailed Gershom a letter in which he informed his youngest son that he (i.e., Gershom) had until 1 March to leave the family home and was not allowed to return without Arthur's permission. Upon leaving the apartment, his father would give him one hundred marks "in order not to leave you without means." Whether Arthur would support his son's university studies after the war's conclusion "will depend upon your comportment until then."[94]

Gershom received some food from his mother and money from his mother's sister, Käte Hirsch Schiepan, but he rejected his aunt's attempts to foster a rapprochement on his father's terms. He claimed that "the suppression of my Zionist activity" was the unacceptable price of his father's aid.[95] Nonetheless, after nearly three months, Gershom wrote to his father, asking for financial support. Arthur replied contemptuously. He scoffed, "I would have been ashamed at the age of 19 and with two healthy arms to have accepted charity." He counseled his son to get a job: "Then you will see how self-earned bread tastes, and it would do your arrogance some good to do some real work. For what you regard as such is really only playing around, and the people who have to pay for your writing and language classes are certainly more than a little enraged inside. Money is something concrete, and people who deal only in abstractions consider it indecent to earn it."[96] Gershom rejected this advice. In the meantime, on the recommendation of a Zionist friend, Gershom moved into the Pension Struck, located in the upper-middle-class suburb of Wilmersdorf. Gershom had entered an entirely new world.

He had grown up in the city center, a short walk from the royal palace and grand museums. Just north of his family's home was a working-class neighborhood with all the picturesque charms and real challenges of life in Berlin's preindustrial core. A few streets south of his family's home was the newspaper district, which bustled with febrile activity. Wilmersdorf had only recently been built up, and it generally appealed to the well-off. While Gershom's childhood neighborhood was populated with old Berliners, who spoke the local dialect, the Pension Struck was popular with migrant Jews from eastern Europe. Many were Zionists, and some were Marxists. They spoke Yiddish or heavily accented German. The food served was kosher. Few German Jews took rooms there. In many ways, it was an island of *Yidishkeyt* and eastern European-style Zionism in a district that was popular with the German-Jewish haute bourgeoisie. In his memoir, written nearly sixty years after the fact, Gershom recalled it as an exciting and intellectually enriching change from the world of his youth. He wrote of meeting Zionist intellectuals and partaking in their endless, internecine debates. However, at the time, Gershom wrote in his diary—in a section subtitled "Truths and Lies of a Young Person and a Zionist"—that the pension was filled with bourgeois types for whom he had no respect, and the pension disgusted him as much as his parents' home. One bright spot during his stay was his new friendship with Zalman Rubashov (later named Zalman Shazar) and S. Y. Agnon. The former became president of Israel, and the latter became one of Israel's greatest writers and the country's first Nobel Prize winner. Rubashov helped Gershom receive a commission for his first paid publication: a translation from Yiddish into German of a book with brief biographies of Zionist pioneer guardsmen killed by Arabs in Palestine.[97]

While Gershom increasingly broke his ties to the Jewish middle class of Berlin, during this era he forged a new, critical friendship with one of the outstanding intellectuals of his generation: Walter Benjamin. Gershom Scholem saw Walter Benjamin for the first time in the autumn of 1913, at a meeting of Berlin youth groups, where Benjamin gave a speech about German and Jewish identity.[98] In 1915, while Gershom was at university in Berlin, the two finally met, and they bonded over a shared love of philosophical inquiry. As close as Gershom felt to his friends from Jung Juda, he acknowledged that "Benjamin was simply of a different caliber."[99] As the historian David Biale has noted, Walter Benjamin had an enormous impact on Gershom Scholem's intellectual development, even without sharing his thoroughly Zionist worldview. They discussed and corresponded intensely about ideas, and Benjamin was often the first to hear and to respond to Gershom's theories. Benjamin's critique of Martin Buber contributed to Gershom's disenchantment with the inspirational thinker.[100]

Walter Benjamin and Gershom Scholem were two of the greatest intellectuals produced by the Jewish bourgeoisie of Berlin, yet they provide a study in contrasts, having grown up in very different milieus, socioeconomically and spatially. The Scholem family, which ran a printshop, was part of the commercial middle class. While the Scholems venerated German high culture in typical German-Jewish bourgeois fashion, they did not circulate in the rarefied world of aesthetes and intellectuals. Moreover, their home was in an economically mixed part of central Berlin. The Benjamin family belonged to the German-Jewish haute bourgeoisie, and Walter's father was a dealer in art and antiques. The family originally lived in the affluent Tiergarten district, adjacent to central Berlin. Later, they moved to the newly developed, wealthy, verdant suburb of Grunewald. Walter spoke only eloquent, proper German, while Gershom often spoke the Berlin dialect—each boy a product of the environment in which he grew up.[101]

Though separated by their university studies and the war, the two remained in contact and visited each other when possible. They inspired each other and intensely debated literary and philosophical issues. In 1917 Benjamin married Dora Pollak and moved to Switzerland, but before his departure, he sent Gershom a secret code to use for writing any sensitive letters to him across the Swiss-German border.[102] By the end of 1917, the two were on a first-name basis, though they still used the formal "Sie" for "you" rather than the informal "Du."[103]

Walter Benjamin was not the only person for whom Gershom developed strong feelings during the course of 1917. He was in the throes of infatuation with several members of the opposite sex. The chief objects of his attention were Meta Jahr, a member of his Zionist circle, and Margarete ("Grete") Brauer, the older sister of his friend Erich. In his diary, he expressed his emotions: "I must not delude myself: am I in love or am I only excited, which ultimately may be purely natural for young people of my age? Recently, I have learned a few things about girls, things that are possible to know only if you have loved."[104] Still, he could not decide which girl was chiefly responsible for his arousal, and soon, greater concerns entered his life.

Even though Gershom was a resolute pacifist, he could not escape the war indefinitely, and in May 1917 he received a conscription notice. On the morning of 18 June, before he entered the gates of the recruitment barracks, his friend Zalman Rubashov presented him with a Hebrew book of Psalms to accompany him as he went to war.[105] He kept the book for the rest of his life, but his time in the army lasted only two months.

In his memoirs, Gershom recalled his military service as "short and stormy, and I do not want to speak about it."[106] In fact, only five weeks after joining the army, Private Gerhard Scholem of the Eighteenth Reserve Infantry Regiment, stationed in Allenstein (today Olsztyn, Poland), was transferred to an army hospital for psychiatric evaluation.[107] Doctors suspected that he suffered from dementia praecox, a diagnosis for conditions that were later labeled as schizophrenia. In letters to his friends, he bemoaned the poor state of his nerves and wrote of sudden seizures. While others at the hospital still went on hiking exercises, Gershom was assigned to clean the barracks and later to sort the mail.[108] Eventually, he was deemed too insane for that duty and ordered merely to supervise the lavatory for two to four hours a day. "Otherwise, I am totally free," he wrote.[109] He spent his days reading, writing, and thinking about philosophy, mathematics, linguistics, and Zionism. His army comrades, who had sympathized with him, soon despised him for avoiding duty—a sentiment that Gershom ascribed to antisemitism.[110] What Gershom did not mention in letters to his friends was that he was feigning illness.

Shortly after his release from active duty, Gershom wrote to Aharon Heller about "the truth about my illness." He noted "that I was not really sick. Rather it was an endless big lie. I am so very *healthy* that at the beginning of this strange undertaking, I did not know what to do. But I thought about it and found a way."[111] He began his act of dissimulation by going into a rage. When he was disciplined by his superior officer, he broke into a "nervous attack" that won him the sympathy of his comrades.[112] His army medical record notes that he entered the hospital on 25 July.[113] He wanted a permanent medical discharge but suspected that even with a diagnosis of psychosis he would be sent to German-occupied Warsaw to work as an army censor. He exclaimed, "Anyway, the Devil take me sideways if I go back to the infantry from here."[114] In fact, on 21 August, barely two months after his induction, the army sent him home as unfit for service.[115]

His mother wrote that although Gershom's family believed him to be "*very healthy*," they "welcomed" the diagnosis "because after that, under no circumstances will you be drafted again, but rather will remain unburdened, and that was still the main thing for you!" Still, his mother reminded him that he was "nervous" and counseled him not to enroll in too many classes.[116] With his parents' renewed financial support, which was an enduring concern, he was able to devote himself full-time to his studies once more.[117] While his brothers faced death on the battlefield, Gershom roamed the streets of Berlin in civilian clothing and contemplated where he should study.[118]

He selected Jena, where his friends from Heidelberg now lived. Although he was concentrating in mathematics, Gershom took a wide range of courses, such as theoretical physics and logic. Interestingly, his professors included Bruno Bauch, who later became an enthusiastic supporter of the Nazis, and Felix Auerbach, a Jew who committed suicide shortly after the Nazis came to power.[119] Gershom also had an active life outside the classroom. On Shabbat, he studied the Torah with local acquaintances, and many other friends came to visit him in Jena. He never suffered from a shortage of discussion and study partners, most of whom were women.[120] During a visit with his friends Erna Michaelis and Meta Jahr, he experienced his first kiss: "I love Meta dearly, and yet I find myself in the same abyss as before. I kissed her and cuddled with her. Was I allowed to do this? She has blossomed like a flower in springtime."[121] And this, despite the fact he had written to her two weeks earlier, "you are not alone in my heart, because my friend and a different girl . . . still dwell there, and always will."[122] The friend was Walter Benjamin, and the other girl was Grete Brauer, older sister of Gershom's friend Erich. In fact, at this time, Gershom and Grete maintained a lively correspondence about Zionism, Judaism, and Bible study.[123]

Gershom, who had just turned twenty, came to idolize Grete, who was five years older. Through letters and visits back to Berlin, he courted her in "his own awkward and bulldozing manner," as one biographer put it.[124] In his diary, he drafted a love letter to her, and a few days later, he actually wrote to her of his love, though very awkwardly and obliquely: "I cannot describe to you what energy it has cost me to write to you, for I know that I have brought my life into a crisis in which it can attain complete purity or shatter. . . . But since there is no one else on Earth to whom I could speak about you, I necessarily have to speak to you. Dear Grete, think about that I cannot write everything that I must write."[125] He added: "That only you have the power to make healthy again my Being, which has become sick from a very terrible mistake in my heart. . . . What should I have done otherwise? You can give back to me [the power of] language in that you do not withdraw your Being. There is no one whose stillest word lifts me up more and heals me more than you."[126]

Grete did not share his passion. And while Gershom preferred to share his feelings through correspondence, Grete wanted to discuss the matter in person. In the end, she had no choice but to break his heart in a letter. She wrote, "It has to be clear and open between us. There cannot be any mis-understanding, and if the knowledge of the truth is also painful for you—I cannot do otherwise. I am subject to a principle, which I cannot withdraw myself from. . . . I want to remain a friend of yours, as I have been up to this point. It is not possible for me to give you more."[127] After Grete's rejection, Gershom suffered a personal crisis and did not even open his mail. As he recovered his equilibrium, he developed a connection to Elsa Burchhardt, known as "Escha." She had grown up in an Orthodox Jewish family in Ham-burg and first met Gershom during a visit to Heidelberg in January 1918. In late March, he began to cultivate his friendship with her more seriously. But he also informed her, "I think very much about Zionist work."[128]

For Gershom, Zionism and intellectual interests remained primary. Dur-ing this time, the Zionist Federation of Germany's Committee for Jewish Cultural Work, led by Salman Schocken, invited young Gershom to join its work. He was allegedly the only youth to receive such an invitation, and he looked forward to meeting Schocken, a department store magnate and later renowned publisher of Judaica.[129] Gershom also expressed an interest in refounding Jung Juda. He and Harry Heymann corresponded about who passed muster for membership in the renewed group.[130] In addition to his Zionist exclusivity, Gershom risked descending into hyperintellectuality. He corresponded intensely with his friends about the minutiae of metaphysics and logic.[131] Even his old friend and Zionist comrade, the law student Kohos Karl Türkischer, began to find Gershom's philosophizing ever more dif-ficult to understand.[132] Meanwhile, Walter Benjamin suggested that Gershom come join him and his wife, Dora, in Bern, Switzerland. In January 1918, an army doctor reviewed Gershom's file and declared him "permanently unfit for military duty; not to be examined further."[133] Now, there was nothing to prevent him from emigrating.

Once final clearance was obtained, Gershom left Germany, and he did not resettle there until after the war had ended. He enrolled at the University of Bern and again took a range of courses in mathematics and physics, with philosophy as his main concentration.[134] He resided in the village of Muri, near the Benjamins' home, and later moved into Bern itself. Before their Swiss reunion in May 1918, Benjamin told Gershom that he (Gershom) was the only person "on the same wavelength" as he was,[135] but rekindling the friendship in person was more difficult. The two men had fierce arguments over philosophy, morality, and ethics. Yet they reconciled sufficiently to read books and journals together, and they jokingly called their intellectual coop-erative the University of Muri.[136] In fact, for long periods of time, Gershom saw no one else aside from Walter and Dora Benjamin.[137] But the solitude began to weigh on him, even as he was acutely aware of his own precocious brilliance. He wrote to a friend, "Admittedly, I have all possibilities here. I can work, think, go for walks, or cry as I please, and I assure you that I have made desperately intensive use of the first two in particular. But I know very well that if I were not assisted by my genius (I can no longer use a lesser word for it), I would be defenseless. I live almost like [I did] last summer, and that is all the more terrifying since I no longer have to defend myself against imaginary madness, but against real madness."[138]

One notable change in Gershom's social life was his blossoming correspondence with Escha Burchhardt. They maintained a very warm, yet slightly formal exchange of letters, and they confided in each other. By November 1918, they used the informal variant of "you" ("Du") with each other, rather than the formal variant ("Sie"), and signed their letters "your Gerhard" and "your Escha."[139] Despite the physical distance between them, he and Escha grew emotionally closer. Gershom returned to Germany in the summer of 1919, continuing his studies in Munich, in part because Escha was there.[140] Indeed, Gershom was still in Switzerland in November 1918, when a revolution broke out in Germany and the war ended. He looked at events in Germany from both a physical and emotional distance. The turmoil in Palestine interested him more than that in Berlin, despite its real impact on his family.[141]

By contrast, the eldest two Scholem brothers had a completely different war experience, serving for the duration of the conflict. Before the outbreak of war, it had been Erich's intention to serve as a one-year volunteer with a Bavarian field artillery regiment. Instead, he served in a unit equipping German aviators. Unlike Werner, who saw frequent combat, Erich remained well behind the front lines, where he suffered from a lack of nutrition, but no enemy attacks.[142] Even Arthur's youngest brother, Georg, participated in the war effort. Despite his lack of previous army service, the forty-year-old doctor served as a staff surgeon in the reserve militia with the rank of captain, for which he was decorated.[143] In fact, nearly half of all German doctors were mobilized.[144]

Throughout the war, Reinhold served with the signal troops, who operated field telephones and laid cables for battlefield communications. Having already served as a one-year volunteer and officer candidate before the war, Reinhold became a platoon commander in a telephone unit early in 1915.[145] In 1916 he was awarded the Iron Cross.[146] By the next summer, Reinhold had been promoted to sergeant (*Vizewachtmeister*), serving in Telephone Division 187 on the Western Front. Though never wounded in action, he was sent back to Berlin in August 1917 with a case of enteritis. He was later transferred to a garrison in Hammerstein in West Prussia (today Czarne, Poland). By January 1918, he was on the Western Front, serving near Verdun.[147]

Though the war had begun with a great display of national unity that portended an end to antisemitism and full integration of Jews into German society, the war had the opposite effect over the long term. Distrust of Jews only increased over time. As frustration grew with the army's inability to win the war and with privations on the home front, the gap that existed between Jewish Germans and non-Jewish Germans before the war threatened to erupt into a chasm. In cities like Berlin, increasing numbers of ordinary Germans began to accept an antisemitic explanation for food shortages. Supposedly, Jewish speculators and commercial middlemen were to blame for the lack of food available to lower- and middle-class Germans. Indeed, the term "Jew" became a byword for anyone allegedly engaging in profiteering, whether the nefarious individual was actually Jewish or not. When the government failed to meet Germans' expectations for the provision of food to civilians, it, too, was accused of being "Jewish" or at least a "defender of Jews."[148]

Antisemites accused German Jews of evading military service, and it became a widespread belief that Jews in war industries used connections unavailable to ordinary Berliners to avoid conscription.[149] Even the Catholic Center Party Reichstag member Matthias Erzberger, who was not an avowed antisemite, demanded a review based on "gender, age liable for military service, connections, [and] religion" of all people involved with the war effort in October 1916.[150] Around the same time, the Prussian war ministry ordered a census of Jews in the army. Although the so-called Jew Census (*Judenzählung*) was carried out, the results were not published, which encouraged rumors that powerful Jews had blocked its publication lest the census's damaging results be known. Only after the war could Jewish scholars prove that the percentage of Jewish frontline soldiers was roughly proportional to their share of the population eligible for military service.[151]

The increase in exclusionary nationalism and the deterioration in the situation for the Jews did not escape the Scholems' notice. Werner reported to Gershom that his old friend Heinz Jansen complained to Emmy about Werner's "unfortunate Jewish way of thinking," while praising the "dear, superb" German people. He referred to Werner as a "Jew" and himself as "we Germans."[152] There was increasing antisemitism in the German army, clearly discernible to Jews who cared about their Jewish identity.[153] In this atmosphere, Werner—who maintained his left-wing socialist position and dedication to Marxism while being fully cognizant of his Jewish roots—began to mull over involvement with the Jewish movement. He had even retreated from a strictly atheist position, decided not to withdraw formally from the Jewish community, and considered raising his future children as Jews.[154]

Werner's relationship to Judaism was a matter of debate for Gershom and his circle. In 1916, Werner told Gershom that "Zionism is itself a sign of life of Judaism, *Die Blauweiße Brille* a sign of life of Jewish youth, and Jewish youth a sign of life of Zionism."[155] Nonetheless, Gershom's good friend Erich Brauer wrote about Werner, "By the way, I do not *believe* that he can be as *Jewish* as us—even though he presents himself so." Gershom strongly disagreed, commenting that Werner was "*on the path*. He went away from us 4 years ago; now he is coming back. . . . I intend *very much* to win him for us later!"[156] Gershom, who viewed the world through indefatigable Jewish lenses, was overly optimistic about his brother, Judaism, and Zionism. Meanwhile, the war had transformed the conditions of daily life in Berlin.

There were privations and changes compared to the years before 1914. Already in 1916, when Werner was convalescing at home, one could see wounded veterans circulating in Berlin. Upon Gershom's release from military service, he returned to Berlin and noticed the seeming emptiness of the city: "Berlin is empty: *everyone*, really everyone has been drafted."[157] Before the war, over two million people lived in Berlin. By the time Gershom made his observation, three hundred thousand fewer people lived in the German capital. Curiously, the phenomenon may have particularly affected his social class. The percentage of Berlin men in the military during World War I was considerably lower than the national average. While 81 percent of all German men of military age served, only 59 percent of Berliners did. This situation resulted from Berlin's disproportionately industrial economy, whose importance to the war effort necessitated keeping workers in the factories and out of the trenches. But Gershom Scholem's world was the bourgeoisie, and soldiers from Berlin were, in fact, generally more middle-class than other German soldiers since industrial workers were often sent back to their factories or not conscripted at all.[158] Additionally, the German government issued a law preventing vital industrial workers from switching employers without permission.

The Scholems' businesses did not have those advantages. They owned printshops, and Berlin's printing industry was one of the most severely affected by the wartime disruptions. By October 1914, the printing industry in southeastern Berlin employed 35 percent as many workers as it had in July 1914, and the paper industry—critical for printers—employed only 23 percent as many workers. Across Berlin, by April 1915, large printing firms employed 54 percent of their prewar workforce. A number of factors created this situation. Without access to their raw materials and with virtually no civilian market for printed items, the paper and printing industries practically collapsed. At the same time, firms in certain industries faced the mobilization of workers, which led to a labor shortage by the spring of 1915.[159] The printing industry refused to raise its contractual wages until 1916, but then they skyrocketed. Before the war, a skilled, married printer in Berlin earned a minimum weekly wage of 34.38 marks. In 1916 that increased to 40.92 marks; 61.46 marks in November 1917; and 76.46 marks by August 1918, according to one source. Moreover, many employers paid considerably more than the minimum.[160] The Scholems were likely caught between these extremes: diminished consumer demand, a lack of both paper stock and skilled printers, and increased wages for those who were available. The war changed the balance of economic power in the city, weakening the owners of small workshops and businesses, who had trouble getting war contracts and keeping workers from going to better-paid war industries.[161]

Inflation affected the economy, and by 1916 there were chronic shortages of consumer goods, especially foodstuffs. Even before the war began, Berlin's population had grown rapidly, but food production in the surrounding rural regions had not kept pace. Once the war began and refugees streamed into the city from Germany's eastern provinces, feeding Berlin's inhabitants became even more difficult. Additionally, German agriculture was hit hard by the war. The military requisitioned farm horses for its own use, and German farmers, who had been heavily dependent on artificial fertilizer, were cut off from Chilean supplies of saltpeter. At the same time, wartime transport inside Germany was unpredictable.[162] As a result of these factors, German cities like Berlin got significantly less food than they needed. Between July 1914 and December 1916, the price of food in Berlin doubled, and it doubled once more by July 1919.[163] The rationing of basic foodstuffs led to a massive diminution in consumption. The authorities did provide more food to workers in critical heavy industries, but for most Germans, the situation was catastrophic. By the period July 1916 to June 1917, meat rations in Germany were roughly 31 percent of prewar consumption. That decreased to 20 percent of prewar levels by the period July 1917 to June 1918, and 12 percent by July 1918 to December 1918. Dietary replacements such as fish, legumes, and rice were nearly impossible to obtain. Cooking fats, including lard, butter, and vegetable oil, were extremely scarce. Only potato rations remained near prewar levels.[164] As early as October 1915, food riots broke out in Berlin, and as the war continued, women's demonstrations occasionally filled the streets with their demands for peace and food. In the summer of 1916, prized factory workers threatened work stoppages over the shortage of food; in January 1918, they went on strike.[165]

The scarcity of food led to a thriving black market, where products were available at greatly inflated prices. Wealthy members of the bourgeoisie could afford to buy food that workers and lower-middle-class burghers could not.[166] Betty Scholem was still able to obtain a goose and fat in November 1917. However, the shadow economy could also disadvantage Jews. While some non-Jewish Berliners who were recent migrants to the city from farms and villages could use family connections to obtain scarce food, most Berlin Jews did not have that option. Jews like the Scholems were not recent arrivals, and even those Jews who had migrated recently to the city usually lacked ties to the German countryside. Betty Scholem's non-Jewish maid, Lydia, arranged food packages for the family, but at times, Betty could not rely on that avenue, and the family ran short of meat and fat. Late in the war, when meat was even scarcer, Betty depended on Lydia, a printshop employee named Boppke, and her son Erich's connections to supply her, "but at what prices!," as she exclaimed. On one occasion, she declined to buy a turkey for one hundred marks, even though she could have fed the family lunch for three days with it.[167] While Gershom was in Jena, his mother sent him food packages and money for food, a sacrifice for the family. Gershom, however, spent his funds on books and travel, incurring his mother's wrath.[168]

With food and heating fuel chronically short, Berlin was ravaged by diseases, such as typhoid, cholera, tuberculosis, and scarlet fever. In the second half of 1918, the worldwide influenza pandemic struck Berlin; however, with military defeat imminent and the government near collapse, the city's public health response was minimal. Educational leaders had to decide whether to close schools and keep children away from potentially infectious peers or to stay open and provide undernourished children with school meals.[169] Some Scholems did find their schools closed, but nearly every member of the extended family eventually caught the flu. Erich had a high fever and hallucinations; Arthur soaked his bed sheets with sweat from his fever. More than 4,700 Berliners died from the flu and respiratory tract diseases during the last three months of 1918. Betty correctly observed that the disease afflicted young adults more severely than the elderly, and their family was fortunate to escape without any flu-related deaths.[170]

In June 1918, the family received some welcome good news: Reinhold had been promoted to the rank of lieutenant in the army reserve. Betty was filled with joy and pride, and Arthur was relieved that Werner's predicament did not adversely affect Reinhold's situation.[171] In fact, Reinhold's appointment was significant for many reasons. Naturally, it was prestigious for the Scholems to have an officer in the family, particularly in an era when the ratio of enlisted men to officers was very high. Additionally, becoming an officer involved successfully navigating a dilatory and byzantine bureaucracy. Not all who attempted the task succeeded.[172] Reinhold's appointment also had meaning for German Jewry as a whole. For decades, thousands of young, educated Jewish men had completed the training and preliminary service required for commission as an officer in the German army reserve, but not a single one had received a commission in a Prussian regiment since 1885.[173] That changed with the war. On account of the greater need for personnel in the army, unbaptized Jews were finally promoted to reserve officer ranks.

In March 1918, three and a half years after the war began, it seemed that the military stalemate was broken. Russia, now under a Bolshevik government, surrendered to the Germans, and Germany could shift men and materiel to the West without concern about the Eastern Front. To exploit its momentary advantage before fresh American troops could shore up French and British forces, Germany made a final bid for victory and launched a series of attacks against Allied forces. After making considerable initial progress, the advance petered out.[174] Reinhold participated in the failed German offensive and remained on the front lines even as German forces suffered reverses.[175] Meanwhile, the home front seethed with discontent, and the army leadership feared mutinies or even revolution in the ranks.

At the beginning of October 1918, Kaiser Wilhelm selected Prince Max von Baden, a presumptive liberal, to serve as imperial chancellor. Under pressure, he undertook modest measures to democratize Germany's government, including the appointment of Social Democrats to high-ranking positions and the abolition of three-class suffrage in Prussia. While not a Socialist, Betty Scholem greeted these measures as a sign of positive change in Germany. She also noted with pride that through his work with the Central Commission for Health Insurance Funds, her husband, Arthur, was personally acquainted with two of the new appointees: Gustav Bauer, state secretary of the Imperial Labor Office (the equivalent of federal minister of labor), and Julius Fräßdorf, minister without portfolio in Saxony's state government.[176] Prince Max's government also began exchanging notes with the American president Woodrow Wilson, trying to agree on terms for an armistice. Betty Scholem welcomed "the peace in sight," particularly after experiencing things so bad that she could not mention them in a letter that the censors might read.[177] Within weeks of her writing those words, in November 1918, the World War ended. However, peace did not mean a return to stability. Political chaos and violence was the order of the day as different groups made claims to power. Betty Scholem soon wrote to Gershom, "We thought that the hard times were behind us; however, it seems as if they are only before us."[178] She was not mistaken. During the next five years, Germans experienced civil war, economic catastrophe, and openly antisemitic violence, all of which directly affected the Scholem family and the Jews of Germany.

CHAPTER 4

Life in the Time of Revolutions

The Early Weimar Republic

By the morning of 9 November 1918, Germany's situation was untenable. Sailors and soldiers inside Germany were mutinying against their commanders and spreading revolution. On the Western Front, German soldiers in rear areas refused to take up forward positions and passively rebelled against the kaiser. The imperial chancellor, Prince Max von Baden, realized that if a civil war broke out, the army would not support the kaiser.[1] In this hopeless situation, the kaiser decided to abdicate the imperial throne, but when he did not make any public declaration of his own, Prince Max simply announced the kaiser's abdication and then resigned as chancellor. He designated Friedrich Ebert, coleader of the Social Democrats, as his successor.[2]

Ebert wanted an elected assembly to write a constitution that would resolve the issue of monarchy or republic; however, events spun out of control within hours. The radical socialist leader Karl Liebknecht intended to proclaim a socialist council (soviet) republic with wide-ranging changes to the political and economic systems. In an attempt to regain the initiative, Philipp Scheidemann, Ebert's coleader of the Social Democrats, addressed a crowd gathered in front of the Reichstag and proclaimed Germany to be a democratic republic. A few hours later, Liebknecht announced his socialist republic from the balcony of Berlin's royal palace.[3] Either way, Germany would be a republic led by a left-wing government, but the scene was now set for a civil war pitting the Center Left against the Far Left.

As residents of central Berlin, the Scholems literally stumbled into the midst of the revolutionary tumult. On the afternoon of 9 November, Betty Scholem took a stroll with her sister, Käte, and they noticed a red flag waving above the palace. They took it to be a sign of the revolution and imminent peace and were seemingly unaware that Karl Liebknecht had just declared the Free Socialist Republic of Germany. After returning home, Betty wrote to Gershom in Switzerland, "Peace is coming; everything will be good!"[4] That same evening, she and Arthur went for a walk near the palace, only to find themselves caught up in a crowd fleeing machine-gun fire. Two days later she wrote, "That should happen to me! My legs are still shaking."[5]

The First World War effectively ended on 11 November 1918, when a delegate appointed by the last imperial German government signed an armistice agreement with the Allies. Even though Germany was now a republic and fighting had ended, revolutionary conditions still reigned in Berlin. Arthur sent his workers home early, so they could participate in political demonstrations. A red placard reading "Public institution! To be protected!" graced the Scholems' printshop, which was protected by soldiers under orders from the revolutionary Workers' and Soldiers' Council.[6] Betty wrote of the chaos in Berlin during the following days: "No one governs, and no one pays attention." Only the "public's sense of order protects the nuts and bolts of public life." Meanwhile, extremists at both ends of the political spectrum concerned her. She feared a revolt by Liebknecht's supporters, known as Spartakists, and she bemoaned the "Jew-baiting" by right-wing parties, "who want to distract the anger of the people—the old historical ruse."[7]

Rather than coming back together after the war, German civil society was fracturing further, with a direct impact on the Scholems and the Jews of Germany. For the brothers Reinhold, Erich, Werner, and Gershom, as well as their parents, formative experiences before and during the war guided the choices they made in this new era. Moreover, the choices made at this time resulted in decisive consequences in the 1930s.

Most German Jews readily embraced the democratic republic that emerged in 1918 and 1919 and maintained their long-standing support for political liberalism. One week after the revolution, the newspaper editor Theodor Wolff, himself a scion of the Jewish bourgeoisie, published an appeal for a new democratic political party. Among his cosigners were Albert Einstein and Rudolf Mosse. A few days later, the German Democratic Party (Deutsche Demokratische Partei) came into being.[8] It became the preferred political party for the vast majority of German Jews, including

Erich Scholem, who spent the postwar months working to implement the transition to a peacetime economy and society.[9] Betty Scholem, an admirer of Wolff and his political moderation during the war, joined the German Democrats almost immediately. Though she had not been politically active during the empire, and even had misgivings about female suffrage, she felt compelled to care about politics at the age of fifty-five.[10] When the Social Democrats took the initiative and democratized Germany, she was full of hope, but one month later, she felt they had no idea what they were doing. They were weak, vacillating, and allowed the Spartakists free rein.[11] Betty had an exceedingly low opinion of those far-left radicals, who were "only criminals, scatterbrains, and young cattle who follow along!"[12]

Werner Scholem did not share his mother and brother's enthusiasm for liberal democracy. He sympathized with the Spartakists, led by Karl Lieb-knecht and Rosa Luxemburg. He deeply regretted that he had not been present in Germany on 9 November 1918: "For the rest of my life, I will never get over it that I did not participate in the revolution in Germany. Such bad luck to have to be stuck during that time far from all those events, while at home every previously halfway [politically] active person became a minister." Instead of receiving a ministerial portfolio, he was still with his army unit, on his way back from France to Burg bei Magdeburg. Once demobilized, he began studying in Berlin, where Emmy had employment, though he preferred to remain in Halle, where he had friends and a "sphere of influence."[13] Emmy threw in her lot with the Spartakists, while Werner was conflicted about whether he should join the new Communist Party that the Spartakists were forming or the Independent Social Democrats, the socialist splinter party that formed one-half of the coalition governing postwar Germany. In 1917 the Independents had broken with the majority Social Democrats over support for the war, but with the conflict over, the Independents were in decline. Meanwhile, many of Emmy and Werner's friends had already joined the Spartakists. For Werner, it was a question of feelings versus reason. His feelings told him to join with the Spartakists, but he recognized "the pointlessness and absurdity" of their policy.[14] Thus, he remained with the Independent Social Democrats for now, though eventually, he, too, would move to the extreme left.

Reinhold also missed the revolution of November 1918 because of his wartime service; however, in contrast to Werner, he strongly opposed the leftist revolutionaries and joined the right-liberal German People's Party (Deutsche Volkspartei).[15] Reinhold was on the Western Front with his division when the war ended. He reached home in December and returned to work at the family printing business within days.[16] In fact, compared to the soldiers serving inside Germany, who helped spread the revolution and expected broad political change, soldiers returning home from the Western Front were generally less concerned with politics and more focused on resuming their old lives.[17] Betty Scholem reported that Reinhold was "like all front-line soldiers, by the way, deeply outraged by the conditions in Berlin, which really are abysmal."[18]

Demonstrations, strikes, assemblies, and political violence became part of everyday life in the German capital. With women's suffrage new, Betty Scholem attended an assembly on how to vote, but a revolutionary soldier addressing the newly enfranchised women spoke pessimistically of the situation in Berlin. Writing to Gershom in quiet Switzerland, Betty related how the Spartakists were involved in shootings around the city, and every morning on her way to work, she noticed red (i.e., socialist or communist) posters on advertising columns. The government required businesses—including Arthur Scholem's printshop—to rehire all their former employees who had left for military service when the war began, though now shifts were limited to eight hours a day. The wish to prevent political instability fostered by unemployment outweighed the need to pay wages out of savings or through loans.[19] However, political transition meant business opportunities as well as potential danger for printers like the Scholems. With Germany now a republic, the former Royal Friedrich Wilhelm University of Berlin hired Arthur Scholem to reprint the school's diplomas, but Berlin's newspapers and printers were also targets for revolutionaries who wished to control the press.[20]

The first postwar government of Germany was the Council of People's Deputies, which was made up of differing Socialists. Despite calls to establish a representative government via a system of councils (or soviets), both revolutionary activists and mainstream politicians steered Germany on a course toward a traditional parliamentary democracy. The initial momentum from early November 1918 that had ended the war and brought Germany to the brink of a soviet-style revolution had been channeled. While this development reassured many bourgeois Germans, not everyone was content.

At the end of December, radical Socialists, including the Spartakists, founded the Communist Party of Germany (Kommunistische Partei Deutschlands). Within days, an open civil war prevailed. Armed workers seized control of several major newspaper offices, only a few blocks from Arthur Scholem's printshop and the family home. Soon, the Communists and even Independent Social Democrats joined the uprising.[21] All manner of demonstrators filled central Berlin's squares. Arthur Scholem's workers left work to join the demonstrations on 6 January; however, when he refused to let them have a second day off from work, his employees called for a workplace assembly. According to Betty Scholem, war veterans spoke in favor of remaining at work while Spartakist employees wanted to join the revolt. Ultimately, Arthur's workers stayed at their printing presses.[22] But the revolt continued.

In the end, the socialist government had to depend on far-right-wing militias and conservative army units to suppress the communist revolt in Berlin. On 15 January, troops arrested, interrogated, and executed Karl Liebknecht and Rosa Luxemburg. His body was deposited at the morgue without identification; hers was dumped into a canal in Berlin's Tiergarten park, not to be found for several months.[23] Throughout the city, militias and army units shot insurgents and suspected Communists.

Other parts of Germany were also aflame with left-wing revolution. In Munich, the Independent Social Democrats, led by Kurt Eisner, who was Jewish, overthrew the Bavarian monarchy even before the kaiser abdicated the imperial throne. Three and a half months later, a right-wing nationalist murdered Eisner, causing Gershom's friend Erich Brauer to despair over the German people.[24] In the political chaos after Eisner's assassination, a communist government came to power in Munich, eventually led by Eugen Leviné, a Russian Jew. Within weeks, right-wing militias and army units defeated the Communists and executed Leviné. His death led to a general strike among the workers of Berlin, and Arthur Scholem's printshop employees were among them. Arthur Scholem was furious that his workers got involved when they had newspapers to print and events in Munich were so far away.[25] Much closer to home, in Berlin, Hugo Haase, a Jewish, left-wing Socialist, who had nominally been cochairman of the German government for seven weeks in 1918, was shot in October 1919.

Many stolidly middle-class German Jews despaired over the fact that Jews were so prominent in the left-wing movements across the country. In Saxony, Anhalt, the Rhineland, the Ruhr valley, northern Germany, and especially Bavaria, Jews were among the revolutionary leadership seeking to transform Germany, not to mention Jewish Communists in governments in Russia and Hungary. Jews were even disproportionately represented among more mainstream governments of the left and center left. Shortly after the revolution of November 1918, the new federal government asked the local Berlin politician Hugo Preuß, a Jew and liberal democrat, to draft a constitution for the republic.[26] Two of the six leaders in republican Germany's first national government were socialist Jews. In February 1919, that government ceded power to a traditional cabinet under the prime minister Philipp Scheidemann. Of the fifteen different men to serve in Scheidemann's cabinet, five were either Jews or Protestants with recent Jewish ancestors, including the ministers of justice, finance, and the interior.[27] The situation was similar in the various state governments. Writing about the Bavarian government in Munich, one Jewish woman proclaimed, "Here, not only were there many Jews among the leaders, but also among all the employees one met in government buildings. It was understood that so many Jews were at the forefront. They were the 'intellectuals.'"[28] Both Jews and antisemites took note of this political-demographic phenomenon. For many Jews, it was a source of anxiety. Indeed, the role of the Jews in the postwar governments moved many antisemites to violence.[29]

In this climate of extreme instability, Germany commenced the work of building a parliamentary democracy. On 19 January, elections were held for a National Assembly to serve as a constitutional convention. For the first time in her life, Betty Scholem voted. She waited in line for an hour and a half to cast her ballot.[30] In fact, over 83 percent of eligible Germans voted in the election, and they rewarded the parties of the center and left who had demanded a reconciliatory end to the war as early as 1917.[31] The Social Democrats received nearly 38 percent of the votes, the Catholic Center Party and its regional allies 19.7 percent, and the German Democrats 18.5 percent. The overwhelming majority of Germany's Jews voted for the German Democrats, including Betty and Erich Scholem. Reinhold's German People's Party won 4.4 percent of the vote. Werner had been a paid campaigner for the Independent Social Democrats, but they won only 7.6 percent.[32]

Nonetheless, the election did not stop the political and social unrest. Betty Scholem wrote to Gershom that every day, another strike broke out, crippling the capital. Even their own printing firm suffered from work stoppages and employment disputes. Additionally, Betty wrote that they still lacked sufficient fats in their diet and heating material for their home. And it was not just the Scholems. She claimed that famine was spreading in the city, the children's mortality rate had doubled, and prices were spiraling upward.[33] Meanwhile, there was gunfire only a few yards from their home.[34] She summed up the first months of peace: "Absolutely, conditions are highly precarious and worrying. By comparison, wartime was golden. Sure, shortages prevailed, but [there was] order. And now violence prevails."[35]

With Berlin still in the throes of unrest, the National Assembly met from February to July 1919 in the city of Weimar. The new constitution that the parliamentarians produced laid the groundwork for what came to be called the Weimar Republic. Signed into effect by the German president Friedrich Ebert on 11 August, the constitution proclaimed, "The German Reich is a republic. The authority of the state comes from the people."[36] This new state also considerably improved the legal basis for the Jews' life in Germany. While previous German laws had guaranteed basic freedom of religion, the Weimar constitution stipulated: "Civil and civic rights and obligations are neither dependent upon nor limited by the exercise of freedom of religion. The enjoyment of civil and civic rights, as well as the admittance to public offices, is independent of religious confession." The republican German state would not sanction discrimination based on religious affiliation. In practical terms, this meant that, in contrast to the state of affairs under the German Empire, Jews would no longer face the de facto discrimination that had precluded them from becoming judges, military officers, and professors at state universities. The new constitution abolished a state church but preserved the rights of religious organizations and guaranteed tax-funded support for religious communities.[37]

While Betty Scholem expressed her concern about the atmosphere of feverish politics and societal uncertainty of early 1919, her son Werner thrived in these conditions. He worked for the *Braunschweiger Volksfreund,* the official newspaper of the Independent Social Democrats in Braunschweig. When the newspaper expanded into Hanover, Werner became local editor. He definitively put his university studies on hold in favor of remunerative employment and politics. As he put it, he worked as a reporter in the morning, as an editor in the afternoon, and as a political speaker in the evening. He bemoaned the lack of cooperation between the Communists and the Independent Social Democrats in Hanover, while they worked "hand in hand" in Braunschweig. He hoped for a united front among the radical Left. Meanwhile, he successfully campaigned for a seat on the Linden city council, where he was the leader of the Independent Social Democratic caucus. It was also his job to organize those "elements disposed to revolution in the city and province of Hanover." He boasted to his brother Gershom about how successful he had been and how annoyed the mainstream Social Democrats were with him.[38] He was the "Independent [Social Democratic] screaming lion of the whole province."[39]

Their Aunt Hedwig hoped to save Werner from the "clutches of professional politics" and implored her husband to give Werner money to study to be a schoolteacher. She had the impression that Werner was not entirely happy as a "publicity crier for his party." In fact, Werner had become an unabashed propagandist for the radical Left. He announced to his family, "from now on, the industrial workers will rule." When his aunt asked what role was open to them, not being factory workers, he replied, "well, naturally you are sitting on your sack of money."[40] He was annoyed that Gershom was not more interested in the revolution and teased his Zionist brother that one day he, too, might find himself in the midst of a revolution "when you establish the Jewish state and your bigwigs make the terrible mistake of establishing a capitalist branch of London there with a Jewish proletariat.

A Jewish-communist proletariat in Palestine. You could really experience something!"[41]

A few months later, Werner changed jobs and cities. Given the choice of serving as party secretary for the Province of Hanover or an editor of the party newspaper in Halle, he resigned from the Linden city council and moved to Halle. Soon Emmy joined him, leaving their daughter behind in Hanover, to be raised by Emmy's mother.[42] Frequently, Werner Scholem, as the anonymous editor or reporter in the field, wrote articles about the remarkable speeches of Werner Scholem, the Independent Social Democratic activist.[43] In a case of the ends justifying the means, his newspaper twisted the truth and even lied to its readers for political purposes. Drafting a letter in his diary, Gershom reproached Werner, "I did know now that Marx had commanded to lie. . . . My hope in your party was false."[44]

While Werner built a new life in the service of the party, his father and oldest brothers became more established in their old lives. Arthur Scholem made Reinhold and Erich junior partners in the family's printing firm and allowed them to make decisions on the company's behalf. With Reinhold and Erich entering the business as his administrative equals, Arthur dissolved Betty's proxy.[45] Arthur, who had long been active in professional organizations and the administration of the local public health insurance fund, continued his voluntary activities, serving on an arbitration board for the graphics industry and working to build a convalescent home for the insurance fund.[46] A Reichstag commission called on him to testify regarding insurance matters, and he consulted at the Labor Ministry.[47] Betty described him as a "bridge-builder in the endless conflict between physicians and insurance companies."[48] Reinhold and Erich spent their leisure time on the water. They had bought a small rowboat, which they christened "Bettychen" (Little Betty) in honor of their mother. They enjoyed rowing along the Zeuthener See and Dahme River, near the southeastern corner of Berlin.[49] Later, in the 1920s, they acquired another hobby and joined the Soncino Society, an association of Jewish bibliophiles. Eventually, Reinhold and Erich printed rare books and special editions on Jewish topics for the society.[50]

Additional changes were soon in store for the Scholem brothers. In the years after the war ended, Germany saw a massive surge in marriages—nearly twice the prewar rate—and Reinhold and Erich were among those marrying. In April 1921, Reinhold married Käthe Wagner, the daughter of a deceased, wealthy businessman, and in September 1921, Erich married Edith Katz, the daughter of a necktie manufacturer.[51] Arthur Scholem seemed pleased with his daughters-in-law, though Aunt Hedwig Scholem did not care for Erich's bride. She did like Reinhold's wife, describing her as "the only thing I could agree with Reinhold about."[52] Ultimately, neither brother had a particularly happy marriage.

The years 1919 and 1920 were especially traumatic and consequential for Germany. On 28 June 1919, five years to the day after the assassination of the Austrian archduke Franz Ferdinand, German officials signed the Treaty of Versailles, officially ending World War I. The treaty reassigned considerable imperial German territory to Poland, Lithuania, France, Belgium, and Denmark. The German army was limited to one hundred thousand men, the navy faced severe restrictions, and the air force was disbanded.[53] Subsequent agreements saddled the Germans with enormous reparations. After various conferences considered sums of 269 billion marks or 248 billion marks in reparations, the Reparations Commission fixed the amount at 132 billion marks, which was almost immediately lowered.[54] To the German people, some of whom never truly accepted the loss of the war, the treaty and reparations demands seemed incredibly harsh. Soon, the Treaty of Versailles and related agreements came to be known as a "Diktat," engendering great bitterness and becoming an object of nationalist fury inside Germany.[55] Even German Jews, who had been restrained in their prowar rhetoric after 1914, were aghast at the treaty, and they joined ranks with their non-Jewish compatriots in opposing it. Along the eastern border with Poland, many Jews joined local German militias to fight against the border changes, and in plebiscites on territorial adjustments, Jews voted overwhelmingly for the German side.[56]

During the first postwar year, as Germany made the turbulent transition from empire to republic, Gershom Scholem remained in Switzerland, where he observed the revolution with some curiosity, in contrast to his earlier indifference to the war.[57] He heard all sorts of rumors about the situation in Germany, and he beseeched his mother for clarification. And as Germany moved toward a new, democratic political order, he applauded the election of the liberal-democratic feminist Gertrud Bäumer to the Reichstag as well as the rumor that university studies would henceforth be free: "That is very nice (then I can enroll in a lot!), but unlikely to be realized."[58]

Gershom Scholem's life in Swiss emigration remained very intellectual, and he maintained a Jewish circle of acquaintances. In his free time, he translated "Ma'oz Tzur" from Hebrew into German for a publication on Hanukkah.[59] As the year came to a close, he hoped to spend Hanukkah with Walter Benjamin and his wife, Dora. Writing to his friend Escha Burchhardt, Gershom commented that while he had a Christmas tree until he was fifteen, Benjamin had one until he was twenty-four. Only Dora broke him of the habit.[60] In the spring, he spent Passover with an extremely religious family.[61] Although Scholem could not be described as Orthodox in terms of his own religious practice, he had a great love of Jewish holidays and a preference for traditional observance. Additionally, after his youth among nominally religious Jews, he had a deep respect for traditional Jewry. He spent Shabbat afternoons with a religious family originally from eastern Europe.[62] His father in Berlin worried that his student son's world was too Jewish. When Gershom Scholem considered traveling to Lausanne or Geneva to learn French, his father opposed the plan by writing, "I have nothing against Lausanne or Geneva, but you may not socialize just with Jews, but rather with Frenchmen. Otherwise, you miss the point [of the trip], and you will learn only Yiddish-Français to go with your Yiddish-German."[63]

When Jewish delegates from eastern Europe passed through Bern on their way to the Paris Peace Conference, Scholem got to know some of them and felt an instant connection to them that transcended his being "from Berlin and a person without a Jewish childhood."[64] He also enjoyed meeting the central European Zionist intellectual Hugo Bergmann. Bergmann, who was born in Prague and circulated among the German-speaking Prague Jewish intelligentsia, which included Franz Kafka and Max Brod, was an early enthusiast of Martin Buber. Scholem told his friend Erich Brauer that Bergmann "completely unexpectedly turned out to be a decent person," and they had a long and frank discussion on a wide range of topics, including Hebrew, Martin Buber, and the Kabbalah.[65] Bergmann wrote to his wife about meeting Scholem: "From an assimilated origin, he has become a total Jew, deeply immersed in the appreciation of the Hebrew spirit. . . . On Friday evening, I will again be the guest of him and his girlfriend."[66] That girlfriend was Escha Burchhardt, who was visiting Scholem in Bern at the time.[67] They married in 1923. Twelve years later, she and Scholem divorced and she married Bergmann.

Although Jung Juda, Gershom Scholem's Zionist club, had dissolved during World War I and Scholem was now relatively isolated in Switzerland, he remained as passionate as ever about Zionism, particularly cultural Zionism. He did not deviate from his belief in the centrality of Hebrew to Zionism and the ability of Zionism—as a cultural movement—to reinvigorate the Jewish people. In fact, he ascribed almost mystical power to the Hebrew language, calling it "the only path."[68] His dislike of the prominent socialist Zionist youth organization Hapoel Hatzair focused on the group's use of language.[69] Additionally—and despite his desire for an all-pervasive revitalization of Judaism and Jewry—Scholem declared that Zionism was not a messianic movement and rejected what he called "radical Zionism." He opposed the application of mysticism to profane politics.[70] However, he imbued Zionism itself with a nearly sacred mission vis-à-vis the Jewish youth of Europe.[71]

Gershom Scholem's family wanted him to return to Germany, in part because Germany's economic situation made it very expensive to support him abroad.[72] Gershom seemed relatively unconcerned about the hardship his plans and peregrinations caused for his family.[73] For him, studies remained his raison d'être. As he wrote to his friend Erich Brauer, "I would be just as little ready to answer the question why I seek or have a relationship to scholarship as the question of God or why I live."[74] But what to study? In April 1919, he explained to his parents that he would study philosophy, math, and Oriental studies, either in Göttingen or Munich. He wanted their approval and did not wish to give the impression that he would live off of their support. He intended to be a professor in Jerusalem, or at least a translator.[75] In November 1919, he wrote to his mother of his future ambitions:

> What will Gerhard Scholem become?
> Well? First he'll become: Gershom Scholem
> Well? Then " " a Ph.D. (hopefully)
> " " " a Jewish philosopher
> " " " an angel in 7th heaven[76]

Not yet twenty-two years old, he already knew that he wanted to earn a doctorate, become a professional scholar and thinker, and immigrate to Palestine.

By autumn 1919, Gershom had returned to Germany. He was ready to take up doctoral studies, and he selected the University of Munich, which was a leader in Semitic studies. Additionally, Escha was studying in Munich, making the city doubly attractive. However, Munich was not only a leading place for the study of Judaic topics, but also a hotbed of radical politics. In early 1919, it was the focal point of the Bavarian Soviet Republic, and after that government's suppression, Bavaria became a stronghold of conservative and far-right political groups, including antisemitic organizations. Reinhold, who was German patriotic, could not help but tease his Zionist, anti-German-nationalist brother Gershom: "Your current stay in Munich shows me that the German idea is still alive and has not perished in the torrent of platitudes from coffeehouse Socialists." He seemed pleased that the Socialists had lost prominence and inquired about antisemitism at the university, particularly as many of the socialist and communist leaders had been Jews.[77] Gershom replied that antisemitism reigned at the university and he did not bother to vote in elections for student government.[78] All around him, he saw signs of rising antisemitism, which only confirmed his desire to leave Germany, but—as he later wrote—he did not understand "the blindness of the Jews, who wanted to know nothing and see nothing of all that," quite possibly a reference to his own family.[79]

At the university, Gershom Scholem began studying philosophy, but soon switched to Semitics. As he later recalled, the university required all philosophy students to have a minor concentration in psychology, which he despised. He also disdained philosophy professors who did not have a historical approach. Thus, he came to study Semitic languages with Fritz Hommel. Meanwhile, Scholem found that his own knowledge of the Talmud, and its traditional interpretation, was better than that of his non-Jewish professors. In general, he had a very low opinion of his non-Jewish professors' Judaic erudition, even calling his doctoral adviser "quite a great ignoramus." Just as he had done in Berlin, Scholem sought Talmud instruction from an Orthodox rabbi outside the university. He also spent much of his time reading Hebrew manuscripts in the Bavarian State Library.[80] Additionally, he studied Hebrew, Greek, Arabic, the Kabbalah, and the Koran, and he spent much time simply philosophizing. Already at this age, Scholem exhibited a wide-ranging interest in mythology, a topic of particular interest for him in his later years.[81] With a large number of subjects to study, he worked so hard that he felt his health was being threatened.[82]

Gershom Scholem's family was less impressed by his scholastic zeal. His letters to his parents from this era frequently mention visits to doctors and give the impression that he was sickly. His father offered to send him on a vacation—under the condition that he "dump all that Judeo-Semitic stuff in the depths of your Munich cabinet and do not take it out until your nerves are all right again."[83] In general, his father had serious misgivings about Gershom's course of study. He even reminded Gershom that their ancestors did their Judaic study alongside another profession.[84] Gershom felt compelled to defend his decision against his father's concerns that it was pointless learning for fun.[85] In fact, Arthur Scholem was both proud of his son's intellect and confused by it. On the one hand, Walter Benjamin reported in 1920 that Arthur Scholem thought his son was a "genius" and "spoke most kindly" of him. On the other hand, over a year later, Arthur read an article that his son wrote and informed him, "At any rate, the accumulated mass of knowledge in this critique is in inverse proportion to its clarity of expression." His father implored him not to study Hebrew and Judaics as his main subjects, but rather to study something more practical, allowing him better career prospects.[86] Gershom even teased his parents by writing: "Lately, the rumor has been going around Munich, I can make mice and elephants through black magic. In reality, for now, I can produce only mistake-free texts, which are incapable of doing mischief to anyone, and with white magic, which is totally allowed without spells! But before final exams, I hope to be able to bring forth the creation of camels and the like!"[87] Even though Scholem occasionally joked that he had become a bona fide practitioner of the Kabbalah, it was chiefly an academic interest, though perhaps not an entirely benign one.

Many scholars believe that Scholem eventually regarded Jewish mysticism as a fortifying or even regenerative force for Judaism. Reading between the lines of his work, they argue that he saw the study of the Kabbalah as facilitating a needed nonnormative and disruptive reading of Jewish tradition. Considering his low opinion of mainstream, liberal German Jewry during his youth and the destruction of European Jewry that he witnessed from afar in the 1940s, such a conclusion seems plausible, though, in the absence of explicit evidence, it remains conjecture. In fact, not every scholar agrees with this interpretation, and it is possible that Scholem regarded the Kabbalah as "primarily a historical phenomenon" and not a contemporary force for seeking truth in Judaism.[88]

At this particular point in Gershom Scholem's life, he was intensely interested in the mythic, as were many of his contemporaries in Germany at this time. The Kabbalah, as Jewish myth, was of particular interest to Gershom. Yet he approached the subject with the exacting methodology of a German university-trained scholar, particularly one interested in philosophy and language. In fact, for his doctoral dissertation, he edited and translated the *Sefer ha-Bahir* (Book of Brilliance), one of the earliest Kabbalistic texts, and compared various historic translations of that collection of epigrams.[89] He submitted his dissertation on 19 January 1922 and passed his oral examination on 3 March 1922, completing his doctorate summa cum laude.[90] As Germany experienced economic and political turmoil in 1922 and 1923, finding a publisher for one's dissertation was no easy feat. Scholem was fortunate to come from a family of printers, and his father's printshop published the first edition.[91] His advisor suggested that he become a lecturer at the University of Munich and work on a *Habilitation*, the postdoctoral degree that would have permitted him to become a tenured faculty member at a German university.[92] In the end, Scholem decided not to pursue an academic career in Germany. Instead, he took his teacher's certification examination in math and studied Hebrew-language math textbooks to prepare for a possible secondary school teaching career in Palestine.[93]

As a student in Munich from 1919 to 1922, Scholem maintained a lively, but very small circle of friends. When he arrived in the city, he rented a room near the university and the Academy of Fine Arts. Among those sharing his apartment was his cousin Heinz Pflaum, who studied Romance languages. When Pflaum moved out, Escha moved in.[94] There was no doubt that this was a very serious relationship for Gershom, and Betty Scholem came to Munich in May 1920 to see her son and his girlfriend.[95] They developed a continuing friendship with the Hebrew-language writer S. Y. Agnon, who lived nearby. Their other friends included Jewish students and bohemians who had moved to the city for studies or for its cultural atmosphere. Depending on the comings and goings of like-minded Jewish students in Munich, he and Escha were occasionally isolated socially.[96] He strongly regretted that he did not have more acquaintances with whom he could speak modern Hebrew. He would have liked best of all to speak only Hebrew with his roommates, who he had hoped would know the language better than he did.[97] However, he did give Hebrew lessons to well-intentioned, if linguistically ungifted Jews.[98] In general, Scholem had little contact with local Munich Jews who did not share his particular Zionist outlook.[99] Just as he had done in Berlin and Jena, he lashed out at the Blau-Weiss Zionist youth in Munich, referring to them as "highly repellent heads" who dominated Jewish fraternity life at the university.[100]

Scholem, not lacking in zeal or self-assuredness, did not hesitate to attack the Zionist leadership. In 1921 Hans Kohn, a prominent central European Zionist leader, and Robert Weltsch, the editor of the German Zionist Federation's newspaper, invited him to collaborate on a book project, but in his reply to them, Scholem excoriated Weltsch and Kohn. He vehemently rejected the notion of *"revolutionary* Zionism" and criticized the Zionist movement's use of this expression, which in his estimation only encouraged actions and words that undermined the Zionist enterprise. Indeed, he was highly critical of "garrulous writers in *galut* [exile, i.e., in the Diaspora] who advertise themselves as 'young workers,'" that is, members of the socialist Zionist movement Hapoel Hatzair (The Young Worker), yet who did not understand what was really happening in Palestine.[101] Scholem and a group of friends wrote a letter to the editor of the *Jüdische Rundschau* in which they ferociously criticized Blau-Weiss and its leader, Walter Moses, essentially depicting his leadership as a cult of personality atop a dictatorship.[102]

In his correspondence with his relatives back in Berlin, Gershom Scholem liked to remind them of how Jewish his life was and how disconnected they were from Jewish tradition. In January 1920, he thanked his parents for their good wishes for the "goyim year."[103] Upon wishing his father a happy birthday in March, he added, "This time, your birthday falls very pleasantly together with Purim—that is tomorrow—so that I will also have occasion here to observe it appropriately."[104] He teased his family by offering his brothers twice-weekly Hebrew grammar lessons, an "unprecedented occasion to use my talents!!"[105]

Walter Benjamin regarded Scholem as a model for his own increasing interest in Judaism. A letter that Scholem had written to Benjamin in June 1920 inspired Benjamin to learn Hebrew, "a decision I would not have dared make on my own," he admitted; and Benjamin began studying with Scholem's friend Erich Gutkind.[106] The following February, Benjamin's wife wrote to Scholem about their friendship, "'I hope with all my heart that we shall meet on the common ground of all things Jewish,'" but Benjamin's other interests and projects continually drew him away from "the world of Judaism."[107] In 1922 Walter and Dora Benjamin asked Gershom to help them participate in a Passover seder "according to strictly Orthodox ritual." Scholem arranged for the Benjamins and his own brother Werner to spend seder at the home of Moses Marx, S. Y. Agnon's brother-in-law and a friend of Gershom.[108]

Not yet twenty-six years old, Gershom Scholem was already well known among the leading German scholars of Judaism. Despite his differences of opinion with Martin Buber, the two men remained close, and Buber promoted Scholem's academic career. Buber helped Scholem make vital connections during his graduate studies and assisted him with early publications. Several years later, Buber recommended Scholem for a lectureship at the new university in Jerusalem.[109] Scholem also had a friendship and sharp feud with Franz Rosenzweig, the director of the Freies Jüdisches Lehrhaus and a renowned Jewish philosopher. Scholem respected Rosenzweig for his translation of *Birkat Hamazon* (grace after meals), but he vehemently attacked Rosenzweig's efforts to bring German Jews closer to Judaism by making Judaism more understandable or palatable to them.[110] Rosenzweig respected Scholem's erudition enough to invite him to teach at the Lehrhaus after completing his doctorate despite his misgivings about Scholem's personality.[111] Scholem, who could be unrelenting and vituperative with his intellectual rivals, later regretted his extreme critique of Rosenzweig, who died of amyotrophic lateral sclerosis (ALS) in 1929.[112] Despite Scholem's strongly critical views of the Zionist Federation of Germany, he was well respected among the German Zionist intelligentsia. In 1920 the Zionist leadership even asked Scholem to take over a new division for Hebrew education.[113] Salman Schocken, a department store magnate and Zionist grandee, also engaged Scholem. Although they had worked on Zionist cultural projects together, the relationship soon took on a private aspect. Schocken was a well-known bibliophile and eventually possessed one of the finest privately held collections of Judaica in the world. As early as 1923, he asked Scholem to help find books for his collection.[114]

While Gershom became fully immersed in a world of Judaism and Zionism, German politics grew ever more chaotic and violent. The formal transformation of the conservative monarchy into an egalitarian republic was too much for many Germans, and in March 1920, right-wing militias and some military units rebelled against the elected federal government in an attempted coup known as the Kapp Putsch. Having seized power in many major cities, they intended to set up a reactionary dictatorship. They detained trade unionists, politicians, and leftist journalists, including Werner Scholem in Halle. Later, he wrote that after his release he led left-wing volunteers in combat against police and army troops—a claim that was disputed by others on the left.[115] In any event, the right-wing revolt stirred up resentments against Jews, and even Gershom, then a student in Munich, informed his mother, "I had a brawl in the street with an antisemite. There was also incitement to pogroms here."[116] The legitimate federal government found itself seemingly impotent. Army units not in open rebellion against the government would not fire on their brother soldiers to suppress the coup. Without the support of the military, the democratic government appeared powerless to stop the revolt and appealed to the people of Germany. Throughout the country, pro-republican workers went on strike and effectively shut down public utilities and operations vital to the success of the coup. Within days, the coup leaders capitulated, and the republic was saved.[117] Still, political uncertainty and violence wracked Germany.

Insurgents from the Kapp Putsch formed the Organisation Consul, a secret society dedicated to the overthrow of the Weimar Republic. Some of the group's members adopted political assassination as their tool, and their most prominent victims were Matthias Erzberger, a leading Catholic politician, who signed the armistice agreement on 11 November 1918 that ended fighting in World War I, and Walther Rathenau, the Jewish foreign minister of Germany, who signed a treaty of cooperation with Soviet Russia.[118]

The far left of the political spectrum also destabilized Germany. In March 1920, armed workers in the Ruhr valley seized power in several cities. Enjoying the support of the Independent Social Democrats and Communists, a network of workers' councils and the so-called Ruhr Red Army soon controlled nearly the whole region. Although the Social Democratic–led federal government was inclined to seek a peaceful resolution to the Ruhr revolt, local units of the army were not. Ultimately, the army and right-wing militias suppressed the uprising and killed hundreds of insurrectionists and their sympathizers.[119]

Around this time, the Independent Social Democrats took up the issue of entry into the Comintern, the international organization of Communist and Left-Socialist parties, founded in Moscow in 1919. The Bolsheviks in Russia wanted to extend their influence to other countries, and Vladimir

Lenin set forth twenty-one conditions that any party had to meet to gain membership in the Comintern. They included changing the party's name, adopting democratic centralism, adhering to a strictly communist program that was both militantly antibourgeois and anti-social-democratic, subjecting the party membership to purges of recalcitrant or uncertain members, and strict adherence to Comintern decisions. While many in the Independent Social Democratic Party opposed this loss of independence, Werner Scholem endorsed compliance and Comintern membership. At a party congress held in Halle in October 1920, a majority of the delegates voted to join the Comintern, but the debate was so divisive that it split the party. Most of the party's active members, including Werner Scholem, joined the Communist Party in December of that year. The remainder, including most of the party's Reichstag representatives, continued the Independent Social Democratic Party until merging with the mainstream Social Democratic Party in 1922.[120]

For two years, the Communist Party had existed on the margins of German political life, with few members and little success. The addition of hundreds of thousands of Independent Social Democrats brought new life to the party, and many of the newcomers quickly rose to prominence as Communists. Among the most successful was Werner Scholem. As early as February 1921, he was elected to the Prussian state legislature—the youngest member of that assembly. Another mark of prestige was his appointment as the figurehead lead editor of *Die Rote Fahne*, the Communist Party's main newspaper. Though Werner did not actually determine the newspaper's editorial line, he bore legal responsibility for it, which soon had serious consequences for him.[121]

Under his nominal editorship, *Die Rote Fahne* published articles encouraging the so-called March Action, an armed uprising in central Germany that the Comintern hoped would spread the world revolution to western Europe. The March Action failed, and both the German federal and Prussian state governments looked to punish the revolutionaries and their supporters. Later that spring, *Die Rote Fahne* claimed that the German army was preparing for a war against Poland, and the state wished to prosecute communist journalists for allegedly revealing military secrets. As the responsible editor, Werner faced two sets of treason charges. The Prussian legislature voted to lift Werner's parliamentary immunity, making him liable for arrest.[122] He went into hiding, but the police caught him in September 1921 after a nationwide manhunt. Some charges were dropped in the summer of 1922 as a result of an amnesty, and the Supreme Court acquitted Werner of the remaining charges the following January. Though he was officially editor of the Communist Party newspaper, the alleged offenses had taken place while he was in hiding and not personally directing content.[123] After his release from detention, he resumed his seat in the Prussian legislature, where he advocated for modernization, secularization, and democratization of the school system, which still bore the imprint of the prewar era. In parliamentary debates, he was a lightning rod for antisemitism.[124] Within the party's internal debates, he soon allied with Ruth Fischer, Arkadi Maslow, and Arthur Rosenberg of the party's left wing and became director of the party organization for the Berlin-Brandenburg district, where Left Communists dominated.[125]

Gershom Scholem was not impressed with his brother's success or prominence. He claimed that the Communist Party of Germany was utterly subservient to the dictates of Moscow, as conveyed by the representative of the Comintern in Germany. He also believed that antisemitism pervaded the Communist Party and alleged that working-class party members referred to Werner as "the Jew" rather than their "comrade."[126] Gershom had no desire to hear his brother orate at communist assemblies or in parliament. Looking back on that time, Gershom recalled, "I could not force myself to go there even once. Our arguments were stormy, although we remained friends."[127]

Of his three brothers, Gershom had the closest relationship with Werner and was most similar to him. Both were quarrelsome intellectuals who rebelled against their parents' German-Jewish bourgeois world, but Gershom chose a different course from Werner. Rather than losing himself in a universalistic class-based struggle or accepting a hybrid German-Jewish identity, he embraced a particularistic Jewish identity. He was certainly not the only young German Jew to espouse Zionism, even over his parents' objections, but he was one of the most extreme Zionists among his peers. Not only had he learned Hebrew, but he also intended to immigrate to Palestine.

By 1923, having formally concluded his university education, Gershom's departure was increasingly becoming reality. His friend Walter Benjamin wrote that he was "very, very sad" to see Gershom leave.[128] Between Rosh Hashanah and Yom Kippur in September 1923, Gershom Scholem departed for Palestine. He traveled by train to Trieste on the Adriatic and, from there, took a ship to Alexandria, Egypt, along with Shlomo Dov (Fritz) Goitein, an orientalist who went on to become one of the greatest authorities on Jews under Islam. After landing in Egypt, the two young scholars continued by coastal steamer to Jaffa, where Escha awaited Gershom. It had not been easy for him to get a visa for Palestine. The British distributed only a limited number of immigration visas, and agricultural pioneers had priority. Only specialists with a guarantee of employment or investors could obtain a visa outside the quota. To facilitate Gershom's immigration, Escha, who had already moved to Palestine, made arrangements with Hugo Bergmann, director of the Jewish National and University Library in Jerusalem. He hired Gershom to serve as director of a nonexistent Hebrew section at the library. Later, Bergmann offered Gershom a real job at the library.[129]

In advance of his own departure, Gershom shipped his personal library of two thousand volumes to Palestine. Although his father no longer wished to support his emigrating son financially, he did lend his employees to pack up the books.[130] Nonetheless, Betty Scholem was very upset with the manner in which her son left Europe. She expected him to write from Trieste, his port of departure, but he did not. His final letter from Munich was simply a card sent with his key and a receipt for photography, which his mother considered expensive. She implored him to remember that she was always waiting to hear from him. Additionally, his uncles were upset that they were not informed of his departure as they had wanted to say goodbye at the train station.[131]

The Germany that Gershom Scholem left was coming apart at the seams. Germany had suffered from inflation since the war's end, but in 1923, the pace increased dramatically. One American dollar was worth approximately 493 German marks in July 1922 (monthly average). The monthly average for January 1923 was nearly 18,000. For July 1923, it was 353,412 marks per dollar, almost 4,620,455 marks in August, and nearly 99 million marks in September. In October, the exchange rate averaged more than 25 billion marks to one dollar. Eventually, the exchange rate hit 4.2 trillion marks to one dollar. The government could not keep pace with the demand for new paper mark bills, and printing presses worked twenty-four hours a day. Eventually, the government resorted to stamping new denominations on old bills. With a stamp, 100,000 marks became 1 billion marks. People who lived on fixed incomes were ruined. Speculators flourished. Savings became utterly worthless in the span of a few days, while mortgages could be paid off with remarkable ease.[132]

As ordinary Germans, the Scholems experienced the hyperinflation the same as their neighbors, but as printers, they were at the center of certain changes in Germany. In September 1923, Betty wrote to Gershom, who had just arrived in Palestine. She exclaimed, "I can imagine that the strangest notions of Germany prevail out there. The reality is even stranger. When you left, the sausage that I gave you, for example, cost 12 million per pound. Today, it is 240 million. Everything has gone up at this [rate] and an even greater rate. The electric tram [costs] 10 million. One can only go shopping with billion bills. The collapse of the economy is complete." Betty was glad that her son was no longer in Germany, but she added that, "we are now also printing money, namely for the government printing office. Great joy and industriousness reigns in the whole workshop since looming dismissal hung over everyone."[133]

Even writing to Gershom became a worrisome expense: "You see, this letter cost 15 million in postage, and starting the day after tomorrow, 30 million. But the price increases last two days at most." Just to pay their employees, Reinhold and Erich engaged in currency speculation. They bought American dollars on Friday and resold them the following Thursday to make payroll.[134] As Betty Scholem put it, "By contrast, day and night, the boys' work consists of financial transactions. They are more like bankers than book printers."[135] In fact, what saved the Scholems was that they were printers. At a time when Germans were not interested in buying or publishing books, the government needed as many printers as possible. Soon, Arthur Scholem's firm employed 130 people and operated four machines in two shifts, but they had fewer individual customers than ever before. Private customers could not pay the ever-rising prices.[136] And as soon as Max Scholem heard that his brother's firm had government work, he rushed to secure a similar contract for his firm, Siegfried Scholem Publishers.[137] Reinhold, Erich, and even Max himself skipped Max's twentieth anniversary party because of their work as money printers.[138]

Meanwhile, the economic turmoil fueled political extremism and instability that culminated in insurrection. Werner Scholem sincerely expected a communist revolution to break out and triumph in Germany in the autumn of 1923. He practically boasted about it to his mother.[139] In fact, in the central German states of Saxony and Thuringia, the German army intervened to forestall a communist uprising; and in Hamburg, the Communist Party tried to seize power, failing dramatically. The Communist Party was temporarily banned, and once again, Werner faced arrest.[140] In Bavaria, a far-right-wing group known as the National Socialist German Workers' Party, or Nazis, led by Adolf Hitler, attempted to seize power. The Bavarian police easily suppressed the Nazi rebellion, but its participants served only minimal prison sentences. Even from the seeming stability of Berlin, Betty expected Germany to fall apart, with the Rhine region seceding and old Prussia left to settle Germany's World War I debt.[141] Public antisemitism also markedly increased in 1923. The Jews were blamed for everything—even the massive increase in pork prices. Georg Scholem's wife, Sophie, could not help but think that Gershom had predicted it before his emigration.[142] On 5 November 1923, Berlin exploded in anti-Jewish violence. Unemployed workers believed a rumor that eastern European Jews living in Berlin had obtained all the emergency food relief funds in order to loan them to non-Jews. The workers soon went on a rampage through the Scheunenviertel, home to thousands of eastern European Jews. They looted shops and assaulted

"Jewish-looking" pedestrians while the police were slow to intervene. After darkness fell, the riots resumed, with the vandals carrying lists of Jewish targets. The police did calm the situation in the Scheunenviertel, but the riot spread to other parts of the city, including upper-middle-class Charlottenburg, home to a large Jewish population.[143] The fact that a food riot could turn antisemitic and xenophobic so quickly did not bode well. Curiously, Betty Scholem wrote to Gershom, "In Berlin there were *no* pogroms," but she added that antisemitism had penetrated the atmosphere of Berlin to such a degree that people cursed the Jews openly and without any sense of shame.[144] By the following spring, Betty wrote, "Now the Jewish question is no longer something to joke about."[145]

In November 1923, Arthur Scholem's contract as a government printer expired, and it was not renewed. Moreover, to replace the devalued paper mark, the German government issued a new, interim currency, the rentenmark, which the Finance Ministry and Reichsbank tightly regulated.[146] Inflation ended, the government balanced its budget, and the new reichsmark was put on the gold standard. By early 1924, Germany's economy stabilized, but not before the printers of Berlin went on strike. Because unemployment remained high, the big printshops and the government printing office simply dismissed and replaced the striking printers.[147]

Some good news for the Scholem family came from Jerusalem: Gershom's engagement and marriage to Escha. The two had known each other for several years and agreed to marry after immigration to Palestine. In fact, they held their wedding on Gershom's twenty-sixth birthday, 5 December 1923. While happy for his son, Arthur looked at the marriage from a practical standpoint. At the time of Gershom and Escha's formal engagement, Arthur wrote that it was Gershom's problem if they tried to start a family with his small salary and Gershom could not expect an allowance from his father. However, Arthur denied Gershom's claims that he (Arthur) had something against Escha: "She comes from a good home, and I consider that so important that I cannot object to this marriage."[148] Betty urged him to secure a dowry before the wedding took place and was upset that Gershom expected her to buy household goods for him in Germany and ship them to Palestine—including a vacuum cleaner. She asked Gershom if he also sent a list of must-have items to Escha's family and noted that his wife's family should send them necessary household goods, not his family.[149] Arthur's attitude in particular may seem surprisingly unsentimental, but at the time, economic background was an important factor for the German-Jewish middle class when seeking a potential spouse.[150] Arthur was concerned with social standing and propriety, and he sent a congratulatory note to Escha's parents in Hamburg, but he was surprised that Escha did not write to him and Betty.[151]

In the midst of the economic and political turmoil of 1923, the Scholem boys in Germany had children. Emmy Scholem, Werner's wife, gave birth to their second daughter, whom they named Renate. Erich's wife, Edith, gave birth to a daughter, named Irene. (Later they had a son, Arthur Junior, known as "Bübi.") Reinhold's wife, Käthe, had given birth to a son, Günter, the previous May. Arthur wrote of the family's great joy with the children.[152] Arthur and Betty had four children in the 1890s, but in the 1920s, those four only had five children of their own. In fact, German-Jewish birthrates were plummeting. In the early 1920s, the birth rate was fourteen live births per thousand, less than half of what it had been forty years earlier, and it would drop further by the early 1930s.[153] German Jewry was facing a looming demographic implosion.

While the younger Scholems were reproducing, Arthur Scholem's health seriously deteriorated. He had had heart trouble for several years, but one day in October 1923, he suffered from heart failure while in Berlin's Lustgarten park. Complete strangers brought him home. Betty, Reinhold, and Erich thought Arthur should go to a spa town to recover, but he was too ill to travel. After he finally returned to work, his firm bought a car so he could get around Berlin more easily.[154] Just before New Year's Day in 1924, Betty and Arthur Scholem traveled to Merano, Italy, so Arthur could rest. Before World War I, this renowned spa town—then known as Meran and part of Austria—was extremely popular with the Jewish bourgeoisie, and it remained so after Italy annexed Merano and the surrounding South Tyrol region after the war.[155] During this vacation, the Scholems were in their element, surrounded by the German-Jewish, middle-aged, upper middle class. They befriended a Jewish lawyer from Hamburg whose physician was Escha's father, and they met a Jewish lawyer from Berlin who had helped Werner's political career.[156] Still, Arthur's health continued its gradual decline, which the Scholems tried to forestall through more visits to spa towns.[157] Meanwhile, relations between Arthur's brothers began to deteriorate. Georg worked as the fiduciary doctor for the printers' insurance fund and held it against Arthur when his own benefit requests were denied.[158] Max and Theobald, business partners in the Siegfried Scholem printing firm, barely spoke to each other. And while Arthur was away convalescing, the family ceased having its Friday night dinners.[159]

The period between late 1918 and early 1924 was one of intense transition for Germany, for Germany's Jews, and for the Scholems. Having weathered the storms of those years, the Scholems were poised for the future. Arthur and his eldest sons, Reinhold and Erich, were established as printers and successful independent businessmen, while Werner's political career was about to take off. It was not long before he became one of the most infamous men in Germany. By contrast, Gershom had left Germany and saw his future and that of the Jewish people in their ancient homeland, the Land of Israel.

CHAPTER 5

The Gold-Plated Twenties and Beyond

Promise, Prosperity, and Depression in Interwar Germany

In 1924, after five years of political unrest and economic catastrophe, Germany turned the corner. The economy recovered from hyperinflation. The country's diplomatic isolation eased, with Germany and France soon embarking on a course of rapprochement. Germany's internal politics were stable, though contentious. A distinct mass culture flourished as new social conventions gained popularity and innovative art, architecture, music, and public entertainment found an audience among progressive Germans. With new or drastically improved technologies, the pace of daily life seemed to go much faster. Indeed, observers of German society spoke both positively and negatively about an Americanization of urban life. From today's perspective, it is possible to see the familiar contours of modern urban life in the years 1924 to 1930, and looking back on those years, particularly after the horrors of Nazism and total war, Germans fondly call them the "Golden Twenties."

Even Jewish culture experienced renewal as a new generation of German Jews came of age. Reacting against their parents' values, they sought new forms of Jewish association and new models for Jewish identity, which did not necessarily involve traditional religious observance. As they reassessed their identities as Jews and Germans, scholars, such as Franz Rosenzweig and Martin Buber, provided frameworks for the effort. In his memoir, Gershom Scholem famously described his brother Reinhold as an avowed assimilationist and characterized his brother Erich as somewhat indifferent, yet they, too, were among those German Jews who reengaged with Jewish religion, culture, and society in this era.[1] Rather than a nadir for German Judaism and the apex of Jewish assimilation in Germany, as has been popularly believed, the stable years of the Weimar Republic held great promise for the Jews.

However, the mid-1920s were a false dawn. Though a variegated and rich Jewishness was visible in Germany by 1928, the specter of social antisemitism still loomed. Then, with the economic collapse of the Great Depression, there was a resurgence of political antisemitism. Still, in 1924, as the crises of the republic's first years passed, the future looked promising to Germans, including Jewish Germans, and even in 1932, no one could foresee the horrors of Buchenwald or Auschwitz.

The hyperinflation of 1923 had depleted the Scholems' capital reserves, but now customers were able to pay for printing services, and things were improving for Arthur and his sons.[2] By November 1925, they were back to their prewar level of business. Betty rejoiced, "That means we have brought the business intact through the war and the inflation. That is something enormous."[3] The other Scholem printing firm, Siegfried Scholem, also recovered, even though the owners, Max and Theobald Scholem, were barely on speaking terms. Max wanted to buy out Theobald, but he did not have the savings, and no one would lend him the money.[4] Betty ascribed the conflict to the Scholems' mercurial nature and Max's delusions of grandeur: "Little Max now sits like the viceroy of India on the elephant of his megalomania."[5] It took many months before the extended family resumed their customary Friday night dinners, and the feud continued until Max's death in 1929.[6] Meanwhile, Siegfried Scholem became printers for Ullstein Verlag, one of Germany's leading newspaper houses.[7]

Founded in 1877 by Leopold Ullstein, who was politically liberal and active in the Jewish community, Ullstein Verlag's publications included the sensationalist tabloid *B. Z. am Mittag*, the highbrow *Vossische Zeitung*, and the mass circulation *Berliner Morgenpost*. In general, Ullstein Verlag represented a progressive, democratic perspective. One of its closest competitors was the Verlag Rudolf Mosse, also owned by a politically liberal, Berlin Jewish family. Mosse's flagship publication was the *Berliner Tageblatt*, edited by Theodor Wolff, a champion of progressive politics. Betty Scholem even complained that, reading the *Tageblatt*, one could get the false impression that all Germans supported republican democracy.[8]

Like most German Jews, Betty Scholem and Erich Scholem voted for the center-left German Democratic Party, the most pro-republican nonsocialist political party. At the time of the Reichstag elections of May 1924—the first since the stabilization—Betty boasted that she had convinced her maid to vote for the Democrats "and with our united powers, we pushed through a couple of manikins in Berlin," namely, the industrialist Carl Friedrich von Siemens and the women's rights activist Marie Elisabeth Lüders.[9] In fact, it seems that Jewish votes decidedly helped the party in certain areas. The German Democratic Party won only 5.7 percent of the vote nationwide but 8.9 percent in Berlin, where Jews made up roughly 5 percent of the population. In districts of the city with a concentrated Jewish population, such as Charlottenburg and Wilmersdorf, the party won 10 to 17 percent of the vote. Conversely, in less Jewish neighborhoods, even affluent ones, such as Zehlendorf, the party fared below average for the city as a whole.[10] The same trend was even more pronounced in Frankfurt, where Jews made up 6.3 percent of the population. There, the German Democrats won 10.2 percent citywide and more than twice that in heavily Jewish districts, such as Westliche Außenstadt and Nordwestliche Außenstadt.[11]

Erich Scholem associated with organizations affiliated with the party, including the liberal Democratic Club in Berlin. Additionally, on Constitution Day, Germany's national holiday and a celebration of the Weimar Republic's values, Erich joined his fellow boating enthusiasts in participating in a pro-republican demonstration.[12] The German Democratic Party also received financial support from many Jewish businessmen and editorial support from the Ullstein and Mosse publishing houses. Not only did the party's support for equality and opposition to antisemitism endear it to Jewish voters and Jewish donors, but it also ran a significant number of Jewish candidates. During the 1920s, between 12.5 and 20 percent of the German Democrats' Reichstag representatives were Jewish. Among the most famous Jewish members of the party were Hugo Preuß, drafter of the Weimar constitution; Walther Rathenau, foreign minister of Germany in 1922; Ludwig Landmann, mayor of Frankfurt; and Bernhard Weiß, vice president (deputy chief) of the Berlin police. The political right wing despised all four for being Jewish and for supporting the republic.[13]

Middle-class and upper-class Jewish voters who did not support the German Democratic Party often voted for the center-right German People's Party. The party endorsed liberal economic policies, anti-Marxism, and German nationalism. However, it was also ambivalent about democracy and republicanism, and its record on antisemitism was mixed. Moreover, not a single self-identified Jew represented the People's Party in the Reichstag or any state legislature.[14] A number of Jewish industrialists, bankers, lawyers, and civil servants did join the party, and possibly the most prominent Jewish member of the party was the Hamburg banker and German patriot Max Warburg.[15] Reinhold Scholem joined the party in 1919 and was an active member in the 1920s.[16] While there is no reason to think that Reinhold disapproved of republican democracy, he was certainly a German patriot.[17]

Overall, the Reichstag elections of May 1924 ended disastrously for the two liberal parties.[18] The German Democrats slumped from 39 representatives to only 28, despite the votes of Betty Scholem and her maid. Similarly, Reinhold's People's Party went from 66 seats to 45 seats. However, as Betty reported to Gershom in Jerusalem, "German Nationalists (read: antisemites) and the Communists received the biggest increase, the Communists from 16 seats to 60."[19] The German Nationalists won 95 seats—24 more than four years previously. The gains made by the Communist Party were even more extreme than Betty described: going from 16 representatives (with only 4 originally elected as Communist Party candidates in 1920) to 62 representatives. One of the new Communists in the Reichstag was Werner Scholem.

His career was nearing its zenith. After the failure of the Communists to mount a successful revolution during the unrest of autumn 1923, Werner Scholem and his allies in the left wing of the party exploited the situation to take over the leadership of the Communist Party. They mobilized the rank and file against party chairman Heinrich Brandler, who belonged to the party's right wing. At the same time, they cultivated important comrades in Moscow, including Grigory Zinoviev, the chairman of the Comintern, and Joseph Stalin, then still an ambitious member of the Russian Communist Party central committee. While Stalin had earlier criticized the Left Opposition, now he sided with it. He proclaimed that the German working class sought true revolutionary leaders—such as Werner Scholem, Max Hesse, and Ruth Fischer—not theoreticians. He specifically criticized Brandler, who enjoyed the patronage of Stalin's rival Karl Radek, the Comintern's representative in Germany.[20] At the German Communist Party's ninth party congress, held in April 1924, one month before Reichstag elections, the so-called Left Opposition came to power.

While Jews comprised a minuscule percentage of the Communist Party's membership, they had been vastly overrepresented in its leadership since the party's establishment in 1919. Moreover, this overrepresentation was never greater than in 1924. Of the fifteen members of the party's new central committee, five came from Jewish families: Werner Scholem, Ruth Fischer, Iwan Katz, Arkadi Maslow, and Arthur Rosenberg. Moreover, all five were university educated, a rarity in a workers' party.[21] In addition to serving in the Reichstag and on the party's central board and politburo, Werner Scholem also directed the party's Organization Bureau, giving him vast power over personnel decisions. As he rebuilt the party's internal structures after the chaos of the previous year, he streamlined the party administration and placed his own allies in staff positions.[22] He was one of the most powerful Communists in Germany, a nationally known political figure.

Betty wanted a ticket to attend the opening session of the Reichstag, but Werner refused to give her one because "I probably would not whistle and make the necessary row, [and] his party has to give the tickets to more reliable people than I unfortunately am!" In fact, when the Reichstag convened, Werner made a spectacle of himself, though he thought himself witty. From his seat in the chamber, he mocked conservative-nationalist parliamentarian Otto von Bismarck, grandson of the founder of modern Germany. Then, when Werner spoke to make a point of order, he took advantage of the opportunity to give "a passionate speech against the government, against the police, [and] against the republic," in the words of one Berlin newspaper. His fellow parliamentarians did not take him seriously, and laughter repeatedly interrupted his speech.[23] The Social Democratic daily *Vorwärts* caricatured Scholem as a baby suckling at the breast of Mother Moscow.[24] However, Werner also touched a raw nerve when he stood in the Reichstag and denounced the judicial system's harsh sentences for activists and insurgents from the political left compared to the leniency shown to those on the political right.[25]

Werner Scholem was an enfant terrible, infamous and despised among his political foes. Betty reported that Werner was rumored to have been punched at the Weimar Republic's annual Constitution Day ceremony.[26] Young Joseph Goebbels took note of Werner Scholem as he ranted about Communist Jews attempting to lead German workers away from nationalism.[27] In a letter to Gershom Scholem, Walter Benjamin wrote, "Europe is full of the representative Scholem. Even the Pan-Germans next to me in the café are speaking of him. He is unleashing everywhere—with reason—mighty storms of antisemitism. His rise to fame and honor makes me rather sad."[28]

Members of the Far Right were not the only ones outraged by Werner. His own family found him off-putting. Betty wrote, "He is acting so dumb in the Reichstag that I am getting terribly angry at him, and the matter is becoming uncongenial to me."[29] Arthur wanted nothing to do with his Communist son, and Uncle Georg thought that being related to Representative Werner Scholem was driving away his patients.[30] When the Reichstag was dissolved in October 1924, Werner Scholem lost his seat in parliament and, critically, his parliamentary immunity, which had shielded him from arrest. Still, Werner maintained his power base. During the next Reichstag election, in December 1924, the Communists lost 17 of their 62 seats, but Werner returned to parliament as one of the 45 Communist representatives.[31]

Nonetheless, Werner Scholem's position within the Communist movement was less secure than it might have seemed. Even as the Left Opposition took power in the party, the Comintern chairman, Zinoviev, warned the German Communists about members of the Left who did not have solid connections to the working class, but who spoke in revolutionary terms. He specifically warned party leaders Ruth Fischer and Arkadi Maslow about Arthur Rosenberg and Werner Scholem.[32] Additionally, within the Communists' ranks, there was a discernible and growing mood of anti-intellectualism and possibly antisemitism, which significantly overlapped. Scholem, Fischer, Katz, and Maslow ran afoul of that sentiment. The leader of the German Comintern delegation called Fischer, Katz, and Scholem "brazen Jewish rascals."[33] Moreover, Moscow sought more control over the European Communist parties, including the German Communist Party.[34] However, Scholem and his closest colleagues fostered more independence from Moscow and ignored Comintern advice.

Then, a critical blunder came in the spring of 1925, when Germany had its first popular election for president, and the Communist Party's policy seemed to tip the election in favor of the political Right. In the second, decisive round of balloting, the leading candidates were the archconservative, monarchist, former field marshal Paul von Hindenburg and the centrist, Catholic politician Wilhelm Marx. However—against the objections of Grigory Zinoviev, Ruth Fischer, and Arkadi Maslow—Werner Scholem insisted that the Communists run their own candidate in the election, rather than endorse a centrist or socialist candidate.[35] Ultimately, Hindenburg received 14,655,641 votes, and Marx received 13,751,605 votes—a difference of barely 900,000 votes. The Communist candidate, Ernst Thälmann, received 1,951,151 votes, more than enough to deprive Marx of the victory.[36] The German republic now had an anti-republican president.

Betty Scholem was livid: "I did not think that there were 14 million such boneheads here. The Communists have caused this with their own candidate. Their two million votes would have pushed Marx through."[37] Even though President von Hindenburg did not actively agitate against the republic, he did little to consolidate support for it, and it remained unpopular among large segments of German society. In 1932, at the age of eighty-four, he was reelected president, and the following year, he appointed Adolf Hitler as chancellor of Germany. Hindenburg died in August 1934, leaving Hitler in sole command of the German state.

Soon after the presidential election of 1925, Werner Scholem's star began to dim.[38] In no uncertain terms, Grigory Zinoviev blamed Scholem and the Ultra-Left for Hindenberg's election and the risk of a monarchist restoration.[39] Even Scholem's previous allies within the party, including Ruth Fischer and Ernst Thälmann, turned against him. Despite election to the central committee at the Communist Party congress in July 1925, a few months later, Scholem was subjected to an internal party investigation and expelled from his leadership positions.[40] Fischer, who had recanted her earlier views and turned against Scholem, could not save her career either. Moscow also arranged to have her replaced as party chairman by Thälmann, who proved a more reliable minion than Fischer.[41] By January 1926, the former party leadership was on the defensive. Stalin said, "Either the Ruth Fischer-Maslow group is smashed, and then the Party will be in a position to overcome the present crisis in the fight against the Scholem group; or the German Communist Party is taken by the diplomatic wiles of the Ruth Fischer-Maslow group, and then the fight will be lost, to the benefit of Scholem."[42]

In fact, as Scholem tried to regain a foothold in the leadership of the German Communist Party, he, too, partook in the shifting alliances between German and Soviet Communists. Though he had once been an ally of Stalin and criticized Zinoviev, Scholem now rallied support for the politically weakened Zinoviev against Stalin, the master tactician who was on the ascendant in the Soviet Union. Concomitantly, Ernst Thälmann was consolidating his position in Germany. In the autumn of 1926, Scholem led central committee members Hugo Urbahns and Hans Weber and hundreds of mid- and low-level German Communist Party functionaries in protesting the suppression of the opposition within the Russian Communist Party, specifically including Grigory Zinoviev, the old Bolshevik leader Lev Kamenev, and Lenin's widow, Nadezhda Krupskaya.[43] The German party leadership ruthlessly attacked the letter's signatories, and in November, Thälmann had Werner Scholem definitively expelled from the Communist Party.[44] By 1929 only two of the sixteen party leaders from 1923–24 still remained in the politburo. At least eleven had been expelled from the party, and nearly half of all leading party functionaries from that era had been expelled or left the party.[45]

The years 1924 and 1925 established the fundamental contours of German politics for the rest of the decade. Atop the German state, there was a reactionary president, whose role was limited but critical in a crisis. In the Reichstag, there was a radical Left, a radical Right, and a spectrum of republican parties from which most cabinet ministers were drawn.[46] Electoral politics were fierce, but there were no more armed insurrections against the state.

Despite the relative stability of the economic and political systems in the mid- to late 1920s, there was still considerable discontent with the republic and its international situation. Betty and Erich's German Democratic Party, the bourgeois political party most associated with the republic, saw its share of the vote shrink significantly. Above all, there was widespread discontent from nearly all sectors of society with the Treaty of Versailles that ended World War I.[47] The concept of the treaty as an imposed burden seeped into German popular consciousness. For example, when Max Scholem agreed to an unfavorable business agreement demanded by Theobald, Max's wife declared, "It is not an agreement, but rather a *Diktat*. It is the Treaty of Versailles!"[48] Stung by the harsh terms of the treaty and encouraged by unapologetic generals and politicians, ordinary Germans claimed that the treaty had driven the country into poverty. Accordingly, Arthur Scholem thought that it was unseemly for Germans, including his wife's wealthy cousin, to travel abroad in great luxury when "Germany goes begging throughout the world for its starving children, publicizes its poverty in every key, and cannot pay any reparations."[49] Despite the Germans' complaints about the Treaty of Versailles, it was considerably less harsh than the treaty that the Germans had planned to impose on the Allies if Germany had won the war. Betty Scholem had a reasonable view of things. She was outraged that the German government spent millions of marks on prestige projects such as zeppelin air travel rather than paying off the reparations and war debts as quickly as possible.[50]

By the mid-1920s, politics were not the only aspect of life altered compared to the prewar years. Jewish religious observance had declined precipitously. Even attendance on the High Holidays, Rosh Hashanah and Yom Kippur, was extremely low, in the opinion of communal officials and observers of religious life. In Berlin, the largest Jewish community in Germany, with approximately 173,000 members total, only 49 percent of adults went to synagogue on Rosh Hashanah and Yom Kippur. The numbers were even lower in Germany's second-largest Jewish community, Frankfurt, where barely 41 percent of the nearly 30,000 Jews attended High Holiday services. By contrast, 58 percent of Jews attended High Holiday services in Breslau, the third-largest community, with 23,240 members. The scholar who assembled these statistics in 1929 ascribed the differences to location, namely, greater interest in Jewish religion farther east.[51]

The situation was varied, and the Scholems' experience illustrates the variety of Jewish religious practice. On the High Holidays, Reinhold, Erich, and their wives attended synagogue "and listened attentively" to the rabbis' sermons, as Betty characterized it.[52] Presumably, she did not go with them, and she did not fast on Yom Kippur.[53] However, that did not mean that Jewish holidays were insignificant to her. She noted that the family was bound "with deeply rooted tradition and sacrosanct connection to Judaism." Rather than celebrating holidays principally through prayer, she marked them "more with good food."[54] In the Scholem family, as in so many German-Jewish families, Shabbat dinners remained a tradition. Betty remarked, "We all love these family evenings very much, and our Judaism is 'anchored' in them, so to speak."[55] As an adult, Reinhold even learned the Friday night *Kiddush* prayer said over wine so that he could lead the family's blessings.[56] They also had Passover seders, ordinarily at the house of their Uncle Theobald, though occasionally Arthur Scholem and family had their own seder.[57] However, a less pervasively observed holiday like Sukkot went completely unnoticed by Betty Scholem and family.[58]

At the same time, the Scholems, like many German Jews in this era, acknowledged Christmas in some way, even if the holiday had no theological significance for them. In December 1924, Betty complained to her Zionist son in Jerusalem, "I have an enormous amount to do to prepare for Christmas, up to the point of going broke."[59] She was not alone. The lead articles in the Berlin Jewish community newsletter for December 1927 were "Hanukkah" and "Judah the Hammerer," but the last page featured an advertisement for Christmas records. Some German Jews had a Hanukkah menorah near their Christmas tree. Many others adopted Christmas cultural traditions for the Jewish holiday, such as baking Hanukkah gingerbread men cookies and Hanukkah fruitcakes.[60]

While Betty Scholem was not exceptional, many Jews like Theobald Scholem chose not to adopt Christian practices as part of acculturation to German society. Theobald and his family did not celebrate Christmas in any way and cultivated an expressly Jewish identity. In contrast to the overwhelming majority of Jewish pupils, who attended state schools, Theobald's daughter Dina attended a Jewish school, though she struggled with Hebrew. Her sister, Eva, attended a Christian boarding school, but she was later active in the Bar Kochba Zionist sports group.[61] As a medical student, she visited Palestine in 1932 and returned full of enthusiasm.[62]

Theobald's family exemplified the generational split between German Zionists. Before 1914, philanthropic Zionism predominated among German Zionists. In the 1920s, the Zionists' rhetoric espousing unapologetic Jewish nationalism and the goal of immigration to Palestine grew more strident, though they comprised only a tiny proportion of the Jewish community in Germany.[63] Theobald Scholem had been active in Jewish national groups for decades, but his wife, Hedwig, could see that he was not serious about leaving Germany.[64] It would take Hitler's persecution to force Theobald to move to Tel Aviv. His daughter Eva expressed scorn for her parents' armchair Zionism and meager Hebrew.[65] For many young Jews, support for Zionism was a wholesale part of the renaissance of Jewish culture in Germany. Other supporters even absorbed theories of Jewish "racial otherness" that shaped their advocacy of Jewish nationalism.[66]

Berlin Jewry, often seen as a paragon of German acculturation, was getting more interested in Palestine during the 1920s, in Betty Scholem's estimation.[67] She and her family were not Zionists, but she also claimed that they were not anti-Zionist. She would occasionally pass on anti-Zionist commentaries to Gershom, her outspoken Zionist son, hoping that he could clarify matters. Instead, he interpreted these views as belonging to Betty and took great offense. In January 1925, Betty replied, "We write you about all these things because we cannot judge them." She added, "I have never made a dumb joke about Zionism or considered it a kind of joke. You know that!"[68] Nonetheless, in September 1930, she wrote to him that she heard someone say, " 'A Zionist is a Jew who uses another Jew's money to send a third Jew to Palestine.' You probably know this definition, but I find it great. That's exactly it, isn't it?"[69] The joke enraged Gershom.[70]

In addition to unreligious or minimally religious German Jews, such as Arthur and Betty, and active Zionist Jews, such as Theobald, there was a sizable minority of German Jews who remained Orthodox. Among them were Max and Martha Burchhardt of Hamburg, the parents of Gershom Scholem's wife. Betty and Arthur did not meet the Burchhardts for nearly a year after Escha and Gershom married, but their first visit was an eye-opener. The Burchhardts consumed only kosher food, including "kosher milk and kosher wine and kosher cookies," as Betty Scholem described it. They said morning prayers in synagogue and recited grace after meals. The Scholems were not familiar with this world from their life in Berlin.[71] However, as religious Jews living in the modern world, the Burchhardts were not unique. A significant minority of all German Jews—between 10 and 20 percent—remained Orthodox in the 1920s.[72]

The Burchhardts espoused modern Orthodoxy, or neo-Orthodoxy as it was known, which sought to strike a balance between traditional Judaism and modern European culture. It advocated active involvement in temporal society, including the practice of a secular profession and involvement in nonsectarian civic life; the adoption of German cultural norms, such as use of the German language, wearing Western clothes, and German patriotism; freedom of conscience; greater rights and religious participation for women; the modernization of Jewish education; and modest liturgical innovations, such as a

German-language sermon and a choir. At the same time, the movement maintained the primacy of *halakhah* (Jewish law), the exclusive use of Hebrew for prayer, and the retention of historic customs.[73] Neo-Orthodox Jews did not see a contradiction between being Jewish and German and fully embraced both identities. Indeed, their lifestyle indicated one way to navigate and connect identities that many other people saw as in competition with each other.

Religious practice was not the only barometer of Jewish affiliation, and by the 1920s, it had ceased to be a primary marker of Jewishness for most German Jews. Nonetheless, they still sought community and other means of giving expression to a Jewish identity. For many German Jews, including some of the Scholems, that desire was realized through affiliation with Jewish social, cultural, and professional organizations. Even as Jewish religious identity abated, Jewish cultural identity remained or even reasserted itself, and in a secular manner.[74] Erich Scholem's wife, Edith, belonged to the League of Jewish Women (Jüdischer Frauenbund).[75] Founded in 1904, this organization combined social welfare and advocacy for women's rights, but it did so in a way that made it palatable to nonworking, middle-class women, and it expressed a strong Jewish identity. Before World War I, it operated vocational training schools and vigorously participated in the campaign to end legalized prostitution and trafficking in women. Its greatest success in the 1920s was winning the vote for women in Jewish communal elections. By 1929, ten years after the German constitution granted women's suffrage in civil elections, women could vote in six of the seven largest Jewish communities, encompassing half of Germany's Jewish population. Women could first vote in Berlin Jewish communal elections in 1926, while the Jewish community of Cologne and many smaller communities continued to resist giving women the vote. The League of Jewish Women had fifty thousand members—more than one-quarter of all Jewish women above thirty years of age and roughly 10 percent of the total Jewish population in Germany.[76] Reinhold, Georg, and Sophie Scholem belonged to the Central Association of German Citizens of the Jewish Faith, the preeminent German-Jewish civic organization. Since 1893 this group had promoted Jewish integration into German society and defended the civil rights of German Jews. Among its members were Rabbi Leo Baeck, constitutional framers Hugo Preuß and Albert Mosse, banker Max Warburg, and several Jewish members of the Reichstag. Walter Benjamin's father, Emil, also belonged.[77] Persistent antisemitism also fostered the growth of Jewish youth groups in the 1920s, and they engaged in fierce debates and competitions; however, compared to the whole of German Jewry, their membership was rather limited in size and centered in large cities.

Another way that German Jews expressed their identity was through combining Jewish interests with the promotion of high culture and education. In formalized settings, bourgeois German Jews applied German standards of art and scholarship to Judaica. Because of this elevation of Jewish culture and the expansion of Jewish educational opportunities, there has been talk of a Jewish renaissance during the Weimar Republic. In fact, Gershom, Reinhold, Erich, and Max Scholem were all part of that movement.

One of the most celebrated manifestations of the Weimar-era Jewish renaissance was the Freies Jüdisches Lehrhaus (Free Jewish House of Learning), under the leadership of Franz Rosenzweig. Growing out of the Society for Jewish Popular Education in Frankfurt, the Lehrhaus offered lecture courses and, above all, study groups and seminars on Jewish topics and the Hebrew language. It appealed to adult learners of all ages and social classes. Although the Lehrhaus began in Frankfurt, Jewish communities in Berlin, Breslau, Hanover, Karlsruhe, Mannheim, Munich, Stuttgart, and Wiesbaden, among others, opened similar institutions. Rosenzweig and his colleagues wished to strengthen Jewish identity within Germany through teaching about Jewish religion, history, and culture. The Lehrhaus applied German standards of erudition, cultivation (*Bildung*), and sophistication to Judaic study.[78] Seeking gifted Jewish intellectuals as teachers for the Lehrhaus, Rosenzweig even hired Gershom Scholem before his emigration from Germany. Rosenzweig commented that the Lehrhaus offered a course on the *Zohar*, a central text of the Kabbalah, "which is taught by Scholem, who is here for the summer and is, as always, *offensive*, but likewise, as always, brilliant." Incidentally, the brilliant, but not infrequently offensive Scholem was astounded that Rosenzweig judged his behavior this way.[79]

Already during World War I, Rosenzweig had written a groundbreaking work of Jewish thought, entitled *The Star of Redemption*. Published in 1921, Gershom Scholem called it "the greatest philosophical accomplishment of recent times."[80] It created a sweeping philosophical system to answer questions about the relationship of the individual to the world and to God through creation, revelation, and redemption. If Rosenzweig's effort to regenerate Jewish life in Germany in the 1920s began with *The Star of Redemption*, it reached its climax with a new translation of the Bible, undertaken with Martin Buber.[81] Their version was accessible to German Jews because it was in German, but it was distinctively Jewish, differing from existing Protestant or Protestant-inspired translations. Rosenzweig and Buber sought to imbue the German-language text with the cadence and archaism of the original Hebrew.

When Gershom Scholem heard about the nascent project, he was astounded and expected the worst. He had a poor opinion of Rosenzweig's earlier translation of Judah Halevi. To his friend Ernst Simon, he confided, "I was always of the secret opinion that a translation of the Bible is the *Xenien* for which the Jews would be guilty before or upon leaving Germany. But will it be that??"[82] Simon liked the translation, despite "individual cases of preciousness . . . and many specific derogations." He added, "Altogether, it seems to me to be a Jewish Luther Bible," that is, a gold-standard translation of the Bible.[83] Scholem strongly disagreed: "I consider the samples as [having a] *decidedly false pathos*, no trace of the Luther Bible." He thought that Rosenzweig and Buber did not have Luther's "feeling for the pitch of language" and were wildly affected in their language.[84] Never shy in Judaic matters, Gershom Scholem shared his opinion directly with Martin Buber.[85]

Rosenzweig died in 1929, and Buber continued the translation and editing alone, which was largely done by 1938 but only fully completed in 1961. Upon that occasion, Gershom Scholem expressed his appreciation and gratitude for the project, and he was tempted to interpret its primary message as "Go forth and learn Hebrew!" Additionally, he could not help but mention the uselessness of such a Bible translation at that point. In his view, a project originally intended to influence German Jews and to improve the German language became "something like a visitor's gift that the German Jews could leave behind for the German people in a symbolic gesture of gratitude upon departing" in the 1930s, which then became "the gravestone of a relationship that was extinguished in unspeakable horror."[86]

At that time, Gershom Scholem had the benefit and bias of hindsight; however, in the late 1920s and early 1930s, German Jews, including Gershom's brothers, continued to build an enriching cultural life for themselves. In early 1933, after many years of preparation, the Jewish community of Berlin opened a museum to showcase its collection of paintings and ritual objects.[87] The Soncino Society of the Friends of the Jewish Book fostered discussion and encouraged collecting special editions that raised Jewish books, including theological books, to the level of European art.[88] This bibliophilic association's membership spanned the spectrum from Zionist to Liberal to Orthodox. As Jews and printers, the Soncino Society had special appeal to the Scholems. Reinhold, Erich, and Max were members, and Max and Erich even served on the society's board. Additionally, the Arthur Scholem lithography firm printed special items for the club.[89] For the Scholems, the Soncino Society was an ideal vehicle to give expression to their Jewishness, which was both cultural and social, but not conventionally religious.

Alongside developments among German Jews, though occasionally intersecting with them, was an explosion of eastern European Jewish cultural activity in Berlin. Many eastern European Jewish intellectuals had come to

Berlin during the World War, and more came during the years of the Weimar Republic. As a result, Berlin became a locus of Hebrew and Yiddish literature, often for export back to eastern Europe.[90] Additionally, many Jews from Poland and Russia came to Berlin to study and contributed to the new forms of Jewish identity and Jewish scholarship emerging in 1920s Berlin.[91] Some of these eastern European Jewish literati, such as Hayim Nahman Bialik and S. Y. Agnon, were friends with Gershom Scholem.

Although the cliché of German Jews in this era is that they fled from Jewish identity and assimilated as thoroughly as possible, such a characterization does not apply to a large portion of German Jewry. They may not have kept kosher and rarely set foot inside a synagogue, but they did seek different and new avenues for their Jewish identity. At the same time, they no longer felt compelled to define being Jewish by what it was not. The Lehrhaus and other groups aimed to make German Jews identify positively with Judaism and Jewish culture rather than basing their Jewish identity solely on the fight against antisemitism.[92]

Amidst all the changes affecting the Scholems in the mid-1920s were two tragedies. First, in December 1924, Kurt, younger son of Georg and Sophie, died of complications from an ear infection. The family was devastated by the loss of the eight-year-old child, and after the funeral, Betty told Gershom to write immediately with his condolences.[93] Then, only a few weeks later, Arthur Scholem died. On the afternoon of 6 February 1925, Arthur Scholem felt poorly and skipped a business lunch, but he insisted on going to his office. Still feeling unwell, he left work early but collapsed on the stairs on his way out of the building. Reinhold and Erich carried him back upstairs, but it was too late. An ambulance took Arthur's body to his home, where his brother Georg, a physician, confirmed the death. Theobald arrived and said the memorial *Kaddish* prayer for his brother. Meanwhile, Betty and Werner were at a café on Potsdamer Platz when Erich suddenly arrived with the news.[94]

The Scholems buried Arthur in a newly purchased family plot in the Berlin-Weißensee Jewish cemetery. Betty and her three sons in Berlin decided to inscribe the plot's wall solely with Arthur's name and birth and death dates. Arthur had often commented negatively when he saw "whole novels on the tombstone," as Betty put it. There would be no Hebrew inscription since only Gershom would be able to read it, and he would rarely visit the grave.[95] Though no one knew it at the time, Arthur Scholem would, in fact, be the only one laid to rest in this tomb. A combination of personal decisions and fate would take Betty, Reinhold, Erich, Werner, and Gershom away from their native city, and they would find their final rest elsewhere.

After Arthur's death, Betty was inundated with notes of condolence and praise for his work. Insurance organizations lauded Arthur in their trade publications. One of his gramophone record label customers from the Arabic music industry even placed a tribute notice in the *Berliner Tageblatt*.[96] Five months after his death, at the dedication ceremony for a new rest home that Arthur had helped establish, all the speakers praised Arthur, and his portrait hung in the boardroom.[97] Gershom also received many expressions of sympathy on the death of his father. Walter Benjamin saw Arthur's obituary in the newspaper and pithily wrote to Gershom in Jerusalem, "Will this cause a change in your [financial] situation?" Benjamin then proceeded to write at great length about his own work.[98] Aunt Sophie, Georg's wife, wrote more sensitively. She noted that Arthur had always been "brotherly and loving" to them, especially after the death of their son Kurt. Georg added, "He really was the head of the family, the exemplary brother. For only now can I speak about it. I have lost a lot with him."[99]

Arthur's death left Betty in a precarious economic state. Her sons urged her to sell her depreciated stocks so as to have some capital, but Betty insisted on holding on to them in the hope that their value might rise once again. Arthur's 100,000-mark life insurance policy was now worthless as a result of the hyperinflation.[100] Arthur Scholem also left behind a striking will. Reinhold, Erich, and Gershom would split the estate in thirds, after the death of their mother, who had unrestricted use of it during her lifetime. No later than September 1921, Arthur had legally disinherited his Communist son Werner. Werner would receive only the minimal share mandated by German law.[101] Reinhold and Erich took over the family printing business and bought out Betty's share. Gershom received his father's cufflinks and his old pocket watch, while Werner received their father's Swiss wristwatch that he wore every day. Werner had wanted the pocket watch for himself, but it had been Arthur's wish that Gershom get to choose the wristwatch or pocket watch, with Werner getting the other. Werner passed the wristwatch on to Reinhold, who was closer to their father, and received another watch in exchange. Betty also sent Gershom a memorial (*Yahrzeit*) calendar, some neckties, and a dozen handkerchiefs.[102]

Despite her own money concerns, Betty continued to subsidize Gershom and Escha's life in Palestine, even as she complained about their spendthrift ways. She could not understand how both of them could have paying jobs, receive money from their parents, and still be chronically in debt. She noted that her ill-paid Communist son earned less than they did and never had debts. Reinhold and Erich poured all their money into the family business. Still, Betty continued to send German marks to Gershom in Jerusalem.[103] In fact, she remained extremely close to her youngest son, even after his emigration. Over the next two decades, they sent hundreds of letters to each other. She frequently admonished Gershom when he did not write, especially on the occasion of family birthdays and celebrations. More curiously, Betty became Gershom's own personal purveyor of German-made consumer goods and delicacies, as he continued to express a marked preference for German food, clothes, and office supplies. His requests fill their correspondence.[104] He specifically demanded German-made sausages and, above all, marzipan, which she dutifully sent to him, despite associating it with Christmas. He even got offended when his mother threatened to cut off his supply.[105] Indeed, this aspect of their correspondence reveals two interesting aspects of Gershom's personality. While he frequently disclaimed any identity as a German Jew, he still felt an attachment to many aspects of German culture.[106] Additionally, he could be extremely sharp, self-important, and simply inconsiderate to those closest to him.

Meanwhile, there was genuine strife in the Scholem family. Reinhold and his wife, Käthe, separated after only a few years of marriage, and he insisted on divorcing—something quite rare at the time.[107] While he moved back in with his parents, Käthe stayed in their apartment and waited for his return. Eventually, she and their son moved in with her sister, leaving Reinhold to pay rent on an empty apartment.[108] Reinhold's marital difficulties had been a frequent subject of discussion between Betty and Arthur, including during Arthur's final days. After Arthur died, Reinhold refused to include Käthe's name among the mourners listed in the obituary, and she attended the funeral with her sister. Nonetheless, Käthe expected them to reconcile at any moment.[109] In the end, Reinhold went back to his wife for the sake of his son: "Only to the child, not to the mother. He thinks that works! Be that as it may, Reinhold has botched his life with this marriage," his mother wrote.[110] Betty suspected that had Arthur still been alive, he would have talked Reinhold out of going back. Erich and Emmy, Werner's wife, also expressed their disapproval in the strongest terms. And after Reinhold returned to his wife, he seemed to be a beaten-down, introspective man, according to Betty and Emmy.[111] Erich was not happily married either. Betty wrote to Gershom, "Both [sons] drag on their wives and wished they did not have them. Is that not unspeakably sad?"[112] Betty was relieved when Erich moved back in with her in the old apartment.[113]

After Arthur's death, Erich and Reinhold took over as the proprietors of the printshop and made it their own, moving the firm to a new space adjacent to Erich's home.[114] In the late 1920s, the lion's share of the Scholems' business was printing labels for gramophone records. Betty remarked that they paid off a significant portion of their bank debts through their record-label printing.[115] Under Reinhold and Erich, the firm also printed a considerable amount of Judaica, and their clients included the Soncino Society of Jewish book collectors and the newspaper *Menorah*. To help them with their Jewish orders, they hired the famous Jewish antiquarian Abraham Horodisch, whom they knew from the Soncino Society. Their Jewish business grew so much that Erich thought they should buy Hebrew type for their printing machines.[116]

To escape from the demands of their work life in Berlin, the Scholems had long rented a small vacation cottage in Zernsdorf, just outside of Berlin. In 1925 the owner wished to sell it, and she let the Scholems have first option on the purchase. Even though the purchase price of 5,000 reichsmarks ($1,200 at the time) was a financial strain for them, Reinhold and Erich jumped at the opportunity. Betty even contributed to the purchase, feeling that it would give her claim to her own room in the house. For Betty, her sons, and their families, it was a haven. They could get away from the tumult of the city and the troubles of their business. They had a garden and a dock for their boat, and they added a veranda and extra rooms to the house. Reinhold cleared the reeds from the lakeshore for swimming.[117] At the time of the Great Depression, when money was especially tight, Betty wrote, "Zernsdorf is true happiness for us. We live modestly there."[118]

Still, in the 1920s, the Scholems could afford some luxuries. In addition to buying a vacation home, they celebrated and traveled. In December 1926, just after Betty Scholem turned sixty, Reinhold and Erich gave her a diamond watch, while Gershom sent her some pillows from Palestine. Her children and grandchildren gathered for a festive breakfast, followed that evening by a large party with speeches, tribute poems, drinking, and dancing until 2 a.m.[119] In 1928 Reinhold finally moved from central Berlin to an upper-middle-class section of Berlin-Schöneberg, where his uncles had long lived. His mother described the modern apartment building: four staircases, an elevator, and lots of sun. While construction on his apartment continued, Reinhold took a fourteen-day vacation in Switzerland.[120]

Betty Scholem also had the travel bug. In 1926 she took a long-awaited trip to Palestine to see Gershom. She stopped in Switzerland en route to Palestine, and on her way back, she visited Egypt, where she rode a camel to see the famous pyramids. She had a wonderful time on her trip, though she was disappointed that her fellow passengers aboard the ocean liner across the Mediterranean did not dress more elegantly. She found Palestine "beautiful" and wished she "had stayed four weeks longer."[121] Upon her return, she distributed gifts to her family and friends, who were full of questions about what it was like there: "People ask the dumbest questions! The most popular is the question, what does one really eat in Palestine! *Everyone* asks that."[122] In 1927 she traveled to Venice with a lady friend and took Italian classes "with a real Italian."[123] In 1930 she wrote about traveling to Sarajevo in Bosnia and Mt. Lovcen in Montenegro en route to Palestine. Her friend worried that they would face "uncivilized food with the runs in its wake," but Betty was willing to risk it.[124] Ultimately, Betty and Erich visited Gershom in Palestine in 1931, traveling by train to Istanbul, then by ship to Beirut, and then overland to Jerusalem.[125] When she returned to Berlin, she told everyone about the modern conditions in which Gershom lived. Berliners "still have the impression it is a sort of Hottentot village and hear with astonishment about the European comforts of your lifestyle."[126]

While Betty traveled through southern Europe and Palestine and Reinhold moved to a more affluent part of Berlin, Werner's situation grew much more precarious. After his expulsion from the Communist Party in 1926, he retained his seat in parliament as an independent member of the Reichstag. However, in late winter 1928, Germany's governing coalition collapsed. President Paul von Hindenburg dissolved the parliament and called for new elections, and Werner lost his seat in the Reichstag. He could not rejoin the Communist Party, and his ambivalent participation in a new Leninist political party yielded no success. His political career was over.

He decided to return to university, this time to study law. At the age of thirty-two, he was much older than most students, and he had a family. Unaccustomed to the demands of university life, he struggled academically, and his mother wondered if he would make it. Gershom noted that older students often did better than younger students since they had a true love of learning, but in Werner's case, he was motivated by hunger. Simply put, he needed a career.[127] While earning a university degree was his best option now, his mother thought, "He absolutely should have stayed with the party, but he definitely did not want that." She wrote that the views that cost him his political career were now, ironically, the party line, though she failed to note Stalin's grip on Russian and German communism and the complete lack of intraparty democracy. As a student, Werner had increased expenses, including course books, and virtually no income.[128] However, the main income for Werner's family was the earnings of his wife, Emmy, who worked as a clerk for a publishing house that specialized in taxation manuals.

Since Arthur's death, Betty had grown closer to her third son and his family, yet she found it hard to relate to her daughter-in-law because of Emmy's working-class and non-Jewish origins. Additionally, Werner and his family lived very differently from the conventionally bourgeois and Jewish Scholems, and Betty regarded them negatively.[129] Indeed, the Scholems could comment very judgmentally about non-Jews. When Emmy experienced health problems after using birth control provided by a Communist, non-Jewish doctor, Betty quipped, "The goys have a hidden way of thinking, a *different* way in any case. I see that often confirmed with both of the Christians in my family."[130] In corresponding with Gershom, and presumably in her everyday speech, Betty used the expression "goyim naches," commonly abbreviated by German Jews as "G.N." This term, literally meaning "Gentile's delight," pejoratively denoted something that gave pleasure to non-Jews but that left Jews unmoved.[131] This sentiment was the product of generations of accreted experiences and a defensive snobbery. The history of negative interactions with non-Jewish Germans reinforced a sense of "our crowd" among German Jews. At the same time, bourgeois German Jews' social class and attendant educational attainments and cultural affinities contributed to a sense of superiority to many non-Jews, a number of whom, incidentally, looked down on Jews.

As a result of these ingrained attitudes, intermarriage remained a controversial topic, even among Jews such as the Scholems, who otherwise considered themselves integrated into the wider German society. At one of the Scholems' Shabbat dinners, Lene Scholem, Max's wife, remarked how negatively she viewed intermarriage—right in front of Emmy.[132] In 1929 Betty Scholem's cousin Else Pflaum converted to Christianity and married a once-divorced man in the Kaiser Wilhelm Memorial Church (Kaiser-Wilhelm-Gedächtniskirche) in Berlin, a veritable monument to German Protestantism, causing great consternation in the family.[133] That year, 27 percent of all German Jewish men and 18 percent of Jewish women who got married had non-Jewish spouses, and the percentage was higher in cities such as Berlin and Hamburg.[134] Statistics do not reveal how many marriages between two Christians involved a recent convert from Judaism. In 1934 Lene and Max Scholem's daughter, Therese, converted to Catholicism and married a non-Jew.[135] The organized Jewish community could not stop the conversions, but it did not let people go quietly. In Berlin, Frankfurt, Dresden, and other cities, Jewish leaders published apostates' names, professions, and addresses in their community newsletters, and Else Pflaum's "withdrawal from Judaism" was duly publicized.[136] When the Nazis banned mixed marriages, Betty applauded the measure and commented that her brother Hans should be relieved that his daughter could not marry her Christian boyfriend.[137]

The inward-looking nature of German Jewish society was partially a legacy of institutional and social barriers to Jewish integration before 1918; however, prejudice against Jews continued during the years of the

Weimar Republic, with particular impact on their social lives. Jewish students attended schools with non-Jews, and Jewish lawyers tried court cases alongside non-Jewish colleagues, but they rarely occupied the same intimate social circles. It was uncommon for middle-class Jews to forge unrestrained personal friendships with non-Jews.[138] In many cases, the profusion of open antisemitism made life positively uncomfortable for German Jews. For example, they could not blithely vacation anywhere they wished, and the Central Association of German Citizens of the Jewish Faith published a list of resort towns and hotels where Jews were not welcome.[139] Even though Werner Scholem had no interest in joining a specifically Jewish organization, his mountain-climbing club was widely considered a "Jewish" club because Jewish alpinists were unwelcome in other German mountaineering associations.[140] Antisemitism and extreme nationalism suffused German academic culture, affecting students' experiences as well as Jewish academics' career prospects.[141] Faced with an exterior world that was lukewarm, if not overtly hostile, many German Jews looked to their extended family and to friends with similar backgrounds for socializing.

The Scholems were a large, tight-knit family. Moreover, for them and German-Jewish families like theirs, the categories of social friend and relative significantly overlapped as they circulated in a world where so many acquaintances, business partners, and neighbors were also distant cousins or relatives-by-marriage. The case of Reinhold Scholem demonstrates the overlapping ties in this society. In 1921 Reinhold married Käthe Wagner, whose sister Anne was married to Arthur Sussmann. Sussmann's sister Sophie was married to Georg Scholem, the youngest brother of Reinhold's father, Arthur. Ten years later, Werner and his family were neighbors with Gertrud Zucker, the sister of Theobald Scholem's wife.

Considering how central the extended family was to the Scholems' world, tragedies reverberated strongly among the immediate families of the four brothers Arthur, Theobald, Max, and Georg. They were deeply shaken when Arthur died suddenly in 1925, and in June 1928, misfortune struck the family again as Georg died at the age of fifty. Suffering from an attack of gallstones, Georg was rushed to the hospital for emergency surgery. He survived another fourteen days before succumbing to pancreatitis. His funeral was especially awful, according to Betty. Sophie, Georg's widow, did not know any of her husband's professional colleagues and did not send them notices of his death. The venerable Berlin rabbi Dr. Samson Weisse conducted the funeral ceremony, but he spoke impersonally and without verve about Georg, a man whose life was both interesting and highly representative of German Jews in his era.[142] Betty predicted that with Georg's death, things were likely to take a turn for the worse within the family: "Since our father's death, Georg was always the mediator in the eternal tales between Theo and Max."

Although brothers Theobald and Max Scholem had not gotten along for years, they warily maintained their partnership as the proprietors of Siegfried Scholem Printers. That détente collapsed in 1928. Max began to act peculiarly. He claimed that someone was extorting him and threatened to throw himself under a moving streetcar. He ran up debts and charged them to the firm, requiring Theobald to pay them off. Theobald then took away Max's rights to contract debts on the firm's behalf. Eventually, Max resigned from the firm, and Theobald publicized the change in management in a popular newspaper.[143] Max then asked Reinhold and Erich to inquire if Theobald would let Max have some of the firm's business to start a new printshop.[144] He also demanded that Theobald pay him off or his whole family would commit suicide.[145]

In fact, Max quickly found a new business. Using money from a settlement with Theobald, he obtained machines from liquidated printshops and hired a large staff. Everyone in the extended family, including Theobald, hoped Max would have success.[146] That goodwill soon dissipated. Max's firm won a contract for a job from the Ullstein media empire. Siegfried Scholem Printers had been doing the work for eight years, but Max was personally friendly with Rudolf Ullstein. Theobald filed a grievance with the printers' association, but it was dismissed as the job was not considered "ongoing work."[147]

Despite winning away one of Siegfried Scholem's prize contracts, Max's firm did not flourish. Once again, Max accrued massive debts.[148] His son Herbert was to join him in the business, but that did not materialize either. Herbert spent three semesters studying at the Master School for Germany's Printers, in Munich, though without much distinction.[149] Herbert lasted only four months at a printshop in Hamburg before being dismissed, and soon the family discovered that he never took his master's examination in Munich. He had used a forged certificate to placate his family.[150]

Max's plight ended spectacularly: he killed himself in a gas explosion. On the evening of 15 November 1929, Max did not come home from work, and his children went looking for him. The night watchman in Max's building escorted them to his firm, and when the watchman opened the door, it triggered an explosion. Max had been lying in the stereotype printshop, with gas on under the melting barrel. The explosion killed Max and severely burned the watchman. Erich was the first relative to arrive on the scene. He could hardly reach the site with three fire engines and thousands of people blocking the way. To prevent embarrassing media coverage, the Scholems relied on their connections to Berlin's press world. They fetched Rudolf Ullstein from his private club, and he and Reinhold drove directly to Ullstein head-quarters. From there, they called Mosse and Scherl, Berlin's other two media empires, but it was too late. Their presses were already running with the news. A reporter from Ullstein's *Berliner Morgenpost* had been on the scene and phoned in his report at 9:30 p.m. By 1 a.m. the newspaper was in print. The various newspaper headlines ranged from strictly factual ("Explosion in a Print Shop," in the highbrow, liberal *Vossische Zeitung*) to sensationalist ("Suicide Victim Causes Serious Gas Explosion," in the popular, conservative *Berliner Lokal-Anzeiger*).[151] The family declined to publish an obituary imme-diately following Max's death. As Betty wrote, "It was publicized enough!"[152]

Max's suicide was part of an increasing trend. More than 10 percent of all German suicides took place in Berlin, and Berlin had one of the highest Jew-ish suicide rates in Europe, if not the highest. In fact, it seemed that Jews took their own lives far more often than members of other religious communities in the German capital. The onset of the Great Depression only increased the number of suicides in Germany, and the rate rose by nearly 14 percent between 1929 and 1932.[153]

After Max's death, the family was deeply concerned about his widow Lene's financial situation. Before his suicide, she had cosigned a promissory note for 7,000 reichsmarks. Fortunately for her, Theobald knew the man and got him to agree to accept a lesser sum.[154] Max's firm went into receivership and was dissolved by early 1931.[155] However, not long after Max's funeral, the Berlin press baron Rudolf Ullstein offered Lene a position managing his company's canteen. She would direct a head chef and a staff of a dozen people to prepare meals for hundreds of company employees, and she would have to source and buy the food, often at 4 a.m., at the bulk market. It seemed an impossible task for a forty-six-year-old woman with no professional experience. The family wished her success and hoped that Ullstein would give her another position if she were not up to the challenge.[156] In the end, however, Lene did prove more than capable at her new job and thrived as a working woman.

Women's participation in the German workforce grew at a tremendous rate in the late 1920s. While the number of women working in the agricul-tural sector decreased significantly, the number of urban, insured women with regular jobs increased dramatically, from five million women in the summer of 1925 to six million in the summer of 1929. Moreover, this increase occurred at a time when there was not full employment in Germany. In addi-tion to more women finding work as unskilled industrial workers, this was an era known for its ubiquitous women salesclerks and secretaries as well as those women working in the entertainment industry. Nonetheless, most German women did not work outside the home.[157]

Barely a year after starting work, Betty Scholem reported that Lene managed to feed three hundred people per day, while Betty struggled to arrange Shabbat dinner for the family. Her salary was 500 reichsmarks, "a giant income for a woman and completely free grub, too," as Betty put it. On days when the cafeteria was closed, she received an additional food allowance.[158] In fact, she still struggled financially and to save money on rent, she gave up her old apartment and moved into a less expensive one.[159] Nonetheless, her professional accomplishment was impressive for a woman with no previous work experience outside the home and exceptional considering the contracting German economy. Soon, thousands more Jewish women like Lene Scholem entered the workforce for the first time or reentered it as their husbands lost jobs because of Nazi antisemitism and the broader economic situation.[160]

The Great Depression came to Germany earlier and more severely than most countries. It is true that during the mid-1920s, national income rose and the balance of trade improved.[161] However, in contrast to almost every major industrialized economy in the world, where share prices generally increased until 1929, share prices in Germany steadily declined starting in the summer of 1927.[162] A lockout in the western German steel industry in November and December 1928 depressed economic production across the economy. Then, the coldest winter in Berlin's recorded history further sapped economic strength, followed by an outflow of investment capital in the spring, owing in part to political conditions. By the summer of 1929, Germany's economy was in severe decline. Even before the New York stock crash in October, German unemployment stood at 1.9 million people, compared to 1.6 million people in the United States, which had a total population twice Germany's size.[163] Moreover, the modernization of German industry and a boom in housing construction had been financed with high-interest foreign loans. If foreign capital markets evaporated, the German economy would collapse.[164]

The German-Jewish middle class was under pressure well before 1929. The vast majority of German Jews worked in commerce, and approximately half of all German Jews were self-employed, compared to 16–17 percent of the population as a whole. While they had much greater freedom to set their work hours and to change the focus of their trade, they also had less of a safety net if their business diminished. Small business owners and pensioners had already seen their income devastated by the inflation of 1923.[165] The economic crises of the early 1930s had a further crushing impact on the commercial middle class, and an increasing number of German-born Jews sought social aid. In fact, the percentage of Jews seeking help was twice as great as the percentage for the overall German population. Among the signs of economic distress was the fact that fewer Jewish families could afford to send their children to university.[166]

The Scholems, too, felt the pinch before the Great Depression began. In 1928 Reinhold and Erich's book-printing business lost so much money that the profitable label-printing business could not make it up. Their earnings initially went toward paying the interest on loans. Because of labor laws, they were unable to dismiss employees summarily, and each time they changed their workers' duties or company policies, their staff filed a grievance.[167] Things only got worse after the Wall Street crash in October 1929.

With the onset of deflation, demand for consumer goods slumped.[168] Small- and medium-sized firms, like the two Scholem printing firms, were particularly affected. In 1931 the world economy suffered a series of shocks that massively deepened the Great Depression. The Austrian Creditanstalt, one of the largest banks in central Europe, crashed in May of that year. In July, the German Darmstädter und Nationalbank collapsed, triggering a run on all major banks. Credit dried up and deflation seemed to spin out of control. While unemployment had been high at 15.7 percent in 1930, it now rose to 23.9 percent and peaked at nearly 31 percent in 1932. Critically for the Scholems and others in the commercial economy, retail sales reached only 63 percent of pre-Depression levels, consumer goods production stood at 78 percent, and total industrial production at 61 percent.[169] Some of the Scholems' biggest customers acquired printing machines and manufactured their own labels. The Scholems received no new contracts and lacked the funds to pay their employees' salaries. Even renting out empty office space in their building was futile. There were simply not enough businesses around. Reinhold was becoming unhinged, and his wife spoke of suicide. Erich managed to keep a level head, but the situation remained extreme. By autumn, they had just enough business to pay salaries, but not enough to make a real profit or to pay their debts. They kept extending their credit with suppliers, but they did not have enough work.[170]

Betty lost her securities, and her sons advised her to withdraw as much money as possible from her bank account and to pay as many bills as possible by check. When her bank closed, she had only 70 marks left from 900 marks. Meanwhile, she opened an account at a more stable, private bank.[171] In 1929, four years after Arthur's death, Betty Scholem finally gave up the apartment where she had lived for over twenty years and moved to a four-room apartment in Erich's apartment building.[172] Her grandchildren loved coming down to her apartment to make mischief.[173] Betty economized when she could and helped Werner out, since he was still studying at university in his thirties.[174] However, she soon faced the reality that she could no longer afford her own apartment. She planned on giving her furniture to Werner and moving in with Erich. She commented, "It's true that my mama was not a rich woman, but at least she died in *her* apartment."[175] The Berlin Scholems were also unable to pay Gershom the subsidy he had enjoyed in Palestine, which only made him indignant. His mother reminded him that he did have his education and a profession of his own choosing.[176] Reinhold owned a well-known business, but he and his wife rented rooms to Japanese diplomats to make ends meet, as did some of their relatives.[177] Emmy Scholem, Werner's wife, had a good job with a printing house until it collapsed, in part because the firm's owner had been stealing from his own company. With the Scholems' help, Emmy joined two other employees in buying the company. They hoped that ownership in a printing firm and Werner's future salary as an attorney would provide the basis for their future.[178]

The poor economic situation soon undermined the political situation. In September 1930, Germany had Reichstag elections, the first national vote since the start of the Great Depression. It was a disaster for the forces of democracy. Betty's German Democratic Party, now known as the German State Party, went from 4.9 percent of the national vote in 1928 to 3.8 percent in 1930. It even lost support in disproportionately Jewish central Berlin and western Berlin. Support for Reinhold's German People's Party dropped nationally from 8.7 percent to 4.5 percent. The Social Democrats remained the largest party in the Reichstag, despite retreating to 24.5 percent from 29.8 percent. Even the reactionary, anti-democratic, nationalist German National People's Party—the second-most successful party for most of the 1920s—saw its share of the vote cut in half, from 14.2 percent to 7 percent. By contrast, extremist parties thrived, chief among them the Nazis. In 1928 the Nazis could muster only 2.6 percent of the national vote. Two years later, they won 18.3 percent, the largest gain of any party. The Communist Party reached 13.1 percent of the vote.[179]

Betty Scholem pithily analyzed the cause: "natural result of unemployment."[180] Betty also fulminated that the nationalist press blamed Germany's economic situation on the World War I reparations and political moderation. She reasoned that, "so long as we are building battleships, no one will believe the nonsense that the reparations are [to blame] for the debacle."[181] Betty reluctantly admitted that Werner had long ago prophesized that capitalism and Germany's political system would collapse.[182]

The economic crisis affected the Jews' position in German society. As demand for retail goods evaporated during the deflation, the Jewish commercial middle class fared especially poorly. Additionally, the Jews incurred the public anger of antisemitic groups. The Nazis hardly needed to point out that, in the cities, Jewish-owned firms dominated the retail clothing trade and department store industry. In the countryside of western Germany, Jewish cattle dealers and grain wholesalers dominated their industries. Although these Jewish businessmen struggled during the Great Depression, their being religiously or culturally different made them suspect, and the Nazis exploited these social divisions and resentments. Even before 1933, Nazis rallied in the streets for boycotts of Jewish businesses and drove many Jews out of business.[183] When Jewish employees lost their jobs, even for purely economic reasons, they were unable to find new positions with non-Jewish firms.[184]

Days after the Nazis' electoral success in 1930, Gershom made light of the situation, writing to his mother, "You seem, however, to have fulfilled your electoral duty only defectively." But he admitted that, "Even here, so far from the blast, it has caused a sensation." In fact, rumors were spreading in Palestine that the Jews of Germany were panicked and "that everyone who could is taking his money over the border as fast as possible," in Gershom's words.[185] In her correspondence with Gershom, Betty downplayed the results of the election and vehemently denied that political circumstances had moved the Jews of Germany to desperate measures: "That 'the Jews are fleeing with bag and baggage to Switzerland' is naturally a big canard. Certainly *not a single Jew* has run away. And why? Not a single riot has occurred. . . . If only the newspapers would refrain from their lies!"[186] However, some Jews were worried. With the two liberal parties—the German Democratic Party / German State Party and the German People's Party—less effectual than ever before, many middle-class Jews looked to the Catholic Center Party as the last bulwark of bourgeois democracy despite that party's overt clericalism. While this was particularly the case after the election of 1930,[187] Georg Kareski, chairman of the Berlin Jewish community and an outspoken Zionist, ran for the Reichstag as a candidate of the Catholic Center Party in 1930. In fact, the Center Party, not the historically pro-Jewish German Democratic Party / German State Party, was the only political party to run an advertisement in the *Israelitisches Familienblatt*.[188]

The Scholem family split over this development. Betty strongly disapproved of Kareski's candidacy and considered it a ploy by the Center Party to win Jewish voters. By contrast, Theobald approved of Kareski. Theobald claimed that "as a Jew, one can only vote Social Democratic or Center Party, and since, however, one cannot vote Social Democratic as an entrepreneur (exploiter and bloodsucker), that leaves only the Center Party!"[189] He was not alone. Large numbers of Jewish voters came to the same conclusion after the 1930 election. While many Jews living in big cities or predominantly Protestant areas voted for the Social Democratic Party, those concerned by the

Socialists' stance on private property and views on religion threw in their lot with the Center Party. In Schöneberg, the middle-class Berlin borough where Theobald lived, Jews made up 7.3 percent of the population by the early 1930s. In 1928, before the crisis, the German Democratic Party/German State Party won 12 percent of the vote in Schöneberg, and the Catholic Center Party won 3.7 percent of the vote. By the summer of 1932, at the height of the Depression, the German State Party won only 2.4 percent compared to 6.3 percent for the Center Party. In upper-middle-class Wilmersdorf, the most Jewish borough of Berlin, the German Democratic Party/German State Party's share of the vote plummeted from 15.4 percent in 1928 to 3.5 percent in July 1932, while the Center Party improved from 3.5 percent to 8.1 percent over the same period—a move partially fueled by Jewish voters changing allegiances. Even the Communists made modest gains in middle-class Jewish areas of Berlin as the fear of Nazism grew, though Reinhold mocked these Jewish burghers and intellectuals as "salon Communists."[190]

Just as Germany experienced political conflict and massive electoral change, political tumult also came to the organized Jewish community. Historically, the assimilationist Liberals dominated Jewish communal affairs in Berlin and throughout Germany. That briefly changed during the last years of Weimar democracy. In 1926 a politically and religiously diverse coalition led by the Jewish People's Party (Jüdische Volkspartei) defeated the Liberals in the Jewish communal elections in Berlin. Nonetheless, the Liberals did not go quietly and filed a legal challenge with the police, alleging election fraud. Some Liberals tried applying political pressure to influence the investigation, while their opponents used parliamentary chicanery to advance their cause. Only in October 1927 could the new leadership enter office, finally breaking the Liberals' long-standing hegemony. As part of the coalition agreement, Jewish People's Party leader Georg Kareski became president of the Berlin community in January 1929. For the first time, a Zionist was head of Germany's largest Jewish community.[191]

For many Berlin Jews, the Jewish People's Party was well suited to the spirit of the times. It sought to create an enhanced communitarian sensibility among Jews. It wanted to focus on cultural, social, and educational institutions; and in religious matters, it supported traditional forms of worship rather than innovations. The party enjoyed particular support from eastern European Jewish immigrants and, later, from downwardly mobile German Jews. The party brought other groups into its orbit through its openness and particular emphases. Among its candidates were the historian Simon Dubnow, the writer Arnold Zweig, and the painter Lesser Ury. When in power, the Jewish People's Party expressed overt solidarity with

Jews elsewhere in the world and gave the community's official newspaper a more national-Jewish outlook. However, the Jewish People's Party also made some concessions to the Liberals, such as opening a synagogue with mixed-gender seating.[192]

Zionist leadership atop the Berlin Jewish community did not last long, and new elections were called for November 1930.[193] Theobald strongly supported the Jewish People's Party and counseled his nephews and sister-in-law to vote for the Berlin Zionists, rather than for the Liberals, whose worldview was closer to Betty, Reinhold, and Erich's. The election led to heated discussions and bad feelings among the Scholems. In the end, the Jewish People's Party's efflorescence was brief. It lost control of the Berlin Jewish community, and the Liberals returned to power.[194] The situation was similar throughout Germany. In cities with large eastern European Jewish populations, the Jewish People's Party enjoyed notable success, but it could never break the Liberals' hold on national leadership.

In contrast to his brothers and mother, Werner was not concerned with Jewish communal politics. He was not involved with the community, even passively, and he attempted to build a new life for himself at the age of thirty-five. In March 1931, he passed the first part of the bar exam and earned the second-highest possible grade, "Completely Satisfactory." In his exam group, three failed and two passed. One of his examiners happened to be August Müller, former state secretary of the Imperial Economics Office (the equivalent of minister of economics), whom Werner called a "Noske socialist," that is, an anti-communist Socialist from the German civil war of 1918–19. As for accusations of antisemitism clouding the examination process, Betty commented at the time, "It is not true that the examiners flunk people simply because they are named Cohn or have a [big] nose."[195]

As a law clerk, Werner stayed in Berlin, which was unusual, but he had a family in the city. He was to work at the district court of Berlin-Pankow, but dubious officials delayed his appointment. They looked for criminal activity in his past; however, the Reichstag had approved an amnesty for political crimes, which exonerated Werner. He planned to take the second part of the bar exam in three years and would become a practicing lawyer, not a judge, and then the politics would begin again. He proclaimed that he would not go over to the bourgeoisie. Rather, he expected that in three or four years, a new, radical workers' movement would arise, and it would be advantageous that he was not a Communist Party official.[196] In the meantime, he remained a political gadfly. While no longer a candidate himself, Werner worked as an election supervisor at a polling station in March 1932, and he could not help but scoff at the upper-class economic status of the voters in his precinct.[197]

On 15 March 1932, Arthur Scholem Printers celebrated its fortieth anniversary. The Scholems had come a long way since twenty-nine-year-old Arthur and twenty-five-year-old Betty opened their printshop in the rear courtyard of a building in central Berlin, but the firm's high-water mark had long passed. Nonetheless, Betty, Reinhold, Erich, Werner, and other relatives held a celebratory dinner at Reinhold's home.[198] From Palestine, Gershom sent his congratulations and expressed his wishes that they all witness the firm's fiftieth anniversary in good health and a good mood.[199] It was not to be. By March 1942, the German Jews' world had collapsed.

In the short term, the firm barely limped along. While they were able to pay their taxes and some outstanding debts, their sales were shrinking. They considered merging the firms of Arthur Scholem and Siegfried Scholem.[200] In the end, Theobald accepted the idea, largely to win Arthur Scholem's label business, but even that commerce shrank to the point that they scarcely used their equipment.[201] After the merger, Theobald dismissed his manager, and Erich took over the position.[202] Around this time, Werner wrote with tremendous and unintended poignancy, "The disintegration of the Jewish bourgeoisie progresses. . . . The decline of the family is taking place very quickly."[203]

In 1932 Gershom contemplated coming to Germany "and then [I] can take a close look at your lives."[204] Betty expressed serious concerns about his taking a trip at this time "with the prevailing testiness, political contagion, and antisemitism."[205] As the Nazi Party moved from electoral triumph to electoral triumph, the Nazis and public perception of them became an increasing part of Gershom's correspondence with his family. In fact, both Betty and Werner expected the Nazis to come to power. Even after Gershom visited Berlin that summer, Betty thought that he underestimated the severity of the economic and political situation. He only saw a façade of middle-class stability.[206] Others saw things more perceptively. The novelist Erich Kästner wrote of this society, "We live provisionally. The crisis never ends!"[207]

Germany's conservative, Catholic chancellor, Franz von Papen, could no longer govern without making use of emergency powers granted to him by President von Hindenburg, and in November 1932, Germany had its fourth national election of the year. While the Nazis were still the largest party in the Reichstag, their share of the national vote declined to 33 percent from 37.4 percent a few months earlier. The Communists, however, saw their vote increase from 14.3 percent to 16.9 percent. One hundred Communists now sat in the Reichstag alongside 196 Nazis out of a total of 584 deputies. Together they commanded a majority in the Reichstag, though neither party was interested in democracy or parliamentary cooperation. By contrast, the Social Democratic Party, German State Party (formerly German Democratic Party), and Center Party—who, collectively, had been known as the Weimar Coalition—controlled only 193 seats.[208] Betty Scholem expected Papen to call for new elections, particularly because of the Communist presence in the Reichstag,[209] but Papen was content to govern through presidential decree.

To prove the Jews' loyalty to Germany, the Jewish veterans' organization, the Reich League of Jewish Frontline Soldiers (Reichsbund jüdischer Frontsoldaten), published a list of every Jewish soldier who died in the German military in World War I.[210] The organization presented the first copy to the German president Paul von Hindenburg and held a ceremony in November 1932 to celebrate the book's publication.[211] The Reich League had long espoused a German patriotic, if not nationalist, position. However, its efforts largely fell on deaf ears in the cacophony of antisemitic invective that consumed the German public by the end of 1932.[212]

There is no disputing that middle- and upper-class German Jews felt a deep attachment to German culture, especially high culture. The *C. V.-Zeitung*, the newspaper of the Central Association of German Citizens of the Jewish Faith, had the subtitle "Pages for Germanness and Judaism" ("Blätter für Deutschtum und Judentum"). Alfred Wiener, the Central Association's general secretary, famously proclaimed, "If there were a Nobel Prize for German sentiments, the German Jews would win it."[213] Germany's national poet, Johann Wolfgang von Goethe, was a particular object of Jewish veneration. On Rosh Hashanah 1928, the Scholems' rabbi gave a sermon on Goethe.[214] In 1932 Jews and Jewish institutions across the country paid homage to Goethe on the one hundredth anniversary of his death. He was the subject of Jewish publications and sermons in Liberal synagogues. Even the strictly Orthodox Jewish high school in Berlin inscribed its diplomas with a quotation from Goethe.[215] The University of Frankfurt, which had a large number of Jewish professors, students, and donors, changed its name to Johann Wolfgang von Goethe University of Frankfurt. An even greater object of affection for German Jewry was Gotthold Ephraim Lessing, whose friendship with Moses Mendelssohn and whose play *Nathan the Wise* symbolized a tradition of tolerance in Germany. In 1929 Jewish groups celebrated the two hundredth anniversary of his birth and, two years later, commemorated the one hundred and fiftieth anniversary of his death.[216]

Nonetheless, the German Jews' insistence on being seen as both Jews and Germans increasingly found little sympathy and, indeed, incurred a great deal of hostility. In the early 1930s, political parties that defended republican democracy and equal rights—including for Jews—were on the defensive, and it was not long before the Nazis destroyed democracy and reversed Jewish emancipation through a series of laws, decrees, and violent actions. The florescence of the Golden Twenties had merely been gold-plated.

CHAPTER 6

In the Promised Land

A New Home in Jerusalem

In the late nineteenth century, two new factors prompted increased Jewish immigration from Europe, particularly eastern Europe, to Palestine. First, altered circumstances in the Russian Empire, including pogroms and economic dislocations, convinced many Jews to seek a new life elsewhere. While many of the emigrants opted for America, others chose Palestine, often for prosaic reasons.[1] Second, with the advent of modern Zionism, increasing numbers of Jews moved to Palestine for ideological reasons. These migrants, usually secular, and often socialist, wanted to build up the Jewish settlement in Ottoman Palestine, known as the Yishuv. However, they also saw themselves as engaged in work to transform the Yishuv and to transform Jewry. They believed that manual, agricultural labor would provide the basis for a comprehensive, variegated Jewish society in Palestine and would regenerate the Jews physically and psychologically. Thus, these Zionist pioneers built or joined agrarian settlements.[2]

Between 1881 and the start of the First World War, approximately seventy-five thousand Jews migrated from Europe to Ottoman Palestine, though harsh living conditions and a lack of economic opportunities compelled half of them to return to Europe. World War I completely changed the situation. In 1917, during the war, the British captured Palestine. After the final defeat of the Central Powers, Britain received official control of Palestine as a mandate territory under the League of Nations, and a third great wave of Jewish migration to Palestine—the Third *Aliyah*—began. Beginning in 1920, the British tightly regulated the number of Jewish immigrants permitted to settle in Palestine, in part because they did not wish to exacerbate the nascent conflict between Jews and Arabs and in part because they did not wish to strain the economic capacity of the territory. The Palestine Zionist Executive did have the authority to assign immigration certificates to a limited number of applicants, and specialists in specific categories could also immigrate. Between September 1919 and the end of 1923, over thirty-four thousand Jews settled in the territory.[3] Gershom Scholem was one of them.

It had long been his intent to move to Palestine. As a teenager, he had learned Hebrew with extreme zeal, and by his early twenties, he worked as a Hebrew-German translator.[4] In addition to his university studies of Semitics, he studied mathematics so that he might find a position as a teacher in Palestine.[5] Ultimately, however, his intense love of books and his knowledge of Judaica, not his mathematical abilities, facilitated his immigration to Palestine. Hugo Bergmann, the German-speaking, Prague-born director of the Jewish national library in Jerusalem, offered Gershom a position as director of the library's nonexistent Hebrew division. Bergmann, who had known Scholem since 1919, was deeply impressed by the young man's erudition and eagerly awaited his immigration: "I am looking forward to Scholem, who, at the age of 24, has penetrated so deep in the Kabbalah and from whom I will learn much. His Hebrew letters to Escha are music."[6]

Not long after Gershom's arrival in Jerusalem, Bergmann offered him a concrete position in the new Hebrew division of the library. The institution tendering employment to Gershom Scholem had begun in 1892 as the Midrash Abarbanel Library, established by B'nai B'rith as Jerusalem's first free public library. By 1914 it had thirty-two thousand volumes, including ten thousand in Hebrew. After World War I, B'nai B'rith transferred the collection to the World Zionist Organization with the aim of establishing a national library. Indeed, in 1925, with the opening of the Hebrew University of Jerusalem, the library moved to the university campus on Mount Scopus and was renamed the Jewish National and University Library. Despite misgivings about the salary, Gershom took the position, and his contribution to the library was soon indispensable. Bergmann described him as "finally a person on whom I can depend."[7] Indeed, Gershom had a systematic knowledge of Hebrew bibliography, and once in Jerusalem, he set about reorganizing the entire Judaica collection of the library. He even invented a library classification system expressly for Jewish studies books—a system that is still used by many libraries for their Judaica collections.[8] He saw his library work as preparation for his "great academic work," which would serve as part of "the reconstruction of the Holy Land by Jewish hands."[9] In fact, young as he was, Gershom was already known in Zionist intellectual circles. Max Scholem had heard Gershom called "Palestine's hope," which was a source of pride for Betty Scholem.[10]

Library work was only a provisional occupation for Gershom. The Zionist leadership and the intelligentsia of the Yishuv were establishing a Hebrew-language university in Jerusalem. Though the initial plans for a university dated from the early twentieth century,[11] no serious progress was achieved until after World War I. Under the leadership of Chaim Weizmann, a Russian-born British chemistry professor and president of the World Zionist Organization, and Judah Magnes, a German-educated American Reform rabbi living in Palestine, the proposal became reality. Albert Einstein lent strong support, and the banker Felix Warburg took charge of the finances. In April 1925, the Hebrew University of Jerusalem formally opened its campus on Mount Scopus, overlooking the Old City. Weizmann became chairman of the board, and Magnes served as chancellor.[12]

Betty Scholem wanted to know if her son had a chance of landing a position there and if the university would adopt the German system of employment and promotion. In fact, it was fully Gershom's intention to strive for a position there.[13] Moreover, it was his hope that the university would become a leading international center for Jewish studies—if not *the* leading academic center for Jewish studies—and inspire Jewish learning throughout the world. The university's Institute of Jewish Studies took a German-Jewish institution as its model.[14] However, in contrast to the case at German universities, Gershom would not have to obtain a postdoctoral qualification (*Habilitation*) or work as an adjunct lecturer (*Privatdozent*) to climb the academic ladder in Jerusalem. In the autumn of 1925, only a few months after the Hebrew University opened, Magnes arranged for Gershom to receive an appointment as an instructor in the Institute of Jewish Studies, which had begun operation in 1924.[15] Two and a half years later, he received a long-term contract from the university.[16]

While Gershom got along very well with the university chancellor, he had a strong dislike for some of his colleagues, most notably Joseph Klausner.[17] The Russian-born Klausner—twenty-three years older than Scholem and having lived in Palestine since 1919—was a supporter of Revisionist Zionism, which Scholem disdained. Moreover, one of Klausner's academic specialties was the history of Jewish messianism, with a focus on the eras of the First Temple and Second Temple. He argued that historically there was a connection between the Jews' spiritual yearning for messianic redemption and their political goal of sovereignty, and he encouraged the modern Zionist movement to take up the mantle of conjoined aspirations. Scholem, also a specialist on the history of Jewish messianism, though with a focus on later eras, denounced the idea of Zionism appropriating religious messianism. Moreover, in terms of Klausner's scholarship, Scholem considered it to be "a disgrace to appoint such a girls' school teacher [i.e., an academic mediocrity] to the University of Jerusalem."[18]

Gershom had certain advantages and disadvantages as he commenced his academic career. His written Hebrew was exceptional; however, his spoken Hebrew still bore an unmistakable German accent, whereas most Ashkenazi Jews in Palestine spoke Hebrew with an eastern European accent.[19] He also had the advantage of writing about texts originally written in Hebrew. He did not need to make the mental conversion from French, English, or even scientific formulae into Hebrew-language pedagogy and scholarship.

However, the growth and concomitant modernization of the Jewish national home, with Hebrew as its official language, led to a paradox. While the reanimation of the ancient language of the Jews in the Land of Israel was commendable, classical Hebrew, with its roots in the Bible, was insufficient for the needs of modern life. Hebrew speakers in Mandate-era Palestine needed not only words for modern inventions such as typewriters, skyscrapers, and locomotives, but also colloquialisms for their quotidian lives. This change in the Hebrew language—historically known as "the Holy Tongue" (*Lashon Hakodesh*)—pained Gershom Scholem. He commented, "With the migration of the language from the Book into [daily] life, the 'soul' was lost."[20] No longer was Hebrew inherently imbued with religious or higher meaning, and its contemporary use was actually a danger to Hebrew speakers, in his estimation. As he wrote to Franz Rosenzweig, "The ghostly Volapük that we speak in the streets here indicates exactly that expressionless linguistic world to which the 'secularization' of the language can only lead." He added, "Every word that does not have to be created new, but rather is taken from the 'good old' treasury, is brimming."[21] Even more harshly, he commented, "We have not resuscitated Hebrew, but only a Golem of it, an Esperanto. In other words, we have even accomplished something negative."[22]

In his fanaticism for Hebrew, Scholem also refused to learn to speak Yiddish, even to conduct business with ultra-Orthodox Ashkenazi Jews in Jerusalem, who spoke Yiddish as their primary language and were among the principal vendors of books on the Kabbalah, which he needed for his research. As a result, he paid over the odds for his books.[23] In any event, Scholem's devotion to Hebrew unequivocally associated him with a certain subset within the broader Zionist movement: those who held Hebrew, and Hebrew alone, to be the language of the Jewish future in Palestine. Moreover, unlike Scholem, most of the other champions of Hebrew had grown up speaking Yiddish, the European Jewish language par excellence. Indeed, just as Gershom Scholem had been an exceptional figure among Zionists in Germany—themselves exceptional among German Jewry as a whole—in Palestine, he remained an exceptional figure among both Ashkenazi Jewry and Hebrew-oriented Zionists.

The transformation of Hebrew was not the only aspect of life in the Yishuv to disappoint Scholem, who, for many years, had idolized and idealized Palestine as the Jewish homeland and a place that would serve as the glowing nucleus of a Jewish renaissance. He discovered that the Jews there did not always live up to his high standards. He called the Jewish literati of the land *"remarkably* stupid" and remarked that the Yishuv was full of "decorative dolls in Hebrew" in addition to "the last Kabbalists."[24] He was extremely critical of other recent arrivals in Palestine, particularly those coming from Poland, who did not share his noble motives for immigration.[25] During the Fourth *Aliyah*, from 1924 through 1928, thirty to forty thousand Jews left Poland for Palestine, but most did so because of poor economic conditions exacerbated by antisemitism, not Zionist ideology.[26] Not only did many of the immigrants choose Palestine simply because the United States no longer welcomed them, but the new arrivals also generally settled in cities and towns, rather than agricultural settlements and frontier outposts. They dramatically increased the Jewish populations of Jerusalem and Haifa, both religiously mixed cities, and they built up Tel Aviv into a real city.[27] In doing so, they created the basis for an urban economy and society in the Yishuv. They also had a middle-class or lower-middle-class, capitalist outlook. As a result, many Zionists shared Scholem's critical view of the immigrants. No less a figure than the Zionist Organization president Chaim Weizmann scoffed that they were re-creating petty-bourgeois Jewish Warsaw in Tel Aviv.[28]

Even with restrictions on immigration, the 1920s saw tremendous growth in the Jewish population in Palestine. Jews went from 9.7 percent of the population in 1919 to 13.5 percent in 1923, the last year of the Third *Aliyah* and the year of Scholem's arrival, to 18.9 percent in 1929, when the Fourth *Aliyah* ended. With a population between 154,000 and 165,000,[29] they maintained their own society, complete with regulations, customs, and civic rituals. The Jewish festival calendar and Jewish law largely determined the rhythm of ordinary life in the Yishuv. Gershom advocated for this return to a national heritage for the Jews as a people. He had a deep love of Jewish traditions and rituals, including those associated with religious holidays and life-cycle events. For example, he expressly preferred traditional Jewish weddings, and during the festival of Sukkot, he had a sukkah at home, even though he was not traditionally Orthodox himself. Writing from Berlin, his mother commented on the disparity between his observance of Jewish rituals and his lack of attendance in synagogue.[30] Ultimately, he was a man who was neither traditionally religious nor secular.[31] As such, he fell between two stools in the Yishuv. Yet Palestine was his home. In 1926 he renounced his German citizenship and adopted Palestinian citizenship once the British made it available to everyone with two years' permanent residence in Palestine.[32]

As a young man in Germany, Gershom had extremely strong opinions about Zionism and expressed his disapproval of contrary views. He and his closest circle of friends impugned coffeehouse Zionism that did not entail active preparation for emigration and the study of the Hebrew language. They also opposed political Zionism that promoted the establishment of Jewish sovereignty over Palestine. Once in Palestine, Gershom was no less critical of other varieties of Zionism, or of those Jews who passed themselves off as Zionists but failed to match his vision of true Zionism.[33] Indeed, he was constantly worried about Zionism and what it had become, and he confided that Zionism had become a "farce."[34] While he was critical of a wide range of Zionist groups, his greatest vituperation was reserved for the Revisionist Zionists, led by Ze'ev Jabotinsky. He considered their militant, maximalist Zionism to be dangerous, and he organized Yishuv intellectuals—including Hugo Bergmann, Hans Kohn, Judah Magnes, and Rabbi Binyamin—against Jabotinsky's demands for a Jewish Legion.[35]

Over time, Gershom Scholem became one of the leading figures in a small, but controversial and important Yishuv political movement known as Brit Shalom (Covenant of Peace). Founded in 1925, largely through the efforts of Arthur Ruppin, a sociologist and prominent Zionist functionary who was raised and educated in Germany before moving to Palestine, the group's official membership never numbered more than a hundred, but its echo was far-reaching.[36] In stark contrast to most Zionists, Brit Shalom rejected the notion of Jewish political sovereignty over Palestine. Rather, its members wanted Jews and Arabs to live together in a binational state, and Ruppin wanted ongoing economic development of the country to consider both peoples. Initially, the core of Brit Shalom's leadership consisted of eastern European–born Palestine academics, but over time, German-speaking, central European–born intellectuals became more prominent. Among them were Hugo Bergmann, Martin Buber, Hans Kohn, and Gershom Scholem. The American-born, German-educated chancellor of the Hebrew University, Judah Magnes, was an unaffiliated sympathizer.[37] Brit Shalom's ideas had great resonance for many German Zionists, and the *Jüdische Rundschau*, the

leading German-language Zionist newspaper, became one of the chief venues for publicizing the group's views.[38]

Scholem, in particular, was deeply influenced by the ideas of Ahad Ha'am,
who saw Zionism as a movement for a Jewish national renaissance, focusing on
culture. In Gershom Scholem's vision, Palestine was to become the center for a
worldwide Jewish renewal, not a Jewish nation-state. Hans Kohn summarized
Brit Shalom's position, "We are all against the concept of a Jewish state because
there is something exclusive about it, because there can be two national homes
in a Palestinian state of some type, an Arab one and a Jewish one. By contrast,
in a Jewish state, as the name implies, the Arabs can only play a secondary
role." For Kohn, Scholem, and their associates, "Our rejection of the Jewish
state does not ensue from coincidental economic crises or the interplay of
politically favorable or unfavorable moments, but rather from a fundamental
attitude that dominates our entire reasoning. We believe that it is necessary to
change the Jews' fundamental attitude. Only then, for many reasons, is Zionism achievable and only then will there be a Zionism that is achievable."[39]

In the years 1926 to 1929, Scholem focused immense energy on promoting
this cause. He frequently sent essays for publication to the Zionist newspaper
editor Robert Weltsch, even when he was speaking solely for himself and not
for Brit Shalom. He acknowledged Arab fears that Jews would take mosques
or Muslim property in the Old City of Jerusalem. And while he blamed Jewish extremists for stoking the Arabs' anxiety, he also considered the Arabs
less capable than the Jews of moderation and restraint: "They [reactionary
Zionists] have stirred up the most evil instincts of a nation that is more primitive than the Jewish one, and unrestrained nationalism from them is to be
expected and excused." At the same time, he felt, "We are not far superior to
this primitive brother nation." In his view, there were two options: the path
of reconciliation with the Arabs or the path of the Revisionist Zionists, who,
he claimed, would not recoil from the rape of the local inhabitants if it meant
getting a Jewish state, which, in that case, "would be nothing other than the
complete downfall of Zionism."[40] Later, he noted the dramatic rise in lit-
eracy rates among Palestinian Arabs and, thus, rejected the argument that it
would be a long time before the Arabs would reach a level of civilization that
would enable them to claim a desire for self-rule as a genuine expression of
popular will.[41] In 1929, when the group's activities reached fever pitch, Hugo
Bergmann confided to Weltsch, "I found Brit Shalom in very eventful activity. The most active is Scholem, who has completely become a politician and
more extreme in his views than he was before."[42] The following year, Scholem demanded that the group adopt "'a clear political line.'" Otherwise, it
had "'no right to exist.'"[43]

Scholem was propelled to this level of activity by a serious and violent crisis for the Yishuv. Starting with Yom Kippur in 1928, the Jewish and Muslim communities had engaged in a fierce argument about Jewish prayer at the Western Wall, with the British Mandate authorities in the middle. By August 1929, chauvinists on both sides were employing nationalist and religious rhetoric to radicalize public opinion. The end result was that on 23 August 1929, armed Arab mobs attacked Jewish neighborhoods in Jerusalem.[44] A particular focus of the attack was the ultra-Orthodox Jewish quarter Mea Shearim. Gershom Scholem reflected, "all that only two minutes away from my apartment, in the heart of Jerusalem. Since that time, naturally, we have not really gotten any peace."[45] In the meantime, the violence spread throughout the territory. It reached its apogee in Hebron, where mobs stormed synagogues, private homes, a school, and even a hospital. They massacred dozens of Jews, including many who had lived side by side with their Arab neighbors for decades. Writing to his mother in Berlin, Gershom Scholem reported that no Arab village or neighborhood had been attacked and that Arabs had only attacked places like Hebron and Safed, home to unarmed, non-Zionist, ultra-Orthodox communities, and not armed Jewish agricultural settlements.[46] In fact, there had been some retaliatory attacks by Jews, and Arab groups had attacked Jewish outposts, though with varying success.[47]

Betty Scholem wanted to know what was really happening in Palestine and claimed that her Berlin newspaper "usually lies" about such matters. She thought that reports of hundreds dead might be false, as had been similar reports about the unrest in Berlin in 1919. After a few weeks, however, she realized that the situation in Palestine was more serious than she had thought, and her sister-in-law Hedwig Scholem could not imagine "that there would be a beneficial coexistence with the Arabs if both sides carried a revolver (be it secretly or openly) in their pocket and looked upon each other with mistrust."[48] In the wake of the riots, Arthur Ruppin left Brit Shalom; however, a nucleus of members continued to maintain their belief in binationalism and expressed their dismay with the direction the Zionist movement was taking. They saw themselves in a struggle against militarism and nationalism and for the true essence of Zionism.[49] While these Brit Shalom members often positioned themselves as outsiders, in fact, they were insiders in Yishuv society, members of the Jewish academic elite in Jerusalem, with ties to the Zionist leadership. Despite their opposition to a Jewish-controlled state in Palestine, they were able to find a place within the Zionist establishment because "political statehood" was not the official goal of the Zionist movement until the 1940s. While many Zionists certainly did favor the establishment of a Jewish state in Palestine in the 1920s, at the time, the movement endorsed the vague notion of a "Jewish National Home."[50]

Nonetheless, to say that most Yishuv Zionists did not have sympathy for Brit Shalom and its political stance after the riots would be an understatement. Despite Bergmann and Scholem's long-standing friendship with Berl Katznelson, the powerful leader of Histradut, the Yishuv's general labor union, Katznelson assailed Brit Shalom's members. He considered them out of touch and hinted at their roots among the assimilated Jews of central Europe rather than among eastern European Jewry with its Jewish popular culture. *Davar*, a prominent workers' daily newspaper edited by Katznelson, stopped printing Brit Shalom statements. Meanwhile, *Davar*'s editorials harshly criticized Bergmann and Brit Shalom for not prioritizing the Jewish people in Palestine.[51] The socialist Zionist leader Meir Ya'ari and the right-wing professor Joseph Klausner both condemned the group, as did Menachem Ussishkin, an early Zionist leader and head of the Jewish National Fund.[52] Many German-speaking Zionists in Palestine, and even some in Germany, openly opposed the Zionist Federation of Germany and the *Jüdische Rundschau* for sympathizing with Brit Shalom. At a German Zionist congress in Jena in 1930, Nahum Goldmann proclaimed, "Brit Shalom is now the most dangerous point in the Zionist political front."[53] Scholem reported to his mother, "The thorns in which Dr. Bergmann has sat are not so bad. In any event, I sit [there] constantly and am proud of it. . . . We Scholems are a combative race."[54]

In February 1930, Scholem and a few other members of Brit Shalom authored a report that they submitted to the Zionist Executive in London and the Jewish Agency. They advocated a binational state characterized as "a free Palestinian commonwealth composed of two peoples, each free in the administration of their own respective domestic affairs, but united in their common political interests, on the basis of complete equality of the rights of each."[55] They also felt that "if the Arab masses realize that the economic policy of the Jewish Agency is to the benefit of the whole of Palestine, anti-Jewish propaganda will have less effect on them."[56] That economic policy included the purchase of land from Arab landowners, draining of swamps to increase arable land, introduction of modern methods of agriculture, and immigration of Jews.

Considering Brit Shalom's advocacy of binationalism, many Jews must have wondered if the organization supported the Haganah, the Yishuv's self-defense militia. Scholem, Ernst Simon, and Hugo Bergmann wrote a letter clarifying their position on the Haganah. "All of us, who were here in the critical days, must testify that the comportment of the H[aganah] is to be judged completely positively." The group was disciplined and provided purely defense. Not only did the militia not participate in revenge actions, but it also actively combated such impulses. Scholem and his colleagues felt that the Haganah had prevented a catastrophe. Moreover, they endorsed the idea of an underground, illegal organization protecting the Jews and supported the Haganah as it was then. They expressly did not promise unconditional support in the future.[57] Similar to their pronounced moderation and equivocation with the Haganah, Brit Shalom was critical of both the British government and the National Council (Va'ad Leumi), the Yishuv's protogovernment. In fact, the National Council appointed a committee to tout the Jews' historic religious claim to the Western Wall, and Scholem expressly refused to lend his scholarly assistance to the committee. He regarded the violence of 1929 as a political conflict, not a religious one. As such, it required a negotiated political solution and not a judgment from above, adjudicating competing religious claims.[58]

The British launched a series of investigations into the unrest. The first inquest culminated with the Shaw Report, named for the commission chairman Walter Shaw. The report held the Arabs responsible for the violence, but rationalized the attacks as the fruit of the Arabs' frustrated national aspirations, especially as Jewish immigration and land purchases continued.[59] Thus, the Shaw Commission recommended that the British reconsider their policy, a suggestion wholly supported by the British high commissioner in Palestine, John Chancellor.[60] To examine the issues of Jewish immigration and settlement, land ownership, and economic development mentioned in the Shaw Report, the British government sent John Hope-Simpson to Palestine. He, too, recommended curbing Jewish immigration and restricting Jewish land purchases. In October 1930, the British colonial secretary, Lord Passfield, issued a white paper, establishing a new British policy in Palestine that limited Jewish immigration based on its affect on the Arab or all-Palestinian economy, not just the Jewish sector of the economy.[61]

The white paper stunned Jewish observers, who interpreted it as a contravention of the terms of the British Mandate from the League of Nations and the Balfour Declaration. Chaim Weizmann, the president of the Zionist Organization, resigned his office in protest. Brit Shalom was publicly critical of both the Passfield White Paper and the Yishuv's National Council, but in Gershom Scholem's estimation, people paid attention to the latter criticism.[62] Ultimately, Prime Minister Ramsay MacDonald significantly amended or abrogated most of the Passfield White Paper with an additional policy statement, and John Chancellor left office as high commissioner.[63]

In 1931 the Zionist Organization met in Basel for the Seventeenth Zionist Congress, the first congress since the violence of 1929. It was also the first congress for the new socialist alliance, Mapai (Mifleget Poalei Eretz Yisrael, or Workers' Party of the Land of Israel), increasingly led by David Ben-Gurion. However, the Seventeenth Zionist Congress has also become known for the theatrics of Ze'ev Jabotinsky and his right-wing Revisionist Zionists. The Revisionists demanded that the assembly officially proclaim the establishment of a sovereign state with a Jewish majority—on both sides of the Jordan River, no less—as the ultimate goal of Zionism. When the delegates rejected this proposal, Jabotinsky angrily stormed out of the conference.[64] The delegates did, however, approve a resolution that Zionism desired "to bring about in Eretz Yisrael the solution to the Jewish question. The homeless, landless people, forced to emigrate, wants to overcome its economic, spiritual, and political misery through setting down roots anew in its historic homeland by means of uninterrupted immigration and settlement and [wants] to renew in Eretz Yisrael its national existence equipped with all the characteristics of a normal national life."[65]

Not only did Gershom Scholem vigorously oppose this "resolution about the 'ultimate aim' of Zionism," he also interpreted it as "openly directed against us [i.e., Brit Shalom]," as he explained to Walter Benjamin. He elaborated, "Yes, a fantastically reactionary resolution was passed against Magnes and the teachers of the university who, to put it succinctly, are carrying the banner of Ahad Ha'am."[66] Scholem had long resisted the ideal of the "normalization of the Jews." The Jews were not, and should not be, a people like others, in his view.[67] The idea that a Jewish state or Jewish political sovereignty over territory would make the Jews like other peoples was only another reason for him to oppose political Zionism. However, by 1931 political Zionism was mainstream within the broader Zionist movement. Summing up the development of Zionism between the riots of August 1929 and the Seventeenth Zionist Congress in 1931, Scholem wrote that a "radical split" had grown between his own notion of Zionism—"a religious-mystical quest for a regeneration of Judaism"—and empirical Zionism, which claimed to have a "political 'solution to the Jewish Question.'" Previously, there had always been a place within the movement for men like him, but recently, "the purely reactionary forces in Zionism have asserted themselves in their way, both politically and morally," and he wondered about his place in the Zionist movement.[68]

Brit Shalom was doomed to fail. Even in the best of times, it had no real Arab partner. Scholem naively thought that a moderate Zionist program would foster the creation of moderate Arab groups, who wanted to negotiate.[69] At the time, he seemed unable to believe that the Arabs were prepared to go into unremitting, permanent opposition to the Jews' presence in Palestine. Looking back on Brit Shalom nearly fifty years later, he compared the Jewish-German dialogue to the Jewish-Arab dialogue. He felt that, in both cases, well-meaning or hopeful Jews were talking, but no one on the other side was listening.[70] Concurrently, Jewish groups dismissed Brit Shalom's ideology as idealist or even antithetical to Zionism at a time when Arab violence threatened the Yishuv and claimed Jewish lives. The group ceased organized activity altogether in the 1930s.[71]

While Gershom Scholem became politically engaged, he remained, above all, a man of scholarship. The years following his appointment at the Hebrew University witnessed a torrent of lectures and publications on a wide range of Judaic topics, but, above all, on the Kabbalah. His inaugural lecture upon taking up his lectureship at the university in 1925 dealt with the origins of the *Zohar*. He staked out a position claiming the antiquity of parts of the text, but he publicly reversed course thirteen years later. In 1928 he wrote an article on the theology of Sabbateanism, his first publication on a subject that would occupy him for many more decades. While some observers have regarded Scholem's early interest in the seventeenth-century false messiah Shabbetai Zevi as "romantic enthusiasm for iconoclasm and charismatic albeit deluded figures," in the words of one biographer, it is likely that Gershom Scholem considered Sabbateanism to be a historical warning. He looked with dismay at Zionist politics in Palestine in the 1920s and worried about Zionism styling itself as a (false) messianic movement.[72]

Incidentally, as Scholem moved forward with his new scholarly life, he did not relinquish ties to his old life. Notably, he continued to publish in German under the name "Gerhard Scholem."[73] His family also published some of his scholarly works, which allowed him to control many aspects of the printing. When they printed his seminal essay "Zur Frage der Entstehung der Kabbala" ("On the Question of the Emergence of Kabbalah"), he told his mother, "I place *great value* on this work," as he hoped to expand his reputation and reach a wider audience.[74] In fact, in this article he revisited and accentuated some themes from his dissertation, and it was clear that Scholem situated the Kabbalah in the history of religion rather than the history of philosophy.

In 1927 the university gave Scholem a semester's leave to study Kabbalistic manuscripts in England and France. A highlight of his time in Europe was seeing his old friend Walter Benjamin. In Paris, Scholem did research in the Bibliothèque Nationale during the day, and he spent his evenings and weekends with Benjamin in the cafés of Montparnasse or the cinema. They discussed philosophy, literature, and the Kabbalah at great length, while Benjamin was reluctant to discuss his new interest in Marxism. Scholem also accompanied Benjamin to a demonstration against the execution of Sacco and Vanzetti, where they were caught in the fray as policemen charged on horseback.[75]

In contrast to some years before, when it seemed that Scholem was drifting into the unknown and Benjamin about to start a brilliant academic career, it was now Scholem who was the established professor and Benjamin who was adrift. Scholem arranged for Benjamin to meet Judah Magnes, the chancellor of the Hebrew University of Jerusalem, who was then in Paris. After an engaging two-hour conversation, Magnes seemed inclined to bring Benjamin to Jerusalem for a one-year trial.[76] Scholem helped shepherd Benjamin's application for a position and discussed the financial details with Magnes, who gave Benjamin money to pay for Hebrew lessons. For a time, Benjamin seemed serious about going to Palestine. He even proclaimed, "My trip to Palestine is a settled matter, as is my intention to strictly observe the course of study prescribed by Your Hierojerusalemitic Excellency."[77] But soon another influence exerted itself on Benjamin.

He began a liaison with Asja Lācis, a Latvian actress and enthusiastic communist. While Benjamin ascribed his inability to travel to Palestine to his ongoing work on *The Arcades Project*, it later became clear that Benjamin's "Russian lady friend" had actively and successfully campaigned against the trip.[78] Eventually, Scholem reproached his friend for his inability to commit to the Palestinian project, even after Scholem had secured funding for him.[79] In the end, Benjamin never traveled to Palestine, did not take up a professorship in Jerusalem, and kept the money that Magnes had given him. Benjamin stayed in Europe and became increasingly engaged with Marxist theory. But his decision not to leave Europe had more significant consequences after the Nazis came to power.

In Jerusalem, Gershom integrated into society, and based on his exchange of letters with his mother, it seems that he and Escha circulated in some of the most prestigious social circles in the Yishuv. They were friends with the famous eye doctor Avraham Ticho and his wife, the artist Anna Ticho, who regularly entertained academics, artists, and British Mandate officials in their garden home, which later became a museum and restaurant in Jerusalem. In fact, Escha was with Anna when a Palestinian assailant stabbed Dr. Ticho during the 1929 riots.[80] Adding to the indignation caused by the attack was the fact that Dr. Ticho was known throughout Palestine for being a Jewish doctor who treated poor Arab patients for no charge. In addition to Gershom's ties to the university's luminaries, he was friendly with Hayim Nahman Bialik, Palestine's leading Hebrew poet and children's author.[81]

Nonetheless, despite his devotion to Zionism and the Land of Israel, Gershom Scholem remained culturally German. He spoke and wrote German much more often than one might expect for a man whose immigration and immersion in Hebrew culture was so ideological. He expressed a clear desire for German delicacies and German products.[82] He continued to dress like a member of the German bourgeoisie, regularly wearing coats and ties, a stark contrast to the casual mode of dress among non-Orthodox Jews in the Yishuv.[83] The Columbia University professor Fritz Stern, who was born in Germany, commented that even decades later, Scholem's home "resembled a German academic home of long ago, more 'German' than anything I had ever seen in postwar Germany."[84] As the historian David Biale has written, Gershom Scholem "never severed himself from German culture, even as he rejected Germany."[85]

From Palestine, Gershom conducted a lively exchange of letters with his mother in Berlin, though their correspondence also often casts Gershom in a negative light. Despite having a good job in Palestine, he still demanded that his mother in Berlin supply him with everything from neckties to household goods, crime novels to academic books, and, above all, European delicacies.[86] He complained about his financial situation and commented, "for not only are books expensive, but also life, even and especially Escha's illness with doctors[,] nurses, hospitals, and medicines, and I myself need two suits this winter."[87] When his mother chided him about her provisioning him, he grew testy with her, even though Escha had warned Gershom not to be too demanding. Unconcerned, he felt that future generations would understand how much his mother loved giving him gifts and how much he loved receiving them. Ironically, he added that in any event, "who thinks right away about publication" of their correspondence?[88] He unabashedly relied on his mother's generosity and admitted that he was spoiled. He noted that Escha chided him for his poor marriage skills, and he claimed that it would take more than five years of marriage to undo the results of twenty years.[89]

While he cloaked his self-absorption in a veil of jocularity, more than once a note of sexism evinced itself. Escha complained to her mother-in-law, "Be assured that this person, your son, shamelessly exploits me, which is unpleasant for me. Long ago, I grasped that Woman must serve."[90] In discussing a vacation, Gershom wrote that he and Escha wanted to visit Vienna, "for me scholarly, for Escha, who is superficial like all women, a target of curiosity."[91] Later, Escha temporarily became his nominal supervisor at a library where he had an honorary position, "which does not suit me at all. Wives should not have a career, at least not mine."[92] He even preferred not to discuss politics with his mother, asking "What gentleman gladly talks politics with ladies," though he made an exception for Escha.[93] In fact, five years after his nuptials, he was happily married.[94]

When Gershom wrote about the financial burden of Escha's illnesses, he was quite serious. She had poor health and suffered from sciatica. As a result, she frequently went to Tiberias, Palestine's spa town, which strained their budget.[95] Escha's doctor encouraged her to keep moving. Thus, when she was in Jerusalem, she spent hours walking around the city, always the same time and same route. Sometimes, Gershom would meet her at a café along her walk. But he particularly liked the café because it was next door to a German bookstore, where he could browse or borrow books.[96] He also used Escha's illness as a pretext to get his mother to send him delicacies, writing, "Therefore, it would be nice of you if you would assist Escha's convalescence at least through small and regular packages of marzipan and meat products."[97]

Gershom's health also suffered, namely, from eyestrain from reading manuscripts.[98] His eye doctor had him wear special eyeglasses, with one clear lens and one opaque lens to train one eye and let the other rest.[99] Other times, he sat in a dark room to rest both eyes, and he special-ordered a magnifying glass from Germany to facilitate his reading.[100] In one case, he asked a journal editor to pay for him to have a scribe assist him with his work.[101]

Nonetheless, his scholarly career flourished as he carved out a niche for himself in the academic world of the Yishuv, and this seemingly apolitical Zionist entered into the fray of Yishuv politics. In the coming years, his renown would spread throughout the Jewish world. He would be famous for his pioneering work on Jewish mysticism and infamous for his devotion to conciliation with the Arabs in Palestine.

CHAPTER 7

The Maelstrom

Jewish Life in Nazi Germany

As 1933 began, desperation gripped Germany. In a country of 65 million people, nearly 6 million were out of work, while less than 12 million were gainfully employed, compared to only one million unemployed and 19 million working in 1929.[1] Fourteen different parties were represented in the Reichstag, and none commanded more than one-third of the seats. Germany had not had a chancellor backed by a parliamentary majority for over two years. Instead, President Paul von Hindenburg and three successive chancellors relied on emergency decrees to enact legislation. While this mode of governance effectively destroyed parliamentarianism, it could have continued without Nazi participation in the cabinet. Still, to many Germans, including Betty Scholem, there seemed to be something inevitable about Hitler becoming the head of government. Nonetheless, in late 1932, she commented, "However, he can't do things any differently. We are almost already indifferent."[2] Little did she realize that Hitler would not play by the rules once in power.

As a result of wrangling between two competing non-Nazi politicians, Hindenburg appointed Adolf Hitler chancellor on 30 January 1933.[3] The appointment led to jubilation among many Germans and panic among others. Betty Scholem was attending a performance of *Faust* that evening. During the first intermission, she stepped outside and saw a celebratory torchlight parade down the Unter den Linden, Berlin's central boulevard. One hour later, during the second intermission, the parade was still going on. She remarked, "Where did the Nazis get 20,000 torch-bearers so quickly?" She also reported that the family's printshop had received no business and there was a run on nonperishable goods in the following days.[4] People feared strikes, and in the succeeding weeks, republican civil servants were dismissed and newspapers were shut down, but Betty claimed, "For the moment, the Jews have nothing to fear."[5]

By and large, German Jews did not panic. Rather, encouraged by many of their leaders, they opted for an attitude of wait-and-see matched by an expectation that they should and could defend their rights.[6] That was a misunderstanding of the situation. In the weeks after Hitler became chancellor in a coalition government, SA men (Nazi Party storm troopers) in many localities defaced Jews' businesses, unabashedly intimidated Jews, and assaulted them on the streets, especially recognizable eastern European Jews.[7] Nazis could now act with impunity to settle scores with Jews who had crossed them in the past.

However, the new regime primarily targeted its political opponents, namely, Socialists and Communists, which mollified Betty Scholem.[8] By contrast, Werner Scholem was beside himself. Visiting Werner at home only days after Hitler became chancellor, Betty reported that his predictions of gloom and doom were "in high bloom."[9] Although the Nazis did not target apolitical Jews initially, politically active Jews immediately recognized the danger posed by the Nazis, and communist and socialist Jews faced a double menace.[10] Werner saw that the political situation was extremely serious, with disastrous consequences for himself, though "if he were still in the party, it would certainly be *even* worse for him!," Betty wrote.[11]

Ultimately, Werner's nonmembership in the Communist Party was moot. On 27 February 1933, an arsonist set the Reichstag building ablaze. The most likely culprit was a Dutch Communist who was found in the building, and the police used the fire as a pretext to arrest communist politicians and intellectuals, including Werner Scholem. His family was bewildered since Werner had not been in the public eye for many years. Nonetheless, news of his arrest made the front page of Berlin's leading liberal newspaper.[12] Not long after the police took Werner into custody, they paid a visit to Reinhold and Erich Scholem's printshop, searching for evidence of communist publications. They were polite as Erich led them around the premises, and in the end, they left only with a copy of the Zionist newspaper *Jüdische Rundschau*. But Betty now found herself self-censoring her letters to Gershom since emergency decrees suspended civil liberties, including habeas corpus, freedom of speech, freedom of assembly, and the privacy of mail and telephone calls. She advised Gershom to get his news from foreign newspapers.[13]

While incarcerated, Werner gave a formal statement that he was neither a member of parliament nor a member of the Communist Party, and less than ten days after his arrest, he was let go. In fact, after his release, he was very calm and claimed not to understand his family's distress. He said that he had experienced worse treatment during the war.[14] Soon, he resumed his work as a lawyer.[15] He even made a brief trip to Prague to explore potential educational and professional opportunities. Comrades who had already fled to Czechoslovakia urged him to remain abroad, but he returned to Germany.[16] He seemed to think that his position in Germany was safe. Events soon proved him wrong.

The Reichstag fire and the perceived threat of a communist insurrection provided the pretext the Nazis needed to demand absolute power. On 23 March 1933, the Reichstag approved the Enabling Act, which granted Hitler the power to issue laws without Reichstag approval. The Nazis left little to chance, however. The vote took place in the presence of Nazi storm troopers, and in the weeks before the vote, they arrested literally dozens of Communist and Social Democratic members of the Reichstag, while many others fled abroad. Nonetheless, even non-Marxist politicians who had supported parliamentarianism, including members of the Center Party and the German State Party, voted for the bill. Only the diminished Social Democratic caucus voted against the bill.[17]

On 1 April, the Nazis organized a boycott of Jewish-owned stores. It was intended as a sop to the hard core in the Nazi Party as well as an economic attack on the representatives of the supposed Jewish conspiracy in Germany. The highly staged nature of the boycott reflected the Nazis' intended goal. SA men gathered outside Jewish-owned stores, often carrying placards that read, "Germans! Defend yourselves! Don't buy from Jews!" In Berlin, Nazi picketers carried bilingual signs, in German and in English, with the caption, "Germans defend yourselves against Jewish atrocity propaganda. Buy only at German shops!" Clearly, they intended for the foreign press to report that Germans were boycotting Jewish-owned stores only as an aggrieved reaction to the Jews having spread lies about Nazis abusing Jews. The Nazi leadership also placed great importance on the boycott being orderly, and Joseph Goebbels wrote in his diary, "Exemplary discipline. An impressive spectacle. Everything proceeds with complete calm."[18] Nonetheless, in many places, the boycott degenerated into open violence as Nazi storm troopers used the boycott as an occasion to beat up anyone on the street who looked like a Jew to them. Some Jewish business owners who complained about the demonstrations were abused or worse. However, in other places, staged protests failed to materialize. Many Jewish-owned stores simply closed early that day or did not open at all, and there were some cases of non-Jewish customers continuing to patronize the businesses they always had, despite the protests. On the occasion of the boycott, the liberal *Frankfurter Zeitung* even dared to criticize the Nazis' governance, though very mildly considering the Nazis' extreme disrespect for the rule of law.[19] The April boycott failed in its grand objective to end Jewish participation in the German economy. At the same time, it alienated many potential supporters. And then, there were the hard facts of economics.[20]

Even if the Nazis did wish to close all Jewish-owned business, it simply was not feasible. The largest Jewish-owned firms, including department store chains, contributed too much to the German economy. They provided jobs to thousands of non-Jewish employees. They kept suppliers in business and provided essential goods and services to non-Jewish Germans. They owed money to banks, which could not afford to write off the loans. They could be publicly demonized and their owners harassed, but the regime could not easily dissolve them.[21] The head of the National Socialist Workers Union at the Jewish-owned Ullstein media conglomerate wrote to the Reich Chancellery to protest the anti-Jewish boycott being undertaken against Ullstein. The boycott, which hurt Ullstein economically, had led to mass firings. At the same time, some employees were not being allowed to join the Nazi Party because they worked for Ullstein. In an attempt to mitigate the Nazis' fury, the petitioner explained, "All the Jewish editors were fired and Christians hired in their place."[22] SA men arrested Heinz Ullstein, a member of the board of directors and son of the firm's managing partner. The Nazis also harassed the Ullstein general director Hans Schäffer, threatened him with arrest, and forced his resignation.[23] Among the employees dismissed from Ullstein was Lene Scholem, Max's widow, who had successfully supported herself economically since his suicide in 1929.[24]

The boycott of 1 April 1933 was only the beginning of a longer-term effort to "Aryanize" the German economy. While Jewish-owned department stores and large banks presented a challenge to Nazi planners, smaller Jewish-owned businesses were more susceptible to the new dangers. Nazi ruffians could smash up Jewish-owned stores with little risk of prosecution. Pressure from local Nazis wore away the bonds between Jewish businessmen and their customers, especially in rural areas. Greed was also a major factor in "Aryans" turning against Jews in Nazi Germany.[25] Non-Jewish competitors exploited the weak position of Jews to intimidate them into selling their businesses for less than full value or used denunciations to get them out of the way.[26]

One week after the boycott, the German government issued the so-called Law for the Restoration of the Professional Civil Service to purge the state bureaucracy of any potentially disloyal elements, including Socialists, Communists, and Jews. Similar decrees limited the number of Jews attending public secondary schools and universities, restricted the practice of Jewish physicians, and withdrew Jews' law licenses, though combat veterans of World War I were exempted.[27] Despite losing so many talented professionals, German society did not erupt in protest. Betty Scholem perceptively explained the situation, "I don't grasp that there are not 10,000 or only 1,000 decent Christians who do not participate and protest loudly. What is happening initially now to the jurists, who have been deprived of their livelihood from one day to the next, can happen tomorrow to the doctors. It won't work so quickly with businessmen since Christian suppliers do not want to let their customers go immediately."[28] In fact, she was right. Jewish attorneys could be pushed out of the legal profession, but completely extracting Jews from the German economy proved more difficult and required a combination of economic, legal, and extralegal mechanisms.

The Nazis were especially keen to rid German cultural institutions of Jewish influence, which they deemed both foreign and nefarious. Already in the first months after Hitler became chancellor, Nazi officials and their sympathizers made sure that orchestras stopped employing Jewish musicians and conductors, including Otto Klemperer and Bruno Walter. Theaters and museums dismissed Jewish employees. The Prussian Academy of Arts required its members to affirm loyalty to the Nazi regime, and the academy's numerous Jewish and politically progressive members were excluded or compelled to resign. The exorcism of Jews and progressives from German culture achieved its most visible expression on 10 May 1933. That evening, Nazi students all across Germany consigned books by Jews, Socialists, Communists, pacifists, and others to the flames of bonfires, often directly in front of the university libraries where they had found the offending books.[29]

The increase in antisemitism was palpable, and Jewish Germans began to find themselves socially isolated. Restaurants, hotels, and entire towns posted signs announcing that Jews were not welcome. Non-Jewish Germans felt no compunction about making antisemitic statements in public.[30] When Betty Scholem asked a bus driver to stop at the top of her street rather than at the official bus stop so she would not have to walk so far—something she had done for years—her fellow passengers yelled, "Oh, I see, for a pack of Jews you make an extra stop!!"[31] The expressions "Jew boy," "Jewish lout," and simply "Jew" became insults that antisemitic Berliners hurled at each other regardless of the object's actual religion.[32]

German Jews encountered antisemitism or simple ostracism from long-standing acquaintances. Non-Jewish Germans often ceased greeting their

Jewish neighbors, asked or told Jews not to frequent their clubs, counseled their children not to play with Jewish schoolmates, and caused problems for their Jewish employers. They stopped shopping at Jewish-owned stores and stopped patronizing Jewish lawyers, doctors, and other professionals they had once supported. The Berlin rabbi Joachim Prinz likened it to life in a medieval ghetto and added, "We would not feel all of this so painfully if we did not have the feeling that we once had neighbors."[33] Jewish society turned inward, and many Jews avoided venues that might turn unpleasant or even dangerous for them.[34]

For many German Jews, previously among the most integrated in the world, emigration unexpectedly became a pressing concern. As early as March 1933, Betty wrote, "Now suddenly everyone wants to be in Palestine!! When I think what a clamor went up among German Jewry when Zionism began!" They had insisted on their Germanness in defiance of the Zionists. "Now we are being informed that we are *not* Germans!"[35] Gershom discouraged his sixty-six-year-old, non-Zionist mother from immigrating to Palestine: "Only we don't consider it right to advise you to do it unless no other alternative is left. Palestine is a land of young people and for young people, and away from all the relationships and people who are familiar to you, you would feel uprooted there over time." Additionally, in his characterization of the situation, there was no place for many German Jews in Palestine: "The country is too small for a large crowd of intellectuals. Reorientation to agriculture is not easy and is only possible in those rare cases where people have their own funds."[36] Ironically, Gershom found his place in Palestine as a professor, not as an agriculturist. Moreover, he was highly successful as a scholar expressly because he was living in Palestine. His communist brother Werner commented, "You have achieved something because you renounced wanting to become something in Germany. If you had become a professor here, you could now be wandering like so many of my acquaintances and law school teachers."[37]

Meanwhile, Georg's son Ernst managed to flee to Paris but returned once he realized that his school credentials would not be recognized in France. The impulse to leave seemed even stronger in the family of the Zionist Theobald. His daughter Dina was on a school exchange program in France, and the family encouraged her to stay there. In fact, Betty wrote, "Theo is completely of the opinion that eventually *all* of us will need to get out." His other daughter Eva had to finish her studies in Bern, Switzerland, after she was compelled to leave university in Berlin.[38] Later, both girls immigrated to Palestine. Theobald even intended to move to Palestine, though he wondered how he would fare there at his age. He asked Gershom to help him secretly transfer money out of Germany and put it aside in Palestine.[39] However, a few months later, Theobald claimed that sticking it out in Germany was more heroic than emigration and that the misery of German Jewish émigrés in Paris was tremendous.[40] Representatives of German Liberal Judaism vigorously tried to convince Jews not to emigrate, painting a bleak picture of their prospects abroad and arguing that they had to renew the process of emancipation.[41] Nonetheless, thirty-seven thousand Jews left Germany in 1933, with the vast majority going to other European countries, particularly France, Czechoslovakia, and the Netherlands, which were culturally familiar to them and could be reached with relatively little expense.[42] In many cases, it was wives and mothers who pushed their families to emigrate, not husbands whose livelihoods or sense of identity bound them to Germany.[43]

Lene Scholem, Max's widow, did not emigrate immediately, but she did find a job as a buyer and director of a Jewish community welfare kitchen not long after her dismissal from Ullstein. She received only 120 marks for the work, but was glad to have it. However, within a year, she lost that position as the Jewish community did not have the funds to keep the cafeteria open. She prepared to immigrate to Brazil, where her son, Herbert, was living.[44] Her daughter, Therese (known as "Esi"), had converted to Catholicism and married a Christian, though unhappily in Betty's estimation.[45] The family also began to worry about what would happen to Betty Scholem's sister, Käte Hirsch Schiepan, if she lost her medical license. She would be completely dependent on her non-Jewish husband, who was allegedly experiencing professional difficulties for having a Jewish-born wife.[46]

Passover seder in April 1933 was the first since the Nazis had come to power. "Beforehand, Theo gave a lovely speech, and he said that Judaism would also overcome this persecution," Betty wrote, but she continued, "Judaism certainly—but the German Jews?"[47] She was more prophetic than she realized. Meanwhile, the experience of oppression and marginalization brought German Jews closer to their Jewish identity. Synagogue attendance increased dramatically, and not just on Rosh Hashanah and Yom Kippur. Jewish adult education courses were heavily subscribed, and many organizations and communities emulated the model established in the 1920s by the Lehrhaus. Although Jews could no longer participate in "Aryan" orchestras and theater troupes, they formed their own groups under the aegis of the Jewish Culture League, whose branches around Germany entertained thousands of Jews with performances of symphonies, operas, and plays written by Jews or specific non-Jewish composers.[48] Many intellectuals, who previously had little use for their Jewishness, felt a connection to Jews and Judaism as a result of the Nazis' persecution. The writer Gertrud Kolmar, who had grown up in

The Old Synagogue in Berlin, ca. 1795. When Marcus and Mathias Scholem moved to Berlin around 1817, one or possibly both of them lived across from this synagogue. Nearly one hundred years later, Gershom Scholem chose to worship here rather than in the Liberal synagogue near his parents' home. Engraving by Friedrich August Calau. Landesarchiv Berlin, F Rep. 250–01, Nr. C 340–1.

Amalie Scholem in Karlsbad, July 1889. As the Scholems gained affluence, they were able to take vacations in central European spa towns, such as Karlsbad in Austria. Even on vacation, their social circle was almost exclusively German-Jewish. Nearly everyone in this photo is Jewish and from Berlin, Posen, Oppeln, or Beuthen in Silesia. Amalie Scholem is third from left. David Scholem Collection.

Airship over the Berlin City Palace, ca. 1910. The airship *Gross II* flies over the kaiser's palace in central Berlin. Imperial pomp and technological innovation characterized life in Berlin in the early twentieth century. Landesarchiv Berlin, F Rep. 290, Nr. 0293407.

Old Berlin, 1903. The Scholems lived in central Berlin, amid old houses and narrow streets, including the Friedrichsgracht quay. Gershom Scholem was born in the house at the far right of the photo. In the background is St. Peter's Church (Petrikirche), built 1847–1853. In the foreground is the wooden Grünstrasse Bridge (Grünstraßenbrücke), which was replaced by a stone bridge one year after this photo was taken. Photo by Waldemar Titzenthaler. Landesarchiv Berlin, F Rep. 290, Nr. II04062.

The Scholem brothers, 1904. From left: Reinhold, Erich, Werner, and Gershom. National Library of Israel, ARC. 4*1599/10/04, 003800360.

Neue Grünstrasse, Berlin, August 1907. Gershom Scholem and his brothers grew up in the last house visible on the right side of the street. The Berlin of their youth was a city undergoing massive transformation. The construction at the end of their street was for a new subway line, which both accommodated and facilitated the city's rapid growth. The first automobiles and horse-drawn carriages competed for space in the streets, and spike-helmeted policemen, like these two standing on the corner of Neue Grünstrasse and Wallstrasse, kept order. Landesarchiv Berlin, F Rep. 290, Nr. 0325452.

The Scholem brothers, November 1904. The Scholem boys are dressed to perform a play written by Betty Scholem for Theobald Scholem's wedding party. From left: Gershom dressed as an Indian, Reinhold as an Arab, Erich as a Chinese, and Werner as a Jewish shepherd in Palestine. National Library of Israel, ARC. 4*1599/10/05, 003800374.

Fifty Years of Siegfried Scholem Printers. In addition to printing newspapers, the Siegfried Scholem firm specialized in lithography in the art nouveau style of the era. This postcard commemorates the firm's fiftieth anniversary celebrations, held just months before the outbreak of World War I. From left: Max, Siegfried, and Theobald Scholem. David Scholem Collection.

Siegfried Scholem printshop, early twentieth century. This photo originally appeared in a prospectus for Siegfried Scholem Printers. David Scholem Collection.

The Scholem family on vacation, May 1913. Arthur Scholem and his family spent the Pentecost holiday in 1913 in Schierke, a health resort town in the Harz Mountains in central Germany. Back row, from left: Arthur, Betty, Reinhold, and Gershom Scholem. In the front row are unidentified friends. National Library of Israel, ARC. 4*1599/10/08, 003800443.

Portrait of Gershom Scholem, age fifteen. Gershom Scholem had this photograph taken in Giessbach, Switzerland, during the summer of 1913. As a young man, he frequently visited tranquil mountain towns for restorative purposes on the recommendation of his doctors. National Library of Israel, ARC. 4*1599/10/09, 003800444.

Berliners celebrate the declaration of war, August 1914. Crowds of middle- and upper-class Germans stand outside the royal palace and acclaim the declaration of war in August 1914. Many expected the war to be over by Christmas. It lasted four years, and over thirteen million men served in the German armed forces, including Reinhold, Erich, Werner, Gershom, and Georg Scholem. Landesarchiv Berlin, F Rep. 290, Nr. II6182.

Mobile soup kitchen in Berlin, 1916. During World War I, this mobile soup kitchen offered Berliners a modest-sized hot lunch for thirty-five pfennigs. Though many Germans greeted the outbreak of war with great enthusiasm, mass mobilization and the Allied blockade led to an extreme shortage of foodstuffs in German cities. The scarcity of food contributed to the fraying of social cohesion and an increase in antisemitism. Library of Congress, LC-B2–4340–9 (P&P).

Dr. Georg Scholem and his family during World War I. Though he was already thirty-seven years old and married with a child, Dr. Georg Scholem was conscripted as a medical officer during World War I. From left: Georg, Ernst, and Sophie Scholem. David Scholem Collection.

Gershom Scholem in the German army, 1917. In 1917 Gershom Scholem was conscripted into the German army, but his service lasted only two months before he was discharged as mentally unfit. Gershom is in the front row, second from left. National Library of Israel, ARC. 4*1599/10/199, 003868494.

Kapp Putsch, Berlin, March 1920. Political violence marked the early years of the Weimar Republic. In March 1920, German marines and far-right-wing militias attempted to overthrow the democratic government of Germany. They occupied Berlin and other major cities until a general strike by workers ended their coup. Here, Kapp forces stand guard on a Berlin street, outside a corset shop. Library of Congress, LC-B2–5164–6 (P&P).

Communist demonstration in Berlin, ca. 1924. Communists demonstrate in the Lustgarten park in central Berlin. They carry red flags and a banner that proclaims, "We will protect the Soviet Union with our bodies!" At this time, Werner Scholem was the second most powerful member of the German Communist Party. Landesarchiv Berlin, F Rep. 290, Nr. 0097002.

Werner Scholem and the Independent Social Democrats, October 1920. Werner Scholem, in the center of the photo, marked with a white X, was a member of the Independent Social Democratic Party after World War I. However, at the Independents' party congress in Halle in October 1920, a majority of delegates, including Scholem, voted to join the Comintern and submit to Moscow's dictates. Soon thereafter, he and hundreds of thousands of Independent Social Democrats joined the Communist Party. Deutsches Historisches Museum, Bildarchiv F 52/3330.

WERNER SCHOLEM   6234-2

Werner Scholem, Member of the Reichstag, 1924. Werner Scholem was not yet thirty years old when he was elected to serve as a member of the German Reichstag for the Communist Party. Library of Congress, LC-B2–6234–2 (P&P).

Gershom and Escha Scholem in a sukkah, Jerusalem, September 1926. Gershom Scholem and his first wife, Escha, relax in a sukkah in Jerusalem. Though Gershom was not conventionally Orthodox, he loved Jewish rituals and holidays, including Sukkot. At the time of this photograph, Gershom and Escha had been married for nearly three years. National Library of Israel, ARC. 4*1599/10/23, 003800658.

Laying the Cornerstone of the Jewish National and University Library, Jerusalem, July 1926. Hebrew University of Jerusalem chancellor Judah Magnes prepares the cornerstone for the Jewish National and University Library on Mt. Scopus in Jerusalem while workers and Gershom Scholem, third from left, in the white fedora, look on. Scholem had a lifelong affiliation with the Jewish National and University Library, now known as the National Library of Israel. His first job after arriving in Palestine in 1923 was at the library, and he held the position until he became a university lecturer. Later, he willed his enormous and priceless personal library to the national library, which still preserves his books as a discrete collection within the library. National Library of Israel, ARC. 4*1599/10/22, 003800656.

The Rehavia neighborhood in Jerusalem, March 1935. With its modern buildings and clean, tree-lined streets, Rehavia quickly became the neighborhood of choice for German-Jewish émigrés in Jerusalem, as well as Jerusalem's Jewish intellectual, economic, and political elites. Gershom Scholem, Hugo Bergmann, and their circle lived there. Photo by Zoltan Kluger. National Photo Collection of Israel, D403–094.

Gershom and Fania Scholem at home, Jerusalem, 1939. Gershom Scholem and
Fania Freud Scholem, his second wife, pose in their apartment in Jerusalem. For
over forty-five years, their home was famous for its book-lined walls, in addition
to its European-style furnishings. After visiting Gershom in 1979, the German-
born American historian Fritz Stern commented that the apartment "resembled a
German academic home of long ago, more 'German' than anything" he had seen in
Germany since the 1930s. National Library of Israel, ARC. 4*1599/10/45, 003802799.

German Jews at a Berlin travel agency, January 1939. By January 1939, two months after Kristallnacht, it was clear that every Jew needed to flee Germany. Here, a crowd of hopeful emigrants lines up outside the Palestine & Orient Lloyd agency in Berlin-Charlottenburg. Bundesarchiv, Bild 183-E01073.

The Scholem brothers, Montreal, June 1938. Erich and Reinhold Scholem immigrated to Australia via Canada in the summer of 1938. In Montreal, they were able to see Gershom who came up from New York, where he was a visiting scholar. It was the last time these three brothers were together. From left: Erich, Gershom, and Reinhold Scholem. National Library of Israel, ARC. 4*1599/10/47, 003802801.

Scholem family reunion in Tel Aviv, circa 1941. Gershom and Fania Scholem visit his uncle Theobald Scholem and aunt Hedwig Scholem, and Hedwig's sister, Gertrud Zucker, after Theobald and Hedwig fled to Palestine. The older Scholems had been lifelong Zionists, but only left Germany in 1938. They settled in Tel Aviv. Zucker lived in Jerusalem, where she ran a guesthouse. From left: Hedwig Scholem, Gertrud Zucker, Gershom Scholem (seated on the floor), Theobald Scholem, and Fania Scholem. David Scholem Collection.

Gershom and Fania Scholem at home, Jerusalem, early 1960s. Gershom and Fania Scholem in their Jerusalem home. David Scholem Collection.

The Scholem family tomb, Berlin Weissensee Cemetery. Arthur Scholem was buried in this grave in 1925. No other member of the family is interred there, and the other names were added later. Collection of the author.

a family with almost no Jewish identity, was similar to many artists in this era. In her prose and poetry, she expressed a desire to reconnect with her Jewish heritage, writing "I did not know Judaism, my faith," and "I would like to prepare for an expedition to my own ancient land."[49]

The Scholems and their extended family were part of this renewed community. Previously, Betty's cousin had seen himself primarily as a German and only secondarily as a Jew, but now he was "inconsolable about the Jewish catastrophe."[50] Reinhold and Erich began learning Hebrew as early as the summer of 1933. While Erich could not lead the Passover seder the following spring, he was soon able to say the traditional Friday night blessings.[51] However, one Friday night, the Scholems had a stark reminder of their earlier ambivalent religiosity. Upon closely examining their *Kiddush* cup, they noticed that under the Hebrew inscription were the words "Christmas 1921." The cup had been a gift to Erich from his brother-in-law. Betty commented that at the time, "No one took offense at that inscription. In contrast to today!!" In fact, for Erich's birthday in 1934, she gave him a challah cover with the Hebrew year 5695 stitched in. At Hanukkah time, the Scholems ceremoniously lit the menorah and said the blessings. Their children knew the holiday songs and celebrated each night of the holiday at a different Hanukkah party. It was similar in other families. "One duly sees how the children will once again become the bearers of Judaism," in Betty's estimation.[52] Reinhold's son, Günter, celebrated his bar mitzvah in September 1935. In fact, bar mitzvahs had become extremely common. The Berlin rabbi Manfred Swarsensky had trouble scheduling them because he had so many boys under his tutelage.[53] Previously assimilated Jews sought consolation in traditions, liturgy, and spirituality long since discarded. Yet some still remained ambivalent about Jewish identity.

During the Nazi years, Werner Scholem, who had married a non-Jewish woman and belonged to an officially atheist political party, expressed mixed feelings about his family's Jewish identity. On the one hand, he worried about his "half-Jewish" children denying that part of their heritage.[54] On the other hand, he did not want them actually adopting the Jewish religion, which he viewed very negatively: "In no way is my sympathy for the Jewish religion greater than that for any other superstition. Just the opposite. If I were a believer, I would be Catholic; they have at least 1000 saints from which a person can choose in any situation. The Jewish religion is no real religion, for it is lacking in a belief in the hereafter. It is nothing other than a popular ritual. Given the choice between Christmas and Hanukkah, I am for the first since we are Germans, despite everything that is said against it."[55] He expressly opposed his daughter going to Jewish religious school or learning Hebrew after she left Germany and settled in England.[56] Nonetheless, questions of Jewish identity were the least of Werner's concerns under Nazi dictatorship.

Early on the morning of Sunday, 23 April 1933, the police rang the bell at the apartment of Werner and Emmy Scholem. Assuming that Werner was away, they interrogated Emmy. As their questions grew more aggressive and even unseemly, Werner emerged from his hiding spot to defend his wife. "'Well, well,' said the policeman. 'We thought you were in Zurich. We gave you the visa, after all.'" He called the police station and was told to bring in Emmy and Werner.[57] Things had been looking positive for Werner. He was making plans to resume his legal studies in Switzerland and had intended to leave the very day he was arrested.[58] Instead, the couple was charged with high treason or subversion, and Werner was transferred to Spandau prison. Their daughters found shelter with Werner's family in Berlin and Emmy's family in Hanover.[59] For a moment in July, it seemed that the police would release Werner from headquarters on Berlin's Alexanderplatz, but it failed to happen.

Additionally, no lawyer would take Werner's case because of his political past. Soon, Betty was spending all her time dealing with the situation.[60] She was not alone in undertaking such an urgent task. It became common in Nazi Germany for Jewish women, who may never have worked outside the home or dealt with the authorities before, to fight for the release of their husbands and fathers from incarceration.[61] While deeply concerned about his brother and sister-in-law, Gershom could not help but think that Werner and Emmy were partially to blame for their predicament since "they seem to have acted with a carelessness totally incomprehensible to anyone else and without the slightest feeling for the situation created by Hitler's seizure of power—operating instead on the assumption that things under fascism would be much as they had been," as he explained to Walter Benjamin.[62]

Investigators accused Werner of participating in a conspiratorial cell of Communist Party members with the goal of subverting the army. Allegedly, ordinary laborers and intellectuals, including former Reichstag representatives, met with soldiers in a Berlin pub to incite them to insubordination. One bright spot for Emmy and Werner was that their case remained within the traditional judicial system. Regular police detained and interrogated them rather than the Gestapo, and an examining magistrate supervised the entire matter. A lawyer with access to Werner's case file secretly told Erich that Werner and Emmy had been arrested with a group of approximately twenty coconspirators. According to Betty, the lawyer claimed that Emmy was the active one, and Werner was merely arrested along with her. Betty was furious at Emmy for remaining active in the Communist Party after her husband had been expelled and at Werner for coming back from Prague after he had been arrested already once by the Nazis.[63] She also commented that Werner and Emmy were in denial "that the Nazis are now doing exactly what the Communists would have done if *they* had taken over the reins." Meanwhile, Betty was keeping Werner's papers, and the whole family was under suspicion.[64] Emmy and Werner were not even allowed to correspond with each other while in jail.[65] Now that Werner was in custody for a second time in three months, Gershom was incredulous: "I truly cannot fathom my brother's behavior . . . specifically, why he didn't put the border behind him the minute they released him from custody the first time."[66]

Werner acknowledged, "I am doubly affected, as a Jew and as a former politician." He felt that his six years of legal study and internship were for naught and never imagined that he would face a treason trial after being expelled from the Communist Party back in 1926. By October, he had been incarcerated for half a year and expected to wait another half year until he had a trial. Although he was fully innocent, he had no expectation of release in the foreseeable future. He wrote that, for the children's sake, they would have to emigrate because of all the laws against "Jews and other non-whites (prohibition of mixed marriages, etc.)."[67] Indeed, Emmy's jailors put considerable pressure on her to divorce her Jewish husband.[68]

In November Emmy was released from investigative custody, with the proviso that she report to the police twice a week, which was intended to preclude her flight.[69] That did not stop her. In February 1934, Emmy disappeared without saying a word to the Scholems.[70] Unbeknownst to them, she had fled to Prague, where she had friends.[71] Even before her release and flight, she had received help from Heinz Hackebeil (or Wiegel-Hackebeil), a young apprentice in the firm where she had worked and, more importantly, a convinced Nazi and sergeant (*Obertruppführer*) in the Nazis' SA paramilitary. His involvement with an arrested Communist endangered his own position, if not his life, and he fled with Emmy when she crossed the frontier to Czechoslovakia. Soon, after her own encounter with the police, fifteen-year-old Edith escaped custody, hiked over the border, and joined her mother and her mother's lover in Prague.

Emmy's disappearance exacerbated Werner's situation. Betty reported that Werner was sitting in jail "wail[ing] like a child that he hears nothing from his wife. *We* should find out where she is!" Moreover, now that Emmy had violated the terms of her pretrial release, it was improbable that the authorities would provisionally release Werner. And without money to pay his lawyer, he agreed to sell his furniture and books for a pittance.[72] Werner Scholem was only one of many Jews desperate for money in the shadow of Nazi oppression.

With the assistance of other exiled German Communists, Emmy made her way to England, got settled in a two-room apartment, and found a job in advertising. She also finally wrote to Werner, Betty, and Werner's lawyer.[73] At this time, their younger daughter, Renate, was happily living in Hanover with Emmy's mother and going to school under an assumed name. Eventually, she came to Britain with Heinz Hackebeil's assistance, and both daughters attempted to build new lives for themselves.[74] With Werner in jail and Emmy in London, Betty served as go-between for their correspondence, even as they feuded over his legal representation.[75]

Emmy and Heinz, no longer romantically involved, operated two businesses. Emmy claimed that he had needed to flee because he, a Nazi, had helped a Communist so much, and she looked after him in London.[76] She noted, "It has certainly not been easy for Heinz to separate himself from his party, for which he fought for many years, and even today he remains true to his ideals. But he did not separate himself at all; he was separated."[77] She also wrote to Werner, "I will wait for you for as long as it will be necessary. Everything that I am building up here, I am building for us both and for the children."[78] She insisted that she had only fled because she had no other choice and she would never leave Werner in the lurch.[79] Earlier, when Werner learned about the circumstances of Emmy's life in London, he asked his mother, "has she [Emmy] been afflicted with something like the spirit of voracious capitalism?" He also asked if Heinz was still living with her.[80]

The Scholems' financial situation appreciably deteriorated after the Nazis came to power. Despite the refuge provided by their vacation property in Zernsdorf, they had to sell part of it. Betty wanted to use the proceeds to build up a nest egg in Palestine, but she found it nearly impossible to get much of her savings out of the country and needed Gershom's help with the endeavor.[81] Gershom either did not understand his mother's financial woes or was insensitive to them. For example, he used her own money to buy her a birthday present, and he requested that she ship books to him in Palestine, both for his own use and for the National Library.[82] In fact, the Scholems' print house suffered a crippling loss of business, while their "Aryan" competitors were expanding. After twenty years, it looked as if the German Geological Society would no longer have the Scholems print their journals. "Geology is a purely Christian field. It seems that the Jews did not participate in the building up of the Earth," Betty sarcastically wrote.[83] The Scholems were utterly reliant on their Jewish customers, chief among them the *Jüdische Rundschau*, the principal Zionist newspaper in Germany. However, gaining new Jewish customers was proving nearly impossible, and when the *Rundschau* was temporarily banned, the Scholems had to dismiss employees.[84]

As tumultuous as the Jewish publishing trade was, it became critical as German Jews alternatively sought distraction from the world around them and information about the changes in that world. Jewish books helped educate and entertain Jews and fueled a doomed reflorescence of Jewish cultural life. Jewish newspapers informed them about changes in the law and options for emigration.[85] In fact, during the early years of Nazi rule, Schocken Books managed to publish two hundred titles with tens of thousands of individual books printed, including its popular *Almanach* and the Schocken Library of classical and contemporary Jewish literature.[86] In a time of great oppression, the Jews of Germany also experienced cultural richness.

Two years after the Nazis took power, rather than fleeing or even making plans for an orderly emigration from Germany, the Scholems continued to vacation abroad: Betty in northern Italy; Erich in Croatia; and Hedwig, Theobald's wife, in Switzerland. Betty visited Werner's wife in London, and Theobald attended the Nineteenth Zionist Congress, in Lucerne, Switzerland.[87] Even after the Nuremberg laws of September 1935 dramatically defined the social chasm between Jewish Germans and non-Jewish Germans, Betty assumed that she would always be able to join Gershom in Palestine if things truly became unbearable for the Jews in Germany, not realizing that emigrating from Nazi Germany or immigrating to British-controlled Palestine would become increasingly difficult.[88]

Eva Scholem, Theobald's daughter, was fortunate to be able to study abroad, in Bern, Switzerland. Over time, she began to feel at home there and could even speak the local dialect like a native.[89] Nonetheless, she still intended to settle in Palestine once she completed her doctorate. Her father helped her with the financial requirements for immigration, she obtained one of the invaluable immigration certificates in 1935, and it looked as if she would be able to practice medicine in Palestine before new limits on immigrant physicians took effect.[90] Her sister, Dina, had already moved to Palestine and, Betty reported, worked taking care of chickens on a kibbutz.[91] Later, Dina married an Italian immigrant to Palestine and took Italian citizenship, which pleased her parents, presumably because it was better than German citizenship. However, Betty wondered why Dina, being such an enthusiastic Zionist, did not take Palestinian citizenship.[92] Eva embarked on a successful medical career in Palestine, and after living in Jerusalem for a few years, she moved to a kibbutz and married in 1939.[93]

While Werner remained in pretrial custody, first in Moabit prison and then in Plötzensee prison, Emmy and their daughters settled into life in England.[94] From London, Emmy wrote to the investigating magistrate in Germany to explain why she had to flee the country. She claimed that the only evidence against her and Werner was a statement by Marie Luise Hammerstein, the communist daughter of a leading German general, and she cited people who could speak in her defense. She disavowed any political activity and now had a job working for an advertising firm. In a second letter to the magistrate, she explained their relationship with Hammerstein, who had joined the Communist Party against Emmy's advice and who had had no contact with the Scholems since the summer of 1928, according to Emmy. Emmy also denied ever having met Hammerstein's powerful father or discussed his profession with the daughter.[95]

At last, on 4 March 1935, Werner and his codefendants came before the People's Court (Volksgerichtshof), a special tribunal created to try political crimes. Far from an independent judicial body, Hitler staffed the court with loyal Nazis and fellow travelers who abandoned traditional legal standards in the name of Nazi justice. And it was here that Werner faced trial for allegedly plotting against the state and attempting to subvert the army. Ironically, the proceedings took place in the very same room of the former Prussian state legislature building where the Communist Party's legislators used to meet, and it was in this room that Werner was expelled from the party's central committee in October 1925. "Well, that is a particular joke of fate," Werner wrote. He claimed that it would be sufficient for his exoneration if the walls of the room could repeat everything they had heard about the name Scholem.[96]

During the five-day trial, the allegations against Werner fell apart. The prosecution's key witness claimed that in the spring of 1932, he had seen Werner in a Berlin pub, attempting to convince soldiers not to shoot at workers if deployed against them. However, by his own admission, the witness was in prison until late June. Werner's defense proved that after the man's release from prison, Werner was on vacation in the Alps or busy preparing for his trip. Moreover, the witness did not even know who Werner Scholem was until presented with his photo during the investigation. While the judges were still highly suspicious of Werner, remarkably they acknowledged that the evidence was insufficient to convict him of the charges specified in the indictment and declared him not guilty. However, rather than release Werner from prison as expected, he was immediately taken into "protective custody," which Nazi-era police used as a euphemism for extralegal incarceration.[97] Appeals to the Gestapo, even in writing from Werner's lawyer, were in vain.[98] Werner was sent to the Columbia concentration camp in Berlin (also known as Columbia-Haus) and later to the Lichtenburg concentration camp.[99]

Why was Werner Scholem arrested and not released, despite his own exclusion from the Communist Party? One possible reason was initially unknown to his mother and the wider public.[100] In the late 1920s, Werner had reportedly had an affair with Marie Luise Hammerstein, daughter of General Kurt von Hammerstein-Equord, head of the Army Command. Marie Luise later worked for the Communist Party's intelligence service. Her sister Helga was also active as a spy, in collaboration with her Jewish, communist husband, Leo Roth.[101] The authorities might have feared that Werner knew about secret military plans and would reveal them to Germany's enemies should he remain free and be able to flee abroad. In fact, such a concern was misplaced. Werner had not been active in the Communist Party's intelligence service, and when Marie Luise began her espionage work, her ties to the discredited, heterodox Communist ended. Despite Emmy Scholem's claims, there is no evidence that Marie Luise denounced Werner, and they were investigated completely separately—he by the regular police and she by the Gestapo. Nonetheless, when Betty heard of her communist son's involvement with a general's daughter, she exclaimed, "He is really a jackass of fantastic proportions!"[102]

Another possible reason why the Nazis did not release Werner was simply his infamy. During his active political career, he was a vitriolic public opponent of the Nazis, who also despised him as a Jew and a Communist.[103] Long before the Nazis came to power and Joseph Goebbels became the minister for public enlightenment and propaganda, he had Werner Scholem in his sights, and it is possible that he used his influence to prevent Werner's release from the concentration camps.[104] Additionally, Werner Scholem served as the exemplar of the degenerate Jewish, communist intellectual, who must be imprisoned. As early as October 1933, a Berlin newspaper published a propagandistic exposé about detainees inside a Nazi prison, and the author focused on a "small, restless Jew . . . a thin, unspeakably ugly person. Lurking, inwardly torn, perpetually moving eyes, big protruding ears. A walking Ahasver. Perpetually fighting against the laws of moral order." Even more offensive in the eyes of the journalist, this Jew's wife was a "tall, blond, petty Aryan of good Friesian blood" who had been turned communist by her husband. This former Reichstag representative had been expelled from the Communist Party, but still attempted to infiltrate the German army. This unnamed enemy of the German people could have been none other than Werner Scholem.[105] When the Nazis staged their massive propaganda exhibition "The Eternal Jew" ("Der ewige Jude") in 1937 and 1938, they displayed a bust of Werner Scholem to demonstrate what they considered to be typically Jewish physical features.[106] Werner Scholem was possibly too prominent, too despised by leading Nazis, and too useful as a propaganda tool to release.

From Werner's letters to his wife and family, it is possible to gain some sense of his experience in Nazi prisons and concentration camps. When possible, he preferred not to have a cellmate, despite the loneliness. He had a low opinion of his fellow prisoners: "rogues and conmen."[107] Writing on Concentration Camp Lichtenberg letterhead, Werner informed his family that prisoners could receive two four-page letters per month from relatives, as well as Nazi newspapers. They could also send him thirty reichsmarks per month, and he was allowed to correspond directly with Emmy.[108] When Werner did not receive his two letters from Emmy, he grew despondent and angry.[109] However, there was much that went unsaid in his letters. Because of censorship, he could not write about the poor and crowded living conditions in the fortress converted into a concentration camp. He did not mention the strictly regimented life, pervasive antisemitism and disdain of intellectuals, or cliquish nature of prison life. He did not write that camp inmates who were Stalinist Communists ostracized and persecuted dissenting Communists like him. Nor did he depict the degradation and torture of prisoners that marked concentration camp life.

Unable to correspond with his lawyer, Werner wrote to Emmy in London for news about his case and to ask her to smooth things over with the Gestapo regarding her life in London. The longer Werner was in prison, the farther away his former life receded. He thought he was doing well considering the conditions, and he worked in the camp laundry, where he operated a wringer machine. "It is a very pleasant job. When I come to you, I will bring extensive specialized knowledge in running a laundry," he joked. Later, he became supervisor of a team of sock darners; however, a vindictive camp official transferred Werner to the sewage removal team, a job so vile that it was reserved for Jewish inmates.[110] In his limited free time, Werner practiced English in the hope that he would be released and could join Emmy in Britain.[111] On 17 January 1936, Werner marked an anniversary: his one thousandth day in custody. "I have the comforting feeling that I will not experience the 10,000th! One has to take the long view. Then, everything isn't so bad."[112] Indeed, Werner was deeply depressed about his situation as the days dragged on and no end was in sight.[113]

Werner's situation and the situation of all Jews in Germany deteriorated considerably in the autumn of 1935. In September, in conjunction with the annual Nazi Party congress in Nuremberg, the Nazis issued the Law for the Protection of German Blood and German Honor and the Reich Citizenship Law, collectively known as the Nuremberg Laws. Jews and non-Jews could not enter into marriages or maintain nonmarital sexual relationships. Jews could no longer employ non-Jewish domestic help under the age of forty-five, and many Jewish families had to dismiss their long-serving maids, as Betty noted to Gershom.[114] Critically, the laws also demoted German Jews to the status of "subjects of the state," rather than citizens, who enjoyed certain rights.

While the legal situation had always been bad for people deemed "full Jews" by the Nazis, the Nuremberg Laws changed the situation of so-called partial Jews—people with only one or two Jewish grandparents. In a society where being classified as Jewish had negative ramifications for one's career prospects or ability to gain an education, approximately two hundred thousand more Germans now faced discrimination.[115] German government bureaucrats, in conversation with Nazi Party officials, worked out the details of two new categories, first-degree and second-degree *Mischlinge* (people of mixed racial ancestry), whose partial Jewishness determined how integrated into German society or how excluded from German society they would be. Even having one less Jewish grandparent enabled a person to enjoy a greater range of opportunities and to escape increased persecution. For millions of Germans, having an impeccably un-Jewish family tree was indispensable. For hundreds of thousands of Jewish Germans like the Scholems, an already precarious situation deteriorated further. However, for Werner Scholem—Jewish and communist—the situation grew even worse.

The Nazis' two great opponents were the Jews and communism. Moreover, in the minds of Nazi ideologues, they were inextricably linked. At the Nazi party congress in 1935, Propaganda Minister Joseph Goebbels gave a speech in which he explicitly attributed the creation and realization of communism to the Jews. He enumerated at tremendous length a litany of Jews or supposed Jews who had promoted Marxism in Russia and Germany. Among those whom he attacked by name were "the Jews [Ernst] Meyer, [August] Thalheimer, [Werner] Scholem, [and Paul] Friedlaender," who controlled "the Press of the German Communist Party in Berlin." The prisoners in Werner's concentration camp heard the speech broadcast live on the radio and turned toward him when his name was mentioned.[116] Being publicly singled out by one of the top Nazis worsened Werner's situation in the camp and diminished his chances of release from the clutches of the Gestapo. As Betty noted, "This institution exists without right and law. With them, there are no proceedings, no appeal, nothing."[117]

The Scholems did occasionally receive uncensored word of Werner's life in the camps. One day during the summer of 1935, a former concentration camp prisoner calling himself "Mr. Schulz" visited Reinhold with news of Werner. Schulz, a homosexual, had been imprisoned for four months and subjected to Nazi "reeducation." Now, he risked being rearrested for spreading information about the camps, but he had promised Werner that he would visit the Scholems. Schulz claimed that the commandant was humane and worked for the release of long-held prisoners. However, Betty was disgusted to learn that the Lichtenberg camp was increasingly filled with homosexuals.[118] In Palestine, Gershom received a report about Werner written by Gerhard Pinthus, a Communist and musicologist, who had been released from incarceration.[119] Pinthus arrived in Lichtenberg in August 1936 and shared a cell with Werner. He claimed that conditions were not terrible and only after their later transfer to Dachau did they face the full concentration camp experience. There, Jews had to work much more than non-Jews, often twelve hours or more per day. They were subject to additional harassment, such as barracks detention and smoking bans. Pinthus and Werner worked in the same labor battalion, transporting cement, stones, and sand, which severely taxed their energy. But the situation grew worse after their transfer to the Buchenwald concentration camp, where they worked thirteen hours a day, received terrible food, and were subjected to unpredictable treatment by the guards. The regular receipt of money was essential for the prisoners because one would starve if one tried to live on the normal rations. Werner was extremely parsimonious with money and permitted himself to buy only essentials, but even the thriftiest prisoners would run out of money without receiving new sums. Werner's health held up decently, but he was seriously ill twice: with diphtheria around Christmas 1937 and with a phlegmon on his right hand in April 1938. Ultimately, the only thing that sustained long-imprisoned Jewish inmates was the comradeship among themselves.[120]

While Werner was still in Lichtenberg, located two hours from Berlin, Betty occasionally visited him, and his whole family began working for Werner's release for the purpose of immigration to Palestine. Gershom used his connections to ensure that Werner would be admitted.[121] In fact, the government of Palestine granted Werner and his family entry permits valid until 30 June 1936. However, the Gestapo had long ago confiscated his passport.[122] Just when Werner expected his release and emigration, the Nazis did not release him. Gershom shared the devastating news with his friend Walter Benjamin and postulated, "Goebbels needs to keep a couple of Jews on hand in order to demonstrate that he has stamped out bolshevism and my brother is apparently among those selected to play the part." He further wrote, "At the time when the final decision had to be made, it came to light that a list existed of people who could be freed only with Goebbels's permission and that the Gestapo had known all the time that my brother was on this list."[123]

In February 1937, the Nazis transferred Werner from Lichtenberg to the Dachau concentration camp.[124] Joining Werner in both camps was Ludwig Bendix, a Jewish lawyer from Berlin. Bendix recorded his recollections of Werner, who already stood out in Lichtenberg through his personal comportment and his persecution by his jailers. For Bendix and other Jewish prisoners, the transfer to Dachau entailed a happy reunion with many former colleagues and former fellow prisoners; however, for Werner it was a disaster. The kapo of the camp's block for Jews, himself a Jewish Communist, exploded when he heard the name Scholem: "Here, you will have no opportunity to confuse people and forge your old plots! Mark my words! Here, you will join the ranks like everyone else!" However, Werner was not treated like any other prisoner. He was under extra scrutiny and subject to particularly harsh treatment. Bendix wanted to intervene on Scholem's behalf, even though they did not get along. He thought that politics should not play a role in the prisoners' relations since they were all victims in the camp; however, other prisoners warned him against doing anything for Scholem. Ultimately, Bendix and Scholem joined Hans Litten, who had famously put Hitler on the stand during a trial in 1931, in giving legal advice to their fellow prisoners in Dachau, though there were limits as to what they could do. Moreover, Scholem's obsessive need for order and his imperious behavior eventually alienated Bendix.[125]

Another inmate, Ernst Federn, a Jewish Trotskyite from Vienna, also recalled Werner in his memoirs. Werner was among the prisoners selected to work on the infamous Moor Express, a cargo wagon pulled by a team of human laborers. Federn lauded Werner's immense strength in the task, which Werner also had later in Buchenwald. Werner's fellow prisoners in Dachau considered him to be undiplomatic, humorless, and an incorrigible misanthrope: "People said: 'The increase of pessimism was Scholemism.'" Additionally, he did not adjust well to changes, becoming anxious. In one instance, he refused to donate a single mark for another inmate because he could not deviate from his strict budget, further worsening his reputation inside the camp. Nonetheless, the inmates of Dachau respected him for his bravery. One day, a young guard decided to mock Werner by making him sing, "I am a dirty Jew with a big nose." Werner, long renowned for his loud voice, sang so loudly that the wives of SS men opened up their windows and began watching the scene, embarrassing the young SS guard, who then ordered Scholem to be quiet. "Werner could triumph, and the others with him," recalled Federn. Over time, however, Werner's political past became an issue as Stalinist Communists arrayed against him. Trotskyite Communists were allegedly not welcome in the camp's underground, which was dominated by mainstream (i.e., Stalinist) Communist Party members.[126]

Meanwhile, Emmy disappeared from Werner's life. She stopped writing. She stopped sending money.[127] And this at a time when Werner needed money, including for dental surgery.[128] Unbeknownst to Werner, Emmy and her lover, Isak Aufseher, a Jewish Communist from Austrian Galicia (later eastern Poland), had gone to Spain, which was in the throes of a civil war. Fascist nationalists in the army, supported by the Catholic Church and aristocracy, had risen up against the left-wing government. Soon, Socialists and Communists from all over Europe and the Americas traveled to Spain, usually via France, to join the Loyalist side in the Spanish Civil War. Emmy's Spanish adventure ended roughly three months after it began, but she remained in Paris with her lover for several more months.[129] Meanwhile, someone from the Jewish Refugees Committee wrote to Gershom in Jerusalem that Emmy's business had collapsed and now she wanted to immigrate to Ecuador with her younger daughter, Renate. The committee had been supporting Emmy, including her older daughter Edith's training as a radiographer. The correspondent also wrote, "Mrs. Scholem's desire to emigrate to Ecuador is mainly based on the hope that once she is in that country, it will be possible for her to get her husband out of the concentration camp."[130]

Under the impact of the ongoing economic crisis and, above all, the effects of Nazi persecution, the Scholems were no longer able to continue their Berlin printing businesses. In 1934 Reinhold and Erich were able to sell their firm's printshop to another publisher, and two years later, they formally dissolved the firm of Arthur Scholem.[131] At the end of 1935, Theobald received a notice from the Reich Chamber of Literature that he was no longer "suited" to be in a "profession disseminating culture." He was thereby expelled from the League of Reich German Booksellers and the Reich Chamber of Literature, and he was encouraged to liquidate the firm or to transfer it to an "Aryan person."[132] In the meantime, Siegfried Scholem existed as one of less than a hundred Jewish printers and publishers allowed in Germany and was limited to exclusively Jewish publications for a Jewish audience, which was an ever-shrinking market.[133] Ultimately, in 1938, the venerable firm of Siegfried Scholem effectively came to an end. Theobald sold the company's inventory, accounts, publishing rights, and name to the Max Lichtwitz printing house for "the laughable contribution of 15,000 RM," in the words of the family's lawyer after the war.[134] Nonetheless, by some measures, the Scholems were lucky. Most Jewish-owned businesses were worthless by late 1938 and could not be sold at any price. The owners simply ceased operations, and to deregister their firms, they had to pay a fee to the Nazi state and run a paid announcement in the Nazis' own *Völkischer Beobachter* newspaper. In Berlin alone, 2,869

Jewish businesses were struck from the city's commercial registry between 1933 and 1937.[135]

The fate of the Siegfried Scholem printshop matched that of thousands of Jewish-owned firms. It was part of a process that has become known as Aryanization. The Nazis had long wanted to remove Jews from the German economy, and intimidation of Jewish merchants and their non-Jewish customers drove most medium and small business owners out of the market. Roughly 60 to 70 percent of firms owned by Jews when the Nazis came to power were no longer under Jewish control by 1938.[136] Theobald Scholem was lucky to have survived the earlier waves of economic disintegration. In contrast to the situation with small businesses, closing many of the large Jewish-owned firms or reordering their management was potentially disruptive to the German economy as it began its recovery from the depths of the Great Depression. In 1933 and 1934, the Nazis "Aryanized" relatively few large firms, though they did target Jewish-owned newspaper concerns, including Mosse and Ullstein. By 1938 Germany's economic situation had improved, with consumer spending power reaching pre-Depression levels.[137] At the same time, Nazi political leaders and German business elites no longer feared a supposed Jewish backlash, and conservative, non-Nazi government officials had been pushed aside. Through a combination of harassment and intimidation—including the threat and use of imprisonment in concentration camps—and complicated financial arrangements (particularly in the case of large firms with subsidiaries and international holdings), the Nazis succeeded in transferring ownership of businesses to "Aryans," usually loyal Nazi Party members or non-Jews who needed to be mollified for various reasons. They also succeeded in creating an impoverished class of residents whose poverty only decreased their chances of emigration.

Just as the Nazis pushed Jewish businessmen out of the commercial economy, they pushed Jewish professionals out of their fields. A notable case is that of Jewish physicians. In 1933, nearly 11 percent of male physicians and more than 13 percent of female physicians in Germany were Jews—4,970 men and 587 women—with the percentages much higher in Berlin.[138] The Nazis attempted to prohibit Jewish physicians from treating patients with public health insurance, forcing them to accept only private patients, but the Nazis could not simply revoke the licenses of all Jewish physicians without disrupting the country's health care system. However, they could demand the expulsion of Jews from professional organizations, such as the League of Doctors in Germany and the German Women Doctors' Association (Verband der Ärzte Deutschlands and Deutscher Ärtzinnenbund). As the Nazis' antisemitic measures increased in quantity and severity, the number of Jewish physicians remaining in Germany drastically decreased.[139] In July 1938, the Nazis decreed that Jews could not practice as fully licensed medical doctors, though a few hundred—expressly calling themselves "treaters of the sick" (Krankenbehandler) and not physicians (Ärzte)—could continue to provide medical treatment to ill Jews.[140] Betty Scholem's sister, Käte Hirsch Schiepan, was among those squeezed out of the medical profession. Despite losing her publicly insured patients, she was able to maintain a minimal practice until 1938, when she lost that right and became fully reliant on her non-Jewish husband.[141] A few months after she and other Jewish physicians saw the end of their careers, Jewish dentists, pharmacists, and even veterinarians lost their licenses as well. By 1939, barely 15 percent of all German Jews were gainfully employed.[142]

Indeed, the Nazis and their collaborators worked to exclude Jews from nearly all areas of German society, with the number of regulations increasing after the Nuremberg Laws of 1935 and increasing again after Kristallnacht in 1938. Authorities banned Jews from public swimming pools, playgrounds, parks, cinemas, theaters, concert halls, and sports facilities. Jews could no longer serve in the army, not even combat veterans from the World War. Jews were not permitted to use public libraries. Jewish students from Germany were not permitted to earn doctorates in 1937 and were barred from universities altogether after Kristallnacht. Jews could no longer have driver's licenses. They could not have carrier pigeons. Eventually, they could not have house pets of any kind. Cities renamed streets that had been named after Jews.[143] Hitler's government forced Jews to rename themselves: any Jew whose name was not immediately identifiable as Jewish had to take the middle name "Sara" or "Israel."[144]

By 1937 it was clear that the Scholems could no longer remain in Germany; however, emigration depended as much on the will of foreign governments as it did on that of the Nazi government. For nearly every destination in the world, German Jews needed entry permits or visas, and they needed funds to take with them. Some foreign governments simply did not want Germany's Jews, and in most cases, the Nazis did not let emigrants take their assets with them. Complicating matters for the disproportionately middle- and upper-middle-class Jews of Germany, many countries did not want immigrant professionals and businessmen competing with their own native university graduates and mercantile class. At the same time, German Jewish doctors, lawyers, and architects worried about the transferability of their credentials.[145]

Even though Zionism had never had a mass following in Germany, Palestine was a common immigration destination for German Jews fleeing Nazi persecution, though it was not the only destination. By July 1938, nearly 150,000 Jews had left Germany, and approximately 44,000 of them had gone to Palestine, 27,000 to the United States, 7,600 to South Africa, 7,500 to Brazil, and 1,000 to Australia—all future destinations for members of the extended Scholem family.[146]

Reinhold and Erich decided to immigrate to Australia, but they could not realize their plan without Gershom's assistance. To apprise Gershom of his role in the operation, Betty and Erich took a dangerous one-day trip across the Czechoslovak border and sent him detailed instructions. Australia required immigrants to bring at least 200 pounds with them. Reinhold had saved up money, but he had only enough for three people: himself, his wife, and his son. Therefore, Gershom was to send Erich the critical funds out of Betty's savings in Palestine—around 300 pounds—which she had been building up in small installments since 1933 in case she had to flee Germany. The little money that Erich already had would remain with his family in Berlin. Once Reinhold and Erich had arrived in Australia and begun working, Erich would send the money back to Gershom in Palestine. Betty and Erich provided Gershom precise instructions on how to transfer the money to a family friend in London and gave Gershom a secret code to use to confirm the transfer. Under no circumstances was he to write the word "emigration."[147]

Knowing her youngest son's inability to deal with unforeseen circumstances and sudden situations, Betty repeatedly impressed on Gershom the urgency of the matter and her determination to provide Erich this "vital opportunity to emigrate." She added, "There can be no discussion about it. We have neither the time nor the opportunity for that as the matter is tremendously urgent. I want it."[148] For nearly fifteen years, Betty Scholem had sent German delicacies, clothes, and books to Gershom in Jerusalem, at his explicit request. Even as his Berlin family suffered under the twin burdens of the Great Depression and Nazi persecution, he had sent them requests. Now, he would have to do something for them—something vital for their lives. For that reason, Betty provided extremely detailed instructions and repeatedly assured Gershom that the transfer would not require much effort on his part; the bank would take care of everything.

At last, after many delays, Reinhold, Erich, and Reinhold's family were able to leave Germany. They traveled to Britain, where they boarded a ship for Canada. In Montreal, they briefly visited with Gershom who was already in North America for research, before continuing to Vancouver. From there, they sailed across the Pacific Ocean to their new home, Sydney, Australia, arriving on 1 July 1938. A few months later, Reinhold wrote to his brother

Gershom, "I can only say that since then, I have been glad every day to be out of Germany."[149]

Though Reinhold and Erich had reached safety, their mother and Erich's family remained behind in Berlin. Even before the horror of Kristallnacht, Reinhold informed Gershom, "The general situation in Berlin has now developed such that it is apparently very necessary that Mom gets out as soon as possible."[150] Even Werner, writing from the Buchenwald concentration camp, urged his mother to emigrate.[151] Betty considered her options: Palestine or Australia. Reinhold had applied to get Betty an Australian entry permit, and she wanted to pursue a Palestinian immigration certificate, even if only as a temporary measure before going to Sydney. She was inclined to settle in Palestine since she had relatives there and could speak German with many residents, but she was worried about the unrest between Arabs and Jews and how her health would fare in the Palestinian climate.[152] As Australian immigration seemed ever more likely, she planned to visit Gershom in Palestine on her way to Sydney, explaining, "It is now allowed inside the [British] Empire."[153]

However, immigration remained controversial among Australians. Australian trade unions claimed that immigrants were taking jobs away from Australians. The unions had suffered major financial losses through failed strikes and feared that an influx of immigrants would break their power. Erich Scholem worried that if the Australian Labour Party returned to power, they would end immigration.[154] Antisemitism was also a significant factor, and in June 1938 the Australian government introduced a quota of three hundred landing permits for Jews per month, expressed a preference for Germans over Poles, and asked the Australian Jewish Welfare Society to screen applicants. At the Évian Conference, held in July 1938 to discuss the Jewish refugee problem, the French delegate asked the Australian delegate how Australia could be so restrictive when it was built on immigration and seemed to need more population. The Australian made it perfectly clear that his country wanted only British immigration.[155] Even Australian Jewish organizations discouraged mass immigration and encouraged new arrivals to adopt Australian customs as quickly as possible.[156]

Late 1938 and early 1939 were dark times for the Jews of Germany, which now also included Austria and the Sudetenland of Czechoslovakia. On the night of 9–10 November, the Nazis unleashed a wave of terror that surpassed anything undertaken in the previous six years. It has become known as Kristallnacht. Mobs of storm troopers and their associates ransacked Jewish property with virtually no restraint. Thousands of shops owned by German Jews had their windows smashed or were destroyed. Nearly thirty thousand

Jews were rounded up and sent to jails or concentration camps. Many Jews were simply killed in their homes or in prisons with no culpability. By the time the violence ended, over 250 synagogues had been burned. In most large cities, the fire departments had been called, but only to prevent the fires from spreading to non-Jewish property.[157] The police reported that many non-Jewish Berliners were outraged by the wanton violence and destruction, but they formed a distinct minority compared to those supporting the action, indifferent to it, or too cowed to comment.[158]

The Nazis eventually released most of the Jews sent to concentration camps right after Kristallnacht. For many of the prisoners, the conditions of their discharge included promises to emigrate from Germany as soon as possible, to transfer their property to a non-Jewish owner, and never to discuss their experiences in the camps.[159] Meanwhile, Nazi officials met with representatives of the insurance industry to decide what to do about claims for damages. Because of a change in German law, insurance companies were not obliged to cover damage from domestic unrest, but not paying claims might damage the industry's international reputation. Hermann Göring wished to confiscate the insurance payments for the German state. In any event, the Jews had to repair the damage of Kristallnacht at their own expense, and the government levied on them an additional fine of 1 billion reichsmarks.[160] Hermann Göring, who was largely responsible for this policy, commented, "I would not like to be a Jew in Germany."[161]

Indeed, after Kristallnacht, it was clear to all Jews that they had to leave Germany. Economic oppression and legal harassment had evolved into indiscriminate physical violence. Even the most optimistic German Jews realized that their situation was not going to improve under the Nazis. In the days after the pogrom, Betty wrote, "My son, I am despondent like never before, but the hope to be across the border one day keeps me going."[162]

Although remaining in Germany was unthinkable, departing Germany was no easy matter. First of all, one needed money to pay exploitative emigration taxes, buy steamship or airplane tickets, and pay for entry visas and other required paperwork. Jews could not export their assets, and Betty Scholem pawned her silver and jewelry for a pittance.[163] Even though, after Kristallnacht, the Australian government announced its willingness to take fifteen thousand refugees over three years, Erich still had trouble getting an Australian entry permit for his wife and family, who remained behind in Berlin, because he had not earned the necessary capital. The family worried that Erich's wife might have to immigrate as a domestic servant and his teenage daughter as a factory worker.[164] Naturally, one needed a valid passport, which for Jews was valid only for emigration and only issued with an entry permit for another country. Additionally, Betty needed a medical certificate. The examining doctor did not want her going to Palestine unless it was the only place she could go, and he also did not want her traveling alone. She then mentioned the possibility of going to Sydney with Erich's wife, Edith, and their children, and the doctor insisted on it. Rather than a prolonged stay with Gershom in Jerusalem, he would meet her at Port Said as her ship stopped en route to Australia.[165]

Moreover, new difficulties presented themselves: Edith and Erich were going to divorce. Still, Erich wanted Edith and the children to flee with Betty in early 1939. Not until Betty landed in Sydney did she learn the full truth about Erich's private life. Meanwhile, Betty got her passport and permission to emigrate before Edith and the children, who also had permits to enter Australia.[166] Eventually, permission was secured and tickets purchased.

At last, on 12 March 1939, Betty Scholem left Berlin forever. The first leg of her journey took her from Berlin to London. On her way, she would have to sleep sitting upright in her seat: "Jews are no longer permitted to travel in sleeping cars (!!), but I will also survive that night!" In London, she saw Werner's wife, Emmy. Five days after having left Berlin, Betty and Erich's family set sail for Sydney on the P&O Line's *Comorin*. Their six-week journey to the other side of the globe included ports of call at Gibraltar, Tangiers, Marseille, Port Said, Aden, Bombay, Colombo, Freemantle, Adelaide, and Melbourne.[167] As planned, in Port Said, Betty visited with Gershom and his second wife, Fania, who had come from Jerusalem. As he described it, "This is likely to be our last meeting by human reckoning."[168] At last, on 27 April, four months before the start of the Second World War, the *Comorin* sailed into Sydney harbor. Betty Scholem was safe.

The fortune that shone on her did not extend to Werner, who was still incarcerated. In September 1938, the Nazis transferred him once again, this time to the relatively new Buchenwald concentration camp, near the historic city of Weimar.[169] Work and living conditions in the new camp were even worse than those in Dachau, but the letters he received from his mother were a "source of strength" for him.[170] To secure Werner's release and emigration, Betty turned to the Aid Association of German Jews (Hilfsverein der Deutschen Juden) and an official there who had been acquainted with Werner's case.[171] This organization, founded in 1901, had provided aid to Jews living under oppressive political and economic conditions in eastern Europe; however, during the Nazi era, the organization turned inward, to help German Jews emigrate. It was able to assist ninety thousand Jews in leaving Germany for other countries, but, ultimately, Werner Scholem was not one of them.[172]

By the time Werner entered Buchenwald, there was new urgency to secure his release. His relatives were leaving Germany, if they could. The international political situation was deteriorating, war seemed imminent, and the Nazis' persecution of Jews reached new extremes. Moreover, after Kristallnacht, Jewish men were let out of the concentration camps only if they could immediately emigrate from Germany, adding to the complexity of arranging their release. Under these circumstances, the Scholems mounted an ever more frantic and bewildered campaign to get Werner discharged from the camps. Emmy turned to Karl Korsch, the famed German Marxist theorist who had settled in the United States, and others from their days as politically active Communists.[173] Edith Scholem, Erich's wife, who had not yet left Germany in January 1939, turned to the American consulate in Berlin.[174] Betty continued to work for Werner's release, though with little hope: "But I, unfortunately, do not believe there will be success, although he has to fill out all the applications. Their [the Nazis'] hunger for revenge is boundless."[175] After Betty and Edith left for Australia, Betty's brother Hans Hirsch remained in Berlin, and he tried Shanghai, China, as a destination for Werner.[176] Werner also gave power-of-attorney to Sophie Scholem, Uncle Georg's widow, to work for his release. She took care of all the necessary preparations, but Werner needed to retrieve his passport in person from the police, so she appealed to the camp authorities for his release. With a passport, he could get a visa, and with a visa, he could book passage on a ship.[177] There was a glimmer of hope. Then, the Nazis denied Werner's request for release without explanation. Hans and Sophie gave up on arranging transport to China as well as their attempts for Colombia.[178] Gerhard Pinthus, who ended up in Palestine after his own release from the concentration camps, told Gershom that he had the impression that Jewish prisoners might be released if their emigration papers were completed: "Lately, the State Police are causing no problems, even releasing political prisoners to go there [Palestine]." But time was of the essence. As the number of Jewish prisoners in Buchenwald decreased, the conditions for those remaining deteriorated.[179]

Some German Jews could get out, and some could not. Betty, Reinhold, and Erich made their new home in Sydney, Australia. Theobald and his wife, Hedwig, fled Germany in 1938, settling in Tel Aviv.[180] Theobald had been a Zionist for nearly four decades, and Hedwig's enthusiasm for Zionism and the Yishuv had long surpassed his. Betty wrote that Hedwig's "longing for 30 years has been fulfilled."[181] A cousin named Max Borchardt escaped to Shanghai. Sophie Scholem made it out as late as March 1940. After a harrowing wartime sea voyage from Rotterdam to South Africa, she settled in Johannesburg, before later going to Australia.[182] Betty's brother Hans Hirsch looked to his international connections for succor. In 1939 the *Bulletin of the American Ceramic Society* printed an article entitled "Hans Hirsch Must Leave Germany," and detailed Hirsch's many professional accomplishments, presumably in the hope that some American ceramics manufacturer would want to secure his services and facilitate his immigration.[183] Ultimately, he made it to Brazil, but Betty's sister, Käte Hirsch Schiepan, was among the approximately 164,000 Jews, mainly women, remaining in Germany in October 1941 when the Nazis banned Jewish emigration from Germany.[184]

In 1938, not long after losing her medical license during the final Aryanization of the German medical profession, Käte's non-Jewish husband announced he was divorcing her "because of racial reasons." Though the majority of intermarried couples persevered under the difficult circumstances, the case of Walter Schiepan and Käte Hirsch Schiepan was not unique. Indeed, for such couples, social ostracism was common, and the non-Jewish partner frequently faced professional difficulties because of the mixed marriage. The regime cajoled, bribed, and even punished non-Jews into divorcing their Jewish spouses, and the courts made it exceedingly easy for non-Jews to divorce their Jewish wives or husbands.[185] However, race was not the only factor for the Schiepans. Käte's husband was having an affair with a much younger woman and claimed that he wanted a new life, including children.[186]

In her case, as in so many others, the divorce had devastating consequences for the Jewish partner. Divorced from her non-Jewish husband, who might have afforded her some protection from the worst persecution, Käte faced deportation to the unknown. Finally, in 1942 the Nazis sent her to Theresienstadt, a former Austrian (later Czechoslovak) fortress turned into a ghetto/concentration camp. Even then, the family maintained hope. The Nazis touted Theresienstadt as the model camp. After temporarily cleaning up the camp and feeding the surviving inmates better, the Nazis allowed a Red Cross inspection, which was closely managed. The elaborate hoax worked, even among Jews. In November 1944, Gershom wrote to his mother that it was some consolation that Käte had been sent to the model concentration camp, which even the Red Cross could visit, unlike other deportation destinations. He commented, "Some minimum of minimum will still be maintained there." He promised to inquire if he could send his aunt a package.[187] In fact, when he wrote those lines, she had been dead for over a year. Though Käte continued to work as a nurse after her arrival in Theresienstadt, her own health deteriorated rapidly, and she died in July 1943.[188] Her ex-husband lived with his new wife in Berlin, but he suffered fatal injuries from a bomb explosion during the battle for Berlin in late April 1945.[189]

In 1940 Werner was the last of the Scholems in Germany, imprisoned in the Buchenwald concentration camp with no chance of release. Additionally, most of his fellow Marxists in Buchenwald—particularly the Stalinist Communists—ostracized him as a Trotskyite, and he did nothing to diminish their animosity. Although the Nazis were the ultimate arbiters of life and death, many communist inmates had tremendous power within the camp. For years, the Communists had competed with the criminal inmates for control of inmate society. Once in control, the Communists even maintained a court to try those who threatened their determination of camp order or worked as SS informers.[190] Communist kapos were known to terrorize other concentration camp inmates, and they also had some influence with the Nazi guards who operated the camp, which was perilous for Werner Scholem.[191]

According to the camp survivor Ernst Federn, repeating what he had heard directly from Werner Scholem, one day in early July 1940, Buchenwald's Moor Express received a new foreman, who switched Werner from pushing the wagon to pulling the wagon, a much more onerous task. Werner became enraged and accused the new headman of acting out of political motivation. The perplexed foreman sought clarification from the supervising kapo, a Stalinist Communist, who then had Werner sent to work in the Buchenwald quarry.[192]

For most prisoners, quarry work was a death sentence. They worked cutting immense blocks of stone and transported them uphill without machinery. Even more grotesque, since the stone could not be sold to local construction companies to build buildings, it was merely ground up for use as gravel. The supervising kapos at the quarry were among the most brutal in Buchenwald. Deadly accidents, fatal beatings, and shootings were daily occurrences at the quarry.[193] Werner would have known that before his transfer.

Werner was luckily not set to work lifting heavy stones. However, some days later, on 17 July, two SS men, Eduard Hinkelmann and Johann Blank, went to Werner and said that they needed someone for work outside the guards' cordon. Blank took him beyond the security line and shot him with his revolver.[194] On Werner Scholem's concentration camp registration card, someone wrote, "Shot while trying to escape, 17 July 1940."[195]

Why did the SS murder Werner Scholem after seven years in the concentration camps? While the actual murder was strictly the work of the SS, is it possible that Hinkelmann and Blank were acting on a denunciation from the Communists? Ernst Federn clearly accused the "Stalinist prisoners' organization in the camp" of inciting the guards to murder Werner. Additionally, in Federn's view, the timing of Werner's death might not have been an accident.

Writing forty years after the fact, Federn noted that Stalin had Leon Trotsky murdered in 1940, though it strains belief to think that the long-standing attempt to murder Stalin's great rival might have been connected with the murder of this one oppositional Communist in the concentration camps.[196] Nonetheless, based on Federn's testimony, one scholar wrote, "The politically abandoned Werner Scholem was the victim of a vendetta in the camp, although I consciously leave it open who was most responsible for his murder: the SS or the camp's Communists."[197] Four decades later, when details of the story of Werner's death and the Communists' alleged role in it reached Gershom in Jerusalem, he was very skeptical. He reported to a cousin, "Emmy [Werner's widow] told me that once again, Werner personally stood rather good with people who remained in the Communist Party, also in the concentration camp, or especially in the concentration camp. And she received several messages about it from trustworthy sources."[198] While Emmy's view did not correspond to the reality of Werner's experience in the camps, she may have been correct about the Communists' noninvolvement in his death. Various scholars dispute the connection between vengeful Stalinist Communists and the SS man who pulled the trigger. Ultimately, it is possible that there was no instigation for Werner's death. By 1940 gratuitous murders were an everyday occurrence in Buchenwald.[199] Simply put, it remains unclear to this day exactly why Werner Scholem was murdered in July 1940.

Word of Werner's death, without any specific details, reached Betty Scholem in mid-September from her cousin Arthur Hirsch, who lived in Zurich. Betty shared the news with Emmy in London: "So is our Werner dead."[200] Betty was stunned. The whole time, she had never given up hope that he would be released. She wrote to Gershom, "The only thing that can console me is that I never deserted him and did everything humanly possible for his release. The conflict because of Werner goes back 30 years like a black thread through my life, and I always stuck by him, and now it ends so!"[201] Three years later, when Emmy Scholem applied for British citizenship, she was rejected. The justification was that she could not petition for naturalization in her own name because she was married and there was no evidence of a divorce or death of her husband.[202]

The story of the Scholems in the 1930s, like that of most German Jews, was one of dispersal or destruction. For Werner Scholem, Käte Hirsch Schiepan, and many other Germans of Jewish descent, there was no escape—only a journey of imprisonment, ending in death. For Betty, Reinhold, Erich, and most Jews living in Germany in 1933, their flight from the Nazis took them to countries of cold refuge around the world. Some waited for the Third Reich's defeat in the hope of returning home, but most built new lives for themselves in places as diverse as Australia, Brazil, Britain, Cuba, Palestine, South Africa, or the United States, to name a few. Indeed, it was in New York, Los Angeles, Tel Aviv, Jerusalem, London, and Sydney that the remnants of historic German Jewry lived on, even as Jewish life in Germany and the long German-Jewish century came to an end.

CHAPTER 8

Cresting of the Fifth Wave

Gershom Scholem's Palestine in the 1930s

By the 1930s, Palestine was no longer marginal to the Jewish world, though it was not quite the center of Jewish life, as Gershom Scholem insisted it was or should be. The Jewish population of the British Mandate of Palestine—officially 174,610 people in 1931—was approximately only 1 percent of the worldwide Jewish population, but it was growing rapidly and had doubled its proportion in a decade.[1] Regardless, the Jewish settlement in Palestine was symbolically important. It was a place where the so-called normalization and regeneration of the Jewish people would take place. Rather than occupying a narrow range of professions, as they historically had in Europe, Jews practiced every profession in Palestine. Guided by Labor Zionist ideology, sallow urban intellectuals from Europe re-created themselves as healthy agriculturalists in Palestine, often living on collective farms. Palestine also represented an attempt to reestablish Jewish political sovereignty after nineteen hundred years. Even if Jewish statehood was not within sight as the decade began, the Yishuv had representative institutions, health care infrastructure, and a school system. In Tel Aviv, nearly an entirely Jewish city, Jews actually did control the mechanisms of government, which used Hebrew, no less. In practical terms, Palestine seemed to offer a haven to oppressed European Jews, especially after the United States effectively ceased accepting eastern European immigrants in 1924. Throughout the 1930s, the Palestine question became increasingly crucial to Jewish communities around the world. What had been something of a curiosity and even an experiment in 1923, when Gershom immigrated, was important in 1933 and critical by 1938.

The growth of Palestine's Jewish population necessitated new infrastructure. Tel Aviv grew rapidly, from 2,000 inhabitants in 1919 to 40,000 at the end of the 1920s to 160,000 by the end of the 1930s.[2] The Jewish population of Jerusalem, the territory's administrative capital, also grew rapidly. While only 33,391 Jews lived in Jerusalem in 1922, by 1931, 51,222 Jews did. Only four years later, an estimated 70,000 Jews lived there, out of a total population of approximately 120,000.[3] The historic residential quarters clustered around the walled Old City were no longer sufficient for the city's burgeoning Jewish professional and administrative class. Meanwhile, several coinciding factors facilitated the construction of new neighborhoods. The Greek Orthodox Patriarchate of Jerusalem was compelled to sell some of its property outside the Old City to settle its enormous debts. Thus, land became available. Additionally, improvements in transportation and construction techniques made it possible to build in remote areas and on the hilly terrain in West Jerusalem.[4] As a result, developers built new residential quarters, one of which became inextricably associated with Gershom Scholem and his circle.

In November 1932, after living for years near Mea Shearim, a centrally situated, ultra-Orthodox neighborhood, in an old house without running water or electricity, Gershom and Escha moved to Rehavia, a neighborhood on the western edge of Jerusalem, featuring modern houses, budding greenery, and refined cafés. It became famous in the 1930s as the Jerusalem district of choice for educated, secular, and liberal Jews from central Europe.[5] Their homes were known for heavy bourgeois furniture, sideboards filled with porcelain dishes, book-lined shelves, and often pianos—a stark contrast to the Spartan aesthetic encouraged by socialist Zionism. Among Rehavia's residents were the Scholems, the scholars Hugo Bergmann and Shlomo Dov Goitein, Zionist officials Kurt Blumenfeld and Arthur Ruppin, and the writer Else Lasker-Schüler. In time, Rehavia became more than merely the name of a residential district. In the words of one former resident and an expert on urban planning in Jerusalem, Rehavia stood "for a political status symbol, for an Ashkenazi-secular elitism, and for the left-bourgeois 'nobility,' an affluent and arrogant aristocracy."[6] Here, according to the legend, leaders of commerce, banking, the judiciary, academia, medicine, and culture lived side by side. In fact, the Scholems and the Bergmanns built a duplex together—immortalized by Lasker-Schüler in her travelogue *Das Hebräerland* (Land of the Hebrews)—and the Scholems paid for their share with Escha's money, though they still had to cut corners on the construction, opting for concrete instead of stone. Nonetheless, Gershom had a lovely home library built. Indeed, the plans and description of the house at 53 Rambam Street formed a notable part of Gershom's correspondence with his mother that year, even though he originally forgot to mention the move to her and she heard about it from friends.[7] Walter Benjamin wrote to Gershom, "I trust that your life in your own house will get off to a happy start." In Gershom's own words, "These wishes were unfortunately not fulfilled, and I left the house to my first wife, Elsa (Escha) Burchhardt (1896–1978) when we divorced in 1936."[8]

In 1933, as dark clouds gathered over Germany, the shadow extended to Palestine. Everyone there with relatives in Germany was urgently concerned about their loved ones, for the "sad prognoses about the fate of the German Jews are not only fulfilled, but rather have been exceeded a thousand-fold," as Gershom wrote—and this was still years before the Holocaust.[9] In March, he confided to Walter Benjamin, "People are generally unsure, both here and in Germany, whether or not to expect a strong wave of emigration from Germany." He added that the government preferred that German Jews immigrate rather than Polish or Romanian Jews, but he stressed that Palestine needed manual laborers and not more university graduates, even though doctors, lawyers, and professors were expected. "The only profession likely to do well under these circumstances will be that of the Hebrew teacher!"[10] By June, he reported to his friend, "My German acquaintances are meanwhile streaming here in growing numbers, to say nothing of people I do not know." Gershom did not view this development positively: "One hears German spoken on the streets to such an extent here, and even more conspicuously in Tel Aviv . . . that it makes people like me feel even more like withdrawing into Hebrew."[11] He actively discouraged his relatives from immigrating to Palestine. In his estimation, Palestine was a land for young, Hebrew-speaking immigrants, and it did not need more German-language printers. Yet ever more Germans came to Palestine, including many acquaintances of Gershom and Escha.[12]

In his correspondence with family and friends, Gershom did not shy away from harsh criticism of German Jewry, despite its tragic situation. Contrasting the Jews of Germany in 1933 with the Jews of Spain in 1492, he noted that "there were no 'Spanish nationalist' Jews who continued to lick the boot that kicked them."[13] Even those who fled to the Jewish national home came in for criticism: "The Germans perceived the Jews to be foreigners and even a portion of the Jews felt alien in Germany. But here the Jews, who are overwhelmingly from eastern Europe, perceive the German Jews as foreigners. They notice more German than Jewish in them."[14] He illustrated his point with a telling anecdote: "On one of the last ships, there arrived a district court judge, who explained to the relief committee that he is ready to do any kind of work, demands only a minimum wage (nonetheless approximately RM 200), and would *even*, if it were necessary, give up his title. For this gentleman such a proclamation is surely an expression of the most extreme sacrifice; for a local Jew, it is an incomprehensible curiosity."[15] He expected the esteemed Jewish studies scholar Martin Buber to experience a crisis when he moved from Germany to Palestine and had to converse regularly in Hebrew.[16] Indeed, Gershom Scholem felt only a little guilty about bursting the German Jews' bubble and sharing his highly Zionist, "uncharitable analysis of the dream world German Jews have been living in," as he explained it to Walter Benjamin.[17] And he was not alone. A key aspect of Zionist ideology was the negation of the Diaspora: the belief that Jewish life outside of the Land of Israel was wracked by discrimination and assimilation in the short term and doomed to destruction in the long term. According to this view of Jewish history and contemporary Jewish life, only Israel offered a solution to the Jews' problem.

Despite Gershom Scholem's Zionism—or perhaps because of his prominence among Zionist intellectuals—he was renowned in Jewish Germany. University-educated German Jews wrote to him, asking if he knew of any employment for them in their professions in Palestine, and he helped some of his old friends according to their qualifications.[18] Sophie Scholem, Georg's widow, got lost looking for Reinhold, Erich, and Betty's vacation home outside Berlin. She asked a stranger for directions, and he replied, "Are you perhaps related to Prof. Sch. in Jerusalem!" The man knew Gershom's work from reading the *Jüdische Rundschau*.[19] Reinhold had a similar conversation with a Berlin rabbi.[20] Sophie's son Ernst wanted to read in the library of the Lehranstalt für die Wissenschaft des Judentums (School for Jewish Studies), and he was told that he needed someone to vouch for him. When he said his name, they immediately asked, "Oh! Are you perhaps . . . etc.? Then you don't need a guarantor!"[21]

With increasing persecution and economic distress in Germany, ever more Jews sought refuge in Palestine, where their presence was symbolically and practically meaningful. At the end of 1935, Gershom wrote to his mother that Gertrud Zucker, sister of Theobald Scholem's wife, Hedwig, was in Palestine. Zucker claimed that all the good things in Palestine resulted from the arrival of new German-Jewish immigrants. Because of them, there were new streets and stores that sold elegant goods for which old settlers should be grateful. Gershom could not convince her that Palestine did not need luxury shops. He explained that the early settlers had come to a wilder, stranger land without connections.[22] In fact, it is illuminating to examine the impact that the newcomers had on life in the Yishuv.

Between 1933 and 1941, approximately sixty thousand Jews from central Europe came to Palestine.[23] So many arrived that the Fifth *Aliyah* is largely associated with them, even though they made up less than half of the new-comers during that wave of Jewish immigration to Palestine. Despite Ger-shom Scholem's understandable skepticism and Gertrud Zucker's boasting, the central European migrants—often undifferentiatedly considered Ger-mans (or "Yekkim" in Hebrew slang)—did significantly alter Palestine and Zionism itself.

As part of its mission and self-understanding, Yishuv Zionism intended to transform "unhealthy," European Jews and Jewry into a nation of healthy, vigorous settlers with an organic connection to the land. The movement dis-proportionately emphasized agricultural settlements, and its predominant political variant in Palestine was socialism as championed by Labor Zionist political parties and labor unions. However, the arrival of so many bourgeois, liberal, urban-oriented Jews from central Europe challenged that narrative, and even if they did not achieve political control over the Zionist movement, they succeeded in transforming the quotidian culture of the Yishuv.

Thousands of Jewish immigrants from Germany, especially those older than thirty, did not opt for life on a kibbutz, preferring to settle in cities. Many German immigrants had capital for investment in commercial enterprises, which contributed to a burgeoning European-style consumer culture in the Yishuv.[24] In 1933 the Jewish Agency for Palestine and the Zionist Federation of Germany concluded the Haavara (or Transfer) Agreement with Nazi Ger-many's Ministry of Economics, permitting German Jews to use their assets to purchase German-made goods for export to Palestine, which could then be redeemed for local currency. Though very controversial, it helped foster the Yishuv economy and mitigated the plight of German-Jewish immigrants to Palestine, who might have otherwise been destitute.[25] Soon, these immi-grants founded and patronized cafés, restaurants, guesthouses, cinemas, and fancy food shops that one would expect to find in upper-middle-class neigh-borhoods in European cities.[26] Gertrud Zucker and her husband, Ludwig, operated a boardinghouse in Jerusalem. Immigrants from Germany signifi-cantly upgraded medical and scientific research institutions. They opened industrial firms and supplied farms with modern agricultural products. Even lawyers, physicians, and shopkeepers who became farmers established middle-class villages rather than Spartan collective farms. Nonetheless, many German Jews saw Palestine as a significant drop in their quality of life, materially and culturally.[27]

German Jews also made significant contributions to the establishment of the judiciary, the state bureaucracy, and academia. Many of them had experience in the German judiciary and civil service. Their training in law and political science inculcated them with respect for the rule of law and a responsive state. They wished to re-create German standards of public services and order in the Yishuv; however, in the face of opposition from entrenched interests, they were only partially successful. The German-Jewish immigrants found it even harder to affect Yishuv politics. The existing political parties, dominated by eastern European Jews, did not enthusiastically welcome German-Jewish members. Even dedicated, longtime Zionists from Germany found it hard to break into the ranks of the Zionist leadership in Palestine. Additionally, non-Zionist and tepidly Zionist immigrants from Germany disproportionately espoused liberal political views and did not view the non-Jewish state, including the British Mandate administration, with hostility. In 1932 German Jews formed their own representation group, the Hitachdut Olei Germania (Association of Immigrants from Germany), which later expanded to include Austrian Jews. This group ultimately split into a social welfare organization, Irgun Olei Merkaz Europa (Organization of Immigrants from Central Europe), and a political party, Aliyah Hadasha (New Immigration). The latter achieved great success during the war years, but soon declined and merged with other nonsocialist political parties.[28]

It was very difficult for many German-Jewish immigrants to adapt to their new lives.[29] Most of them came to Palestine because they had to, not because they wanted to, and before 1933, they had not been dyed-in-the-wool Zionists. A popular joke told of two immigrants who met in Palestine, and one said to the other, "Are you coming from conviction or from Germany?"[30] Indeed, they were often out of place. They brought with them European clothes unsuited to the climate and European attitudes on dress, food, and comportment that were out of step with conventions in the Yishuv. Many struggled to find enduring jobs that had any relation to their old professions. Hence the story about laborers with doctorates: "Here is your next brick, Herr Doktor." "Thank you, Herr Doktor." "You're welcome, Herr Doktor."[31] They struggled with the language, and in the 1930s, one could hear German ubiquitously spoken in parts of Tel Aviv, Haifa, and Jerusalem, which Hebrew-oriented Zionist settlers found offensive. Even worse in the eyes of some, the German Jews persisted in celebrating "Christian" holidays, such as New Year's Day on 1 January.[32] In general, they did not fit in with the prevailing culture or the Labor Zionist–inflected collectivist ethos. In the words of one German immigrant, their new life was "a difficult break, which has never really ended."[33] Younger immigrants, who were still of school age or just starting careers, integrated more easily. And the immigrants' children and grandchildren, educated in Hebrew and socialized by Yishuv or Israeli institutions, adopted the norms and values of the dominant society. Decades later, many of the immigrants fully regarded Israel as home, but had an unreconciled German-Israeli identity.

In the short run, the Fifth *Aliyah* increased the Jewish proportion of the total population in Palestine to the point that British Mandate leaders could not ignore Jewish concerns. The refugees' successful accommodation proved the Yishuv's capacity to absorb massive numbers of immigrants and to create a variegated society, which abetted the absorption of future waves of immigrants. Zionist leaders could foresee a time when Palestine would have a Jewish majority, based purely on immigration trends.[34]

Language was a focal point of the German-Jewish immigrants' practical difficulties, and even Gershom Scholem, living in Jerusalem since 1923, wrestled with the theoretical question of language. As he planned a big, introductory book on the Kabbalah, he was reluctant to write it in German; however, his German was more refined than his Hebrew, which he also spoke fluently. He debated writing and publishing the book in Hebrew and then rewriting it in German or writing it in German and having the publisher translate it into Hebrew for simultaneous publication. If he published the book in German first, given the chance to publish it in Hebrew, he would be accused of disloyalty.[35] He told Walter Benjamin that he wanted to publish it first in Hebrew "for moral reasons."[36] Moreover, Scholem's most important scholarly article of this era was written and first published in Hebrew. Later translated into English as "Redemption through Sin," it was an illumination and reconsideration of Sabbateanism in the era after Shabbetai Zevi's conversion to Islam. "But this essay, which would be of great interest to you, can only be written in Hebrew anyway, at least if the author is to remain free from apologetic inhibitions," Gershom explained to Benjamin.[37] Thus, the essay's controversial subject, rather than purely linguistic political considerations, influenced the choice of language.

In fact, when it came to the choice of language, Gershom did continue to write many works in German, even in the mid-1930s.[38] It was, after all, his native language, but there was another reason. German-language scholarship was more accessible to an international audience than Hebrew-language scholarship, even among Jewish scholars.[39] Writing for an American Jewish audience some years later, he composed his essays originally in German and had them translated into English.[40] Looking back on the 1930s, Gershom wrote that he maintained contact with the German language until 1933, when Hitler introduced a new phase of German. Thereafter, Gershom considered himself an "old-fashioned author," who used outdated expressions or turns of phrase that had acquired new meaning in the interval. Nonetheless, he had misgivings about modern Hebrew. The Hebrew language had changed dramatically since he had begun studying it, and he seemed disappointed that the language of the Book had become the "language of babbling children."[41]

By the 1930s, Gershom Scholem's career began to take off, a development he noted with his characteristic combination of wit and vanity. Writing about his latest book project, he joked, "I estimate the book to be 250 pages, and the publisher is the finest publishing house in the world, namely the University of Jerusalem Press. Naturally, there are publishers galore here. What an idea? We are a civilized people, after all."[42] He realized that his career had the potential to enter a new phase, but a little self-promotion would not hurt. He wrote to his mother, "I think it is time to do something for my professorship. What is Soncino Society really there for??," meaning the Jewish bibliophile society in which his brothers were very active.[43] He knew that his family in Berlin basked in his reflected fame, which had spread to Germany.[44] However, beyond his control was the fact that the university struggled financially, and at one point, he actually feared losing his position.[45]

In 1932 Gershom was able to take a research leave from the university. Among his destinations were the Vatican Library and the Biblioteca Casanatense in Rome, where he worked all day, without even a lunch break. His mother chided him that he did not take more time for sightseeing during his European trip. She found it incomprehensible that he could not step back from his manuscripts even to take a day-trip to Naples or to see the Isle of Capri.[46] In fact, it was during this time that Scholem began his long association with the publisher Schocken Books, founded by the department store magnate and Zionist administrator Salman Schocken.[47] Connections were critical for the promotion of one's scholarship, and Martin Buber had informed Schocken about Scholem's research on the Kabbalah.[48] It was not long before the publishing house began to regard Scholem as a very difficult author, someone who promised big things but did not follow through.[49]

Soon, it was unclear exactly what Gershom's future status at the university would be: as a professor of history of religion, Jewish philosophy, or Kabbalistic studies? He agreed to teach Jewish philosophy until the university could hire someone to teach the field, something he feared would take a long time. In fact, "the German catastrophe," as he put it, led to an influx of Jewish academics to Palestine, including Julius Guttmann, who taught philosophy. Gershom Scholem was now free to concentrate on the Kabbalah. In late summer 1933, the university appointed him to a full professorship for the study of Jewish mysticism.[50] Betty was overjoyed to hear the news: "At first, your card fell out of the letter, and as I read Prof. Dr. Scholem, I just had to start bawling and could not read the letter." When she regained her composure, she began calling their acquaintances to share the rare good news. Even if the position did not come with a raise, it still brought honor, "and honor is also worth something, more than money!," in Betty's words.[51]

The university grew dramatically as a result of the political situation in Europe. Dozens of new professors and hundreds more students joined the university. There were always new faces in Scholem's lectures.[52] A faculty of sciences opened in 1935. Scholem found the expansion, and specifically the division of labor in the philosophy program, to his liking. Guttmann, who represented an older European liberal tradition, taught rationalism, and Scholem taught the Kabbalah. Having someone else to teach philosophy also enabled Scholem to be less evenhanded in his presentation of history and philosophy.[53]

Scholem was a prominent figure at the university and a leader of the humanities faculty, serving in the university senate and on many powerful committees.[54] He wanted Judah Magnes to resign as chancellor of the university, and when that did not happen, he supported an effort to reorganize the university in 1935. Magnes received the title of president, but without any significant powers. Real management of the university fell to Salman Schocken as chairman of the Executive Council and to Hugo Bergmann as the rector, the equivalent of provost at an American university. In a letter to his mother, Scholem claimed that he had managed Bergmann's election to the position.[55] A few years later, Scholem became dean of the Faculty of Humanities and later served as head of the Institute of Jewish Studies. In the 1930s, he also worked to bring Martin Buber to Palestine for a position at the university, finally succeeding in May 1938.[56] As Scholem grew famous in the Yishuv intelligentsia in the 1930s, his intellectual pugnaciousness did not abate. He boasted to Walter Benjamin how he launched into a "tempestuous" critique of Franz Rosenzweig at a commemoration for the man's fiftieth birthday.[57]

On one occasion, Gershom Scholem's combination of wit and high self-regard backfired. It had long been a tradition for serious book collectors to print catalogues of their collections. However, in 1936 Gershom commissioned a catalogue of all the desired books *not already* in his collection. The brochure bore the title "Kuntres alu le Shalom," a pun that referred to the Book of Genesis ("Go you up in peace," Gen. 45:17) and to himself ("Go to Scholem"). Gershom hoped that some book dealers might have the items he wanted and would let him know, but he inadvertently drove up the prices of all the books he wanted.[58] His personal library overwhelmed his home, and he resorted to keeping some books in the dining room, in a cabinet that he had painted green to match the furniture.[59]

Life at 53 Rambam Street was not always harmonious, and the Scholems' and Bergmanns' marriages deteriorated in the 1930s, ending with a double divorce and double remarriage: Hugo Bergmann marrying Escha Scholem and Gershom Scholem marrying his student Fania Freud. As early as 1932, Gershom Scholem mentioned Fania Freud to Walter Benjamin, referring to her as "Tom Freud's niece," the latter being an acquaintance of Benjamin.[60] The following year, he mentioned Fania to his mother. Referring to the guests at a birthday party for Escha's cousin, he wrote, "I invited a student of mine who is the same age as her. A catlike young being, about whom one will someday be able to say that she is the first professionally educated female Kabbalist."[61] There is no doubt that Gershom felt drawn to Fania.

Another strain on the Scholems' marriage was Escha's chronically poor health, and she seems to have suffered from depression.[62] Her sciatica necessitated long stays at the spa in Tiberias. These sojourns were costly and meant that she was not working full time, which taxed the Scholems' budget.[63] It is also possible that Gershom did not like having to fend for himself during Escha's incapacitation or absences. He enjoyed being taken care of by women, such as Escha and his mother, rather than having to take care of them. He had also taken to calling her ailment "eschiatica."[64] Incidentally, Hugo Bergmann went to visit Escha during her time in Tiberias, which caused tension with Gershom.[65] Meanwhile, Gershom spent the summer of 1934 in Jerusalem, where he studied the *Zohar* for an hour a day with a group of devoted students, including Fania.[66]

In late 1934 or early 1935, matters came to a head. Gershom learned that Escha and Bergmann were having an affair. Gershom and Escha discussed a divorce, while Hugo Bergmann wanted to divorce his wife, Else. From Tiberias, where Escha was physically convalescing and perhaps seeking a respite from the tumult of her life in Jerusalem, she and Gershom entered into negotiations on the particulars of their divorce. Their correspondence on the matter descended into recriminations and indignant defenses. Nonetheless, Escha declared her enduring affection for Gershom and continued to ask tenderly after his well-being and professional activity.[67] Meanwhile, Hugo Bergmann's divorce—which affected the Scholems' divorce and remarriages—depended on the consent of Mrs. Bergmann, who kept changing her mind about the matter. She even felt she was being blackmailed into divorcing and hired a Tel Aviv lawyer to represent her.[68] After learning that Gershom had initiated the Scholems' divorce, she accused Hugo of feeling "obligated" to marry Escha and doing it unwillingly.[69]

As things dragged on, Gershom hesitated to inform either his mother or close friend Walter Benjamin what was happening. Eventually, Betty

Scholem learned about Gershom and Escha's divorce, but not about Hugo Bergmann. Escha also went to pains to prevent her family from learning the complete truth of the situation.[70] Even as her own divorce seemed certain, Escha was indecisive about marrying Bergmann, and she expressed sincere concerns about Gershom marrying Fania.[71] Gershom Scholem had been the center of Escha's world for nearly fifteen years, and as their marriage dissolved, she maintained tender and grateful feelings toward him. She wrote, "You have been so unspeakably much to me—my husband and also the child that I was not allowed to bear—and though it ends so bitterly and in such anguish, let me thank you once again and call you 'My Dear' without you withdrawing into yourself."[72]

Additionally, as the divorces moved forward, the dispensation of the joint house became a serious issue, and Escha and Gershom went back and forth over who would keep the house and furniture. She promised Gershom, "not to squeeze you like a lemon and not to hunt and torment you."[73] Nonetheless, she was adamant that it was primarily her money that had paid for their half of the duplex at 53 Rambam Street. She informed the lawyer Felix Rosenblüth that she was willing to pay back the hundred pounds, plus interest, that Gershom had invested in the house.[74] Gershom was extremely concerned about the financial ramifications of his divorce—namely, supporting two households if Escha remained unmarried.[75] In fact, Escha married Hugo Bergmann and later had two daughters, Chana and Nechama. Bergmann's first wife left Jerusalem.[76] By contrast, Gershom moved to a pension at 28 Abarbanel Street, only a two-minute walk from his old house. The boardinghouse, owned and operated by Helene Cohn, was very popular with German-speaking visitors to Jerusalem. Additionally, both Gershom's old home and his new residence had been designed by Helene's sister, the architect Lotte Cohn. The Cohn sisters were from Steglitz, a suburb of Berlin, and had come to Jerusalem in 1921.[77]

Gershom's life as a bachelor was short-lived. On 4 December 1936, the day before his thirty-ninth birthday, he married Fania. He had wanted to get married on his birthday, but it fell on Shabbat. Among the guests at the wedding were many members of Jerusalem's intelligentsia as well as his cousin Eva, Theobald's daughter.[78] Betty Scholem was happy that her son had remarried, but the family was also full of questions: When did Gershom and Fania's friendship turn into love? Could Fania cook? What about the rabbi who married them? Betty expressed surprise that Fania's family, from Poland, had opposed her Zionism. Betty had thought that only assimilated Jews in the West had opposed Zionism.[79] A few months later, replying to a letter in which Gershom mentioned that Fania was sick, Betty scolded her son for his financial mismanagement: "For ten years, I have only heard from you how much money illnesses cost and you do not have a red cent, and now you are carrying on like this?! At the same time, it is on my mind, why don't you economize?" She noted that all their married friends regularly dined at home, but Gershom and Fania seemed to eat out all the time.[80]

Escha did not evince bitterness about the turn of events. Writing a letter to Gershom from New York, where she had gone with Hugo Bergmann only months after the weddings, she expressly included, "best greetings also to Fanja [sic]."[81] Incidentally, her marriage to Bergmann met with approval from their friend Martin Buber, who told Bergmann that Bergmann and Escha belonged together. Buber added that in any other country, it would not matter if they were married, but Palestine was a glass house and he was rector of the university. Thus, they had to marry to live together.[82] Gershom wanted to bring Fania to Europe to meet his family, but she was unable to receive a visa for Germany, and the trip was canceled.[83]

Gershom Scholem also had the fate of friends in Europe on his mind. Throughout the 1930s, and especially after the Nazis came to power in Germany, he tried to help Walter Benjamin. Benjamin was facing financial disaster and, unbeknownst to Scholem, contemplating suicide. Many years later, Scholem came across a will that Benjamin had written at the time, granting all his manuscripts to Scholem. He wanted Scholem to preserve these writings in the university library in Jerusalem or the Prussian State Library. He also gave Scholem the rights to publish anything he had written. He wanted "about 40–60%" of the profits to go to his son Stefan. However, in 1932, Benjamin's desire to live prevailed.[84] The two men continued to correspond intensely, but they did not see each other again for several years, being unable to coordinate their work plans and travel schedules. Indeed, their separation affected their correspondence and led to circumspection.

As Scholem worked to foster his relationship with the Jewish publishing patron Salman Schocken, he tried to get Schocken interested in Benjamin. Benjamin was working on a book about Franz Kafka and asked Scholem to get him a commission for it.[85] Scholem suggested that Schocken Books have Benjamin publish an essay on Kafka for the Schocken *Almanach*, but the press declined, not wanting to offend Max Brod, Kafka's close friend, future biographer, and literary executor, who was publishing Kafka's complete works with Schocken.[86] By the late 1930s, Scholem was firmly in Schocken's stable of authors, and his affiliation with Schocken coincided with his ties to the intelligentsia of the Yishuv, many of whom also published with Schocken and were also born or educated in Germany or Austria. When *Die Geheimnisse der Schöpfung* (The Secret of Creation) came out, Gershom asked

Salman Schocken to send copies to the novelist S. Y. Agnon, historian Fritz (Yitzhak) Baer, philosopher Hugo (Shmuel) Bergmann, architect Lotte Cohn, philosopher Hans Jonas, jurist Felix Rosenblüth (Pinchas Rosen), pedagogue Ernst (Akiva) Simon, physicist Samuel (Shmuel) Sambursky, and artist Anna Ticho, among others.[87]

Scholem was not just a man of pure scholarship. He was also deeply concerned about the nature of Zionism and the fate of the Yishuv. As the conflict between Arabs and Jews in Palestine intensified, Gershom Scholem found himself alienated from the Zionist movement. Already at the time of the Arab riots in 1929 and the stormy Seventeenth Zionist Congress in 1931, Gershom Scholem advocated a policy of Arab-Jewish reconciliation and, even more controversially, binationalism. By the 1930s, he saw the Zionist movement as self-defeating, largely because of its political nature. While Scholem had always been a Zionist, his Zionism was chiefly cultural.[88] But the movement was increasingly intensely political. In June 1933, Haim Arlosoroff, a socialist member of the Zionist Executive and director of the Jewish Agency's Political Department, was assassinated while walking along the beach in Tel Aviv with his wife. Although the police arrested three Revisionist Zionists for the murder, they were eventually acquitted, and the murder remains a mystery to this day.[89] Gershom Scholem had been friends with Arlosoroff during his Berlin Zionist days and, in a letter to his mother, blamed "Jews of an extreme revisionist tendency" for this "very evil political murder."[90] Later that year, the Palestinian Arab leadership declared a one-day general strike against Jewish immigration and the sale of property to Jews, and there were bloody battles between the British Mandate police and some Arabs.[91] However, that was only a mere hint of the violence to erupt in 1936.

For years, an increasing stream of Jewish immigration from Europe enlarged the population of the Yishuv and inflamed Arab nationalists. In the spring of 1936, Palestinian Arabs rose up in armed protest that escalated into a large-scale rebellion. Arab insurgents began ambushing British police and Jewish travelers on the roads and launched coordinated attacks on isolated Jewish settlements. But they also employed many of the tactics of modern terrorism: seemingly indiscriminate attacks on urban civilian targets, such as cafés and schools, with the goal of inciting mass fear that would lead to capitulation.[92]

There was a curfew at night, but Gershom was unable to rest or work quietly. From his home in the Rehavia district of Jerusalem, he could hear the nightly sound of gunfire in the countryside.[93] He reported to Walter Benjamin that Arab towns were forced by militants to observe a general strike. The Jews had kept their nerve and maintained the political and moral high ground. Scholem hoped that they would continue to do so.[94] Months later, he commented that Jerusalem was still under a virtual state of siege. Every evening the sounds of gunfire filled the air. One of his colleagues was murdered while reading in his study, there were frequent bombings, and a sense of fatalism pervaded daily life. Still, urban life was safer than rural life in Gershom's estimation.[95]

The revolt posed a quandary for the Yishuv: How should it respond? The Jewish population of Palestine was too big for the Arabs to destroy completely, but the Yishuv was too small to defend itself without British assistance. The Yishuv's principal paramilitary force, the Haganah, was still loosely organized and had no directing general staff, though it essentially adhered to the policy of self-restraint advocated by the Yishuv's primary political leaders, including David Ben-Gurion. While Arab fighters viewed every single Jew in Palestine as the enemy, Jewish leaders sought to differentiate between Arab leaders and the masses and between combatants and noncombatants. However, renegade Haganah soldiers and other Jewish militias, such as the Revisionists' National Military Organization (colloquially known as Etzel or Irgun), undertook revenge attacks and perpetrated their own atrocities. Still, such incidents were generally rare, and most Jews abhorred wanton attacks on Arab civilians.[96]

Meanwhile, the revolt accelerated the trend of disentanglement, or voluntary segregation, of the two communities. Fearing for their safety, many Jews moved from mixed neighborhoods to exclusively Jewish ones. The Arabs' general strike spurred the development of a solely Jewish economy as the Yishuv developed its own production and supply facilities. Among the most significant actions was the shutdown of the Jaffa port. Rather than use Jewish labor to operate Jaffa's port—a temporary expedient and a physically dangerous one for Jewish longshoremen—the Zionist leadership had a rudimentary port constructed in Tel Aviv. Moreover, the long-term segregation of Jews and Arabs gained impetus from the maintenance of a distinct Hebrew school system for Jewish children, where they absorbed lessons about the Jews' historic connection to Palestine.[97]

Gershom Scholem wrote to Walter Benjamin in June 1936 with his political analysis of the Arab revolt. He explained that the uprising had "undoubtedly begun in the expectation of being able to force the English government into suspending Jewish immigration by these rather overly oriental methods." He continued, "This has proved to be a total miscalculation up to now, and the government has remained uncompromising." However, Scholem expected the government to make concessions to the Arabs after suppressing the revolt. And he was essentially correct. Even while condemning the

Arabs for the violence and moving vigorously to suppress it, in 1939, after the end of the revolt, the British granted a highly desired concession: a near total cessation of Jewish immigration to Palestine. Scholem also accurately noted that the stakes were greater than during the last Arab mass revolt, in 1929. Since then, hundreds of thousands of Jewish immigrants, including many from Germany, had bolstered the population of the Yishuv. In 1928 Jews formed less than one-fifth of Palestine's total population. By 1939 they were nearly one-third. Despite the violence, Jews felt more confident as they knew how difficult it would be to dislodge them from the territory.[98]

In late 1936, the British government formed a commission under Lord William Peel, ostensibly to study the situation in Palestine without any prejudices or plans, but really to devise an exit strategy for the British. Peel and his commission conducted long hearings in-country and interviewed the most prominent Jewish and Arab leaders before issuing a report. The report's authors admitted the failure of the mandate and recommended the partition of Palestine. After population and land-ownership transfers, it was foreseen that a Jewish state would exist in the Galilee and along the northern coast, excluding Jaffa. An Arab political entity would take shape among the southern coast, in the Negev, along the west bank of the Jordan River, and in the Judean hill country. Additionally, Jerusalem, the Christian holy places Bethlehem and Nazareth, and a corridor to the Mediterranean Sea were to remain a British mandate under international supervision.[99]

The report, occasioned by an Arab revolt against the Jewish presence in Palestine, brought renewed urgency to a long-smoldering debate among Zionists: What was the ultimate aim of Zionism? For the first time, the idea of a Jewish state in Palestine seemed feasible, but that option did not meet with universal acclaim. Indeed, there was widespread diversity of opinion on the matter, some born of ideology and some resulting from purely practical concerns.[100] Some political Zionists welcomed the establishment of any Jewish state in the Holy Land, no matter how small. Others protested that the movement had aspired to a Jewish or Jewish-led state on the whole of the territory and that the area allotted by the Peel Commission was simply too small to be viable or defensible. Above all, the provisions concerning Jerusalem were offensive to many, particularly considering that the majority of Jerusalem's inhabitants were Jews. After much debate and arm-twisting by David Ben-Gurion and Chaim Weizmann, the Twentieth Zionist Congress voted to accept the Peel Commission's report as a basis for negotiations, particularly regarding the proposed borders of the Jews' state.[101]

Gershom Scholem, too, yielded to reality and decided that half a loaf was better than none. He was opposed to partition in theory, but he thought that the Peel Commission's plan was worth pursuing: "Like many others, I am personally against partition as such, since I believe that joint Arab-Jewish sovereignty in the whole of Palestine to be the more ideal solution, but this opportunity is one we will probably never be granted." And so, "after many debates and long deliberation, I joined the 'cantonists,'" that is, those supporting dividing Palestine into Jewish and Arab cantons.[102] When the plan for partition did not come to fruition, Gershom considered it a missed opportunity.

The Peel Commission did not have the last word. Its successor, the Woodhead Commission, reviewed the first report with an eye toward its implementation. John Woodhead and his fellow investigators modified the proposed partition plan to avoid massive population transfers, particularly of Arabs from the designated Jewish area. Under the Woodhead Commission's preferred plan, known as Plan C, the Jewish area was especially small—485 square miles—and many Jewish settlements and Jewish-owned properties were outside the area's proposed boundaries.[103]

In 1939 the British organized a conference in London to deal with the conflict in Palestine. Arab representatives to the conference refused to sit in the same room as Jewish representatives to the conference, which degenerated into a series of separate meetings with the British colonial secretary Malcolm MacDonald. In the end, the Arabs refused to accept partition of the territory or a continued British mandate. Jewish representatives were willing to accept both, though with notable reservations and modifications to the proposed plans. They rejected an end to Jewish immigration and the idea of the Jews having protected minority status in an Arab state. In any event, the conference failed.[104]

Without the approval of either side, in May 1939, the British issued a white paper in which they announced a radical diminution in the number of Jewish immigrants permitted to enter Palestine, an Arab veto on all Jewish immigration after five years, a virtual prohibition of land sales to Jews, and an endorsement of eventual independence for the unified territory, that is, an Arab-majority state.[105] The decision to cease permitting large-scale Jewish immigration to Palestine could not have come at a worse time for the Jews of Europe, who faced catastrophe. The Zionist leader Robert Weltsch, who largely sympathized with the members of Brit Shalom, called the white paper the "Jewish Munich," making reference to Britain's craven capitulation to Hitler's demands at the Munich conference in 1938.[106] However, so-called illegal immigration continued, and Gershom Scholem thought that the British Mandate government tolerated it, if not actively supported it. He essentially accused the British of playing a double game in which they told the

Arabs that they were not giving the Jews any more visas and they told the Jews not to complain so long as the Jews could continue to bring young people to Palestine. Meanwhile, Gershom had been trying to get an entrance visa for his mother.[107]

Even before the London conference collapsed, Scholem prognosticated that British intransigence would only fan the flames of Jewish radicalism. He wrote: "Feelings are running very high, since the Jews believe (and rightly so, to some extent) that they have been sold out, and the willingness to answer terror with terror is extraordinarily high. That would be very stupid, of course, since our situation is very different from that of the Arabs, and terrorist activities from Jewish quarters can be countered much more easily. But the mood is now such that the possibility must be taken into account."[108] Indeed, Etzel, the Revisionist Zionists' militia, did engage in anti-Arab and eventually anti-British terrorism in Palestine. The drift toward radicalism greatly disheartened Scholem: "The chance of salvaging a viable Palestinian settlement over the course of the next world war is being endangered just as much by us as by the Arabs and the English. Abominable things occur from among our ranks as well, and I shudder when I try to consider what the sole consequence must be. We are living in terror; the capitulation of the English in the face of this terror leads the fools among us to believe that terror is the only weapon with which we, too, can achieve something, not withstanding special circumstances."[109]

To his relief, an uneasy peace settled between Jews and Arabs once the Second World War broke out, but Scholem worried about the effect of Nazi propaganda on the Arabs.[110] He also hoped that the Allies would permit the Jews to fight in the war as Jews. He reasoned, "After all, we are the ones against whom war has been waged all these years, and it would be a good thing if we did our part to bring about the downfall of Hitlerism."[111] In Scholem's own sphere, things were improving. The university reopened, and with local students unable to study abroad, enrollments had increased—even for courses on particularly difficult or obscure subjects, such as those taught by Scholem, including the history of the Sabbatean movement and the book of Bahir.[112]

Scholem's international reputation was growing by the late 1930s. Henry Corbin, a French scholar of Islam, asked Scholem to contribute something for his journal *Hermes*.[113] When the Nazis forced the Schocken *Almanach* to cease publication, the Schocken staffer Moritz Spitzer went to great lengths to get a contribution from Scholem for the final edition. Scholem's initial submission, which was exceptionally long and very scholarly, left Spitzer practically apoplectic, but the publisher wanted to conciliate the scholar. He wrote, "After all, Scholem cannot be missing from the last almanac from Schocken Books!"[114] Arguably the turning point for Gershom Scholem's reputation outside of strictly academic circles was his book *Major Trends in Jewish Mysticism*. The book itself grew out of a series of lectures Scholem had given in America in 1938.

In the summer of 1937, the prominent New York rabbi and Zionist leader Stephen Wise invited Scholem to speak at New York's Jewish Institute of Religion the following year. Scholem was to give several lectures in English, and one in Hebrew, on the topic of "major trends in Jewish mysticism." The institute intended to publish the lectures. In exchange, Scholem would receive an honorarium of $1,200, worth approximately $21,000 in today's money.[115] With the trip providing him an opportunity to view Kabbalistic manuscripts in New York and Cincinnati—something he had wanted to do for years—and to visit Walter Benjamin en route to New York, Scholem eagerly agreed.[116]

Since Scholem felt his English was not good enough simply to write the lectures in English, he wrote them in German and then worked with a translator to put them into English. He found writing for English-language delivery very challenging: "That is a very unfamiliar task and costs a lot of time. The art of composing short sentences is not something that attracted my attention in the past. I will have to make up for it."[117] In advance of his trip, he had his mother, already dealing with the Great Depression and Nazi persecution, scour Berlin for a travel guide to New York. The most recent Baedeker guidebook for the United States was from 1909, making it woefully outdated, and neither the Thomas Cook nor American Express travel agencies were allowed to carry English guidebooks for America. Betty did get some maps and brochures at American Express, where the staff was surprised that Gershom could not get what he wanted in Jerusalem.[118]

As planning proceeded, not everything went smoothly. Gershom Scholem's publisher, Schocken Books, noted that it was publishing a book whose theme overlapped with his lectures. Schocken wanted Scholem to tell Wise that his obligation to Schocken took priority.[119] After the lectures, Wise wrote that if Schocken published the lectures, the Jewish Institute of Religion would not subsidize the publication, but it would buy many copies for distribution. In fact, after a few delays, in 1941 Schocken Publishing House of Jerusalem published the first edition of *Major Trends in Jewish Mysticism*.[120] Its chapter headings were almost identical to the titles of Scholem's lectures.

Scholem tied together several strands of his earlier research and presented an intriguing continuity of Jewish history. The sixteenth-century Kabbalah of Isaac Luria and his followers in Safed was derived from centuries of earlier mystical traditions. Moreover, it was a response to the tragedy of the Jews' expulsion from Spain. Critically, the Lurianic Kabbalah fostered a belief that the Jews' exile could be mystically brought to an end, and this belief smoldered until it flared into messianism in the form of Sabbateanism. Indeed, elements of the established Kabbalistic tradition made Sabbateanism virtually inevitable.[121] Additionally, Scholem claimed, Hasidic Judaism was also an outgrowth of the Lurianic Kabbalah, and it was no "accident that the Hasidic movement made its first appearance in the regions where Sabbatianism [sic] had taken strongest root," in his view. He called the Lurianic Kabbalah, Sabbateanism, and Hasidic Judaism "three stages of the same process," but Hasidism represented a taming of messianic impulses compared to the explosion that was Sabbateanism.[122] Ultimately, by overthrowing traditional rabbinic authority, Sabbateanism opened the door for Jewish modernity.[123] In addition to presenting this startling theory of Jewish history, Scholem also weighed in on the controversy over authorship of the *Zohar*, the most important text of the Kabbalah. He revised his earlier opinion and stated that the *Zohar* was a pseudepigraphical text written by Moses de Léon, and solely by him, in the late thirteenth century.[124]

Introducing his work to a new audience and doing research in American archives and libraries were not the only enticements for Scholem to cross the Atlantic. America was a different environment for him, and he very much wanted to gain some understanding of it. He wrote to Walter Benjamin, "I am learning quite a lot here, and I am using every opportunity to explore this strange world a bit."[125] After an initial stay in New York, he traveled to Cleveland and Cincinnati, the latter being the home of Hebrew Union College. In Cincinnati, he spent Passover seder with his old Berlin friend Moses Marx, who was a bibliographer at Hebrew Union College. Scholem recalled a seder fifteen years earlier with Marx and Walter Benjamin. Scholem then drove with acquaintances back to New York and acknowledged a reality of American life: "Trying to see something of the country without a car is a project doomed to failure, so I am dependent on the few car owners I have access to." Scholem also complained that Americans ate dinner too early. In New York City, he wrote, "I'm trying to gain a general impression of New York Jewry (two million in one city!), and that brings me together with diverse people."[126]

Reflecting later on his time in the New World, Scholem wrote, "The air is still freer over there, and . . . the intellectual atmosphere is better than we in Europe are accustomed to presume. There is widespread openness to and interest in matters Americans aren't supposed to be interested in." Nonetheless, he worried about Americans' lack of concern with the problems of other continents. Additionally, for Scholem, America did not represent "unlimited opportunity" for the Jews, as a common German saying went. It was a place where "insuperable barriers" still existed and divided Jews from the rest of the nation. "I would be very happy to spend a whole year there sometime, but I imagine it would be unbearable in the long run." He also predicted that Walter Benjamin would find New York "especially difficult to bear," despite the cultural diversity of the city and the large number of European intellectuals living there."[127]

While in New York, Scholem could draw on the rare experience of having spent time recently with Benjamin. When Scholem passed through Paris on his way to America in February 1938, he saw his friend for the first time in eleven years. Benjamin's Marxist orientation was the focus of their discussions and often heated arguments. Benjamin affiliated with the Institute for Social Research, and Scholem was troubled by the institute's Marxism, Benjamin's strong ties to Bertolt Brecht, and the issue of Stalinism versus anti-Stalinism in the years of the purges. Indeed, Benjamin was hesitant to condemn the show trials underway in Moscow. Scholem also felt that Benjamin's attachment to France led to his ambivalence about seeking refuge in America or Britain, both of which he viewed with some antipathy.[128] When Gershom Scholem returned to Paris in late summer 1938, accompanied by his wife, Fania, Benjamin was too busy with work in Denmark to visit them. Scholem, for his part, was doubly annoyed because the Left Bank hotel that Theodor Adorno and Benjamin had recommended, the Hôtel Le Littré, was frequented by the Action Française, an extreme right-wing, Catholic movement. The concierge and other guests looked askance at the Scholems.[129] After leaving Paris, he did not write to Benjamin for some months. He was exhausted, commenting, "I let myself sink into a comfortable, or lazy, state of lethargy on our way back" to Palestine through Europe. Then he had eye trouble and had to undergo an operation.[130]

Benjamin asked Scholem to peruse the January 1940 issue of the Institute for Social Research's Zeitschrift für Sozialforschung because he had two essays in it and because he wanted Scholem's opinion on Max Horkheimer's essay "Die Juden und Europa" ("The Jews and Europe"). Scholem and his friend vehemently disagreed about Horkheimer's argument. Moreover, Scholem could not understand Benjamin's slavish self-subordination to the institute. In February Scholem sent Benjamin a long critique of the essay. It was his last letter to Benjamin.[131] Seven months later, Benjamin was dead.

The German-Jewish philosopher Hannah Arendt was also a part of this circle of friends. Although Hannah Arendt and Gershom Scholem had a bitter falling-out in the 1960s over the trial of Adolf Eichmann, in the 1930s and early 1940s they were close. During Scholem's visit to Benjamin in Paris in 1938, he spent time with Arendt, who told him about her in-progress biography of Rahel Varnhagen. The following year, he praised the work, though he interpreted her underlying argument differently from her intended emphasis. He even commented on her manuscript, "Pity, I don't see how the book will ever find a publisher." It did and became a classic.[132] She also denounced the Stalinist show trials. In 1941 he referred to her as "one of my good friends" and "a wonderful woman and excellent Zionist."[133] It was from Arendt that Scholem learned of the death of Walter Benjamin, who committed suicide on the French-Spanish border in September 1940 when it seemed that he would not gain entry to Spain and might be handed over to the Nazis by Vichy French authorities. Gershom reflected, "It is a terrible blow, and there is no recovery from it."[134]

By the end of 1940, most of the moorings of Gershom Scholem's old life had been cut. His closest brother, Werner, and his dear friend, Walter Benjamin, were both dead. His surviving brothers and mother no longer lived in Germany, a country that had consigned its Jewish heritage to destruction. Yet even without access to Germany, Gershom Scholem took many of the intellectual traditions of central Europe and transplanted them to Jerusalem. He advocated rigorous norms for academic scholarship in Judaic studies as he pioneered a new discipline and built up a Hebrew-language university. He struggled for multicultural understanding between peoples in Palestine. Yet world events compelled him to reconsider politics and even the world of scholarship. Scholem, a binationalist, accepted the partition of Palestine and supported the creation of a Jewish state. More consequential for his reputation and legacy, he transcended the world of academia and became a public intellectual, operating on a worldwide stage. While he would continue to visit Europe for research and conferences and renewed ties there, he began to address audiences in America, as well as Israel, on issues of political and religious importance and historical interest.

CHAPTER 9

Afterlives

Sydney and Jerusalem

Sydney, Australia, was a long way from Berlin, both geographically and culturally. The Scholems' old home had been a cosmopolitan metropolis of over four million inhabitants in the heart of Europe, while their new home was a city with a little over one million residents, ten thousand miles from Europe. Nonetheless, Reinhold extolled its modernity.[1] Australia was a country of immigrants, but primarily from the British Isles, and many Australians were uncomfortable with immigrants unlike themselves. There was a Jewish community, but in 1933, it numbered only 23,000 out of a total Australian population of over 6,600,000.[2]

In the 1920s, Jews were very integrated into Australian society. In fact, high rates of intermarriage, low reproduction rates, and tremendous cultural assimilation were setting up the Jewish community for demographic implosion.[3] Despite some regeneration through immigration from Poland, the Anglicized Jewish community leadership had become sclerotic and neglected Jewish education for the youth.[4] Nonetheless, many German Jews looked to Australia as a refuge from Nazi persecution. That need became acute by the late 1930s, and between 1938 and 1940, nine thousand immigrant Jews reached Australia. Faced with widespread anti-immigrant and antisemitic attitudes, Jewish community officials pressured the newcomers not to make themselves conspicuous and to adopt Australian culture as quickly as possible. They were not to congregate in large groups and, above all, not to speak German in public.[5]

For the Scholem brothers, starting their lives over in Australia was a struggle. Not long after arriving, Erich settled in the suburb of Woollahra, where he bought a small general store. He worked seven days a week and closed only on Sunday morning, while his customers were at church. Betty seemed amazed that Erich offered everything from chicken feed to butter and eggs. He stocked sewing articles as well as thirty-six kinds of cookies. He had wanted to work for a firm, but Australian nativism made it almost impossible. Self-employment was the only viable option in his opinion, and his little shop did quite well for a time. Reinhold ran a store near the train station in the town of Como, about twenty miles from central Sydney. The property also had a gas station where his son, Günter, worked, and his wife, Käthe, worked in the shop. Betty commented that Reinhold's store stocked even more wares than Erich's. In addition to fishing gear, cement, and kitchenware, he had fifty-eight varieties of cheese. However, unseasonable weather wreaked havoc on his business as vacationers stayed away.[6] Moreover, the lifestyle took a toll on him. Betty wrote, "In the long run he cannot endure the ceaseless hard work without a day off, restless and irregular meals, too little sleep, and everything else that goes with it."[7]

Reinhold and Erich were safe in Australia, but their private lives were in turmoil. Reinhold, who had never been truly happy in his marriage, fought with his wife, especially after Betty arrived and moved in with them.[8] Erich's life was also tumultuous. Even before bringing his wife and their children to Australia, he had decided to divorce his wife.[9] In fact, he immigrated with a new companion, Hildegard ("Hilde") Samuel, whom Gershom had met when he saw his brothers in Montreal as they passed through on their way to Australia and as he took a break from his research in the United States. No one had mentioned Hilde to Betty until Betty disembarked in Sydney. When Betty finally asked Erich why he was divorcing his wife at this point, rather than sooner or later, he commented that he had not done it in Germany for the sake of the children, but he wanted to start his life anew in Australia.[10] Additionally, it was common for unhappy Jewish couples in Nazi Germany to stay together legally until after immigrating to a safe country. Erich and Hilde married in 1939. The following year, his ex-wife, Edith, married an Australian widower with grown children.[11]

The strains of economic struggle only exacerbated tensions within the family. When Betty arrived in Australia, the family did not have money for her to have her own apartment or a room in a boardinghouse. Therefore, she lived with Reinhold's family, but Betty and Käthe frequently quarreled. Erich did not have space for Betty either, and it was not long before she was frequently sleeping over at the home of Erich's ex-wife, while their son, Arthur, slept on the floor so that his grandmother could have his bed. Betty seriously contemplated joining Gershom in Palestine.[12] Gershom complained to Walter Benjamin that he might have to support Betty financially in Australia.[13]

In Australia, the Scholems connected with the Jewish community, but with mixed emotions and mixed results. Erich came to know the local Zionists shortly after arriving, and he wrote, "The Zionists here are a funny group. [They] know terribly little about Jewish things, and an assimilationist from Germany is a scholar in comparison."[14] Erich's daughter, Irene, joined a youth club, but found it to be an unsatisfying experience. "The Australians take care to withdraw as soon as the refugees increase," Betty commented.[15] For German-Jewish immigrants, including the Scholems, involvement with the established Jewish community had the potential to facilitate and ease integration. It could have been a place to engage with and learn from native Australians while remaining in a half-familiar environment, but that promise was only partially realized.

In fact, in terms of Jewish communal affiliation, many immigrants went their own way, which led to a diversification of Australian Judaism. Before the 1930s, nominal Orthodoxy dominated all aspects of religious life. The central European Jews, including the Scholems, supported a new Reform temple founded in Sydney in 1938. Reinhold was enthusiastically active in the men's club.[16] For the next few decades, only about one-fifth of Jews affiliated with progressive synagogues, and progressive Judaism in Australia remained largely associated with immigrants from Germany and Austria.[17]

However, the Scholems' German origin seemed to be ever more problematic during the war years. German Jews were classified as enemy aliens, whose movements were highly regulated. For a time, Betty even needed a special permit to travel to her doctor in another part of town, and their legal status had a negative impact on Reinhold's business.[18] When Erich became ill, he did not want his mother to visit him in the hospital because she might speak German with him, which would cause additional problems.[19] As Betty wrote to Gershom during one of the darkest years of the war, "That devil Hitler hunted us there because we are Jews, and everywhere in the world we are now Germans, even here in this far-flung land."[20]

In fact, one of the most interesting aspects of the Scholems' lives in Australia was the persistence or diminution of their identification as German. Erich overtly rejected Germanness, even as it was an indelible part of who he was. He was the first in the family to gain Australian citizenship.[21] When he was nearly fifty years old, he enlisted in the Australian army.[22] While he was not assigned to an overseas combat unit, his willingness to fight for his new country—or against his old country—is noteworthy. Even after the defeat of

Germany and the establishment of a democratic government there, Erich's disdain scarcely abated. He first returned to Germany in 1960, twenty-two years after fleeing, and he found the people to be pushy, argumentative, and self-centered.[23] It enraged him when ordinary Germans told him that they had known nothing about what really transpired under the Nazis and, instead, complained about the Allies' bombardment of German cities. Moreover, they invariably denied having supported the Nazis. "It was always the others," Erich facetiously wrote. After departing Germany, he told Gershom, "I must say that I feel considerably better outside the German borders. The longer I was there, the more they got on my nerves."[24] German culture seemed not to appeal to him either, and he regarded himself as an Anglophile, a sentiment confirmed by his trip to Germany.[25] Nonetheless, he felt that culture in Australia was second-rate compared to Europe. "Despite its two million inhabitants, Sydney is the largest village in the Southern Hemisphere and correspondingly provincial," he wrote.[26]

Reinhold, who emigrated shortly before turning forty-seven and lived another forty-seven years in Australia, had a more positive relationship to Germany and his German identity. He refused to let Hitler define for him what it meant to be German.[27] In his correspondence with Gershom, throughout the 1960s and 1970s, he defended the historic place of the Jews in German society and maintained that before Hitler came to power, they had been well integrated in Germany. Gershom insisted that the German Jews had simply been deluding themselves, and their epistolary debate grew quite heated at times.[28] By the early 1970s, Reinhold made plans to return to Germany for the first time since his emigration. A decade after Erich's unhappy visit to Germany, Reinhold visited Düsseldorf for business and did not express the same apprehension or bitterness that marked Erich's letters.[29] At the same time, his German deteriorated over time. Though he spoke German with his immediate family and his cousins in Australia, he commonly inserted English words into German.[30] Unlike Gershom, whose professional life necessitated the use of German and who visited Germany frequently, Reinhold truly was losing contact with Germany and Germanness.

Among the Australian Scholems, the most curious case of enduring or renewed ties to Germany involved Erich's son, Arthur. In 1952 he hurriedly married a woman whom he met while traveling through East Germany.[31] Arthur's first cousin Renate (Werner's daughter) commented, "It seems strange somehow that Arthur Scholem should have been able to make this marriage so easily and quickly when he himself was a victim of the Germans."[32] Even more surprising, after living and working in Africa for many years, Arthur returned permanently to Germany, settling in the Harz

Mountains. His father could not stand the Germans and felt uncomfortable in Germany, but Arthur married a non-Jewish German and returned permanently to Germany.

After the war ended, the family in Australia still faced considerable challenges. Betty's health deteriorated, and Reinhold and Erich were under severe financial strain. In desperation, Reinhold wrote to Gershom in March 1946 because Betty still had some money in Palestine, and he wanted to use those funds for their mother's care.[33] A few weeks after that exchange of letters, Betty died, never having left Australia after her immigration. For years after her death, interpersonal conflicts prevented her family from erecting a suitable headstone for her.[34]

Just as Betty, Reinhold, and Erich spent the war years confined to Australia, Gershom Scholem spent the war years in Palestine. By 1942 the nature of the catastrophe befalling European Jewry was known to the Jews of the Yishuv. Some intellectuals bewailed the Zionist movement's failure to heed the warnings of prophetic Zionist leaders to bring the Jews out of Europe posthaste; however, Gershom protested that no one could have foreseen the attempted wholesale destruction of the Diaspora. Moreover, with the tragedy still unfolding, he felt it was too early to reflect on the disaster.[35] Meanwhile, through his correspondence with friends and relatives abroad, he learned of his own losses in the Holocaust, including the murder of his brother Werner and the suicide of his friend Walter Benjamin. In other cases, little was known definitively about the fate of those left behind in Europe. For example, he awaited the war's end to learn information about the death of his cousin Loni, and in 1944, he believed that his aunt Käte was still alive.[36]

However, the tragic dispersion of German Jewry did lead to one happy occasion: a reunion with his uncle Theobald and aunt Hedwig. As a boy, Gershom looked to them as his patrons within the family, even though he could privately be very critical of Theobald. His uncle had been an early Zionist, and his aunt had even dreamed of immigrating to Palestine. Gershom and his family had spent Jewish holidays such as Hanukkah and Passover at their home. Gershom left Germany for Palestine in 1923, while his aunt and uncle immigrated to Palestine only when the effects of Nazi persecution were too great. Once Theobald and Hedwig settled in Tel Aviv, Gershom spent Passover with them as he had twenty-five or thirty years earlier.[37]

During the war years, Scholem served as a dean at the Hebrew University of Jerusalem, where he wrestled with tremendous institutional challenges. Mobilization affected the number of students enrolled at the university.[38] Meanwhile, politics increasingly permeated university life. The philosophy professor Ernst Simon was under attack for his views in favor of cooperation with the Arabs and hesitation about a Jewish-majority state. There were calls for his dismissal, and Scholem feared that protesters would disrupt Simon's classes. Scholem hoped that the university would not tolerate such actions.[39] In fact, Simon remained at the university and was eventually promoted to full professor. In 1940 Scholem's publisher and patron Salman Schocken, who had helped administer the university since the Bergmann coup of 1935, left for America to raise funds for the institution. When he decided to remain in America, he lost his influence and position at the university.[40]

During the war, from a great distance, Gershom Scholem watched his reputation spread in America. After *Major Trends in Jewish Mysticism* came out, Scholem eagerly awaited, and criticized, the reviews. Among the more amusing exchanges was one he had with Adolph S. Oko, editor of the *Contemporary Jewish Record*, the predecessor of *Commentary* magazine. Scholem was enraged by the magazine's review of the book, written by Hans Kohn, who was well known to Scholem from Brit Shalom. Scholem attacked Kohn: "You might have written whatever you like about or against my book, and I would have enjoyed it much more than I will ever be able to take pleasure in the unsignificant [sic] 'schmus' of that everlasting 'Ober-Quatscher' [Chief Blatherer] who is known by the name of Hans Kohn. By Jove, that would have been the last man to make him write a review on my book." Scholem was annoyed that no one in America had taken up the challenge presented by his book, which implicitly attacked all previous American work on Jewish mysticism.[41] In fact, the problem that Oko faced was that no one in academia really had any expertise on this topic other than Scholem himself. In the end, Oko and Scholem agreed that Scholem could write an article of four to five thousand words on Jewish mysticism for the magazine. Moreover, Scholem insisted that he be allowed to write it in German and Oko would have to translate it.[42]

The war in Europe ended in May 1945. It was followed by a time of taking stock, especially for Gershom Scholem. In his diary, he confided his feelings of despair, desperation, and loneliness. He did not know how he or the Jewish people would find their way forward. Similarly, in a letter to the scholar Shalom Spiegel, he wrote that it was hard to celebrate the defeat of Nazi Germany when the Jews had been defeated. Yet, citing Psalm 82, he expressed tempered joy that no longer did their "enemies rage and . . . haters raise their heads." It was possible to fight for the Good, and the balance between Good and Evil had been restored.[43]

One of the most significant changes wrought by the war and the Holocaust was the destruction of European Jewry and the permanent transfer of leadership in the Jewish world to America and Palestine (soon Israel). This development directly affected Gershom Scholem. As he explained to Leo Baeck, formerly a rabbi in Berlin, "The opinion of the [Hebrew] University is that Jerusalem should be considered the central spiritual heir and successor of the institutions of central European Jewry destroyed in our people's catastrophe."[44] The university administration sent Scholem and a librarian to Europe to collect ownerless Jewish books and ship them back to Jerusalem.[45] However, a number of challenges confronted Scholem in his task. First of all, the Allies tightly controlled access to occupied Germany, and all countries required visas. He would need a series of permissions and, ultimately, need to wear a military uniform while working in Germany. Second, the Americans intended to return Jewish libraries, confiscated by the Nazis, to the governments of their countries of origin. If their source could not be identified, the Americans would send them to the United States. Moreover, both the Library of Congress and American Jewish seats of learning wanted the ownerless Jewish books. While the Joint Distribution Committee (JDC) helped Scholem with his mission in small ways, he had the distinct impression that the JDC wanted the books for American Jewry and did not do as much as it could have to assist him.[46]

Once he received the necessary visas and permits, Scholem traveled through Czechoslovakia and Germany, inquiring after books. There was a modest collection in Prague and a massive accumulation of books in Offenbach, Germany, in the American zone of occupation. Scholem succeeded in getting the books in Prague, which had originated in Germany before transfer to the Theresienstadt concentration camp, sent to Jerusalem with the consent of the Prague Jewish community. The books in Offenbach were a different story. There were hundreds of thousands of them from across Europe, and they had been picked over before Scholem's arrival or consisted of insignificant items. Nonetheless, Scholem succeeded in finding a small number of interesting Hebrew books and manuscripts. The American military authorities would not let Scholem have them. Ultimately, an American army Jewish chaplain arranged for their shipment to Jerusalem without Scholem's prior knowledge. When the controversy over the theft calmed down, the Hebrew University library was allowed to keep the items.[47] Some German libraries housed valuable collections of Hebrew manuscripts that survived the war. So Scholem negotiated with the German authorities, telling them that surrendering these collections "might be an important moral gesture . . . as a symbolic act towards the Jewish people and as a first step toward bridging the awful abyss that has been created between the two peoples."[48] It is hard to tell whether Scholem sincerely meant this or whether he just wanted the manuscripts for Jerusalem. Moreover, his travels through Europe, which was now seemingly devoid of Jewish life and learning, angered and depressed him. He called that time "some of the bitterest months of my life."[49]

He reported on the situation of the Jews living in German cities and the lives of Jewish displaced persons in United Nations camps.[50] Zionist leaders wanted them to go to Palestine. Despite the manifest need to do something for the displaced persons, Scholem felt that the Yishuv was unprepared for such an influx and their sudden arrival would lead to a "catastrophe." He also complained about the poor economic situation in Palestine and credited a rise in crime to increased inflation. He openly worried about thieves taking his rare and valuable library.[51]

In these years, as Israel achieved independence and built a new society, Scholem wrote one of his most intriguing short essays, a rumination on the history of the Star of David. Indeed, the timing was no accident since the Israeli national flag was prominently emblazoned with the six-pointed star. Rather than being an ancient symbol of Judaism, Scholem argued, it gained its association with Judaism largely as a medieval or early modern talismanic element. It was also used as an occasional symbol of the Jewish community of Prague. Later, in the nineteenth century, European Jews sought a decorative element that they could use similarly to the way that Christians used crosses, and the Star of David enjoyed widespread popularity. Near the century's end, the Zionists adopted it as their hallmark, in part because it was a popular design and not a religious symbol. However, in Scholem's view, the six-pointed star only gained its "sacredness" through its use as a badge of Jewish degradation during the Holocaust, after which it was reappropriated with hope and pride by the Jews.[52] One cannot help but see in this scholarly essay the personal views of a man who had long viewed political Zionism skeptically and whose family had suffered tragedy during the Holocaust.

Among the many intellectuals who maintained a dialogue with Scholem, one of his most noted and fiercest interlocutors was Hannah Arendt, who, like Scholem, was a brilliant intellectual of German-Jewish origin. Although they had been good friends and shared many views on the situation of European Jewry after the war, they clashed over the nature and future of Zionism in the postwar era.[53] Arendt posited that the Revisionists had taken over the Zionist movement in principle, if not in fact, and she railed against the movement's inherent elitism and alienation from the masses as it cultivated ties to the Great Powers in an effort to achieve its goals. In her understanding, at that time, a Jewish state would exist "within an imperial sphere of interest," that is, under the protection of the world's main powers and without the consent of its Arab neighbors—conditions that were unacceptable to her. Indeed, she castigated the Zionist leadership of the 1940s for not showing concern for the Arabs' political aspirations. She also attacked the Zionists' interpretation of antisemitism, which, as she saw it, regarded hatred of Jews as something innate and eternal rather than as a political phenomenon tied to nationalism. She claimed that the Zionist leadership instrumentalized antisemitism to gain support instead of actively combatting it.[54] Utterly incensed, Gershom Scholem called her article "a spirited reissue of a communist critique of a strictly anti-Zionist nature mixed with a diffuse, enduring Diaspora nationalism." While he conceded her point that even left-wing Zionism had grown more nationalist in character and did not prioritize Arab-Jewish reconciliation, he counseled her to accept the reality of the situation, as he had done. He, once an unabashed partisan of a binational Palestine, now supported partition of the territory largely out of frustration with the Arabs' unwillingness to accept reasonable political solutions to the Palestine problem. As for Arendt, in Scholem's eyes, she had the temerity to criticize the Zionist movement and Jewish settlement in Palestine without expressing sufficient support for Zionism and the Yishuv.[55] While he did not wish this quarrel to end their friendship, it was not the last dispute between these two intellectual giants.

Seventeen years later, in the wake of the trial of Adolf Eichmann in Jerusalem, Scholem and Arendt publicly clashed and then ended their friendship. At issue was Arendt's attitude toward Jewish victims and survivors of the Holocaust. In the pages of the *New Yorker* and in the first edition of her book *Eichmann in Jerusalem*, Arendt characterized Jewish leaders as collaborators with the Nazis. She specifically referred to Rabbi Leo Baeck, titular head of all German-Jewish organizations under Nazi rule and an elder in the Theresienstadt concentration camp, as the "Jewish Führer." This characterization was so explosive that Arendt omitted it in later editions of *Eichmann in Jerusalem*.[56] Scholem, who self-identified wholly as a Jew and whose family had suffered greatly in the Holocaust, wrote of her "heartless, frequently almost sneering and malicious tone" and her "flippancy," made worse by the fact that she was not there and did not face the daily moral dilemmas of those in the camps. He found Arendt lacking in pathos for her fellow Jews, what he called "Ahabath Israel" ("love of Israel," also rendered "Ahavat Yisrael"). She replied, "You are quite right—I am not moved by any 'love' of this sort, and for two reasons: I have never in my life 'loved' any people or collective—neither the German people, nor the French, nor the American, nor the working class or anything of that sort." She claimed only love for individuals. In any event, "this 'love of the Jews' would appear to me, since I am myself Jewish, as something rather suspect. I cannot love myself or anything which I know is part and parcel of my own person." She then dissected his letter in light of how she interpreted her book *Eichmann in Jerusalem* and in light of her earlier philosophical work.[57] The exchange, which was published in the main newsletter for German-Jewish émigrés in Israel and later in the main Zurich newspaper and *Encounter* magazine, was too much for the friendship to bear. In no small part, Scholem and Arendt were too strong-willed, self-righteous, and argumentative to tolerate differences of opinion on matters of such importance to them. They did not speak again after 1964.

Scholem's relationship with Martin Buber also experienced severe strains. In 1961, he gave vent to long-held negative opinions of Buber's scholarship. Both in public lectures and in the press, Scholem excoriated the esteemed philosopher of religion for his ahistorical interpretation of Hasidism. Buber published a reply to Scholem's critique, which prompted a response by Scholem.[58] Nonetheless, Scholem was asked to speak at Buber's funeral in June 1965. It was only with Fania's help that he was able to compose a speech that navigated between false praise and revealing his true feelings about Buber.[59] Despite Scholem's opinion of Buber as a scholar, he esteemed his colleague's efforts toward fostering reconciliation between Arabs and Jews. In the 1950s, Scholem participated in a campaign to win the Nobel Peace Prize for Buber.[60]

In the decades after the Second World War, Scholem, once a Young Turk, became an éminence grise in international academic circles. Naturally, he won immense respect for having pioneered the academic field of Kabbalah studies. His graduate students went on to become noted scholars in their own right and expanded academic research of the Kabbalah into nearly all of its facets. What was once a radical, fringe field of Judaic study that was looked upon askance or seen as almost dangerously vibrant had become a perfectly ordinary academic discipline.[61] As a new generation researched the Kabbalah and Sabbateanism, many of Scholem's conclusions were contradicted or reversed, yet his stature in the field still obliged scholars to respond to him. In the estimation of many who knew him, he utterly dominated the life and work of the humanities at the Hebrew University of Jerusalem. He was immensely influential and even feared within Israel's community of Jewish studies academics.[62] At one point, he was considered for the presidency of the Hebrew University.[63] Yet his reputation went far beyond his own discipline and his own institution.[64]

Gershom Scholem's publications directly or indirectly addressed issues of wide interest in history and religion, and he participated in scholarly conversations across genres. His work remains the subject of study by scholars in disciplines such as German literature and comparative literature, political science, philosophy, history, and history of religions, in addition to Jewish studies. In his own lifetime, Scholem and Henry Corbin, a French scholar of Islam, developed a friendship and took a leading role in the Eranos conferences, which dealt with psychology, mythology, philosophy, and spirituality in different faith traditions.[65] After Scholem's retirement, he had visiting professorships and guest lectureships at many universities, and he received honorary doctorates from Yale University, Brandeis University, and the University of Zurich.

By the 1960s and 1970s, Gershom Scholem enjoyed a remarkable reputation among the international literati. Numerous writers and scholars made pilgrimages to his home in Jerusalem, including the literary critic Leslie Fiedler; historian Lucy Dawidowicz; novelists Mark Mirsky, Cynthia Ozick, and Norma Rosen; and Spanish-language writer Jorge Luis Borges.[66] Borges even wrote a poem that made direct reference to Scholem.[67] Years before winning the Nobel Prize in Literature, the Australian novelist Patrick White drew inspiration for *Riders in the Chariot* from Scholem's work.[68] Chaim Potok modeled a character in the novel *The Book of Lights* on Scholem.[69]

Scholem also became a public intellectual with a following in the United States. His work spoke to an audience that sought insights into the "dark chambers" of the universe. In Cynthia Ozick's words, "Gershom Scholem is a historian who has remade the world. He has remade it the way Freud is said to have remade it—by breaking open the shell of the rational to uncover the spiraling demons inside."[70] The *New York Times* reviewed Scholem's books and reported on his visit to New York City in 1975.[71] His contributions to *Commentary* magazine, an important journal of Jewish thought and public affairs through much of the Cold War era, treated highbrow American readers to a taste of "the foremost Jewish scholar living today," in the words of *Commentary*'s editor.[72] In that same publication, the literary scholar Robert Alter traced Scholem's career with deep admiration.[73]

Even in Germany, an audience for Gershom Scholem's scholarship developed, and many of his books appeared in German before they appeared in English. In 1960 he published a German-language edition of *On the Kabbalah and Its Symbolism*. A version of his Hebrew-language book on the origins of the Kabbalah appeared in German in 1966. English editions of both books appeared only later.[74] In the words of one biographer, citing Jürgen Habermas, "all the beacons of the German intellectual world treated Scholem with so much respect and humility."[75] Starting in the late 1950s, Scholem frequently gave guest lectures at German universities, was interviewed or was the subject of examination in the German-language press, and received numerous prizes and honors in Germany. He spoke extensively on German radio about his life and work. Shortly before his death, he was elected to membership in the exclusive Pour le Mérite order of merit, Germany's highest civilian honor.[76] For a man who had spent most of his life disclaiming a German identity, he maintained a vigorous connection to Germany, a country whose language and customs he knew intimately. Indeed, despite the burden of German history and his intense feelings about discussing the past with Germans, it is likely that Gershom Scholem still felt more comfortable in Germany than in America.[77]

Interestingly, he also seemed to have a special relationship with Switzerland, which was a largely German-speaking country that was not directly implicated in the Holocaust. Scholem regularly attended the Eranos conferences in Ascona, Switzerland, beginning in 1949. There, he lectured in German and reacclimated to using German for scholarship after a hiatus of over a decade.[78] He frequently visited or passed through Zurich, where a number of his books were published and where the university awarded him an honorary doctorate, an honor denied to Winston Churchill, Scholem crowed.[79] Even Erich Scholem, as a tourist, came across his brother's work advertised and celebrated in Zurich.[80]

Within Israel, Gershom Scholem's stature was also recognized. When the Weizmann Institute inaugurated one of its earliest computers, in 1965, he spoke at its dedication and named the machine "Golem."[81] In 1958, soon after publishing his magisterial biography of Shabbetai Zevi, he won the Israel Prize. Eleven years later, he received the Yakir Yerushalayim prize as an honored citizen of Jerusalem, as well as many awards and honorary doctorates from Israeli universities. In 1968 he became president of the Israel Academy of Sciences and Humanities, serving for six years. He was personally acquainted with Israeli prime ministers, and the Israeli president and government ministers celebrated his birthday.[82] At the same time, he did not back away from his own left-wing position in Israeli politics. He opposed the execution of Adolf Eichmann after the latter's conviction for crimes against the Jewish people and crimes against humanity.[83] He was strongly critical of David Ben-Gurion's political machinations in the early 1960s.[84] After the Six-Day War, he was one of the first public figures to reject annexation of the occupied territories, adding his name to a manifesto published in the liberal daily newspaper *Haaretz*.[85] Indeed, after the stunning Israeli victory, he commented that since the people of Israel had "the memory of the situation of the defeated, as well as the living, human feeling of the victor—we should be able to attain some balance in our experience." He hoped that there would be peace for the Arabs and the Jews.[86] By the

1970s, he supported the secular, left-wing, pro-peace Movement for Civil Rights and Peace, commonly known as Ratz.[87] His scholarly views were also regarded controversially. In the late 1950s, he published his magnum opus, an 850-page biography of Shabbetai Zevi that became the subject of intense debate among Israeli intellectuals.[88]

Despite his fame within and outside academia, Gershom Scholem's true inner life remained something of a mystery. Moreover, he cultivated an air of unknowability.[89] Harold Bloom thought that Scholem masqueraded as a historical researcher, but was really a "hidden theologian of Jewish Gnosis."[90] Despite knowing Scholem rather well, George Steiner could not discern if Scholem believed in God and knew that Scholem would not say. Indeed, Scholem seemed to delight in others' puzzlement over his character. Steiner remarked, "The quizzicalities in Scholem's smile and the hints of a deep-lying Voltairean merriment were legion."[91] Cynthia Ozick visited Scholem in Jerusalem and asked, "Does the scholar of Kabbalah possess a hidden self?" Was there a "shadow-Scholem"? Fania Scholem told Ozick that she knew the answer, but refused to say, to her husband's amusement. When Ozick inquired, "How much of Professor Scholem is theater?," he replied, "Ask Mrs. Scholem," who answered, "One hundred percent."[92]

While Gershom participated in both scholarly and political controversies, his brothers in Sydney faced very different challenges. Though Reinhold and Erich had traveled to Australia together, their paths began to diverge in the postwar years. Reinhold took over a plastics molding business, which eventually brought him prosperity and comfort. By the 1960s, he was able to afford a luxury automobile and vacations in Europe.[93] Reinhold also had very firm convictions regarding Australian politics, supporting the Liberal Party, which became popular with Sydney Jewry.[94] Käthe, his wife of forty-nine years, died in 1971, but it was not long before Reinhold found love with a septuagenarian German-Jewish widow.[95] Reinhold, who had been open to friendships with non-Jewish Germans during his youth, still found his closest circle among Jews.

While Reinhold seemed to find a secure place for himself in Australia, Erich's life remained difficult. Business success eluded him. He tried various enterprises, including a sandwich shop and a cane furniture factory, but he never found real stability.[96] Moreover, he had a contentious relationship with his grown children. Erich's son, Arthur, was a mechanic in the mining industry and lived in Zambia for many years before returning to Germany.[97] Additionally, Erich quarreled with Reinhold, and they went for long periods of time without any contact.[98] Erich's health was also frail. In the 1950s, he survived intestinal cancer and lung cancer.[99]

Erich Scholem died on a February night in 1965. He had gone to dinner and a lecture by himself when his heart failed. Erich's widow indicated that he had wanted a rabbi at his funeral. Reinhold, who handled the arrangements, assumed Erich had meant someone from the liberal North Shore Temple Emanuel in Sydney. In fact, for some time, Erich had been a member of the Orthodox North Shore Synagogue. Erich's daughter, Irene, and one of her children attended the funeral. Reinhold, as male next of kin, was asked to recite the memorial *Kaddish*. He told Gershom that Erich's quick death, without a long preceding illness, was lucky, and he wished the same for himself. Reinhold and Erich, the oldest two Scholem brothers, had grown up together, worked together for several decades, and emigrated together. Reinhold had lost his closest brother and a friend: "In Berlin, not only were we friends in business, but personally, too."[100] In contrast, Gershom seemed not to have been close to Erich at all. He remembered having shared a bedroom with Erich when they were boys, but "since he went into the army 50 years ago, I have had hardly any close contact with him and received very little correspondence from him." His image of his brother remained frozen in time, "almost entirely shaped by the impressions and experiences of our youth."[101]

Even more surprising than Erich's belated embrace of Orthodox Judaism, Emmy Wiechelt Scholem, Werner's non-Jewish widow, found her path to Judaism. In 1958 she moved back to Germany, settling initially in a small town in southwestern Germany. Later, she returned to Hanover, where she became active in the Jewish community and had a leadership role at the Jewish retirement home.[102] In 1968, thirty-three years after Werner had implored her not to give their children a Jewish education, Emmy converted to Judaism and took the Hebrew name Miriam. Writing about it some years later, Gershom claimed that Emmy converted "because she wanted at least to be buried among Jews."[103]

By the 1960s, Gershom, who was an internationally famous historian of Judaism, began writing a series of reminiscences of his youth that culminated in his memoir, *From Berlin to Jerusalem*. Beyond shaping public understanding of Jewish mysticism and messianism, as he did with his scholarship, he was now molding public perception of modern German-Jewish history. In 1962 he wrote one of his best-known essays, "Wider den Mythos vom deutsch-jüdischen 'Gespräch'" (Against the Myth of a German-Jewish "Dialogue"), which was published two years later.[104] He insisted that the historic dialogue between Jews and Germans had been a mere monologue: the Jews had spoken, but received no response, or none that was positive. When the

Jews contributed to German culture or society, their contributions were ignored or denigrated, he claimed.

Not every émigré who had once been a part of the German-Jewish bourgeoisie shared Gershom's view, much to his dismay. When American historians Peter Gay, born in Berlin in 1923, and Fritz Stern, born in Breslau in 1926, presented a different view of German-Jewish life, Gershom became irritated.[105] Even though Reinhold was proud of his brother's accomplishments as a scholar, Gershom's publications on the era of their youth drew his ire. The two brothers also feuded over which writers were "Jewish" and which were "German," categories that Gershom seemed to regard as mutually exclusive.[106]

However, Gershom also worked actively for dialogue and even reconciliation, though he had doubts about the success of the project.[107] In 1966, at the meeting of the World Jewish Congress in Brussels, he spoke on relations between Jews and Germans, a topic that had occupied his thoughts for fifty years, as he put it.[108] Incidentally, among the most notable speakers at that international Jewish conference was Eugen Gerstenmaier, president (speaker) of the German Bundestag, who had opposed the Nazis when he was a young man. Gershom Scholem also increasingly visited Germany, making the tour of German universities and cultural institutions.[109] He promoted the publication of his work in German, though he was extremely selective about who would be allowed to publish his work in Germany, and he ultimately developed a close working relationship with Suhrkamp Verlag.[110] While he had claimed that there had been no true German-Jewish dialogue, he was, in fact, engaging in a selective dialogue with Germans about the past.

Despite their fervent disagreements over politics, culture, and religion, Gershom and Reinhold remained in frequent contact. Reinhold's age began to catch up with him, and he was injured in a fall, which led to surgery. He later moved into an assisted living home.[111] His health recovered such that he could get around, and he hoped that Gershom would come to Australia for his ninetieth birthday party in August 1981. However, the distance was too great, and Gershom's schedule was too busy.[112] Ultimately, instead of a trip to Sydney, Gershom vacationed in Sils Maria, Switzerland. Soon thereafter, he traveled to Berlin, a city to which he still felt emotionally and culturally attached. He joined the first class of fellows at the Wissenschaftskolleg zu Berlin, an institution modeled on the Institute for Advanced Study in Princeton, New Jersey. A few months after his arrival in Berlin, he injured his hip in a fall, which delayed a planned short trip back to Jerusalem. Once his hip began healing well, he went to Jerusalem to complete his convalescence. However, he developed abdominal pains that evaded medical explanation.

Rather than returning to Berlin, he remained in Jerusalem, where he died on 21 February 1982, a few months past his eighty-fourth birthday.[113]

Yet Gershom Scholem, the towering intellectual with an international audience, was not the last Scholem of his generation. Reinhold—a man with German, Jewish, and Australian identities to varying degrees—outlived his youngest brother by nearly four years. He died on 19 November 1985 at the age of ninety-four.

Conclusion

By the time that Gershom Scholem died in 1982, the German-Jewish century had long been over. Even the attenuated afterlife of the German-Jewish bourgeoisie in exile was drawing to a close. However, for more than 120 years, beginning with Frederick William III's emancipation edict in 1812, Jews had found a place in German society. The beacons of rights and economic opportunities drew Jews to German cities, where they embarked on a journey of social ascent. Within two generations, German Jewry had undergone a complete transformation.

Around 1817, a poor baker from Glogau named Marcus Scholem migrated to Berlin. At the time, approximately 3,500 Jews lived in Berlin. At the start of the nineteenth century, other cities had similarly small Jewish communities: 3,000 Jews lived in Frankfurt am Main, 2,900 in Breslau, and 6,400 in Hamburg. In total, nearly 330,000 Jews lived throughout the German lands, and most of them—especially in Prussia—inhabited towns or rural areas.[1] It was not possible to speak of German Jewry as a predominantly urban group. Even after migration to the cities began in earnest, most urban Jews, including Marcus Scholem and his wife, were situated among the lower tiers of the bourgeoisie or the working class.

By the time Marcus's son Siegfried died in 1901, the situation was different. German Jewry was urban to an exceptional degree. During that decade, more than half of all Jews in Germany lived in major metropolises compared to barely 20 percent of the general population. Nearly 145,000 Jews lived in greater Berlin alone. Frankfurt and Breslau each had Jewish populations of 20,000 or more, and Hamburg was close behind.[2] While many Jews were too poor to be assessed income tax, the vast majority of Jews discernibly belonged to the middle class or upper middle class. In fact, Jews were twice as likely as the general population to belong to the tax-paying strata of society.[3] Germany's Jews formed a large, visible, and important, though not entirely integrated, part of the urban middle class.

Moreover, the German-Jewish bourgeoisie constituted a unique subculture, with specific occupational, cultural, and political characteristics. Far more than non-Jewish members of the middle class, bourgeois German Jews worked in commerce or trade. It is no surprise that for three generations, the Scholems were independent businessmen, namely, printshop owners. Nonetheless, by the time of the First World War, a significant number of German Jews had salaried positions in commerce.[4] Naturally, many Jews aspired to the liberal professions, including Georg, Gershom, and Werner Scholem. In fact, the Jewish bourgeoisie's emphasis on education facilitated this movement into the professions. Even though Arthur Scholem and his two oldest brothers were not going to attend university, they did attend a Realgymnasium, a modern university-preparatory secondary school. Similarly, all four of Arthur's sons studied at a Realgymnasium, though Reinhold and Erich were destined to take over the family printing business and only Werner and Gershom studied at a university.

For the Scholems and many Jews in Germany in the early twentieth century, secondary education was an end in itself, not merely a means to acquire credentials for higher education. Both in Gymnasium and through their vocational travels throughout western Europe, Reinhold and Erich acquired the familiarity with culture that marked members of the upper middle class. However, the Jews of Germany also had a special relationship to German culture, tied to a notion of personal cultivation, elevation, and liberal civilization. They venerated German high culture, and they situated it in a liberal and tolerant worldview. Young Gershom Scholem accompanied his mother to performances of plays by Friedrich Schiller, and Reinhold and Erich heard their rabbi deliver sermons on Johann Wolfgang von Goethe. Later, as German society and culture turned more exclusionary, many German Jews contended that they were the true inheritors of the traditions of German high culture, which had been open to the world.

During the years of the Weimar Republic, the Jews' appreciation for German high culture provided a model for the transformation of Jewish culture. As traditional religious observance diminished, many German Jews, including the Scholems, sought other means of giving expression to their Jewish identity. They founded or participated in cultural organizations that venerated and studied aspects of Jewish heritage, but did so using a modern, German framework rather than a traditionally Jewish one. The most famous example is Franz Rosenzweig's Lehrhaus, which offered continuing education courses on Jewish topics, including one course taught by Gershom Scholem before his emigration. Erich and Reinhold Scholem were active in the Soncino Society for Jewish bibliophiles. Their firm even printed special editions of Jewish books for Soncino Society members to collect. Although Gershom Scholem characterized his family as little interested in Judaism, the Scholems were integrally part of the renaissance of Jewish culture and the recasting of Jewish identity in interwar Germany.

While German Jews had a sense of themselves as German, they also recognized that they were different. Even if they celebrated Christmas as a "German" holiday rather than a Christian one, they rarely purged all traces of their Jewish heritage from their lives. In the late nineteenth century, many Jews formed their own social clubs, fraternities, and welfare associations, both to represent their interests and in response to their exclusion from general groups. Alternatively, expressly liberal and tolerant associations, such as Werner Scholem's mountaineering club, came to be known informally as "Jewish" clubs because of the proportion of Jewish members. Another interesting manifestation of the Jews' sense of self was their fraught social intercourse with non-Jewish Germans. The Scholems moved mainly in Jewish social circles. Resulting perhaps from a history of social separation and antisemitism, it was not uncommon for German Jews such as Betty Scholem or her sister-in-law Lene Scholem to look down on non-Jews and regard their ways as peculiar.

Turning to politics, Germany's Jews were remarkable both for their political cohesion and their diversity. The vast majority of German Jews voted for liberal democratic, or left-liberal, political parties, namely, the Progressive People's Party under the German Empire and the German Democratic Party during the Weimar Republic. Indeed, Betty Scholem was an avowed supporter of the German Democrats, and her son Erich joined like-minded organizations. With the Jewish middle and upper middle class concentrated in certain residential districts of Berlin, Frankfurt, and other cities, Jewish votes notably helped the German Democrats in limited areas. While most Jews and many of their communal leaders supported liberal democratic parties, some Jewish voters preferred national liberal, or right-liberal, parties. The small-business owner Reinhold Scholem and the banker Max Warburg joined the German People's Party.

By contrast, many Jews espoused leftist politics, including social democracy and communism. Though some middle-class Jews, such as Theobald Scholem, shied away from the Social Democrats, their party's share of the Jewish vote grew during the early twentieth century, not least of all because the party proved to be the principal bulwark against Nazism. For other Jews, particularly intellectuals who no longer affiliated with the Jewish community, the Social Democrats were not radical enough. Werner Scholem and his comrades embraced communism as the solution to society's problems. Although Jewish intellectuals formed only a small portion of the Communist Party membership, their right-wing enemies attacked the party with antisemitic invective. Coincidentally, in 1924, Werner and several Jewish intellectuals did come to power in the party, though a pro-Stalin, anti-intellectual, and possibly antisemitic wave swept them from power within a few years. Finally, a distinct minority of German Jews sought political and social solutions to the problems of their community elsewhere altogether, and they became Zionists. Although German Zionists were relatively few in number, for many years, particularly before the First World War, they had notable influence in the Zionist movement. Moreover, Zionism offered an alternative for young German Jews who were frustrated with their parents' liberalism and German patriotism at a time when the promise of liberal democracy in Germany remained unfulfilled. Gershom Scholem, then still known as Gerhard, circulated among a community of young German Zionists, though he was an extremist in that he learned fluent Hebrew while living in Germany and took active steps to immigrate to Palestine.

The choices made by the brothers Reinhold, Erich, Werner, and Gershom Scholem reflect the options that German Jews saw available to them in the years immediately following the First World War. Erich's path was the most typical, yet Reinhold, Werner, and Gershom each represent a distinct and significant community of German Jews. Moreover, their experiences provide a case study of how political choices and their attendant worldviews led to specific fates, including reluctant emigration during the Nazi era, imprisonment and death in concentration camps, voluntary immigration to Palestine, and the construction of new identities.

One of the most remarkable facets of the German-Jewish bourgeoisie's story is that, even after the German Jews' century came to an end, there existed a distinct, transnational German-Jewish diaspora. Like many immigrants of different nationalities, the émigré generation remained only partially integrated into the society and culture of their new homes. A man like Reinhold Scholem found himself suspended between two spheres, German and Australian. Even Gershom Scholem, who did not wish to be seen as a German Jew, lived a life that was quintessentially part of the story of the German-Jewish bourgeoisie. Long after settling in the Land of Israel, he retained innumerable aspects of the culture and education he had absorbed in Germany.

Fritz Stern wrote that historians are like seabirds that move along with the current while consistently facing backward.[5] As the current of time races forward and landscapes and cultures change, it is worth looking at the historic world of the German-Jewish bourgeoisie from today's perspective. What remains of that specific milieu? What has become of the Scholems' Berlin?

In March 1929, Betty Scholem's cousin Else, a recent convert to Christianity, got married in Berlin's Kaiser Wilhelm Memorial Church. Directly opposite was the Romanisches Café, frequented by Jewish writers and artists such as Elias Canetti, Alfred Döblin, Joseph Roth, Else Lasker-Schüler, and Billy Wilder, among others. Just to the east was the Kaufhaus des Westens department store, founded by the Jewish entrepreneur Adolf Jandorf and owned by the Jewish firm Hermann Tietz & Co. Just to the west was the Fasanenstrasse Synagogue, where Rabbi Leo Baeck frequently officiated. The surrounding streets were home to tens of thousands of middle-class and upper-class Berlin Jews. The church where Betty's cousin married was emblematic of the Protestant establishment, but it was situated in a neighborhood—perhaps *the* neighborhood—associated with the German-Jewish bourgeoisie. Where is that world today?

The old Romanisches Café is gone, destroyed in an aerial attack during the Second World War. The Kaufhaus des Westens still exists, having been rebuilt after the war, and is now owned by a Thai department store conglomerate. The Fasanenstrasse Synagogue, a symbol of bourgeois, liberal Berlin Jewry, was devastated during Kristallnacht on the express orders of Joseph Goebbels, and Allied bombs essentially completed the destruction. However, since 1959, a Jewish communal center has stood on the site, providing services and administration for the Jews of West Berlin.

Arthur Scholem and his family lived in central Berlin, barely fifteen minutes away on the subway. Today, they would scarcely recognize the neighborhood. Much of the picturesque Fischerinsel neighborhood, where Gershom was born, survived the war, only to be demolished by East German urban planners in the 1960s. They even eradicated the historic layout of the area's streets before erecting high-rise apartment buildings. Just across the Spree River, a number of original buildings remain, but the house at Neue Grünstrasse 26, where Gershom grew up and Betty lived until 1929, disappeared long ago. In its place sits a contemporary office building. For many decades, there was nothing at the site of Siegfried Scholem's home. That stretch of

Sebastianstrasse was raked clean and lay adjacent to the Berlin Wall in the so-called Death Strip. After German reunification, it remained vacant. Only in the 2010s did developers rebuild the area with modern apartments. Above all, there is no indication that this neighborhood was once home to a large Jewish population. Not a single monument or plaque recalls families like the Scholems.

Walking north through central Berlin, one passes a mix of historic buildings, empty lots, unattractive constructions from the East German era, and contemporary architecture in glass and stone. Entire streets that once shaped the city no longer exist. A guidebook from the 1920s will not serve a pedestrian well. Coming to the edge of the Scheunenviertel, once the heart of working-class and eastern European Jewry in Berlin, there are numerous vestiges of Jewish life: memorials, museums, and historic sites. But there is also a renewed Jewish presence, including communal institutions, kosher and kosher-style cafés, galleries for Jewish art or Jewish artists, and stores that offer Judaica. However, it is questionable how much of this cultural renaissance is for local Jewish consumption and how much is for the tourist trade. In any event, Gershom Scholem would find neither the Old Synagogue, where he formerly prayed, nor the scores of Hebraica bookstores, where he spent his pocket money on books. Above all, the greatest absence is Jews.

The core Jewish population of Germany is now approximately 116,000, less than one-fifth of its pre-Holocaust peak. Even more incongruous is that the largest Jewish group in Germany today is Russian-speaking Jews born in the former Soviet Union, followed by Israeli expatriates and the descendants of eastern European Holocaust survivors who settled in Germany. The pre-1933 German Jews are gone. The unfortunate among them fell victim to the Nazis; the lucky ones escaped to Palestine, America, or other countries of exile. Even after the war ended, most German-Jewish refugees remained abroad.

Remarkably, many of the institutions that Jews founded, funded, or directed for the common good in pre-Holocaust Germany still exist. It is through the efforts of Jewish patrons that Frankfurt has an important university, the Goethe University, and Munich has the largest natural science and technology museum in the world, the Deutsches Museum. Rudolf Mosse funded an archaeological expedition for Berlin's Egyptian Museum and donated many objects to that collection. Visitors can see paintings by Titian, Manet, and Cézanne, donated to Berlin museums by Eduard Arnhold. Berlin and Hamburg still have Jewish hospitals with roots in the eighteenth and nineteenth centuries. Jewish publishers no longer dominate the Berlin press, but many of their corporations live on, and almost every middle-class German home has books published by Fischer Verlag or Ullstein Verlag. On a more quotidian level, Jewish expressions and Yiddish words pepper the modern German language without most speakers even knowing the origins of "mischpoche," "chuzpe," and "meschugge" (to use the German spellings).

On a broader level, the specific subculture of the German Jews has dissipated nearly into nothingness. While they took their habits and traditions with them into exile, their descendants have fully become Israelis, Americans, Australians, and Britons. Many Jews of German descent support the Leo Baeck Institute in New York, London, or Jerusalem, but few of them speak German. Even fewer of them cook German-Jewish culinary specialties, such as Berches (German challah), or pray at synagogues that follow the traditional German rite. Those who have retained a Jewish identity have blended in with the predominant eastern European–inflected Ashkenazi tradition. Concomitantly, the Reform Jewish movement in America, founded and long led by German Jews, is now dominated by Jews of eastern European descent.

Neither the Scholems' Berlin nor their specific German-Jewish subculture still exists, but do they still have a presence in the historical memory of their former homeland? Today's Germany has made an effort to remember the Jews who were once at home in German society. Streets, squares, schools, and other institutions are named for German Jews, particularly locally notable victims of the Holocaust. Lübeck has named a school for the Prenski siblings, while Essen has a school named for suffragist Frida Levy. In Berlin, a gymnasium commemorates the Olympic gymnasts Alfred and Gustav Flatow. Similarly, Munich has Elisabeth-Kohn-Strasse, Frankfurt Otto-Loewe-Strasse, and Hamburg Joseph-Carlebach-Platz, to name a few examples. Curiously, however, many older "Jewish" street names removed by the Nazis in the 1930s have not been restored.

Like many cities, Berlin has honored its famous Jewish residents in visible ways. Blue-and-white porcelain plaques indicate the former homes of the composers Arnold Schönberg and Kurt Weill, architect Erich Mendelsohn, painter Felix Nussbaum, poets Nelly Sachs and Else Lasker-Schüler, publishers Rudolf Mosse and Hans Ullstein, police vice president (deputy chief) Bernhard Weiß, and numerous others. The James Simon Gallery serves as the central visitors' center for Berlin's Museum Island. One can walk along the Rahel-Varnhagen-Promenade or relax in Henriette-Herz-Park. There are streets named for Cora Berliner, Gertrud Kolmar, and Leo Baeck.

Germany and Berlin have certainly not forgotten Hannah Arendt. The Technical University of Dresden has a Hannah Arendt Institute, while the

University of Oldenburg has a Hannah Arendt Center. A plaque recalls the house in Berlin where she lived before her emigration, and a Berlin school is named in her memory—one of many throughout Germany. More than a dozen cities in Germany have named streets for Arendt, but none is more prominent than Berlin's Hannah-Arendt-Strasse, immediately adjacent to the national Memorial to the Murdered Jews of Europe. Public memory of Walter Benjamin, a native son who wrote a memoir entitled *Berlin Childhood around 1900*, is much lighter. A plaque commemorates the building in Berlin-Wilmersdorf where he lived in the early 1930s and partially wrote his memoir, though not the house in Berlin-Grunewald where he spent his childhood. Conservative politicians and local residents in Grunewald prevented authorities from naming a street after Benjamin in the 1990s.[6] After years of construction, in 2001, the city opened the colonnade-lined Walter-Benjamin-Platz, close to the Kurfürstendamm, West Berlin's luxury shopping boulevard.

In contrast to Arendt and Benjamin, no blue-and-white porcelain plaque indicates where Werner Scholem lived or worked in Berlin. Perhaps his time as a leader of the Communist Party was too brief to warrant recognition by the city's historical commission and the local government. Moreover, as an anti-Stalinist Communist, the former East German regime was not going to acknowledge him with a memorial. Yet he is not entirely forgotten in the German capital. Embedded in the pavement near the location of his no-longer-extant home in Berlin's Hansa Quarter is a small brass plate, known in German as a *Stolperstein*, inscribed with the year of his arrest and the date of his murder in Buchenwald. This marker, only a few inches large, was sponsored by the neighborhood's Catholic church in 2004. Werner Scholem did serve in the Reichstag, a notable accomplishment, and he was killed by the Nazis. Thus, his name is one of ninety-six on the Memorial to the Murdered Members of the Reichstag, situated just outside the imposing parliament building. His name also appears on an art installation inside the building, alongside those of 4,780 other democratically elected members of Germany's federal legislature between 1919 and 1999.

Even those modest tributes are more than one finds for Gershom Scholem. No research institute or school in Germany bears his name. Despite an effort made shortly after his death, there are no streets or plazas named for him in his native city.[7] No one has erected a plaque at the site of his childhood home. To find a physical monument to Gershom Scholem in Berlin, one has to leave the bustle of the city center and travel to one of the quietest spots in the city: the Jewish cemetery of Berlin-Weißensee.

It is the largest Jewish cemetery in Europe and the final resting place of more than 115,000 German Jews. In the 1920s, a large staff maintained its 106 acres of landscaped terrain divided in neat rows.[8] Today, much of the cemetery is overgrown with ivy and brush, and it is hard to locate specific graves, excepting those of prominent individuals. Near the cemetery's back wall, a long walk from the front gate, is the grave of Arthur Scholem, who died in 1925. In the Jewish memorial tradition, visitors have left small stones along the edges of the tombstone, but it seems unlikely that they are there for Arthur Scholem, a modestly known printshop owner and expert on health insurance funds. In fact, they probably are for Gershom Scholem, who is not buried there.

Translated into English, the full inscription on the funerary monument:

Arthur Scholem
Born 1863 in Berlin Died 1925 in Berlin

Betty Scholem
née Hirsch
Born 1866 in Berlin Died 1946 in Sydney

Werner Scholem
Born 1895 in Berlin
Shot 1942 in Buchenwald

Erich Scholem
Born 1895 in Berlin Died 1965 in Sydney

Gerhard G. Scholem
Born 1897 in Berlin Died 1982 in Jerusalem

This tombstone, which has several inaccuracies, is the only physical remembrance of Gershom Scholem in Berlin.

Perhaps that is the way he would have wanted it. He gladly left Germany in 1923 and chronicled his German youth in a memoir pointedly entitled *From Berlin to Jerusalem*. When he died in Jerusalem in 1982, he was buried in that city's Sanhedria Cemetery, a short walk from both the Old City and the Hebrew University of Jerusalem. The inscription on his gravestone, which is entirely in Hebrew, recalls him as "a man of the Third *Aliyah*," the wave of Jewish immigration to Palestine from 1919 through 1923. Yet he returned to Germany over and over in his later years. Only months before his death, he basked in the affection that attended his time as a fellow at the

Wissenschaftskolleg zu Berlin. The local Jewish community welcomed him with open arms. He led a seminar on the *Zohar* for Berlin scholars. Younger fellows at the Wissenschaftskolleg literally kneeled at his feet to engage in dialogue with him as he sat on a high-backed chair and held forth.[9] Enjoying the respect of his fellow Berlin Jews and the adoration of non-Jewish scholars in Berlin, Gershom Scholem, the man who had so ardently renounced the world of the German-Jewish bourgeoisie, was at home.

ACKNOWLEDGMENTS

My exploration of the Scholem family began while researching for another book on German-Jewish history. In the spring of 1999, I was investigating the former West German chancellor Konrad Adenauer's relations with the Jews. The historian and Adenauer expert Hans Peter Mensing mentioned to me that in the 1920s, when Adenauer was the mayor of Cologne, he had sent a letter of support to a German Zionist committee. The committee published that letter in a pamphlet, a copy of which I found at the library of the Leo Baeck Institute in New York. As I transcribed the pamphlet's bibliographic information, I noticed that it had been printed by the firm of Siegfried Scholem in Berlin. I knew the name Scholem in connection with Gershom Scholem, the great scholar of Jewish mysticism, but I had never heard of Siegfried Scholem. After additional exploration, I learned that Siegfried was Gershom Scholem's grandfather and a publisher of some renown in Berlin. Later, while doing research on the former West German opposition leader Kurt Schumacher, I came across an encyclopedia entry for Werner Scholem, Gershom's brother, who was a leading Communist politician in the 1920s. Turning to Gershom Scholem's memoir, *From Berlin to Jerusalem*, I read about his other two brothers, characterized as a liberal centrist and a German nationalist. Though I was slightly acquainted with Gershom Scholem's work, I had not realized that he had come from such an interesting family. I was intrigued. I mentioned the Scholems' diverse politics to the Jewish historian Paula Hyman, for whom I was working as an assistant. She immediately made the comparison to the sociologist Robert Brym's theory of Jewish family origins and politicization, and she encouraged me to investigate the Scholems further. Many years later, here I am.

I owe a debt of gratitude to Hans Peter Mensing for indirectly starting me on this project and to the late Paula Hyman for repeatedly encouraging me to continue with it.

A research project like the one that culminated in this book requires tremendous support. I am deeply grateful to the Gerda Henkel Stiftung, which awarded me a fellowship for archival research in Germany. I am also grateful to Case Western Reserve University and the University of Tulsa for their financial support for this project. At Case Western Reserve University, particular thanks go to the Baker-Nord Center for the Humanities, the Office of Research and Technology Management, and the Samuel Rosenthal Professorship of Judaic Studies, with the support of Charlotte R. Kramer, Jane Horvitz, and their families.

The assistance of innumerable archivists, librarians, and scholars was also needed. I wish to acknowledge a few in particular: the late Margot Cohn, Alexander Gordin, Zvi Leshem, Stefan Litt, Paul Maurer, Rachel Misrati, Dani Reiss, and Aviad Stollman in Jerusalem; Michael Buckmiller in Hanover; Kerstin Bötticher in Berlin; Stephen Poppel in New York; Jessica Suzanne Mosher, MD, in Boston; Jennifer Starkey in Cleveland; Holger König of the Verein Historische Uniformen des Deutschen Kaiserreiches 1871–1918 e. V.; and the leaders of the Berliner-Turner-Verein von 1850 e. V. William Claspy deserves extra thanks for facilitating so much of my library research in Cleveland. Thanks also go to additional staff members of the National Library of Israel, particularly the Archives Department and the Gershom Scholem Library; the Central Archive for the History of the Jewish People; the Bundesarchiv (German Federal Archives) in Berlin; the Bibliothek für Bildungsgeschichtliche Forschung (Library for Education History Research); the Center for Jewish History and Leo Baeck Institute in New York; McFarlin Library at the University of Tulsa; and Kelvin Smith Library at Case Western Reserve University. Anja Schnabel assisted me greatly with my research in Jerusalem. Bill Rebiger, who has studied Gershom Scholem's Berlin, was a kind host and interlocutor.

I want to thank the Scholem family for offering assistance. The late David Scholem, Adam Scholem, Peter Scholem, and Woody Lewenstein shared family documents with me. Irene Scholem Ellison, Liesel Scholem, and Stephen Scholem shared their memories with me. It was a delight to meet Renee Goddard (née Renate Scholem) in London.

After having completed the bulk of my research on the Scholems, I was fortunate to be able to present my findings at several scholarly venues. Michael Berkowitz and Markham Geller kindly invited me to speak at the Institute of Jewish Studies, University College London. Those remarks became a chapter in a volume edited by Mirjam Zadoff and Noam Zadoff. I also delivered papers on Gershom Scholem at the annual conference of the German Studies Association, the Center for Jewish Studies at the University of Minnesota, and the Henry A. Turner Memorial Colloquium at Yale University. At each of those events, I received valuable feedback from audience members and fellow panelists.

A number of scholars aided me in shaping this narrative. Two readers for Cornell University Press provided exceptional feedback and helped improve the manuscript immensely. Marsha Rozenblit gave it a close read and made many suggestions for refinement. Marion Kaplan's work on the social history of German Jewry and Steven Aschheim's work on Gershom Scholem have been an inspiration since I began researching the Scholems and their world. The Scholem scholars Mirjam Zadoff and Noam Zadoff have followed this project for many years and offered criticism as they read earlier versions of this text. Ralf Hoffrogge was helpful with archival sources on Werner Scholem. David Biale, Gershom Scholem's first biographer, was very generous with his time and knowledge. I appreciate all the assistance and insights from these scholars.

Historians ask questions, research ideas, and write down their conclusions. However, turning a manuscript into a book requires a different skill set—that of an editor. I have been fortunate to work with Emily Andrew, senior editor at Cornell University Press. She has guided me in refining my exposition and argumentation. She helped me highlight those aspects that needed emphasis and was always open to hearing new ideas. My additional gratitude goes to Mahinder Kingra, editor in chief at Cornell University Press. His suggestions for the introduction and conclusion made me rethink the role of an academic historian as a storyteller. In sum, they have helped build a book. I cannot thank them enough.

Many friends have helped me in so many ways as I pondered and wrote about the Scholems. Rachel Gordan has always been willing to discuss Jewish history, the discipline of Judaic studies, and the world of academic publishing. Leslie Morris and William Gray were sounding boards as the project developed. At Case Western Reserve University, my colleagues have shared their thoughts and offered support, and special thanks go to Kenneth Ledford, David Hammack, Alan Rocke, Peter Haas, Susanne Vees-Gulani, and Cyrus Taylor. Samantha Lettieri provided extraordinary assistance in preparing the manuscript. Perach Kodish helped me with translations from Hebrew. Sabina Shcherbakova made it possible for me to have time to write the manuscript.

For as long as I can remember, the Geller family has delighted in my scholarly endeavors. I appreciate it immensely, though my joy in completing this book is tempered by the fact that my father did not live to see it. The Glauberg family has been intrigued as I researched this story, which closely resembles their own. This project has been a part of Mira, Sarah, and Louis's lives from the beginning. I have treasured their youthful interest in my work. During the many years that it took to research and write the Scholems' story,

I was accompanied by Valerie from Jerusalem to Berlin and beyond. She has done more than anyone else to help me turn an idea into reality. Thank you.

Finally, this book is dedicated to the memory of Selma Glauberg, Recha Glauberg Linick, Markus Linick, Paul Linick, Lucie Linick Gottlieb, and Heinz Gottlieb—members of the German-Jewish bourgeoisie, a family of printers, and six of the six million.

NOTES

The following abbreviations are used in the notes:

BArch   Bundesarchiv, Berlin
Correspondence-
  WBGS   Walter Benjamin and Gershom Scholem. *The Correspondence*
                    of Walter Benjamin and Gershom Scholem. Edited by Gershom
                    Scholem. Translated by Gary Smith and André Lefevere.
                    Cambridge, Mass.: Harvard University Press, 1992.
GJHMT   Michael A. Meyer, ed. *German-Jewish History in Modern Times.*
                    4 vols. New York: Columbia University Press, 1996–1998.
LAB   Landesarchiv Berlin
LBIYB   *Leo Baeck Institute Year Book*
LUH, IPW   Leibniz Universität Hannover, Institut für Politische Wissenschaft
MuSiB   Betty Scholem and Gershom Scholem. *Mutter und Sohn im*
                    Briefwechsel 1917–1946. Edited by Itta Shedletzky. Munich: C. H.
                    Beck, 1989.
NLI   National Library of Israel
SAPMO   Stiftung Archiv der Parteien und Massenorganisationen der DDR
VBnJ   Gershom Scholem. *Von Berlin nach Jerusalem. Jugenderinnerungen.*
                    Rev. ed. Translated by Michael Brocke and Andrea Schatz.
                    Frankfurt: Jüdischer Verlag, 1994.
WBTSF   Gershom Scholem. *Walter Benjamin: The Story of a Friendship.*
                    Translated by Harry Zohn. Philadelphia: Jewish Publication
                    Society of America, 1981. Reprint, New York: New York Review
                    Books, 2003.

Introduction

1. On cultural identity and social class as determinants of political views among Russian Jewish families, see Robert J. Brym, *The Jewish Intelligentsia and Russian Marxism: A Sociological Study of Intellectual Radicalism and Ideological Divergence* (New York: Schocken, 1978).

2. Gershom Scholem, *From Berlin to Jerusalem: Memories of My Youth*, trans. Harry Zohn (New York: Schocken, 1980), 42.

3. Shulamit Volkov, *Germans, Jews, and Antisemites: Trials in Emancipation* (Cambridge: Cambridge University Press, 2006), 30.

4. Reinhold Scholem to Gershom Scholem, 29 February 1972, Gershom Scholem Collection, Archive Department, National Library of Israel (hereafter cited as NLI), ARC. 4*1599/01/3031.

5. On the Jews and German politics, see, among others, Jacob Toury, *Die politischen Orientierungen der Juden in Deutschland. Von Jena bis Weimar* (Tübingen: Mohr Siebeck, 1966); Ernest Hamburger, *Juden im öffentlichen Leben Deutschlands. Regierungsmitglieder, Beamte und Parlamentarier in der monarchischen Zeit 1848–1918* (Tübingen: Mohr Siebeck, 1968); Donald L. Niewyk, *The Jews in Weimar Germany* (Baton Rouge: Louisiana State University Press, 1980); Ernest Hamburger and Peter Pulzer, "Jews as Voters in the Weimar Republic," *LBIYB* 30 (1985): 3–66; Peter Pulzer, *Jews and the German State: The Political History of a Minority, 1848–1933* (Oxford: Blackwell, 1992); Ludger Heid and Arnold Paucker, eds., *Juden und deutsche Arbeiterbewegung bis 1933. Soziale Utopien und religiös-kulturelle Traditionen* (Tübingen: J. C. B. Mohr [Paul Siebeck], 1992); and Martin Liepach, *Das Wahlverhalten der jüdischen Bevölkerung. Zur politischen Orientierung der Juden in der Weimarer Republik* (Tübingen: J. C. B. Mohr [Paul Siebeck], 1996). On Jewish communal politics, see, among others, Jacob Toury, "Organizational Problems of German Jewry: Steps towards the Establishment of a Central Organization (1893–1920)," *LBIYB* 13 (1968): 57–90; Stephen M. Poppel, *Zionism in Germany, 1897–1933: The Shaping of a Jewish Identity* (Philadelphia: Jewish Publication Society of America, 1977); Marjorie Lamberti, *Jewish Activism in Imperial Germany* (New Haven, Conn.: Yale University Press, 1978); Marion A. Kaplan, *The Jewish Feminist Movement in Germany: The Campaigns of the Jüdischer Frauenbund, 1904–1938* (Westport, Conn.: Greenwood, 1979); Hagit Lavsky, *Before Catastrophe: The Distinctive Path of German Zionism* (Detroit, Mich.: Wayne State University Press, 1996); Avraham Barkai, *"Wehr Dich!" Der Centralverein deutscher Staatsbürger jüdischen Glaubens 1893–1938* (Munich: C. H. Beck, 2002); and Stefan Vogt, *Subalterne Positionierungen. Der deutsche Zionismus im Feld des Nationalismus in Deutschland 1890–1933* (Göttingen: Wallstein, 2016).

6. Arthur Prinz, *Juden im Deutschen Wirtschaftsleben. Soziale und wirtschaftliche Struktur im Wandel 1850–1914*, ed. Avraham Barkai (Tübingen: Mohr Siebeck, 1984); Werner E. Mosse, *Jews in the German Economy: The German-Jewish Economic Élite, 1820–1935* (Oxford: Clarendon Press, 1987); Tillmann Krach, *Jüdische Rechtsanwälte in Preußen. Über die Bedeutung der freien Advokatur und ihre Zerstörung durch den Nationalsozialismus* (Munich: C. H. Beck, 1991); John M. Efron, *Medicine and the German Jews: A History* (New Haven, Conn.: Yale University Press, 2001).

7. Selected essays in Werner E. Mosse and Arnold Paucker, eds., *Juden im Wilhelminischen Deutschland 1890–1914. Ein Sammelband* (Tübingen: Mohr Siebeck, 1971); Michael Brenner, *The Renaissance of Jewish Culture in Weimar Germany* (New Haven, Conn.: Yale University Press, 1998); Michael Brenner and Derek Jonathan Penslar, eds., *In Search of Jewish Community: Jewish Identities in Germany and Austria, 1918–1933* (Bloomington: Indiana University Press, 1998); Simone Lässig, *Jüdische Wege ins Bürgertum. Kulturelles Kapital und sozialer Aufstieg im 19. Jahrhundert* (Göttingen: Vandenhoeck & Ruprecht, 2004); Benjamin Maria Baader, *Gender, Judaism, and Bourgeois Culture in Germany, 1800–1870* (Bloomington: Indiana University Press, 2006).

8. Siegmund Kaznelson, ed., *Juden im deutschen Kulturbereich. Ein Sammelwerk*, 3rd ed. (Berlin: Jüdischer Verlag, 1962); Julius H. Schoeps, ed., *Juden als Träger bürgerlicher Kultur in Deutschland* (Stuttgart: Burg, 1989). Cf. Peter Gay, *Freud, Jews and Other Germans: Masters and Victims in Modernist Culture* (New York: Oxford University Press, 1978).

9. Cf. Amos Elon, *The Pity of It All: A History of the Jews in Germany, 1743–1933* (New York: Metropolitan, 2002). The book was republished as *The Pity of It All: A Portrait of the German-Jewish Epoch, 1743–1933*. On Jewish emancipation, see, among

others, Jacob Katz, *Out of the Ghetto: The Social Background of Jewish Emancipation, 1770–1870* (Cambridge, Mass.: Harvard University Press, 1973); Annegret H. Brammer, *Judenpolitik und Judengesetzgebung in Preussen 1812 bis 1847 mit einem Ausblick auf das Gleichberechtigungsgesetz des Norddeutschen Bundes von 1869* (Berlin: Schelzky & Jeep, 1987); and Marion Schulte, *Über die bürgerlichen Verhältnisse der Juden in Preussen. Ziele und Motive der Reformzeit (1787–1812)* (Berlin: Walter de Gruyter, 2014). On Jewish integration, see George L. Mosse, *German Jews beyond Judaism* (Bloomington: Indiana University Press, 1985); Deborah Hertz, *Jewish High Society in Old Regime Berlin* (New Haven, Conn.: Yale University Press, 1988; reprint, Syracuse, N.Y.: Syracuse University Press, 2005); David Sorkin, *The Transformation of German Jewry, 1780–1840* (New York: Oxford University Press, 1987); Steven M. Lowenstein, *The Berlin Jewish Community: Enlightenment, Family, and Crisis* (New York: Oxford University Press, 1994); and Deborah Hertz, *How Jews Became Germans: The History of Conversion and Assimilation in Berlin* (New Haven, Conn.: Yale University Press, 2007).

10. Diary entry, 22 February 1913, in Gershom Scholem, *Tagebücher nebst Aufsätzen und Entwürfen bis 1923*, vol. 1, *1913–1917*, ed. Karlfried Gründer and Friedrich Niewöhner (Frankfurt: Jüdischer Verlag, 1995), 13–14.

11. E.g., Elon, *Pity of It All*; and Marion A. Kaplan, ed., *Jewish Daily Life in Germany, 1618–1945* (New York: Oxford University Press, 2005).

12. Saul Friedländer, *Nazi Germany and the Jews*, vol. 1, *The Years of Persecution, 1933–1939* (New York: HarperCollins, 1997), 291.

13. Yoav Gelber, *Moledet hadashah. Aliyat Yehude merkaz Eropah u-kelitatam 1933–1948* (Jerusalem: Makon Leo Baeck, 1990); Moshe Zimmermann and Yotam Hotam, eds., *Zweimal Heimat. Die Jeckes zwischen Mitteleuropa und Nahost* (Frankfurt: beerenverlag, 2005); Joachim Schlör, *Endlich im Gelobten Land? Deutsche Juden unterwegs in eine neue Heimat* (Berlin: Aufbau, 2003); Gisela Dachs, *Die Jeckes* (Frankfurt: Jüdischer Verlag, 2005); Claudia Sonino, *German Jews in Palestine, 1920–1948: Between Dream and Reality*, trans. Juliet Haydock (Lanham, Md.: Lexington Books, 2016).

14. Tobias Brinkmann, *Migration und Transnationalität* (Paderborn: Ferdinand Schöningh, 2010); Jay Howard Geller and Leslie Morris, eds., *Three-Way Street: Jews, Germans, and the Transnational* (Ann Arbor: University of Michigan Press, 2016). Hagit Lavsky has examined the push and pull factors that fostered Jewish emigration from Germany in the interwar years. Hagit Lavsky, *The Creation of the German-Jewish Diaspora: Interwar German-Jewish Immigration to Palestine, the USA, and England* (Berlin: Walter de Gruyter, 2017).

15. Among the best thematic surveys of German-Jewish history are Trude Maurer, *Die Entwicklung der jüdischen Minderheit in Deutschland (1780–1933). Neuere Forschungen und offene Fragen* (Tübingen: Max Niemeyer, 1992); Michael A. Meyer, ed., *German-Jewish History in Modern Times*, vol. 1, *Tradition and Enlightenment, 1600–1780*, vol. 2, *Emancipation and Acculturation, 1780–1871*, vol. 3, *Integration in Dispute, 1871–1918*, vol. 4, *Renewal and Destruction, 1918–1945* (New York: Columbia University Press, 1996, 1997, 1997, 1998) (hereafter cited as *GJHMT*); and Kaplan, *Jewish Daily Life in Germany*.

16. Marion A. Kaplan, *The Making of the Jewish Middle Class: Women, Family and Identity in Imperial Germany* (New York: Oxford University Press, 1991); Marion A. Kaplan, *Between Dignity and Despair: Jewish Life in Nazi Germany* (New York: Oxford University Press, 1998).

17. E.g., Niall Ferguson, *The House of Rothschild: Money's Prophets, 1798–1848* (New York: Viking Penguin, 1998); Niall Ferguson, *The House of Rothschild: The World's Banker, 1849–1998* (New York: Viking Penguin, 1999); Ron Chernow, *The Warburgs: The Twentieth-Century Odyssey of a Remarkable Jewish Family* (New York: Random House, 1993); Elisabeth Kraus, *Die Familie Mosse. Deutsch-jüdisches Bürgertum im 19. und 20. Jahrhundert* (Munich: C. H. Beck, 1999); Erica Fischer and Simone Ladwig-Winters, *Die Wertheims. Geschichte einer Familie* (Berlin: Rowohlt-Berlin, 2004); and Sigrid Bauschinger, *Die Cassirers. Unternehmer, Kunsthändler, Philosophen: Biographie einer Familie*, 2nd ed. (Munich: C. H. Beck, 2016).

18. Till van Rahden, *Jews and Other Germans: Civil Society, Religious Diversity, and Urban Politics in Breslau, 1860–1925*, trans. Marcus Brainard (Madison: University of Wisconsin Press, 2008), 8 and 9.

19. Fritz Stern, *Five Germanys I Have Known* (New York: Farrar, Straus and Giroux, 2006), 82. In his study of Jewish society in Breslau, Till van Rahden notes the high level of Jewish integration in Breslau and claims a precipitous deterioration of the Jews' situation after 1916. Rahden, *Jews and Other Germans*, 231–238.

20. Dolores L. Augustine, "Arriving in the Upper Class: The Wealthy Business Elite of Wilhelmine Germany," in *The German Bourgeoisie: Essays on the Social History of the German Middle Class from the Late Eighteenth to the Early Twentieth Century*, ed. David Blackbourn and Richard J. Evans (New York: Routledge, 1991), 56–60.

21. Gershom Scholem, *Von Berlin nach Jerusalem. Jugenderinnerungen* (Frankfurt: Suhrkamp, 1977), in English as *From Berlin to Jerusalem: Memories of My Youth*, trans. Harry Zohn (New York: Schocken, 1980); revised as *Mi-Berlin li-Yerushalayim. Zikhronot ne'urim* (Tel Aviv: Am Oved, 1982) and *Von Berlin nach Jerusalem. Jugenderinnerungen*, trans. Michael Brocke and Andrea Schatz (Frankfurt: Jüdischer Verlag, 1994) (hereafter cited as *VBnJ*).

22. Cynthia Ozick, "The Mystic Explorer," *New York Times*, 21 September 1980.

23. Ozick, "Mystic Explorer," *New York Times*, 21 September 1980.

24. Cf. Michael Brenner, "A Tale of Two Families: Franz Rosenzweig, Gershom Scholem and the Generational Conflict around Judaism," *Judaism: A Quarterly Journal of Jewish Life and Thought* 42, no. 3 (Summer 1993): 349; and Jay Howard Geller, "The Scholem Brothers and the Paths of German Jewry, 1914–1939," *Shofar: An Interdisciplinary Journal of Jewish Studies* 30, no. 2 (Winter 2012): 52–73.

25. David Biale, "The Demonic in History: Gershom Scholem and the Revision of Jewish Historiography" (PhD diss., University of California, Los Angeles, 1977), published as David Biale, *Gershom Scholem: Kabbalah and Counter-History* (Cambridge, Mass.: Harvard University Press, 1979).

26. See, among others, David Biale, *Gershom Scholem: Kabbalah and Counter-History*, 2nd ed. (Cambridge, Mass.: Harvard University Press, 1982); Harold Bloom, ed., *Gershom Scholem* (New York: Chelsea House, 1987); Joseph Dan, *Gershom Scholem and the Mystical Dimension of Jewish History* (New York: New York University Press, 1987); Paul Mendes-Flohr, ed., *Gershom Scholem: The Man and His Work* (Albany: State University of New York Press, 1994); Peter Schäfer and Gary Smith, eds., *Gershom Scholem. Zwischen den Disziplinen* (Frankfurt: Suhrkamp, 1995); Elisabeth Hamacher, *Gershom Scholem und die allgemeine Religionsgeschichte* (New York: Walter de Gruyter, 1999); Steven M. Wasserstrom, *Religion after Religion: Gershom Scholem, Mircea Eliade, and Henry Corbin at Eranos* (Princeton, N.J.: Princeton University Press, 1999);

Stéphane Mosès and Sigrid Weigel, eds., *Gershom Scholem. Literatur und Rhetorik* (Cologne: Böhlau, 2000); Daniel Weidner, *Gershom Scholem. Politisches, esoterisches und historiographisches Schreiben* (Munich: Wilhelm Fink, 2003); Steven E. Aschheim, "The Metaphysical Psychologist: On the Life and Letters of Gershom Scholem," *Journal of Modern History* 76, no. 4 (December 2004): 903–933; Bill Rebiger, "'Das Wesentliche spielt sich nicht auf der Leipziger Straße ab, sondern . . . im Geheimen'—Gershom Scholem und Berlin," *European Association for Jewish Studies Newsletter* 16 (Spring 2005): 81–99; [Michael Brenner, ed.], "Zur Historischen Gestalt Gershom Scholems," special issue of *Münchner Beiträge zur Jüdischen Geschichte und Kultur* 1, no. 2 (2007); Benjamin Lazier, *God Interrupted: Heresy and the European Imagination between the World Wars* (Princeton, N.J.: Princeton University Press, 2009); Moshe Idel, *Old Worlds, New Mirrors: On Jewish Mysticism and Twentieth-Century Thought* (Philadelphia: University of Pennsylvania Press, 2010); Joseph Dan, *Al Gershom Scholem. Teresar ma'amarim* (Jerusalem: Merkaz Zalman Shazar le-toldot Yisrael, 2010); Enrico Lucca, "Una visione dialettica della storia ebraica: Gershom Scholem e l'eredità del messianismo" (PhD diss., Università degli Studi di Milano, 2012); Ronny Miron, *The Angel of Jewish History: The Image of the Jewish Past in the Twentieth Century* (Brighton, Mass.: Academic Studies Press, 2014); David Biale, "Gershom Scholem, *Einst und Jetzt*: Zionist Politics and Kabbalistic Historiography," in *Against the Grain: Jewish Intellectuals in Hard Times*, ed. Ezra Mendelsohn, Stefani Hoffman, and Richard I. Cohen (New York: Berghahn Books, 2014), 51–63; Zohar Maor, "Death or Birth: Scholem and Secularization," in Mendelsohn, Hoffman, and Cohen, *Against the Grain*, 64–85; Gerold Necker, Elke Morlok, and Matthias Morgenstern, eds., *Gershom Scholem in Deutschland. Zwischen Seelenverwandtschaft und Sprachlosigkeit* (Tübingen: Mohr Siebeck, 2014); Bill Rebiger, "Auch eine Berliner Kindheit um Neunzehnhundert. Zur Biographie des jungen Gershom Scholem bis 1915," in Necker, Morlok, and Morgenstern, *Gershom Scholem in Deutschland*, 19–36; Paul Reitter, *Bambi's Jewish Roots and Other Essays on German-Jewish Culture* (New York: Bloomsbury Academic, 2015), 11–27; and Mirjam Zadoff and Noam Zadoff, eds., *Scholar and Kabbalist: The Life and Work of Gershom Scholem* (Leiden: Brill, 2019).

27. Among others: Jürgen Habermas, *Philosophical-Political Profiles*, trans. Frederick G. Lawrence (Cambridge, Mass.: MIT Press, 1983), 129–164, 171–188, and 199–210; Harold Bloom, *The Strong Light of the Canonical: Kafka, Freud, and Scholem as Revisionists of Jewish Culture and Thought* (New York: City College, 1987); Robert Alter, *Necessary Angels: Tradition and Modernity in Kafka, Benjamin, and Scholem* (Cambridge, Mass.: Harvard University Press, 1991); Susan A. Handelman, *Fragments of Redemption: Jewish Thought and Literary Theory in Benjamin, Scholem, and Levinas* (Bloomington: Indiana University Press, 1991); Steven E. Aschheim, *Scholem, Arendt, Klemperer: Intimate Chronicles in Turbulent Times* (Bloomington: Indiana University Press, 2001); Eric Jacobson, *Metaphysics of the Profane: The Political Theology of Walter Benjamin and Gershom Scholem* (New York: Columbia University Press, 2003); Steven E. Aschheim, *Beyond the Border: The German-Jewish Legacy Abroad* (Princeton, N.J.: Princeton University Press, 2007); Gabriele Guerra, *Judentum zwischen Anarchie und Theokratie. Eine religionspolitische Diskussion am Beispiel der Begegnung zwischen Walter Benjamin und Gershom Scholem* (Bielefeld: Aisthesis, 2007); Bram Mertens, *Dark Images, Secret Hints: Benjamin, Scholem, Molitor and the Jewish Tradition* (New York: Peter Lang, 2007); Stéphane Mosès, *The Angel of History: Rosenzweig, Benjamin, Scholem*, trans.

Barbara Harshav (Stanford, Calif.: Stanford University Press, 2008); Carl Djerassi, *Four Jews on Parnassus—a Conversation: Benjamin, Adorno, Scholem, Schönberg* (New York: Columbia University Press, 2008). See also Gershom Scholem, *Walter Benjamin: The Story of a Friendship*, trans. Harry Zohn (Philadelphia: Jewish Publication Society of America, 1981; reprint, New York: New York Review Books, 2003) (hereafter cited as *WBTSF*); and Walter Benjamin and Gershom Scholem, *The Correspondence of Walter Benjamin and Gershom Scholem, 1932–1940*, ed. Gershom Scholem, trans. Gary Smith and André Lefevere (Cambridge, Mass.: Harvard University Press, 1992) (hereafter cited as *Correspondence-WBGS*).

28. Amir Engel, *Gershom Scholem: An Intellectual Biography* (Chicago: University of Chicago Press, 2017); George Prochnik, *Stranger in a Strange Land: Searching for Gershom Scholem and Jerusalem* (New York: Other Press, 2017); Noam Zadoff, *Gershom Scholem: From Berlin to Jerusalem and Back; An Intellectual Biography*, trans. Jeffrey Green (Waltham, Mass.: Brandeis University Press, 2018); David Biale, *Gershom Scholem: Master of the Kabbalah* (New Haven, Conn.: Yale University Press, 2018).

29. Ralf Hoffrogge, *Werner Scholem. Eine politische Biographie (1895–1940)* (Konstanz: UVK Verlagsgesellschaft, 2014); Mirjam Zadoff, *Der rote Hiob. Das Leben des Werner Scholem* (Munich: Carl Hanser, 2014). See also Michael Buckmiller and Pascal Nafe, "Die Naherwartung des Kommunismus—Werner Scholem," in *Judentum und politische Existenz. Siebzehn Porträts deutsch-jüdischer Intellektueller*, ed. Michael Buckmiller, Dietrich Heimann, and Joachim Perels (Hanover: Offizin, 2000), 61–82.

30. Diary entry, n.d. [winter 1913], in Gershom Scholem, *Tagebücher*, 1:9; Gershom Scholem, *VBnJ*, 9.

31. Jacob Borut, "The Province versus Berlin?: Relations between Berlin and the Other Communities as a Factor in German Jewish Organisational History at the End of the Nineteenth Century," *LBIYB* 44 (1999): 127–142; Reinhard Rürup, "Jewish History in Berlin—Berlin in Jewish History," *LBIYB* 45 (2000): 50.

1. Origins

1. Klaus Klöppel, *Breslau. Niederschlesien und seine tausendjährige Hauptstadt*, 5th ed. (Berlin: Trescher Verlag, 2016), 212–214; Franz D. Lucas and Margret Heitmann, *Stadt des Glaubens. Geschichte und Kultur der Juden in Glogau*, 2nd ed. (Hildesheim: Georg Solms, 1992), 379.

2. Tobias Schenk, "Das Emanzipationsedikt—Ausdruck 'defensiver Modernisierung' oder Abschluss rechtsstaatlicher Entwicklungen des '(aufgeklärten) Absolutismus'?," in *Das Emanzipationsedikt von 1812 in Preußen. Der lange Weg der Juden zu "Einländern" und "preußischen Staatsbürgern*," ed. Irene A. Diekmann (Berlin: Walter de Gruyter, 2013), 38.

3. Mordechai Breuer, "The Early Modern Period," in Meyer, *GJHMT*, 1:147–151.

4. Prussia, *Gesetz-Sammlung für die Königlichen Preußischen Staaten 1812* (Berlin: Georg Decker, [1812]), 17–22, reprinted in Moritz Veit, *Der Entwurf einer Verordnung über die Verhältnisse der Juden und das Edikt vom 11. März 1812* (Leipzig: F. A. Brockhaus, [1847]), 22–31.

5. Stefi Jersch-Wenzel, "Legal Status and Emancipation," in Meyer, *GJHMT*, 2:24–30 and 38–49.

6. Gershom Scholem, *VBnJ*, 9.

7. "Verzeichnis der am 24. März 1812 in Glogau lebenden Familien," in Lucas and Heitmann, *Stadt des Glaubens*, 552. She does not appear on the "Allgemeiner Nachweis der Ao. 1812 angenommenen Familien-Namen und der damaligen Minorennen der Hiesigen Gemeinde," Lucas and Heitmann, 524–525.

8. On Abraham Scholem, born in Krakow, family tree and private correspondence between Peter Scholem and the author. On Abraham Scholem in Brandenburg, Geheimes Staatsarchiv Preußischer Kulturbesitz, I. HA Geheimer Rat, Rep. 49 Fiscalia E, Strafsachen, 1763–1771. It is not clear that this Scholem was an ancestor of Gershom Scholem, but the latter did note that his surname was exceptionally uncommon. Gershom Scholem, *VBnJ*, 9.

9. Stefi Jersch-Wenzel, "Population Shifts and Occupational Structure," in Meyer, *GJHMT*, 2:55–57.

10. Bernhard Brilling to Gershom Scholem, 5 April 1978, NLI, ARC. 4*1599/01/0365.

11. Bernhard Brilling, "Geschichte des jüdischen Goldschmiedegewerbes in Schlesien," *Hamburger Mittel- und Ostdeutsche Forschungen* 6 (1967): 181 and 204. There is some confusion over Marcus's date of birth. Bernhard Brilling reported his birth date as 20 February 1798; however, Berlin city records provided 20 February 1789, and Marcus's tombstone read 1800. Bernhard Brilling to Gershom Scholem, 6 December 1977, NLI, ARC. 4*1599/01/0365; Gershom Scholem to Reinhold Scholem, 4 July 1973, NLI, ARC. 4*1599/01/3031; Jacob Jacobson, *Die Judenbürgerbücher der Stadt Berlin 1809–1851* (Berlin: Walter de Gruyter, 1962), 187 and 364–365; photograph of Marcus Scholem's grave, taken by Reinhold Scholem ca. 1937, David Scholem Collection.

12. Jersch-Wenzel, "Population Shifts and Occupational Structure," in Meyer, *GJHMT*, 2:55–57.

13. Friedrich Nicolai, *Beschreibung der Königlichen Residenzstädte Berlin und Potsdam, aller daselbst befindlicher Merkwürdigkeiten, und der umliegenden Gegend*, 3rd ed. (Berlin: Friedrich Nicolai, 1786), 240.

14. Claudia-Ann Flumenbaum, "From the Beginnings until 1789," in Nachama, Schoeps, and Simon, *Jews in Berlin*, 16–17.

15. Lowenstein, *Berlin Jewish Community*, 10–11 and 14; Richard Borrmann, *Die Bau- und Kunstdenkmäler von Berlin* (Berlin: Julius Springer, 1893), 257; David Joseph, "Stiftshütte, Tempel- und Synagogenbauten (Schluss)," *Ost und West* 1, no. 11 (November 1901): 845; Bill Rebiger, *Das jüdische Berlin. Kultur, Religion und Alltag gestern und heute*, 3rd ed. (Berlin: Jaron, 2007), 70.

16. Breuer, "Early Modern Period," in Meyer, *GJHMT*, 1:151; Nicolai, *Beschreibung der Königlichen Residenzstädte Berlin und Potsdam*, 240.

17. Lowenstein, *Berlin Jewish Community*, 35–41, 78–79, and 104–110; Hertz, *Jewish High Society*.

18. Lowenstein, *Berlin Jewish Community*, 136–137, 99–100, and 120–133; Hertz, *Jewish High Society*, 204–250.

19. Michael A. Meyer, "The Religious Reform Controversy in the Berlin Jewish Community, 1814–1823," *LBIYB* 24 (1979): 150.

20. Lowenstein, *Berlin Jewish Community*, 136–140, 126, 144, and 7.

21. E. F. W. Wegener, ed., *Haus- und General-Adressbuch der Königl. Haupt- und Residenzstadt Berlin auf das Jahr 1822* (Berlin: E. F. W. Wegener, 1822), 124; J. W. Boicke, ed., *Allgemeiner Wohnungsanzeiger für Berlin auf das Jahr 1827* (Berlin: J. W. Boicke, 1827), n.p.

22. Lowenstein, *Berlin Jewish Community*, 16–18 and 142.

23. Jacobson, *Die Judenbürgerbücher der Stadt Berlin*, 187 and 364.

24. Jacobson, *Die Judenbürgerbücher der Stadt Berlin*, 187 and 364.

25. Steven M. Lowenstein, "The Beginning of Integration, 1780–1870," in Kaplan, *Jewish Daily Life in Germany*, 109–110.

26. Jacobson, *Die Judenbürgerbücher der Stadt Berlin*, 187 and 364; Wegener, ed., *Haus- und General-Adressbuch* (1822), 124; Boicke, ed., *Allgemeiner Wohnungsanzeiger* (1827), n.p.; E. Winckler, ed., *Adress-Buch für Berlin mit Einschluß der nähern Umgegend und Charlottenburg auf das Jahr 1835* (Berlin: H. A. W. Logier, 1835), 301.

27. Jersch-Wenzel, "Population Shifts and Occupational Structure," in Meyer, *GJHMT*, 2:79–81.

28. Königlicher Polizei-Rath Winckler, ed., *Allgemeiner Wohnungsanzeiger für Berlin, Charlottenburg und Umgebungen auf das Jahr 1842* (Berlin: Veit und Comp., 1842), 1:393 and 4:133; Königlicher Polizei-Rath Winckler, ed., *Allgemeiner Wohnungsanzeiger für Berlin, Charlottenburg und Umgebungen auf das Jahr 1846* (Berlin: Veit und Comp., 1846), 421 and 775; Kaplan, *Making of the Jewish Middle Class*, 154–155.

29. Gershom Scholem, *VBnJ*, 11.

30. Steven M. Lowenstein, "The Pace of Modernization of German Jewry in the Nineteenth Century," *LBIYB* 21 (1976): 41–56.

31. Gershom Scholem, *VBnJ*, 12; certificate ("Bescheinigung") from the Gesamtarchiv der Juden in Deutschland, 15 August 1938, David Scholem Collection; last will and testament of Siegfried Scholem, 20 January 1901, NLI, ARC. 4*1599/02/1; Lowenstein, "Pace of Modernization," *LBIYB* 21 (1976): 46.

32. Lowenstein, *Berlin Jewish Community*, 180; Lowenstein, "Pace of Modernization," *LBIYB* 21 (1976): 43–44; Steven M. Lowenstein, "The Community," in Meyer, *GJHMT*, 3:135.

33. Michael Brenner, "Between Revolution and Legal Equality," in Meyer, *GJHMT*, 2:301.

34. Lowenstein, "Beginning of Integration, 1780–1870," in Kaplan, *Jewish Daily Life in Germany*, 138–139.

35. "Zeugnis für den Buchdruckergehülfen Solm Marcus Scholem," 4 October 1859, NLI, ARC. *1599/02/2; Friedrich Heimbertsohn Hinze, *Poetische Schriften*, ed. Friedrich Meyer von Waldeck (Berlin: A. Duncker, 1859); last will and testament of Siegfried Scholem, 20 January 1901, NLI, ARC. 4*1599/02/1.

36. E.g., *Talmud Bavli* (Berlin: Julius Sittenfeld, 1861–1868).

37. Lowenstein, *Berlin Jewish Community*, 180–181; Hertz, *Jewish High Society*, 229.

38. Marion A. Kaplan, "For Love or Money: The Marriage Strategies of Jews in Imperial Germany," *LBIYB* 28 (1983): 263–300.

39. Last will and testament of Siegfried Scholem, 20 January 1901 (copy dated 5 September 1972), David Scholem Collection; Jacobson, *Die Judenbürgerbücher der Stadt Berlin*, 535; Gershom Scholem, *VBnJ*, 15 and 45.

40. Data on self-employment is from 1871. Brenner, "Between Revolution and Legal Equality," in Meyer, *GJHMT*, 2:306.

41. Last will and testament of Siegfried Scholem, 20 January 1901 (copy dated 5 September 1972), David Scholem Collection.

42. Siegfried Scholem, ed., *Fest-Programm für den Einzug der siegreichen Krieger in Berlin am 16. Juni 1871* (Berlin: Siegfried Scholem, [1871]).

43. Brenner, "Between Revolution and Legal Equality," in Meyer, *GJHMT*, 2:301.

44. Frank B. Tipton, *A History of Modern Germany since 1815* (London: Continuum, 2003), 141 and 143.

45. Photograph of Amalie Scholem in Karlsbad, July 1889, David Scholem Collection.

46. Photograph of Sebastianstrasse 20, n.d., David Scholem Collection.

47. Steven M. Lowenstein, "Ideology and Identity," in Meyer, *GJHMT*, 3:281–304, esp. 282–290.

48. Lowenstein, "Community," in Meyer, *GJHMT*, 3:135.

49. Köllnisches Gymnasium zu Berlin, *Jahresbericht über das Schuljahr 1895–96* (Berlin: Felgentreff, 1896), 27; "Die zweite Lesung der Besoldungsvorlage in der Budgetskommission des Abgeordnetenhauses," *Wochenschrift für deutsche Bahnmeister* 14, no. 11 (14 March 1897): 98–99.

50. Luisenstädtisches Realgymnasium, *Bericht über das Schuljahr 1886–1887* (Berlin: Otto Elsner, 1887), 21; James C. Albisetti and Peter Lundgreen, "Höhere Knabenschulen," in *Handbuch der deutschen Bildungsgeschichte*, vol. 4, *1870–1918, Von der Reichsgründung bis zum Ende des Ersten Weltkrieges*, ed. Christa Berg (Munich: C. H. Beck, 1991), 247; Marion A. Kaplan, "As Germans and as Jews in Imperial Germany," in Kaplan, *Jewish Daily Life in Germany*, 202.

51. Luisenstädtisches Realgymnasium, *Bericht über das Schuljahr 1886–1887*, 18 and 24; Luisenstädtisches Realgymnasium, *Bericht über das Schuljahr 1901–1902* (Berlin: Naucksche Buchdruckerei, 1902), 28.

52. Max is the only son for whom there is an extant archival record that he left the school for an apprenticeship. Luisenstädtisches Realgymnasium Jahrgänge 1852–1897 Schülerverzeichnis, Landesarchiv Berlin, A Rep. 020–04, 147, entry no. 6227 (hereafter cited as LAB).

53. Gershom Scholem, *VBnJ*, 12–13; Reinhold Scholem to Gershom Scholem, 10 February 1978, NLI, ARC. 4*1599/01/3031.

54. Kaplan, "As Germans and as Jews," in Kaplan, *Jewish Daily Life in Germany*, 191 and 210; Gershom Scholem, *VBnJ*, 27; Victor Klemperer, *Curriculum Vitae: Jugend um 1900*, vol. 1 (Berlin: Siedler Verlag, 1989), 599–600.

55. Claudia Huerkamp, *Der Aufstieg der Ärzte im 19. Jahrhundert. Vom gelehrten Stand zum professionellen Experten: Das Beispiel Preußens* (Göttingen: Vandenhoeck & Ruprecht, 1985), 81–85; Monika Richarz, "Occupational Distribution and Social Structure," in Meyer, *GJHMT*, 3:57.

56. Georg Scholem attended the Luisenstädtisches Realgymnasium from 4 September 1883 to 1 October 1889. Luisenstädtisches Realgymnasium Jahrgänge 1852–1897 Schülerverzeichnis, LAB, A Rep. 020–04, 147, entry no. 6515. He passed his school-leaving examination with respectable, but not extraordinary grades. "Verzeichnis der Ober-Primaner am Köllnischen Gymnasium zu Berlin, welche sich für den Michaelis-Termin 1895 zur Abiturienten-Prüfung gemeldet haben" and "Ergebnisse der Abiturienten-Prüfung an dem Köllnischen Gymnasium zu Berlin Michaelis 1895," LAB, A Rep. 020–09, 176.

57. Köllnisches Gymnasium zu Berlin, *Jahresbericht über das Schuljahr 1895–96*, 22–23.

58. Friedrich-Wilhelms-Universität zu Berlin, *Amtliches Verzeichnis des Personals und der Studierenden der Königlichen Friedrich-Wilhelms-Universität zu Berlin* (Berlin: Gustav Schade, 1895), 140; Friedrich-Wilhelms-Universität zu Berlin, *Amtliches Verzeichnis des Personals und der Studierenden der Königlichen Friedrich-Wilhelms-Universität zu Berlin* (Berlin: Gustav Schade, 1899), 173; "Georg und Phiechens Werdegang," David Scholem Collection; Georg Scholem, "Über Unguentum hydrargyri colloidalis (Mercurcolloid), seine Anwedungsweise und Wirkung" (Dr.med. diss., Universität Leipzig, 1901).

59. Hans Hirsch, "Über Kondensationen halogenierter ß-Naphtochinone mit Methylenderivaten" (Dr.phil. diss., Friedrich-Wilhelms-Universität zu Berlin, 1900); Käte Hirsch, "Zur Frage der Frühoperation der Membrana Descemeti bei eitriger Keratitis" (Dr.med. diss., Albert-Ludwigs-Universität zu Freiburg im Breisgau, 1904).

60. Betty Scholem to Gershom Scholem, 20 September 1925, NLI, ARC. 4*1599/ 01/3082.

61. Ugo D'Orazio, "Angst vor 'Fräulein Doktor.' Die Diskussion über das medizinische Frauenstudium in Deutschland," in *Geschlechterdifferenz im interdisziplinären Gespräch*, ed. Doris Ruhe (Würzburg: Königshausen & Neumann, 1998), 91; Eduard Seidler, *Die Medizinische Fakultät der Albert-Ludwigs-Universität Freiburg im Breisgau. Grundlagen und Entwicklung*, rev. ed. (Berlin: Springer-Verlag, 1993), 234–235; Harriet Pass Freidenreich, *Female, Jewish, and Educated: The Lives of Central European University Women* (Bloomington: Indiana University Press, 2002), 9 and 52–57; Kaplan, "As Germans and as Jews," in Kaplan, *Jewish Daily Life in Germany*, 231.

62. Theodor Heuss to Georg Friedrich Knapp, 6 August 1910, in Theodor Heuss, *Aufbruch im Kaiserreich. Briefe 1892–1917*, ed. Frieder Günther (Munich: K. G. Saur, 2009), 302–303.

63. Max Pflaum of Pflaum & Co., succeeded by his son Georg. Gershom Scholem, *VBnJ*, 15; Max Plowden-Pflaum to Gershom Scholem, 31 January 1978, NLI, ARC. 4*1599/01/3018; *Berliner Adressbuch für das Jahr 1875*, ed. A. Ludwig (Berlin: Societät der Berliner Bürger-Zeitung, 1875), 661; *Berliner Adressbuch für das Jahr 1889*, ed. A. Ludwig (Berlin: W. & S. Loewenthal, 1889), 1:709 and 2:871.

64. Betty Scholem, "Ex Oriente Lux," in *Divided Passions: Jewish Intellectuals and the Experience of Modernity*, by Paul Mendes-Flohr (Detroit, Mich.: Wayne State University Press, 1991), 111–121.

65. Reinhold Scholem to Gershom Scholem, 18 July and 23 November 1977, NLI, ARC. 4*1599/01/3031; Berlin Museum, *Synagogen in Berlin*, vol. 2, *Zur Geschichte einer zerstörten Architektur*, ed. Rudolf Bothe (Berlin: Willmuth Arenhövel, 1983), 22–23; Ernst Heinrich, *Berlin und seine Bauten*, vol. 6, *Sakralbauten* (Berlin: Ernst & Sohn, 1997), 286.

66. Gershom Scholem, *VBnJ*, 17.

67. Marion A. Kaplan, "Redefining Judaism in Imperial Germany: Practices, Mentalities, and Community," *Jewish Social Studies* 9, no. 1 (Fall 2002): 10.

68. Gershom Scholem, *VBnJ*, 17.

69. Gershom Scholem, *VBnJ*, 32.

70. "Darwinistisches," *Schlemiel. Illustriertes jüdisches Witzblatt* 2, no. 1 (1 January 1904): 3; Jüdisches Museum Berlin, *Stories of an Exhibition: Two Millennia of German Jewish History* (Berlin: Stiftung Jüdisches Museum Berlin, 2001), 81.

71. Gershom Scholem, *VBnJ*, 32; Kaplan, *Making of the Jewish Middle Class*, 76.

72. Gershom Scholem, *VBnJ*, 32–33 and 27–28.

73. Hedwig Scholem to Gershom Scholem, 19 August 1916, 16 August 1917, 28 July 1917, 29 September 1917, 29 November 1918, and 4 January 1919, NLI, ARC. 4*1599/01/3032.

74. Kaplan, *Making of the Jewish Middle Class*, 76.

75. Peter Gay, *My German Question: Growing Up in Nazi Berlin* (New Haven, Conn.: Yale University Press, 1999), 53.

76. Gershom Scholem, *VBnJ*, 17; Betty Scholem, "Aufzeichnung von Mutter," in Betty Scholem and Gershom Scholem, *Mutter und Sohn im Briefwechsel 1917–1946*, ed. Itta Shedletzky (Munich: C. H. Beck, 1989), 530 (hereafter cited as *MuSiB*); Gershom Scholem to Reinhold Scholem, 20 February 1978, NLI, ARC. 4*1599/01/3031.

77. [Jüdische Gemeinde zu Berlin], *Verzeichnis der wahlfähigen Mitglieder der jüdischen Gemeinde zu Berlin im Jahre 1895* (Berlin: Jacoby, [1895]), 46; [Jüdische Gemeinde zu Berlin], *Verzeichnis der wahlfähigen Mitglieder der jüdischen Gemeinde zu Berlin im Jahre 1907* (Berlin: Jacoby, [1907]), 160.

78. Gershom Scholem, *VBnJ*, 17.

79. Monika Richarz, "Demographic Developments," in Meyer, *GJHMT*, 3:14; Kaplan, "As Germans and as Jews," in Kaplan, *Jewish Daily Life in Germany*, 264.

80. Gershom Scholem, *VBnJ*, 33–34; Reinhold Scholem to Gershom Scholem, 10 February 1978, NLI, ARC. 4*1599/01/3031; Werner Scholem to Gershom Scholem, 29 July 1918, NLI, ARC. 4*1599/01/3034.

81. Augustine, "Arriving in the Upper Class," in Blackbourn and Evans, *The German Bourgeoisie*, 56 and 80n34; Christof Biggeleben, *Das "Bollwerk des Bürgertums." Die Berliner Kaufmannschaft 1870–1920* (Berlin: C. H. Beck, 2006), 119.

82. Rürup, "Jewish History in Berlin," *LBIYB* 45 (2000): 37–50, quote on 44.

83. Theodor Fontane to Herr und Frau Guttmann, 25 January 1890, in Theodor Fontane, *Briefe Theodor Fontanes*, 2nd collection, 2nd ed., ed. Otto Pniower and Paul Schlenther, vol. 2 (Berlin: F. Fontane, 1910), 245.

84. Theobald Scholem, "Zur 50. Wiederkehr des Todestages von Friedrich Ludwig Jahn," *Jüdische Turnzeitung* 3, no. 10 (October 1902): 166–167; Michael Brenner, "From Subject to Citizen," in Meyer, *GJHMT*, 2:272.

85. Arthur Scholem, *Allerlei für Deutschlands Turner* (Berlin: Arthur Scholem, 1885); Theobald Scholem, *Geschichte des Berliner Turner-Vereins 1850–1900* (Berlin: Siegfried Scholem, 1900); Stammrolle, entry nos. 1024 and 1068, Berliner Turner-Verein von 1850 e. V. Georg was even a member for one month. Stammrolle, entry no. 1204, Berliner Turner-Verein von 1850 e. V.

86. Stammrolle, entry no. 1024, Berliner Turner-Verein von 1850 e. V.

87. Gershom Scholem, *VBnJ*, 28; "Satzung der Jüdischen Turnerschaft," *Jüdische Turnzeitung* 6, nos. 5/6 (May/June 1905): 91–95; "Gründung der 'Jüdischen Turnerschaft,'" in *Dokumente zur Geschichte des deutschen Zionismus 1882–1933*, ed. Jehuda Reinharz (Tübingen: J. C. B. Mohr, 1981), 79n1; "Der zweite Jüdische Turntag," *Ost und West* 5, no. 5 (May 1905): 359–360, quote on 360.

88. "Die Stelle der 'Jüdischen Turnerschaft' zum Zionismus," *Jüdische Turnzeitung* 6, nos. 5/6 (May/June 1905): 99–100.

89. Todd Samuel Presner, *Muscular Judaism: The Jewish Body and the Politics of Regeneration* (London: Routledge, 2007), 106–154.

90. Michael Brenner, "Introduction: Why Jews and Sports?," in *Emancipation through Muscles: Jews and Sports in Europe*, ed. Michael Brenner and Gideon Reuveni (Lincoln: University of Nebraska Press, 2006), 5; Daniel Wildmann, "Jewish Gymnasts and Their Corporeal Utopias in Imperial Germany," in Brenner and Reuveni, *Emancipation through Muscles*, 27, 30–31, and 40n23; George Eisen, "Zionism, Nationalism and the Emergence of the Jüdische Turnerschaft," *LBIYB* 28 (1983): 247–262.

91. Gershom Scholem, *VBnJ*, 13; Peter Fritzsche, *Reading Berlin 1900* (Cambridge, Mass.: Harvard University Press, 1996).

92. Werner E. Mosse, "Rudolf Mosse and the House of Mosse, 1867–1920," *LBIYB* 4 (1959): 237–259.

93. Betty Scholem to Gershom Scholem, 20 August 1929; Gershom Scholem to Betty Scholem, 5 September 1929; Betty Scholem to Gershom Scholem, 26 September 1933; all in *MuSiB*, 195, 200, and 330.

94. Betty Scholem to Gershom Scholem, 19 November 1929, in *MuSiB*, 211.

95. "Konkursverfahren," 18 November 1899, "Konkursverfahren," 13 July 1900, and "Tabelle," LAB, A Rep. 342–02, Nr. 42380.

96. Kaplan, "As Germans and as Jews," in Kaplan, *Jewish Daily Life in Germany*, 228; Paul Lerner, *The Consuming Temple: Jews, Department Stores, and the Consumer Revolution in Germany, 1880–1940* (Ithaca, N.Y.: Cornell University Press, 2015), 151–157.

97. Gershom Scholem, *VBnJ*, 35–36; Reinhold Scholem to Gershom Scholem, 18 July 1977 and 10 February 1978, NLI, ARC. 4*1599/01/3031; Betty Scholem to Gershom Scholem, 15 June 1926, NLI, ARC. 4*1599/01/3083.

2. Berlin Childhood around 1900

1. Paul M. Kennedy, *The Rise and Fall of the Great Powers: Economic Change and Military Conflict from 1500 to 2000* (New York: Random House, 1987), 200.

2. Stefan Zweig, *Die Welt von Gestern. Erinnerungen eines Europäers* (Stockholm: Bermann-Fischer, 1942), 136–137. The Viennese journalist and aphorist Karl Kraus also preferred the progressive modernity of Berlin to Austria, while the Nobel Peace Prize winner and writer Alfred Hermann Fried noted how insecure Viennese felt vis-à-vis Berlin. Karl Kraus, "Notizen," *Das Rendez-vous*, no. 5 (3 September 1892): 9; Karl Kraus, "Länder und Leute," in *Sprüche und Widersprüche* (Munich: Albert Langen, 1909), 195–216; Alfred H. Fried, *Wien-Berlin. Ein Vergleich* (Vienna: Josef Lenobel Verlagsbuchhandlung, 1908), 2.

3. [Walther Rathenau], "Die schönste Stadt der Welt," *Die Zukunft* 26, [no. 1] (7 January 1899): 39.

4. Borut, "The Province versus Berlin?," *LBIYB* 44 (1999): 127–131.

5. "Stand der Bevölkerung," in Berlin, Statistisches Bureau der Stadt Berlin, *Berliner Städtisches Jahrbuch für Volkswirthschaft und Statistik*, vol. 1, ed. H. Schwabe (Berlin: Leonhard Simion, 1874), 86; "Volkszählung-Ergebnisse. Religionsbekenntnis," in Berlin, Statistisches Amt der Stadt Berlin, *Statistisches Jahrbuch der Stadt Berlin*, vol. 27, *Enthaltend die Statistik der Jahre 1900 bis 1902*, ed. E. Hirschberg (Berlin: P. Stankiewicz' Buchdruckerei, 1903), 30; Jacob Segall, "Die Juden in Groß-Berlin," *Zeitschrift für Demographie und Statistik der Juden* 10, no. 9/10 (September/October 1914): 121.

6. Ulrich Eckhart and Andreas Nachama, *Jüdische Orte in Berlin* (Berlin: Nicolaische Verlagsbuchhandlung, 2005), 11–37; Rebiger, *Das jüdische Berlin*, 190–193.

7. Segall, "Die Juden in Groß-Berlin," 123.

8. Betty Scholem to Gershom Scholem, 18 June 1928, in *MuSiB*, 170.

9. See Erdmann Graeser, *Spreelore* (Berlin: Das Neue Berlin, 1950).

10. Gershom Scholem, *VBnJ*, 19.

11. Christian Simon, *Schöneberg im Wandel der Geschichte. "Es war in Schöneberg im Monat Mai"* (Berlin: be.bra-Verlag, 1998).

12. Segall, "Die Juden in Groß-Berlin," 121.

13. Hermann Ebling, *Friedenau erzählt. Geschichten aus einem Berliner Vorort 1871 bis 1914* (Berlin: Edition Friedenauer Brücke, 2007).

14. Segall, "Die Juden in Groß-Berlin," 121.

15. Marion Kaplan, *"Unter Uns:* Jews Socialising with Other Jews in Imperial Germany," *LBIYB* 48 (2003): 43.

16. Mendes-Flohr, *Divided Passions*, 109–110; Betty Scholem, "Ex Oriente Lux," in Mendes-Flohr, *Divided Passions*, 111–121.

17. "Georg und Phiechens Werdegang" and "Zum 70. Geburtstag unserer lieben Mutter Amalie Scholem am 9. Juli 1907," David Scholem Collection; Betty Scholem, "Aufzeichnung von Mutter," in *MuSiB*, 527.

18. Gershom Scholem to Reinhold Scholem, 24 May 1976 and 8/11 September 1976, NLI, ARC. 4*1599/01/3031.

19. Gershom Scholem, *VBnJ*, 23, 38–39, and 25; Reinhold Scholem to Gershom Scholem, 29 February 1972, NLI, ARC. 4*1599/01/3031.

20. Reinhold Scholem to Gershom Scholem, 29 February 1972, NLI, ARC. 4*1599/01/3031.

21. Gershom Scholem to Reinhold Scholem, 29 May 1972, NLI, ARC. 4*1599/01/3031; Gershom Scholem, *VBnJ*, 20–22; S. Schachnowitz, "Eine Würdigung Schillers vom Standpunkte des Judentums," *Der Israelit* 46, no. 36 (4 May 1905), no. 37 (8 May 1905), and no. 38 (11 May 1905): 779–781, 791–792, and 819–820; Raphael Breuer, "Zum Schillertag," *Der Israelit* 46, no. 36 (4 May 1905): 755–759 and 771–774; Nathan Rosenstreich, "Gershom Scholem's Conception of Jewish Nationalism," in Mendes-Flohr, *Gershom Scholem*, 110.

22. Richarz, "Occupational Distribution and Social Structure," in Meyer, *GJHMT*, 3:55; Thomas Nipperdey, *Deutsche Geschichte 1866–1918*, vol. 1, *Arbeitswelt und Bürgergeist* (Munich: C. H. Beck, 1994), 400.

23. Wolf Gruner, "Einleitung," in *Die Verfolgung und Ermordung der europäischen Juden durch das nationalsozialistische Deutschland 1933–1945*, vol. 1, *Deutsches Reich 1933–1937*, ed. Wolf Gruner (Munich: R. Oldenbourg, 2008), 18.

24. Luisenstädtisches Realgymnasium Schülerverzeichnis 1897–1944, LAB, A. Rep. 020–04, 149, entry nos. 8625, 9029, 9124, and 9387.

25. Kaplan, "As Germans and as Jews," in Kaplan, *Jewish Daily Life in Germany*, 203.

26. Certificate, 24 March 1914, Zeugnisse über die wissenschaftliche Befähigung für den einjährigen freiwilligen Militärdienst, LAB, A. Rep. 020–04, 91.

27. Ute Frevert, *A Nation in Barracks: Modern Germany, Military Conscription and Civil Society* (Oxford: Berg, 2004), 159–160; Werner T. Angress, "Prussia's Army and the Jewish Reserve Officer Controversy before World War I," *LBIYB* 17 (1972): 19–42.

28. Kaplan, "As Germans and as Jews," in Kaplan, *Jewish Daily Life in Germany*, 206.

29. Aschheim, *Scholem, Arendt, Klemperer*, 22–23.

30. Richarz, "Demographic Developments," in Meyer, *GJHMT*, 3:10.

31. Gershom Scholem, *VBnJ*, 19–20, 24, 37; Kaplan, "As Germans and as Jews," in Kaplan, *Jewish Daily Life in Germany*, 192.

32. Kaplan, "As Germans and as Jews," in Kaplan, *Jewish Daily Life in Germany*, 188.

33. Kaplan, *Making of the Jewish Middle Class*, 154–155.

34. Gershom Scholem, *VBnJ*, 23.

35. Luisenstädtisches Realgymnasium Schülerverzeichnis 1897–1944, LAB, A. Rep. 020–04, 149, entry nos. 8625 and 9029.

36. Marion A. Kaplan, "*Unter Uns*," *LBIYB* 48 (2003): 50.

37. Reinhold Scholem to Gershom Scholem, 29 February 1972 and 10 February 1978, NLI, ARC. 4*1599/01/3031.

38. Richarz, "Occupational Distribution and Social Structure," in Meyer, *GJHMT*, 3:38 and 60.

39. Kenneth F. Ledford, "Jews in the German Legal Professions: Emancipation, Assimilation, Exclusion," in *Jews and the Law*, ed. Ari Mermelstein, Victoria Saker Woeste, Ethan Zadoff, and Marc Galanter (New Orleans, La.: Quid Pro Quo, 2014), 13–36; Angress, "Prussia's Army," *LBIYB* 17 (1972); Pulzer, *Jews and the German State*, 85–96.

40. Volkov, *Germans, Jews, and Antisemites*, 65–155.

41. Norbert Kampe, "Jews and Antisemites at Universities in Imperial Germany (I): Jewish Students: Social History and Social Conflict," *LBIYB* 30 (1985): 357–394; Lisa Swartout, "Facing Antisemitism: Jewish Students at German Universities, 1890–1914," *Leipziger Beiträge zur jüdischen Geschichte und Kultur* 2 (2004): 149–165.

42. Walter Laqueur, *The Changing Face of Antisemitism: From Ancient Times to the Present Day* (Oxford: Oxford University Press, 2008), 91–106.

43. Lamberti, *Jewish Activism in Imperial Germany*; Barkai, "*Wehr Dich!*," 19–54.

44. Diary entry, 18 February 1913, in Gershom Scholem, *Tagebücher*, 1:11.

45. Luisenstädtisches Realgymnasium Schülerverzeichnis 1897–1944, LAB, A. Rep. 020–04, 149, entry no. 9124; Hoffrogge, *Werner Scholem*, 30–34.

46. Gershom Scholem, *VBnJ*, 36.

47. Gershom Scholem, "With Gershom Scholem: An Interview," in *On Jews and Judaism in Crisis: Selected Essays*, ed. Werner J. Dannhauser (New York: Schocken, 1976), 3; Werner Scholem to Gershom Scholem, 2 December 1914, NLI, ARC. 4*1599/01/3034.

48. Bureau des Reichstages, *Reichstags-Handbuch, II. Wahlperiode 1924* (Berlin: Reichsdruckerei, 1924), 516.

49. Hamburger and Pulzer, "Jews as Voters," *LBIYB* 30 (1985): 4 and 32–43; Peter Pulzer, "The Response to Antisemitism," in Meyer, *GJHMT*, 3:274–276.

50. Gershom Scholem, *VBnJ*, 46.

51. M. Zadoff, *Der rote Hiob*, 20–25.

52. Ernst Jünger to Gershom Scholem, 20 April 1975, NLI, ARC. 4*1599/01/1307.

53. Betty Scholem, "Aufzeichnung von Mutter," in *MuSiB*, 530; Gershom Scholem, *VBnJ*, 12, 17, and 41; "Einsegnung im Monat Dezember 1911. Synagoge Lindenstraße," *Gemeindeblatt der Jüdischen Gemeinde zu Berlin* 2, no. 1 (12 January 1912): 11.

54. Gershom Scholem to Reinhold Scholem, 14 October 1976, NLI, ARC. 4*1599/01/3031; Gershom Scholem, *VBnJ*, 16 and 32.

55. Gershom Scholem, *VBnJ*, 40–43; diary entry, 24 February 1913, in Gershom Scholem, *Tagebücher*, 1:16.

56. Gershom Scholem, *VBnJ*, 48–52, 56–57, and 63; Maor, "Death or Birth," in Mendelsohn, Hoffman, and Cohen, *Against the Grain*, 67; Gershom Scholem to Vorstand der Jugendgruppe der Agudass Jissroël in Berlin, 10 May 1914, *Briefe*, vol. 1, *1914–1947*, ed. Itta Shedletzky (Munich: C. H. Beck, 1994), 3 (hereafter cited as *Briefe*).

57. Gershom Scholem, *VBnJ*, 44–45 and 52–54.

58. Gershom Scholem, *VBnJ*, 48–52; Steven E. Aschheim, *Brothers and Strangers: The East European Jew in German and German Jewish Consciousness, 1800–1923* (Madison: University of Wisconsin Press, 1982), 121–138, esp. 134–135.

59. Gideon Shimoni, *The Zionist Ideology* (Hanover, N.H.: Brandeis University Press, 1995), 88–100.

60. Lowenstein, "Ideology and Identity," in Meyer, *GJHMT*, 3:299–304.

61. Chana C. Schütz, "The Imperial Era (1871–1918)," in Nachama, Schoeps, and Simon, *Jews in Berlin*, 127.

62. Poppel, *Zionism in Germany*, 21–67.

63. Schütz, "Imperial Era (1871–1918)," in Nachama, Schoeps, and Simon, *Jews in Berlin*, 127–128; Lowenstein, "Community," in Meyer, *GJHMT*, 3:143.

64. Engel, *Gershom Scholem*, 29.

65. Gershom Scholem, *VBnJ*, 61–62.

66. E. Jacobson, *Metaphysics of the Profane*, 56–61.

67. Gershom Scholem to Reinhold Scholem, 29 May 1972, NLI, ARC. 4*1599/01/3031.

68. Diary entry, 22 February 1913, in Gershom Scholem, *Tagebücher*, 1:13–14.

3. Things Fall Apart

1. Modris Eksteins, *Rites of Spring: The Great War and the Birth of the Modern Age* (Boston, Mass.: Houghton Mifflin, 1989), 56–62; "Die Stunde der Abrechnung. Begeisterung in Berlin und Wien," *Neue Preußische Zeitung (Kreuz-Zeitung)* no. 345 (26 July 1914, morning edition): [1].

2. "Strassenkundgebungen in Berlin," *Vossische Zeitung*, no. 374 (26 July 1914, morning edition): [5].

3. "Eröffnungssitzung im Weißen Saale des Königlichen Schlosses zu Berlin am Dienstag den 4. August 1914. Thronrede.," *Verhandlungen des Reichstags, XIII. Legislaturperiode. II. Session*, vol. 306, *Stenographische Berichte. Von der Eröffnungssitzung am 4. August 1914 bis zur 34. Sitzung am 16. März 1916* (Berlin: Norddeutsche Buchdruckerei und Verlags-Anstalt, 1916), 2.

4. "An die deutschen Juden!," *Im deutschen Reich* 20, no. 9 (September 1914): 339.

5. "Deutsche Juden!," *Jüdische Rundschau* 19, no. 32 (7 August 1914): 1.

6. Sarah Panter, *Jüdische Erfahrungen und Loyalitätskonflikte im Ersten Weltkrieg* (Göttingen: Vandenhoeck & Ruprecht, 2014), 39–52.

7. Tim Grady, *The German-Jewish Soldiers of the First World War in History and Memory* (Liverpool: Liverpool University Press, 2011), 3 and 25.

8. Panter, *Jüdische Erfahrungen und Loyalitätskonflikte*, 40.

9. Grady, *German-Jewish Soldiers*, 27, 37, and 69.

10. Gershom Scholem, *VBnJ*, 25.

11. Certification from Dieter Dureck, Landesamt für Gesundheit und Soziales Berlin, Versorgungsamt-Krankenbuchlager, 10 June 2008.

12. Reinhold Scholem to Gershom Scholem, 10 February 1978, NLI, ARC. 4*1599/01/3031.

13. Ernst Jünger to Gershom Scholem, 20 April 1975, NLI, ARC. 4*1599/01/1307.

14. Gershom Scholem to Werner Scholem, 7 September 1914, and Werner Scholem to Gershom Scholem, 8 September 1914, in *Briefe*, 1:5 and 1:7 ; diary entry, "Notizen meiner Wenigkeit," 4 December 1914, in Gershom Scholem, *Tagebücher*, 1:70; Gershom Scholem, *VBnJ*, 92.

15. Werner Scholem to Gershom Scholem, 8 September 1914, NLI, ARC. 4*1599/01/3034; diary entry, "Notizen meiner Wenigkeit," 4 December 1914, in Gershom Scholem, *Tagebücher*, 1:70; Carl E. Schorske, *German Social Democracy, 1905–1917: The Development of the Great Schism* (Cambridge, Mass.: Harvard University Press, 1955), 285–291 and 296–302.

16. Werner Scholem to Gershom Scholem, 22 September 1914, NLI, ARC. 4*1599/01/3034.

17. Gershom Scholem to Werner Scholem, 7 September 1914, in *Briefe*, 1:5; Werner Scholem to Gershom Scholem, 8 September 1914, in *Briefe*, 1:6 and 1:10; Werner Scholem to Gershom Scholem, 22 September 1914, NLI, ARC. 4*1599/01/3034.

18. Gershom Scholem, *VBnJ*, 59; diary entries, "Aus der Werkstatt des Geistes," 20 January and 2 February 1915, in Gershom Scholem, *Tagebücher*, 1:79 and 1:88; diary entry, 18 December 1915, in Gershom Scholem, *Tagebücher*, 1:207.

19. Werner Scholem to Gershom Scholem, 22 September 1914, NLI, ARC. 4*1599/01/3034.

20. Werner Scholem to Gershom Scholem, 14 November 1914, NLI, ARC. 4*1599/01/3034.

21. Luisenstädtisches Realgymnasium in Berlin, *Bericht über das Schuljahr 1914–1915* (Berlin: Naucksche Buchdruckerei, 1915), 21.

22. Luisenstädtisches Realgymnasium in Berlin, *Bericht über das Schuljahr 1914–1915*, 13.

23. Gershom Scholem to Werner Scholem, 13 September 1914, NLI, ARC. 4*1599/01/3034.

24. Diary entry, "Notizen meiner Wenigkeit," 26 November 1914, in Gershom Scholem, *Tagebücher*, 1:61.

25. Gershom Scholem to Werner Kraft, 19 August 1917, in *Briefe*, 1:101.

26. Heinrich Margulies, "Der Krieg der Zurückbleibenden," *Jüdische Rundschau* 20, no. 6 (5 February 1915): 47.

27. Stefan Vogt, "The First World War, German Nationalism, and the Transformation of German Zionism," *LBIYB* 57 (2012): 267–291, esp. 269–275.

28. Gershom Scholem et al. to the *Jüdische Rundschau*, 20 February 1915, in "Aus der Werkstatt des Geistes," in Gershom Scholem, *Tagebücher*, 1:89–90, quote on 90.

29. Gershom Scholem to Martin Buber, 10 July 1916, in *Briefe*, 1:348n8.

30. Hedwig Scholem to Gershom Scholem, n.d. [1915], NLI, ARC. 4*1599/01/3032.

31. Gershom Scholem, *VBnJ*, 66–67; diary entries, "Buch der Eitelkeit. Metaphysischen Geschichten eines physischen Ichs," 4, 17, and 18 October 1915, in Gershom Scholem, *Tagebücher*, 1:171 and 1:173–174; Königstädtisches Realgymnasium, Zeugnis der Reife, 18 October 1915, NLI, ARC. 4*1599/02/5.

32. Diary entry, "Randbemerkungen zum täglichen Erlebnisbuch. Siddur Scheli!," n.d., in Gershom Scholem, *Tagebücher*, 1:185–187.

33. Königliche Friedrich-Wilhelms-Universität zu Berlin, Abgangs-Zeugnis, 30 August 1917, NLI, ARC. 4*1599/02/7; paragraph 3 of the "Vorschriften für die Studierenden der Landesuniversitäten vom 1. Oktober 1879," in Friedrich-Wilhelms-Universität zu Berlin, *Vorschriften für die Studierenden der Königlichen Friedrich-Wilhelms-Universität zu Berlin* (Berlin: Universitäts-Buchdruckerei von Gustav Schade, 1912), 7; Friedrich-Wilhelms-Universität zu Berlin, *Amtliches Verzeichnis des Personals und der Studierenden der Königlichen Friedrich-Wilhelms-Universität zu Berlin* (Berlin: Universitäts-Buchdruckerei von Gustav Schade, 1915), 202 (matriculation number 2068); Erich Brauer to Gershom Scholem, 30 September 1917, NLI, ARC. 4*1599/01/0356.2.

34. E.g., Friedrich-Wilhelms-Universität zu Berlin, *Amtliches Verzeichnis des Personals und der Studierenden der Königlichen Friedrich-Wilhelms-Universität zu Berlin auf das Winterhalbjahr vom 16. Oktober 1915 bis 15. März 1916* (Berlin: Arthur Scholem, 1915).

35. Biale, *Gershom Scholem* (2018), 14 and 16.

36. Gershom Scholem to Erich Brauer, 21 and 7 June 1916, NLI, ARC. 4*1599/01/0356.3; Gershom Scholem, *VBnJ*, 80–83; Gershom Scholem, "95 Thesen über Judentum und Zionismus," 15 July 1918, NLI, ARC. 4*1599/07/277.1.15.

37. [Das Jüdische Volksheim Berlin], *Das Jüdische Volksheim Berlin. Erster Bericht, Mai/Dezember 1916* (Leipzig: Oscar Brandstetter, n.d. [1916 or 1917]); Gershom Scholem to Siegfried Lehmann, 4 and 9 October 1916, in *Briefe*, 1:43–46 and 1:53–56; Gershom Scholem to Harry Heymann, 12 November 1916, in *Briefe*, 1:59; Siegfried Lehmann to Gershom Scholem, n.d. [autumn 1916], NLI, ARC. 4*1599/01/1543.

38. Gershom Scholem to Edgar Blum, 26 October 1916, NLI, ARC. 4*1599/01/0297.2.

39. Gershom Scholem to Siegfried Weitzmann, 9 June 1916, Gershom Scholem to Max Fischer, 20 June 1916, in *Briefe*, 1:32 and 1:33–34; Gerhard Scholem, "Zum Problem der Uebersetzung [*sic*] aus dem Jidischen," *Jüdische Rundschau* 22, no. 2 (12 January 1917): 16–17.

40. Gershom Scholem to Erich Brauer, 21 June 1916, NLI, ARC. 4*1599/01/0356.3.

41. Gershom Scholem to Harry Heymann, 12 November 1916, NLI, ARC. 4*1599/01/1144.

42. Gershom Scholem to Edgar Blum, 26 October 1916, NLI, ARC. 4*1599/01/0297.2.

43. Gershom Scholem to Harry Heymann, 12 November 1916, NLI, ARC. 4*1599/01/1144.

44. Gershom Scholem to Harry Heymann, 21 November 1917, NLI, ARC. 4*1599/01/1144.

45. Gerhard [Gershom] Scholem, "Jüdische Jugendbewegung," *Der Jude* 1, no. 12 (March 1917): 822.

46. Gerhard [Gershom] Scholem, "Al Chet . . . ," *Jüdische Rundschau* 23, no. 39 (27 September 1918): 303–304. See Walter Laqueur, "The German Youth Movement and the 'Jewish Question,'" *LBIYB* 6 (1961): 193–205; Chanoch Rinott, "Major Trends in Jewish Youth Movements in Germany," *LBIYB* 19 (1974): 77–95.

47. Gerhard [Gershom] Scholem, "Jüdische Jugendbewegung," 822.

48. Gerhard [Gershom] Scholem, "Jugendbewegung, Jugendarbeit und Blau-Weiß," *Blau-Weiß-Blätter (Führernummer)* 1, no. 2 (August 1917): 26–30, esp. 28; Rinott, "Major Trends in Jewish Youth Movements," *LBIYB* 19 (1974): 88–90.

49. Gershom Scholem to Meta Jahr, 14 October 1917, in *Briefe*, 1:115.

50. Erna Michaelis to Gershom Scholem, 3 October 1917, NLI, ARC. 4*1599/ 01/1790; Bernhard Bartfeld to Gershom Scholem, 21 October 1917, NLI, ARC. 4*1599/01/0163.

51. Diary entry, "Aus der Werkstatt des Geistes," 20 January 1915, in Gershom Scholem, *Tagebücher*, 1:81.

52. Hannah Weiner, "Gershom Scholem and the Jung Juda Youth Group in Berlin, 1913–1918," *Studies in Zionism* 5, no. 1 (1984): 29–42.

53. Gershom Scholem to Harry Heymann, 15 January 1918, in *Briefe*, 1:137.

54. G.S. [Gershom Scholem], "Jugendbewegung," *Die Blauweiße Brille*, no. 1 (Av 5675 [July 1915]).

55. G.S. [Gershom Scholem], "Ideologie," *Die Blauweiße Brille*, no. 3 (Tevet 5675 [December 1915]).

56. Karl Glaser, "Oratio pro Domo," *Blau-Weiß-Blätter (Führernummer)* 1, no. 2 (August 1917): 35; Gershom Scholem to Harry Heymann, 19 May 1917, NLI, ARC. 4*1599/01/1144.

57. Alfred Kupferberg, "Der Wert des Historizismus. Eine Betrachtung zum Jugendtag," *Jüdische Rundschau* 23, no. 42 (18 October 1918): 326.

58. Julie Schächter to Gershom Scholem, 21 October 1915, NLI, ARC. 4*1599/ 01/2292.

59. "Sapienti Sat!," letter from Walter Roth to the board of Jung Juda, 4 September 1915, *Die Blauweiße Brille*, no. 2 (Tishrei 5675 [September 1915]).

60. Gershom Scholem to Zentralcomitée der Zionistischen Vereinigung für Deutschland, 10 December 1916, NLI, ARC. 4*1599/01/2985.

61. Hedwig Scholem to Gershom Scholem, 10 January 1916, NLI, ARC. 4*1599/ 01/3032.

62. Hedwig Scholem to Gershom Scholem, 19 August 1916, 28 July 1917, 16 August 1917, 29 September 1917, 4 November 1917, 20 January 1918, and 27 October 1918, NLI, ARC. 4*1599/01/3032.

63. Gershom Scholem, *VBnJ*, 76–78.

64. Stephanie Rothstein to Gershom Scholem, 14 and 25 November 1915, 2 and 14 December 1915, 15 January 1916, 15 May 1916, and 12 June 1916, NLI, ARC. 4*1599/01/2233; diary entry, "Randbemerkungen zum täglichen Erblebnisbuch. Siddur Scheli," 5 December 1915, in Gershom Scholem, *Tagebücher*, 1:192.

65. Certification from Dieter Dureck, Landesamt für Gesundheit und Soziales Berlin, Versorgungsamt-Krankenbuchlager, 10 June 2008.

66. Norman Stone, *The Eastern Front, 1914–1917* (London: Penguin, 1975), 227–231.

67. Certification from Dieter Dureck, Landesamt für Gesundheit und Soziales Berlin, Versorgungsamt-Krankenbuchlager, 10 June 2008; Werner Scholem to Gershom Scholem, 19 June 1916, NLI, ARC. 4*1599/01/3034.

68. Certification from Dieter Dureck, Landesamt für Gesundheit und Soziales Berlin, Versorgungsamt-Krankenbuchlager, 10 June 2008; Werner Scholem to Gershom Scholem, 22 August 1916, NLI, ARC. 4*1599/01/3034.

69. Werner Scholem to Gershom Scholem, 2 and 22 August 1916, NLI, ARC. 4*1599/01/3034.

70. Werner Scholem to Gershom Scholem, 22 August 1916, NLI, ARC. 4*1599/ 01/3034.

71. Werner Scholem to Gershom Scholem, 31 August 1916, NLI, ARC. 4*1599/01/3034.

72. Werner Scholem to Gershom Scholem, 7 July 1916 and 23 June 1916, NLI, ARC. 4*1599/01/3034.

73. Werner Scholem to Gershom Scholem, 13 October 1916, NLI, ARC. 4*1599/01/3034.

74. Werner Scholem to Gershom Scholem, 5 February 1917, NLI, ARC. 4*1599/01/3034; Gershom Scholem, *VBnJ*, 92; Karl Heinz Jahnke et al., *Geschichte der deutschen Arbeiterjugendbewegung 1904–1945* (Berlin: Neues Leben, 1973), 140.

75. Werner Scholem to Gershom Scholem, 17 June and 22 August 1917, NLI, ARC. 4*1599/01/3034.

76. Werner Scholem to Gershom Scholem, 12 August 1917, NLI, ARC. 4*1599/01/3034.

77. Gershom Scholem, *VBnJ*, 92 and 109–110; Emmy Wiechelt Scholem to Gershom Scholem, 5 February 1918, NLI, ARC. 4*1599/01/3023.

78. Werner Scholem to Gershom Scholem, 3 June 1917, NLI, ARC. 4*1599/01/3034.

79. Werner Scholem to Gershom Scholem, 17 June and 1 July 1917, NLI, ARC. 4*1599/01/3034.

80. Marriage certificate, 31 December 1917, Leibniz Universität Hannover, Institut für Politische Wissenschaft (hereafter cited as LUH, IPW), Nachlass Werner Scholem, 1712310; Gershom Scholem to Harry Heymann, 28 December 1917, NLI, ARC. 4*1599/01/1144.

81. Werner Scholem to Gershom Scholem, 12 and 22 August and 9 December 1917, NLI, ARC. 4*1599/01/3034; Gershom Scholem to Werner Kraft, 28 December 1917, in *Briefe*, 1:135.

82. Werner Scholem to Gershom Scholem, 7 and 13 July 1916, NLI, ARC. 4*1599/01/3034.

83. Werner Scholem to Gershom Scholem, 9 December 1917 and 10 February 1918, NLI, ARC. 4*1599/01/3034.

84. Emmy Wiechelt Scholem to Gershom Scholem, 5 February 1918, NLI, ARC. 4*1599/01/3023.

85. Werner Scholem to Gershom Scholem, 20 February and 11 April 1918, NLI, ARC. 4*1599/01/3034.

86. Werner Scholem to Gershom Scholem, 20 February 1918, NLI, ARC. 4*1599/01/3034.

87. Gershom Scholem, *Tagebücher nebst Aufsätzen und Entwürfen bis 1923*, vol. 2, *1917–1923*, ed. Friedrich Niewöhner, Karlfried Gründer, and Herbert Kopp-Oberstebrink (Frankfurt: Jüdischer Verlag, 2000), 147.

88. Emmy Wiechelt Scholem to Gershom Scholem, 3 December 1919, NLI, ARC. 4*1599/01/3023.

89. Werner Scholem to Gershom Scholem, 13 and 15 April 1918, NLI, ARC. 4*1599/01/3034.

90. Werner Scholem to Gershom Scholem, 21 April 1918, 15 May 1918 (quote), 29 June 1918, and 1 and 29 September 1918, NLI, ARC. 4*1599/01/3034.

91. Werner Scholem to Gershom Scholem, 26 December 1918, NLI, ARC. 4*1599/01/3034.

92. Emmy Wiechelt Scholem to Gershom Scholem, 14 October 1918, NLI, ARC. 4*1599/01/3023.

93. Hedwig Scholem to Gershom Scholem, 20 February 1919, NLI, ARC. 4*1599/01/3032.

94. Arthur Scholem to Gershom Scholem, 15 February 1917, in *MuSiB*, 13.

95. Gershom Scholem to Käte Hirsch Schiepan, 6 June 1917, NLI, ARC. 4*1599/01/3019; Gershom Scholem to Reinhold Scholem, 1 August 1977, NLI, ARC. 4*1599/01/3031.

96. Arthur Scholem to Gershom Scholem, 12 May 1917, in *MuSiB*, 13.

97. Gershom Scholem, *VBnJ*, 92–107; "Exemplum non datum. Das nicht gegebene Beispiel. Wahrheiten und Lügen eines jungen Menschen und Zionisten (Zionisten-Menschen) namens Gerhard Scholem," 19 May 1917, in Gershom Scholem, *Tagebücher*, 2:18; *Jiskor. Ein Buch des Gedenkens an gefallene Wächter und Arbeiter im Lande Israel*, trans. N. N. [Nomen Nescio] (Berlin: Jüdischer Verlag, 1918).

98. Gershom Scholem, *WBTSF*, 7.

99. Gershom Scholem, *VBnJ*, 76.

100. Biale, *Gershom Scholem* (2018), 25.

101. Gershom Scholem, *WBTSF*, 14–15.

102. Gershom Scholem, *WBTSF*, 51.

103. Walter Benjamin to Gershom Scholem, 6 September 1917, in Walter Benjamin, *Gesammelte Briefe*, vol. 1, *1910–1918*, ed. Christoph Gödde and Henri Lonitz (1995; reprint Frankfurt: Suhrkamp, 2016), 379.

104. Diary entry, "Über Metaphysik, Logik und einige nicht dazugehörende Gebiete phänomenologischer Besinning," 5 November 1917, in Gershom Scholem, *Tagebücher*, 2:75, and in Gershom Scholem, *Lamentations of Youth: The Diaries of Gershom Scholem, 1913–1919*, ed. and trans. Anthony David Skinner (Cambridge, Mass.: Belknap Press of Harvard University Press, 2007), 195.

105. Gershom Scholem, *VBnJ*, 103; diary entry, 5 December 1957, in Schmuel Hugo Bergman, *Tagebücher und Briefe*, vol. 2, *1948–1975*, ed. Miriam Sambursky (Königstein: Jüdischer Verlag bei Athenäum, 1985), 264–265.

106. Gershom Scholem, *VBnJ*, 108.

107. Certification from Dieter Dureck, Landesamt für Gesundheit und Soziales Berlin, Versorgungsamt-Krankenbuchlager, 10 June 2008.

108. Gershom Scholem to Aharon Heller, 8 July 1917, Gershom Scholem to Werner Kraft, 14 July 1917, and Gershom Scholem to Erich Brauer, 15 July 1917, in *Briefe*, 1:70, 1:77, and 1:77–79.

109. Gershom Scholem to Aharon Heller, 17 July 1917, in *Briefe*, 1:82–83.

110. Gershom Scholem to Erich Brauer, 15 July 1917, Gershom Scholem to Gerda Goldberg, 6 August 1917, in *Briefe*, 1:77–79 and 1:88.

111. Gershom Scholem to Aharon Heller, 15 August 1917, in *Briefe*, 1:97 and 1:99.

112. Gershom Scholem to Erich Brauer, 25 June or July [month unclear] 1917, NLI, ARC. 4*1599/01/0356.3.

113. Certification from Dieter Dureck, Landesamt für Gesundheit und Soziales Berlin, Versorgungsamt-Krankenbuchlager, 10 June 2008.

114. Gershom Scholem to Aharon Heller, 17 July 1917, in *Briefe*, 1:83.

115. Certification from Dieter Dureck, Landesamt für Gesundheit und Soziales Berlin, Versorgungsamt-Krankenbuchlager, 10 June 2008.

116. Betty Scholem to Gershom Scholem, 16 November 1917, in *MuSiB*, 17–18.

117. Betty Scholem to Gershom Scholem, 2 October 1917, NLI, ARC. 4*1599/01/3077.

118. Gershom Scholem to Harry Heymann, 25 August 1917, NLI, ARC. 4*1599/01/1144; Gershom Scholem to Harry Heymann, 14 August 1917, in *Briefe*, 1:96.

119. Großherzoglich und Herzoglich Sächsische Gesamt-Universität Jena, Abgangs-Zeugnis, 25 April 1918, NLI, ARC. 4*1599/02/7; Gershom Scholem, *VBnJ*, 110–111.

120. Gershom Scholem to Harry Heymann, 4 and 28 December 1917, in *Briefe*, 1:129 and 1:133; Gershom Scholem, *VBnJ*, 111–112.

121. Diary entry, 19 December 1917, in Gershom Scholem, *Lamentations of Youth*, 206.

122. Diary entry with a copy of a letter from Gershom Scholem to Meta Jahr, 5 December 1917, in Gershom Scholem, *Lamentations of Youth*, 204.

123. E.g., Grete Brauer to Gershom Scholem, 11 July [1917?] and 25 October 1917, NLI, ARC. 4*1599/01/0357.

124. Anthony David Skinner, "The Idiot: January 1917–April 1918," in Gershom Scholem, *Lamentations of Youth*, ed. and trans. Anthony David Skinner, 163.

125. Typescript "Aus dem Tagebüchern von Gerschom [*sic*] Scholem" kept with correspondence to/from Grete Brauer, 2 March 1918, NLI, ARC. 4*1599/01/0357; Gershom Scholem to Grete Brauer, 7 March 1918, in *Briefe*, 1:142–143.

126. Gershom Scholem to Grete Brauer, 7 March 1918, in *Briefe*, 1:144.

127. Grete Brauer to Gershom Scholem, 11 March 1918, NLI, ARC. 4*1599/01/0357.

128. Gershom Scholem to Escha Burchhardt, 24 March 1918, in *Briefe*, 1:147.

129. Salman Schocken, Ausschuss für Jüdische Kulturarbeit, December 1917, NLI, ARC. 4*1599/01/3050; Gershom Scholem to Salman Schocken, 18 January 1918, Gershom Scholem to Harry Heymann, 1 March 1918, in *Briefe*, 1:138 and 1:141.

130. Gershom Scholem to Escha Burchhardt, 24 March 1918, Gershom Scholem to Harry Heymann, 9 April 1918, in *Briefe*, 1:147 and 1:153.

131. Aharon Heller to Gershom Scholem, 18 February 1918, NLI, ARC. 4*1599/01/1110.

132. Kohos Türkischer to Gershom Scholem, 2 January 1918, NLI, ARC. 4*1599/01/2677.

133. Gershom Scholem to Harry Heymann, 15 January 1918, in *Briefe*, 1:136.

134. Universität Bern, Abgangs-Zeugnis, 21 July 1919, NLI, ARC. 4*1599/02/7; Gershom Scholem, *VBnJ*, 123.

135. Walter Benjamin to Gershom Scholem, 13 January 1918, in Walter Benjamin, *The Correspondence of Walter Benjamin, 1910–1940* (Chicago: University of Chicago Press, 1994), 110.

136. Gershom Scholem, *WBTSF*, 66–67, 72–83, among others.

137. Gershom Scholem to Erich Brauer, 16 June 1918, NLI, ARC. 4*1599/01/0356.3.

138. Gershom Scholem to Aharon Heller, 23 June 1918, in *Briefe*, 1:161.

139. Gershom Scholem to Escha Burchhardt, 24 March, 21 June, 26 October, and 23 November 1918, in *Briefe*, 1:146–148, 1:158–160, 1:176–178, and 1:184–188; e.g.,

Escha Burchhardt to Gershom Scholem, [5 March 1918], [15 June 1918], [4 July 1918], 25 October 1918, and 18 November 1918, NLI, ARC. 4*1599/01/3065.

140. Gershom Scholem to Werner Kraft, 6 July 1919, in *Briefe*, 1:206; Gershom Scholem, *VBnJ*, 133. On his continued admiration for Grete Brauer, see Gershom Scholem to Meta Jahr, 12 August 1918, NLI, ARC. 4*1599/01/1259; diary entry, 11 December 1918, in Gershom Scholem, *Lamentations of Youth*, 277.

141. Gershom Scholem to Escha Burchhardt, 23 November 1918, in *Briefe*, 1:184; Gershom Scholem, *WBTSF*, 96.

142. Diary entry, "Aus dem Werkstatt des Geistes," 27 March 1915, in Gershom Scholem, *Tagebücher*, 1:95; Betty Scholem to Gershom Scholem, 4 September 1918, NLI, ARC. 4*1599/01/3078.

143. Photo of Georg Scholem and family, n.d., David Scholem Collection; Betty Scholem to Gershom Scholem, 5 November 1917, NLI, ARC. 4*1599/01/3077.

144. Catherine Rollet, "The 'Other War' I: Protecting Public Health," in Winter and Robert, *Capital Cities at War*, 433, citing Otto Lentz, *Die Seuchenbekämpfung in Preußen während des Krieges und ihr Ergebnis bis Ende 1915*, Veröffentlichungen aus dem Gebiete der Medizinalverwaltung, vol. 6, no. 3 (Berlin: Schoetz, 1916), 4.

145. Reinhold Scholem to Gershom Scholem, 20 June 1976, NLI, ARC. 4*1599/01/3031.

146. Reinhold Scholem to Gershom Scholem, 19 June 1916, NLI, ARC. 4*1599/01/3031.

147. Certification from Dieter Dureck, Landesamt für Gesundheit und Soziales Berlin, Versorgungsamt-Krankenbuchlager, 10 June 2008; Betty Scholem to Gershom Scholem, 19 October 1917 and 26 January 1918, NLI, ARC. 4*1599/01/3077 and 3078.

148. Belinda J. Davis, *Home Fires Burning: Food, Politics, and Everyday Life in World War I Berlin* (Chapel Hill: University of North Carolina Press, 2000), 132–133 and 135.

149. Davis, *Home Fires Burning*, 134.

150. Quoted in Egmont Zechlin, *Die deutsche Politik und die Juden im Ersten Weltkrieg* (Göttingen: Vandenhoeck & Ruprecht, 1969), 525.

151. Franz Oppenheimer, *Die Judenstatistik des preußischen Kriegsministeriums* (Munich: Verlag für Kulturpolitik, 1922); Jacob Segall, *Die deutschen Juden als Soldaten im Kriege 1914–1918. Eine statistische Studie* (Berlin: Philo-Verlag, 1922); Werner T. Angress, "The German Army's 'Judenzählung' of 1916: Genesis—Consequences—Significance," *LBIYB* 23 (1978): 117–138; Jacob Rosenthal, *"Die Ehre des jüdischen Soldaten." Die Judenzählung im Ersten Weltkrieg und ihre Folgen* (Frankfurt: Campus, 2007).

152. Werner Scholem to Gershom Scholem, 19 June 1916, NLI, ARC. 4*1599/01/3034.

153. Diary entry, 14 August 1916, in Gershom Scholem, *Tagebücher*, 1:358–359.

154. Werner Scholem to Gershom Scholem, 7 July 1916, NLI, ARC. 4*1599/01/3034.

155. Werner Scholem to Gershom Scholem, 23 June 1916, NLI, ARC. 4*1599/01/3034.

156. Erich Brauer to Gershom Scholem, 15 July 1916, and Gershom Scholem to Erich Brauer, 17 July 1916, in *Briefe*, 1:349n7 and 1:42.

157. Gershom Scholem to Harry Heymann, 25 August 1917, NLI, ARC. 4*1599/01/1144.

158. Adrian Gregory, "Lost Generations: The Impact of Military Casualties on Paris, London, and Berlin," in Winter and Robert, *Capital Cities at War*, 58–59 and 71.

159. Jon Lawrence, "The Transition to War in 1914," in Winter and Robert, *Capital Cities at War*, 141, 160, and 157; Thierry Bonzon, "Transfer Payments and Social Policy," in Winter and Robert, *Capital Cities at War*, 286.

160. Waldemar Zimmermann, "Die Veränderung der Einkommens- und Lebensverhältnisse der deutschen Arbeiter durch den Krieg," in *Die Einwirkung des Krieges auf Bevölkerungsbewegung, Einkommen und Lebenshaltung in Deutschland*, ed. Rudolf Meerwarth, Adolf Günther, and Waldemar Zimmermann (Stuttgart: Deutsche Verlags-Anstalt, 1932), 404–406.

161. Jon Lawrence, "Material Pressures on the Middle Classes," in Winter and Robert, *Capital Cities at War*, 247.

162. Thierry Bonzon and Belinda Davis, "Feeding the Cities," in Winter and Robert, *Capital Cities at War*, 306–307, 311–313, and 317.

163. Jonathan Manning, "Wages and Purchasing Power," in Winter and Robert, *Capital Cities at War*, 259; cf. Zimmermann, "Die Veränderung der Einkommens- und Lebensverhältnisse," in Meerwarth, Günther, and Zimmermann, *Die Einwirkung des Krieges*, 428. Zimmermann indicates a 72 percent increase between January–July 1914 and December 1915, while Manning cites a 36 percent increase between July 1914 and December 1915.

164. Zimmermann, "Die Veränderung der Einkommens- und Lebensverhältnisse," in Meerwarth, Günther, and Zimmermann, *Die Einwirkung des Krieges*, 457.

165. Davis, *Home Fires Burning*, 80–88, 118, and 225.

166. Davis, *Home Fires Burning*, 222–223.

167. Betty Scholem to Gershom Scholem, 16 November 1917, 25 February 1918, and 26 October 1918, in *MuSiB*, 18, 20, and 21.

168. Betty Scholem to Gershom Scholem, 16 November 1917 and 21 January 1918, in *MuSiB*, 18 and 19.

169. Catherine Rollet, "The 'Other War' II: Setbacks in Public Health," in Winter and Robert, *Capital Cities at War*, 484.

170. Hedwig Scholem to Gershom Scholem, 6 July 1917, and 24 October, 29 November, and 4 January 1918, NLI, ARC. 4*1599/01/3032; Betty Scholem to Gershom Scholem, 26 October and 18 November 1918, in *MuSiB*, 20–21 and 24; Rollet, "'Other War' II," in Winter and Robert, *Capital Cities at War*, 482.

171. Betty Scholem to Gershom Scholem, 21 and 24 June 1918, NLI, ARC. 4*1599/01/3078.

172. David J. Fine, *Jewish Integration in the German Army in the First World War* (Berlin: Walter de Gruyter, 2012), 100–105 and 119.

173. Angress, "Prussia's Army," *LBIYB* 17 (1972).

174. John Keegan, *The First World War* (New York: Knopf, 1999), 392–412.

175. Betty Scholem to Gershom Scholem, 16 July and 11 September 1918, NLI, ARC. 4*1599/01/3078.

176. Betty Scholem to Gershom Scholem, 26 October 1918, NLI, ARC. 4*1599/01/3078.

177. Betty Scholem to Gershom Scholem, 13 October 1918, NLI, ARC. 4*1599/01/3078.

178. Betty Scholem to Gershom Scholem, 11 November 1918, in *MuSiB*, 23.

4. Life in the Time of Revolutions

1. Maximilian, Prince of Baden [Prinz Max von Baden], *Erinnerungen und Dokumente*, ed. Golo Mann and Andreas Burckhardt (Stuttgart: Ernst Klett, 1968), 595.

2. Heinrich August Winkler, *Weimar 1918–1933. Die Geschichte der ersten deutschen Demokratie* (Munich: C. H. Beck, 1993), 31.

3. Philipp Scheidemann, *Memoiren eines Sozialdemokraten* (Hamburg: Severus, 2010), 2:244–249; Winkler, *Weimar 1918–1933*, 33.

4. Betty Scholem to Gershom Scholem, 9 November 1918, in *MuSiB*, 22–23, quote on 23.

5. Betty Scholem to Gershom Scholem, 11 November 1918, in *MuSiB*, 23.

6. Betty Scholem to Gershom Scholem, 11 November 1918, in *MuSiB*, 23.

7. Betty Scholem to Gershom Scholem, 11 December 1918, NLI, ARC. 4*1599/01/3078.

8. "Die große demokratische Partei," *Berliner Tageblatt* 47, no. 587 (16 November 1918, morning edition): [1]; "Die deutsche demokratische Partei," *Vossische Zeitung*, no. 595 (21 November 1918, morning edition): [2].

9. Erich Scholem to Gershom Scholem, 20 April 1960, NLI, ARC. 4*1599/01/3024; Reinhold Scholem to Gershom Scholem, 18 July 1977, NLI, ARC. 4*1599/01/3031; Betty Scholem to Gershom Scholem, 11 December 1918, NLI, ARC. 4*1599/01/3078.

10. Betty Scholem to Gershom Scholem, 18 November 1918, in *MuSiB*, 25.

11. Betty Scholem to Gershom Scholem, 11 December 1918, NLI, ARC. 4*1599/01/3078.

12. Betty Scholem to Gershom Scholem, 25 January 1919, NLI, ARC. 4*1599/01/3079.

13. Werner Scholem to Gershom Scholem, 26 December 1918, NLI, ARC. 4*1599/01/3034.

14. Hedwig Scholem to Gershom Scholem, 4 January 1919, NLI, ARC. 4*1599/01/3032; Werner Scholem to Gershom Scholem, 26 December 1918, NLI, ARC. 4*1599/01/3034.

15. Werner Scholem to Gershom Scholem, 7 February 1919, NLI, ARC. 4*1599/01/3034; Reinhold Scholem to Gershom Scholem, 25 November 1919, in *MuSiB*, 58.

16. Betty Scholem to Gershom Scholem, 29 November 1918, 23 December 1918, and 1 January 1919, NLI, ARC. 4*1599/01/3078 and 3079.

17. Richard Bessel, *Germany after the First World War* (Oxford: Clarendon Press, 1993), 83.

18. Betty Scholem to Gershom Scholem, 23 December 1918, NLI, ARC. 4*1599/01/3078.

19. Betty Scholem to Gershom Scholem, 18 and 29 November, 11 and 23 December 1918, in *MuSiB*, 24–25, 26, 27, and 29; Bessel, *Germany after the First World War*, 115–116 and 160.

20. Betty Scholem to Gershom Scholem, 18 November 1918 and 9 January 1919, in *MuSiB*, 25 and 31.

21. Winkler, *Weimar 1918–1933*, 58; Mark Jones, *Founding Weimar: Violence and the German Revolution of 1918–1919* (Cambridge: Cambridge University Press, 2016), 180 and 332; Wolfram Pyta, *Die Weimarer Republik* (Berlin: Landeszentrale für politische Bildung, 2004), 29.

22. Betty Scholem to Gershom Scholem, 7/9 January 1919, in *MuSiB*, 30.

23. J. P. Nettl, *Rosa Luxemburg* (London: Oxford University Press, 1966), 2:772–775.

24. Bernhard Grau, *Kurt Eisner 1867–1919. Eine Biographie* (Munich: C. H. Beck, 2001), 343–448; Erich Brauer to Gershom Scholem, 20 February 1919, NLI, ARC. 4*1599/01/0356.2.

25. Betty Scholem to Gershom Scholem, 8 June 1919, in *MuSiB*, 49–50.

26. Ernest Hamburger, "Hugo Preuß: Scholar and Statesman," *LBIYB* 20 (1975): 179–206.

27. Liepach, *Das Wahlverhalten der jüdischen Bevölkerung*, 16–26.

28. Rahel Straus, *Wir lebten in Deutschland. Erinnerungen einer deutschen Jüdin 1880–1933*, ed. Max Kreutzberger (Stuttgart: Deutsche Verlags-Anstalt, 1961), 225.

29. Heinrich August Winkler, *Der lange Weg nach Westen*, vol. 1, *Deutsche Geschichte vom Ende des Alten Reiches bis zum Untergang der Weimarer Republik* (Munich: C. H. Beck, 2000), 429.

30. Betty Scholem to Gershom Scholem, 22 January 1919, in *MuSiB*, 34.

31. Winkler, *Weimar 1918–1933*, 69.

32. Hedwig Scholem to Gershom Scholem, 4 January 1919, NLI, ARC. 4*1599/01/3032.

33. Betty Scholem to Gershom Scholem, 13 February, 19 June, and 24 March 1919, NLI, ARC. 4*1599/01/3079.

34. Betty Scholem to Gershom Scholem, 7 March 1919, NLI, ARC. 4*1599/01/3079.

35. Betty Scholem to Gershom Scholem, 13 February 1919, NLI, ARC. 4*1599/01/3079.

36. Article 1, "Die Verfassung des Deutschen Reiches," 11 August 1919, in *Reichsgesetzblatt* 1919, no. 152, 1383.

37. Articles 136–141, "Die Verfassung des Deutschen Reiches," 11 August 1919, in *Reichsgesetzblatt* 1919, no. 152, 1408–1410, quote from Article 136 on 1408.

38. Werner Scholem to Gershom Scholem, 7 February and 30 March 1919, NLI, ARC. 4*1599/01/3034.

39. Gershom Scholem to Werner Kraft, 10 April 1919, in *Briefe*, 1:202.

40. Hedwig Scholem to Gershom Scholem, 20 February 1919, NLI, ARC. 4*1599/01/3032.

41. Werner Scholem to Gershom Scholem, 30 March 1919, NLI, ARC. 4*1599/01/3034.

42. Werner Scholem to Gershom Scholem, 4 June 1919, NLI, ARC. 4*1599/01/3034.

43. M. Zadoff, *Der rote Hiob*, 129.

44. Diary entry, "An Werner über das *Volksblatt*," Gershom Scholem to Werner Scholem, 10 August 1919, in Gershom Scholem, *Tagebücher*, 2:508–509.

45. Arthur Scholem to Amtsgericht Berlin-Mitte, Handelregisterabteilung A, 30 December 1919, Arthur, Reinhold, and Erich Scholem to Amtsgericht (Registergericht), 10 January 1920, LAB, A Rep. 342–02, Nr. 42380.

46. Betty Scholem to Gershom Scholem, 25 May 1919, and Arthur Scholem to Gershom Scholem, 25 July 1920, NLI, ARC. 4*1599/01/3079; Arthur Scholem to Gershom Scholem, 13 August 1919, in *MuSiB*, 51.

47. Arthur Scholem to Gershom Scholem, 9 October 1923, in *MuSiB*, 84.

48. Betty Scholem to Gershom Scholem, 20 May 1924, NLI, ARC. 4*1599/01/3081.

49. Betty Scholem to Gershom Scholem, 24 March, 5 April, and 25 May 1919, NLI, ARC. 4*1599/01/3079.

50. Reinhold Scholem to Gershom Scholem, 21 February 1927, NLI, ARC. 4*1599/01/3031; Erich Scholem to Gershom Scholem, 25 January 1930, NLI, ARC. 4*1599/01/3024.

51. Reinhold Scholem to Gershom Scholem, 14 October 1976, NLI, ARC. 4*1599/01/3031; "Personalien," *Ministerial-Blatt der Handels- und Gewerbe-Verwaltung* 6, no. 3 (12 February 1906): 71; *Berliner Adressbuch 1921* (Berlin: August Scherl, 1921), 1:1366; "Eheschließungen, Geborene und Gestorbene im Gebiete des Deutschen Reichs in den Jahren 1851 bis 1926," in Germany, Statistisches Reichsamt, *Statistisches Jahrbuch für das Deutsche Reich*, vol. 46, *1927* (Berlin: Reimar Hobbing, 1927), 28.

52. Hedwig Scholem to Gershom Scholem, 19 March 1921, NLI, ARC. 4*1599/01/3032.

53. "Treaty of Peace with Germany (Treaty of Versailles, 1919)," in United States, *Treaties and Other International Agreements of the United States of America, 1776–1949*, vol. 2, *Multilateral, 1918–1930*, ed. Charles I. Bevans (Washington, D.C.: Department of State, 1969), 43–240.

54. Sally Marks, "Reparations Reconsidered: A Reminder," *Central European History* 2, no. 4 (December 1969): 356–365.

55. Detlev J. K. Peukert, *The Weimar Republic: The Crisis of Classical Modernity*, trans. Richard Devenson (New York: Hill and Wang, 1993), 42–46.

56. Niewyk, *Jews in Weimar Germany*, 109.

57. Gershom Scholem to Escha Burchhardt, 23 November 1918, in *Briefe*, 1:184.

58. Gershom Scholem to Betty Scholem, 11 January 1919 and 2 February 1919, NLI, ARC. 4*1599/12/3000.

59. Gershom Scholem to Betty Scholem, 9 April 1919, in *MuSiB*, 42; Gershom Scholem to Escha Burchhardt, 23 November 1918, in *Briefe*, 1:185; *Moaus zur. Ein Chanukkahbuch* (Berlin: Jüdischer Verlag, 1918).

60. Gershom Scholem to Escha Burchhardt, 23 November 1918, in *Briefe*, 1:185.

61. Gershom Scholem to Betty Scholem, 9 April 1919, in *MuSiB*, 43.

62. Gershom Scholem to Betty Scholem, 17 February 1919, NLI, ARC. 4*1599/12/3000.

63. Arthur Scholem to Gershom Scholem, 25 January 1919, in *MuSiB*, 35–36.

64. Gershom Scholem to Werner Kraft, 10 April 1919, in *Briefe*, 1:201.

65. Gershom Scholem to Erich Brauer, 15 March 1919, NLI, ARC. 4*1599/01/0356.3.

66. Hugo Bergmann to Else Bergmann, 12 March 1919, in Schmuel Hugo Bergman, *Tagebücher und Briefe*, vol. 1, *1901–1948*, ed. Miriam Sambursky (Königstein: Jüdischer Verlag bei Athenäum, 1985), 118.

67. Gershom Scholem to Escha Burchhardt, 23 November 1918, and Gershom Scholem to Werner Kraft, 10 April 1919, in *Briefe*, 1:185 and 1:201.

68. "Wenn man erzählen könnte, wie wir Zionisten wurden," 1919, NLI, ARC. 4*1599/07/277.1.31.

69. Gershom Scholem to Ludwig Strauss, 22 July 1919, NLI, ARC. 4*1599/01/2572.

70. Gershom Scholem to Albert Baer, 28 April 1920, NLI, ARC. 4*1599/07/277.1.41.

71. Gershom Scholem, "Die Wahrheit," NLI, ARC. 4*1599/07/277.1.50.

72. Arthur Scholem to Gershom Scholem, 1 August 1919, in *MuSiB*, 50–51.

73. Betty Scholem to Gershom Scholem, 11 February and 23 October 1919, NLI, ARC. 4*1599/01/3079.

74. Gershom Scholem to Erich Brauer, 25 April 1919, NLI, ARC. 4*1599/01/0356.3.

75. Gershom Scholem to Betty and Arthur Scholem, 26 April 1919, in *MuSiB*, 45–46.

76. Gershom Scholem to Betty and Arthur Scholem, 23 November 1919, in *MuSiB*, 58.

77. Reinhold Scholem to Gershom Scholem, 25 November 1919, NLI, ARC. 4*1599/01/3031.

78. Gershom Scholem to Betty and Arthur Scholem, 6 December 1919, in *MuSiB*, 59.

79. Gershom Scholem, *VBnJ*, 153.

80. Gershom Scholem to Erich Brauer, 14 December 1920, NLI, ARC. 4*1599/01/0356.3; Gershom Scholem, *VBnJ*, 141–142 and 144–146.

81. Gershom Scholem to Erich Brauer, winter 1919 and 3 March 1920, NLI, ARC. 4*1599/0356.3.

82. Gershom Scholem to Meta Jahr, 1 July 1920, NLI, ARC. 4*1599/01/1259.

83. Arthur Scholem to Gershom Scholem, 25 July 1920, NLI, ARC. 4*1599/01/3079.

84. Arthur Scholem to Gershom Scholem, 15 December 1921, NLI, ARC. 4*1599/01/3079.

85. Gershom Scholem to Betty Scholem, 29 March 1920, NLI, ARC. 4*1599/12/3000.

86. Walter Benjamin to Gershom Scholem, 17 April 1920, in Gershom Scholem, *A Life in Letters, 1914–1982*, ed. and trans. Anthony David Skinner (Cambridge, Mass.: Harvard University Press, 2002), 112; Arthur Scholem to Gershom Scholem, 3 December 1921, in *MuSiB*, 79–80.

87. Gershom Scholem to Betty and Arthur Scholem, 14 June 1920, in *MuSiB*, 74.

88. See Engel, *Gershom Scholem*, 9–20 among others, quote on 17.

89. Gershom Scholem to Erich Brauer, 6 June and 14 December 1920, NLI, ARC. 4*1599/01/0356.3.

90. Betty Scholem to Gershom Scholem, 4 March 1922, NLI, ARC. 4*1599/01/3079; David A. Rees, "Fritz Hommels Gutachten zu Gerhard Scholems Dissertation," *Münchner Beiträge zur Jüdischen Geschichte und Kultur* 2 (2007): 87.

91. Gershom Scholem, *VBnJ*, 175; Gerhard [Gershom] Scholem, *Das Buch Bahir. Sepher Ha-Bahir. Ein Text aus der Frühzeit der Kabbala auf Grund eines kritischen Textes ins Deutsche übersetzt und kommentiert* (Berlin: Arthur Scholem, 1923), reprinted as *Das Buch Bahir. Ein Schriftdenkmal aus der Frühzeit der Kabbala auf Grund der kritischen Neuausgabe* (Leipzig: W. Drugulin, 1923).

92. Gershom Scholem to Betty and Arthur Scholem, 6 March 1922, NLI, ARC. 4*1599/12/3000.

93. Gershom Scholem, *VBnJ*, 175.

94. Gershom Scholem, *VBnJ*, 140–141 and 150.

95. Betty Scholem to Gershom Scholem, 30 May 1920, in *MuSiB*, 71.

96. Gershom Scholem to Erich Brauer, 6 June 1920, NLI, ARC. 4*1599/01/0356.3.

97. Gershom Scholem to Meta Jahr, 1 July 1920, NLI, ARC. 4*1599/01/1259.

98. Gershom Scholem to Erich Brauer, 14 December 1920, NLI, ARC. 4*1599/01/0356.3.

99. Gershom Scholem, *VBnJ*, 147–153.

100. Gershom Scholem to Erich Brauer, 6 June 1920, NLI, ARC. 4*1599/01/0356.3.

101. Gershom Scholem to Robert Weltsch and Hans Kohn, 30 July 1921, in *Briefe*, 1:216–217.

102. "Erklärung," *Jüdische Rundschau* 27, no. 97 (8 December 1922): 638.

103. Gershom Scholem to Betty Scholem, 6 January 1920, NLI, ARC. 4*1599/12/3000.

104. Gershom Scholem to Arthur Scholem, 3 March 1920, NLI, ARC. 4*1599/12/3000.

105. Gershom Scholem to Betty and Arthur Scholem, 14 August 1920, in *MuSiB*, 79.

106. Walter Benjamin to Gershom Scholem, 23 July 1920, in *The Correspondence of Walter Benjamin, 1910–1940*, 165; Gershom Scholem, *WBTSF*, 110.

107. Gershom Scholem, *WBTSF*, 112.

108. Gershom Scholem, *WBTSF*, 140.

109. Gershom Scholem, *VBnJ*, 156–157 and 236.

110. Gershom Scholem to Franz Rosenzweig, 7 March 1921, in *Briefe*, 1:214; Walter Benjamin to Gershom Scholem, 30 December 1922, in Walter Benjamin, *Gesammelte Briefe*, vol. 2, *1919–1924*, ed. Christoph Gödde and Henri Lonitz (Frankfurt: Suhrkamp, 1996), 300.

111. Franz Rosenzweig to Joseph Prager, 30 May 1923, in Franz Rosenzweig, *Briefe*, ed. Edith Rosenzweig (Berlin: Schocken, 1935), 482.

112. Gershom Scholem, "With Gershom Scholem: An Interview," in Scholem, *On Jews and Judaism in Crisis*, 21.

113. Erna Michaelis to Gershom Scholem, 1 July 1920, NLI, ARC. 4*1599/01/1790.

114. Handwritten notes on Scholem's relationship with Schocken, 15 June 1923, NLI, ARC. 4*1599/01/3050.

115. Frank Hirschinger, *"Gestapoagenten, Trotzkisten, Verräter." Kommunistische Parteisäuberungen in Sachsen-Anhalt 1918–1953* (Göttingen: Vandenhoeck & Ruprecht, 2005), 28; "Herr Scholem berichtigt," *Vorwärts* 41, no. 392 (21 August 1924, morning edition): [2].

116. Gershom Scholem to Betty Scholem, 19 March 1920, in *MuSiB*, 68.

117. Winkler, *Weimar 1918–1933*, 119–127.

118. Howard Stern, "The Organisation Consul," *Journal of Modern History* 35, no. 1 (March 1963): 20–32.

119. Winkler, *Weimar 1918–1933*, 131–134.

120. Werner Scholem to Gershom Scholem, 6 August 1919, NLI, ARC. 4*1599/01/3034; Hedwig Scholem to Gershom Scholem, 3 December 1920, NLI, ARC. 4*1599/01/3032; David W. Morgan, *The Socialist Left and the German Revolution: A History of the German Independent Social Democratic Party, 1917–1922* (Ithaca, N.Y.: Cornell University Press, 1975), 364–367 and 372–438.

121. "Verantwortlicher Redakteur: Werner Scholem, Berlin," *Die Rote Fahne* 4, no. 104 (3 March 1921, evening edition): [4].

122. "Gemeinsame Sitzung des Reichskabinetts mit dem Preußischen Staatsministerium vom 28. März 1921, 11 Uhr," 28 March 1921, Bundesarchiv, R 43

I/1366, p. 351 (hereafter cited as BArch); "Beratung des Antrages des Justizministers auf Erteilung der Genehmigung zur strafgerichtlichen Verfolgung des Abgeordneten Scholem wegen Hochverrats," 2 June 1921, in Prussia (Germany), Landtag, *Sitzungsberichte des Preußischen Landtags. 1. Wahlperiode. 1. Tagung: begonnen am 10. März 1921*, vol. 1 (Berlin: Preußische Verlagsanstalt, 1922), 1435–1506; "Vermerk," 26 June 1922, BArch, R 3003/11 J 16/21, Bd. 2; Hermann Weber, "Zum Verhältnis von Komintern, Sowjetstaat und KPD," in *Deutschland, Russland, Komintern*, vol. 1, *Überblicke, Analysen, Diskussionen*, ed. Hermann Weber, Jakov Drabkin, Bernhard H. Bayerlein, and Aleksandr Galkin (Berlin: Walter de Gruyter, 2014), 9–139.

123. Various documents, including "Beschluß," 19 August 1922, BArch, R 3003/11 J 16/1921, Bd. 1; "Anklageschrift" and "Im Namen des Volkes," n.d. [after 22 January 1923], BArch, R 3003/6 J 34/22, Bd. 2.

124. Hoffrogge, *Werner Scholem*, 197–217.

125. Buckmiller and Nafe, "Die Naherwartung des Kommunismus," in Buckmiller, Heimann, and Perels, *Judentum und politische Existenz*, 67.

126. Gershom Scholem, *VBnJ*, 180.

127. Gershom Scholem, *VBnJ*, 181.

128. Walter Benjamin to Gershom Scholem, 1 February 1923, in Benjamin, *Gesammelte Briefe*, 2:312.

129. Gershom Scholem, *VBnJ*, 199–202 and 207–208.

130. Gershom Scholem to Salman Schocken, 8 September 1923, in *Briefe*, 1:218–219; Gershom Scholem, *VBnJ*, 200–201; Saverio Campanini, "*Alu im Shalom.* Die Bibliothek Gershom Scholems vor der Auswanderung," in Necker, Morlok, and Morgenstern, *Gershom Scholem in Deutschland*, 73–96.

131. Betty Scholem to Gershom Scholem, 21 September 1923, in *MuSiB*, 80–81.

132. Gordon A. Craig, *Germany, 1866–1945* (New York: Oxford University Press, 1978), 450–451; Peukert, *Weimar Republic*, 66.

133. Betty Scholem to Gershom Scholem, 9 October 1923, in *MuSiB*, 83.

134. Betty Scholem to Gershom Scholem, 15 October 1923, in *MuSiB*, 84–85.

135. Betty Scholem to Gershom Scholem, 23 October 1923, in *MuSiB*, 88.

136. Betty Scholem to Gershom Scholem, 23 and 30 October 1923, NLI, ARC. 4*1599/01/3080.

137. Betty Scholem to Gershom Scholem, 15 October 1923, in *MuSiB*, 86.

138. Betty Scholem to Gershom Scholem, 30 October 1923, NLI, ARC. 4*1599/01/3080.

139. Betty Scholem to Gershom Scholem, 15 October 1923, in *MuSiB*, 86.

140. Winkler, *Weimar 1918–1933*, 213–216 and 225–227; Betty Scholem to Gershom Scholem, 27 March and 17 July 1928, in *MuSiB*, 160–161 and 174. The Damoclean sword was lifted on 13 July 1928 through a general amnesty.

141. Betty Scholem to Gershom Scholem, 23 October 1923, in *MuSiB*, 88.

142. Sophie Scholem to Gershom Scholem, 12 November 1923, NLI, ARC. 4*1599/01/3027.

143. David Clay Large, "'Out with the Ostuden': The Scheunenviertel Riots in Berlin, November 1923," in *Exclusionary Violence: Antisemitic Riots in Modern German History*, ed. Christhard Hoffmann, Werner Bergmann, and Helmut Walser Smith (Ann Arbor: University of Michigan Press, 2002), 123–140.

144. Betty Scholem to Gershom Scholem, 20 November 1923, NLI, ARC. 4*1599/01/3080.

145. Betty Scholem to Gershom Scholem, 31 March 1924, NLI, ARC. 4*1599/01/3081.

146. Betty Scholem to Gershom Scholem, 12 November 1923, NLI, ARC. 4*1599/01/3080; Winkler, *Weimar 1918–1933*, 237–238.

147. Betty Scholem to Gershom Scholem, 20 November 1923, NLI, ARC. 4*1599/01/3080.

148. Arthur Scholem to Gershom Scholem, 1 November 1923, in *MuSiB*, 91.

149. Betty Scholem to Gershom Scholem, 2 November 1923, in *MuSiB*, 93–94.

150. Trude Maurer, "From Everyday Life to a State of Emergency: Jews in Weimar and Nazi Germany," in Kaplan, *Jewish Daily Life in Germany*, 284.

151. Betty Scholem to Gershom Scholem, 2/4 November 1923, in *MuSiB*, 92–93.

152. Betty Scholem to Gershom Scholem, 9 October 1923, and Arthur Scholem to Gershom Scholem, 9 October 1923, in *MuSiB*, 82 and 84.

153. Arthur Ruppin, *Soziologie der Juden*, vol. 1, *Die Soziale Struktur der Juden* (Berlin: Jüdischer Verlag, 1930), 170; Avraham Barkai, "Population Decline and Economic Stagnation," in Meyer, *GJHMT*, 4:31.

154. Hedwig Scholem to Gershom Scholem, 19 March 1921, NLI, ARC. 4*1599/01/3032; Betty Scholem to Gershom Scholem, 23 October, 12 and 24 November 1923, NLI, ARC. 4*1599/01/3080.

155. Annie Sacerdoti, *The Guide to Jewish Italy* (New York: Rizzoli, 2004), 94; Ferruccio Delle Cave and Eva Maria Baur, *Literatur und Kur. Ein literarischer Themenweg durch die Kurstadt Meran* (Merano: Gemeinde Meran, 2012), 6–7, 21, and 27.

156. Betty Scholem to Gershom Scholem, 30 December 1923 and 2 January 1924, NLI, ARC. 4*1599/01/3080 and 3081.

157. Betty Scholem to Gershom Scholem, 22 and 29 July 1924, NLI, ARC. 4*159 901/3081.

158. Betty Scholem to Gershom Scholem, 30 September 1923, NLI, ARC. 4*1599/01/3080.

159. Betty Scholem to Gershom Scholem, 24 March 1924, NLI, ARC. 4*1599/01/3081.

5. The Gold-Plated Twenties and Beyond

1. Gershom Scholem, *VBnJ*, 47.

2. Betty Scholem to Gershom Scholem, 24 March 1924, NLI, ARC. 4*1599/01/3081.

3. Betty Scholem to Gershom Scholem, 10 November 1925, NLI, ARC. 4*1599/01/3081.

4. Betty Scholem to Gershom Scholem, 24 March and 1 April 1924, NLI, ARC. 4*1599/01/3081.

5. Betty Scholem to Gershom Scholem, 13 April 1924, NLI, ARC. 4*1599/01/3081.

6. Betty Scholem to Gershom Scholem, 21 October 1924, 7 May and 5 November 1929, NLI, ARC. 4*1599/01/3081 and 3086.

7. Betty Scholem to Gershom Scholem, 29 December 1925, NLI, ARC. 4*1599/01/3081.

8. Betty Scholem to Gershom Scholem, 12 August 1929, NLI, ARC. 4*1599/01/3081.

9. Betty Scholem to Gershom Scholem, 5 May 1924, NLI, ARC. 4*1599/01/3081.

10. "Die Wohnbevölkerung nach der Religion am 16. Juni 1925," in Berlin, Statistisches Amt der Stadt Berlin, *Statistisches Jahrbuch der Stadt Berlin*, vol. 3, *1927* (Berlin: Otto Stollberg, Verlag für Politik und Wirtschaft, 1927), 6–7; "Reichstagswahlen am 4. Mai 1924," in Berlin, Statistisches Amt der Stadt Berlin, *Statistisches Taschenbuch der Stadt Berlin 1924* (Berlin: Otto Stollberg, Verlag für Politik und Wirtschaft, 1924), 111; "Die Wahlen zum Deutschen Reichstag von 1871 bis 1924," in Germany, Statistisches Reichsamt, *Statistisches Jahrbuch für das Deutsche Reich*, 46:497.

11. "Die Wohnbevölkerung nach dem Religionsbekenntnis am 16. Juni 1925," "Die auf die Wahlvorschläge entfallenden Stimmen und Abgeordneten," and "Abstimmungsergebnisse der Wahl zum Deutschen Reichstag vom 4. Mai 1924 nach Stadtteilen und Wahlvorschlägen," in Frankfurt am Main (Germany), Statistisches Amt, *Statistisches Handbuch der Stadt Frankfurt a. M.*, 2nd ed., *Enthaltend die Statistik der Jahre 1906/07 bis 1926/27* (Frankfurt am Main: August Osterrieth, 1928), 69, 447, and 448.

12. Gershom Scholem to Reinhold Scholem, 8/11 September 1976 and 1 August 1977, and Reinhold Scholem to Gershom Scholem, 18 July 1977, NLI, ARC. 4*1599/01/3031; Betty Scholem to Gershom Scholem, 12 August 1929, NLI, ARC. 4*1599/01/3086; Brenner, "Tale of Two Families," 350.

13. Unsigned editorial, "Wählt überall die demokratische Liste!"; Rudolf Oeser, "Wahltag"; and Ludwig Haas, "Gedanken zum Wahltag"; all in *Berliner Tageblatt 53*, no. 212 (4 May 1924, morning edition): [1]; Hamburger and Pulzer, "Jews as Voters," *LBIYB* 30 (1985): 9–14.

14. Hamburger and Pulzer, "Jews as Voters," *LBIYB* 30 (1985): 14–23; P. B. Wiener, "Die Parteien der Mitte," in *Entscheidungsjahr 1932. Zur Judenfrage in der Endphase der Weimarer Republik*, ed. Werner E. Mosse and Arnold Paucker, 2nd ed. (Tübingen: J. C. B. Mohr, 1965), 314–321.

15. Hamburger and Pulzer, "Jews as Voters," *LBIYB* 30 (1985): 21; Gershom Scholem to Betty Scholem, dated "eve of Passover" [24 April 1929], NLI, ARC. 4*1599/12/3001.

16. Reinhold Scholem to Gershom Scholem, 25 November 1919, NLI, ARC. 4*1599/01/3031; Reichsklub der Deutschen Volkspartei e. V., *Mitgliederverzeichnis April 1923* (Berlin: n.p., [1923]), 56.

17. Gershom Scholem, *VBnJ*, 47.

18. "Gesamtergebnis der Wahlen zum Reichstag am 4. Mai 1924," in Germany, Statistisches Reichsamt, *Statistisches Jahrbuch für das Deutsche Reich*, vol. 44, *1924/25* (Berlin: Verlag für Politik und Wirtschaft, 1925): 390–391.

19. Betty Scholem to Gershom Scholem, 5 May 1924, NLI, ARC. 4*1599/01/3081.

20. Joseph V. Stalin, "Die deutsche Revolution und die Fehler des Genossen Radek. Aus dem Bericht auf dem Plenum des Zentralkomitees der RKP(b)," 15 January 1924, in *Deutscher Oktober 1923. Ein Revolutionsplan und sein Scheitern*, ed. Bernhard H. Bayerlein, Leonid G. Babicenko, Fridrich I. Firsov, and Aleksandr Ju. Vatlin (Berlin: Aufbau, 2003), 448–449.

21. Hamburger and Pulzer, "Jews as Voters," *LBIYB* 30 (1985): 43–45.

22. Betty Scholem to Gershom Scholem, 1 April 1924, NLI, ARC. 4*1599/01/3081; "Referat Scholem auf Konferenz pol. u. org. Sekretäre und Chefredakture 4./9.24,"

4 September 1924, Bundesarchiv, Stiftung Archiv der Parteien und Massenorganisationen der DDR, RY 1/I 2/2/4 (hereafter cited as BArch-SAPMO); "Protokoll der Sitzung der Zentrale vom 14. April 1924," 14 April 1924, BArch-SAPMO, RY 1/I 2/2/16.

23. Betty Scholem to Gershom Scholem, 3 June 1924, NLI, ARC. 4*1599/01/3081; "Kommunistische Obstruktion," *Vossische Zeitung*, no. 252 (28 May 1924, morning edition): [1–2].

24. "Kommunistische Spitzenkandidaten," *Vorwärts* 41, no. 163 (5 April 1924): [2nd insert, n.p.].

25. "10. Sitzung," 24 June 1924, *Verhandlungen des Reichstags. II. Wahlperiode 1924*, vol. 381, *Stenographische Berichte (von der 1. Sitzung am 27. Mai 1924 bis zur 29. Sitzung am 30. August 1924)* (Berlin: Verlag der Reichsdruckerei, 1924), 240–246.

26. Betty Scholem to Gershom Scholem, 2 September 1924, in *MuSiB*, 109–110.

27. Diary entry, 14 July 1924, in Joseph Goebbels, *Die Tagebücher von Joseph Goebbels*, ed. Elke Fröhlich, pt. 1, *Aufzeichnungen 1923–1941*, vol. 1/I, *Oktober 1923– November 1925* (Munich: K. G. Saur, 2004), 169.

28. Walter Benjamin to Gershom Scholem, 13 June 1924, in Benjamin, *Gesammelte Briefe*, 2:468.

29. Betty Scholem to Gershom Scholem, 16 June 1924, NLI, ARC. 4*1599/01/3081.

30. Betty Scholem to Gershom Scholem, 20 May and 3 June 1924, NLI, ARC. 4*1599/01/3081.

31. "Gesamtergebnis der Wahlen zum Reichstag am 7. Dezember 1924," in Germany, Statistisches Reichsamt, *Statistisches Jahrbuch für das Deutsche Reich*, 46:498–499.

32. "Artikel des Genossen Sinowjew," in Kommunistische Partei Deutschlands, *Bericht über die Verhandlungen des IX. Parteitages der Kommunistischen Partei Deutschlands (Sektion der Kommunistischen Internationale) abgehalten in Frankfurt a. M. vom 7. bis 10. April 1924* (Berlin: Vereinigung Internationaler Verlagsanstalten, 1924), 78–85; Grigory Zinoviev to Arkadi Maslow and Ruth Fischer, 31 March 1924, in *Deutschland, Russland, Komintern*, vol. 2, *Dokumente (1918–1943)*, pt. 1, ed. Hermann Weber, Jakov Drabkin, and Bernhard H. Bayerlein (Berlin: Walter de Gruyter, 2015), 372–374, esp. 374.

33. Rosa Aschenbrenner to Josef Eisenberger, 1 August 1929, in "Ein Briefwechsel," *Gegen den Strom. Organ der KPD (Opposition)* 2, no. 34 (24 August 1929): 14.

34. Hermann Weber, "The Stalinization of the KPD: Old and New Views," in *Bolshevism, Stalinism and the Comintern: Perspectives on Stalinization, 1917–53*, ed. Norman LaPorte, Kevin Morgan, and Matthew Worley (New York: Palgrave Macmillan, 2008), 22–23; Hermann Weber, *Die Wandlung des deutschen Kommunismus. Die Stalinisierung der KPD in der Weimarer Republik* (Frankfurt: Europäische Verlagsanstalt, 1969).

35. "Diskussion über das Referat 'Die weltpolitische Lage und die Aufgaben der Komintern' und den Bericht der Zentrale. Scholem," in Zentrale der Kommunistischen Partei Deutschlands, *Bericht über die Verhandlung des X. Parteitages der Kommunistischen Partei Deutschlands* (Berlin: Vereinigung Internationaler Verlagsanstalten, 1925), 392–393; Weber, *Die Wandlung des deutschen Kommunismus*, 106–107.

36. "Gesamtergebnis der Wahl des Reichspräsidenten (I. und II. Wahlgang) am 29. März und 26. April 1925," in Germany, Statistisches Reichsamt, *Statistisches Jahrbuch für das Deutsche Reich*, vol. 45, 1926 (Berlin: Reimar Hobbing, 1926), 450–451.

37. Betty Scholem to Gershom Scholem, 26 April 1925, NLI, ARC. 4*1599/01/3082.

38. Weber, "Stalinization of the KPD," in LaPorte, Morgan, and Worley, *Bolshevism, Stalinism and the Comintern*, 22–44.

39. "Brief des Exekutivkomitees der Komintern an den X. Parteitag der Kommunistischen Partei Deutschlands," in Kommunistische Partei Deutschlands, *Beschlüsse des X. Parteitages der Kommunistischen Partei Deutschlands* (Berlin: Zentralkomitee der K.P.D., 1925), 83.

40. "1. Reichskonferenz der KPD," "Bericht der Scholem-Kommission," 1 November 1925, BArch-SAPMO, RY 1/I 1/2/4; Förster to Grigory Zinoviev et al., 3 November 1925, in Weber, *Deutschland, Russland, Komintern* 2/1:478–481, esp. 479.

41. Joseph Stalin to Nikolai Bucharin, 25 July 1925, in Weber, *Deutschland, Russland, Komintern* 2/1:462–464.

42. Joseph V. Stalin, "The Fight against Right and 'Ultra-Left' Deviations: Two Speeches Delivered at a Meeting of the Presidium of the E.C.C.I.," 22 January 1926, in *Works*, vol. 8, *January–November 1926* (Moscow: Foreign Languages Publishing House, 1954), 5.

43. "Rebellion in der KPD. Erklärung von 700 Funktionären gegen die Zentrale," *Vorwärts* 43, no. 431 (no. 213, edition B) (13 September 1926): 1; "Erklärung von 700 KPD-Mitgliedern zur russischen Frage und gegen die Verfolgung der Linken Opposition in der Sowjetunion ('Brief der 700')," 1 September 1929, in Weber, *Deutschland, Russland, Komintern* 2/1:531–538; Pierre Broué, "Gauche allemande et Opposition russe de 1926 à 1928," *Cahiers Leon Trotsky*, no. 22 (June 1985): 4–25.

44. Wilhelm Pieck, "Auf zur revolutionären Arbeit—gegen ihre Saboteure!," *Die Rote Fahne* 9, no. 203 (14 September 1926): 12; "Protokoll der Sitzung des Polbüros vom 2. November 1926" and "Beschlüsse der Sitzung des Polbüros vom 2. November 1926," 2 November 1926, BArch-SAPMO, RY 1/I 2/3/6; unknown [illegible signature] to Deutsche Vertretung beim EKKI, 6 November 1926, BArch-SAPMO, RY 1/I 2/5/33b; Broué, "Gauche allemande et Opposition russe," 8.

45. Weber, "Stalinization of the KPD," in LaPorte, Morgan, and Worley, *Bolshevism, Stalinism and the Comintern*, 32.

46. Peukert, *Weimar Republic*, 208.

47. Winkler, *Weimar 1918–1933*, 96.

48. Betty Scholem to Gershom Scholem, 11 March 1929, NLI, ARC. 4*1599/01/3086.

49. Betty Scholem to Gershom Scholem, 19 February 1924, NLI, ARC. 4*1599/01/3081.

50. Betty Scholem to Gershom Scholem, 13 April 1929, NLI, ARC. 4*1599/01/3086.

51. R. E. May, "Der Prozentsatz der Teilnahme der Juden Groß-Berlins am Gottesdienst der hohen Feiertage," *Gemeindeblatt der Jüdischen Gemeinde zu Berlin* 19, no. 6 (June 1929): 292–293.

52. Betty Scholem to Gershom Scholem, 18 September 1928 and 9 October 1929, NLI, ARC. 4*1599/01/3085 and 3086.

53. Betty Scholem to Gershom Scholem, 6 October 1930, NLI, ARC. 4*1599/01/3087.

54. Betty Scholem to Gershom Scholem, 20 September 1925, NLI, ARC. 4*1599/01/3082.

55. Betty Scholem to Gershom Scholem, 20 November 1928, NLI, ARC. 4*1599/01/3085; Maurer, "From Everyday Life to a State of Emergency," in Kaplan, *Jewish Daily Life in Germany*, 327.

56. Betty Scholem to Gershom Scholem, 2 February 1926, NLI, ARC. 4*1599/01/3083.

57. Betty Scholem to Gershom Scholem, 20 April 1924, NLI, ARC. 4*1599/01/3081.

58. Betty Scholem to Gershom Scholem, 28 October 1928, NLI, ARC. 4*1599/01/3085.

59. Betty Scholem to Gershom Scholem, 16 December 1924, NLI, ARC. 4*1599/01/3081.

60. "Chanukah," "Judas, der Hämmerer," and "Zum Weichnachtsfest Odeon Electric Musikplatten," *Gemeindeblatt der Jüdischen Gemeinde zu Berlin* 17, no. 12 (2 December 1927): [287] and 314; Maurer, "From Everyday Life to a State of Emergency," in Kaplan, *Jewish Daily Life in Germany*, 328.

61. Betty Scholem to Gershom Scholem, 3 April 1929, NLI, ARC. 4*1599/01/3086.

62. Betty Scholem to Gershom Scholem, 11 January 1926 and 28 April 1932, NLI, ARC. 4*1599/01/3083 and 3089.

63. On their numbers, see Poppel, *Zionism in Germany*, 176–177; cf. Lavsky, *Before Catastrophe*, 33.

64. Betty Scholem to Gershom Scholem, 15 February 1927, NLI, ARC. 4*1599/01/3084.

65. Betty Scholem to Gershom Scholem, 28 April 1932, NLI, ARC. 4*1599/01/3089.

66. Niewyk, *Jews in Weimar Germany*, 129–132.

67. Betty Scholem to Gershom Scholem, 23 July 1928, NLI, ARC. 4*1599/01/3085.

68. Betty Scholem to Gershom Scholem, 12 January 1925, in *MuSiB*, 117.

69. Betty Scholem to Gershom Scholem, 2 September 1930, NLI, ARC. 4*1599/01/3087.

70. Gershom Scholem to Betty Scholem, 11 September 1930, NLI, ARC. 4*1599/12/3001.

71. Betty Scholem to Gershom Scholem, 16 September 1924, NLI, ARC. 4*1599/01/3081.

72. Kurt Wilhelm, "The Jewish Community in the Post-Emancipation Period," *LBIYB* 2 (1957): 70; cf. Paul Mendes-Flohr, "Jewish Cultural and Spiritual Life," in Meyer, *GJHMT*, 4:154.

73. David Rudavsky, *Emancipation and Adjustment: Contemporary Jewish Religious Movements, Their History and Thought* (New York: Diplomatic Press, 1967), 218–248.

74. Brenner, *Renaissance of Jewish Culture*, 3–5.

75. Betty Scholem to Gershom Scholem, 15 September 1931, in *MuSiB*, 251; Avraham Barkai, "Jewish Life in Its German Milieu," in Meyer, *GJHMT*, 4:68.

76. Kaplan, *Jewish Feminist Movement*; Tobias Metzler, *Tales of Three Cities: Urban Jewish Cultures in London, Berlin, and Paris (c. 1880–1940)* (Wiesbaden: Harrassowitz, 2014), 211.

77. Centralverein deutscher Staatsbürger jüdischen Glaubens, *Mitglieder-Verzeichnis 1908* (Berlin: Das Vereinsbureau, 1908), 10, 56, 67, 158, 170; *Mitglieder-Verzeichnis des Verbandes Groß-Berliner Ortsgruppen* (Berlin: Centralverein deutscher Staatsbürger jüdischen Glaubens, 1919), 22, 38, 98, 108, and 213.

78. Brenner, *Renaissance of Jewish Culture*, 69–99.

79. Franz Rosenzweig to Joseph Prager, 30 May 1923, in Rosenzweig, *Briefe*, 481–482; Gershom Scholem to Edith Rosenzweig, 29 May 1935, in *Briefe*, 1:259.

80. Gershom Scholem to Edith Rosenzweig, 20 February 1930, in *Briefe*, 1:242.

81. Mara H. Benjamin, *Rosenzweig's Bible: Reinventing Scripture for Jewish Modernity* (Cambridge: Cambridge University Press, 2009).

82. Gershom Scholem to Ernst Simon, 22 December 1925, in *Briefe*, 1:230.

83. Ernst Simon to Gershom Scholem, 2 January 1926, in *Briefe*, 1:404–405n4, quotes on 405.

84. Gershom Scholem to Ernst Simon, n.d. [January 1926], in *Briefe*, 1:231–232.

85. Gershom Scholem to Martin Buber, 27 April 1926, in *Life in Letters*, 153.

86. Gershom Scholem, "An einem denkwürdigen Tage," in *Judaica*, vol. 1 (1963; reprint, Frankfurt: Suhrkamp, 1997), 209–210 and 213–215.

87. Max Osborn, "Jüdisches Museum," *Vossische Zeitung*, no. 42 (25 January 1933, evening edition): [6].

88. Brenner, *Renaissance of Jewish Culture*, 173–176.

89. Betty Scholem to Gershom Scholem, 15 November 1926, 14 August 1928, and 25 January 1930, NLI, ARC. 4*1599/01/3083, 3085, and 3087; Erich Scholem to Gershom Scholem, 27 March 1928, NLI, ARC. 4*1599/01/3024; Frank Schlöffel, "Zionismus und Bibliophilie. Heinrich Loewe und die neuen 'Soncinaten,'" *Soncino—Gesellschaft der Freunde des jüdischen Buches. Ein Beitrag zur Kulturgeschichte*, ed. Karin Bürger, Ines Sonder, and Ursula Wallmeier (Berlin: Walter de Gruyter, 2014), 33n35; Martin Münzel, "Zwischen Ökonomie und Bibliophile. Unternehmer und Verleger als Mitglieder der Soncino-Gesellschaft," in Bürger, Sonder, and Wallmeier, *Soncino*, 78–79 and 93; Ines Sonder, "Neun Holzschnitte zum Buch Jesus Sirach. Jakob Steinhardt und die neunte Publikation der Soncino-Gesellschaft von 1929," in Bürger, Sonder, and Wallmeier, *Soncino*, 96–97.

90. Gennady Estraikh, "Vilna on the Spree: Yiddish in Weimar Berlin," *Aschkenas. Zeitschrift für Geschichte und Kultur der Juden* 16, no. 1 (March 2006): 103–127; Gennady Estraikh and Mikhail Krutikov, eds., *Yiddish in Weimar Berlin: At the Crossroads of Diaspora Politics and Culture* (London: Legenda, 2010); Jeffrey A. Grossman, "Yiddish Writers/German Models in the Early Twentieth Century," in Geller and Morris, *Three-Way Street*, 66–90.

91. Alan T. Levenson, "The 'Triple Immersion': A Singular Moment in Modern Jewish Intellectual History?," in Geller and Morris, *Three-Way Street*, 46–65.

92. Brenner, *Renaissance of Jewish Culture*, 76.

93. Betty Scholem to Gershom Scholem, 21 and 28 December 1924, NLI, ARC. 4*1599/01/3081.

94. Betty Scholem to Gershom Scholem, 9 February 1925, NLI, ARC. 4*1599/01/3082; Sophie Scholem to Gershom Scholem, 6 February 1925, NLI, ARC. 4*1599/01/3027.

95. Betty Scholem to Gershom Scholem, 26 April 1925, in *MuSiB*, 130.

96. Betty Scholem to Gershom Scholem, 17 and 24 February 1925, in *MuSiB*, 120 and 122; "Familien-Anzeigen," *Berliner Tageblatt* 54, no. 66 (8 February 1925, morning edition): [10].

97. Betty Scholem to Gershom Scholem, 28 July 1925, NLI, ARC. 4*1599/01/3082.

98. Walter Benjamin to Gershom Scholem, 19 February 1925, in *Correspondence of Walter Benjamin, 1910–1940*, 262.

99. Sophie Scholem to Gershom Scholem, 6 February 1925, NLI, ARC. 4*1599/01/3027.

100. Betty Scholem to Gershom Scholem, 24 February and 9 March 1925, NLI, ARC. 4*1599/01/3082.

101. Last will and testament of Arthur Scholem, 18 February 1925, originally notarized 24 September 1921, LUH, IPW, Nachlass Werner Scholem.

102. Betty Scholem to Gershom Scholem, 9 February, 3 March, and 20 April 1925, NLI, ARC. 4*1599/01/3082.

103. Betty Scholem to Gershom Scholem, 30 March and postscript 31 March 1925, and 16 June 1925, NLI, ARC. 4*1599/01/3082.

104. See Gershom Scholem to Betty Scholem, 31 January 1928, 13 April 1928, 6 September 1928, 4 October 1928, 8 January 1932, 26 January 1936, 7 March 1936, NLI, ARC. 4*1599/12/3001 and 3002; Betty Scholem to Gershom Scholem, 11 August 1925, 4 October 1925, 14 December 1925, 31 January 1928, and 6 January 1931, NLI, ARC. 4*1599/01/3082, 3085, and 3088.

105. Betty Scholem to Gershom Scholem, 11 and 25 August 1925, NLI, ARC. 4*1599/01/3082; Betty Scholem to Gershom Scholem, 31 January 1928, and Gershom Scholem to Betty Scholem, 31 January 1928, in *MuSiB*, 154 and 156.

106. Jay Howard Geller, "From Berlin and Jerusalem: On the Germanness of Gershom Scholem," *Journal of Religious History* 35, no. 2 (June 2011): 211–232.

107. Ruppin, *Soziologie der Juden*, 1:232–233.

108. Betty Scholem to Gershom Scholem, 1 April 1924, 20 and 27 January 1925, 3 and 17 February 1925, and 3 March 1925, NLI, ARC. 4*1599/01/3081 and 3082.

109. Betty Scholem to Gershom Scholem, 9 and 17 February, and 17 March 1925, NLI, ARC. 4*1599/01/3082.

110. Betty Scholem to Gershom Scholem, 26 April 1925, NLI, ARC. 4*1599/01/3082.

111. Betty Scholem to Gershom Scholem, 5 May and 24 November 1925, NLI, ARC. 4*1599/01/3082; Emmy Scholem to Gershom Scholem, 25 June 1951, NLI, ARC. 4*1599/01/3023.

112. Betty Scholem to Gershom Scholem, 18 August 1924, NLI, ARC. 4*1599/01/3081.

113. Betty Scholem to Gershom Scholem, 26 January 1926, NLI, ARC. 4*1599/01/3083.

114. Betty Scholem to Gershom Scholem, 11 November 1926, NLI, ARC. 4*1599/01/3083; Betty, Reinhold, and Erich Scholem to Amtsgericht Handelsregister A 330, 26 June 1925, and Arthur Scholem Buchdruckerei to Amtsgericht Berlin-Mitte, 2 April 1927, LAB, A Rep. 342–02, Nr. 42380.

115. Betty Scholem to Gershom Scholem, 22 May 1928 and 27 January 1930, NLI, ARC. 4*1599/01/3085 and 3087.

116. Erich Scholem to Gershom Scholem, 27 March 1928, NLI, ARC. 4*1599/01/3024; Betty Scholem to Gershom Scholem, 11 June and 18 September 1928, NLI, ARC. 4*1599/01/3085.

117. Betty Scholem to Gershom Scholem, 20 April 1924, 3 June 1924, 26 August 1924, 6 June 1925, 30 June 1925, and 17 August 1928, NLI, ARC. 4*1599/01/3081, 3082, and 3085.

118. Betty Scholem to Gershom Scholem, 27 May 1932, NLI, ARC. 4*1599/01/3089.

119. Betty Scholem to Gershom Scholem, 7 December 1926, NLI, ARC. 4*1599/01/3083.

120. Betty Scholem to Gershom Scholem, 22 May 1928, NLI, ARC. 4*1599/01/3085.

121. Betty Scholem to Gershom Scholem, 23 February, 7 and 12 May, and 17 August 1926, in *MuSiB*, 139, 140, 141–142, and 146, quote on 146.

122. Betty Scholem to Gershom Scholem, 1 June 1926, NLI, ARC. 4*1599/01/3083.

123. Betty Scholem to Gershom Scholem, 31 January and 15 February 1927, NLI, ARC. 4*1599/01/3084.

124. Betty Scholem to Gershom Scholem, 21 January 1930, NLI, ARC. 4*1599/01/3087.

125. Betty Scholem to Gershom Scholem, 6 June 1931, in *MuSiB*, 228.

126. Betty Scholem to Gershom Scholem, 10 June 1931, in *MuSiB*, 238.

127. Gershom Scholem to Betty Scholem, 6 September 1928, in *MuSiB*, 176.

128. Betty Scholem to Gershom Scholem, 18 September 1928, in *MuSiB*, 178.

129. E.g., Betty Scholem to Gershom Scholem, 2 September 1924, in *MuSiB*, 110.

130. Betty Scholem to Gershom Scholem, 18 September 1928, in *MuSiB*, 178.

131. Betty Scholem to Gershom Scholem, 12 March 1930, in *MuSiB*, 217; Gay, *My German Question*, 50.

132. Betty Scholem to Gershom Scholem, 1 March 1932, NLI, ARC. 4*1599/01/3089.

133. Betty Scholem to Gershom Scholem, 18 June and 8 July 1928, and 25 March 1929, NLI, ARC. 4*1599/01/3085 and 3086. Else Pflaum was related to Betty by marriage and was the widow of Betty's cousin Richard Pflaum.

134. "Die Religionszugehörigkeit der Eheschließenden im Jahre 1929," in Germany, Statistisches Reichsamt, *Statistisches Jahrbuch für das Deutsche Reich*, vol. 50, *1931* (Berlin: Reimar Hobbing, 1931), 30; Barkai, "Jewish Life in Its German Milieu," in Meyer, *GJHMT*, 4:57.

135. Betty Scholem to Gershom Scholem, 7 March 1934, in *MuSiB*, 353.

136. Betty Scholem to Gershom Scholem, 7 January 1930, NLI, ARC. 4*1599/01/3087; "Austritte aus dem Judentum. Else Alfermann geb. Baruch. Charlottenburg, Uhlandstraße 175," *Gemeindeblatt der Jüdischen Gemeinde zu Berlin* 20, no. 1 (January 1930): 32. Else Pflaum's second husband was Rudolf Alfermann, an industrialist from western Germany.

137. Betty Scholem to Gershom Scholem, 5 October 1935, in *MuSiB*, 402.

138. Wolfgang Benz, "The Legend of German-Jewish Symbiosis," *LBIYB* 37 (1992): 98–99; Maurer, "From Everyday Life to a State of Emergency," in Kaplan, *Jewish Daily Life in Germany*, 334.

139. David Clay Large, *The Grand Spas of Central Europe: A History of Intrigue, Politics, Art, and Healing* (Lanham, Md.: Rowman & Littlefield, 2015), 294–295.

140. Klaus Kundt, "'Juden und Mitglieder der Sektion Donauland unerwünscht.' Der Deutsche Alpenverein (DAV) hat mit der Aufarbeitung seiner antisemitischen Vergangenheit begonnen," *Gedenkstättenrundbrief* 117 (2004): 19–28.

141. Niewyk, *Jews in Weimar Germany*, 61–68.

142. Betty Scholem to Gershom Scholem, 18 and 25 June 1928, NLI, ARC. 4*1599/01/3085.

143. Betty Scholem to Gershom Scholem, 18 and 29 December 1928, and Betty Scholem to Escha Scholem, 14 January 1929, NLI, ARC. 4*1599/01/3085 and 3086; "Handelsregister," *Vossische Zeitung*, no. 613 (29 December 1928, morning edition): [7]; Max Scholem, Theobald Scholem, and Ludwig Zucker to Amtsgericht Berlin-Mitte, Abteilung für Handelsregistersachen, 21 December 1928, LAB, A Rep. 342–02, Nr. 44488.

144. Betty Scholem to Gershom Scholem, 29 December 1928, NLI, ARC. 4*1599/01/3085.

145. Betty Scholem to Gershom Scholem, 6 January 1929, NLI, ARC. 4*1599/01/3086.

146. Industrie- und Handelskammer zu Berlin to Amtsgericht Berlin-Mitte, 12 February 1929, LAB, A Rep. 342–02, Nr. 41918; Betty Scholem to Gershom Scholem, 29 January and 28 October 1929, NLI, ARC. 4*1599/01/3086.

147. Betty Scholem to Gershom Scholem, 13 April and 7 May 1929, NLI, ARC. 4*1599/01/3086.

148. Betty Scholem to Gershom Scholem, 28 October and 16 December 1929, NLI, ARC. 4*1599/01/3086.

149. Betty Scholem to Gershom Scholem, 8 February 1927 and 23 July 1928, NLI, ARC. 4*1599/01/3084 and 3085.

150. Betty Scholem to Gershom Scholem, 3 December 1929, and 17 March and 15 April 1930, NLI, ARC. 4*1599/01/3086 and 3087.

151. E.g., "Explosion in einer Druckerei," *Vossische Zeitung*, no. 542 (16 November 1929, morning edition): [5]; "Gas-Explosion am Elisabeth-Ufer," *Berliner Morgenpost*, no. 274 (16 November 1929): [5]; and "Selbstmörder verursacht schwere Gasexplosion," *Berliner Lokal-Anzeiger* 47, no. 542 (16 November 1929, morning edition): [3].

152. Betty Scholem to Gershom Scholem, 19 November 1929, in *MuSiB*, 212.

153. "Jüdische Selbstmordstatistik," *Jüdische Rundschau* 32, nos. 83/84 (21 October 1927): 594; "Ursache der Sterbefälle im Jahre 1929 nach Ländern und Landesteilen," in Germany, Statistisches Reichsamt, *Statistisches Jahrbuch für das Deutsche Reich*, 50:37; "Die Ursachen der Sterbefälle im Jahre 1932," in Germany, Statistisches Reichsamt, *Statistisches Jahrbuch für das Deutsche Reich*, vol. 53, 1934 (Berlin: Reimar Hobbing, 1934), 42–43; cf. Moritz Föllmer, "Suicide and Crisis in Weimar Berlin," *Central European History* 42, no. 2 (June 2009): 196.

154. Betty Scholem to Gershom Scholem, 24 November 1929, NLI, ARC. 4*1599/01/3086.

155. Various registry records, LAB, A Rep. 342–02, Nr. 41918.

156. Betty Scholem to Gershom Scholem, 24 November 1929, NLI, ARC. 4*1599/01/3086.

157. Tim Mason, "Women in Germany, 1925–1940: Family, Welfare and Work. Part I," *History Workshop* 1, no. 1 (Spring 1976): 81–82.

158. Betty Scholem to Gershom Scholem, 18 February 1931, NLI, ARC. 4*1599/01/3088.

159. Betty Scholem to Gershom Scholem, 2 February 1932, NLI, ARC. 4*1599/01/3089.

160. Kaplan, *Between Dignity and Despair*, 28–30; Maurer, "From Everyday Life to a State of Emergency," in Kaplan, *Jewish Daily Life in Germany*, 319.

161. Karl Hardach, *The Political Economy of Germany in the Twentieth Century* (Berkeley: University of California Press, 1980), 31–33.

162. Figure 6, "Share Prices in Selected Markets, Monthly, 1926–35," in Charles P. Kindleberger, *The World in Depression, 1929–1939* (1973; reprint Berkeley: University of California Press, 2013), 121. German share prices had a modest rally between January and June 1928, but the overall trend between June 1927 and January 1931 was sharply downward.

163. Kindleberger, *World in Depression*, 116–117; cf. Hans-Ulrich Wehler, *Deutsche Gesellschaftsgeschichte*, vol. 4, *1914–1949*, 2nd ed. (Munich: C. H. Beck, 2003), 258.

164. Hardach, *Political Economy of Germany*, 37.

165. Barkai, "Population Decline and Economic Stagnation," in Meyer, *GJHMT*, 4:34–35 and 38.

166. Ludwig [*sic*, probably Leo] Baeck, "Die jüdischen Gemeinden," in *Zehn Jahre deutsche Geschichte 1918–1928* (Berlin: Otto Stollberg, 1928), 440; Julius Roth- holz, "Rückgang der jüdischen Studierenden Preussens," *C. V.-Zeitung* 5, no. 27 (2 July 1926): 359–360; Margot Melchior, "Die Zahl der jüdischen Studierenden nimmt ab," *C. V.-Zeitung* 10, no. 5 (30 January 1931): 47; Barkai, "Population Decline and Economic Stagnation," in Meyer, *GJHMT*, 4:38–39.

167. Betty Scholem to Gershom Scholem, 6 January 1929, NLI, ARC. 4*1599/01/3086.

168. Christoph Kreutzmüller, *Final Sale in Berlin: The Destruction of Jewish Commer- cial Activity, 1930–1945*, trans. Jane Paulick and Jefferson Chase (New York: Berghahn Books, 2015), 60.

169. Wolfram Fischer, "Wirtschaftsgeschichte Deutschlands 1919–1945," in *Handwörterbuch der Wirtschaftswissenschaft*, vol. 9, *Wirtschaft und Politik bis Zölle, Nachtrag*, ed. Willi Albers et al. (Stuttgart: Gustav Fischer, 1982), 85; cf. Hardach, *Political Economy of Germany*, 39.

170. Betty Scholem to Gershom Scholem, 30 June, 19 July, 28 July, 12 October, and 17 November 1931, and 23 May 1932, NLI, ARC. 4*1599/01/3088 and 3089.

171. Betty Scholem to Gershom Scholem, 11 August 1931, NLI, ARC. 4*1599/01/3088.

172. Betty Scholem to Gershom Scholem, 11 and 18 March 1929, NLI, ARC. 4*1599/01/3086.

173. Betty Scholem to Gershom Scholem, 31 December 1929, NLI, ARC. 4*1599/01/3086.

174. Betty Scholem to Gershom Scholem, 28 July 1931, NLI, ARC. 4*1599/01/3088.

175. Betty Scholem to Gershom Scholem, 4 August 1931, in *MuSiB*, 243.

176. Gershom Scholem to Betty Scholem, 5 August 1931, and Betty Scholem to Gershom Scholem, 18 August 1931, NLI, ARC. 4*1599/12/3002.

177. Betty Scholem to Gershom Scholem, 4 November 1931, NLI, ARC. 4*1599/01/3088.

178. Betty Scholem to Gershom Scholem, 10 November 1931 and 4 January 1932, NLI, ARC. 4*1599/01/3088 and 3089.

179. "Gesamtergebnis der Wahlen zum Reichstag am 20. Mai 1928," in Germany, Statistisches Reichsamt, *Statistisches Jahrbuch für das Deutsche Reich*, vol. 49, *1930* (Berlin: Reimar Hobbing, 1930), 562–563; "Gesamtergebnis der Wahlen zum Reichstag am 14. September 1930," in Germany, Statistisches Reichsamt, *Statistisches Jahrbuch für das Deutsche Reich* 50:546–547.

180. Betty Scholem to Gershom Scholem, 16 September 1930, NLI, ARC. 4*1599/01/3087.

181. Betty Scholem to Gershom Scholem, 16 June 1931, NLI, ARC. 4*1599/01/3088.

182. Betty Scholem to Gershom Scholem, 11 August and 29 October 1931, NLI, ARC. 4*1599/01/3088.

183. Barkai, "Population Decline and Economic Stagnation," in Meyer, *GJHMT*, 4:40–42.

184. Maurer, "From Everyday Life to a State of Emergency," in Kaplan, *Jewish Daily Life in Germany*, 308.

185. Gershom Scholem to Betty Scholem, 18 September 1930, NLI, ARC. 4*1599/12/3001.

186. Betty Scholem to Gershom Scholem, 6 October 1930, NLI, ARC. 4*1599/01/3087.

187. Hamburger and Pulzer, "Jews as Voters," *LBIYB* 30 (1985): 55–60.

188. *Israelitisches Familienblatt* 32, no. 37 (11 September 1930): 12.

189. Betty Scholem to Gershom Scholem, 6 October 1930, NLI, ARC. 4*1599/01/3087.

190. "Die Bevölkerung Berlins nach Religionszugehörigkeit 1925 und 1933," "Bezirk Wilmersdorf: Wahlstatistik 1921–1933," and "Bezirk Schöneberg: Wahlstatistik 1921–1933," in *Berlin Demokratie 1919–1945*, vol. 1, *Berlin als Hauptstadt der Weimarer Republik 1919–1933*, ed. Otto Büsch and Wolfgang Haus (Berlin: Walter de Gruyter, 1987), 321, 414, and 426; Reinhold Scholem to Gershom Scholem, 20 June 1976, NLI, ARC. 4*1599/01/3031.

191. Metzler, *Tales of Three Cities*, 211–224; Michael Brenner, "The Jüdische Volkspartei: National-Jewish Communal Politics during the Weimar Republic," *LBIYB* 35 (1990): 238–239.

192. Metzler, *Tales of Three Cities*, 182; Brenner, "Jüdische Volkspartei," *LBIYB* 35 (1990): 220–226 and 239–241.

193. Metzler, *Tales of Three Cities*, 223–224; cf. Brenner, "Jüdische Volkspartei," *LBIYB* 35 (1990): 239.

194. Betty Scholem to Gershom Scholem, 16 November and 2 December 1930, NLI, ARC. 4*1599/01/3087; Brenner, "Jüdische Volkspartei," *LBIYB* 35 (1990): 239.

195. Certificate from Kammergericht, 2 March 1931, LUH, IPW, Nachlass Werner Scholem; Betty Scholem to Gershom Scholem, 4 March 1931, NLI, ARC. 4*1599/01/3088; Werner Scholem to Gershom Scholem, 23 March 1931, NLI, ARC. 4*1599/01/3034.

196. Werner Scholem to Gershom Scholem, 23 March 1931, NLI, ARC. 4*1599/01/3034.

197. Betty Scholem to Gershom Scholem, 18 March 1932, in *MuSiB*, 259.

198. Betty Scholem to Gershom Scholem, 18 March 1932, NLI, ARC. 4*1599/01/3089.

199. Gershom Scholem to Betty Scholem, 22 March 1932, in *MuSiB*, 262.

200. Betty Scholem to Gershom Scholem, 1 June 1932, NLI, ARC. 4*1599/01/3089.

201. Betty Scholem to Gershom Scholem, 15 November 1932, in *MuSiB*, 269.

202. Betty Scholem to Gershom Scholem, 17 January 1933, NLI, ARC. 4*1599/01/3090.

203. Werner Scholem to Gershom Scholem, 14 November 1932, NLI, ARC. 4*1599/01/3034.

204. Gershom Scholem to Betty Scholem, 8 January 1932, in *MuSiB*, 253.

205. Betty Scholem to Gershom Scholem, 9 February 1932, in *MuSiB*, 256.

206. Betty Scholem to Gershom Scholem, 9 February 1932, Betty Scholem to Gershom Scholem, 28 April 1932, Gershom Scholem to Betty Scholem, 1 May 1932, and Betty Scholem to Gershom Scholem, 20 November 1932, in *MuSiB*, 256, 265, 266, and 270; Betty Scholem to Escha Scholem, 10 October 1932, NLI, ARC. 4*1599/01/3089; Werner Scholem to Gershom Scholem, 14 November 1932, NLI, ARC. 4*1599/01/3034.

207. Erich Kästner, *Fabian. Die Geschichte eines Moralisten* (Stuttgart: Deutsche Verlags-Anstalt, 1931), 80.

208. "Gesamtergebnis der Wahlen zum Reichstag am 31. Juli 1932," in Germany, Statistisches Reichsamt, *Statistisches Jahrbuch für das Deutsche Reich*, vol. 51, *1932* (Berlin: Reimar Hobbing, 1932), 542–543; "Die Wahlen zum Deutschen Reichstag von 1919 bis 1933," in Germany, Statistisches Reichsamt, *Statistisches Jahrbuch für das Deutsche Reich*, vol. 52, *1933* (Berlin: Reimar Hobbing, 1933), 539.

209. Betty Scholem to Gershom Scholem, 15 November 1932, NLI, ARC. 4*1599/01/3089.

210. Reichsbund jüdischer Frontsoldaten, ed., *Die jüdischen Gefallenen des deutschen Heeres, der deutschen Marine und der deutschen Schutztruppen 1914–1918. Ein Gedenkbuch* (Berlin: "Der Schild," 1932).

211. Barkai, *"Wehr Dich!,"* 441n13.

212. Ulrich Dunker, *Der Reichsbund jüdischer Frontsoldaten 1919–1938. Geschichte eines jüdischen Abwehrvereins* (Düsseldorf: Droste, 1977); Tim Grady, "Fighting a Lost Battle: The *Reichsbund jüdischer Frontsoldaten* and the Rise of National Socialism," *German History* 28, no. 1 (March 2010): 1–20.

213. "Thüringen," *Der Israelit* 71, no. 26 (26 June 1930): 2.

214. Betty Scholem to Gershom Scholem, 18 September 1928, NLI, ARC. 4*1599/01/3085.

215. Mendes-Flohr, "Between Germanism and Judaism, Christians and Jews," in Meyer, *GJHMT*, 4:158; Albert Meyer, "Eine jüdische Idealgemeinde," in *Adass Jisroel. Die jüdische Gemeinde in Berlin (1869–1942): Vernichtet und Vergessen*, ed. Mario Kessler (Berlin: Museumspädagogischer Dienst Berlin, 1986), 210.

216. Mendes-Flohr, "Between Germanism and Judaism, Christians and Jews," in Meyer, *GJHMT*, 4:157–160.

6. In the Promised Land

1. Gur Alroey. *An Unpromising Land: Jewish Migration to Palestine in the Early Twentieth Century* (Stanford, Calif.: Stanford University Press, 2014).

2. Howard M. Sachar, *A History of Israel: From the Rise of Zionism to Our Time*, 3rd ed. (New York: Alfred A. Knopf, 2010), 26–35 and 71–80.

3. "Monthly Trend of Immigration," in *Ten Years of Jewish Immigration into Palestine, 1919–1928*, ed. Palestine Zionist Executive, Immigration Department (Jerusalem: s.n., 1929), 11, reproduced in *The Rise of Israel*, ed. Aaron S. Klieman, vol. 15, *Practical Zionism, 1920–1939* (New York: Garland, 1987), 106.

4. E.g., Chaim Nachman Bialik, "Halacha und Aggada," trans. Gerhard [Gershom] Scholem, *Der Jude* 4, nos. 1–2 (1919): 61–77.

5. Gershom Scholem, *WBTSF*, 101.

6. Hugo Bergmann to Else Bergmann, 17 July 1923, in Bergman, *Tagebücher und Briefe*, 1:181.

7. Hugo Bergmann to Else Bergmann, 3 October 1923, in Bergman, *Tagebücher und Briefe*, 1:184.

8. Malachi Beit-Arié, "Gershom Scholem as Bibliophile," in Mendes-Flohr, *Gershom Scholem*, 124.

9. Gershom Scholem to Fritz Hommel, 18 July 1924, in *Briefe*, 1:220.

10. Betty Scholem to Gershom Scholem, 2 November 1923, postscript 4 November 1923, in *MuSiB*, 93.

11. Chaim Weizmann, "Project for a Jewish University," July 1902, in *The Letters and Papers of Chaim Weizmann*, vol. 1, ser. B, *August 1898–July 1931*, ed. Barnet Litvinoff (New Brunswick: Transaction Books, 1983), 13–34.

12. Hebrew University of Jerusalem, *The Hebrew University, Jerusalem: Its History and Development* (Jerusalem: s.n., 1939), 1–9.

13. Betty Scholem to Gershom Scholem, 3 and 21 December 1924, NLI, ARC. 4*1599/01/3081.

14. N. Zadoff, *Gershom Scholem*, 17–19.

15. Werner Scholem to Gershom Scholem, 4 October 1925, in *MuSiB*, 132; Gershom Scholem to Ernst Simon, 22 December 1925, in *Briefe*, 1:229; Daniel P. Kotzin, *Judah L. Magnes: An American Jewish Nonconformist* (Syracuse, N.Y.: Syracuse University Press, 2010), 200; cf. Assaf Selzer, *The History of the Hebrew University of Jerusalem: Who's Who Prior to Statehood; Founders, Designers, Pioneers*, trans. Jenni Tsafrir (Jerusalem: Magnes Press, 2015), 228.

16. Betty Scholem to Gershom Scholem, 31 January 1928, in *MuSiB*, 154.

17. Gershom Scholem to Ernst Simon, 22 December 1925, in *Briefe*, 1:229–230.

18. Engel, *Gershom Scholem*, 118–121; Gershom Scholem to Ernst Simon, 22 December 1925, in *Briefe* 1:230.

19. Gershom Scholem, *VBnJ*, 208.

20. Gershom Scholem, untitled essay on language, n.d., NLI, ARC. 4*1599/08/277.1.56. See Weidner, *Gershom Scholem*, 124–144; and Lina Barouch, *Between German and Hebrew: The Counterlanguages of Gershom Scholem, Werner Kraft and Ludwig Strauss* (Berlin: Walter de Gruyter, 2016), 66.

21. "Bekenntnis über unsere Sprache," 7 Tevet 5687 [12 December 1926], NLI, ARC. 4*1599/08/277.1.56. See William Cutter, "Ghostly Hebrew, Ghastly Speech: Scholem to Rosenzweig, 1926," *Prooftexts* 10, no. 3 (September 1990): 413–433; and

Annabel Herzog, "'Monolingualism' or the Language of God: Scholem and Derrida on Hebrew and Politics," *Modern Judaism* 29, no. 2 (May 2009): 226–238.

22. Gershom Scholem, untitled essay on language, n.d., NLI, ARC. 4*1599/08/277.1.56.

23. Gershom Scholem, *VBnJ*, 218.

24. Gershom Scholem to Werner Kraft, 17 December 1924, in *Briefe*, 1:222.

25. Gershom Scholem to Ernst Simon, 2 September 1925, in *Briefe*, 1:228.

26. "Distribution by Citizenship," in Palestine Zionist Executive, Immigration Department, *Ten Years of Jewish Immigration*, 16, reproduced in Klieman, *Rise of Israel*, 15:111; cf. Ben Halpern and Jehuda Reinharz, *Zionism and the Creation of a New Society* (New York: Oxford University Press, 1998), 198.

27. Palestine, *Report and General Abstracts of the Census of 1922*, ed. J. B. Barron (Jerusalem: Greek Convent Press, 1923), 14, 20, and 33; E. Mills, *Census of Palestine 1931* (Jerusalem: Greek Convent and Goldberg Presses, 1932), 15, 40, and 91.

28. Weizmann, "Shedding Some Illusions," 23 August 1925, in *Letters and Papers of Chaim Weizmann*, vol. 1, ser. B., 454.

29. "Estimate of Settled Population by Religions," in Palestine Zionist Executive, Immigration Department, *Ten Years of Jewish Immigration*, 6–7, reproduced in Klieman, *Rise of Israel*, 15:101–102; cf. Palestine, *Report and General Abstracts of the Census of 1922*, 5, and Mills, *Census of Palestine 1931*, n.p.

30. Betty Scholem to Gershom Scholem, 7 and 29 September 1926, and 18 October 1926, NLI, ARC. 4*1599/01/3083.

31. Gershom Scholem, "With Gershom Scholem: An Interview," in Scholem, *On Jews and Judaism in Crisis*, 46.

32. Editorial comment by Gershom Scholem, in Benjamin and Scholem, *Correspondence-WBGS*, 45n12.

33. Gershom Scholem to Ernst Simon, 2 September 1925, in *Briefe*, 1:228–229.

34. "Die Verzweiflung der Siegenden," 12 April 1926, NLI, ARC. 4*1599/07/277.1.57; "Auszüge aus meinem Tagebuch," 1926, NLI, ARC. 4*1599/02/277.1.60.

35. Gershom Scholem to Ernst Simon, 12 May 1926, in *Briefe*, 1:233; "Erklärung," 9 April 1926, *Jüdische Rundschau* 31, no. 31 (23 April 1926): 231.

36. Lavsky, *Before Catastrophe*, 167–170; Susan Lee Hattis, *The Bi-National Idea in Palestine during Mandatory Times* (Haifa: Shikmona, 1970), 38–40.

37. Hagit Lavsky, "German Zionists and the Emergence of Brit Shalom," in *Essential Papers on Zionism*, ed. Jehuda Reinharz and Anita Shapira (New York: New York University Press, 1996), 652; Kotzin, *Judah L. Magnes*, 198–199.

38. Lavsky, *Before Catastrophe*, 170; Lavsky, "German Zionists," in Reinharz and Shapira, *Essential Papers on Zionism*, 657.

39. Hans Kohn to M. Beilinson, [8 July 1927], NLI, ARC. 4*1599/01/1440.

40. Gershom Scholem to Robert Weltsch, 7 November 1928, NLI, ARC. 4*1599/01/2851; Gerhard [Gershom] Scholem, "Ist Verständigung mit den Arabern gescheitert?," *Jüdische Rundschau* 33, no. 92 (20 November 1928): 644.

41. Gerhard [Gershom] Scholem, "Zur Frage des Parlaments," *Jüdische Rundschau* 36, no. 11 (8 February 1929): 65.

42. Hugo Bergmann to Robert Weltsch, 19 September 1929, in Bergman, *Tagebücher und Briefe*, 1:289.

43. Quoted in Hattis, *Bi-National Idea*, 47.

44. Tom Segev, *One Palestine, Complete: Jews and Arabs under the British Mandate*, trans. Haim Watzman (New York: Metropolitan Books, 2000), 295–313.

45. Gershom Scholem to Betty Scholem, 29 August 1929, NLI, ARC. 4*1599/12/3001.

46. Gershom Scholem to Betty Scholem, 12 September 1929, NLI, ARC. 4*1599/12/3001.

47. Segev, *One Palestine, Complete*, 314–327; Hillel Cohen, *Year Zero of the Arab-Israeli Conflict: 1929*, trans. Haim Watzman (Waltham, Mass.: Brandeis University Press, 2015).

48. Betty Scholem to Gershom Scholem, 20 and 27 August and 11 September 1929, NLI, ARC. 4*1599/01/3086.

49. Shalom Ratzabi, *Between Zionism and Judaism: The Radical Circle in Brith Shalom, 1925–1933* (Leiden: Brill, 2002), 142–143.

50. Aschheim, *Beyond the Border*, 9.

51. Anita Shapira, *Berl: The Biography of a Socialist Zionist; Berl Katznelson, 1887–1944* (Cambridge: Cambridge University Press, 1984), 171; M. Beilinson, "From Binationalism to Liquidation" [Hebrew], *Omer Poalei Eretz Yisrael* [*Davar*, no. 1347] (5 November 1929): 2, reprinted as "Von der Binationalität zur Liquidierung," in M[oshe] Beilinson, *Zum Jüdisch-Arabischen Problem. Eine Aufsatzreihe* (Tel Aviv: Verlag "Dawar," 1930), 47–52.

52. Ratzabi, *Between Zionism and Judaism*, 145–146; Steven E. Aschheim, *At the Edges of Liberalism: Junctions of European, German, and Jewish History* (New York: Palgrave Macmillan, 2012), 45.

53. Gerda Arlosoroff to Gershom Scholem, 28 October 1929, NLI, ARC 4*1599/01/923; Gershom Scholem et al. to the Geschäftsführender Ausschuss der Zionistischen Vereinigung für Deutschland, 21 October 1929, NLI, ARC. 4*1599/01/2985; "Die politische Debatte in Jena," *Jüdische Rundschau* 35, no. 2 (7 January 1930): 13.

54. Gershom Scholem to Betty Scholem, 30 January 1930, in *MuSiB*, 215–216.

55. Brit Shalom, *Memorandum by the "Brith Shalom" Society on an Arab Policy for the Jewish Agency* (Jerusalem: Azriel Press, 1930), 3; Hattis, *Bi-National Idea*, 51–52.

56. Brit Shalom, *Memorandum by the "Brith Shalom" Society*, 7.

57. Gershom Scholem, Ernst Simon, and Hugo Bergmann to Robert Weltsch, 22 September 1929, NLI, ARC. 4*1599/01/2851.

58. Ratzabi, *Between Zionism and Judaism*, 154; Biale, *Gershom Scholem* (1982), 102; Biale, *Gershom Scholem* (2018), 99–100; Jewish Telegraphic Agency, "Jewish Rights at Wailing Wall," *Daily News Bulletin* 12, no. 55 (6 March 1931): 3–4.

59. Great Britain, *Report of the Commission on the Palestine Disturbances of August, 1929* (London: His Majesty's Stationery Office, 1930), particularly 157–168, reproduced in *The Rise of Israel*, ed. Aaron S. Klieman, vol. 18, *The Turn toward Violence, 1920–1929* (New York: Garland, 1987), 341–352.

60. Martin Kolinsky, *Law, Order and Riots in Mandatory Palestine, 1928–35* (London: St. Martin's Press, 1993), 80–82.

61. Segev, *One Palestine, Complete*, 335–336.

62. Diary entries, 25 and 27 October 1930, in Bergman, *Tagebücher und Briefe*, 1:318 and 320.

63. Segev, *One Palestine, Complete*, 336–338.

64. Zionist Organization, *Stenographisches Protokoll der Verhandlungen des XVII. Zionistenkongresses und der Zweiten Tagung des Council der Jewish Agency für Palästina* (London: Zentralbureau der Zionistischen Organisation, 1931), 386 and 397–398; Yaacov Shavit, *Jabotinsky and the Revisionist Movement, 1925–1948* (London: Frank Cass, 1988), 60, 185–186, and 211.

65. Zionist Organization, *Stenographisches Protokoll der Verhandlungen des XVII. Zionistenkongresses*, 386 and 397.

66. Gershom Scholem to Walter Benjamin, 1 August 1931, in Gershom Scholem, *WBTSF*, 218.

67. Gershom Scholem to Walter Benjamin, 1 August 1931, in Gershom Scholem, *WBTSF*, 218; Gershom Scholem, "With Gershom Scholem: An Interview," in Scholem, *On Jews and Judaism in Crisis*, 34.

68. Gershom Scholem to Walter Benjamin, 1 August 1931, in Gershom Scholem, *WBTSF*, 217.

69. Diary entry, 7 December 1929, in Bergman, *Tagebücher und Briefe*, 1:298.

70. Gershom Scholem to Reinhold Scholem, 8/11 September 1976, NLI, ARC. 4*1599/01/3031.

71. Hattis, *Bi-National Idea*, 138.

72. Engel, *Gershom Scholem*, 122; Gerhard [Gershom] Scholem, "Über die Theologie des Sabbatianismus im Lichte Abraham Cardozos," *Der Jude* 10, no. 1 (March 1928): 123–139, esp. 139.

73. E.g., Gerhard [Gershom] Scholem, "Alchemie und Kabbala. Ein Kapitel aus der Geschichte der Mystik," *Monatsschrift für Geschichte und Wissenschaft des Judentums* 69, nos. 1/2 (January/February 1925): 13–30.

74. Gershom Scholem to Betty Scholem, 8 November 1928, in *MuSiB*, 183; Gerhard [Gershom] Scholem, "Zur Frage der Entstehung der Kabbala," *Korrespondenzblatt des Vereins zur Gründung und Erhaltung einer Akademie für die Wissenschaft des Judentums* 9 (1928): 4–26.

75. Gershom Scholem, *WBTSF*, 158, 161–164, and 169–170.

76. Gershom Scholem, *WBTSF*, 166–168.

77. Gershom Scholem, *WBTSF*, 188–192, 195–196, and 198; Walter Benjamin to Gershom Scholem, 30 January, 11 March, 23 April, 24 May, 18 June, and 1 August 1928, in *Correspondence of Walter Benjamin, 1910–1940*, 321–322, 327, 332–333, 335, 337, and 339, quote on 339.

78. Gershom Scholem, *WBTSF*, 196–198.

79. Gershom Scholem to Walter Benjamin, 20 February 1930, in *Correspondence of Walter Benjamin, 1910–1940*, 362.

80. Gershom Scholem to Betty Scholem, 23 August 1928, 29 November 1929, and 11 December 1929, NLI, ARC. 4*1599/12/3001.

81. Gershom Scholem to Betty Scholem, 17 July 1934, NLI, ARC. 4*1599/12/3002.

82. Jay Howard Geller, " 'I Have Been a Stranger in a Foreign Land': The Scholem Brothers and German-Jewish Émigré Identity," in Geller and Morris, *Three-Way Street*, 129–130.

83. See Anat Helman, *A Coat of Many Colors: Dress Culture in the Young State of Israel* (Boston, Mass.: Academic Studies Press, 2011), 25.

84. Stern, *Five Germanys I Have Known*, 368.

85. Biale, *Gershom Scholem* (1982), 110–111.

86. Betty Scholem to Gershom Scholem, 4 October 1925, 31 January 1928, and 6 January 1931, NLI, ARC. 4*1599/01/3082, 3085, and 3088; Gershom Scholem to Betty Scholem, 18 April, 6 September, and 8 November 1928, NLI, ARC. 4*1599/12/3001.

87. Gershom Scholem to Betty Scholem, 21 November 1928, NLI, ARC. 4*1599/12/3001.

88. Gershom Scholem to Betty Scholem, 31 January and 10 May 1928, NLI, ARC. 4*1599/12/3001.

89. Gershom Scholem to Betty Scholem, 4 October 1928, in *MuSiB*, 182.

90. Escha Scholem to Betty Scholem, 13 April 1928, in *MuSiB*, 161.

91. Gershom Scholem to Betty Scholem, 4 October 1928, in *MuSiB*, 181.

92. Gershom Scholem to Betty Scholem, 22 August 1929, in *MuSiB*, 196.

93. Gershom Scholem to Betty Scholem, 30 January 1930, in *MuSiB*, 215.

94. Gershom Scholem to Betty Scholem, 8 November 1928, in *MuSiB*, 183.

95. Gershom Scholem to Betty Scholem, 12 April 1934 and 21 November 1935, NLI, ARC. 4*1599/12/3002.

96. Gershom Scholem to Betty Scholem, 28 August and 18 September 1930, in *MuSiB*, 218 and 219.

97. Gershom Scholem to Betty Scholem, 21 November 1928, NLI, ARC. 4*1599/12/3001.

98. Gershom Scholem to Julius Guttmann, 2 August 1928, NLI, ARC. 4*1599/01/1019.

99. Gershom Scholem to Betty Scholem, 23 August 1928, NLI, ARC. 4*1599/12/3001.

100. Betty Scholem to Gershom Scholem, 27 August and 5 November 1929, in *MuSiB*, 197 and 208.

101. Gershom Scholem to Julius Guttmann, 2 August 1928, NLI, ARC. 4*1599/01/1019.

7. The Maelstrom

1. Detlev Humann, statistical appendix to *"Arbeitsschlacht." Arbeitsbeschaffung und Propaganda in der NS-Zeit 1933–1939* (Göttingen: Wallstein, 2011), 10.

2. Betty Scholem to Gershom Scholem, 20 November 1932, in *MuSiB*, 270.

3. Henry Ashby Turner, *Hitler's Thirty Days to Power* (Boston, Mass.: Addison-Wesley, 1996).

4. Betty Scholem to Gershom Scholem, 7 February 1933, in *MuSiB*, 274.

5. Betty Scholem to Gershom Scholem, 20 February 1933, in *MuSiB*, 276–277, quote on 277.

6. Ludwig Holländer, "Die neue Regierung," *C. V.-Zeitung* 12, no. 5 (2 February 1933): 33–34; Friedländer, *Nazi Germany and the Jews*, 1:14–17.

7. Avraham Barkai, "Exclusion and Persecution: 1933–1938," in Meyer, *GJHMT*, 4:198–199; Friedländer, *Nazi Germany and the Jews*, 1:18–19.

8. Betty Scholem to Gershom Scholem, 27 March 1933, in *MuSiB*, 287.

9. Betty Scholem to Gershom Scholem, 14 February 1933, in *MuSiB*, 275.

10. Kaplan, *Between Dignity and Despair*, 18.

11. Betty Scholem to Gershom Scholem, 14 February 1933, in *MuSiB*, 275.

12. Nikolaus Wachsmann, *KL: A History of the Nazi Concentration Camps* (New York: Farrar, Straus and Giroux, 2015), 28–29; "Neue Notverordnung in Sicht. Hunderte von Verhaftungen," *Vossische Zeitung*, no. 100 (28 February 1933, evening edition): [1]; Betty Scholem to Gershom Scholem, 28 February 1933, in *MuSiB*, 278–279.

13. Betty Scholem to Gershom Scholem, 5 March 1933, in *MuSiB*, 281.

14. Betty Scholem to Gershom Scholem, 5 March 1933, in *MuSiB*, 281.

15. Betty Scholem to Gershom Scholem, 27 March 1933, in *MuSiB*, 286.

16. Betty Scholem to Gershom Scholem, 18 April 1933, in *MuSiB*, 293.

17. Wolfgang Benz, *A Concise History of the Third Reich*, trans. Thomas Dunlap (Berkeley: University of California Press, 2006), 26–28.

18. Diary entry, 2 April 1933, in Joseph Goebbels, *Die Tagebücher von Joseph Goebbels*, ed. Elke Fröhlich, pt. 1, *Aufzeichnungen 1923–1941*, vol. 2/III, *Oktober 1932–März 1934* (Munich: K. G. Saur, 2006), 160.

19. "Gedanken zum 1. April," *Frankfurter Zeitung* 77, no. 247 (1 April 1933, second morning edition): [1].

20. Kreutzmüller, *Final Sale in Berlin*, 105–110; Kaplan, *Between Dignity and Despair*, 21–23.

21. Richard J. Evans, *The Third Reich in Power* (New York: Penguin, 2005), 15 and 379–382.

22. National Socialist Workers Union of Ullstein to Reich Chancellery, 21 June 1933, in *Archives of the Holocaust*, vol. 20, *Bundesarchiv of the Federal Republic of Germany, Koblenz and Freiburg*, ed. Henry Friedlander and Sybil Milton (New York: Garland, 1993), 26–27.

23. Martin Münzel, *Die jüdischen Mitglieder der deutschen Wirtschaftselite 1927–1955. Verdrängung, Emigration, Rückkehr* (Paderborn: Ferdinand Schöningh, 2006), 394–407, esp. 397.

24. Betty Scholem to Gershom Scholem, 27 June 1933, in *MuSiB*, 312.

25. Barkai, "Exclusion and Persecution," in Meyer, *GJHMT*, 4:227–229.

26. Kaplan, *Between Dignity and Despair*, 21–24.

27. Friedländer, *Nazi Germany and the Jews*, 1:27–31; Barkai, "Exclusion and Persecution," in Meyer, *GJHMT*, 4:201–203.

28. Betty Scholem to Gershom Scholem, 9 April 1933, in *MuSiB*, 291.

29. Friedländer, *Nazi Germany and the Jews*, 1:10–11 and 57–58.

30. Kaplan, *Between Dignity and Despair*, 36–38 and 45.

31. Betty Scholem to Gershom Scholem, 18 April 1933, in *MuSiB*, 294.

32. Wolf Gruner, "Die Berliner und die NS-Judenverfolgung. Eine mikrohistorische Studie individueller Handlungen und sozialer Beziehungen," in *Berlin im Nationalsozialismus. Politik und Gesellschaft 1933–1945*, ed. Rüdiger Hachtmann, Thomas Schaarschmidt, and Winfried Süß (Göttingen: Wallstein, 2011), 65.

33. Joachim Prinz, "Das Leben ohne Nachbarn," *Jüdische Rundschau* 40, nos. 31–32 (17 April 1935): 3; cf. Gruner, "Die Berliner und die NS-Judenverfolgung," in Hachtmann, Schaarschmidt, and Süß, *Berlin im Nationalsozialismus*, 87.

34. Kaplan, *Between Dignity and Despair*, 34–46.

35. Betty Scholem to Gershom Scholem, 19 March 1933, in *MuSiB*, 285.

36. Gershom Scholem to Betty Scholem, 20 April 1933, in *MuSiB*, 294 and 295.

37. Werner Scholem to Gershom Scholem, 5 October 1933, in *MuSiB*, 334–335.

38. Betty Scholem to Gershom Scholem, 18 and 25 April, 9 July, and 19 November 1933, in *MuSiB*, 293, 296, 317, and 351.

39. Theobald Scholem to Gershom Scholem, 22 June 1933, NLI, ARC. 4*1599/01/3032.

40. Theobald Scholem to Gershom Scholem, 4 September 1933, NLI, ARC. 4*1599/01/3032.

41. Gtz [George Goetz], "Emigranten," *Jüdisch-liberale Zeitung* 13, no. 6 (15 June 1933): [3].

42. Werner Rosenstock, "Exodus 1933–1939: A Survey of Jewish Emigration from Germany," *LBIYB* 1 (1956): 377 and 379–380.

43. Kaplan, *Between Dignity and Despair*, 63–64.

44. Betty Scholem to Gershom Scholem, 9 July 1933, and 14 May and 17 July 1934, in *MuSiB*, 318, 361, and 362.

45. Betty Scholem to Gershom Scholem, 7 March 1934, in *MuSiB*, 353.

46. Betty Scholem to Gershom Scholem, 18 April and 3 November 1933, in *MuSiB*, 293 and 344–345.

47. Betty Scholem to Gershom Scholem, 19 April 1933, in *MuSiB*, 294.

48. Lily E. Hirsch, *A Jewish Orchestra in Nazi Germany: Musical Politics and the Berlin Jewish Culture League* (Ann Arbor: University of Michigan Press, 2010); Rebecca Rovit, *The Jewish Kulturbund Theatre Company in Nazi Berlin* (Iowa City: University of Iowa Press, 2012).

49. Gertrud Kolmar, "Susanna," in *Das Leere Haus. Prosa jüdischer Dichter*, ed. Karl Otten (Stuttgart: Cotta-Verlag, 1959), 299; Gertrud Chodziesner [Gertrud Kolmar], "Die Jüdin," *Blätter der jüdischen Buchvereinigung* 3, no. 2 (September 1936): 7.

50. Betty Scholem to Gershom Scholem, 5 November 1933, in *MuSiB*, 345.

51. Betty Scholem to Gershom Scholem, 26 September and 3 October 1933, 6 March and 4 December 1934, in *MuSiB*, 330, 332, 355, and 375.

52. Betty Scholem to Gershom Scholem, 4 December 1934, in *MuSiB*, 374–376, quotes on 375.

53. Betty Scholem to Gershom Scholem, 14 August and 18 September 1935, in *MuSiB*, 395 and 397.

54. Werner Scholem to Emmy Scholem, 20 December 1933, LUH, IPW, Nachlass Werner Scholem, 3312200.

55. Werner Scholem to Emmy Scholem, 29 January 1935, LUH, IPW, Nachlass Werner Scholem, 3501290.

56. Werner Scholem to Emmy Scholem, 29 January 1935, LUH, IPW, Nachlass Werner Scholem, 3501290; cf. M. Zadoff, *Der rote Hiob*, 233.

57. Betty Scholem to Gershom Scholem, 23 October 1933, in *MuSiB*, 341.

58. Betty Scholem to Gershom Scholem, 25 April 1933, in *MuSiB*, 295–296.

59. Betty Scholem to Gershom Scholem, 28 May, 18 June, and 18 September 1933, in *MuSiB*, 303–304, 309, and 329.

60. Betty Scholem to Gershom Scholem, 18 and 7 June 1933, in *MuSiB*, 308–309 and 305.

61. Kaplan, *Between Dignity and Despair*, 60–61.

62. Gershom Scholem to Walter Benjamin, 4 September 1933, in Benjamin and Scholem, *Correspondence-WBGS*, 75.

63. "Anklageschrift!," 18 October 1934, BArch, R 3017/13 J 195/33; Betty Scholem to Gershom Scholem, 1 August 1933, in *MuSiB*, 320–321.

64. Betty Scholem to Gershom Scholem, 1 August 1933, in *MuSiB*, 322.

65. Untersuchungsrichter des Reichsgerichts to Emmy Scholem, 28 June 1933, LUH, IPW, Nachlass Werner Scholem, 3306280.

66. Gershom Scholem to Walter Benjamin, 4 May 1933, in Benjamin and Scholem, *Correspondence-WBGS*, 43.

67. Werner Scholem to Gershom Scholem, 5 October 1933, in *MuSiB*, 335.

68. M. Zadoff, *Der rote Hiob*, 221.

69. "Beschluß," 23 November 1933, LUH, IPW, Nachlass Werner Scholem, 3311231.

70. Emmy Scholem to Landgerichtsdirektor Dr. Zimmer, Untersuchungsrichter beim Reichsgericht, 29 June 1934, LUH, IPW, Nachlass Werner Scholem, 3406290.

71. Emmy Scholem to Werner Scholem, 9 January 1935, LUH, IPW, Nachlass Werner Scholem, 3501090.

72. Betty Scholem to Gershom Scholem, 6/7 March 1934, in *MuSiB*, 352–353.

73. Betty Scholem to Gershom Scholem, 8 April and 17 July 1934, in *MuSiB*, 356–358 and 361–363.

74. M. Zadoff, *Der rote Hiob*, 230–231.

75. Betty Scholem to Escha Scholem, 8 October 1934, in *MuSiB*, 369.

76. Betty Scholem to Gershom Scholem, 12 August and 8 October 1934, and 1 October 1935, in *MuSiB*, 367, 371, and 399.

77. Emmy Scholem to Heinrich Reinefeld, 20 January 1935, LUH, IPW, Nachlass Werner Scholem, 3501200.

78. Emmy Scholem to Werner Scholem, 9 January 1935, LUH, IPW, Nachlass Werner Scholem, 3501090.

79. Emmy Scholem to Reinhold Scholem, 31 May 1935, NLI, ARC. 4*1599/01/3023.

80. Werner Scholem to Betty Scholem, 29 November 1934, LUH, IPW, Nachlass Werner Scholem, 3411290.

81. Betty Scholem to Gershom Scholem, 28 May, 19 August, and 10, 23, and 30 October 1933, in *MuSiB*, 305, 323–325, 337, 339–341, and 342.

82. Betty Scholem to Gershom Scholem, 5 November 1933, Gershom Scholem to Betty Scholem, 7 November 1933, and Betty Scholem to Gershom Scholem, 16 July 1937, in *MuSiB*, 345, 346–349, and 431.

83. Betty Scholem to Gershom Scholem, 27 March 1933, in *MuSiB*, 287.

84. Theobald Scholem to Gershom Scholem, 24 March and 11 July 1934, NLI, ARC. 4*1599/01/3032; Betty Scholem to Gershom Scholem, 14 August 1935, in *MuSiB*, 394.

85. Mendes-Flohr, "Jewish Cultural Life under National Socialism," in Meyer, *GJHMT*, 4:303–312.

86. Stephen M. Poppel, "Salman Schocken and the Schocken Verlag," *LBIYB* 17 (1972): 93 and 112–113.

87. Betty Scholem to Gershom Scholem, 27 April, 14 August, and 14 October 1935, in *MuSiB*, 385–386, 394, and 403.

88. Betty Scholem to Gershom Scholem, 27 April and 18 September 1935, in *MuSiB*, 386–387 and 397.

89. Eva Scholem to Gershom Scholem, 25 December 1934, NLI, ARC. 4*1599/01/3032.

90. Eva Scholem to Gershom Scholem, 28 August 1935, NLI, ARC. 4*1599/01/3032; Betty Scholem to Gershom Scholem, 14 August 1935, in *MuSiB*, 395; Doron Niederland, "The Emigration of Jewish Academics and Professionals from Germany in the First Years of Nazi Rule," *LBIYB* 33 (1988): 298.

91. Betty Scholem to Gershom Scholem, 14 August 1935, in *MuSiB*, 395.

92. Betty Scholem to Gershom Scholem, 6 December 1937, in *MuSiB*, 443.

93. Betty Scholem to Gershom Scholem, 5 January 1938 and 29 December 1939, in *MuSiB*, 445 and 481.

94. Emmy Scholem to Gershom Scholem, 16 August 1934, NLI, ARC. 4*1599/01/3023.

95. Emmy Scholem to Landgerichtsdirektor Dr. Zimmer, Untersuchungsrichter beim Reichsgericht, 29 June and 9 July 1934, LUH, IPW, Nachlass Werner Scholem, 3406290 and 3407090.

96. Werner Scholem to Emmy Scholem, 15 February 1935, LUH, IPW, Nachlass Werner Scholem, 3502150.

97. Judgment of the Volksgerichtshof, n.d. [ca. 5 March 1935], BArch, R 3017/13J 195/33; Betty Scholem to Gershom Scholem, 12 March 1935, in *MuSiB*, 380–382.

98. Betty Scholem to Gershom Scholem, 29 March 1935, in *MuSiB*, 384.

99. Report from Emmy Scholem, n.d. [1935], LUH, IPW, Nachlass Werner Scholem, XXXXXX7.

100. Buckmiller and Nafe, "Die Naherwartung des Kommunismus," in Buckmiller, Heimann, and Perels, *Judentum und politische Existenz*, 77–78.

101. Ruth Fischer to Franz Jung, 18 August 1960, in Ruth Fischer and Arkadij Maslow, *Abtrünnig wider Willen. Aus Briefen und Manuskripten des Exils*, ed. Peter Lübbe (Munich: R. Oldenbourg, 1990), 335; Reinhard Müller, "Hitlers Rede vor der Reichswehr- und Reichsmarineführung am 3. Februar 1933," *Mittelweg 36* 10, no. 4 (February/March 2000): 74–90; Andreas Wirsching, "'Man kann nur Boden germanisieren.' Eine neue Quelle zu Hitlers Rede vor den Spitzen der Reichswehr am 3. Februar 1933," *Vierteljahrshefte für Zeitgeschichte* 49, no. 3 (July 2001): 517–550.

102. Betty Scholem to Gershom and Escha Scholem, 11 May 1935, in *MuSiB*, 388.

103. Kim Wünschmann, *Before Auschwitz: Jewish Prisoners in the Concentration Camps* (Cambridge, Mass.: Harvard University Press, 2015), 23–25.

104. Diary entry, 14 July 1924, in Goebbels, *Tagebücher*, 1/1/I:169; Gershom Scholem to Walter Benjamin, 19 April 1936, in Benjamin and Scholem, *Correspondence-WBGS*, 177.

105. "16 Tage Moabit. Erlebnisse in Untersuchungshaft von Nr. 1621," *Berliner Illustrierte Nachtausgabe* (27 October 1933), in NLI, ARC. 4*1599/02/4.

106. BArch, Bild 119–04–29–36 and Bild 119–04–29–38.

107. Werner Scholem to Emmy Scholem, 13 December 1934, LUH, IPW, Nachlass Werner Scholem, 3412130.

108. Werner Scholem to "Meine Lieben," 1 May 1935, LUH, IPW, Nachlass Werner Scholem, 3505010.

109. Werner Scholem to Emmy Scholem, 14 June 1935, LUH, IPW, Nachlass Werner Scholem, 3506140.

110. Werner Scholem to Emmy Scholem, 20 June (quote) and 21 August 1935, LUH, IPW, Nachlass Werner Scholem, 3506200 and 3508210; Ludwig Bendix, a.k.a. Reversus, "Konzentrationslager Deutschland und andere Schutzhafterinnerungen 1933–1937," Leo Baeck Institute (Center for Jewish History), ME 40, MM 7, 4:19–22 and 4:26.

111. Betty Scholem to Gershom Scholem, 14 October 1935, in *MuSiB*, 404.

112. Werner Scholem to Emmy Scholem, 8 January 1936, LUH, IPW, Nachlass Werner Scholem, 3601080.

113. Werner Scholem to Emmy Scholem, 5 March 1936, LUH, IPW, Nachlass Werner Scholem, 3603050.

114. Betty Scholem to Gershom Scholem, 18 September 1935, in *MuSiB*, 397.

115. Friedländer, *Nazi Germany and the Jews*, 1:151.

116. Joseph Goebbels, *Communism with the Mask Off: Speech Delivered in Nürnberg on September 13th, 1935 at the Seventh National Socialist Party Congress* (Berlin: M. Müller & Sohn K. G., [1935]), 28; Betty Scholem to Gershom Scholem, 1 October 1935, in *MuSiB*, 398.

117. Betty Scholem to Gershom Scholem, 5 October 1935, in *MuSiB*, 400.

118. Betty Scholem to Gershom Scholem, 14 October 1935, in *MuSiB*, 404–405.

119. See Knut Bergbauer, Sabine Fröhlich, and Stefanie Schüler-Springorum, *Denkmalsfigur. Biographische Annäherung an Hans Litten 1903–1938* (Göttingen: Wallstein Verlag, 2008), 289–290 and 300.

120. Gershom Scholem to Emmy Scholem, 25 August 1939, LUH, IPW, Nachlass Werner Scholem, 3908250.

121. Gershom Scholem to Betty Scholem, 18 February 1936, NLI, ARC. 4*1599/12/3002.

122. Werner Scholem to Emmy Scholem, 24 March 1936, LUH, IPW, Nachlass Werner Scholem, 3603240.

123. Gershom Scholem to Walter Benjamin, 19 April 1936, and editorial comment by Gershom Scholem, in Benjamin and Scholem, *Correspondence-WBGS*, 177 and 177n2.

124. Werner Scholem to "Meine Lieben," 6 February 1937, LUH, IPW, Nachlass Werner Scholem, 3702060.

125. Bendix, "Konzentrationslager Deutschland und andere Schutzhafterinnerungen 1933–1937," Leo Baeck Institute (Center for Jewish History), ME 40, MM 7, 4:19–22, 4:80, 5:6, 4:75–78.

126. Quoted in Bernhard Kuschey, *Die Ausnahme des Überlebens. Ernst und Hilde Federn. Eine biographische Studie und eine Analyse der Binnenstrukturen des Konzentrationslagers* (Gießen: Psychosozial-Verlag, 2003), 1:361–365 and 357, quotes on 361 and 362.

127. Werner Scholem to Betty Scholem, 19 June 1937, LUH, IPW, Nachlass Werner Scholem, 3706190; Betty Scholem to Gershom Scholem, 16 July 1937, in *MuSiB*, 430.

128. Werner Scholem to "Meine Lieben," 4 and 18 July 1937, LUH, IPW, Nachlass Werner Scholem, 3707040 and 3707180.

129. Werner Portmann and Siegbert Wolf, "Isak Aufseher (1905–1977). Luftmensch und Spanienkämpfer," in *"Ja, ich kämpfte." Von Revolutionsträumen, "Luftmenschen" und Kindern des Schtetls. Biographien radikaler Jüdinnen und Juden* (Münster: Unrast, 2006), 47.

130. Jewish Refugees Committee to Gershom Scholem, 19 November 1937, NLI, ARC. 4*1599/01/3023.

131. Reinhold Scholem and Erich Scholem to Amtsgericht Berlin, 27 March 1936, LAB, A Rep. 342–02, Nr. 42380; Erich Scholem to Gershom Scholem, 18 February 1934, NLI, ARC. 4*1599/01/3024.

132. Hans Münzer to Wiedergutmachungskammer Berlin-Wilmersdorf, 17 December 1952, LAB, B Rep. 025–03, Nr. 34 WGA 2000/51.

133. Jan-Pieter Barbian, *The Politics of Literature in Nazi Germany: Books in the Media Dictatorship* (New York: Bloomsbury Academic, 2013), 178–179; Volker Dahm, "Jewish Publishing in Nazi Germany, 1933–1938," in *Jewish Book Annual*, vol. 46, 1988–1989/5749, ed. Jacob Kabakoff (New York: Jewish Book Council, 1988), 7–19; cf. Kreutzmüller, *Final Sale in Berlin*, 214; and Mendes-Flohr, "Jewish Cultural Life under National Socialism," in Meyer, *GJHMT*, 4:303–312.

134. "Abschrift," 31 March 1938, LAB, B Rep. 025–03, Nr. 34 WGA 2000/51; Theobald Scholem to Amtsgericht Berlin Handelsregister, 18 August 1938, "Verfügung," 27 August 1938, LAB A Rep. 342–02, Nr. 44488; Hans Münzer to Wiedergutmachungskammer Berlin-Wilmersdorf, 17 December 1952, LAB, B Rep. 025–03, Nr. 34 WGA 2000/51.

135. Kreutzmüller, *Final Sale in Berlin*, 175 and 213.

136. Avraham Barkai, *From Boycott to Annihilation: The Economic Struggle of German Jews, 1933–1943*, trans. William Templer (Hanover, N.H.: University Press of New England, 1989), 111.

137. Karl A. Schleunes, *The Twisted Road to Auschwitz: Nazi Policy toward German Jews, 1933–1939* (Urbana: University of Illinois Press, 1970), 143–148.

138. Claudia Huerkamp, "Jüdische Akademikerinnen in Deutschland 1900–1938," *Geschichte und Gesellschaft* 19 (1993): 319.

139. Friedländer, *Nazi Germany and the Jews*, 1:30 and 225.

140. Efron, *Medicine and the German Jews*, 264.

141. Betty Scholem to Gershom Scholem, 5 January and 27 September 1938, in *MuSiB*, 445 and 449.

142. Bruno Blau, "Die Juden in Deutschland von 1933 bis 1945," *Judaica* 7 (1951): 280.

143. Friedländer, *Nazi Germany and the Jews*, 1:117, 122–123, 229–230, and 285; diary entry, 15 May 1942, in Victor Klemperer, *I Will Bear Witness: A Diary of the Nazi Years, 1942–1945*, trans. Martin Chalmers (New York: Random House, 1999), 52.

144. Diary entry, 24 August 1938, in Victor Klemperer, *I Will Bear Witness: A Diary of the Nazi Years, 1933–1941*, trans. Martin Chalmers (New York: Random House, 1998), 264.

145. Kaplan, *Between Dignity and Despair*, 70–72.

146. Werner Rosenstock, "Exodus 1933–1939," 387.

147. Erich and Betty Scholem to Gershom Scholem, 21 November 1937, in *MuSiB*, 438–441; Michael Blakeney, "Australia and the Jewish Refugees from Central Europe: Government Policy, 1933–1939," *LBIYB* 29 (1984): 108; Ernst G. Löwenthal,

Philo-Atlas. Handbuch für die jüdische Auswanderung (Berlin: Philo G.m.b.H., Jüdischer Buchverlag, 1938), 17 and 271.

148. Erich and Betty Scholem to Gershom Scholem, 21 November 1937, in *MuSiB*, 438.

149. Reinhold Scholem to Gershom Scholem, 18 October 1938, NLI, ARC. 4*1599/01/3031.

150. Reinhold Scholem to Gershom Scholem, 18 October 1938, NLI, ARC. 4*1599/01/3031.

151. Werner Scholem to Betty Scholem, 28 August 1938, LUH, IPW, Nachlass Werner Scholem, 3808280.

152. Betty Scholem to Gershom Scholem, 12 October 1938, in *MuSiB*, 450–451.

153. Betty Scholem to Gershom Scholem, 25 October and 19 November 1938, in *MuSiB*, 451 and 455, quote on 451.

154. Erich Scholem to Gershom Scholem, 6 November 1938, NLI, ARC. 4*1599/01/3024.

155. Blakeney, "Australia and the Jewish Refugees," *LBIYB* 29 (1984): 106, 111, and 115–116.

156. Blakeney, "Australia and the Jewish Refugees," *LBIYB* 29 (1984): 109.

157. Alan E. Steinweis, *Kristallnacht 1938* (Cambridge, Mass.: Harvard University Press, 2009), 56–98; Friedländer, *Nazi Germany and the Jews*, 1:269–270 and 274–277.

158. Gruner, "Die Berliner und die NS-Judenverfolgung," in Hachtmann, Schaarschmidt, and Süß, *Berlin im Nationalsozialismus*, 70–73.

159. Steinweis, *Kristallnacht 1938*, 112–114.

160. Steinweis, *Kristallnacht 1938*, 103–107.

161. "Stenographic Report of the Meeting on the 'Jewish Question' under the Chairmanship of Field Marshal Goering in the Reichs Air Force," 12 November 1938, in Office of the United States Chief Counsel for Prosecution of Axis Criminality, *Nazi Conspiracy and Aggression*, vol. 4 (Washington, D.C.: United States Government Printing Office, 1946), 455.

162. Betty Scholem to Gershom Scholem, 13 November 1938, in *MuSiB*, 454.

163. Betty Scholem to Gershom Scholem, 4 March 1939, in *MuSiB*, 463.

164. Betty Scholem to Gershom Scholem, 13 November 1938, in *MuSiB*, 454; Blakeney, "Australia and the Jewish Refugees," *LBIYB* 29 (1984): 121–124.

165. Betty Scholem to Gershom Scholem, 16 December 1938, in *MuSiB*, 456–457; Gershom Scholem to Walter Benjamin, 2 March 1939, in Benjamin and Scholem, *Correspondence-WBGS*, 247.

166. Betty Scholem to Gershom Scholem, 22 January, and 7 and 15 February 1939, in *MuSiB*, 458–460; Erich Scholem to Gershom Scholem, 1 December 1938, NLI, ARC. 4*1599/01/3024.

167. Betty Scholem to Gershom Scholem, 4 March 1939, in *MuSiB*, 463; alien passengers manifest for *Comorin*, Ancestry.com, *UK, Outward Passenger Lists, 1890–1960* [database on-line] (Provo: Ancestry.com Operations, 2012), originally Board of Trade: Commercial and Statistical Department and successors: Outwards Passenger Lists, BT27, Records of the Commercial, Companies, Labour, Railways and Statistics Departments, Records of the Board of Trade and of successor and related bodies, National Archives, Kew, Richmond, Surrey, England.

168. Gershom Scholem to Walter Benjamin, 20 March 1939, in Benjamin and Scholem, *Correspondence-WBGS*, 251.

169. Betty Scholem to Gershom Scholem, 27 September 1938, in *MuSiB*, 449.

170. Werner Scholem to Betty Scholem, 28 August 1938, LUH, IPW, Nachlass Werner Scholem, 3808280.

171. Betty Scholem to Gershom Scholem, 25 October 1938, in *MuSiB*, 452.

172. Betty Scholem to Gershom Scholem, 13 November 1938, in *MuSiB*, 453.

173. Emmy Scholem to Karl Korsch, 4 November 1938, LUH, IPW, Nachlass Werner Scholem, 3811040.

174. Edith Scholem to American Consulate General, Berlin, 9 January 1939, LUH, IPW, Nachlass Werner Scholem, 3901090.

175. Betty Scholem to Gershom Scholem, 4 March 1939, in *MuSiB*, 463.

176. Hans Hirsch to Emmy Scholem, 5 March 1939, LUH, IPW, Nachlass Werner Scholem, 3903050.

177. Werner Scholem to Sophie Scholem, 2 April 1939, and Sophie Scholem to Concentration Camp Weimar-Buchenwald, 5 April 1939, LUH, IPW, Nachlass Werner Scholem, 3904020 and 3904050.

178. Hans Hirsch to Emmy Scholem, 24 June and 21 August 1939, LUH, IPW, Nachlass Werner Scholem, 3906240 and 3908210.

179. Gershom Scholem to Emmy Scholem, 25 August 1939, LUH, IPW, Nachlass Werner Scholem, 3908250.

180. Betty Scholem to Gershom Scholem, 27 September 1938, in *MuSiB*, 449.

181. Betty Scholem to Gershom Scholem, 7 February 1939, in *MuSiB*, 460.

182. Sophie Scholem, "Meine Reise nach Süd-Afrika," Adam Scholem Collection.

183. "Hans Hirsch Must Leave Germany," *Bulletin of the American Ceramic Society* 18, no. 2 (February 1939): 76.

184. Kaplan, *Between Dignity and Despair*, 132 and 138–143.

185. Kaplan, *Between Dignity and Despair*, 88–89.

186. Betty Scholem to Gershom Scholem, 27 September 1938, in *MuSiB*, 449.

187. Gershom Scholem to Betty Scholem, 19 November 1944, in *MuSiB*, 517.

188. "Abschrift aus einem Brief von Grete Lichtwitz," appended to letter from Hans Hirsch to Gershom Scholem, 29 May 1946, NLI, ARC. 4*1599/01/3012; Freie Universität Berlin, Zentralinstitut für sozialwissenschaftliche Forschung, ed., *Gedenkbuch Berlins. Der jüdischen Opfer des Nationalsozialismus* (Berlin: Edition Hentrich, 1995).

189. "Abschrift aus einem Brief von Grete Lichtwitz," appended to letter from Hans Hirsch to Gershom Scholem, 29 May 1946, NLI, ARC. 4*1599/01/3012; Gershom Scholem to Reinhold Scholem, 5 March 1978, NLI, ARC. 4*1599/01/3031.

190. Benedikt Kautsky, *Teufel und Verdammte. Erfahrungen und Erkenntnisse aus sieben Jahren in deutschen Konzentrationslagern* (Zürich: Büchergilde Gutenberg, 1946), 236–237.

191. Lutz Niethammer, ed., *Der "gesäuberte" Antifaschismus. Die SED und die roten Kapos von Buchenwald* (Berlin: Akademie, 1994).

192. t.n. [Ernst Federn], "In Memoriam: Werner Scholem," *Die Internationale. Theoretische Zeitschrift der Gruppe Internationale Marxisten (GIM), Deutsche Sektion der IV. Internationale*, no. 16 (June 1981): 119.

193. Gedenkstätte Buchenwald, ed., *Buchenwald Concentration Camp, 1937–1945: A Guide to the Permanent Historical Exhibition* (Göttingen: Wallstein, 2004), 118.

194. t.n. [Ernst Federn], "In Memoriam: Werner Scholem," 119; Kuschey, *Die Ausnahme des Überlebens*, 1:512–514; cf. *The Buchenwald Report*, ed. and trans. David A. Hackett (Boulder, Colo.: Westview, 1995), 184.

195. "Auf Flucht erschossen 17.7.40," Werner Scholem file, document no. 10748285#1, International Tracing Service, Bad Arolsen.

196. t.n. [Ernst Federn], "In Memoriam: Werner Scholem," 117–120, quote on 118.

197. Kuschey, *Die Ausnahme des Überlebens*, 2:564.

198. Gershom Scholem to Dina Waschitz (née Scholem), 2 August 1981, in *Briefe*, vol. 3, *1971–1982*, ed. Itta Shedletzky (Munich: C. H. Beck, 1999), 240 (hereafter cited as *Briefe*).

199. M. Zadoff, *Das rote Hiob*, 294; Hoffrogge, *Werner Scholem*, 444–445.

200. Betty Scholem to Emmy Scholem, 18 September 1940, LUH, IPW, Nachlass Werner Scholem, 4009180.

201. Betty Scholem to Gershom Scholem, 27 September 1940, in *MuSiB*, 492.

202. Home Office, Nationality Division to Emmy Scholem, 17 September 1943, LUH, IPW, Nachlass Werner Scholem, 4309170.

8. Cresting of the Fifth Wave

1. E. Mills, "Summary for Palestine," in *Census of Palestine 1931*, unnumbered page before page 1; Harry S. Linfield, "Statistics of Jews," *American Jewish Year Book* 24 (1922–23): 300 and 303; Harry S. Linfield, "Statistics of Jews," *American Jewish Year Book* 33 (1931–32): 281 and 285.

2. Anat Helman, *Young Tel Aviv: A Tale of Two Cities*, trans. Haim Watzman (Waltham, Mass.: Brandeis University Press, 2010), 2.

3. Palestine, *Report and General Abstracts of the Census of 1922*, 14; E. Mills, *Census of Palestine 1931*, 40; I. Ben-Zwi [Yitzhak Ben-Zvi], *Jerusalem* (Jerusalem: Goldberg's Press, 1936), [4], reproduced in *The Rise of Israel*, ed. Aaron S. Klieman, vol. 16, *The Jewish Yishuv's Development in the Interwar Period* (New York: Garland, 1987), 308.

4. Ruth Kark and Michal Oren-Nordheim, *Jerusalem and Its Environs: Quarters, Neighborhoods, Villages, 1800–1948* (Detroit, Mich.: Wayne State University Press, 2001), 151–152 and 156–159.

5. David Kroyanker, "Rehavia—Das 'Jeckenland' von Jerusalem," in Zimmermann and Hotam, *Zweimal Heimat*, 260–266; Thomas Sparr, *Grunewald im Orient. Das deutsch-jüdische Jerusalem* (Berlin: Berenberg, 2018).

6. Kroyanker, "Rehavia," in Zimmermann and Hotam, *Zweimal Heimat*, 260–266 and 263, quote on 263.

7. Else Lasker-Schüler, "Das Hebräerland," in *Gesammelte Werke*, vol. 2, *Prosa und Schauspiele*, ed. Friedhelm Kemp (Munich: Kösel-Verlag, 1962), 801–803; Betty Scholem to Gershom Scholem, 10 March 1932, Gershom Scholem to Betty Scholem, 19 April 1932, Betty Scholem to Gershom Scholem, 28 April 1932, Gershom Scholem to Betty Scholem, 1 May 1932, Betty Scholem to Gershom Scholem, 14

August 1932, Gershom Scholem to Betty Scholem, 25 October 1932, all in NLI, ARC. 4*1599/12/3002.

8. Walter Benjamin to Gershom Scholem, 25 October 1932, editorial comment by Gershom Scholem, in Benjamin and Scholem, *Correspondence-WBGS*, 20 and 20n1.

9. Gershom Scholem to Ulrich Gerhardt, 3 May 1933, in *Briefe*, 1:252.

10. Gershom Scholem to Walter Benjamin, ca. 20 March 1933, in Benjamin and Scholem, *Correspondence-WBGS*, 33.

11. Gershom Scholem to Walter Benjamin, 15 June 1933, in Benjamin and Scholem, *Correspondence-WBGS*, 56.

12. Gershom Scholem to Betty Scholem, 20 April, 10 May, and 22 June 1933, NLI, ARC. 4*1599/12/3002.

13. Gershom Scholem to Ulrich Gerhardt, 3 May 1933, in *Briefe*, 1:252–253.

14. Gershom Scholem to Betty Scholem, 26 April 1933, in *MuSiB*, 297.

15. Gershom Scholem to Betty Scholem, 26 April 1933, in *MuSiB*, 297.

16. Gershom Scholem to Walter Benjamin, 29 December 1936, in Benjamin and Scholem, *Correspondence-WBGS*, 189–190.

17. Gershom Scholem to Walter Benjamin, 15 June 1933, in Benjamin and Scholem, *Correspondence-WBGS*, 56.

18. E.g., S. B. Bamberger to Gershom Scholem, 23 April 1933, NLI, ARC. 4*1599/01/0136; Biale, *Gershom Scholem* (2018), 114–115.

19. Betty Scholem to Escha Scholem, 8 October 1934, in *MuSiB*, 370.

20. Betty Scholem to Gershom Scholem, 12 October 1930, NLI, ARC. 4*1599/12/3001.

21. Betty Scholem to Gershom Scholem, 19 November 1934, in *MuSiB*, 372.

22. Gershom Scholem to Betty Scholem, 26 December 1934, in *MuSiB*, 377.

23. Yoav Gelber, "The Historical Role of Central European Immigration to Israel," *LBIYB* 38 (1993): 326n6.

24. Dan Horowitz and Moshe Lissak, *Origins of the Israeli Polity: Palestine under the Mandate*, trans. Charles Hoffman (Chicago: University of Chicago Press, 1978), 5 and 237n3.

25. Avraham Barkai, "German Interests in the Haavara-Transfer Agreement 1933–1939," *LBIYB* 35 (1990): 245–266; Yehuda Bauer, *Jews for Sale?: Nazi-Jewish Negotiations, 1933–1945* (New Haven, Conn.: Yale University Press, 1994), 5–29.

26. Nachum Gross, "Entrepreneure: Einwanderer aus Mitteleuropa in der Wirtschaft Palästinas," in Zimmermann and Hotam, *Zweimal Heimat*, 133.

27. Interviews with Uri Rapp, Erna Jacob, and Gabriel Walter, in *Wir sind die Letzten. Fragt uns aus. Gespräche mit den Emigranten der dreißiger Jahre in Israel*, ed. Anne Betten and Miryam Du-nour, 3rd ed. (Gerlinger: Bleicher, 1998), 287–289.

28. Gelber, "Historical Role," *LBIYB* 38 (1993): 335 and 332.

29. Schlör, *Endlich im Gelobten Land?*, 106–207.

30. Diary entry, 22 May 1933, in Klemperer, *I Will Bear Witness . . . 1933–1941*, 18.

31. Interview with James Springer, in Betten and Du-nour, *Wir sind die Letzten*, 167; Ruth Gruber, *Israel Without Tears* (New York: A. A. Wyn, 1950), 86.

32. Interviews with Friedel Loewenson, Uri Rapp, Iwan Lilienfeld, and Esriel Hildesheimer, in Betten and Du-nour, *Wir sind die Letzten*, 161–162, 310–311, and 328; Moaz Azaryahu, *Tel Aviv: Mythography of a City* (Syracuse, N.Y.: Syracuse University Press, 2007), 89 and 82.

33. Interview with Chaim Sela, in Betten and Du-nour, *Wir sind die letzten*, 170.

34. Anita Shapira, *Land and Power: The Zionist Resort to Force, 1881–1948*, trans. William Templer (Oxford: Oxford University Press, 1992), 211–212.

35. Gershom Scholem to Moritz Spitzer, 17 December 1934, NLI, ARC. 4*1599/01/3059.

36. Gershom Scholem to Walter Benjamin, 28 June 1935, in Benjamin and Scholem, *Correspondence-WBGS*, 161.

37. Gershom Scholem to Walter Benjamin, 18 December 1935, in Benjamin and Scholem, *Correspondence-WBGS*, 174; Gershom Scholem, "A Commandment Fulfilled by Means of a Transgression" [Hebrew], *Knesset* 2 (1937): 347–392; Gershom Scholem, "Redemption through Sin," trans. Hillel Halkin, in *The Messianic Idea in Judaism and Other Essays on Jewish Spirituality* (New York: Schocken, 1971), 78–141.

38. Gershom Scholem to Walter Benjamin, 20 June 1934, in Benjamin and Scholem, *Correspondence-WBGS*, 118.

39. Gershom Scholem to Walter Benjamin, 1 August 1931, in Gershom Scholem, *WBTSF*, 217.

40. Gershom Scholem to Adolph S. Oko, 26 March 1944, in *Briefe*, 1:292.

41. Gershom Scholem, "Sprache," n.d., NLI, ARC. 4*1599/08/277.1.56.

42. Gershom Scholem to Betty Scholem, 20 March 1930, NLI, ARC. 4*1599/12/3001.

43. Gershom Scholem to Betty Scholem, 22 May 1930, NLI, ARC. 4*1599/12/3001.

44. Betty Scholem to Gershom Scholem, 12 October 1930, NLI, ARC. 4*1599/12/3001.

45. Gershom Scholem to Betty Scholem, 29 March 1933, NLI, ARC. 4*1599/12/3002.

46. Gershom Scholem to Betty Scholem, 8 January 1932; Betty Scholem to Gershom Scholem, 18 March 1932; Gershom Scholem to Betty Scholem, 22 March 1932; Gershom Scholem to Betty Scholem, 19 April 1932; all in *MuSiB*, 253, 259, 261–262, and 262–263.

47. Siegfried Moses, "Salman Schocken—His Economic and Zionist Activities," *LBIYB* 5 (1960): 86.

48. Lambert Schneider, Schocken Verlag, to Gershom Scholem, 26 January 1933, NLI, ARC. 4*1599/01/3058.

49. Handwritten notes on Gershom Scholem's relationship with Schocken Verlag, 19 and 20 November 1934, NLI, ARC. 4*1599/01/3050.

50. Editorial comment by Gershom Scholem, and Gershom Scholem to Walter Benjamin, ca. 20 March 1933, 4 and 19 September 1933, in Benjamin and Scholem, *Correspondence-WBGS*, 24n6, 32, 75 (quote), and 79; Gershom Scholem to Betty Scholem, 19 October 1933, in *MuSiB*, 338.

51. Gershom Scholem to Betty Scholem, 26 September 1933, in *MuSiB*, 330.

52. Gershom Scholem to Betty Scholem, 30 August 1933 and 21 November 1934, in *MuSiB*, 327 and 373–374.

53. Gershom Scholem to Walter Benjamin, 22 November 1934, in Benjamin and Scholem, *Correspondence-WBGS*, 147.

54. Gershom Scholem to Betty Scholem, 27 November 1933, NLI, ARC. 4*1599/12/3002.

55. Diary entries, 20 May 1933 and 17 June 1934, in Bergman, *Tagebücher und Briefe*, 1:344 and 1:366; Gershom Scholem to Betty Scholem, 21 November and 11 December 1935, NLI, ARC. 4*1599/12/3002; Gershom Scholem to Walter Benjamin, 18 December 1935, in Benjamin and Scholem, *Correspondence-WBGS*, 173.

56. Selzer, *History of the Hebrew University of Jerusalem*, 229; Gershom Scholem to Martin Buber, 24 August 1933, in Gershom Scholem, *Life in Letters*, 247; Gershom Scholem to Hebrew University Survey Committee, 27 December 1933, and Gershom Scholem to Martin Buber, 1 February 1938, in *Briefe*, 1:254–256 and 1:263.

57. Gershom Scholem to Walter Benjamin, 29 December 1936, in Benjamin and Scholem, *Correspondence-WBGS*, 190.

58. Gershom Scholem to Betty Scholem, 17 March 1936, in *MuSiB*, 414; Beit-Arié, "Gershom Scholem as Bibliophile," in Mendes-Flohr, *Gershom Scholem*, 123.

59. Gershom Scholem to Betty Scholem, 13 December 1934, NLI, ARC. 4*1599/12/3002.

60. Editorial comment by Gershom Scholem, in Benjamin and Scholem, *Correspondence-WBGS*, 24n5.

61. Gershom Scholem to Betty Scholem, 30 August 1933, in *MuSiB*, 328.

62. Gershom Scholem to Walter Benjamin, early February 1934 and 6 February 1935, in Benjamin and Scholem, *Correspondence-WBGS*, 98 and 150.

63. Gershom Scholem to Walter Benjamin, 20 June 1934, in Benjamin and Scholem, *Correspondence-WBGS*, 118; Gershom Scholem to Betty Scholem, 21 November 1935, NLI, ARC. 4*1599/12/3002.

64. Gershom Scholem to Walter Benjamin, 11 April 1934, in Benjamin and Scholem, *Correspondence-WBGS*, 104.

65. Escha Scholem to Gershom Scholem, 21 March 1934, NLI, ARC. 4*1599/01/3074.

66. Gershom Scholem to Walter Benjamin, 20 September 1934, in Benjamin and Scholem, *Correspondence-WBGS*, 142–143.

67. Escha Scholem to Gershom Scholem, 8 January, n.d. [document 345], 15 February, and 8 August 1935, NLI, ARC. 4*1599/01/3075; diary entry, 10 October 1935, in Bergman, *Tagebücher und Briefe*, 1:411.

68. Escha Scholem to Gershom Scholem, 14 January 1935, 12 February 1936, and undated letters [documents 338 and 339], NLI, ARC. 4*1599/01/3075 and 3076.

69. Escha Scholem to Gershom Scholem, n.d. [1936?, document 384], NLI, ARC. 4*1599/01/3076.

70. Gershom Scholem to Betty Scholem, 7 March 1936, in *MuSiB*, 410; Gershom Scholem to Walter Benjamin, 18 December 1935 and 19 April 1936, in Benjamin and Scholem, *Correspondence-WBGS*, 172 and 176; Escha Scholem to Gershom Scholem, 28 January 1936 and April 1936 [document 408], NLI, ARC. 4*1599/01/3076.

71. Escha Scholem to Gershom Scholem, 27 December 1935 and n.d. [1936?, document 381], NLI, ARC. 4*1599/01/3075 and 3076.

72. Escha Scholem to Gershom Scholem, n.d. [1936?, document 383], NLI, ARC. 4*1599/01/3076.

73. Escha Scholem to Gershom Scholem, 3 January 1936, NLI, ARC. 4*1599/01/3076.

74. Escha Scholem to Felix Rosenblüth, 5 February 1936, NLI, ARC. 4*1547/01/68.

75. Gershom Scholem to Walter Benjamin, 19 April 1936, in Benjamin and Scholem, *Correspondence-WBGS*, 176.

76. Gershom Scholem to Walter Benjamin, 29 December 1936, in Benjamin and Scholem, *Correspondence-WBGS*, 188; Miriam Sambursky, "Einleitung 1929–1938," in Bergman, *Tagebücher und Briefe*, 1:278.

77. Gershom Scholem to Betty Scholem, 22 November 1936, in *MuSiB*, 417; Ines Sonder, "Bauen für ein neues Land. Die Architektin Lotte Cohn zwischen Berlin und Erez Israel," in *Salondamen und Frauenzimmer. Selbstemanzipation deutsch-jüdischer Frauen in zwei Jahrhunderten*, ed. Elke-Vera Kotowski (Berlin: Walter de Gruyter, 2016), 116; Sparr, *Grunewald im Orient*, 29–32.

78. Gershom Scholem to Betty Scholem, 4 December 1936, in *MuSiB*, 418.

79. Betty Scholem to Gershom Scholem, 6 January 1937, in *MuSiB*, 421–422.

80. Betty Scholem to Gershom Scholem, 3 August 1937, in *MuSiB*, 433.

81. Escha Scholem Bergmann to Gershom Scholem, 12 April 1937, NLI, ARC. 4*1599/01/3077.

82. Diary entry, 9 September 1939, in Bergman, *Tagebücher und Briefe*, 1:430.

83. Betty Scholem to Gershom Scholem, 3 August 1937, in *MuSiB*, 433.

84. Gershom Scholem, *WBTSF*, 231 and 237, quote on 237.

85. Walter Benjamin to Gershom Scholem, [28 February 1933], *Correspondence of Walter Benjamin, 1910–1940*, 403.

86. Poppel, "Salman Schocken and the Schocken Verlag," *LBIYB* 17 (1972): 102–103; Moritz Spitzer, Schocken Verlag, to Gershom Scholem, 16 June 1934, NLI, ARC. 4*1599/01/3058.

87. Handwritten notes on Gershom Scholem's relationship with Schocken Verlag, 21 May 1936, NLI, ARC. 4*1599/01/3050; Gershom Scholem, *Die Geheimnisse der Schöpfung. Ein Kapitel aus dem Sohar* (Berlin: Schocken, 1935).

88. Gershom Scholem, "Nach der Entscheidung," June 1930, NLI, ARC. 4*1599/07/277.1.70; Gershom Scholem, "Um was geht der Streit?," November 1931, NLI, ARC. 4*1599/07/277.1.73, published in the newsletter of the German section of Hechalutz, *Informationsblatt* 4, no. 39 (November 1931): 15–19.

89. Mitchell Cohen, *Zion and State: Nation, Class, and the Shaping of Modern Israel* (New York: Columbia University Press, 1992), 158–159; Gerald Cromer, *A War of Words: Political Violence and Public Debate in Israel* (London: Frank Cass, 2004), 118–119.

90. Gershom Scholem to Betty Scholem, 22 June 1933, NLI, ARC. 4*1599/12/3002.

91. Betty Scholem to Gershom Scholem, 30 October 1933, and Gershom Scholem to Betty Scholem, 16 November 1933, in *MuSiB*, 343 and 350.

92. Segev, *One Palestine, Complete*, 367.

93. Gershom Scholem to Betty Scholem, 9 June 1936, in *MuSiB*, 412–413.

94. Gershom Scholem to Walter Benjamin, 6 June 1936, in Benjamin and Scholem, *Correspondence-WBGS*, 180.

95. Gershom Scholem to Walter Benjamin, 26 August 1936, in Benjamin and Scholem, *Correspondence-WBGS*, 183–184.

96. Segev, *One Palestine, Complete*, 382–383; Shapira, *Land and Power*, 235–243.

97. Segev, *One Palestine, Complete*, 386–390; Shapira, *Land and Power*, 220 and 258.

98. Gershom Scholem to Walter Benjamin, 6 June 1936, in Benjamin and Scholem, *Correspondence-WBGS*, 180.

99. Great Britain, Palestine Royal Commission, *Report* (London: His Majesty's Stationery Office, 1937), 363–364 and 380–397, reproduced in *The Rise of Israel*, ed. Aaron S. Klieman, vol. 24, *The Royal Commission Report, 1937* (New York: Garland, 1987), 424.

100. Shapira, *Land and Power*, 219.

101. Sachar, *History of Israel*, 207–208.

102. Gershom Scholem to Walter Benjamin, 10 July 1937, and editorial comment by Gershom Scholem, in Benjamin and Scholem, *Correspondence-WBGS*, 200 and 196n5.

103. Great Britain, Palestine Partition Commission, *Report* (London: His Majesty's Stationery Office, 1938).

104. Sachar, *History of Israel*, 220.

105. Great Britain, Colonial Office, *Palestine. Statement of Policy* (London: His Majesty's Stationery Office, 1939), reproduced in *The Rise of Israel*, ed. Aaron S. Klieman, vol. 27, *The Darkest Year, 1939* (New York: Garland, 1987), 302–313.

106. Shapira, *Land and Power*, 233.

107. Gershom Scholem to Shalom Spiegel, 1 January 1939, in *Briefe*, 1:267–268.

108. Gershom Scholem to Walter Benjamin, 2 March 1939, in Benjamin and Scholem, *Correspondence-WBGS*, 247.

109. Gershom Scholem to Walter Benjamin, 30 June 1939, in Benjamin and Scholem, *Correspondence-WBGS*, 255–256.

110. Gershom Scholem to Walter Benjamin, 15 December 1939, in Benjamin and Scholem, *Correspondence-WBGS*, 261. On that topic, see Jeffrey Herf, *Nazi Propaganda for the Arab World* (New Haven, Conn.: Yale University Press, 2009).

111. Gershom Scholem to Walter Benjamin, 11 September 1939, in Benjamin and Scholem, *Correspondence-WBGS*, 258.

112. Gershom Scholem to Walter Benjamin, 15 December 1939, in Benjamin and Scholem, *Correspondence-WBGS*, 261.

113. Henry Corbin to Gershom Scholem, 31 August 1937, NLI, ARC. 4*1599/01/5017.

114. Moritz Spitzer, Schocken Verlag, to Gershom Scholem, n.d. [1938, document 34], NLI, ARC. 4*1599/01/3058.

115. Stephen Wise to Gershom Scholem, 28 June 1937, NLI, ARC. 4*1599/01/2896.

116. Gershom Scholem to Walter Benjamin, 10 July 1937, in Benjamin and Scholem, *Correspondence-WBGS*, 201; Gershom Scholem, *WBTSF*, 257–258; Gershom Scholem to Stephen Wise, 16 August and 22 September 1937, NLI, ARC. 4*1599/01/2896.

117. Gershom Scholem to Walter Benjamin, 12 August and 29 November 1937, in Benjamin and Scholem, *Correspondence-WBGS*, 205 and 210, quote on 210.

118. Betty Scholem to Gershom Scholem, 26 October 1937, in *MuSiB*, 435.

119. Moritz Spitzer, Schocken Verlag, to Gershom Scholem, 7 December 1937, NLI, ARC. 4*1599/01/3058.

120. Stephen S. Wise to Gershom Scholem, 15 June 1938, NLI, ARC. 4*1599/01/2896; Gershom Scholem, *Major Trends in Jewish Mysticism* (Jerusalem: Schocken, 1941). The actual printing was done in Tel Aviv by Haaretz, which was owned by the Schocken family.

121. Gershom Scholem, *Major Trends in Jewish Mysticism* (1941 edition), 255–256 and 283.

122. Gershom Scholem, *Major Trends in Jewish Mysticism* (1941 edition), 325–329, quotes on 326 and 323.

123. Robert Alter, foreword to *Major Trends in Jewish Mysticism*, by Gershom Scholem (New York: Schocken, 1995), xviii-xx.

124. Gershom Scholem, *Major Trends in Jewish Mysticism* (1941 edition), 186–190.

125. Gershom Scholem to Walter Benjamin, 25 March 1938, in Benjamin and Scholem, *Correspondence-WBGS*, 214.

126. Gershom Scholem to Walter Benjamin, 6 May 1938, in Benjamin and Scholem, *Correspondence-WBGS*, 219.

127. Gershom Scholem to Walter Benjamin, 6–8 November 1938, in Benjamin and Scholem, *Correspondence-WBGS*, 234–235.

128. Gershom Scholem, *WBTSF*, 257–258 and 263–268.

129. Gershom Scholem to Walter Benjamin, 14 June 1938, and Walter Benjamin to Gershom Scholem, 8 July 1938, in Benjamin and Scholem, *Correspondence-WBGS*, 229 and 230; Gershom Scholem, *WBTSF*, 271.

130. Gershom Scholem to Walter Benjamin, 6–8 November 1938, in Benjamin and Scholem, *Correspondence-WBGS*, 232.

131. Gershom Scholem, *WBTSF*, 277–280; Max Horkheimer, "Die Juden und Europa," *Zeitschrift für Sozialforschung* 8, nos. 1–2 (1939): 115–137.

132. Gershom Scholem, *WBTSF*, 267–268; Gershom Scholem to Walter Benjamin, 30 June 1939, in Benjamin and Scholem, *Correspondence-WBGS*, 257; Hannah Arendt, *Rahel Varnhagen: The Life of a Jewess*, trans. Richard Winston and Clara Winston (London: East and West Library, 1957).

133. Gershom Scholem to Shalom Spiegel, 17 July 1941, in *Briefe*, 1:285.

134. Gershom Scholem to Shalom Spiegel, 8 January 1941, in *Briefe*, 1:284.

9. Afterlives

1. Reinhold Scholem to Gershom Scholem, 18 October 1938, NLI, ARC. 4*1599/01/3031.

2. Suzanne D. Rutland, *The Jews in Australia* (Cambridge: Cambridge University Press, 2005), 51.

3. Suzanne D. Rutland, *Edge of the Diaspora: Two Centuries of Jewish Settlement in Australia*, 2nd ed. (New York: Holmes and Meier, 1997), 142–143.

4. Rutland, *Edge of the Diaspora*, 166–167.

5. Rutland, *Jews in Australia*, 51 and 62–63; W. D. Rubinstein, *The Jews in Australia: A Thematic History*, vol. 2, *1945 to the Present* (Melbourne: William Heinemann, 1991), 51.

6. Betty Scholem to Gershom Scholem, 9 and 24 May and 29 December 1939, in *MuSiB*, 469–471, 473–474, and 482.

7. Betty Scholem to Gershom Scholem, 27 September 1940, in *MuSiB*, 493.

8. Betty Scholem to Gershom Scholem, 5 December 1939, in *MuSiB*, 479–480.

9. Betty Scholem to Gershom Scholem, 22 January 1939, in *MuSiB*, 458.

10. Betty Scholem to Gershom Scholem, 9 May 1939, in *MuSiB*, 470–471.

11. Betty Scholem to Gershom Scholem, 15 June 1941, in *MuSiB*, 501; Kaplan, *Between Dignity and Despair*, 88.

12. Betty Scholem to Gershom Scholem, 29 and 5 December 1939, in *MuSiB*, 479–482.

13. Gershom Scholem to Walter Benjamin, 2 March 1939, in Benjamin and Scholem, *Correspondence-WBGS*, 247.

14. Erich Scholem to Gershom Scholem, n.d. [1938], NLI, ARC. 4*1599/01/3024.

15. Betty Scholem to Gershom Scholem, 26 April 1941, in *MuSiB*, 499.

16. Betty Scholem to Gershom Scholem, 25 March 1945, in *MuSiB*, 523.

17. Rubinstein, *Jews in Australia*, 2:18.

18. Betty Scholem to Gershom Scholem, 26 April 1941 and 14 October 1942, in *MuSiB*, 497 and 511–512.

19. Betty Scholem to Gershom Scholem, 17 May 1944, in *MuSiB*, 512–513.

20. Betty Scholem to Gershom Scholem, 10 November 1940, in *MuSiB*, 495.

21. Betty Scholem to Gershom Scholem, 17 May 1944, in *MuSiB*, 512.

22. Betty Scholem to Gershom Scholem, 5 November 1944 and 25 March 1945, in *MuSiB*, 514, and 524.

23. Erich Scholem to Gershom Scholem, 15 May 1960, NLI, ARC. 4*1599/01/3024.

24. Erich Scholem to Gershom Scholem, 10 July 1960, NLI, ARC. 4*1599/01/3024.

25. Erich Scholem to Gershom Scholem, 15 May 1960, NLI, ARC. 4*1599/01/3024.

26. Erich Scholem to Gershom Scholem, 20 April 1960, end of December 1963, and 24 December 1961, NLI, ARC. 4*1599/01/3024.

27. Gershom Scholem, *VBnJ*, 47.

28. Reinhold Scholem to Gershom Scholem, 10 October 1965 and 29 February 1972, and Gershom Scholem to Reinhold Scholem, 16 November 1965 and 29 May 1972, NLI, ARC. 4*1599/01/3031.

29. Reinhold Scholem to Gershom Scholem, 22 April and 9 May 1971, NLI, ARC. 4*1599/01/3031.

30. E-mail message from Liesel Scholem and Stephen Scholem to the author, 25 April 2017; Reinhold Scholem to Gershom Scholem, 30 May 1973 and 19 April 1975, NLI, ARC. 4*1599/01/3031.

31. Arthur Scholem Jr. to Gershom Scholem, 8 July 1952, NLI, ARC. 4*1599/01/3020.

32. Renate Goddard-Scholem to Gershom Scholem, 16 August 1952, NLI, ARC. 4*1599/01/3010.

33. Reinhold Scholem to Gershom Scholem, 12 March 1946, NLI, ARC. 4*1599/01/3031.

34. Arthur Scholem Jr. to Gershom Scholem, 6 July 1951 and 20 April 1952, NLI, ARC. 4*1599/01/3020; Therese ("Esi") Lacher-Pogany to Gershom Scholem, 5 February 1951, NLI, ARC. 4*1599/01/3013.

35. N. Zadoff, *Gershom Scholem*, 77–79.

36. Gershom Scholem to Betty Scholem, 19 November 1944, in *MuSiB*, 517.

37. Betty Scholem to Gershom Scholem, 26 April 1941, in *MuSiB*, 496.

38. Gershom Scholem to Salman Schocken, 5 June 1941, NLI, ARC. 4*1599/01/3051.

39. Gershom Scholem to Salman Schocken, 9 October 1941, NLI, ARC. 4*1599/01/3051.

40. Moses, "Salman Schocken," *LBIYB* 5 (1960): 97–99.

41. Hans Kohn, "The Jewish Mystic," *Contemporary Jewish Record* 6, no. 6 (December 1943): 665–667; Gershom Scholem to Adolph S. Oko, 26 March 1944, in *Briefe*, 1:292.

42. Adolph S. Oko to Gershom Scholem, 25 May 1944 and 13 December 1943, and Gershom Scholem to Adolph S. Oko, 26 March 1944, in *Briefe*, 1:439n2, 1:438n1, and 1:292–293.

43. N. Zadoff, *Gershom Scholem*, 93–94; Gershom Scholem to Shalom Spiegel, 8 May 1945, in *Briefe*, 1:297.

44. Gershom Scholem to Leo Baeck, 2 June 1946, in *Briefe*, 1:314.

45. Gershom Scholem to Gustav Schocken, 31 January 1946, NLI, ARC. 4*1599/01/3055; Noam Zadoff, "Travelling to the Past, Creating the Future: Gershom Scholem's Journey to Germany in 1946," *Jewish Culture and History* 11, nos. 1–2 (2009): 199–208; N. Zadoff, *Gershom Scholem*, 95–141.

46. Gershom Scholem to David Werner Senator, 24 April 1946, NLI, ARC. 4*1599/02/23.

47. N. Zadoff, *Gershom Scholem*, 134–141.

48. Gershom Scholem to the Hebrew University of Jerusalem, 29 July 1946, in *Briefe*, 1:320.

49. Gershom Scholem to Rudolf Hagelstange, 22 June 1952, in *Briefe*, vol. 2, *1948–1970*, ed. Thomas Sparr (Munich: C. H. Beck, 1995), 32 (hereafter cited as *Briefe*).

50. Gershom Scholem, "Besuch bei den Juden in Deutschland," NLI, ARC. 4*1599/07/277.1.89.

51. Gershom Scholem to Hannah Arendt, 16 December 1945, in *Briefe*, 1:307 (quote); Gershom Scholem to Betty Scholem, 27 February 1945, in *MuSiB*, 520.

52. Gershom Scholem, "The Curious History of the Six-Pointed Star," *Commentary* 8, no. 3 (September 1949): 243–251, quote on 251.

53. Amnon Raz-Krakotzkin, "Binationalism and Jewish Identity: Hannah Arendt and the Question of Palestine," in *Hannah Arendt in Jerusalem*, ed. Steven E. Aschheim (Berkeley: University of California Press, 2001), 165–180; Marie-Luise Knott, "Hannah Arendt—Gershom Scholem. Die Konstellation," in *Hannah Arendt and Gershom Scholem, Der Briefwechsel: 1939–1964*, ed. Marie-Luise Knott (Frankfurt: Jüdischer Verlag im Suhrkamp Verlag, 2010), 608–642.

54. Hannah Arendt, "Zionism Reconsidered," *Menorah Journal* 32, no. 2 (October–December 1945): 162–196, quote on 194.

55. Gershom Scholem to Hannah Arendt, 28 January 1946, in *Briefe*, 1:309–314, quote on 309.

56. Hannah Arendt, "Eichmann in Jerusalem—III," *New Yorker*, 2 March 1963, 42; Hannah Arendt, *Eichmann in Jerusalem: A Report on the Banality of Evil* (New York: Viking, 1963), 105.

57. Gershom Scholem to Hannah Arendt, 23 June 1963, Hannah Arendt to Gershom Scholem, 24 July 1963, published as "'Eichmann in Jerusalem' (An Exchange of Letters)," *Encounter* 22, no. 1 (January 1964): 51–56, Scholem quotes on 51 and 52, Arendt quotes on 54. Originally published as "Ein Briefwechsel über Hannah Arendts Buch," *MB: Wochenzeitung des Irgun Olej Merkas Europa* 31, no. 33 (16 August 1963): 3–5, and "Ein Briefwechsel über Hannah Arendts Buch 'Eichmann in Jerusalem,'" *Neue Zürcher Zeitung* 184, no. 4247 (20 October 1963, Sonntagausgabe): n.p.

58. Gershom Scholem, "Martin Buber's Hasidism: A Critique," *Commentary* 32, no. 4 (October 1961): 305–316; Gershom Scholem, "Martin Bubers Deutung des Chassidismus I.," *Neue Zürcher Zeitung* 183, no. 2013 (20 May 1962, Sonntagausgabe): n.p.; Gershom Scholem, "Martin Bubers Deutung des Chassidismus II.," *Neue Zürcher Zeitung* 183, no. 2121 (27 May 1962, Sonntagausgabe): n.p.; Martin Buber, "Interpreting Hasidism," *Commentary* 36, no. 3 (September 1963): 218–225; Gershom Scholem, "Martin Buber's Interpretation of Hasidism," in *The Messianic Idea in Judaism,* 228–250.

59. Gershom Scholem to Theodor Adorno, 20 June 1965, in *Briefe,* 2:139.

60. Diary entry, 22 January 1959, in Bergman, *Tagebücher und Briefe,* 2:299.

61. Biale, *Gershom Scholem* (1982), 147.

62. Prochnik, *Stranger in a Strange Land,* 410–417; N. Zadoff, *Gershom Scholem,* xviii.

63. Biale, *Gershom Scholem* (2018), 170.

64. Amos Funkenstein, "Gershom Scholem: Charisma, *Kairos* and the Messianic Dialectic," *History and Memory* 4, no. 1 (Spring/Summer 1992): 124; Daniel Weidner, "Reading Gershom Scholem," *Jewish Quarterly Review* 96, no. 2 (Spring 2006): 203.

65. Wasserstrom, *Religion after Religion.*

66. Ozick, "Mystic Explorer," *New York Times,* 21 September 1980.

67. Jorge Luis Borges, "El Golem," in *El Otro, el Mismo* (Buenos Aires: Emecé Editores, 1969), 47–49.

68. Edgar L. Chapman, "The Mandala Design of Patrick White's *Riders in the Chariot,*" *Texas Studies in Literature and Language* 21, no. 2 (Summer 1979): 201n31.

69. Joseph Dan, ed., *The Heart and the Fountain: An Anthology of Jewish Mystical Experiences* (Oxford: Oxford University Press, 2002), 288n8.

70. Ozick, "Mystic Explorer," *New York Times,* 21 September 1980.

71. E.g., Cynthia Ozick, "Slouching toward Smyrna," review of *Sabbatai Sevi: The Mystical Messiah, 1626–1676,* by Gershom Scholem, *New York Times,* 24 February 1974; Arthur A. Cohen, "Passionate Scholar," review of *On Jews and Judaism in Crisis,* by Gershom Scholem, *New York Times,* 11 September 1977; Eleanor Blau, "Scholars Laud Reviver of Jewish Mystic Past," *New York Times,* 18 October 1975.

72. Editor's biographical comment on Gershom Scholem, "Jews and Germans," *Commentary* 42, no. 6 (November 1966): 31.

73. Robert Alter, "The Achievement of Gershom Scholem," *Commentary* 55, no. 4 (April 1973): 69–77.

74. Gershom Scholem, *Zur Kabbala und ihrer Symbolik* (Zurich: Rhein-Verlag, 1960); cf. Gershom G. Scholem, *On the Kabbalah and Its Symbolism,* trans. Ralph Manheim (London: Routledge and Kegan Paul, 1965); Gershom Scholem, *Ursprung und Anfänge der Kabbala* (Berlin: Walter de Gruyter, 1962); cf. Gershom Scholem, *Origins of the Kabbalah,* ed. R. J. Zwi Werblowsky, trans. Allan Arkush (Philadelphia: Jewish Publication Society, 1987).

75. N. Zadoff, *Gershom Scholem,* xvii.

76. Gershom Scholem to Reinhold Scholem, 25 May 1968, 4 July 1973, and 8 July and 31 August 1981, NLI, ARC. 4*1599/01/3031; Gershom Scholem to Hans-Georg Gadamer, 7 March 1969, in *Briefe,* 2:220–221; Gershom Scholem to Hellmut Becker, 2 July 1981, in *Briefe,* 3:236–237; Gershom Scholem, "Mein Weg zur Kabbala," *Süddeutsche Zeitung,* Feuilleton section, 20/21 July 1974; comments on Hessischer

Rundfunk, Frankfurt am Main, 1967, released as an audio CD: Gershom Scholem, *Die Erforschung der Kabbala* (Cologne: supposé, 2006).

77. Gershom Scholem to Walter Benjamin, 25 March, 6 May, and 6–8 November 1938, in Benjamin and Scholem, *Correspondence-WBGS*, 214, 219, and 234–235.

78. Gershom Scholem, "My Way to Kabbalah (1974)," in *On the Possibility of Jewish Mysticism in Our Time and Other Essays*, ed. Avraham Shapira, trans. Jonathan Chipman (Philadelphia: Jewish Publication Society, 1997), 24; Wasserstrom, *Religion after Religion*.

79. Gershom Scholem to Reinhold Scholem, 25 May 1968, NLI, ARC. 4*1599/01/3031.

80. Erich Scholem to Gershom Scholem, 6 December 1960, NLI, ARC. 4*1599/01/3024.

81. Gershom Scholem, "The Golem of Prague and the Golem of Rehovoth," *Commentary* 41, no. 1 (January 1966): 62–65.

82. Diary entry, 28 March 1961, in Bergman, *Tagebücher und Briefe*, 2:366; Gershom Scholem to Reinhold Scholem, 25 May 1968, NLI, ARC. 4*1599/01/3031.

83. Gershom Scholem, "On Sentencing Eichmann to Death," *Journal of International Criminal Justice* 4, no. 4 (September 2006): 859–861; Fania Scholem to Reinhold Scholem, 17 December 1961, NLI, ARC. 4*1599/01/3031.

84. Diary entry, 28 March 1961, in Bergman, *Tagebücher und Briefe*, 2:366.

85. "Security and Peace—yes, Annexation—no" [Hebrew], *Haaretz*, 15 December 1967.

86. Gershom Scholem, "A Lecture About Israel (1967)," in *On the Possibility of Jewish Mysticism*, 39.

87. Gershom Scholem to Reinhold Scholem, 1 August 1977, NLI, ARC. 4*1599/01/3031.

88. Gershom Scholem, *Shabtai Tsevi veha-tenu'ah ha-shabta'it bi-yeme hayav* (Tel Aviv: Am Oved, 1956/1957); Gershom Scholem, *Sabbatai Sevi: The Mystical Messiah, 1626–1676*, trans. R. J. Zwi Werblowsky (Princeton, N.J.: Princeton University Press, 1973); Biale, *Gershom Scholem* (2018), 171–175.

89. Engel, *Gershom Scholem*, 1–5.

90. Harold Bloom, "Scholem: Unhistorischer oder jüdischer Gnostizismus," *Babylon. Beiträge zur jüdischen Gegenwart* 1 (1986): 70, reprinted as "Scholem: Unhistorical or Jewish Gnosticism," in Bloom, *Gershom Scholem*, 207.

91. George Steiner, "The Friend of a Friend," *New Yorker*, 22 January 1990, 134.

92. Ozick, "Mystic Explorer," *New York Times*, 21 September 1980.

93. Reinhold Scholem to Gershom Scholem, 25 November 1946, 31 August 1958, and 22 April 1971, NLI, ARC. 4*1599/01/3031.

94. Reinhold Scholem to Gershom Scholem, 10 February 1978, NLI, ARC. 4*1599/01/3031; Rubinstein, *Jews in Australia*, 2:34.

95. Reinhold Scholem to Gershom Scholem, 28 March 1971, 30 May 1973, and 28 January 1974, NLI, ARC. 4*1599/01/3031.

96. Reinhold Scholem to Gershom Scholem, 28 October 1948, NLI, ARC. 4*1599/01/3031; Therese ("Esi") Lacher-Pogany to Gershom Scholem, 5 February 1951, NLI, ARC. 4*1599/01/3013.

97. Reinhold Scholem to Gershom Scholem, 3 May 1947 and 31 March 1951, NLI, ARC. 4*1599/01/3031; Arthur Scholem Jr. to Gershom Scholem, 6 July 1951, 20 April and 8 July 1952, and 12 February 1970, NLI, ARC. 4*1599/01/3020.

98. Reinhold Scholem to Gershom Scholem, 31 March 1951 and 11 April 1960, NLI, ARC. 4*1599/01/3031; Erich Scholem to Gershom Scholem, end of December 1963, NLI, ARC. 4*1599/01/3024.

99. Reinhold Scholem to Gershom Scholem, 5 September 1954 and 9 December 1956, NLI, ARC. 4*1599/01/3031; Erich Scholem to Gershom Scholem, 24 December 1959, NLI, ARC. 4*1599/01/3024.

100. Reinhold Scholem to Gershom Scholem, 4 March 1965, NLI, ARC. 4*1599/01/3031.

101. Gershom Scholem to Reinhold Scholem, 26 February 1965, NLI, ARC. 4*1599/01/3031; Gershom Scholem to Hilde Scholem, 26 February 1965, NLI, ARC. 4*1599/01/3024.

102. Emmy Wiechelt Scholem to Gershom Scholem, 3 October 1958 and 7 February 1967, NLI, ARC. 4*1599/01/3023.

103. Emmy Wiechelt Scholem to Gershom Scholem, 12 April 1968, NLI, ARC. 4*1599/01/3023; Gershom Scholem, VBnJ, 35.

104. Gershom Scholem, "Wider den Mythos vom deutsch-jüdischen 'Gespräch,'" in Auf gespaltenem Pfad, ed. Manfred Schlösser (Darmstadt: Erato-Presse, 1964), 229–232.

105. Gay, Freud, Jews and Other Germans, x-xi; Gershom Scholem to Robert Alter, 29 October 1978, and Gershom Scholem to George Steiner, 9 July 1980, in Briefe, 3:193–194 and 3:209; Stern, Five Germanys I Have Known, 367–368.

106. Reinhold Scholem to Gershom Scholem, 29 February 1972 and 10 October 1965, NLI, ARC. 4*1599/01/3031.

107. Gershom Scholem to Lisl Mühlstein, 7 November 1966, in Briefe, 2:152.

108. Gershom Scholem to Reinhold Scholem, 26 July 1966, and Reinhold Scholem to Gershom Scholem, 21 August 1966, NLI, ARC. 4*1599/01/3031.

109. Gershom Scholem to Reinhold Scholem, 25 May 1968, NLI, ARC. 4*1599/01/3031.

110. Gershom Scholem to Südwest Verlag, 13 September 1966, NLI, ARC. 4*1599/01/2584; correspondence with Suhrkamp Verlag, 1953–82, NLI, ARC. 4*1599/01/3040–3048.

111. Günter Scholem to Gershom Scholem, 22 April 1979, NLI, ARC. 4*1599/01/3028; Reinhold Scholem to Gershom Scholem, 11 March and 10 December 1978, and 28 February and 9 May 1979, NLI, ARC. 4*1599/01/3031.

112. Reinhold Scholem to Gershom Scholem, 26 June and 10 September 1981, and n.d. [document 129, August or September 1981], NLI, ARC. 4*1599/01/3031; Gershom Scholem to Irmgard and Arthur Scholem Jr., 12 November 1980, in Briefe, 3:220.

113. Gershom Scholem to Reinhold Scholem, 15 December 1981, NLI, ARC. 4*1599/01/3031; Gershom Scholem to Peter Wapnewski, 31 January 1982, in Briefe, 3:252–254; "Gershom Scholem, Professor of Jewish Mysticism, Is Dead," New York Times, 22 February 1982.

Conclusion

1. Jersch-Wenzel, "Population Shifts and Occupational Structure," in Meyer, GJHMT, 2:54–57; Lowenstein, Berlin Jewish Community, 3 and 16. "German lands"

refs to states within the future borders of the German Empire as well as Austrian Bohemia, Moravia, Lower Austria, Upper Austria, Styria, Carinthia, Salzburg, Tyrol, and Vorarlberg.

2. Data from 1910, Richarz, "Demographic Developments," in Meyer, *GJHMT*, 3:26–30.

3. Richarz, "Occupational Distribution and Social Structure," in Meyer, *GJHMT*, 3:61.

4. Richarz, "Occupational Distribution and Social Structure," in Meyer, *GJHMT*, 3:60.

5. Stern, *Five Germanys I Have Known*, 11.

6. Jürgen Karwelat, "Antisemit, Kriegshetzer. Soll nach Reinhold Seeberg auch in Zukunft eine Straße im Grunewaldviertel benannt sein?," *Die Tageszeitung*, 7 October 1996; "Seebergsteig behält seinen Namen," *Der Tagesspiegel*, 16 October 1996.

7. Freunde der Hebräischen Universität Jerusalem in Berlin e. V. to Eberhard Diepgen, 7 February 1985, NLI, ARC. 4*1599/02/270.

8. Alfred Etzold, *Ein Berliner Kulturdenkmal von Weltgeltung. Der jüdische Friedhof Berlin-Weissensee* (Berlin: Hentrich und Hentrich, 2006), 37 and 82.

9. Hartmut von Hentig, *Mein Leben—bedacht und bejaht*, vol. 2, *Schule, Polis, Gartenhaus* (Munich: Carl Hanser, 2007), 570–571; N. Zadoff, *Gershom Scholem*, 236–240.

BIBLIOGRAPHY

Unpublished Primary Sources

Berliner Turner-Verein von 1850 e. V.
Stammrolle

Bundesarchiv, Berlin-Lichterfelde
Kommunistische Partei Deutschlands
Nationalsozialistische Justiz
Oberreichsanwalt beim Reichsgericht
Oberreichsanwalt beim Volksgerichtshof
Reichsministerium des Innern

Geheimes Staatsarchiv Preußischer Kulturbesitz, Berlin
Strafsachen, 1763–71

International Tracing Service, Bad Arolsen
Werner Scholem file

Landesarchiv Berlin
Handelsregister, Amtsgericht Charlottenburg
Köllnisches Gymnasium
Luisenstädtisches Gymnasium
Standesamtsbestände
Wiedergutmachungsämter

Landesamt für Gesundheit und Soziales, Berlin
Versorgungsamt-Krankenbuchlager

Leo Baeck Institute, Center for Jewish History, New York
Ludwig Bendix Papers

Leibniz Universität Hannover, Institut für Politische Wissenschaft
Nachlass Werner Scholem

National Archives, Kew, Richmond, Surrey, England

National Library of Israel, Archive Department, Jerusalem
Escha Bergman Collection
Gershom Scholem Collection

Adam Scholem Collection

David Scholem Collection

Interviews and private communications between the author and Adam Scholem, David Scholem, Irene Scholem Ellison, Liesel Scholem, Peter Scholem, Stephen Scholem, and Renee Goddard (née Renate Scholem)

Published Primary Sources

"An die deutschen Juden!" *Im deutschen Reich* 20, no. 9 (September 1914): 339.

Arendt, Hannah. *Eichmann in Jerusalem: A Report on the Banality of Evil.* New York: Viking, 1963.

Arendt, Hannah. "Eichmann in Jerusalem—III." *New Yorker*, 2 March 1963, 40–91.

Arendt, Hannah. *Rahel Varnhagen: The Life of a Jewess.* Translated by Richard Winston and Clara Winston. London: East and West Library, 1957.

Arendt, Hannah. "Zionism Reconsidered." *Menorah Journal* 32, no. 2 (October– December 1945): 162–196.

Beilinson, M[oshe]. *Zum Jüdisch-Arabischen Problem. Eine Aufsatzreihe.* Tel Aviv: Verlag "Dawar," 1930.

Benjamin, Walter. *The Correspondence of Walter Benjamin, 1910–1940.* Chicago: University of Chicago Press, 1994.

Benjamin, Walter. *Gesammelte Briefe.* Vol. 1, *1910–1918.* Edited by Christoph Gödde and Henri Lonitz. 1995. Reprint, Frankfurt: Suhrkamp, 2016.

Benjamin, Walter. *Gesammelte Briefe.* Vol. 2, *1919–1924.* Edited by Christoph Gödde and Henri Lonitz. Frankfurt: Suhrkamp, 1996.

Benjamin, Walter, and Gershom Scholem. *The Correspondence of Walter Benjamin and Gershom Scholem, 1932–1940.* Edited by Gershom Scholem. Translated by Gary Smith and André Lefevere. Cambridge, Mass.: Harvard University Press, 1992.

Ben-Zwi, I. [Yitzhak Ben-Zvi]. *Jerusalem.* Jerusalem: Goldberg's Press, 1936.

Bergman, Schmuel Hugo. *Tagebücher und Briefe.* Vol. 1, *1901–1948.* Edited by Miriam Sambursky. Königstein: Jüdischer Verlag bei Athenäum, 1985.

Bergman, Schmuel Hugo. *Tagebücher und Briefe.* Vol. 2, *1948–1975.* Edited by Miriam Sambursky. Königstein: Jüdischer Verlag bei Athenäum, 1985.

Berlin (Germany). Statistisches Amt der Stadt Berlin. *Statistisches Jahrbuch der Stadt Berlin.* Vol. 3, *1927.* Berlin: Otto Stollberg, Verlag für Politik und Wirtschaft, 1927.

Berlin (Germany). Statistisches Amt der Stadt Berlin. *Statistisches Jahrbuch der Stadt Berlin.* Vol. 27, *Enthaltend die Statistik der Jahre 1900 bis 1902.* Edited by E. Hirschberg. Berlin: P. Stankiewicz' Buchdruckerei, 1903.

Berlin (Germany). Statistisches Amt der Stadt Berlin. *Statistisches Taschenbuch der Stadt Berlin 1924.* Berlin: Otto Stollberg, Verlag für Politik und Wirtschaft, 1924.

Berlin (Germany). Statistisches Bureau der Stadt Berlin. *Berliner Städtisches Jahrbuch für Volkswirthschaft und Statistik.* Vol. 1. Edited by H. Schwabe. Berlin: Leonhard Simion, 1874.

Berliner Adressbuch für das Jahr 1875. Edited by A. Ludwig. Berlin: Societät der Berliner Bürger-Zeitung, 1875.

Berliner Adressbuch für das Jahr 1889. Edited by A. Ludwig. 2 vols. Berlin: W. & S. Loewenthal, 1889.

Berliner Adressbuch 1921. Vol. 1. Berlin: August Scherl, 1921.

Betten, Anne, and Miryam Du-nour, eds. *Wir sind die Letzten. Fragt uns aus. Gespräche mit den Emigranten der dreißiger Jahre in Israel.* 3rd ed. Gerlinger: Bleicher, 1998.

Bialik, Chaim Nachman. "Halacha und Aggada." Translated by Gerhard Scholem. *Der Jude* 4, nos. 1–2 (1919): 61–77.

Boicke, J. W., ed. *Allgemeiner Wohnungsanzeiger für Berlin auf das Jahr 1827*. Berlin: J. W. Boicke, 1827.

Borges, Jorge Luis. "El Golem." In *El Otro, el Mismo*, 47–49. Buenos Aires: Emecé Editores, 1969.

"Brief des Exekutivkomitees der Komintern an den X. Parteitag der Kommunistischen Partei Deutschlands." In Kommunistische Partei Deutschlands, *Beschlüsse des X. Parteitages der Kommunistischen Partei Deutschlands*, 77–87. Berlin: Zentralkomitee der K.P.D., 1925.

Brit Shalom. *Memorandum by the "Brith Shalom" Society on an Arab Policy for the Jewish Agency*. Jerusalem: Azriel Press, 1930.

Buber, Martin. "Interpreting Hasidism." *Commentary* 36, no. 3 (September 1963): 218-225.

Bureau des Reichstages. *Reichstags-Handbuch, II. Wahlperiode 1924*. Berlin: Reichsdruckerei, 1924.

Centralverein deutscher Staatsbürger jüdischen Glaubens. *Mitglieder-Verzeichnis 1908*. Berlin: Das Vereinsbureau, 1908.

Centralverein deutscher Staatsbürger jüdischen Glaubens. *Mitglieder-Verzeichnis des Verbandes Groß-Berliner Ortsgruppen*. Berlin: Centralverein deutscher Staatsbürger jüdischen Glaubens, 1919.

"Diskussion über das Referat 'Die weltpolitische Lage und die Aufgaben der Komintern' und den Bericht der Zentrale: Scholem." In Zentrale der Kommunistischen Partei Deutschlands, *Bericht über die Verhandlung des X. Parteitages der Kommunistischen Partei Deutschlands*, 391–396. Berlin: Vereinigung Internationaler Verlagsanstalten, 1925.

"'Eichmann in Jerusalem' (An Exchange of Letters)." *Encounter* 22, no. 1 (January 1964): 51–56.

Federn, Ernst [t.n.]. "In Memoriam: Werner Scholem." *Die Internationale. Theoretische Zeitschrift der Gruppe Internationale Marxisten (GIM), Deutsche Sektion der IV. Internationale*, no. 16 (June 1981): 117–120.

Fischer, Ruth, and Arkadij Maslow. *Abtrünnig wider Willen. Aus Briefen und Manuskripten des Exils*. Edited by Peter Lübbe. Munich: R. Oldenbourg, 1990.

Fontane, Theodor. *Briefe Theodor Fontanes*. 2nd collection. 2nd ed. Edited by Otto Pniower and Paul Schlenther. Vol. 2. Berlin: F. Fontane, 1910.

Frankfurt am Main (Germany). Statistisches Amt. *Statistisches Handbuch der Stadt Frankfurt a. M.*, 2nd ed., *Enthaltend die Statistik der Jahre 1906/07 bis 1926/27*. Frankfurt am Main: August Osterrieth, 1928.

Freie Universität Berlin, Zentralinstitut für sozialwissenschaftliche Forschung, ed. *Gedenkbuch Berlins. Der jüdischen Opfer des Nationalsozialismus*. Berlin: Edition Hentrich, 1995.

Fried, Alfred H. *Wien-Berlin. Ein Vergleich*. Vienna: Josef Lenobel Verlagsbuchhandlung, 1908.

Friedlander, Henry, and Sybil Milton, ed., *Archives of the Holocaust*. Vol. 20, *Bundesarchiv of the Federal Republic of Germany, Koblenz and Freiburg*. New York: Garland, 1993.

Friedrich-Wilhelms-Universität zu Berlin. *Amtliches Verzeichnis des Personals und der Studierenden der Königlichen Friedrich-Wilhelms-Universität zu Berlin*. Berlin: Gustav Schade, 1895.

Friedrich-Wilhelms-Universität zu Berlin. *Amtliches Verzeichnis des Personals und der Studierenden der Königlichen Friedrich-Wilhelms-Universität zu Berlin*. Berlin: Gustav Schade, 1899.

Friedrich-Wilhelms-Universität zu Berlin. *Amtliches Verzeichnis des Personals und der Studierenden der Königlichen Friedrich-Wilhelms-Universität zu Berlin*. Berlin: Universitäts-Buchdruckerei von Gustav Schade, 1915.

Friedrich-Wilhelms-Universität zu Berlin. *Amtliches Verzeichnis des Personals und der Studierenden der Königlichen Friedrich-Wilhelms-Universität zu Berlin auf das Winterhalbjahr vom 16. Oktober 1915 bis 15. März 1916*. Berlin: Arthur Scholem, 1915.

Friedrich-Wilhelms-Universität zu Berlin. *Vorschriften für die Studierenden der Königlichen Friedrich-Wilhelms-Universität zu Berlin*. Berlin: Universitäts-Buchdruckerei von Gustav Schade, 1912.

Germany. Reichstag. *Verhandlungen des Reichstags, XIII. Legislaturperiode. II. Session*. Vol. 306, *Stenographische Berichte. Von der Eröffnungssitzung am 4. August 1914 bis zur 34. Sitzung am 16. März 1916*. Berlin: Norddeutsche Buchdruckerei und Verlags-Anstalt, 1916.

Germany. Reichstag. *Verhandlungen des Reichstags. II. Wahlperiode 1924*. Vol. 381, *Stenographische Berichte (von der 1. Sitzung am 27. Mai 1924 bis zur 29. Sitzung am 30. August 1924)*. Berlin: Verlag der Reichsdruckerei, 1924.

Germany. Statistisches Reichsamt. *Statistisches Jahrbuch für das Deutsche Reich*. Vol. 44, *1924/25*. Berlin: Verlag für Politik und Wirtschaft, 1925.

Germany. Statistisches Reichsamt. *Statistisches Jahrbuch für das Deutsche Reich*. Vol. 45, *1926*. Berlin: Reimar Hobbing, 1926.

Germany. Statistisches Reichsamt. *Statistisches Jahrbuch für das Deutsche Reich*. Vol. 46, *1927*. Berlin: Reimar Hobbing, 1927.

Germany. Statistisches Reichsamt. *Statistisches Jahrbuch für das Deutsche Reich*. Vol. 49, *1930*. Berlin: Reimar Hobbing, 1930.

Germany. Statistisches Reichsamt. *Statistisches Jahrbuch für das Deutsche Reich*. Vol. 50, *1931*. Berlin: Reimar Hobbing, 1931.

Germany. Statistisches Reichsamt. *Statistisches Jahrbuch für das Deutsche Reich*. Vol. 51, *1932*. Berlin: Reimar Hobbing, 1932.

Germany. Statistisches Reichsamt. *Statistisches Jahrbuch für das Deutsche Reich*. Vol. 52, *1933*. Berlin: Reimar Hobbing, 1933.

Germany. Statistisches Reichsamt. *Statistisches Jahrbuch für das Deutsche Reich*. Vol. 53, *1934*. Berlin: Reimar Hobbing, 1934.

Goebbels, Joseph. *Communism with the Mask Off: Speech Delivered in Nürnberg on September 13th, 1935 at the Seventh National Socialist Party Congress*. Berlin: M. Müller & Sohn K. G., [1935].

Goebbels, Joseph. *Die Tagebücher von Joseph Goebbels*. Edited by Elke Fröhlich. Pt. 1, *Aufzeichnungen 1923–1941*. Vol. 1/I, *Oktober 1923–November 1925*. Munich: K. G. Saur, 2004.

Goebbels, Joseph. *Die Tagebücher von Joseph Goebbels*. Edited by Elke Fröhlich. Pt. 1, *Aufzeichnungen 1923–1941*. Vol. 2/III, *Oktober 1932–März 1934*. Munich: K. G. Saur, 2006.

Graeser, Erdmann. *Spreelore*. Berlin: Das Neue Berlin, 1950.

Great Britain. Colonial Office. *Palestine. Statement of Policy*. London: HMSO, 1939.

Great Britain. Palestine Partition Commission. *Report*. London: HMSO, 1938.

Great Britain. Palestine Royal Commission. *Report*. London: HMSO, 1937.

Great Britain. *Report of the Commission on the Palestine Disturbances of August, 1929*. London: HMSO, 1930.

Gruber, Ruth. *Israel Without Tears*. New York: A. A. Wyn, 1950.

"Gründung der 'Jüdischen Turnerschaft.'" In *Dokumente zur Geschichte des deutschen Zionismus 1882–1933*, edited by Jehuda Reinharz, 79–80. Tübingen: J. C. B. Mohr, 1981.

Hackett, David A., ed. and trans. *The Buchenwald Report*. Boulder, Colo.: Westview, 1995.

"Hans Hirsch Must Leave Germany." *Bulletin of the American Ceramic Society* 18, no. 2 (February 1939): 76.

Hentig, Hartmut von. *Mein Leben—bedacht und bejaht*. Vol. 2, *Schule, Polis, Gartenhaus*. Munich: Carl Hanser, 2007.

Heuss, Theodor. *Aufbruch im Kaiserreich. Briefe 1892–1917*. Edited by Frieder Günther. Munich: K. G. Saur, 2009.

Hinze, Friedrich Heimbertsohn. *Poetische Schriften*. Edited by Friedrich Meyer von Waldeck. Berlin: A. Duncker, 1859.

Hirsch, Hans. "Über Kondensationen halogenierter ß-Naphtochinone mit Methylenderivaten." Dr.phil. diss., Friedrich-Wihelms-Universität zu Berlin, 1900.

Hirsch, Käte. "Zur Frage der Frühoperation der Membrana Descemeti bei eitriger Keratitis." Dr.med. diss., Albert-Ludwigs-Universität zu Freiburg im Breisgau, 1904.

Honigmann, Barbara. *Roman von einem Kinde. Sechs Erzählungen*. Darmstadt: Luchterhand, 1986.

Horkheimer, Max. "Die Juden und Europa." *Zeitschrift für Sozialforschung* 8, nos. 1–2 (1939): 115–137.

Jacobson, Jacob. *Die Judenbürgerbücher der Stadt Berlin 1809–1851*. Berlin: Walter de Gruyter, 1962.

Jiskor. Ein Buch des Gedenkens an gefallene Wächter und Arbeiter im Lande Israel. Translated by N. N. [Nomen Nescio]. Berlin: Jüdischer Verlag, 1918.

[Jüdische Gemeinde zu Berlin]. *Verzeichnis der wahlfähigen Mitglieder der jüdischen Gemeinde zu Berlin im Jahre 1895*. Berlin: Jacoby, [1895].

[Jüdische Gemeinde zu Berlin]. *Verzeichnis der wahlfähigen Mitglieder der jüdischen Gemeinde zu Berlin im Jahre 1907*. Berlin: Jacoby, [1907].

[Das Jüdische Volksheim Berlin]. *Das Jüdische Volksheim Berlin. Erster Bericht, Mai/ Dezember 1916*. Leipzig: Oscar Brandstetter, [1916 or 1917].

Kästner, Erich. *Fabian. Die Geschichte eines Moralisten*. Stuttgart: Deutsche Verlags-Anstalt, 1931.

Kautsky, Benedikt. *Teufel und Verdammte. Erfahrungen und Erkenntnisse aus sieben Jahren in deutschen Konzentrationslagern*. Zürich: Büchergilde Gutenberg, 1946.

Klemperer, Victor. *Curriculum Vitae. Jugend um 1900*. Vol. 1. Berlin: Siedler Verlag, 1989.

Klemperer, Victor. *I Will Bear Witness: A Diary of the Nazi Years, 1933–1941*. Translated by Martin Chalmers. New York: Random House, 1998.

Klemperer, Victor. *I Will Bear Witness: A Diary of the Nazi Years, 1942–1945*. Translated by Martin Chalmers. New York: Random House, 1999.

Klieman, Aaron S., ed. *The Rise of Israel*. Vol. 15, *Practical Zionism, 1920–1939*. New York: Garland, 1987.

Klieman, Aaron S., ed. *The Rise of Israel*. Vol. 16, *The Jewish Yishuv's Development in the Interwar Period*. New York: Garland, 1987.

Klieman, Aaron S., ed. *The Rise of Israel*. Vol. 18, *The Turn toward Violence, 1920–1929*. New York: Garland, 1987.

Klieman, Aaron S., ed. *The Rise of Israel*. Vol. 24, *The Royal Commission Report, 1937*. New York: Garland, 1987.

Klieman, Aaron S., ed. *The Rise of Israel*. Vol. 27, *The Darkest Year, 1939*. New York: Garland, 1987.

Kohn, Hans. "The Jewish Mystic." *Contemporary Jewish Record* 6, no. 6 (December 1943): 665–667.

Köllnisches Gymnasium zu Berlin. *Jahresbericht über das Schuljahr 1895–96*. Berlin: Felgentreff, 1896.

Kolmar, Gertrud. "Susanna." In *Das Leere Haus. Prosa jüdischer Dichter*, ed. Karl Otten, 291–336. Stuttgart: Cotta-Verlag, 1959.

Kommunistische Partei Deutschlands. "Artikel des Genossen Sinowjew." In *Bericht über die Verhandlungen des IX. Parteitages der Kommunistischen Partei Deutschlands (Sektion der Kommunistischen Internationale) abgehalten in Frankfurt a. M. vom 7. bis 10. April 1924*, 79–85. Berlin: Vereinigung Internationaler Verlagsanstalten, 1924.

Kraus, Karl. *Frühe Schriften 1892–1900*. Vol. 1, *1892–1896*. Edited by Joh. J. Braakenburg. Munich: Kösel-Verlag, 1979.

Kraus, Karl. "Länder und Leute." In *Sprüche und Widersprüche*, 195–216. Munich: Albert Langen, 1909.

Kuschey, Bernhard. *Die Ausnahme des Überlebens. Ernst und Hilde Federn. Eine biographische Studie und eine Analyse der Binnenstrukturen des Konzentrationslagers*. Gießen: Psychosozial-Verlag, 2003.

Lasker-Schüler, Else. "Das Hebräerland." In *Gesammelte Werke*, vol. 2, *Prosa und Schauspiele*, edited by Friedhelm Kemp, 785–971. Munich: Kösel-Verlag, 1962.

Löwenthal, Ernst G. *Philo-Atlas. Handbuch für die jüdische Auswanderung*. Berlin: Philo G.m.b.H, Jüdischer Buchverlag, 1938.

Luisenstädtisches Realgymnasium. *Bericht über das Schuljahr 1886–1887*. Berlin: Otto Elsner, 1887.

Luisenstädtisches Realgymnasium. *Bericht über das Schuljahr 1901–1902*. Berlin: Naucksche Buchdruckerei, 1902.

Luisenstädtisches Realgymnasium in Berlin. *Bericht über das Schuljahr 1914–1915*. Berlin: Naucksche Buchdruckerei, 1915.

Maximilian, Prince of Baden [Baden, Prinz Max von]. *Erinnerungen und Dokumente*. Edited by Golo Mann and Andreas Burckhardt. Stuttgart: Ernst Klett, 1968.

Mills, E. *Census of Palestine 1931*. Jerusalem: Greek Convent and Goldberg Presses, 1932.

Moaus zur. Ein Chanukkahbuch. Berlin: Jüdischer Verlag, 1918.

Nicolai, Friedrich. *Beschreibung der Königlichen Residenzstädte Berlin und Potsdam, aller daselbst befindlicher Merkwürdigkeiten, und der umliegenden Gegend*. 3rd ed. Berlin: Friedrich Nicolai, 1786.

Office of the United States Chief Counsel for Prosecution of Axis Criminality. *Nazi Conspiracy and Aggression*. Vol. 4. Washington, D.C.: United States Government Printing Office, 1946.

Ozick, Cynthia. *Art and Ardor*. New York: Alfred A. Knopf, 1983.

Palestine. *Report and General Abstracts of the Census of 1922*. Edited by J. B. Barron. Jerusalem: Greek Convent Press, 1923.

Palestine Zionist Executive, Immigration Department, ed. *Ten Years of Jewish Immigration into Palestine, 1919–1928*. Jerusalem: s.n., 1929.

Plessner, Salomon, ed. *Dat Moshe ve-yehudit oder Jüdisch-Mosaischer Religionsunterricht für die israelitische Jugend. Ein für den öffentlichen, auch Privat- und Selbstunterricht sich eignendes Lehrbuch der Hauptreligionswahrheiten und Lehren des Judenthums*. Berlin: L. Fernbach, jun., 1838.

Prussia (Germany). *Gesetz-Sammlung für die Königlichen Preußischen Staaten 1812*. Berlin: Georg Decker, [1812].

Prussia (Germany). Landtag. *Sitzungsberichte des Preußischen Landtags. 1. Wahlperiode. 1. Tagung: begonnen am 10. März 1921*. Vol. 1. Berlin: Preußische Verlagsanstalt, 1922.

Reichsbund jüdischer Frontsoldaten, ed. *Die jüdischen Gefallenen des deutschen Heeres, der deutschen Marine und der deutschen Schutztruppen 1914–1918. Ein Gedenkbuch*. Berlin: "Der Schild," 1932.

Reichsklub der Deutschen Volkspartei e. V. *Mitgliederverzeichnis April 1923*. Berlin: n.p., [1923].

Rosenzweig, Franz. *Briefe*. Edited by Edith Rosenzweig. Berlin: Schocken, 1935.

"Satzung der Jüdischen Turnerschaft." *Jüdische Turnzeitung* 6, nos. 5/6 (May/June 1905): 91–95.

Scheidemann, Philipp. *Memoiren eines Sozialdemokraten*. Vol. 2. Hamburg: Severus, 2010.

Scholem, Arthur. *Allerlei für Deutschlands Turner*. Berlin: Arthur Scholem, 1885.

Scholem, Betty. "Aufzeichnung von Mutter." In B. Scholem and G. Scholem, *Mutter und Sohn im Briefwechsel 1917–1946*, 527–531.

Scholem, Betty. "Ex Oriente Lux." In *Divided Passions: Jewish Intellectuals and the Experience of Modernity*, by Paul Mendes-Flohr, 111–121. Detroit, Mich.: Wayne State University Press, 1991.

Scholem, Betty, and Gershom Scholem. *Mutter und Sohn im Briefwechsel 1917–1946*. Edited by Itta Shedletzky. Munich: C. H. Beck, 1989.

Scholem, Georg. "Über Unguentum hydrargyri colloidalis (Mercurcolloid) seine Anwendungsweise und Wirkung." Dr.med. diss., Universität Leipzig, 1901.

Scholem, Gerhard [Gershom]. "Alchemie und Kabbala. Ein Kapitel aus der Geschichte der Mystik." *Monatsschrift für Geschichte und Wissenschaft des Judentums* 69, nos. 1/2 (January/February 1925): 13–30.

Scholem, Gerhard [Gershom]. *Das Buch Bahir. Ein Schriftdenkmal aus der Frühzeit der Kabbala auf Grund der kritischen Neuausgabe*. Leipzig: W. Drugulin, 1923.

Scholem, Gerhard [Gershom]. *Das Buch Bahir. Sepher Ha-Bahir. Ein Text aus der Frühzeit der Kabbala auf Grund eines kritischen Textes ins Deutsche übersetzt und kommentiert*. Berlin: Arthur Scholem, 1923.

Scholem, Gerhard [Gershom]. "Ideologie." *Die Blauweiße Brille*, no. 3 (Tevet 5675 [December 1915]): n.p.

Scholem, Gerhard [Gershom]. "Jüdische Jugendbewegung." *Der Jude* 1, no. 12 (March 1917): 822–825.

Scholem, Gerhard [Gershom]. "Jugendbewegung." *Die Blauweiße Brille*, no. 1 (Av 5675 [July 1915]): n.p.

Scholem, Gerhard [Gershom]. "Jugendbewegung, Jugendarbeit und Blau-Weiß." *Blau-Weiß-Blätter (Führernummer)* 1, no. 2 (August 1917): 26–30.

Scholem, Gerhard [Gershom]. "Über die Theologie des Sabbatianismus im Lichte Abraham Cardozos." *Der Jude* 10, no. 1 (March 1928): 123–139.

Scholem, Gerhard [Gershom]. "Zur Frage der Entstehung der Kabbala." *Korrespondenzblatt des Vereins zur Gründung und Erhaltung einer Akademie für die Wissenschaft des Judentums* 9 (1928): 4–26.

Scholem, Gershom. "95 Thesen über Judentum und Zionismus." In *Gershom Scholem. Zwischen den Disziplinen*, edited by Peter Schäfer and Gary Smith, 287–295. Frankfurt: Suhrkamp, 1995.

Scholem, Gershom. "An einem denkwürdigen Tage." In *Judaica*, 1:207–215. 1963. Reprint, Frankfurt: Suhrkamp, 1997.

Scholem, Gershom. *Briefe*. Vol. 1, *1914–1947*. Edited by Itta Shedletzky. Munich: C. H. Beck, 1994.

Scholem, Gershom. *Briefe*. Vol. 2, *1948–1970*. Edited by Thomas Sparr. Munich: C. H. Beck, 1995.

Scholem, Gershom. *Briefe*. Vol. 3, *1971–1982*. Edited by Itta Shedletzky. Munich: C. H. Beck, 1999.

Scholem, Gershom. "A Commandment Fulfilled by Means of a Transgression" [Hebrew]. *Knesset* 2 (1937): 347–392.

Scholem, Gershom. "The Curious History of the Six-Pointed Star." *Commentary* 8, no. 3 (September 1949): 243–251.

Scholem, Gershom. *Die Erforschung der Kabbala*. Cologne: supposé, 2006.

Scholem, Gershom. *From Berlin to Jerusalem: Memories of My Youth*. Translated by Harry Zohn. New York: Schocken, 1980.

Scholem, Gershom. *Die Geheimnisse der Schöpfung. Ein Kapitel aus dem Sohar*. Berlin: Schocken, 1935.

Scholem, Gershom. "The Golem of Prague and the Golem of Rehovoth." *Commentary* 41, no. 1 (January 1966): 62–65.

Scholem, Gershom. *Judaica*. Vol. 2. 1970. Reprint, Frankfurt: Suhrkamp, 1995.

Scholem, Gershom. *Lamentations of Youth: The Diaries of Gershom Scholem, 1913–1919*. Edited and translated by Anthony David Skinner. Cambridge, Mass.: Belknap Press of Harvard University Press, 2007.

Scholem, Gershom. "A Lecture About Israel (1967)." In *On the Possibility of Jewish Mysticism*, 35–39.

Scholem, Gershom. *A Life in Letters, 1914–1982*. Edited and translated by Anthony David Skinner. Cambridge, Mass.: Harvard University Press, 2002.

Scholem, Gershom. "Martin Buber's Hasidism: A Critique." *Commentary* 32, no. 4 (October 1961): 305–316.

Scholem, Gershom. "Martin Buber's Interpretation of Hasidism." In *The Messianic Idea in Judaism and Other Essays on Jewish Spirituality*, 228–250. New York: Schocken, 1971.

Scholem, Gershom. *Major Trends in Jewish Mysticism*. Jerusalem: Schocken, 1941.

Scholem, Gershom. *The Messianic Idea in Judaism and Other Essays on Jewish Spirituality*. New York: Schocken, 1971.

Scholem, Gershom. *Mi-Berlin li-Yerushalayim. Zikhronot ne'urim*. Tel Aviv: Am Oved, 1982.

Scholem, Gershom. "My Way to Kabbalah (1974)." In *On the Possibility of Jewish Mysticism*, 20–24.

Scholem, Gershom. *On the Kabbalah and Its Symbolism*. Translated by Ralph Manheim. London: Routledge and Kegan Paul, 1965.

Scholem, Gershom. *On the Possibility of Jewish Mysticism in Our Time and Other Essays*. Edited by Avraham Shapira. Translated by Jonathan Chipman. Philadelphia: Jewish Publication Society, 1997.

Scholem, Gershom. "On Sentencing Eichmann to Death." *Journal of International Criminal Justice* 4, no. 4 (September 2006): 859–861.

Scholem, Gershom. *Origins of the Kabbalah*. Edited by R. J. Zwi Werblowsky. Translated by Allan Arkush. Philadelphia: Jewish Publication Society, 1987.

Scholem, Gershom. "Redemption through Sin." Translated by Hillel Halkin. In *The Messianic Idea in Judaism and Other Essays on Jewish Spirituality*, 78–141. New York: Schocken, 1971.

Scholem, Gershom. *Sabbatai Sevi: The Mystical Messiah, 1626–1676*. Translated by R. J. Zwi Werblowsky. Princeton, N.J.: Princeton University Press, 1973.

Scholem, Gershom. *Shabtai Tsevi veha-tenu'ah ha-shabta'it bi-yeme hayav*. Tel-Aviv: Am Oved, 1956/1957.

Scholem, Gershom. *Tagebücher nebst Aufsätzen und Entwürfen bis 1923*. Vol. 1, *1913–1917*. Edited by Karlfried Gründer and Friedrich Niewöhner. Frankfurt: Jüdischer Verlag, 1995.

Scholem, Gershom. *Tagebücher nebst Aufsätzen und Entwürfen bis 1923*. Vol. 2, *1917–1923*. Edited by Friedrich Niewöhner, Karlfried Gründer, and Herbert Kopp-Oberstebrink. Frankfurt: Jüdischer Verlag, 2000.

Scholem, Gershom. *Ursprung und Anfänge der Kabbala*. Berlin: Walter de Gruyter, 1962.

Scholem, Gershom. *Von Berlin nach Jerusalem. Jugenderinnerungen*. Frankfurt: Suhrkamp, 1977.

Scholem, Gershom. *Von Berlin nach Jerusalem. Jugenderinnerungen*. Rev. ed. Translated by Michael Brocke and Andrea Schatz. Frankfurt: Jüdischer Verlag, 1994.

Scholem, Gershom. "Walter Benjamin." *Leo Baeck Institute Year Book* 10 (1965): 117–136.

Scholem, Gershom. *Walter Benjamin: Die Geschichte einer Freundschaft*. Frankfurt: Suhrkamp, 1975.

Scholem, Gershom. *Walter Benjamin: The Story of a Friendship*. Translated by Harry Zohn. Philadelphia: Jewish Publication Society of America, 1981. Reprint, New York: New York Review of Books, 2003.

Scholem, Gershom. "Wider den Mythos vom deutsch-jüdischen 'Gespräch.'" In *Auf gespaltenem Pfad*, edited by Manfred Schlösser, 229–232. Darmstadt: Erato-Presse, 1964.

Scholem, Gershom. "With Gershom Scholem: An Interview." In *On Jews and Judaism in Crisis: Selected Essays*, edited by Werner J. Dannhauser, 1–48. New York: Schocken, 1976.

Scholem, Gershom. *Zur Kabbala und ihrer Symbolik.* Zurich: Rhein-Verlag, 1960.

Scholem, Siegfried, ed. *Fest-Programm für den Einzug der siegreichen Krieger in Berlin am 16. Juni 1871.* Berlin: Siegfried Scholem, [1871].

Scholem, Theobald. *Geschichte des Berliner Turner-Vereins 1850–1900.* Berlin: Siegfried Scholem, 1900.

Scholem, Theobald. "Zur 50. Wiederkehr des Todestages von Friedrich Ludwig Jahn." *Jüdische Turnzeitung* 3, no. 10 (October 1902): 166–167.

Stalin, Joseph V. "Die deutsche Revolution und die Fehler des Genossen Radek. Aus dem Bericht auf dem Plenum des Zentralkomitees der RKP(b)," 15 January 1924. In *Deutscher Oktober 1923. Ein Revolutionsplan und sein Scheitern,* edited by Bernhard H. Bayerlein, Leonid G. Babicenko, Fridrich I. Firsov, and Aleksandr Ju. Vatlin, 443–450. Berlin: Aufbau, 2003.

Stalin, Joseph V. "The Fight against Right and 'Ultra-Left' Deviations: Two Speeches Delivered at a Meeting of the Presidium of the E.C.C.I.," 22 January 1926. In *Works,* vol. 8, *January–November 1926,* 1–10. Moscow: Foreign Languages Publishing House, 1954.

"Die Stelle der 'Jüdischen Turnerschaft' zum Zionismus." *Jüdische Turnzeitung* 6, nos. 5/6 (May/June 1905): 98–103.

Stern, Fritz. *Five Germanys I Have Known.* New York: Farrar, Straus and Giroux, 2006.

Straus, Rahel. *Wir lebten in Deutschland. Erinnerungen einer deutschen Jüdin 1880–1933.* Edited by Max Kreutzberger. Stuttgart: Deutsche Verlags-Anstalt, 1961.

Talmud Bavli. Berlin: Julius Sittenfeld, 1861–68.

United States. "Treaty of Peace with Germany (Treaty of Versailles, 1919)." In *Treaties and Other International Agreements of the United States of America, 1776–1949,* vol. 2, *Multilateral, 1918–1930,* edited by Charles I. Bevans, 43–240. Washington, D.C.: Department of State, 1969.

Veit, Moritz. *Der Entwurf einer Verordnung über die Verhältnisse der Juden und das Edikt vom 11. März 1812.* Leipzig: F. A. Brockhaus, [1847].

Weber, Hermann, Jakov Drabkin, and Bernhard H. Bayerlein, eds. *Deutschland, Russland, Komintern.* Vol. 2, *Dokumente (1918–1943).* Pt. 1. Berlin: Walter de Gruyter, 2015.

Wegener, E. F. W., ed. *Haus- und General-Adressbuch der Königl. Haupt- und Residenzstadt Berlin auf das Jahr 1822.* Berlin: E. F. W. Wegener, 1822.

Weizmann, Chaim. *The Letters and Papers of Chaim Weizmann.* Vol. 1, ser. B, *August 1898–July 1931.* Edited by Barnet Litvinoff. New Brunswick: Transaction Books, 1983.

Weizmann, Chaim. "Project for a Jewish University." In *Letters and Papers of Chaim Weizmann,* vol. 1, ser. B, 13–34.

Weizmann, Chaim. "Shedding Some Illusions." In *Letters and Papers of Chaim Weizmann,* vol. 1, ser. B, 451–468.

Winckler, E., ed. *Adress-Buch für Berlin mit Einschluß der nähern Umgegend und Charlottenburg auf das Jahr 1835.* Berlin: H. A. W. Logier, 1835.

Winckler, Königlicher Polizei-Rath, ed. *Allgemeiner Wohnungsanzeiger für Berlin, Charlottenburg und Umgebungen auf das Jahr 1842.* Vol. 1. Berlin: Veit, 1842.

Winckler, Königlicher Polizei-Rath, ed. *Allgemeiner Wohnungsanzeiger für Berlin, Charlottenburg und Umgebungen auf das Jahr 1842.* Vol. 4. Berlin: Veit, 1842.

Winckler, Königlicher Polizei-Rath, ed. *Allgemeiner Wohnungsanzeiger für Berlin, Charlottenburg und Umgebungen auf das Jahr 1846.* Berlin: Veit, 1846.

Zionist Organization. *Stenographisches Protokoll der Verhandlungen des XVII. Zionistenkongresses und der Zweiten Tagung des Council der Jewish Agency für Palaestina.* London: Zentralbureau der Zionistischen Organisation, 1931.

Zweig, Stefan. *Die Welt von Gestern. Erinnerungen eines Europäers.* Stockholm: Bermann-Fischer, 1942.

"Der zweite Jüdische Turntag." *Ost und West* 5, no. 5 (May 1905): 359–360.

Primary Source Periodicals

American Jewish Year Book
Babylon. Beiträge zur jüdischen Gegenwart
Berliner Illustrierte Nachtausgabe
Berliner Lokal-Anzeiger
Berliner Morgenpost
Berliner Tageblatt
Blau-Weiß-Blätter (Führernummer)
Die Blauweiße Brille
Blätter der jüdischen Buchvereinigung
Bulletin of the American Ceramic Society
Contemporary Jewish Record
Commentary
C. V.-Zeitung
Daily News Bulletin (Jewish Telegraphic Agency)
Davar
Der Israelit
Encounter
Frankfurter Zeitung
Gegen den Strom. Organ der KPD (Opposition)
Gemeindeblatt der Jüdischen Gemeinde zu Berlin
Haaretz
Im deutschen Reich
Informationsblatt
Israelitisches Familienblatt
Journal of International Criminal Justice
Der Jude
Jüdisch-liberale Zeitung
Jüdische Rundschau
Jüdische Turnzeitung
MB: Wochenzeitung des Irgun Olej Merkas Europa
Menorah Journal
Ministerial-Blatt der Handels- und Gewerbe-Verwaltung
Monatsschrift für Geschichte und Wissenschaft des Judentums
Neue Preußische Zeitung (Kreuz-Zeitung)
Neue Zürcher Zeitung

New York Times
New Yorker
Ost und West
Preußische Jahrbücher
Reichsgesetzblatt
Das Rendez-vous
Die Rote Fahne
Schlemiel. Illustriertes jüdisches Witzblatt
Süddeutsche Zeitung
Der Tagesspiegel
Die Tageszeitung
Vorwärts
Vossische Zeitung
Wochenschrift für deutsche Bahnmeister
Zeitschrift für Demographie und Statistik der Juden
Zeitschrift für Sozialforschung
Die Zukunft

Secondary Sources

Albisetti, James C., and Peter Lundgreen. "Höhere Knabenschulen." In *Handbuch der deutschen Bildungsgeschichte*, vol. 4, *1870–1918, Von der Reichsgründung bis zum Ende des Ersten Weltkrieges*, edited by Christa Berg, 228–278. Munich: C. H. Beck, 1991.

Alexander, Gabriel E. "Die Entwicklung der jüdischen Bevölkerung in Berlin zwischen 1871 und 1945." *Tel Aviver Jahrbuch für deutsche Geschichte* 20 (1991): 287–314.

Alroey, Gur. *An Unpromising Land: Jewish Migration to Palestine in the Early Twentieth Century*. Stanford, Calif.: Stanford University Press, 2014.

Alter, Robert. "The Achievement of Gershom Scholem." *Commentary* 55, no. 4 (April 1973): 69–77.

Alter, Robert. Foreword to *Major Trends in Jewish Mysticism*, by Gershom Scholem, xi–xxiv. New York: Schocken, 1995.

Alter, Robert. *Necessary Angels: Tradition and Modernity in Kafka, Benjamin, and Scholem*. Cambridge, Mass.: Harvard University Press, 1991.

Angress, Werner T. "The German Army's 'Judenzählung' of 1916: Genesis—Consequences—Significance." *Leo Baeck Institute Year Book* 23 (1978): 117–138.

Angress, Werner T. "Prussia's Army and the Jewish Reserve Officer Controversy before World War I." *Leo Baeck Institute Year Book* 17 (1972): 19–42.

Aschheim, Steven E. *At the Edges of Liberalism: Junctions of European, German, and Jewish History*. New York: Palgrave Macmillan, 2012.

Aschheim, Steven E. *Beyond the Border: The German-Jewish Legacy Abroad*. Princeton, N.J.: Princeton University Press, 2007.

Aschheim, Steven E. *Brothers and Strangers: The East European Jew in German and German Jewish Consciousness, 1800–1923*. Madison: University of Wisconsin Press, 1982.

Aschheim, Steven E. "The Metaphysical Psychologist: On the Life and Letters of Gershom Scholem." *Journal of Modern History* 76, no. 4 (December 2004): 903–933.

Aschheim, Steven E. *Scholem, Arendt, Klemperer: Intimate Chronicles in Turbulent Times.* Bloomington: Indiana University Press, 2001.

Augustine, Dolores L. "Arriving in the Upper Class: The Wealthy Business Elite of Wilhelmine Germany." In *The German Bourgeoisie: Essays on the Social History of the German Middle Class from the Late Eighteenth to the Early Twentieth Century,* edited by David Blackbourn and Richard J. Evans, 46–86. New York: Routledge, 1991.

Azaryahu, Moaz. *Tel Aviv: Mythography of a City.* Syracuse, N.Y.: Syracuse University Press, 2007.

Baader, Benjamin Maria. *Gender, Judaism, and Bourgeois Culture in Germany, 1800–1870.* Bloomington: Indiana University Press, 2006.

Baeck, Ludwig [sic, probably Leo]. "Die jüdischen Gemeinden." In *Zehn Jahre deutsche Geschichte 1918–1928,* 439–444. Berlin: Otto Stollberg, 1928.

Barbian, Jan-Pieter. *The Politics of Literature in Nazi Germany: Books in the Media Dictatorship.* New York: Bloomsbury Academic, 2013.

Barkai, Avraham. "Exclusion and Persecution: 1933–1938." In Meyer, *GJHMT,* 4:197–230.

Barkai, Avraham. *From Boycott to Annihilation: The Economic Struggle of German Jews, 1933–1943.* Translated by William Templer. Hanover, N.H.: University Press of New England, 1989.

Barkai, Avraham. "German Interests in the Haavara-Transfer Agreement, 1933–1939." *Leo Baeck Institute Year Book* 35 (1990): 245–266.

Barkai, Avraham. "Jewish Life in Its German Milieu." In Meyer, *GJHMT,* 4:45–71.

Barkai, Avraham. "Population Decline and Economic Stagnation." In Meyer, *GJHMT,* 4:30–44.

Barkai, Avraham. *"Wehr Dich!" Der Centralverein deutscher Staatsbürger jüdischen Glaubens 1893–1938.* Munich: C. H. Beck, 2002.

Barouch, Lina. *Between German and Hebrew: The Counterlanguages of Gershom Scholem, Werner Kraft and Ludwig Strauss.* Berlin: Walter de Gruyter, 2016.

Bauer, Yehuda. *Jews for Sale?: Nazi-Jewish Negotiations, 1933–1945.* New Haven, Conn.: Yale University Press, 1994.

Bauschinger, Sigrid. *Die Cassirers. Unternehmer, Kunsthändler, Philosophen: Biographie einer Familie.* 2nd ed. Munich: C. H. Beck, 2016.

Beit-Arié, Malachi. "Gershom Scholem as Bibliophile." In Mendes-Flohr, *Gershom Scholem,* 120–127.

Beling, Eva. *Die gesellschaftliche Eingliederung der deutschen Einwanderer in Israel. Eine soziologische Untersuchung der Einwanderung aus Deutschland zwischen 1933 und 1945.* Frankfurt: Europäische Verlagsanstalt, 1967.

Benjamin, Mara H. *Rosenzweig's Bible: Reinventing Scripture for Jewish Modernity.* Cambridge: Cambridge University Press, 2009.

Benz, Wolfgang. *A Concise History of the Third Reich.* Translated by Thomas Dunlap. Berkeley: University of California Press, 2006.

Benz, Wolfgang. "The Legend of German-Jewish Symbiosis." *Leo Baeck Institute Year Book* 37 (1992): 95–102.

Benz, Wolfgang, Arnold Paucker, and Peter Pulzer. *Jüdisches Leben in der Weimarer Republik*. Tübingen: Mohr Siebeck, 1998.

Bergbauer, Knut, Sabine Fröhlich, and Stefanie Schüler-Springorum. *Denkmalsfigur. Biographische Annäherung an Hans Litten 1903–1938*. Göttingen: Wallstein Verlag, 2008.

Berkowitz, Michael. *Zionist Culture and West European Jewry before the First World War*. Cambridge: Cambridge University Press, 1993. Reprint, Chapel Hill: University of North Carolina Press, 1996.

Berlin Museum. *Synagogen in Berlin*. Vol. 2, *Zur Geschichte einer zerstörten Architektur*, edited by Rudolf Bothe. Berlin: Willmuth Arenhövel, 1983.

Bessel, Richard. *Germany after the First World War*. Oxford: Clarendon Press, 1993.

Biale, David. "The Demonic in History: Gershom Scholem and the Revision of Jewish Historiography." PhD diss., University of California, Los Angeles, 1977.

Biale, David. "Gershom Scholem, *Einst und Jetzt*: Zionist Politics and Kabbalistic Historiography." In Mendelsohn, Hoffman, and Cohen, *Against the Grain*, 51–63.

Biale, David. *Gershom Scholem: Kabbalah and Counter-History*. Cambridge, Mass.: Harvard University Press, 1979.

Biale, David. *Gershom Scholem: Kabbalah and Counter-History*. 2nd ed. Cambridge, Mass.: Harvard University Press, 1982.

Biale, David. *Gershom Scholem: Master of the Kabbalah*. New Haven, Conn.: Yale University Press, 2018.

Biggeleben, Christof. *Das "Bollwerk des Bürgertums." Die Berliner Kaufmannschaft 1870–1920*. Berlin: C. H. Beck, 2006.

Blakeney, Michael. "Australia and the Jewish Refugees from Central Europe: Government Policy, 1933–1939." *Leo Baeck Institute Year Book* 29 (1984): 103–133.

Blau, Bruno. "Die Juden in Deutschland von 1933 bis 1945." *Judaica* 7 (1951): 270–284.

Bloom, Harold, ed. *Gershom Scholem*. New York: Chelsea House, 1987.

Bloom, Harold. "Scholem: Unhistorical or Jewish Gnosticism." In Bloom, *Gershom Scholem*, 207–220.

Bloom, Harold. *The Strong Light of the Canonical: Kafka, Freud, and Scholem as Revisionists of Jewish Culture and Thought*. New York: City College, 1987.

Bonzon, Thierry. "Transfer Payments and Social Policy." In Winter and Robert, *Capital Cities at War*, 286–302.

Bonzon, Thierry, and Belinda Davis. "Feeding the Cities." In Winter and Robert, *Capital Cities at War*, 305–341.

Borrmann, Richard. *Die Bau- und Kunstdenkmäler von Berlin*. Berlin: Julius Springer, 1893.

Borut, Jacob. "The Province versus Berlin?: Relations between Berlin and the Other Communities as a Factor in German Jewish Organisational History at the End of the Nineteenth Century." *Leo Baeck Institute Year Book* 44 (1999): 127–142.

Brammer, Annegret H. *Judenpolitik und Judengesetzgebung in Preußen 1812 bis 1847 mit einem Ausblick auf das Gleichberechtigungsgesetz des Norddeutschen Bundes von 1869*. Berlin: Schelzky & Jeep, 1987.

Brenner, Michael. "Between Revolution and Legal Equality." In Meyer, *GJHMT*, 2:279–318.

Brenner, Michael. "From Subject to Citizen." In Meyer, *GJHMT*, 2:251–276.

Brenner, Michael. "Introduction: Why Jews and Sports?" In Brenner and Reuveni, *Emancipation through Muscles*, 1–9.

Brenner, Michael. "The Jüdische Volkspartei: National-Jewish Communal Politics during the Weimar Republic." *Leo Baeck Institute Year Book 35* (1990): 219–243.

Brenner, Michael. *The Renaissance of Jewish Culture in Weimar Germany*. New Haven, Conn.: Yale University Press, 1998.

Brenner, Michael. "A Tale of Two Families: Franz Rosenzweig, Gershom Scholem and the Generational Conflict around Judaism." *Judaism: A Quarterly Journal of Jewish Life and Thought 42*, no. 3 (Summer 1993): 349–361.

[Brenner, Michael, ed.] "Zur Historischen Gestalt Gershom Scholems." Special issue, *Münchner Beiträge zur Jüdischen Geschichte und Kultur 1*, no. 2 (2007).

Brenner, Michael, and Derek Jonathan Penslar, eds. *In Search of Jewish Community: Jewish Identities in Germany and Austria, 1918–1933*. Bloomington: Indiana University Press, 1998.

Brenner, Michael, and Gideon Reuveni, eds. *Emancipation through Muscles: Jews and Sports in Europe*. Lincoln: University of Nebraska Press, 2006.

Breuer, Mordechai. "The Early Modern Period." In Meyer, *GJHMT*, 1:147–151.

Brilling, Bernhard. "Geschichte des jüdischen Goldschmiedegewerbes in Schlesien." *Hamburger Mittel- und Ostdeutsche Forschungen 6* (1967): 163–221.

Brinkmann, Tobias. *Migration und Transnationalität*. Paderborn: Ferdinand Schöningh, 2010.

Brock, Peter. "Confinement of Conscientious Objectors as Psychiatric Patients in World War I." *Peace & Change 23*, no. 3 (July 1998): 247–264.

Broué, Pierre. "Gauche allemande et Opposition russe de 1926 à 1928." *Cahiers Leon Trotsky*, no. 22 (June 1985): 4–25.

Brym, Robert J. *The Jewish Intelligentsia and Russian Marxism: A Sociological Study of Intellectual Radicalism and Ideological Divergence*. New York: Schocken, 1978.

Buckmiller, Michael, and Pascal Nafe. "Die Naherwartung des Kommunismus—Werner Scholem." In *Judentum und politische Existenz. Siebzehn Porträts deutsch-jüdischer Intellektueller*, edited by Michael Buckmiller, Dietrich Heimann, and Joachim Perels, 60–81. Hanover: Offizin, 2000.

Bürger, Karin, Ines Sonder, and Ursula Wallmeier, eds. *Soncino—Gesellschaft der Freunde des jüdischen Buches. Ein Beitrag zur Kulturgeschichte*. Berlin: Walter de Gruyter, 2014.

Büsch, Otto, and Wolfgang Haus, eds. *Berlin Demokratie 1919–1945*. Vol. 1, *Berlin als Hauptstadt der Weimarer Republik 1919–1933*. Berlin: Walter de Gruyter, 1987.

Campanini, Saverio. "Alu im Shalom. Die Bibliothek Gershom Scholems vor der Auswanderung." In Necker, Morlok, and Morgenstern, *Gershom Scholem in Deutschland*, 73–96.

Chapman, Edgar L. "The Mandala Design of Patrick White's *Riders in the Chariot*." *Texas Studies in Literature and Language 21*, no. 2 (Summer 1979): 186–202.

Chernow, Ron. *The Warburgs: The Twentieth-Century Odyssey of a Remarkable Jewish Family*. New York: Random House, 1993.

Cohen, Hillel. *Year Zero of the Arab-Israeli Conflict: 1929*. Translated by Haim Watzman. Waltham, Mass.: Brandeis University Press, 2015.

Cohen, Mitchell. *Zion and State: Nation, Class, and the Shaping of Modern Israel*. New York: Columbia University Press, 1992.

Craig, Gordon A. *Germany, 1866–1945*. New York: Oxford University Press, 1978.

Cromer, Gerald. *A War of Words: Political Violence and Public Debate in Israel*. London: Frank Cass, 2004.

Cutter, William. "Ghostly Hebrew, Ghastly Speech: Scholem to Rosenzweig, 1926." *Prooftexts* 10, no. 3 (September 1990): 413–433.

Dachs, Gisela. *Die Jeckes*. Frankfurt: Jüdischer Verlag, 2005.

Dahm, Volker. "Jewish Publishing in Nazi Germany, 1933–1938." In *Jewish Book Annual*, vol. 46, *1988–1989/5749*, edited by Jacob Kabakoff, 7–19. New York: Jewish Book Council, 1988.

Dan, Joseph. *Al Gershom Scholem. Teresar ma'amarim*. Jerusalem: Merkaz Zalman Sha-zar le-toldot Yisrael, 2010.

Dan, Joseph. *Gershom Scholem and the Mystical Dimension of Jewish History*. New York: New York University Press, 1987.

Dan, Joseph, ed. *The Heart and the Fountain: An Anthology of Jewish Mystical Experiences*. Oxford: Oxford University Press, 2002.

Davis, Belinda J. *Home Fires Burning: Food, Politics, and Everyday Life in World War I Berlin*. Chapel Hill: University of North Carolina Press, 2000.

Delle Cave, Ferruccio, and Eva Maria Baur. *Literatur und Kur. Ein literarischer Themen-weg durch die Kurstadt Meran*. Merano: Gemeinde Meran, 2012.

Djerassi, Carl. *Four Jews on Parnassus—a Conversation: Benjamin, Adorno, Scholem, Schönberg*. New York: Columbia University Press, 2008.

D'Orazio, Ugo. "Angst vor 'Fräulein Doktor.' Die Diskussion über das medizinische Frauenstudium in Deutschland." In *Geschlechterdifferenz im interdisziplinären Gespräch*, edited by Doris Ruhe, 91–116. Würzburg: Königshausen & Neumann, 1998.

Dunker, Ulrich. *Der Reichsbund jüdischer Frontsoldaten 1919–1938. Geschichte eines jüdischen Abwehrvereins*. Düsseldorf: Droste, 1977.

Ebling, Hermann. *Friedenau erzählt. Geschichten aus einem Berliner Vorort 1871 bis 1914*. Berlin: Edition Friedenauer Brücke, 2007.

Eckhart, Ulrich, and Andreas Nachama. *Jüdische Orte in Berlin*. Berlin: Nicolaische Verlagsbuchhandlung, 2005.

Efron, John M. *Medicine and the German Jews: A History*. New Haven, Conn.: Yale University Press, 2001.

Eisen, George. "Zionism, Nationalism and the Emergence of the Jüdische Turner-schaft." *Leo Baeck Institute Year Book* 28 (1983): 247–262.

Eksteins, Modris. *Rites of Spring: The Great War and the Birth of the Modern Age*. Boston, Mass.: Houghton Mifflin, 1989.

Elon, Amos. *Founder: A Portrait of the First Rothschild and His Time*. New York: Viking, 1996.

Elon, Amos. *The Pity of It All: A History of the Jews in Germany, 1743–1933*. New York: Metropolitan, 2002.

Engel, Amir. *Gershom Scholem: An Intellectual Biography*. Chicago: University of Chicago Press, 2017.

Estraikh, Gennady. "Vilna on the Spree: Yiddish in Weimar Berlin." *Aschkenas. Zeitschrift für Geschichte und Kultur der Juden* 16, no. 1 (March 2006): 103–127.

Estraikh, Gennady, and Mikhail Krutikov, eds. *Yiddish in Weimar Berlin: At the Cross-roads of Diaspora Politics and Culture*. London: Legenda, 2010.

Etzold, Alfred. *Ein Berliner Kulturdenkmal von Weltgeltung. Der jüdische Friedhof Berlin-Weissensee*. Berlin: Hentrich und Hentrich, 2006.

Evans, Richard J. *The Third Reich in Power*. New York: Penguin, 2005.

Ferguson, Niall. *The House of Rothschild: Money's Prophets, 1798–1848*. New York: Viking Penguin, 1998.

Ferguson, Niall. *The House of Rothschild: The World's Banker, 1849–1998*. New York: Viking Penguin, 1999.

Fine, David J. *Jewish Integration in the German Army in the First World War*. Berlin: Walter de Gruyter, 2012.

Fischer, Erica, and Simone Ladwig-Winters. *Die Wertheims. Geschichte einer Familie*. Berlin: Rowohlt-Berlin, 2004.

Fischer, Wolfram. "Wirtschaftsgeschichte Deutschlands 1919–1945," in *Handwörterbuch der Wirtschaftswissenschaft*, vol. 9, *Wirtschaft und Politik bis Zölle, Nachtrag*, ed. Willi Albers, Karl Erich Born, Ernst Dürr, Helmut Hesse, Alfons Kraft, Heinz Lampert, Klaus Rose, Hans-Heinrich Rupp, Harald Scherf, Kurt Schmidt, and Waldemar Wittmann, 83–100. Stuttgart: Gustav Fischer, 1982.

Flumenbaum, Claudia-Ann. "From the Beginnings until 1789." In Nachama, Schoeps, and Simon, *Jews in Berlin*, 9–52.

Föllmer, Moritz. "Suicide and Crisis in Weimar Berlin." *Central European History* 42, no. 2 (June 2009): 195–221.

Freidenreich, Harriet Pass. *Female, Jewish, and Educated: The Lives of Central European University Women*. Bloomington: Indiana University Press, 2002.

Frevert, Ute. *A Nation in Barracks: Modern Germany, Military Conscription and Civil Society*. Oxford: Berg, 2004.

Friedländer, Saul. *Nazi Germany and the Jews*. Vol. 1, *The Years of Persecution, 1933–1939*. New York: HarperCollins, 1997.

Friedländer, Saul. *Nazi Germany and the Jews, 1939–1945: The Years of Extermination*. New York: HarperCollins, 2007.

Fritzsche, Peter. *Reading Berlin 1900*. Cambridge, Mass.: Harvard University Press, 1996.

Funkenstein, Amos. "Gershom Scholem: Charisma, *Kairos* and the Messianic Dialectic." *History and Memory* 4, no. 1 (Spring/Summer 1992): 123–140.

Gay, Peter. *Freud, Jews and Other Germans: Masters and Victims in Modernist Culture*. New York: Oxford University Press, 1978.

Gay, Peter. *My German Question: Growing Up in Nazi Berlin*. New Haven, Conn.: Yale University Press, 1999.

Gedenkstätte Buchenwald, ed. *Buchenwald Concentration Camp, 1937–1945: A Guide to the Permanent Historical Exhibition*. Göttingen: Wallstein, 2004.

Gelber, Yoav. "The Historical Role of Central European Immigration to Israel." *Leo Baeck Institute Year Book* 38 (1993): 323–339.

Gelber, Yoav. *Moledet hadashah. Aliyat Yehude merkaz Eropah u-kelitatam 1933–1948*. Jerusalem: Makon Leo Baeck, 1990.

Geller, Jay Howard. "From Berlin and Jerusalem: On the Germanness of Gershom Scholem." *Journal of Religious History* 35, no. 2 (June 2011): 211–232.

Geller, Jay Howard. " 'I Have Been a Stranger in a Foreign Land': The Scholem Brothers and German-Jewish Émigré Identity." In Geller and Morris, *Three-Way Street*, 125–143.

Geller, Jay Howard. "The Scholem Brothers and the Paths of German Jewry, 1914–1939." *Shofar: An Interdisciplinary Journal of Jewish Studies* 30, no. 2 (Winter 2012): 52–73.

Geller, Jay Howard, and Leslie Morris, eds. *Three-Way Street: Jews, Germans, and the Transnational.* Ann Arbor: University of Michigan Press, 2016.

Grab, Walter, and Julius H. Schoeps, eds. *Juden in der Weimarer Republik. Skizzen und Porträts.* 2nd ed. Darmstadt: Wissenschaftliche Buchgesellschaft, 1998.

Grady, Tim. *A Deadly Legacy: German Jews and the Great War.* New Haven, Conn.: Yale University Press, 2017.

Grady, Tim. "Fighting a Lost Battle: The *Reichsbund jüdischer Frontsoldaten* and the Rise of National Socialism." *German History* 28, no. 1 (March 2010): 1–20.

Grady, Tim. *The German-Jewish Soldiers of the First World War in History and Memory.* Liverpool: Liverpool University Press, 2011.

Grau, Bernhard. *Kurt Eisner 1867–1919. Eine Biographie.* Munich: C. H. Beck, 2001.

Gregory, Adrian. "Lost Generations: The Impact of Military Casualties on Paris, London, and Berlin." In Winter and Robert, *Capital Cities at War*, 57–103.

Gross, Nachum. "Entrepreneure: Einwanderer aus Mitteleuropa in der Wirtschaft Palästinas." In Zimmermann and Hotam, *Zweimal Heimat*, 132-136.

Grossman, Jeffrey A. "Yiddish Writers / German Models in the Early Twentieth Century." In Geller and Morris, *Three-Way Street*, 66–90.

Gruner, Wolf. "Die Berliner und die NS-Judenverfolgung. Eine mikrohistorische Studie individueller Handlungen und sozialer Beziehungen." In *Berlin im Nationalsozialismus. Politik und Gesellschaft 1933–1945*, edited by Rüdiger Hachtmann, Thomas Schaarschmidt, and Winfried Süß, 57–87. Göttingen: Wallstein, 2011.

Gruner, Wolf. "Einleitung." In *Die Verfolgung und Ermordung der europäischen Juden durch das nationalsozialistische Deutschland 1933–1945*, vol. 1, *Deutsches Reich 1933–1937*, edited by Wolf Gruner, 13–50. Munich: R. Oldenbourg, 2008.

Guerra, Gabriele. *Judentum zwischen Anarchie und Theokratie. Eine religionspolitische Diskussion am Beispiel der Begegnung zwischen Walter Benjamin und Gershom Scholem.* Bielefeld: Aisthesis, 2007.

Habermas, Jürgen. *Philosophical-Political Profiles.* Translated by Frederick G. Lawrence. Cambridge, Mass.: MIT Press, 1983.

Halpern, Ben, and Jehuda Reinharz. *Zionism and the Creation of a New Society.* New York: Oxford University Press, 1998.

Hamacher, Elisabeth. *Gershom Scholem und die allgemeine Religionsgeschichte.* New York: Walter de Gruyter, 1999.

Hamburger, Ernest. "Hugo Preuß: Scholar and Statesman." *Leo Baeck Institute Year Book* 20 (1975): 179–206.

Hamburger, Ernest. *Juden im öffentlichen Leben Deutschlands. Regierungsmitglieder, Beamte und Parlamentarier in der monarchischen Zeit 1848–1918.* Tübingen: Mohr Siebeck, 1968.

Hamburger, Ernest, and Peter Pulzer. "Jews as Voters in the Weimar Republic." *Leo Baeck Institute Year Book* 30 (1985): 3–66.

Handelman, Susan A. *Fragments of Redemption: Jewish Thought and Literary Theory in Benjamin, Scholem, and Levinas.* Bloomington: Indiana University Press, 1991.

Hardach, Karl. *The Political Economy of Germany in the Twentieth Century.* Berkeley: University of California Press, 1980.

Hattis, Susan Lee. *The Bi-National Idea in Palestine during Mandatory Times.* Haifa: Shikmona, 1970.

Hebrew University of Jerusalem. *The Hebrew University, Jerusalem: Its History and Development.* Jerusalem: s.n., 1939.

Hecht, Cornelia. *Deutsche Juden und Antisemitismus in der Weimarer Republik.* Bonn: J. H. W. Dietz Nachf., 2003.

Heid, Ludger, and Arnold Paucker, eds. *Juden und deutsche Arbeiterbewegung bis 1933. Soziale Utopien und religiös-kulturelle Traditionen.* Tübingen: J. C. B. Mohr (Paul Siebeck), 1992.

Heinrich, Ernst. *Berlin und seine Bauten.* Vol. 6, *Sakralbauten.* Berlin: Ernst & Sohn, 1997.

Heinrichs, Helmut, Harald Franzki, Klaus Schmalz, and Michael Stolleis, eds. *Deutsche Juristen jüdischer Herkunft.* Munich: C. H. Beck, 1993.

Helman, Anat. *A Coat of Many Colors: Dress Culture in the Young State of Israel.* Boston, Mass.: Academic Studies Press, 2011.

Helman, Anat. *Young Tel Aviv: A Tale of Two Cities.* Translated by Haim Watzman. Waltham, Mass.: Brandeis University Press, 2010.

Herf, Jeffrey. *Nazi Propaganda for the Arab World.* New Haven, Conn.: Yale University Press, 2009.

Hertz, Deborah. *How Jews Became Germans: The History of Conversion and Assimilation in Berlin.* New Haven, Conn.: Yale University Press, 2007.

Hertz, Deborah. *Jewish High Society in Old Regime Berlin.* New Haven, Conn.: Yale University Press, 1988. Reprint, Syracuse, N.Y.: Syracuse University Press, 2005.

Herzog, Annabel. "'Monolingualism' or the Language of God: Scholem and Derrida on Hebrew and Politics." *Modern Judaism* 29, no. 2 (May 2009): 226–238.

Hett, Benjamin Carter. *Burning the Reichstag: An Investigation into the Third Reich's Enduring Mystery.* New York: Oxford University Press, 2014.

Hirsch, Lily E. *A Jewish Orchestra in Nazi Germany: Musical Politics and the Berlin Jewish Culture League.* Ann Arbor: University of Michigan Press, 2010.

Hirschinger, Frank. *"Gestapoagenten, Trotzkisten, Verräter." Kommunistische Parteisäuberungen in Sachsen-Anhalt 1918–1953.* Göttingen: Vandenhoeck & Ruprecht, 2005.

Hoffrogge, Ralf. *Werner Scholem. Eine politische Biographie (1895–1940).* Konstanz: UVK Verlagsgesellschaft, 2014.

Horowitz, Dan, and Moshe Lissak. *Origins of the Israeli Polity: Palestine under the Mandate.* Translated by Charles Hoffman. Chicago: University of Chicago Press, 1978.

Huerkamp, Claudia. *Der Aufstieg der Ärzte im 19. Jahrhundert. Vom gelehrten Stand zum professionellen Experten: Das Beispiel Preußens.* Göttingen: Vandenhoeck & Ruprecht, 1985.

Huerkamp, Claudia. "Jüdische Akademikerinnen in Deutschland 1900–1938." *Geschichte und Gesellschaft* 19 (1993): 311–331.

Humann, Detlev. *"Arbeitsschlacht." Arbeitsbeschaffung und Propaganda in der NS-Zeit 1933–1939.* Göttingen: Wallstein, 2011.

Idel, Moshe. *Old Worlds, New Mirrors: On Jewish Mysticism and Twentieth-Century Thought.* Philadelphia: University of Pennsylvania Press, 2010.

Jacobson, Eric. *Metaphysics of the Profane: The Political Theology of Walter Benjamin and Gershom Scholem.* New York: Columbia University Press, 2003.

Jahnke, Karl Heinz, Rudolf Falkenberg, Bernd Ferchland, Werner Lamprecht, Horst Pietschmann, and Siegfried Scholze. *Geschichte der deutschen Arbeiterjugendbewegung 1904–1945.* Berlin: Neues Leben, 1973.

Jersch-Wenzel, Stefi. "Legal Status and Emancipation." In Meyer, *GJHMT*, 2:7–49.

Jersch-Wenzel, Stefi. "Population Shifts and Occupational Structure." In Meyer, *GJHMT*, 2:50–89.

Jones, Mark. *Founding Weimar: Violence and the German Revolution of 1918–1919.* Cambridge: Cambridge University Press, 2016.

Joseph, David. "Stiftshütte, Tempel- und Synagogenbauten (Schluss)." *Ost und West* 1, no. 11 (November 1901): 831–848.

Jüdisches Museum Berlin. *Stories of an Exhibition: Two Millennia of German Jewish History.* Berlin: Stiftung Jüdisches Museum Berlin, 2001.

Kampe, Norbert. "Jews and Antisemites at Universities in Imperial Germany (I): Jewish Students: Social History and Social Conflict." *Leo Baeck Institute Year Book* 30 (1985): 357–394.

Kaplan, Marion A. "As Germans and as Jews in Imperial Germany." In Kaplan, *Jewish Daily Life in Germany*, 173–269.

Kaplan, Marion A. *Between Dignity and Despair: Jewish Life in Nazi Germany.* New York: Oxford University Press, 1998.

Kaplan, Marion A. "For Love or Money: The Marriage Strategies of Jews in Imperial Germany." *Leo Baeck Institute Year Book* 28 (1983): 263–300.

Kaplan, Marion A., ed. *Jewish Daily Life in Germany, 1618–1945.* New York: Oxford University Press, 2005.

Kaplan, Marion A. *The Jewish Feminist Movement in Germany: The Campaigns of the Jüdischer Frauenbund, 1904–1938.* Westport, Conn.: Greenwood, 1979.

Kaplan, Marion A. *The Making of the Jewish Middle Class: Women, Family and Identity in Imperial Germany.* New York: Oxford University Press, 1991.

Kaplan, Marion A. "Redefining Judaism in Imperial Germany: Practices, Mentalities, and Community." *Jewish Social Studies* 9, no. 1 (Fall 2002): 1–33.

Kaplan, Marion A. "*Unter Uns*: Jews Socialising with Other Jews in Imperial Germany." *Leo Baeck Institute Year Book* 48 (2003): 41–65.

Kark, Ruth, and Michal Oren-Nordheim. *Jerusalem and Its Environs: Quarters, Neighborhoods, Villages, 1800–1948.* Detroit, Mich.: Wayne State University Press, 2001.

Katz, Jacob. *Out of the Ghetto: The Social Background of Jewish Emancipation, 1770–1870.* Cambridge, Mass.: Harvard University Press, 1973.

Kaznelson, Siegmund, ed. *Juden im deutschen Kulturbereich. Ein Sammelwerk.* 3rd ed. Berlin: Jüdischer Verlag, 1962.

Keegan, John. *The First World War.* New York: Alfred A. Knopf, 1999.

Kennan, George F. *The Decline of Bismarck's European Order: Franco-Russian Relations, 1875–1890.* Princeton, N.J.: Princeton University Press, 1979.

Kennedy, Paul M. *The Rise and Fall of the Great Powers: Economic Change and Military Conflict from 1500 to 2000.* New York: Random House, 1987.

Kindleberger, Charles P. *The World in Depression, 1929–1939*. 1973. Reprint, Berkeley: University of California Press, 2013.

Klöppel, Klaus. *Breslau. Niederschlesien und seine tausendjährige Hauptstadt*. 5th ed. Berlin: Trescher Verlag, 2016.

Knott, Marie-Luise. "Hannah Arendt—Gershom Scholem. Die Konstellation." In Hannah Arendt and Gershom Scholem, *Der Briefwechsel 1939–1964*, edited by Marie-Luise Knott, 608–642. Frankfurt: Jüdischer Verlag im Suhrkamp Verlag, 2010.

Krach, Tillmann. *Jüdische Rechtsanwälte in Preußen. Über die Bedeutung der freien Advokatur und ihre Zerstörung durch den Nationalsozialismus*. Munich: C. H. Beck, 1991.

Kraus, Elisabeth. *Die Familie Mosse. Deutsch-jüdisches Bürgertum im 19. und 20. Jahrhundert*. Munich: C. H. Beck, 1999.

Kreutzmüller, Christoph. *Final Sale in Berlin: The Destruction of Jewish Commercial Activity, 1930–1945*. Translated by Jane Paulick and Jefferson Chase. New York: Berghahn Books, 2015.

Kolinsky, Martin. *Law, Order and Riots in Mandatory Palestine, 1928–35*. London: St. Martin's Press, 1993.

Kotzin, Daniel P. *Judah L. Magnes: An American Jewish Nonconformist*. Syracuse, N.Y.: Syracuse University Press, 2010.

Kroyanker, David. "Rehavia—Das 'Jeckenland' von Jerusalem." In Zimmermann and Hotam, *Zweimal Heimat*, 260–266.

Kundt, Klaus. "'Juden und Mitglieder der Sektion Donauland unerwünscht.' Der Deutsche Alpenverein (DAV) hat mit der Aufarbeitung seiner antisemitischen Vergangenheit begonnen." *Gedenkstättenrundbrief* 117 (2004): 19–28.

Lamberti, Marjorie. *Jewish Activism in Imperial Germany*. New Haven, Conn.: Yale University Press, 1978.

Laqueur, Walter. *The Changing Face of Antisemitism: From Ancient Times to the Present Day*. Oxford: Oxford University Press, 2008.

Laqueur, Walter. "The German Youth Movement and the 'Jewish Question.'" *Leo Baeck Institute Year Book* 6 (1961): 193–205.

Large, David Clay. *The Grand Spas of Central Europe: A History of Intrigue, Politics, Art, and Healing*. Lanham, Md.: Rowman & Littlefield, 2015.

Large, David Clay. "'Out with the Ostuden': The Scheunenviertel Riots in Berlin, November 1923." In *Exclusionary Violence: Antisemitic Riots in Modern German History*, edited by Christhard Hoffmann, Werner Bergmann, and Helmut Walser Smith, 123–140. Ann Arbor: University of Michigan Press, 2002.

Lässig, Simone. *Jüdische Wege ins Bürgertum. Kulturelles Kapital und sozialer Aufstieg im 19. Jahrhundert*. Göttingen: Vandenhoeck & Ruprecht, 2004.

Lavsky, Hagit. *Before Catastrophe: The Distinctive Path of German Zionism*. Detroit, Mich.: Wayne State University Press, 1996.

Lavsky, Hagit. *The Creation of the German-Jewish Diaspora: Interwar German-Jewish Immigration to Palestine, the USA, and England*. Berlin: Walter de Gruyter, 2017.

Lavsky, Hagit. "German Zionists and the Emergence of Brit Shalom." In *Essential Papers on Zionism*, edited by Jehuda Reinharz and Anita Shapira, 648–670. New York: New York University Press, 1996.

Lawrence, Jon. "Material Pressures on the Middle Classes." In Winter and Robert, *Capital Cities at War*, 229–254.

Lawrence, Jon. "The Transition to War in 1914." In Winter and Robert, *Capital Cities at War*, 135–163.

Lazier, Benjamin. *God Interrupted: Heresy and the European Imagination between the World Wars*. Princeton, N.J.: Princeton University Press, 2009.

Ledford, Kenneth F. "Jews in the German Legal Professions: Emancipation, Assimilation, Exclusion." In *Jews and the Law*, edited by Ari Mermelstein, Victoria Saker Woeste, Ethan Zadoff, and Marc Galanter, 13–36. New Orleans, La.: Quid Pro Quo, 2014.

Lerner, Paul. *The Consuming Temple: Jews, Department Stores, and the Consumer Revolution in Germany, 1880–1940*. Ithaca, N.Y.: Cornell University Press, 2015.

Lentz, Otto. *Die Seuchenbekämpfung in Preußen während des Krieges und ihr Ergebnis bis Ende 1915*. Veröffentlichungen aus dem Gebiete der Medizinalverwaltung, vol. 6, no. 3. Berlin: Schoetz, 1916.

Levenson, Alan T. "The 'Triple Immersion': A Singular Moment in Modern Jewish Intellectual History?" In Geller and Morris, *Three-Way Street*, 46–65.

Liepach, Martin. *Das Wahlverhalten der jüdischen Bevölkerung. Zur politischen Orientierung der Juden in der Weimarer Republik*. Tübingen: J. C. B. Mohr (Paul Siebeck), 1996.

Linfield, Harry S. "Statistics of Jews." *American Jewish Year Book* 24 (1922–23): 298–322.

Linfield, Harry S. "Statistics of Jews." *American Jewish Year Book* 33 (1931–32): 271–304.

Lowenstein, Steven. M. "The Beginning of Integration, 1780–1870." In Kaplan, *Jewish Daily Life in Germany*, 93–171.

Lowenstein, Steven M. *The Berlin Jewish Community: Enlightenment, Family, and Crisis*. New York: Oxford University Press, 1994.

Lowenstein, Steven M. "The Community." In Meyer, *GJHMT*, 3:125–152.

Lowenstein, Steven M. "Epilogue: The German-Jewish Diaspora." In Meyer, *GJHMT*, 4:393–402.

Lowenstein, Steven M. "Ideology and Identity." In Meyer, *GJHMT*, 3:281–304.

Lowenstein, Steven M. "The Pace of Modernization of German Jewry in the Nineteenth Century." *Leo Baeck Institute Year Book* 21 (1976): 41–56.

Lucas, Franz D., and Margret Heitmann. *Stadt des Glaubens. Geschichte und Kultur der Juden in Glogau*. 2nd ed. Hildesheim: Georg Solms, 1992.

Lucca, Enrico. "Una visione dialettica della storia ebraica: Gershom Scholem e l'eredità del messianismo." PhD diss., Università degli Studi di Milano, 2012.

Manning, Jonathan. "Wages and Purchasing Power." In Winter and Robert, *Capital Cities at War*, 255–285.

Maor, Zohar. "Death or Birth: Scholem and Secularization." In Mendelsohn, Hoffman, and Cohen, *Against the Grain*, 64–85.

Marks, Sally. "Reparations Reconsidered: A Reminder." *Central European History* 2, no. 4 (December 1969): 356–365.

Mason, Tim. "Women in Germany, 1925–1940: Family, Welfare and Work. Part I." *History Workshop* 1, no. 1 (Spring 1976): 74–113.

Maurer, Trude. *Die Entwicklung der jüdischen Minderheit in Deutschland (1780–1933). Neuere Forschungen und offene Fragen*. Tübingen: Max Niemeyer, 1992.

Maurer, Trude. "From Everyday Life to a State of Emergency: Jews in Weimar and Nazi Germany." In Kaplan, *Jewish Daily Life in Germany*, 271–373.

Meerwarth, Rudolf, Adolf Günther, and Waldemar Zimmermann, eds. *Die Einwirkung des Krieges auf Bevölkerungsbewegung, Einkommen und Lebenshaltung in Deutschland*. Stuttgart: Deutsche Verlags-Anstalt, 1932.

Mendelsohn, Ezra, Stefani Hoffman, and Richard I. Cohen, eds. *Against the Grain: Jewish Intellectuals in Hard Times*. New York: Berghahn Books, 2014.

Mendes-Flohr, Paul. "Between Germanism and Judaism, Christians and Jews." In Meyer, *GJHMT*, 4:157–169.

Mendes-Flohr, Paul. *Divided Passions: Jewish Intellectuals and the Experience of Modernity*. Detroit, Mich.: Wayne State University Press, 1991.

Mendes-Flohr, Paul, ed. *Gershom Scholem: The Man and His Work*. Albany: State University of New York Press, 1994.

Mendes-Flohr, Paul. "Jewish Cultural and Spiritual Life." In Meyer, *GJHMT*, 4:127–156.

Mertens, Bram. *Dark Images, Secret Hints: Benjamin, Scholem, Molitor and the Jewish Tradition*. New York: Peter Lang, 2007.

Metzler, Tobias. *Tales of Three Cities: Urban Jewish Cultures in London, Berlin, and Paris (c. 1880–1940)*. Wiesbaden: Harrassowitz, 2014.

Meyer, Albert. "Eine jüdische Idealgemeinde." In *Adass Jisroel. Die jüdische Gemeinde in Berlin (1869–1942): Vernichtet und Vergessen*, edited by Mario Kessler, 210–211. Berlin: Museumspädagogischer Dienst Berlin, 1986.

Meyer, Michael A., ed. *German-Jewish History in Modern Times*. Vol. 1, *Tradition and Enlightenment, 1600–1780*. New York: Columbia University Press, 1996.

Meyer, Michael A., ed. *German-Jewish History in Modern Times*. Vol. 2, *Emancipation and Acculturation, 1780–1871*. New York: Columbia University Press, 1997.

Meyer, Michael A., ed. *German-Jewish History in Modern Times*. Vol. 3, *Integration in Dispute, 1871–1918*. New York: Columbia University Press, 1997.

Meyer, Michael A., ed. *German-Jewish History in Modern Times*. Vol. 4, *Renewal and Destruction, 1918–1945*. New York: Columbia University Press, 1998.

Meyer, Michael A. "The Religious Reform Controversy in the Berlin Jewish Community, 1814–1823." *Leo Baeck Institute Year Book* 24 (1979): 139–155.

Miron, Guy. *Mi-"sham" le-"khan" be-guf r'ishon: Zikhronoteihem shel yoz'ei Germania be-Yisrael*. Jerusalem: Magnes, 2004.

Miron, Ronny. *The Angel of Jewish History: The Image of the Jewish Past in the Twentieth Century*. Brighton, Mass.: Academic Studies Press, 2014.

Morgan, David W. *The Socialist Left and the German Revolution: A History of the German Independent Social Democratic Party, 1917–1922*. Ithaca, N.Y.: Cornell University Press, 1975.

Morton, Frederic. *The Rothschilds: A Family Portrait*. New York: Atheneum, 1961.

Moses, Siegfried. "Salman Schocken—His Economic and Zionist Activities." *Leo Baeck Institute Year Book* 5 (1960): 73–104.

Mosès, Stéphane. *The Angel of History: Rosenzweig, Benjamin, Scholem*. Translated by Barbara Harshav. Stanford, Calif.: Stanford University Press, 2008.

Mosès, Stéphane, and Sigrid Weigel, eds. *Gershom Scholem. Literatur und Rhetorik*. Cologne: Böhlau, 2000.

Mosse, George L. *German Jews beyond Judaism*. Bloomington: Indiana University Press, 1985.

Mosse, Werner E. *Jews in the German Economy: The German-Jewish Economic Élite, 1820–1935.* Oxford: Clarendon Press, 1987.

Mosse, Werner E. "Rudolf Mosse and the House of Mosse, 1867–1920." *Leo Baeck Institute Year Book* 4 (1959): 237–259.

Mosse, Werner E., and Arnold Paucker, eds. *Juden im Wilhelminischen Deutschland 1890–1914. Ein Sammelband.* Tübingen: Mohr Siebeck, 1971.

Mosse, Werner E., Arnold Paucker, and Reinhard Rürup, eds. *Revolution and Evolution: 1848 in German-Jewish History.* Tübingen: J. C. B. Mohr, 1981.

Müller, Reinhard. "Hitlers Rede vor der Reichswehr- und Reichsmarineführung am 3. Februar 1933." *Mittelweg 36* 10, no. 4 (February/March 2000): 74–90.

Münzel, Martin. *Die jüdischen Mitglieder der deutschen Wirtschaftselite 1927–1955. Verdrängung, Emigration, Rückkehr.* Paderborn: Ferdinand Schöningh, 2006.

Münzel, Martin. "Zwischen Ökonomie und Bibliophile. Unternehmer und Verleger als Mitglieder der Soncino-Gesellschaft." In Bürger, Sonder, and Wallmeier, *Soncino,* 75–94.

Nachama, Andreas, Julius H. Schoeps, and Hermann Simon, eds. *Jews in Berlin.* Translated by Michael S. Cullen. Berlin: Henschel, 2002.

Necker, Gerold, Elke Morlok, and Matthias Morgenstern, eds. *Gershom Scholem in Deutschland. Zwischen Seelenverwandtschaft und Sprachlosigkeit.* Tübingen: Mohr Siebeck, 2014.

Nettl, J. P. *Rosa Luxemburg.* Vol. 2. London: Oxford University Press, 1966.

Niederland, Doron. "The Emigration of Jewish Academics and Professionals from Germany in the First Years of Nazi Rule." *Leo Baeck Institute Year Book* 33 (1988): 285–300.

Niethammer, Lutz, ed. *Der "gesäuberte" Antifaschismus. Die SED und die roten Kapos von Buchenwald.* Berlin: Akademie, 1994.

Niewyk, Donald L. *The Jews in Weimar Germany.* Baton Rouge: Louisiana State University Press, 1980.

Nipperdey, Thomas. *Deutsche Geschichte 1866–1918.* Vol. 1, *Arbeitswelt und Bürgergeist.* Munich: C. H. Beck, 1994.

Oppenheimer, Franz. *Die Judenstatistik des preußischen Kriegsministeriums.* Munich: Verlag für Kulturpolitik, 1922.

Panter, Sarah. *Jüdische Erfahrungen und Loyalitätskonflikte im Ersten Weltkrieg.* Göttingen: Vandenhoeck & Ruprecht, 2014.

Paucker, Arnold. *Der jüdische Abwehrkampf gegen Antisemitismus und Nationalsozialismus in den letzten Jahren der Weimarer Republik.* Hamburg: Leibniz, 1968.

Peukert, Detlev J. K. *The Weimar Republic: The Crisis of Classical Modernity.* Translated by Richard Devenson. New York: Hill and Wang, 1993.

Poppel, Stephen M. "Salman Schocken and the Schocken Verlag." *Leo Baeck Institute Year Book* 17 (1972): 93–113.

Poppel, Stephen M. *Zionism in Germany, 1897–1933: The Shaping of a Jewish Identity.* Philadelphia: Jewish Publication Society of America, 1977.

Portmann, Werner, and Siegbert Wolf. "Isak Aufseher (1905–1977). Luftmensch und Spanienkämpfer." In *"Ja, ich kämpfte." Von Revolutionsträumen, "Luftmenschen" und Kindern des Schtetls. Biographien radikaler Jüdinnen und Juden,* 27–70. Münster: Unrast, 2006.

Presner, Todd Samuel. *Muscular Judaism: The Jewish Body and the Politics of Regeneration*. London: Routledge, 2007.

Prinz, Arthur. *Juden im Deutschen Wirtschaftsleben. Soziale und wirtschaftliche Struktur im Wandel 1850–1914*. Edited by Avraham Barkai. Tübingen: Mohr Siebeck, 1984.

Prochnik, George. *Stranger in a Strange Land: Searching for Gershom Scholem and Jerusalem*. New York: Other Press, 2017.

Pulzer, Peter. *Jews and the German State: The Political History of a Minority, 1848–1933*. Oxford: Blackwell, 1992.

Pulzer, Peter. "The Response to Antisemitism." In Meyer, *GJHMT*, 3:252–280.

Pyta, Wolfram. *Die Weimarer Republik*. Berlin: Landeszentrale für politische Bildung, 2004.

Rahden, Till van. *Jews and Other Germans: Civil Society, Religious Diversity, and Urban Politics in Breslau, 1860–1925*. Translated by Marcus Brainard. Madison: University of Wisconsin Press, 2008.

Ratzabi, Shalom. *Between Zionism and Judaism: The Radical Circle in Brith Shalom, 1925–1933*. Leiden: Brill, 2002.

Raz-Krakotzkin, Amnon. "Binationalism and Jewish Identity: Hannah Arendt and the Question of Palestine." In *Hannah Arendt in Jerusalem*, edited by Steven E. Aschheim, 165–180. Berkeley: University of California Press, 2001.

Rebiger, Bill. "Auch eine Berliner Kindheit um Neunzehnhundert. Zur Biographie des jungen Gershom Scholem bis 1915." In Necker, Morlok, and Morgenstern, *Gershom Scholem in Deutschland*, 19–36.

Rebiger, Bill. *Das jüdische Berlin. Kultur, Religion und Alltag gestern und heute*. 3rd ed. Berlin: Jaron, 2007.

Rebiger, Bill. " 'Das Wesentliche spielt sich nicht auf der Leipziger Straße ab, sondern . . . im Geheimen'—Gershom Scholem und Berlin." *European Association for Jewish Studies Newsletter* 16 (Spring 2005): 81–99.

Rees, David A. "Fritz Hommels Gutachten zu Gerhard Scholems Dissertation." *Münchner Beiträge zur Jüdischen Geschichte und Kultur* 2 (2007): 87–91.

Reinharz, Jehuda. *Fatherland or Promised Land: The Dilemma of the German Jew, 1893–1914*. Ann Arbor: University of Michigan Press, 1975.

Reinharz, Jehuda, and Walter Schatzberg, eds. *The Jewish Response to German Culture: From the Enlightenment to the Second World War*. Hanover, N.H.: University Press of New England, 1985.

Reitter, Paul. *Bambi's Jewish Roots and Other Essays on German-Jewish Culture*. New York: Bloomsbury Academic, 2015.

Richarz, Monika. "Demographic Developments." In Meyer, *GJHMT*, 3:7–34.

Richarz, Monika. "Occupational Distribution and Social Structure." In Meyer, *GJHMT*, 3:35–67.

Rinott, Chanoch. "Major Trends in Jewish Youth Movements in Germany." *Leo Baeck Institute Year Book* 19 (1974): 77–95.

Rollet, Catherine. "The 'Other War' I: Protecting Public Health." In Winter and Robert, *Capital Cities at War*, 421–455.

Rollet, Catherine. "The 'Other War' II: Setbacks in Public Health." In Winter and Robert, *Capital Cities at War*, 456–486.

Rösch, Paul. "Die touristische Speisekarte in Südtirol, ein Spiegelbild der Tourismusentwicklung." *Carinthia I. Zeitschrift für geschichtliche Landeskunde von Kärnten* 193 (2003): 507–529.

Rosenstock, Werner. "Exodus 1933–1939: A Survey of Jewish Emigration from Germany." *Leo Baeck Institute Year Book* 1 (1956): 373–390.

Rosenstreich, Nathan. "Gershom Scholem's Conception of Jewish Nationalism." In Mendes-Flohr, *Gershom Scholem*, 104–119.

Rosenthal, Jacob. *"Die Ehre des jüdischen Soldaten." Die Judenzählung im Ersten Weltkrieg und ihre Folgen.* Frankfurt: Campus, 2007.

Rovit, Rebecca. *The Jewish Kulturbund Theatre Company in Nazi Berlin.* Iowa City: University of Iowa Press, 2012.

Rubinstein, W. D. *The Jews in Australia: A Thematic History.* Vol. 2, *1945 to the Present.* Melbourne: William Heinemann, 1991.

Rudavsky, David. *Emancipation and Adjustment: Contemporary Jewish Religious Movements, Their History and Thought.* New York: Diplomatic Press, 1967.

Ruppin, Arthur. *Soziologie der Juden.* Vol. 1, *Die Soziale Struktur der Juden.* Berlin: Jüdischer Verlag, 1930.

Rürup, Reinhard. *Emanzipation und Antisemitismus. Studien zur "Judenfrage" der bürgerlichen Gesellschaft.* Göttingen: Vandenhoeck & Ruprecht, 1975.

Rürup, Reinhard. "Jewish History in Berlin—Berlin in Jewish History." *Leo Baeck Institute Year Book* 45 (2000): 37–50.

Rutland, Suzanne D. *Edge of the Diaspora: Two Centuries of Jewish Settlement in Australia.* 2nd ed. New York: Holmes and Meier, 1997.

Rutland, Suzanne D. *The Jews in Australia.* Cambridge: Cambridge University Press, 2005.

Sacerdoti, Annie. *The Guide to Jewish Italy.* New York: Rizzoli, 2004.

Sachar, Howard M. *A History of Israel: From the Rise of Zionism to Our Time.* 3rd ed. New York: Alfred A. Knopf, 2010.

Schäfer, Peter, and Gary Smith, eds. *Gershom Scholem. Zwischen den Disziplinen.* Frankfurt: Suhrkamp, 1995.

Schenk, Tobias. "Das Emanzipationsedikt—Ausdruck 'defensiver Modernisierung' oder Abschluss rechtsstaatlicher Entwicklungen des '(aufgeklärten) Absolutismus'?" In *Das Emanzipationsedikt von 1812 in Preußen. Der lange Weg der Juden zu "Einländern" und "preußischen Staatsbürgern,"* edited by Irene A. Diekmann, 23–76. Berlin: Walter de Gruyter, 2013.

Schieb, Roswitha. *Jeder zweite Berliner. Schlesische Spuren an der Spree.* Potsdam: Verlag Kulturforum östliches Europa, 2012.

Schleunes, Karl A. *The Twisted Road to Auschwitz: Nazi Policy toward German Jews, 1933–1939.* Urbana: University of Illinois Press, 1970.

Schlöffel, Frank. "Zionismus und Bibliophilie. Heinrich Loewe und die neuen 'Soncinaten.'" In Bürger, Sonder, and Wallmeier, *Soncino*, 25–40.

Schlör, Joachim. *Endlich im Gelobten Land? Deutsche Juden unterwegs in eine neue Heimat.* Berlin: Aufbau, 2003.

Schoeps, Julius H., ed. *Juden als Träger bürgerlicher Kultur in Deutschland.* Stuttgart: Burg, 1989.

Schorsch, Ismar. *Jewish Reactions to German Anti-Semitism, 1870–1914.* New York: Columbia University Press, 1972.

Schorske, Carl E. *German Social Democracy, 1905–1917: The Development of the Great Schism.* Cambridge, Mass.: Harvard University Press, 1955.

Schulte, Marion. *Über die bürgerlichen Verhältnisse der Juden in Preußen. Ziele und Motive der Reformzeit (1787–1812).* Berlin: Walter de Gruyter, 2014.

Schütz, Chana C. "The Imperial Era (1871–1918)." In Nachama, Schoeps, and Simon, *Jews in Berlin,* 89–136.

Segall, Jacob. *Die deutschen Juden als Soldaten im Kriege 1914–1918. Eine statistische Studie.* Berlin: Philo-Verlag, 1922.

Segall, Jacob. "Die Juden in Groß-Berlin." *Zeitschrift für Demographie und Statistik der Juden* 10, nos. 9/10 (September/October 1914): 121–132.

Segev, Tom. *One Palestine, Complete: Jews and Arabs under the British Mandate.* Translated by Haim Watzman. New York: Metropolitan Books, 2000.

Seidler, Eduard. *Die Medizinische Fakultät der Albert-Ludwigs-Universität Freiburg im Breisgau. Grundlagen und Entwicklung.* Rev. ed. Berlin: Springer-Verlag, 1993.

Selzer, Assaf. *The History of the Hebrew University of Jerusalem: Who's Who Prior to Statehood; Founders, Designers, Pioneers.* Translated by Jenni Tsafrir. Jerusalem: Magnes Press, 2015.

Shapira, Anita. *Berl: The Biography of a Socialist Zionist; Berl Katznelson, 1887–1944.* Cambridge: Cambridge University Press, 1984.

Shapira, Anita. *Land and Power: The Zionist Resort to Force, 1881–1948.* Translated by William Templer. Oxford: Oxford University Press, 1992.

Shavit, Yaacov. *Jabotinsky and the Revisionist Movement, 1925–1948.* London: Frank Cass, 1988.

Shimoni, Gideon. *The Zionist Ideology.* Hanover, N.H.: Brandeis University Press, 1995.

Showalter, Dennis E. *The Wars of Frederick the Great.* London: Longman, 1996.

Simon, Christian. *Schöneberg im Wandel der Geschichte. "Es war in Schöneberg im Monat Mai."* Berlin: be.bra-Verlag, 1998.

Sonder, Ines. "Bauen für ein neues Land. Die Architektin Lotte Cohn zwischen Berlin und Erez Israel." In *Salondamen und Frauenzimmer. Selbstemanzipation deutsch-jüdischer Frauen in zwei Jahrhunderten,* edited by Elke-Vera Kotowski, 111–118. Berlin: Walter de Gruyter, 2016.

Sonder, Ines. "Neun Holzschnitte zum Buch Jesus Sirach. Jakob Steinhardt und die neunte Publikation der Soncino-Gesellschaft von 1929." In Bürger, Sonder, and Wallmeier, *Soncino,* 95–112.

Sonino, Claudia. *German Jews in Palestine, 1920–1948: Between Dream and Reality.* Translated by Juliet Haydock. Lanham, Md.: Lexington Books, 2016.

Sorkin, David. *The Transformation of German Jewry, 1780–1840.* New York: Oxford University Press, 1987.

Sparr, Thomas. *Grunewald im Orient. Das deutsch-jüdische Jerusalem.* Berlin: Berenberg, 2018.

Spector, Scott. *Modernism without Jews?: German-Jewish Subjects and Histories.* Bloomington: Indiana University Press, 2017.

Steiner, George. "The Friend of a Friend." *New Yorker,* 22 January 1990, 133–136.

Steinweis, Alan E. *Kristallnacht 1938.* Cambridge, Mass.: Harvard University Press, 2009.

Stern, Howard. "The Organisation Consul." *Journal of Modern History* 35, no. 1 (March 1963): 20–32.

Stone, Norman. *The Eastern Front, 1914–1917*. London: Penguin, 1975.

Swartout, Lisa. "Facing Antisemitism: Jewish Students at German Universities, 1890–1914." *Leipziger Beiträge zur jüdischen Geschichte und Kultur* 2 (2004): 149–165.

Tipton, Frank B. *A History of Modern Germany since 1815*. London: Continuum, 2003.

Toury, Jacob. "Organizational Problems of German Jewry: Steps towards the Establishment of a Central Organization (1893–1920)." *Leo Baeck Institute Year Book* 13 (1968): 57–90.

Toury, Jacob. *Die politischen Orientierungen der Juden in Deutschland. Von Jena bis Weimar*. Tübingen: Mohr Siebeck, 1966.

Turner, Henry Ashby. *Hitler's Thirty Days to Power*. Boston, Mass.: Addison-Wesley, 1996.

Vogt, Stefan. "The First World War, German Nationalism, and the Transformation of German Zionism." *Leo Baeck Institute Year Book* 57 (2012): 267–291.

Vogt, Stefan. *Subalterne Positionierungen. Der deutsche Zionismus im Feld des Nationalismus in Deutschland 1890–1933*. Göttingen: Wallstein, 2016.

Volkov, Shulamit. *Germans, Jews, and Antisemites: Trials in Emancipation*. Cambridge: Cambridge University Press, 2006.

Volkov, Shulamit. *Die Juden in Deutschland 1780–1918*. 2nd edition. Munich: R. Oldenbourg Verlag, 2000.

Wachsmann, Nikolaus. *KL: A History of the Nazi Concentration Camps*. New York: Farrar, Straus and Giroux, 2015.

Wasserstrom, Steven M. *Religion After Religion: Gershom Scholem, Mircea Eliade, and Henry Corbin at Eranos*. Princeton, N.J.: Princeton University Press, 1999.

Weber, Hermann. "The Stalinization of the KPD: Old and New Views." In *Bolshevism, Stalinism and the Comintern: Perspectives on Stalinization, 1917–53*, edited by Norman LaPorte, Kevin Morgan, and Matthew Worley, 22–44. New York: Palgrave Macmillan, 2008.

Weber, Hermann. *Die Wandlung des deutschen Kommunismus. Die Stalinisierung der KPD in der Weimarer Republik*. Frankfurt: Europäische Verlagsanstalt, 1969.

Weber, Hermann. "Zum Verhältnis von Komintern, Sowjetstaat und KPD." In *Deutschland, Russland, Komintern*, vol. 1, *Überblicke, Analysen, Diskussionen*, edited by Hermann Weber, Jakov Drabkin, Bernhard H. Bayerlein, and Aleksandr Galkin, 9–139. Berlin: Walter de Gruyter, 2014.

Wehler, Hans-Ulrich. *Deutsche Gesellschaftsgeschichte*. Vol. 4, *1914–1949*. 2nd ed. Munich: C. H. Beck, 2003.

Weidner, Daniel. *Gershom Scholem. Politisches, esoterisches und historiographisches Schreiben*. Munich: Wilhelm Fink, 2003.

Weidner, Daniel. "Reading Gershom Scholem." *Jewish Quarterly Review* 96, no. 2 (Spring 2006): 203–231.

Weiner, Hannah. "Gershom Scholem and the Jung Juda Youth Group in Berlin, 1913–1918." *Studies in Zionism* 5, no. 1 (1984): 29–42.

Wiener, P. B. "Die Parteien der Mitte." In *Entscheidungsjahr 1932. Zur Judenfrage in der Endphase der Weimarer Republik*, edited by Werner E. Mosse and Arnold Paucker, 314–321. 2nd ed. Tübingen: J. C. B. Mohr.

Wildmann, Daniel. "Jewish Gymnasts and Their Corporeal Utopias in Imperial Germany." In Brenner and Reuveni, *Emancipation through Muscles*, 27–43.

Wilhelm, Kurt. "The Jewish Community in the Post-Emancipation Period." *Leo Baeck Institute Year Book* 2 (1957): 47–75.

Wirsching, Andreas. "'Man kann nur Boden germanisieren.' Eine neue Quelle zu Hitlers Rede vor den Spitzen der Reichswehr am 3. Februar 1933." *Vierteljahrshefte für Zeitgeschichte* 49, no. 3 (July 2001): 517–550.

Winkler, Heinrich August. *Der lange Weg nach Westen.* Vol. 1, *Deutsche Geschichte vom Ende des Alten Reiches bis zum Untergang der Weimarer Republik.* Munich: C. H. Beck, 2000.

Winkler, Heinrich August. *Weimar 1918–1933. Die Geschichte der ersten deutschen Demokratie.* Munich: C. H. Beck, 1993.

Winter, Jay, and Jean-Louis Robert. *Capital Cities at War: Paris, London, Berlin, 1914–1919.* Cambridge: Cambridge University Press, 1997.

Wünschmann, Kim. *Before Auschwitz: Jewish Prisoners in the Concentration Camps.* Cambridge, Mass.: Harvard University Press, 2015.

Zadoff, Mirjam. *Der rote Hiob. Das Leben des Werner Scholem.* Munich: Carl Hanser, 2014.

Zadoff, Mirjam, and Noam Zadoff, eds. *Scholar and Kabbalist: The Life and Work of Gershom Scholem.* Leiden: Brill, 2019.

Zadoff, Noam. *Gershom Scholem: From Berlin to Jerusalem and Back; An Intellectual Biography.* Translated by Jeffrey Green. Waltham, Mass.: Brandeis University Press, 2018.

Zadoff, Noam. "Travelling to the Past, Creating the Future: Gershom Scholem's Journey to Germany in 1946." *Jewish Culture and History* 11, nos. 1–2 (2009): 199–208.

Zechlin, Egmont. *Die deutsche Politik und die Juden im Ersten Weltkrieg.* Göttingen: Vandenhoeck & Ruprecht, 1969.

Zimmermann, Moshe. *Die deutschen Juden 1914–1945.* Munich: R. Oldenbourg, 1997.

Zimmermann, Moshe, and Yotam Hotam, eds. *Zweimal Heimat. Die Jeckes zwischen Mitteleuropa und Nahost.* Frankfurt: beerenverlag, 2005.

Zimmermann, Waldemar. "Die Veränderung der Einkommens- und Lebensverhältnisse der deutschen Arbeiter durch den Krieg." In *Die Einwirkung des Krieges auf Bevölkerungsbewegung, Einkommen und Lebenshaltung in Deutschland,* edited by Rudolf Meerwarth, Adolf Günther, and Waldemar Zimmermann, 281–474. Stuttgart: Deutsche Verlags-Anstalt, 1932.

"Die zweite Lesung der Besoldungsvorlage in der Budgetskommission des Abgeordnetenhauses." *Wochenschrift für deutsche Bahnmeister* 14, no. 11 (14 March 1897): 98–99.

INDEX

Agnon, S. Y., 61, 86
Agudat Yisrael, 43
Aid Association of German Jews, 166
Aliyah Hadasha, 177
antisemitism
    abolishment of legal,
        40–41
    Aryanization and, 160–62
    and bar exam process, 123
    in Communist Party, 101
    during First World War, 63, 67
    following First World War, 12, 83–84,
        92–93
    under German Empire, 29, 30, 38, 41
    during Great Depression, 120–21
    in gymnastics organizations, 29
    and Kristallnacht, 3, 164–65
    and Nuremberg Laws, 156–57
    reactions to, 4
    and rise of Nazi Party, 143, 144–47
    and strengthened Jewish identity, 148–49
    under Weimar Republic, 79, 90, 114–15
Arab revolt (1936–39), 184–86
Arendt, Hannah, 191–92, 200–202, 215–16
Arlosoroff, Haim, 184
Arthur Scholem Printers, 25, 35, 74, 76–77,
    111–12, 124, 152, 160
Aryanization, 160–62
Auerbach, Felix, 64
Aufseher, Isak, 160
Australia
    challenges in, 197
    immigration to, 163–64, 165–66, 193
    Jewish communal affiliation in, 195
    and Scholems' German identity, 195–97
    Scholems' life in, 194–97, 205–6

Baeck, Rabbi Leo, 106, 199, 201, 213
bar mitzvahs, 42, 149
Bauch, Bruno, 64
Bauer, Gustav, 71

Bäumer, Gertrud, 81
Bebel, August, 42
Beckh, Hermann, 52
Bendix, Ludwig, 159
Benjamin, Dora, 81, 87
Benjamin, Walter
    on Arthur's opinion of Gershom, 84
    death of, 192
    and death of Arthur Scholem, 110
    decides against immigrating to Palestine,
        138–39
    family background of, 62, 106
    on Gershom's childhood, 11
    on Gershom's fame, 100
    on Gershom's home in Rehavia, 174
    Gershom's relationship with, 61–62, 64,
        87, 191
    Gershom tries to help, 183
    Gershom visits, in Switzerland, 65
    plaque commemorating, 216
    religious observance of, 81
Bergmann, Else, 181
Bergmann, Hugo
    and Brit Shalom, 133
    divorce and remarriage of, 181, 182, 183
    employed by Hebrew University of
        Jerusalem, 180
    and Gershom's immigration to Palestine,
        90–91, 128
    on Haganah, 135–36
    meets Gershom, 82
Berlin
    antisemitism in, 92–93, 160–61
    communist revolt in, 76–77
    Eastern European Jews in, 53, 61, 92–93,
        108–9, 122–23
    growth and modernization of, 32–33
    High Holiday attendance in, 103
    Jewish cultural center established in, 53
    Jewish population in, 17–18, 33–34
    mixing of Christians and Jews in, 28

Berlin (continued)
 modern-day, 213–15
 revolutionary conditions in, 74
 Scholem family's history in, 17–22
 Scholems' life in, 19–20, 23, 34–35, 112
 sites honoring Jews in, 215–16
 suburbs of, 35–36
 under Weimar Republic, 76
 World War I's impact on, 68–70
Berliner Tageblatt, 30, 97
Berliner Turner-Verein, 29
Berlin-Weißensee cemetery, 216–17
Bialik, Hayim, 139
Bible, new translation of, 107–8
Bildung, 37
Blank, Johann, 169
Die Blauweiße Brille, 55, 56, 68
Blau-Weiss movement, 54–56, 86
Bleichrode, Isaak, 43
Bloom, Harold, 205
Blum, Edgar, 53–54
Blumenfeld, Kurt, 45
B'nai B'rith lodges, 30
Bodenheimer, Max, 44
Borchardt, Max, 167
Borges, Jorge Luis, 203
Brandler, Heinrich, 99
Brauer, Erich, 68, 77
Brauer, Margarete ("Grete"), 62, 64–65
Braunschweiger Volksfreund, 79
Brit Shalom, 132–33, 134–35, 137–38, 187
Buber, Martin
 on Bergmann's marriage to Escha, 183
 and Bible translation, 107–8
 Gershom impressed by, 44, 52
 Gershom's disenchantment with,
  52–53, 62
 Gershom's relationship with, 52–53, 56,
  87, 202
 immigrates to Palestine, 175
Buchenwald concentration camp, 2–3, 158,
 166–67, 169–70
Burchhardt, Elsa ("Escha")
 courtship of, 65, 66, 85–86
 divorce of, 82, 174, 181–82, 183
 Gershom's treatment of, 140
 health problems of, 140, 141, 181
 home of, in Palestine, 173–74, 182
 immigrates to Palestine, 90–91
 life of, in Palestine, 139
 marriage of, 82, 93–94
 marries Hugo Bergmann, 181
Burchhardt, Martha, 105
Burchhardt, Max, 105

Center Party, 121–22
Central Association of German Citizens of
 the Jewish Faith, 30, 48, 106, 115
Christmas, 26–27, 42, 81, 104, 149, 211
Cohn, Helene, 182
Cohn, Lotte, 182
Cohn, Rabbi Emil Bernhard, 44
Comintern, 88–89
Commentary magazine, 203
Committee for Jewish Cultural Work, 65
Communist Party of Germany, 76, 89,
 99–102, 124–25, 212
communist revolt, 76–77, 88
concentration camps
 Jews sent to, following Kristallnacht,
  164–65
 Käte Hirsch sent to, 168
 Werner's imprisonment in, 2–3, 154–60,
  166–67, 169–70
Corbin, Henry, 188, 203
Council of People's Deputies, 76
cultural refinement, 24, 37, 125–26

Dachau concentration camp, 158, 159
deflation, 119

Ebert, Friedrich, 73, 78
Edict Concerning the Civil Status of the
 Jews in the Prussian State (1812), 6, 15, 16
education
 of Jewish bourgeoisie, 37–38
 of Scholems, 23–25, 37–41, 51–52, 64,
  83–85, 113, 210
Eisner, Kurt, 77
Enabling Act (1933), 144
Erzberger, Matthias, 67, 88

family size, of bourgeois Jews, 39
Federn, Ernst, 159, 169–70
Fischer, Ruth, 90, 99, 101, 102
Flatow, Gustav Felix, 29
Fontane, Theodor, 28
food shortages
 during First World War, 69–70
 following First World War, 78, 92–93
forms, preprinted, 31
France, 15
Franz Ferdinand, Archduke, 47
Fräßdorf, Julius, 71
Frederick II, King, 14
Frederick William I, King, 17–18
Frederick William III, King, 6, 15, 19
Freies Jüdisches Lehrhaus, 107, 211
Freud, Fania, 166, 181, 182–83, 205

Friedenau, 35–36
Friedländer, David, 18, 19

Gay, Peter, 207
German Democratic Party, 74–75, 78, 98–99, 103, 211. *See also* German State Party
German Nationalists, 99
German People's Party, 98–99, 120, 211
German State Party, 120, 122. *See also* German Democratic Party
Gerstenmaier, Eugen, 207
Glaser, Hirsch Simon, 20
Glogau, 14–15, 16–17
Goebbels, Joseph, 100, 144, 155, 157, 158
Goethe, Johann Wolfgang von, 125
Goitein, Shlomo Dov (Fritz), 90
Goldmann, Nahum, 135
Göring, Hermann, 165
Great Depression, 118–22
Gutkind, Erich, 87
Guttmann, Julius, 179, 180
gymnastics, 28–29

Ha'am, Ahad, 133
Haase, Hugo, 57, 77
Haavara Agreement, 176
Hackebeil, Heinz, 151, 152
Haganah, 135–36, 185
Hammerstein, Helga, 155
Hammerstein, Marie Luise, 154, 155
Hammerstein-Equord, Kurt von, 155
Hanukkah, 104, 149
Hasidism, 190
Haskalah, 18
Hebrew language, 130–31, 178–79
Hebrew University of Jerusalem, 129, 179–80, 197–99, 202
Herz, Henriette, 18
Herzl, Theodor, 44, 45, 55
Herzl Club, 56
Heuss, Theodor, 26
Heuss-Knapp, Elly, 26
Heymann, Harry, 53, 65
High Holidays, 42, 103–4
Hindenburg, Paul von, 101, 102, 142
Hinkelmann, Eduard, 169
Hirsch, Hans, 25, 114, 167–68
Hirsch, Hermann, 26
Hirsch, Käte, 25–26, 28, 60, 148, 162, 168, 197
Hirsch, Samson Raphael, 43
Hitachdut Olei Germania, 177
Hitler, Adolf, 92, 101, 142–43
Holländer, Esther, 20–21

Hommel, Fritz, 84
Hope-Simpson, John, 136
Horodisch, Abraham, 112

Independent Social Democratic Party, 58, 75–77, 88–89
inflation, 91–92, 93, 97
influenza pandemic, 70
Institute for Social Research, 191
intermarriage, 28, 114, 168
Irgun Olei Merkaz Europa, 177
Isaac, Feile, 20

Jabotinsky, Ze'ev, 132, 137
Jacobson, Israel, 18
Jahr, Meta, 62, 64
Jansen, Heinz, 67
Jew Census, 67
Jewish Institute of Religion, 189
Jewish National and University Library, 91, 128–29
Jewish organizations, 30, 43–44, 164, 201
Jewish People's Party, 122–23
Jewish renaissance in Germany, 107–9, 148–49
Jüdische Rundschau, 27, 50–51, 132–33, 152
Jünger, Ernst, 42, 49
Jung Juda, 55–56, 65

Kabbalah, 85, 138–39, 189–90, 202
Kapp Putsch, 87–88
Kareski, Georg, 121
Kästner, Erich, 124
Katz, Edith, 80–81, 106, 165–66, 167, 194
Katz, Iwan, 99
Katznelson, Berl, 135
Kautsky, Karl, 42
Klausner, Joseph, 129–30
Kohn, Hans, 86, 133, 198
Köllnisches Gymnasium, 25
Kolmar, Gertrud, 148–49
Korsch, Karl, 167
Kristallnacht, 3, 164–65

Lake Naroch Offensive (1916), 56–57
Landmann, Ludwig, 98
last names, requirement for Jews to take, 16
Law for the Protection of German Blood and German Honor (1935), 156–57
Law for the Restoration of the Professional Civil Service (1933), 145–46
League of Jewish Women, 30, 106
Lehmann, Siegfried, 53
Lenin, Vladimir, 88–89

Lessing, Gotthold Ephraim, 125
Leviné, Eugen, 77
Levy, Hedwig ("Hete")
    flees Germany, 167
    Gershom reunited with, 197
    Gershom's relationship with, 51, 56
    marriage of, 36
    on Reinhold and Erich's brides, 80–81
    religious observance of, 104–5
    and unrest in Palestine, 134
    and Werner's leftist political views, 79
    Zionist sympathies of, 27
Lichtenberg concentration camp, 156,
    157–58
Liebknecht, Karl, 49, 57, 73, 74, 77
Litten, Hans, 159
Lüders, Marie Elisabeth, 98
Luisenstädtisches Realgymnasium, 24–25,
    38, 42
Lurianic Kabbalah, 189–90
Luxemburg, Rosa, 49, 77

MacDonald, Ramsay, 136
Magnes, Judah, 129, 132, 139, 180
March Action (1921), 89
marriage
    intermarriage, 28, 114, 168
    of Jews in Berlin, 20
    post-war surge in, 80
    relationship between husbands and wives
        in Jewish, 39
Marx, Moses, 87, 190
Marx, Wilhelm, 101
Marxism, 49–50, 139, 169, 191
Maslow, Arkadi, 90, 99, 101
Max von Baden, Prince, 71, 73
Mendelssohn, Moses, 18, 125
Michaelis, Erna, 64
Midrash Abarbanel Library, 128
military service, 38, 40, 49, 51–52, 56–60, 63,
    66–67, 70–71
Moor Express in concentration camps,
    159, 169
Moses, Walter, 86
Müller, August, 123

Napoleon, 15
National-Jewish Association, 44
Nazis
    antisemitism under, 3, 121, 143, 144–47,
        156–57, 164–65
    Aryanization under, 160–62
    and end of German-Jewish epoch, 6

Haavara Agreement with, 176
Jewish emigration under, 147–48, 162–66,
    167–68, 170–71
Reinhold and Erich flee, 2, 163–64
rise of, 13, 124–25, 142–44
Scholems' financial situation under,
    152–53
suppression of rebellion of, 92
Werner opposes, 155
Werner's imprisonment under, 2–3,
    150–52, 154–60, 166–67, 169–70
neo-Orthodoxy, 105–6
Nordau, Max, 29
Nuremberg Laws (1935), 156–57

Oko, Adolph S., 198
Old Synagogue (Berlin), 43
Organisation Consul, 88
Orthodox Jews and Judaism in Germany,
    18–19, 43, 48, 105–6, 125
Ozick, Cynthia, 9, 203, 205

Palestine. See also Zionism
    adaptation of German-Jewish immigrants
        to, 177–78
    Arab revolt in, 184–86
    Betty travels to, 112–13
    British regulation of immigration to,
        186–88
    culture and religious observance in,
        131–32
    as destination for Jews fleeing Nazis,
        162–63
    Eva and Dina immigrate to, 153
    Gershom immigrates to, 90–91, 128
    Gershom's home in, 173–74, 181
    Gershom's life in, during war years,
        197–98
    Gershom's profession in, 128–31, 138–39,
        178–80
    Haganah in, 135–36, 185
    impact of German-Jewish immigrants in,
        176–77, 178
    increased Jewish immigration to, 127–28,
        131, 147, 174, 175–76
    Jewish population in, 173
    language of German-Jewish immigrants
        in, 178
    support for binationalism in, 135–36
    symbolic importance of, 172–73
    unrest in, 133–34, 135, 136, 184–88
Papen, Franz von, 124, 125
Passfield White Paper, 136

Peel Commission, 186–87
Pension Struck, 61
Pflaum, Else, 114
Pflaum, Heinz, 85
physicians, Jewish, 161–62
Pinthus, Gerhard, 158, 167
Potok, Chaim, 203
preprinted forms, 31
Preuß, Hugo, 77, 98
Princip, Gavrilo, 47
print media, 21–22, 30–31
Prinz, Joachim, 147
Prussia, status of Jews in, 14–16

Rathenau, Walther, 88
record labels, 31
Rehavia, 173–74
Reich Citizenship Law (1935), 156–57
Reich League of Jewish Frontline
    Soldiers, 125
Reichstag fire, 143, 144
rentenmark, 93
Revisionist Zionism, 129, 132, 133, 137
Revolution (1918–19), German, 73–78
Rosenberg, Arthur, 90, 99, 101
Rosenzweig, Franz, 87, 107–8, 211
Rosh Hashanah, 103–4
Die Rote Fahne, 89–90
Rothstein, Stephanie, 56
Rubashov, Zalman, 61, 63
Ruppin, Arthur, 132, 134
Russian Empire, increased Jewish immigration
    from, 127

Sabbateanism, 138, 178, 190, 202
Samuel, Hildegard ("Hilde"), 194
Schächter, Julie, 55–56
Schäffer, Hans, 145
Scheidemann, Philipp, 73, 77
Schiepan, Walter, 28, 168
Schiller, Friedrich, 37
Schlesinger, Amalie, 22, 23, 35, 36
Schlesinger, David, 22
Schocken, Salman, 65, 87, 179, 180, 198
Schocken Books, 153, 179, 183–84, 188–89
Scholem, Abraham (Adolph), 21
Scholem, Abraham (in Scholem
    genealogy), 16
Scholem, Arthur
    career of, 25, 30–31, 92
    death of, 109–10
    education of, 23–25, 210
    evicts Gershom, 60

on German economy, 103
and Gershom's education, 84
and Gershom's immigration to
    Palestine, 91
and Gershom's marriage, 93–94
grave of, 109, 217
as gymnastics enthusiast, 29
health problems of, 94
personality of, 11
political views of, 30, 42
Reinhold and Erich partner with, 80
religious observance of, 26–27, 42, 104
residence in Berlin, 23, 34
Werner's relationship with, 57, 58
Scholem, Arthur Jr. ("Bübi"), 94, 196–97, 205
Scholem, Betty Hirsch
    on antisemitism, 92–93, 123, 146
    and cultural refinement, 37, 210
    death of, 197
    and death of Arthur, 109–10
    and end of First World War, 71–72
    and establishment of Weimar Republic,
        74, 76
    family background of, 25–26
    and family celebrations, 36
    and food shortages during First World
        War, 70
    on Georg's death, 115–16
    on German economy, 91–92, 103
    on Gershom's feigned mental illness,
        63–64
    and Gershom's immigration to Palestine,
        91, 140–41
    and Gershom's marriage, 93
    Gershom's relationship with, 93, 110–11,
        140–41, 189
    on Gershom's remarriage, 182–83
    on Gershom's university employment,
        129, 179–80
    Great Depression's impact on, 119–20
    health problems of, 3, 164, 166, 197
    immigrates to Australia, 163–64, 165–66
    on intermarriage, 114
    on Jewish emigration, 147
    on Lene's employment, 118
    life of, in Australia, 194–95, 197
    on Nazis' rise to power, 121, 142–43
    on 1925 presidential election, 101
    on Nuremberg Laws, 157
    occupation of, 39
    political views of, 30, 75, 97–98
    religious observance of, 26–27, 42, 103–4
    residence in Berlin, 34

Scholem, Betty Hirsch (*continued*)
  and rise of Nazi Party, 142–43
  sixtieth birthday of, 112
  on sons' marriages, 111
  on surviving inflation, 97
  travels of, 112–13, 153
  and unrest in Palestine, 134
  votes for first time, 78
  on Werner's death, 170
  and Werner's imprisonment, 150–51, 155,
    158, 167
  on Werner's political career, 100
  Werner's relationship with, 113–14
  and Zernsdorf cottage, 112
  on Zionism, 105
Scholem, Dina, 104, 147, 153
Scholem, Edith, 60, 151, 160
Scholem, Erich
  as assimilationist, 97
  career of, 12, 80, 92, 111–12, 160
  death of, 206
  and death of Arthur, 109, 110
  education of, 37, 38, 39–40
  engages in currency speculation, 92
  and family celebrations, 36
  and First World War, 12, 66, 75
  Great Depression's impact on, 119
  identity and perspectives of, 11, 149,
    195–96
  immigrates to Australia, 2, 163–64
  immigration of family of, 165–66
  life of, in Australia, 194, 195–96, 205–6
  marriage of, 80–81, 111, 194
  and Max's death, 116
  military service of, 40, 49, 66
  political views of, 3–4, 39, 97–98
  religious observance of, 39, 103
  views on postwar Germany, 196
  and Zernsdorf cottage, 112
Scholem, Ernst, 147, 175
Scholem, Eva, 104, 105, 147, 153
Scholem, Georg
  career and education of, 23–25
  death of, 115–16
  and death of Arthur, 109, 110
  marriage of, 36
  military service of, 66
  nurses Werner during First World War, 57
  relationship of, with brothers, 94
Scholem, Gershom
  ambitions of, 83
  on Arab revolt, 185–86
  Arendt and, 191–92, 200–202

Betty's relationship with, 110–11
and Brit Shalom, 132–33
Buber's relationship with, 56, 87, 202
career of, 12, 128–31, 138–39, 179–80,
  188–89, 202–5
on Communist Party, 90
criticizes German Jewry, 174–75
as culturally German, 140
and cultural refinement, 210
death of, 207–8
and death of Arthur, 109, 110
discourages Betty from immigrating to
  Palestine, 147
divorce of, 174, 181–82
during early post-war years, 81–83
education of, 37, 38, 51–52, 64, 83–85
engagement of, 50
Erich's relationship with, 206
evicted from family home, 60–61
family background of, 10–11
and family celebrations, 36
on father's Jewish identity, 27
feigns mental illness, 63–64
fellowship at Wissenschaftskolleg zu
  Berlin, 207–8, 217–18
forges friendship with Benjamin, 61–62
and Freies Jüdisches Lehrhaus, 107
From Berlin to Jerusalem, 9, 206, 217
Die Geheimnisse der Schöpfung, 183–84
on German-Jewish reconciliation, 207
grave of, 217
Great Depression's impact on, 120
health problems of, 141
home of, in Palestine, 173–74, 182
identity and perspectives of, 11, 140,
  206–7
immigrates to Palestine, 90–91, 128
and immigration of Scholem family,
  163–64
interest of, in Jewish mysticism, 85
interest of, in own biography and German-Jewish experience, 9, 206–7
on Jewish immigration to Palestine,
  174, 175
On the Kabbalah and Its Symbolism, 203
and Kapp Putsch, 88
on Käte Hirsch's imprisonment, 168
"Kuntres alu le Shalom," 180
life of, in Berlin, 34–35
life of, in Munich, 85–86
Major Trends in Jewish Mysticism,
  189–90, 198
marriage of, 93–94, 182–83

military service of, 51–52, 63
personality of, 11, 56, 87, 111, 140–41, 205
political views and background of, 3–4
and public perception of modern
   German-Jewish history, 206–7
"Redemption through Sin," 178
religious observance of, 81–82, 131–32
relocates to Bern, 65–66
renowned in Jewish Germany, 175
and rise of Nazi Party, 121, 124
romantic life of, 62, 64–65, 66, 181–82
Rosenzweig's relationship with, 87
on Rosenzweig's translation of Bible, 108
scholarship on, 9–10
and Scholems' financial difficulties under
   Nazis, 152
on Star of David, 200
and theoretical question of language,
   178–79
travels in postwar Europe, 198–200
turns toward Judaism, 42–44
and unrest in Palestine, 133–34, 184–88
U.S. lecture series of, 1, 189–91
during war years, 197–98
on Werner's death, 170
and Werner's imprisonment, 150, 151, 158
Werner's relationship with, 90
on World War I, 49–51
on Zionism, 82, 132, 137
Zionism and Jewish identity of, 44–46
"Zur Frage der Entstehung der
   Kabbala," 138
Scholem, Günter, 94, 149
Scholem, Herbert, 116
Scholem, Irene, 94, 195, 206
Scholem, Kurt, 109
Scholem, Lazarus, 17
Scholem, Lene, 114, 117, 118, 145, 148
Scholem, Marcus, 17, 19, 20–21
Scholem, Mathias, 17, 19, 20
Scholem, Max
   death of, 116–17
   education of, 23–25, 210
   and family celebrations, 36
   as gymnastics enthusiast, 29
   moves to suburbs, 35
   prints money for government, 92
   relationship of, with brothers, 94, 97, 116
Scholem, Reinhold
   as assimilationist, 96–97
   career of, 12, 80, 92, 111–12, 160
   death of, 208
   and death of Arthur, 109, 110

education of, 37, 38, 39–40
engages in currency speculation, 92
and establishment of Weimar Republic,
   75–76
and family celebrations, 36
final years of, 207, 208
and First World War, 12, 66–67, 70–71, 75
Gershom's relationship with, 207
Great Depression's impact on, 119, 120
identity and perspectives of, 11, 149,
   196, 207
immigrates to Australia, 2, 163–64
joins German People's Party, 99
life of, in Australia, 194, 196, 205–6
marriage of, 80–81, 111
and Max's death, 117
military service of, 40, 49, 66–67, 70–71
political and religious views of, 3–4, 39
religious observance of, 103, 104
views on postwar Germany, 196
and Zernsdorf cottage, 112
Scholem, Renate, 94, 152, 160, 196
Scholem, Scholem, 16
Scholem, Solm (Siegfried), 21–23, 25
Scholem, Theobald
   considers immigrating to Palestine,
      147–48
   education of, 23–25, 210
   and family celebrations, 36
   flees Germany, 167
   forced out of printing business, 160
   Gershom reunited with, 197
   as gymnastics enthusiast, 29
   marriage of, 36
   Max's relationship with, 116
   moves to suburbs, 35
   and printshop merger, 124
   relationship of, with brothers, 94, 97
   religious observance of, 27, 104–5
   supports Georg Kareski, 121
   supports Jewish People's Party, 123
Scholem, Therese, 114, 148
Scholem, Werner
   arrest and imprisonment of, 2–3, 150–52,
      154–60, 166–67, 169–70
   Betty's relationship with, 113–14
   charged with treason, 89–90, 154
   death of, 169–70
   and death of Arthur, 109, 110
   on disintegration of Jewish
      bourgeoisie, 124
   education of, 38, 41, 113
   elected to Prussian state legislature, 89

Scholem, Werner (*continued*)
  endorses Comintern membership, 89
  and establishment of Weimar
    Republic, 75
  and First World War, 12, 56–57, 58–60, 75
  on Gershom in Palestine, 147
  Gershom's relationship with, 90
  identity and perspectives of, 11
  as law clerk, 123–24
  leftist activism of, 79–80
  marker commemorating, 216
  marriage of, 28, 58
  military service of, 56–57, 58–60, 75
  political and religious views of, 3–4, 39,
    41–42, 57–58, 59, 149–50
  political career of, 12, 89–90, 99–102, 113
  refuses to enlist in army, 49–50
  and rise in antisemitism, 67–68
  and rise of Nazi Party, 143–44
  scholarship on, 10
Scholem, Zipporah, 16–17
Schöneberg, 35, 36, 122
self-employment of Jews, 22–23, 40, 118
Shaw Report, 136
Shazar, Zalman, 61. *See also*
  Rubashov, Zalman
Siegfried Scholem Book and Lithograph
  Printers, 22–23, 35, 92, 94, 97, 116,
  124, 160
Siemens, Carl Friedrich von, 98
Simon, Ernst, 135–36, 197–98
Social Democratic Party, 42, 49, 58, 78,
  120, 212
Soncino Society of the Friends of the Jewish
  Book, 108, 211
Spanish Civil War, 160
Spartakists, 74, 75
Spitzer, Moritz, 188–89
Stalin, Joseph, 99, 102, 170
Star of David, 200
Steiner, George, 205
Stern, Fritz, 8, 140, 207, 213
suicide, 117
Sussmann, Sophie ("Piechen"), 36, 110,
  167, 175
Swarsensky, Manfred, 149

Thälmann, Ernst, 101, 102
Theresienstadt concentration camp, 168
Ticho, Anna, 139
Ticho, Avraham, 139
Treaty of Versailles, 81, 103
Troeltsch, Ernst, 52

Trotsky, Leon, 170
Türkischer, Kohos Karl, 38, 65

Ullstein, Heinz, 145
Ullstein, Rudolf, 116–17
Ullstein Verlag, 97, 116, 145
University of Munich, 83–85

van Rahden, Till, 8
Varnhagen von Ense, Rahel, 18
Vossische Zeitung, 30, 97

Wagner, Käthe, 80–81, 94, 111, 115, 194, 205
Weimar Republic
  appreciation for German high culture
    during, 210–11
  and communist revolt, 76–77
  constitution for, 78–79
  establishment of, 73–74
  Jewish involvement in, 74–75, 77–78
  and Kapp Putsch, 87–88
  Scholems' views on, 75–76
  Werner thrives under, 79–80
Weiß, Bernhard, 98
Weizmann, Chaim, 129, 131, 136
Weltsch, Robert, 86, 187
White, Patrick, 203
White Paper of 1939, 187–88
Wiechelt, Emmy
  arrest of, 150–51
  Betty's relationship with, 113–14
  converts to Judaism, 206
  denied British citizenship, 170
  engagement of, 50
  and establishment of Weimar
    Republic, 75
  flees Germany, 151–52
  gives birth to Edith, 60
  Great Depression's impact on, 120
  immigration plans of, 160
  marriage of, 58
  settles in England, 153–54
  on Werner's military service, 59
Wiener, Alfred, 125
Wilhelm II, Kaiser, 47–48, 71, 73
Wilmersdorf, 61
Wise, Stephen, 189
Wolff, Theodor, 74
women
  education and employment of, 26, 39,
    117–18
  Gershom's views on, 140–41, 181
  League of Jewish Women, 30, 106

women's suffrage, 76, 78, 106
Woodhead, John, 187
Woodhead Commission, 187
World War I
  beginning of, 47–48, 73–74
  end of, 71–72, 74
  German Jews' service during, 53
  Gershom's military service during,
    51–52, 63
  Gershom's views on, 49–51, 53–55
  impact of, 12, 67–70, 78
  inflation following, 91–92, 93, 97
  and integration of Jews into Germany, 48
  and Jewish immigration to Palestine,
    127–28
  and rise in antisemitism, 67–68
  Scholems' service during, 49–50, 66–67
  and Treaty of Versailles, 81, 103
  Werner's military service during, 56–57,
    58–60, 75
  Werner's views on, 57–58

Yom Kippur, 103–4

Zernsdorf cottage, 112, 152
Zinoviev, Grigory, 99, 101, 102
Zionism. See also Palestine
  Brit Shalom and, 132–33, 134–35, 137–38

character of German, 44–45, 132–33
generational split between German
  Zionists, 104–5
German Zionists' influence on, 212
Gershom's concern about, 184–85
and Gershom's Jewish identity, 44–46
Gershom's passion for, 82, 132
Gershom's views on First World War and,
  53–56
and gymnastics, 29
and increased Jewish immigration to
  Palestine, 127
mission of, 176
and negation of Diaspora, 175
resolution on aim of, 137
Revisionist, 129, 132, 133, 137
revolutionary, 86
and unrest in Palestine, 186–88
Werner on, 68
Zionist Congress, First, 44, 45
Zionist Congress, Seventeenth, 137, 184
Zionist Congress, Nineteenth, 153
Zionist Congress, Twentieth, 186
Zionist Federation of Germany, 44, 48, 56,
  65, 135, 176
Zohar, 138, 190
Zucker, Gertrud, 175, 176
Zweig, Stefan, 32–33